PREFACE

As a discipline, criminology must deal not only with the causes of crime—the traditional emphasis of sociologists—but also with the criminal justice system and corrections. With that twofold task in mind, I have written this text in an attempt to combine my training in sociology and in law.

During my years of teaching criminology to undergraduates, I was impressed with their eagerness to learn how law relates to the traditional topics covered in the course, even to the point of their enjoying judicial opinions. Thus, excerpts from appellate opinions have been used to illustrate such concepts as punishment and to demonstrate the role of the courts in the reformation of the criminal justice system. To minimize the need for supplemental materials, the text provides the results of sociological research—both historical and contemporary—on the criminal justice system. Summaries and critiques of classic books on criminology, analyses of recent sociological research, and attention to major sociological theorists who have contributed significantly to the study of crime are also included.

The response to the three previous editions of this text indicates that students and instructors have found the integration of law and social science to be a viable approach to the study of criminal behavior. No less important to users of earlier editions has been the assessment of society's response to criminal behavior. Therefore the basic format has been retained, but with some significant changes.

Each chapter of this edition opens with a short preview indicating the purpose of the chapter, along with an outline of the major topics covered in the chapter. At a glance readers will be alerted to the chapter's coverage and will have, at the same time, a useful tool for review. Other new features are "Highlights" and "Exhibits." Highlights, which are generally taken from popular sources, illustrate how crime is depicted in the mass media. Exhibits focus on scholarly materials. These new features, along with the continued use of tables, figures, cartoons, and photographs, provide variety and image to the text.

In this edition footnotes are grouped together at the end of the text. This change has permitted the retention of the scholarly research that has marked *Crime and Criminology,* while reducing space requirements, thus enabling us to expand discussions in some areas.

The organization of the text remains essentially the same, although there are now five, rather than four, major divisions. Part I introduces the study of criminology, with Chapter 1, "Law and Crime," explaining the concept of crime and analyzing the meaning of that term. The chapter then explores the significance and purpose of the criminal law, concluding with a look at what might happen when the criminal law is used to control morality.

Chapter 2, "The Measurement of Crime and Its Impact," focuses on the accumulation of data on crime. Official as well as unofficial methods of collecting data are considered, and data on crime and on victimization are analyzed in terms of age, race, and sex.

In this edition the chapter on measurement and research has been eliminated to allow more space for discussions of sociological theories in Part II; a brief examination of research, however, is included in Chapter 3.

Part II, "Explanations of Criminal Behavior," examines the causes of crime. Chapter 3, which opens with a brief introduction to the methods of studying crime, explores the historical explanations of criminal behavior that have strongly influenced "modern" developments. The influence of the classical and positive schools of thought are explained, contrasted, and related to current philosophies of punishment and sentencing. The contributions of economists to our understanding of whether punishment deters are also discussed.

Chapter 4, "Biological and Psychological Theories," a new chapter, considers two areas of thought that are becoming more important in our understanding of criminal behavior. After a discussion of psychological and biological theories of causation, we look at their impact on our legal system, especially the insanity defense, used successfully in the trial of John W. Hinckley, Jr., charged with attempting to assassinate President Ronald Reagan.

Part II ends with two chapters on sociological explanations of criminal behavior. These chapters follow the same format as those of the third edition, but the material has been updated, featuring the addition of such topics as the concept of defensible space and routine activity theory.

Part III, "Typologies of Criminal Behavior," is characterized by substantial revision of the two chapters in the third edition, plus the introduction of a new chapter on domestic violence. Chapter 7, "Crimes of Violence," focuses on violent crimes, such as murder, rape, and robbery, that do not necessarily involve family members. Chapter 8 examines violent crimes in the context of domestic violence, as well as such crimes as sexual abuse of children and abuse of elderly parents. Finally, Chapter 9 considers the major property crimes.

Part IV, "The Criminal Justice System," follows the same chapter sequence as the third edition but contains organizational changes. Chapter 10, "The American System of Criminal Justice," deals with the due process rights of defendants and then explores the conflict between those rights and the growing recognition of the rights of victims. The discussions on plea bargaining and the jury system have been moved to Chapter 13, "The Court System." Finally, the chapter on sentencing has been

CRIME AND CRIMINOLOGY

CRIME AND CRIMINOLOGY

Sue Titus Reid, J.D., Ph.D.

George Beto Professor
of Criminal Justice
Sam Houston State University
Huntsville, Texas

FOURTH EDITION

Holt, Rinehart and Winston
NEW YORK   CHICAGO   SAN FRANCISCO   PHILADELPHIA   MONTREAL   TORONTO
LONDON   SYDNEY   TOKYO   MEXICO CITY   RIO DE JANEIRO   MADRID

IN LOVING MEMORY OF
CARL C. NUTLEY
A GREAT TEACHER AND A DEAR FRIEND

Library of Congress Cataloging in Publication Data
Reid, Sue Titus.
    Crime and criminology.

    Includes indexes.
    1. Crime and criminals.   2. Criminal justice,
Administration of.   I. Title.
HV6025.R515   1985   364   84-25176

ISBN 0-03-070752-8

CBS COLLEGE PUBLISHING
Holt, Rinehart and Winston
The Dryden Press
Saunders College Publishing

Acknowledgments

Cover: Ben Shahn, *Bartolomeo Vanzetti and Nicola Sacco.*
From the Sacco-Vanzetti series of twenty-three paintings
(1931–32). Tempera on paper over composition board,
10½ x 14½″ (26.7 x 36.8 cm).   Collection,
© The Museum of Modern Art, New York, 1985.
Gift of Abby Aldrich Rockefeller.

(Continued on p. 707)

combined with that on punishment into Chapter 14, "Disposition of the Convicted Offender."

Part V, "Social Reaction to Crime: Corrections," has been shortened considerably. All of the chapters, however, have been updated with the most current legal and sociological materials available at the time of writing.

Chapter 15, "The Modern Prison," focuses on the problem of overcrowding in our prisons and discusses the implications of that situation for prison management, prison staff, and prison violence. Chapter 16, "The Inmates' World," looks at the inmate social system, prison programs, and treatment of prisoners. Chapter 17, "Corrections in the Community," analyzes the problems inmates face when they leave prison and explores attempts to reintegrate ex-offenders into the community. Release on parole is included in this discussion.

Finally, the Epilogue assesses "where we are" and includes brief discussions of recent material, such as the 1983 data on crime and major Supreme Court decisions in criminal justice, that were not available during the writing of the seventeen chapters of the text.

Technical as well as nontechnical terms are defined in a comprehensive glossary following the text. All glossary items are listed in the index and are boldfaced for easy identification on the pages where they appear.

ACKNOWLEDGMENTS

Writers must assume responsibility for their work, but the success of this text through the second and third editions, as well as the present edition, must be shared with my friend and colleague, Lorna Keltner. In particular, Lorna drafted the revisions of Chapters 15, 16, and 17. But beyond her legal and sociological expertise are the invaluable contributions that she makes on a daily basis—the encouragement and the enthusiasm that are necessary to keep one going when the work is long and tedious.

Under Lorna's guidance, several students assisted with the research at various stages of this edition. Our gratitude goes to Sharon Bell and Patrick Kelley for their work in the earlier stages of the revision, to Michael McGuire and Brenda Lucas who worked with us throughout the project, and to Ronnie Powell, John Decker, and Lyn Markham, who joined us during the later stages of the second draft. June Marler supplied technical accuracy and enthusiasm during numerous hours of typing the manuscript.

My sister Jill Pickett assisted the research as well as typing. She, her family, and our parents continue to provide the support, love, and understanding that are so important to writers, who must of necessity spend many hours alone in the study and who as a result do not "emerge" often enough for social gatherings.

Earl McPeek, Acquisitions Editor, joined the staff at Holt, Rinehart and Winston during the production phase of this book and provided his guidance and support in the later stages. Roz Sackoff, Senior Developmental Editor, once again provided editorial expertise, encouragement, and a tremendous sense of humor to assist me in keeping the work in perspective. Roz has now served as the developmental editor for five of my books, but her enthusiasm has never flagged, and her work continues to be of the highest caliber. Senior Project Editor Françoise Bartlett oversaw and coordinated all of the day-to-day activities that turn a manuscript into a bound book. Mary Root Taucher also contributed immeasurably to this edition.

Numerous reviewers have made editorial suggestions, and to all of them I owe a special thanks. At various stages, the following individuals assisted with this edition: Leo Carroll, University of Rhode Island; Robert Culbertson, Illinois State University; Gilbert Geis, University of California, Irvine; Joan Neff Gurney, University of Richmond; Patricia Harvey, Colorado State University; Jay Livingston, Montclair State University; Terry Norris, Columbus College, Georgia; Joseph Rogers, New Mexico State University; Carol M. Smeja, University of Georgia; Maria Volpe, John Jay College; and Franklin P. Williams III, Sam Houston State University. In particular, I would like to thank Franklin P. Williams III and Marilyn McShane for writing the *Instructor's Manual.*

I am also grateful to my friends and colleagues at the University of Tulsa for their support during the initial stages of this manuscript.

Finally, I would like to express my special appreciation to Victor G. Strecher, Dean of the Criminal Justice Center at Sam Houston State University in Huntsville, Texas. During the final stages of the writing of this edition, and the production of the book, I occupied the George Beto Chair at the Criminal Justice Center. The support of Dean Strecher, his staff, and the faculty and students of Sam Houston's Criminal Justice Center were invaluable during those final days of work on the book. I express my sincere appreciation for the opportunity to have worked with all of them.

Huntsville, Texas   S.T.R.
January 1985

CONTENTS

PART 1

INTRODUCTION TO THE STUDY OF CRIME

CHAPTER 1

Law and crime

The focus of this chapter is on the formal method of law as an instrument for controlling behavior. Specifically, we shall examine the elements of the criminal law, followed by a discussion of the purpose of the criminal law. Clearly, one purpose is to prevent and control *criminal* behavior, but there is considerable debate over what should be considered a crime. We shall study the use of the criminal law to control behaviors that many people consider "private," and therefore "their own business." Alcohol and drug abuse and some types of sexual behavior between consenting adults are discussed to illustrate the problems of the negative effects of attempting to control such behavior by law. At the same time, we note the need to exercise some control over these behaviors when they do infringe on public safety and health.

**THE CONCEPT
OF LAW**

THE IMPORTANCE
OF LAW

Law is important because it touches virtually every area of social interaction. Law is used to protect ownership; to define the parameters of private and public property; to regulate business; to raise revenue; and to provide for redress when agreements are broken—for example, in contract law.

Laws allow civil damages for those who are harmed by others—from injuries caused in automobile accidents to slander and assault and battery. The law is also used to uphold certain institutions, such as the family. Laws regulate marriage and divorce or dissolution, the handling of dependent and neglected children, and the inheritance of property. Laws in some states attempt to protect marriage by providing civil suits for the alienation of the affection of a spouse. Laws are also designed to protect the legal and political system. Laws organize power relationships. They establish who is superordinate and who is subordinate in given situations. Laws maintain the status quo but also provide for needed changes. Finally, laws, especially criminal laws, not only protect private and public interests but also preserve order. Society determines that some interests are so important that the informal social controls and mores are not sufficient, and therefore laws must be passed, giving the state the power of enforcement. Law thus becomes a formal system of social control that may be exercised when other forms of control are not effective.

FORMAL
COMPARED TO
INFORMAL
SOCIAL
CONTROLS

Every society has certain functions that must be performed in order for the society to continue existing. In addition to providing for food, clothing, shelter, and reproduction of its members, societies must have ways to teach the young the social **norms*** of the group. This is accomplished through a process that sociologists call **socialization.**[1] The process of socialization means not only teaching the norms but also providing ways to encourage members to follow those norms. In simple societies, this process of socialization may be carried out by means of informal methods, but in more complex societies, formal methods, such as the criminal law, may be necessary.

*Folkways and
mores as social
controls*

An early sociologist, William Graham Sumner, called the informal methods of social control **folkways** and **mores.**[2] Folkways are the customary or routine ways of doing things, such as gathering wild fruits and vegetables and killing wild animals for a food supply. Likewise, if someone stole your cow, custom might permit you to take the cow back. And if a man raped your daughter, you might even be permitted to kill the person for revenge.

When these customary ways of solving problems become important to the welfare of society, they become mores and are then considered the "right"

*Terms in boldface type are defined in the Glossary.

or "wrong" ways to act. But not all folkways become mores, and thus it may not be important to the society whether you kill wild animals for food or gather wild fruits. It may, however, be very important whether you take action against someone who steals your cow or rapes your daughter. Private revenge, in many cases, was not only acceptable; it was expected, as it was thought that the society's welfare depended on such actions. Mores are not habits or customs that we may choose to avoid but are required behaviors. Mores tell people how to behave. According to Sumner, mores "coerce and restrict a newborn generation."

Among simple societies, mores were often sufficient for controlling behavior. One of the reasons for this was that behavior was easily observable; any deviance would be known. The fear of being socially ostracized by the group was apparently sufficient to "keep people in line." Thus, a disapproving glance, an embarrassed silence, a smile, a nod, a frown—all were effective in controlling most members of society. These informal methods are not as effective, however, in a more complex society. Thus, it is necessary to develop additional social controls, one of which is law. Laws cover various types of behavior; we will be concerned only with the criminal law in this text. But because of the overlap between criminal law and tort law, it is important to distinguish the two types of law.

CRIMINAL LAW AND TORT LAW COMPARED

Torts represent a significant body of law, although "a really satisfactory definition of a tort has yet to be found."[3] Torts include a variety of civil wrongs, ranging from slander and libel to assault and battery. Included are such actions as inflicting emotional distress on another, negligently injuring someone in an automobile, industrial, or another type of accident, false imprisonment, medical malpractice, and trespassing on property.

Many torts grew out of criminal laws. Some actions may be both torts and **crimes.** For example, when several young women were killed in a fiery crash when their Ford Pinto was hit from the rear, the state prosecuted the Ford Motor Company for criminal homicide and the parents of the young women sued Ford for the tort of wrongful death. Although the state lost its case (that is, the company was not found "guilty"), the tort actions resulted in damage awards as high as six million dollars.

The most important difference between criminal prosecution and civil actions is that in a criminal case, the accused is being punished by the state because the criminal act usually has repercussions on members of society in addition to the actual victim of the crime. Because crimes are considered to be more serious than civil actions, our system provides more safeguards and protections for defendants in criminal trials than are available in civil cases. But it is the concept of crime that provides the basis for our study of criminology.

DEFINITIONS OF CRIME The definition of crime must be precise, unambiguous, and usable. That is, the definition must permit us to determine who is and who is not a criminal. Various approaches have been used to define and study crime; some are legal and some are not. This text will emphasize the legal approach, for our system of criminal justice is based on a legal definition of crime.

LEGAL DEFINITION OF CRIME Crime is an act defined by law; unless the elements specified by criminal law are present and proved beyond a reasonable doubt, a person should not be convicted of a crime. The following legal definition will serve as our reference point:

> Crime is an intentional act or omission in violation of criminal law (statutory and case law), committed without defense or justification, and sanctioned by the state as a felony or misdemeanor.[4]

Crime is an intentional act or omission **Requirement of an act or omission of a legal duty.** The first part of the definition embodies some philosophies central to the American system of law: A person may not be punished for his or her thoughts; action must be taken. In some cases, words may be considered acts, as in treason or in aiding or abetting another to commit a crime; these are crimes. In those cases it can reasonably be argued that some "action" has been taken, but an individual cannot be punished under the American system of law for thinking about committing a crime if no elements are put into action toward the commission of that crime. To consider murdering a spouse but to do nothing toward the commission of that act is not a crime. However, hiring someone to murder the spouse is a crime.

The failure to act may also be a crime, but not unless there is a legal duty to act in a particular case. Moral duty will not suffice. Consider, for example, a man who spent the weekend with his mistress. After an argument she took an overdose of morphine tablets, and he did not call a physician to try to save her life. Although he may have been under a moral obligation to try to save her life, he was under no *legal duty*. Therefore his failure to assist her does not constitute crime. In this case, there was no contractual relationship, no statute providing that the man had a legal duty to aid in such a situation, and there was no status relationship that imposed a legal duty, such as the relationship of husband and wife. Finally, the defendant had not assumed such care of the woman that placed her in a position in which she could not get aid from anyone else except him. If he had taken her to an island where they were the only inhabitants, presumably he would have had a legal duty to try to get her to a doctor. In this case, the Michigan Supreme Court ruled that "the fact that this woman was in the house created no such legal duty as exists in law and is due from a husband towards his wife. . . . Such an inference would be very repugnant to our moral sense."[5]

If, however, it had been shown that the man had committed a crime toward the deceased and that that crime had led her to commit suicide, he could have been charged with her death. Consider the case in which a man raped a twelve-year-old child who then jumped or fell into a creek and drowned. He was convicted of second-degree **murder**, as the court ruled that he had a legal duty to try to save her life, because he caused her peril.[6]

Acts or omissions, in order to be criminal, must also have been voluntary, and that presumes that the actor had control over his or her actions. If a person has a heart attack while driving a car and kills another human being, he or she cannot be convicted of the crime of **manslaughter,** as the heart attack was an involuntary act over which the person had no control. The case would be different, however, if the individual had had a series of heart attacks and therefore knew it might be dangerous to drive an automobile.

Requirement of intent An act or the omission of an act is not alone sufficient to constitute a crime. The law requires criminal **intent,** or **mens rea,** the mental element required to establish culpability. This element is extremely important, for in many cases it will be the critical factor in determining whether an act was or was not a crime. It may also determine, in the case of a crime, the type of crime committed (for example, whether a **homicide** is first- or second-degree murder or a type of manslaughter). Despite the importance of *mens rea,* historically the term has not been clearly defined or developed. More recently, the American Law Institute, in its **Model Penal Code**, divided culpability into four mental states, "a person is not guilty of an offense unless he acted purposely, knowingly, recklessly or negligently, as the law may require, with respect to each material element of the offense."[7] The interpretation of these four tiers of culpability has been the subject of considerable dispute. It is clear, however, that one may be held criminally liable for the unintended consequences of an intended act. One may also be held criminally liable for injury or death to a victim other than the intended victim or for a more serious degree of harm than that intended. Consider the following examples.

In the first case, Jones shot at Anders with the intent of killing him, but being a bad shot, he missed Anders and killed Williams instead. Jones, thus, might be held for the death of the victim.

Or consider the case of the unhappy husband who wanted to move to an inexpensive apartment. He could not convince his wife to leave their home, which she wished to refurnish. He thereupon decided to scare her in order to change her mind about living in the house, and so he hired a man to fire several shots into the air while his wife was out walking the dog. This man, too, was a bad shot and killed the woman. Even though there was no specific intent to kill the woman, both men were charged with murder. They had plotted, and one did carry out, an act that a reasonable person should have known could have resulted in serious injury or death. It is possible, of course, that in such a case the charge would be reduced to reckless or negligent homicide. But the point is that the actors could be tried for murder.

In another example, the defendant, upon being asked to treat a woman, represented himself as a physician. He prescribed that she be wrapped in flannel soaked in kerosene oil and that this be kept wet by applying more kerosene every three hours. This was done with the consent of her husand and her attendants, but not of the victim. She later died of burns and blisters caused by the kerosene. The defendant requested that the jury be informed that if they found he had "an honest purpose and intended to cure the disease, he is not guilty of this offense (manslaughter) however gross his ignorance of the quality and tendency of the remedy prescribed, or of the nature of the disease, or of both." The court instructed the jury that "it is not necessary to show an evil intent . . . if by gross and reckless negligence he caused the death, he is guilty of culpable homicide." The jury returned a verdict of guilty of manslaughter.[8]

Exceptions to the requirement of intent. There are exceptions to this "requirement" of a criminal intent. First, under the doctrine of **respondeat superior** ("let the master answer"), a "master" is liable for certain acts of his or her "servants," even if he or she did not know they were committing the acts. **Scienter,** or knowledge of the act, is not required on the part of the superior. This is referred to as the concept of **strict liability** and, in tort law, is aimed mainly at legislation that protects the public. In one case, the president of a drug company was found guilty of violating a provision of the Pure Food and Drug Act that required the proper labeling of drugs. He personally did not know that the drugs had been mislabeled by those of his employees responsible for repackaging and labeling the drugs received from the manufacturer, but the United States Supreme Court upheld the conviction.[9]

A second major exception to the requirement of intent is the **felony-murder** doctrine, under which a person may be held criminally responsible for the death of another when the death is the result of the commission of another **felony** (a felony is a more serious crime than a **misdemeanor**), even though the death was not intended and was not the result of reckless or negligent behavior. Suppose, for example, a person commits the felony of arson by setting fire to a barn and several children playing inside the barn die as a result. The arsonist could be charged with the murder of those children. The doctrine, where applied in the United States, is usually limited to deaths that follow the commission of inherently dangerous felonies such as forcible **rape, robbery, arson,** and **burglary.**[10]

. . . In violation of criminal law To be convicted of a crime, a person must violate the **criminal law.** Criminal law comes from two sources: statutes and court decisions. State legislatures pass statutes that indicate which acts are considered criminal; those statutes then apply to actions in those states. Congress passes statutes that apply to

the commission of federal crimes (such as treason, kidnapping, assassinations of the president, and bank robbery).

In many cases, **statutory law** is a codification of laws that have evolved through custom and prior judicial decisions. The term **common law** is used to refer to laws of this type and comes from the English common law system that developed in England after the Norman Conquest in 1066. Before that time there was no distinction among law, custom, religion, and morality. Decisions might be different in different communities. The Normans, however, wanted to establish some unity, and to do so the king employed representatives to travel to the various jurisdictions. These representatives kept the king informed about the different **jurisdictions** and also carried news to each of what was happening in the others. "The result of all this was that the legal principles being applied began to be similar, or common, in all parts of England. Thus, the terms 'Common Law of England,' and 'Common Law.'"[11]

Because the common law was developed on a case-by-case basis, the term **case law** is often used synonymously with common law and is contrasted with written, or statutory, law. Case law is just as important as statutory law, and the English common law has had a deep influence on the development of law in the United States.

Common law offenses have been kept alive and interpreted by judicial decisions, which are an important part of American law today. Even when state legislatures enact laws to cover the common law offenses, the interpretation of those statutes is often left to common law decisions. This is seen in federal courts, in which a person cannot be punished for a common law crime unless it is enacted by Congress into a statute. Once that occurs and Congress provides a penalty for the offense, the courts may resort to the common law for interpretations of those statutes.

The reality and the importance of the common law was proclaimed by the famous jurist Oliver Wendell Holmes, Jr.:

> The common law is not a brooding omnipresence in the sky, but the articulate voice of some sovereign or quasi-sovereign that can be identified.[12]
>
> The life of the law has not been logic, it has been experience . . . in order to know what it is, we must know what it has been, and what it tends to become. . . . The very considerations which judges most rarely mention, and always with an apology, are the secret root from which the law draws all the juices of life.[13]

Administrative law

One further type of law should be noted, and that is **administrative law.** The legislatures of the states and the Congress of the United States often delegate to administrative agencies—the Federal Trade Commission, parole boards, public universities, human rights commissions, and others—the power to make rules that regulate the governing of those institutions. The rules must be made following certain specified guidelines. When actions, even if they involve violations of the criminal law, are handled by administrative agencies, as opposed to the courts, such actions are not considered in terms of criminal law. The administrative agency, upon report of a violation, will conduct a hearing that does not involve all of the elements of **due process** of a criminal **trial**. The agency may issue certain orders. For example, in the case of a restaurant owner who violates food and drug laws, the agency might issue a "cease and desist" order, but no one thinks of that order as "criminal." If the restaurant owner refuses to obey, the agency may then take the case to court and get a court order, which, if violated, may constitute contempt of court. Even in that case, the **offender** is not looked upon by society in the same negative light with which society typically views persons who are convicted in criminal courts. Data on such administrative decisions are not included in the Federal Bureau of Investigation (FBI) data on crime.

... Committed without defense or justification   The next part of the legal definition of crime is that the act or omission of an act is not a crime if the individual has a legally recognized defense or justification for the act. Individuals are not, then, responsible for all acts that cause harm or injury to others; the law recognizes some extenuating circumstances. But historically, this has not always been the case.

Defenses that may be raised are insanity, intoxication in some cases, mistake of fact, ignorance of the law, duress, consent of the victim, entrapment, and justification. An explanation of all of these and the exceptions involved would require a course in criminal law and procedure, and so only a few examples that, at least in some jurisdictions, might be sufficient to enable the actor to escape conviction of a criminal act, will be considered here.

Justification.   A person faced with the possibility of death from another individual might use the defense of *justifiable homicide* for killing that individual. For example, a police officer, in pursuit of an armed robbery suspect who fires at the officer, may be justified in killing that suspect. It is not required that the officer actually be facing death. It is sufficient that it would be reasonable for the officer to think that the suspect will kill either the officer or another person. People may also be excused from criminal liability for inflicting serious bodily harm on others if they are in danger of being injured by these persons. But people who kill or injure to protect themselves or others may use only the extent of force necessary for that protection.

Mistake of fact.   Mistake of fact may also be a defense to a crime. A rather unusual case illustrates this defense. One evening an eighteen-year-old went to bed and, as was her custom, wore no clothing. The defendant, who was walking on the sidewalk outside the house, saw the nude girl through her open bedroom window. He decided to pay her a social visit. Before climbing onto the windowsill, he removed all his clothing. The young woman, who had been intimate with her boyfriend at the house earlier that evening, held out her arms upon seeing the young man and thereby welcomed him into the room. However, after they had had sexual relations, she decided he was not her boyfriend, turned on the light, and slapped him. In this case, the defendant might have had a defense of mistake of fact. Because the woman held out her arms to him, he could have reasonably thought he was being invited into the room; therefore, he could not be convicted of trespassing. The crucial legal point in this case was where he was when she held out her arms. "[I]f he was on the sill outside the window when he thought that she was inviting him to come in, then he would not have been a trespasser, but, if he had entered the room intending to join her in bed before she held out her arms, then he was a trespasser." This is referred to as a *narrow point of law.*[14]

Entrapment   **Entrapment** is a defense often used in the types of crimes we shall discuss later in this chapter: drugs and sex. The defense may be used successfully when a police officer, or someone acting as the agent of a law enforcement officer, entraps a person to commit a crime. The defense is generally limited to less serious crimes, in most cases to the so-called **victimless crimes** such as solicitation and sale of controlled substances (like narcotics). The defense would not be available for crimes such as rape and murder.

The governmental agent, however, may provide an *opportunity* for someone to commit a crime, and that does not constitute entrapment. "To determine whether entrapment has been established a line must be drawn between the trap for the unwary innocent and the trap for the unwary criminal." Of course, that line is hard to draw, but the Supreme Court recognized the defense in one case involving a government informer who first met the petitioner in a doctor's office where both were undergoing treatment for narcotics addiction. Several accidental meetings followed, either at the doctor's office or at the pharmacy where the two men had their prescriptions filled. Finally, the informer asked the petitioner if he knew of a good source for purchasing illegal narcotics. The petitioner at first ignored the questions, and only after repeated requests in which the informer proclaimed that he was really suffering for lack of drugs, did the petitioner finally acquiesce. After several occasions on which the petitioner sold drugs to the agent, he was arrested. The Supreme Court overturned the conviction, ruling that this petitioner was "induced" by the agent. The brief excerpt from the case below gives the reasons that the Court considered this a case of entrapment.[15]

Sherman v. United States

The case at bar illustrates an evil which the defense of entrapment is designed to overcome. The government informer entices someone attempting to avoid narcotics not only into carrying out an illegal sale but also into returning to the habit of use. Selecting the proper time, the informer then tells the government agent. The set-up is accepted by the agent without even a question as to the manner in which the informer encountered the seller. Thus the Government plays on the weaknesses of an innocent party and beguiles him into committing crimes which he otherwise would not have attempted. Law enforcement does not require methods such as this.

. . . Sanctioned by the state as a felony or misdemeanor

The categories of felony and misdemeanor are important in the legal definition of crime. Initially, in common law, a felony was a crime for which a person could be required to forfeit all property. That was the main distinction between felonies and misdemeanors. Common law felonies were murder, manslaughter, forcible rape, **sodomy**, **larceny**, robbery, arson, and burglary. Over time, other felonies, such as statutory rape, have been added by statute.

Today the distinction between felony and misdemeanor is made mainly in terms of the sentence that may be imposed. Generally, felonies are crimes for which a person may be **sentenced** to death or imprisoned for long periods of time. Misdemeanors are the less serious offenses for which a **fine** or short-term incarceration may be provided. The distinction is important. It determines, for example, how much force the **police** may use in apprehending a suspect. It may also influence police decisions regarding **arrest** and **prosecutors'** prosecutorial decisions concerning **charging** and **plea bargaining**. It may also determine in which court the case may be tried.

NONLEGAL DEFINITIONS OF CRIME

Under the legal definition in American law, a person is or becomes a criminal only when he or she has been convicted of having broken the law by committing an act previously defined in law as a crime.

Some researchers in criminology have, however, taken a broader approach to the study of crime. In many studies the focus is on violations of the criminal law, regardless of the legal disposition of those cases. Thus, one who has violated the law but who has been acquitted by a **jury** in a proper trial, might still be studied as "criminal." The goal is to discover the reasons that most people, not just those who are convicted, violate the law. Consider the following example.

In March 1983, a seventy-nine-year-old Fort Lauderdale, Florida, man went to the hospital to visit his sixty-two-year-old wife, who was suffering from a disease that would eventually make her senile and helpless. The husband had earlier placed his wife in a nursing home because he was unable to care for her, but when she became too ill to be cared for properly in that facility, she was hospitalized. While she was in the hospital, her husband, during his daily visits, placed her in a wheelchair and wheeled her around the floor of the hospital to give her a change of scenery. On the day in question, he wheeled her into a stairwell and shot her in the head, quickly ending her life. According to a neighbor, "He's no murderer. He did it out of love because she was suffering so much."[16]

When he testified before the grand jury that was to consider whether he should be indicted, he said, "I was afraid I missed or something and only hurt her." His lawyer testified, "He had a wife who was a living body with no mind." (She had a mysterious disease that had ravaged her brain several years earlier.) The Florida **grand jury** refused to return an indictment for any crime, although they could have indicted the husband for first-degree murder, a crime that in Florida may result in the death penalty.[17] Consequently, the man was never tried. If we use a strict legal definition of crime, he would not be included. Yet, he killed a person without the benefit of any legally recognized defenses.

One of the best-known proponents of a nonlegal definition of crime is the criminologist Thorsten Sellin. He emphasizes that nonscientists should not be permitted to define the subject matter for scientists—lawyers and legislators should not be permitted to tell social scientists how crime must be defined. He does not claim that there is no place for the legal definition in criminology; rather, "that if a science of human conduct is to develop, the investigator in this field of research must rid himself of shackles which have been forged by the criminal law." Sellin then goes on to discuss the development of what he calls **conduct norms,** ways of doing things that are developed by a group through social interaction. "For every person . . . there is from the point of view of a given group of which he is a member, a normal (right) and an abnormal (wrong) way of reacting, the norm depending upon the social values of the group which formulated it." These conduct norms are socially defined and differ from group to group and are not necessarily codified into law. In the end, Sellin prefers, rather than extend the legal definition of crime, to leave that as it is and refer to violations of conduct norms, which are not illegal, as abnormal conduct.[18]

ANALYSIS OF DEFINITIONS OF CRIME

Paul Tappan maintained that nonlegal definitions were too loose, too ambiguous, and left too much room to the definer to determine what crime was:

> Whether criminology aspires one day to become a science or a repository of reasonably accurate descriptive information, it cannot tolerate a nomenclature

of such loose and variable usage . . . [with regard to definitions of white-collar crime]. The rebel may enjoy a veritable orgy of delight in damning as criminal almost anyone he pleases. . . .

Vague, omnibus concepts defining crime are a blight upon either a legal system or a system of sociology that strives to be objective. They allow judge, administrator, or conceivably sociologist, in an undirected, freely operating discretion, to attribute the status "criminal" to any individual or class which he conceives nefarious. This can accomplish no desirable objective, either politically or sociologically.[19]

The term *crime* should be used only in its strict legal definition and the term *criminal* used only to refer to those who have been convicted in the criminal courts. The terms *crime* and *criminal* have severe implications and repercussions, and they should be used only after proper procedures for establishing which acts are criminal, as in the case of defining *crime,* or, in the case of *criminal,* after the defendant has been through a criminal trial and guilt has been decided by a **judge** or jury. This is not to suggest, however, that the nonlegal definitions are not important. From the point of view of the causes of human behavior, it is important for social scientists to study the behavior of persons who have committed criminal acts but who have not been processed through the criminal justice system to the point of conviction.

THE PURPOSE OF THE CRIMINAL LAW

Clearly, the criminal law should be used to regulate criminal activity. The problem, of course, is to define crime. We have looked at the legal definition of crime and explored the elements of that definition. But that explanation does not resolve the problem of what behavior should be included within those elements.

THE CONTROL OF CRIME

The seriousness of the impact of the criminal law should lead us to question very carefully what kinds of behavior ought to be covered by the reach of the law. Consider a few examples. In 1983, in a bar in New Bedford, Massachusetts, a woman was gang raped while a crowd of drinkers stood by watching. Two men were convicted of aggravated rape, two were convicted of assault with intent to rape, and two were acquitted. No one made any effort to stop the crime. Should those observers have been made criminally responsible for the crime, or should criminal liability be limited only to the perpetrators of the crime? This case raises the issue of whether the criminal law should impose an affirmative duty to act to prevent a crime. In general, the legal answer is no, although there may be an ethical duty to act.

In 1982, an interesting situation arose in Los Angeles, California, when public health officials began throwing into garbage cans "Peking ducks" that they found in restaurants. The Chinese, who have been preparing these ducks for four thousand years, were violating a health regulation concerning refrigeration of food. According to the state code, the duck had to be either chilled to 45 degrees or less or heated to at least 140 degrees, at all times. According to the Chinese, "If we put it in the refrigerator, the skin won't be crispy. If we put it in the heat too long, the meat will be tough and dry. . . . If we cooked it according to the health department, no one would come to buy our duck."

Some health experts said that the method of preparing Peking duck did not pose a health problem, although it did violate the health codes. "This is an old traditional method of preparation . . . and it has never been implicated in any cases of food poisoning." The real issue for our concern, however, was noted by one of the restaurant owners who said,

> If we had a big epidemic, that'd be one thing . . . the spirit of the law is to protect the public. But if you try to enforce to the letter a law which is a bad law you've got to try to change it. I'm for protecting the public. But when food is not contaminated, and you condemn it, it's a sin.[20]

Both of these cases raise the question of how extensive the law should be. Obviously, we need to protect the public health, but do we need to do so in a case that violates the technical law but creates no health problem? Obviously, we should try to prevent rape, but should we do that by imposing on all people who witness a crime, an affirmative duty to help prevent that crime? Must they do so at the risk of danger to themselves? And if we decide to regulate any or all of the above, should we do so by civil or criminal law (or both)? Finally, how should the law respond to activities such as homosexuality, **prostitution,** the use of alcohol or drugs, and suicide? These activities involve what some people call **victimless crimes,** actions that relate only to the person involved. On the other hand, it is argued that we all are harmed by such actions.

Distinction between mala in se *and* mala prohibita *crimes*

The disagreement concerning which acts should be included in the criminal law requires recognizing the difference between acts that are **mala in se** and those that are **mala prohibita.** *Mala in se* refers to acts that are evil in themselves—rape, murder, robbery, arson, aggravated assault, and so on. There is general agreement that such acts are criminal.[21] In contrast, crimes *mala prohibita* are those that are evil because they are forbidden, such as traffic offenses. Until the recent past, the use of contraceptives in some states was illegal, and abortion, except to save the life of the pregnant woman, was illegal. These acts were crimes because they were prohibited; clearly, there is no general agreement that the acts are criminal in themselves.

Historically there has been little difference between *mala in se* and *mala prohibita* crimes, because in primitive societies, morality, sin, and law are usually not distinguished. In both ancient Greece and Egypt "law, morals, and religion were integrated into a single idea."[22] The meaning of the word

---

HIGHLIGHT
CRIMES AGAINST THE PERSON

"'Rape' was not a word much used in Victorian England, and none of the euphemisms so dear to the heart of the nineteenth-century journalist . . . fits this most extreme of sexual crimes—with the exception of sexual murder. 'Outrage' was the favorite, but the roll of indignation-arousing nouns and adjectives was too often exhausted by minor misdemeanours, as witness, the Valentine Baker case of 1876, where a kiss and an arm round a waist was described by a member of parliament as 'one of the most scandalous and atrocious crimes ever committed.'"

Source: Ronald Pearsall, "Perversion," chap. 7 in *The Worm in the Bud: The World of Victorian Sexuality* (Middlesex, England: Penguin Books, 1983), p. 388. (First published by Weidenfeld & Nicolson, 1969.)

---

for crime in different languages can give some indication of how nations view crime and morality. In French and English law, for example, crime simply means a breaking of the law. In Hungarian, crime means not only a legally prohibited act but also a sinful act or evil fault. In Roman law, the word *crime* comes from *crimen,* which meant what was expressed by the earlier word *delictum:* "fault, sinning, an act against morality the fundamentals of which were common to all."[23]

THE CONTROL OF MORALITY

The meshing of sin and crime has led us to conceive of the criminal law as having as one of its purposes the control of morality.[24] This purpose, however, has historically been and today remains an issue of considerable debate. Some argue that the law "overreaches"[25] or "overcriminalizes,"[26] that crimes, such as drug and alcohol abuse and consensual sexual behavior, are actions that harm only the people involved.

Substance abuse: alcohol and drugs

The historical fact, however, is that the law has been and still is being used to attempt to regulate morality and immorality. For example, the use and abuse of alcohol and drugs, and the legal reaction in this country to such abuse,[27] clearly illustrate the successes and problems with attempting to control "moral" behavior by law. It is impossible to separate these two kinds of substance abuse in terms of effect, as many people may be classified as both alcohol and drug abusers. For our purposes of analysis, however, there are some differences both historically and currently; so we shall look first at alcohol and then at drug abuse before discussing the impact of each on criminal behavior.

Alcohol   December 5, 1983, marked the fiftieth anniversary of the repeal of Prohibition, a "celebration" that could be marked by the fact that Americans that year spent $59 billion on alcohol, with an estimated additional $49 billion consumed by alcohol-related work loss, accidents, sickness, and death.[28] Alcohol is also blamed for 100,000 deaths each year, and there are a reported thirteen million alcoholics and problem drinkers in this country.[29] These figures indicate that the effects of alcohol create more than "personal" problems; there are reactions that affect society as well. The result, historically, has been a series of attempts to legislate in this area.

In 1919, we began to legislate liquor in the extreme—by passing the Eighteenth Amendment to the United States Constitution, prohibiting the manufacture, sale, and transportation of intoxicating liquors. According to a columnist writing fifty years after this experiment ended:

> It made life both better and worse. With 170,000 saloons closed, alcohol consumption was cut by as much as half, as were arrests for disorderly conduct and drunkenness. The death rate for cirrhosis of the liver was cut two-thirds . . . [but it also] lessened faith in government, made it adventurous and profitable to dare the law, and human to admire those who did it.[30]

The Eighteenth Amendment did not prohibit drinking liquor—it just attempted to make it more difficult to obtain. Violations of the law were rampant, and bootlegging became acceptable to most people. Thus the experiment failed and national Prohibition was repealed in 1933. The result is that we can legally make, sell, and use liquor, but the criminal law is still used to control public drunkenness as well as driving under the influence of alcohol and regulating the age at which young people may legally buy liquor. The use of the law to regulate in these areas illustrates the need to distinguish between behavior that affects others and behavior that is, for the most part, private. Driving under the influence of alcohol is a serious problem that often results in accidents that kill and injure thousands. There is evidence, as we shall see in a later chapter, that criminalizing this behavior and strictly enforcing these laws, does have a **deterrent** effect.

These two uses of the criminal law to regulate alcohol may very well be an appropriate use of the criminal law, but they must be distinguished from using that law to define as criminal all manufacture and sales of alcohol (as during Prohibition) or public drunkenness. Yet, public drunkenness has been defined as criminal behavior. The public drunk who threatens no one but who is a danger only to himself or herself and an inconvenience to others, accounts for 35 to 50 percent of all arrests on charges of drunkenness.[31]

Many of those arrested for public drunkenness are "homeless, penniless, and beset with acute personal problems."[32] Most are arrested more than once, and many spend so much time in jail that they have been described as serving a life sentence on the installment plan. Such persons are not aided by being placed in jail and, as a result of enforcing criminal laws in this area, the police are diverted from other, more important functions.

Today, the trend with regard to public drunkenness and alcoholism is toward treatment and rehabilitation, not prosecution for criminal behavior.[33] A Georgia statute, passed in 1974, illustrates this trend:

> It is the policy of this State that alcoholics may not be subject to criminal prosecution because of their consumption of alcoholic beverages but rather should be afforded a continuum of treatment in order that they may lead normal lives as productive members of society.[34]

Drugs   The criminal law is used even more extensively in the area of drug use than in attempts to regulate the use of alcohol, but this has not always been the case in the United States. In the latter half of the 1800s and the early part of the 1900s, drugs could be purchased in this country by anyone without penalty. But gradually, laws were passed to regulate the sale and use of drugs. Recently, President Ronald Reagan and his administration declared "war" on drugs, aimed mainly at the sale of drugs, especially drug trafficking by pushers associated with **organized crime.** In early 1982, it was announced that the FBI had been assigned **jurisdiction** to investigate drug offenses. According to Attorney General William French Smith, "For the first time since its establishment over 50 years ago, the full resources of the FBI will be added to our fight against the most serious crime problem facing our nation—drug trafficking." The FBI efforts are coordinated with those of the Drug Enforcement Administration, the United States attorneys, and other agencies in the Department of Justice, as well as other federal agencies.[35]

President Reagan announced in late 1982 that the Justice Department would form twelve special task forces across the country. Composed of agents from various federal agencies, the teams were to concentrate on the large networks of drug distribution. By May of 1983, however, it was reported that the plan for these teams was falling behind schedule, even though Congress had appropriated $127.5 million for the program for the balance of their fiscal year.

Drugs, like alcohol, involve some problems that many people agree should be included in the criminal law. The production and sale of dangerous narcotics are examples. There is not, however, much agreement on the criminalization of the possession of small amounts of drugs such as marijuana, the use of which is considered by many people to be a private matter. That issue is clearly debatable, but the critical issue still remains as to whether the *criminal law* should be used to control this behavior. Is this an effective use of the criminal law? The chief of the Justice Department's organized crime section stated, in emphasizing its lack of success in controlling the general drug problem, "You can't take a problem that is a medical, social and law enforcement problem, and hold law enforcement responsible for solving the whole problem by itself."[36]

Sexual behavior   Another area in which the law attempts to regulate private behavior is illustrated by legislative attempts to regulate consensual sexual behavior. We are not talking about sex by force or sex with children, which will be discussed in later chapters; rather, our discussion will be limited to private, consensual sexual behavior by adults.

Norval Morris and Gordon Hawkins, who have written extensively on using the law to regulate moral behavior, have emphasized that with the possible exception of John Calvin's sixteenth-century Geneva, the United States has the most moralistic criminal law in history. They refer to sex offense laws as possibly designed "to provide an enormous legislative chastity belt encompassing the whole population and proscribing everything but solitary and joyless masturbation and 'normal coitus' inside wedlock."[37]

Fornication. "Prostitution may be our oldest profession; fornication is surely among our oldest crimes."[38] The word **fornication** comes from the Latin word for brothel *(fornix)* and legally means "unlawful sexual intercourse between two unmarried persons." If one of the parties is married and the other unmarried, the latter is committing fornication and the former adultery, a crime that often carries a harsher penalty. In some jurisdictions, however, if either party involved in the illicit relationship is married, the law considers that both parties are committing adultery.[39]

Although with the greater acceptance of cohabitation, defined legally as "living together as man and wife," many states have changed their statutes and now permit sexual relations in private between consenting persons, even though they are not married,[40] some jurisdictions have retained the statutes regarding fornication. The Idaho statute is an example:

> Any unmarried person who shall have sexual intercourse with an unmarried person of the opposite sex shall be deemed guilty of fornication, and, upon conviction thereof, shall be punished by a fine of not more than $300 or by imprisonment for not more than 6 months or both such fine and imprisonment; provided that the sentence imposed or any part thereof may be suspended with or without probation in the discretion of the court.[41]

HIGHLIGHT
THE CONTROL OF MORALITY—THE CHURCH OR THE STATE?

"What we did for Marian" was out of love, so said the elders of the Church of Christ in Collinsville, a small community near Tulsa, Oklahoma. The elders were reacting to the $390,000 damage award—"The Will of the Lord"—decided in favor of Marian Guinn, who sued the elders and the members of the church for invading her privacy and causing her "extreme emotional distress."

Guinn, a young divorced mother of four, had joined the church but was not attending regularly when an elder informed her that she should not be dating the former mayor, a divorced man. "He is not suitable for you," she was told. When the former mayor called one of the elders about another matter, he was asked about his relationship with Guinn, and he admitted that it was an intimate one. The elder confronted Guinn; she admitted that she was having an affair. She was told that she must end the relationship, come back into the church, and repent before all the members. Guinn refused and personally delivered a handwritten letter to the elders. In this letter she indicated that she wished to resign from the church and that the information she gave to the elders about her personal life should be kept confidential. She was assured that it would be, but the letter was later read to the congregation. She was told that she could not resign, "We have to withdraw from you."

The elders claim that it was their duty to inform Marian that by engaging in fornication, she was commiting a sin, that she must stop, and that she must repent. If they did not attempt to "save" her, they too would be guilty for her sin. But Guinn, her attorney, and the jury, took a different view—the elders had invaded Guinn's personal rights.

The Oklahoma case has gained national attention; it has been the subject of "60 Minutes" on television and will become a movie. Shortly after the award was announced, a similar suit was filed in San Jose, California, by a man who confided in a counselor in his church, giving him details of his marital and sexual problems. "That material that I gave to him in confidence, six weeks later, was publicly read before six hundred members of the church."

Although the criminal law may not be the best form of social control of morality, these cases illustrate that the church may not be, either. In exercising what church members consider to be their responsibility, they are invading the rights of their members. Our courts recognize as torts the violation of the right of privacy, as well as the subjecting of others to "extreme emotional distress," for which the individuals who have suffered the "civil wrong" may sue in civil court. In the case of Guinn, the jury awarded actual damages—a measure of money that is to "compensate" the victim for the injury. The jury also awarded punitive damages, "smart money" designed to deter this kind of activity.

Source: Information taken from *Tulsa World,* March 28, 1984, p. 18, col. 2; March 16, 1984, p. 1, col. 1; and March 18, 1984, p. B1, col. 2; and various radio and television accounts of the Guinn lawsuit.

Sodomy statutes. Most typical of the statutes regulating sexual behavior are those prohibiting "deviant sexual acts." Usually these are **sodomy** statutes. Historically, sodomy has referred to both bestiality (intercourse between a human and an animal) and buggery (intercourse by a man with another man or with woman by the anus). In most jurisdictions in the United States, however, this crime has been interpreted to include other sexual acts considered by some to be deviant—for example, oral stimulation of the sexual organs.

The Wisconsin statute defining sexual perversion is an example of a sodomy statute. It provides a penalty of $500 or a prison sentence of not more than five years or both for any person who commits either of the following acts of "sexual perversion":

1. Commits an abnormal act of sexual gratification involving the sex organ of one person and the mouth or anus of another; or
2. Commits an act of sexual gratification involving his sex organ and the sex organ, mouth, or anus of an animal.[42]

But there is little attempt to enforce sodomy statutes except in the case of male homosexuals, and the statutes probably remain on the books for that purpose, with homosexuals claiming that they are often harassed by the police[43] for what they believe to be their own business. Again, the question arises—is this behavior something that we should attempt to regulate by law? Is it any of the "law's business" what people do in private?

In the past, the argument in favor of criminalizing sodomy was that the act was "unnatural," and indeed, many statutes, even today, refer to the crime as a "crime against nature." For example, the Idaho statute that reads, in part, "Every person who is guilty of the infamous crime against nature, committed with mankind or with any animal"[44] has been interpreted to include not only "the common-law crime of sodomy . . . but all unnatural carnal copulations, whether with man or beast, committed per os [mouth] or per anum [anus]."[45]

Another traditional argument for criminalizing sodomy (as well as prostitution) is to prevent the spread of disease. The recent focus on AIDS (acquired immunity deficiency syndrome), a deadly disease first discovered in 1979, has called attention to homosexuality as a health problem, as the incidence of the disease is higher among male homosexuals than any other group. About 40 percent of the people who contract the disease die, and so the public thus argues that it must be protected from the possibility of contracting the deadly disease and that this can be done only by controlling homosexuality. In one city, after people reacted with fear and panic upon hearing that a group of homosexuals had rented a public swimming pool for a party, the city had the pool drained.

Homosexuals claim that the publicity given to AIDS has given police another "reason" for harassing homosexuals.[46] After the initial panic died down, however, some organizations began to emphasize the need for research on AIDS. A private, medical AIDS foundation has been established in New York City, and Cornell University Medical College received a three-year $1.3 million grant by the National Institute of Health to study the disorder. Other medical institutes have also received grants for the study of AIDS, and in August 1983, the mayor of New York City signed into law a bill that provides $5.3 million for research into AIDS and community assistance to its victims.[47]

A few states have also revised their sodomy statutes. In 1961 the Illinois

"What's our official stand on sin?"

© 1985 by Sidney Harris. Reprinted by permission.

Criminal Code reflected this change. Although the new criminal code defines "deviant sexual conduct" as "any act of sexual gratification involving the sex organs of one person and the mouth or anus of another,"[48] the revised code does not prohibit such acts if they are voluntary, between consenting adults, and conducted in private.

Some other states have followed Illinois, but for the most part, we have retained many statutes that were designed to regulate sexual behavior. We have not been willing to accept the argument that these behaviors are personal to the individuals involved and have no "victims."[49] But it is important to distinguish between behavior that may be considered immoral or sinful by some but that has no victims and behavior that does have significant societal repurcussions.

ANALYSIS OF THE USE OF THE CRIMINAL LAW TO REGULATE MORAL BEHAVIOR

The basic argument in favor of using the law to regulate moral behavior is that the state has an interest in preserving the morals of its people. It is assumed that the threat of legal sanction will deter people from violating such laws. However, we have seen in our discussions of laws prohibiting behavior in the areas of alcohol and drug abuse and sexual behavior, that the formal social control of law is not always effective. But, goes the argument, even if the law does not prevent all people from engaging in these behaviors, it also serves as a symbol of morality;[50] it provides moral guidance. The law also creates group cohesion for those who conform.[51] To abolish these laws, it is argued, would give the acts an official stamp of approval, resulting in increased participation. This position is, of course, controversial but perhaps more importantly, it is difficult to measure the degree to which it is accurate. Furthermore, the evidence questions the position that, for example, the use of alcohol and drugs is strictly a private matter.

DRUGS, ALCOHOL, AND CRIME

To argue that the use of drugs and alcohol is a private matter is to ignore the impact that such usage has on the society.

The publication in 1983 of a Department of Justice report on prisoners and alcohol focused on the relationship between the use of alcohol and the commission of criminal activity. The study indicated an "excessive pre-prison involvement with alcohol on the part of a great many inmates." Even if some of the inmates exaggerated their reports of alcohol use, concluded the study, "it is clear that alcohol has played a major role in the lives of many prison inmates." Furthermore, almost one-half of the inmates said they had been drinking just before the commission of the criminal act for which they were incarcerated at the time of the study, with more than three-fifths reporting that they had been drinking heavily. This study was based on a 1979 survey of inmates and was the first such study on a nationwide

Drugs, alcohol, sex—private behavior or behavior that should be regulated by the criminal law?

basis to report drinking habits. "It established a greater degree of involvement with alcohol than had generally been anticipated."[52]

The National Council on Alcoholism reports that approximately 64 percent of murders, 41 percent of assaults, 34 percent of rapes, 29 percent of other sex crimes, 30 percent of suicides, 56 percent of fights or assaults in the home, and 60 percent of the cases of child abuse may be attributed to alcohol misuses. Furthermore, "when alcoholism is treated, associated violent behavior is known to decrease."[53] Such pronouncements should be analyzed carefully, however. The presence of alcohol abuse and crime does not necessarily mean that there is a direct cause-and-effect relationship. On the other hand, it is unreasonable to ignore the possible effect of alcohol abuse, present in so many instances when crimes are committed.

The relationship between drug use and crime was a major interest of Congress when, after amending the Omnibus Crime Control Act in 1976, it directed the National Institute of Law Enforcement and Criminal Justice to collaborate with the National Institute on Drug Abuse to explore the relationship between drug abuse and crime. As a result, an interagency multidisciplinary study team was appointed to review what we know about this relationship. As part of that study, the team produced a review of the literature on drug abuse and crime and concluded, "After reviewing the literature on the criminal behavior patterns of addicts it was difficult to avoid the conclusion that addicts engage in substantial amounts of income-generating crime."[54]

Finally, a sociologist, who has for many years studied the relationships between heroin use and crime, conducted interviews with 356 heroin users who had a long history of drug use. He concluded, "The data on current criminal activity clearly demonstrate not only that most of the heroin users were committing crimes, but also that they were doing so extensively and for the purpose of drug use support."[55]

THE LAW AND
DETERRENCE

Possibly the strongest argument against the laws that attempt to regulate morality is that they do not achieve the main purpose for which they are passed, ostensibly the **deterrence** of behavior.[56] The ineffectiveness of the law in controlling the abuse of alcohol is an example. There is evidence that today young people begin the use and abuse of alcohol at a very early age, even before the age of ten. Substance abuse among young people, as well as increased recognition of the problem, is evidenced by the recently developed centers for the treatment of alcoholism (as well as drug abuse) in young teen-agers. Recent studies have revealed a significant increase in problem drinking among women, particularly younger women, posing serious health problems as well as threats to unborn children. Alcoholic women also run a great risk of rape and unwanted pregnancies. With two out of three women using alcohol, according to a 1981 Gallup poll, the membership of women in Alcoholics Anonymous is the highest ever.[57] Recently, attention has been focused on the problem of alcoholism among priests and nuns, especially nuns, as they are less likely than priests to receive treatment. The National Clergy Council on Alcoholism reported that alcoholism among priests is at least as high as that of the general population.[58]

On the other hand, there is evidence that the increased penalties and the greater probability of arrest and conviction have had an impact on the abuse of alcohol while driving. The movement toward greater efforts to criminalize driving under the influence of alcohol and/or drugs has gained impetus in the past two years with the origin of two grass-roots organizations, MADD (Mothers Against Drunk Drivers), started by a California mother whose son was killed by a drunk driver, and RID (Remove Intoxicated Drivers).

During the recent emphasis on deterring drunk driving, most states have passed statutes stiffening their DUI (driving under the influence) laws and raised the age at which people may begin drinking legally, an age that had been lowered in many states during the past decade. Many jurisdictions have established programs for the treatment and counseling of problem drinkers arrested for DUI,[59] whereas local police, setting up roadblocks and using other methods, have increased the arrest rates, with an average now of 1.2 million arrests each year for drunken driving.

Under pressure from MADD and other similar organizations, in early 1982 the president established a thirty-member commission to work with

---

HIGHLIGHT

JUDGE FREES MAN JWI—JOGGING WHILE INTOXICATED

In November, 1983, a man was arrested for being "under the influence of alcohol and a roadway hazard." The man was jogging home from a bachelor party, thinking it would be better to jog than to drive. The judge agreed, saying "The statute concerns intoxicated pedestrians causing hazards to traffic. He may have been intoxicated, but there is no evidence that he was a hazard . . . I'd certainly rather have him jogging home than driving home."

Tulsa World, November 5, 1983, p. D14, col. 1.

---

state and local governments on the issue of drunk driving. Reagan stated: "Drunk driving and the gruesome toll it takes every day is the most often-committed violent crime in our country and has been allowed to become a national disgrace." Later in 1982, Congress passed a statute, providing seed money for states that enact certain types of laws aimed at controlling and preventing drunk driving. The federal government will provide funds for counseling and rehabilitation programs, with $25 million provided in fiscal year 1983 and $50 million for each of the following two years.[60]

But the authorities do not agree on the analysis of the results of the crackdown on DUI. Numerous states, for example, have reported more arrests and a lower death rate, along with mandatory jail sentences for drunk drivers. But others report that efforts to combat drunk driving are not effective unless accompanied by counseling and other forms of rehabilitation therapy, especially in regard to the chronic drunk, as compared with the social drinker. Still others—like sociologist H. Laurence Ross, who has studied the effects of legislation and other forms of social control on drinking behavior in several countries, including this one—conclude that such legislation has only a short-term effect when the drinking problem is treated as a moral issue rather than a question of safety.[61]

A recent study by the Department of Transportation (DOT) concluded that jailing drunk drivers might not be the most effective deterrent and that mandatory jail terms have proved to be costly and have also exacerbated the severe problem of jail overcrowding. The DOT also found that the more stringent laws are not always rigidly enforced. That is, some judges, who apparently think that the laws are too severe, circumvent them for first offenders, for example, by limiting sentences to the time already spent in jail "sleeping off" the effect of drinking.

The experience of Prohibition as well as the recent studies of the effect of legislation on the use and abuse of alcohol are difficult to interpret because so many other variables are involved in decisions concerning the use of alcohol. But these experiences may illustrate the futility of trying to legislate people's private behavior. They may also tell us that, at least in some cases, when that behavior becomes public to the point of endangering the welfare and lives of others, the strict enforcement of strict laws may be effective. But even if that is the case, the total impact of the law must also be recognized. That is, the enforcement efforts have an impact not only on drunk drivers and their families but also on the system's capacity to process and incarcerate those who are convicted. That total impact, along with alternatives, should be considered carefully before the power of the criminal law is used to regulate the behavior.

REACTIONS OF THE POLICE

In order to gain evidence of violations of statutes regulating morality, police usually must resort to techniques that invade privacy, as these crimes are usually committed in private. Many of the electronic eavesdropping and entrapment cases in American courts have dealt with attempts by the police to get evidence on drug or alcohol abuse, gambling, and sexual offenses. Police have posed as homosexuals, invaded public toilets in person or with electronic devices, and viewed or listened to some of the most private human behaviors in order to secure evidence of a law violation. The attempt to suppress vice often leads to corruption and demoralization of the police force. On occasion the police may become corrupt by joining in the illegal activities. Or they may become frustrated at attempts to "catch" violators and therefore begin to chisel away at procedural rights.

Finally, in attempting to control morality by law, the resources of the criminal justice system are diverted from other areas such as the protection of life and property.

DISCRIMINATION

Laws designed to regulate morality have also left the system of criminal justice wide open for discrimination. Sex discrimination in the enforcement of laws of prostitution is notorious. Laws regulating sodomy are usually enforced only against male homosexuals; such laws have also been used as a measure for deporting aliens, as they may be deported for "immoral behavior."[62] Finally, such laws may be selectively enforced on the basis of social class or other "extralegal" variables.[63]

SUMMARY AND CONCLUSION

In this chapter we have explored the purpose of the criminal law. Because the criminal law defines criminal behavior, thus formulating the basis for the kinds of behavior on which this study of criminology focuses, this discussion is important to setting the stage for the text. Many of the issues that will be raised throughout the text will in some way be related to the central issue of this chapter—what the purpose of the criminal law should be and what kinds of behavior should be included within its reach. The answers to those questions will largely determine who is and who is not a "criminal" and therefore who does and who does not constitute a basis for the study of criminology.

The inclusion or exclusion of morality within the reach of the criminal law will affect all elements of the criminal justice system. The rights of defendants versus the rights of victims and the right of society to be protected from criminal behavior will be affected. Crackdowns on drinking, especially while driving, have exacerbated the already-serious problems of jail and prison overcrowding. Removal of alcohol and drug use from the criminal law requires the provision of other kinds of institutions and facilities for handling such problems. And central to the entire discussion is the underlying theme of deterrence: we impose these sanctions in order to deter people from engaging in the proscribed behavior. Sociological contributions to our understanding of whether or not laws deter will be crucial in our continued analysis of the issue of deterrence.

What, then, should be the purpose of law? It has been argued that the main purpose of the criminal law is to protect persons and property from the abuse of others. "When the criminal law invades the spheres of private morality . . . it exceeds its proper limits at the cost of neglecting its primary tasks. This unwarranted extension is expensive, ineffective, and criminogenic."[64]

What should be included within the province of the criminal law? The president's crime commission, after noting that more research was needed to determine the best way to deal with many problems, concluded that at least enough is now known "to warrant abandonment of the common legislative premise that the criminal law is a sure panacea for all social ailments."[65]

Certainly the criminal law should be used to protect individuals from the use of force in the areas of behavior discussed in this chapter. For example, no person, adult or juvenile, should be forced to engage in any sexual behavior. The criminal law should penalize those who participate in sexual behavior with persons under the age of consent; that is, immature persons should be protected from sexual exploitation. The sexism of laws should be removed, and males as well as females should be protected against the unwilling viewing of sexual behavior; when consenting behavior is permitted, it should be restricted to places where one can reasonably expect privacy.

The law cannot, however, control the behavior of all people in a complex mass society. The law should provide some standards, some goals, some guidelines, a statement of what conduct is so important that it must be formally sanctioned. The law should also provide some moral guidance; but it should not be used to regulate behavior that is more properly regulated by other agencies or by individuals.

Nor should the law interfere with our rights of privacy: "Any attempt to criminalize all wrongful conduct would involve intolerable intrusions into citizens' lives and choices. Much wrongdoing in people's private and working lives should not be legally punishable because it involves areas of behavior which a free society should keep clear of the drastic intervention of the criminal law."[66]

Finally, law is "inherently social. Sociological perspectives and inquiries are necessary if we are to appreciate the social nature of law."[67]

CHAPTER 2

The measurement of crime and its impact

The focus of this chapter is on data on crime. We shall examine the official and unofficial ways in which data are collected on crimes, criminals, and victims of crime. The variables, such as police discretion, methods of reporting, the victims' cooperation or refusal to cooperate, and administrative and bureacratic changes, that may affect the accuracy of data are discussed. With this background on the problems of collecting data, we shall then turn to an analysis of the most recent data, looking at them in terms of the variables of age, race, and sex. The characteristics of victims of crime are considered in terms of race, sex and age variables. Finally, we shall consider whether we need a new perspective on crime data.

In 1968, for the first time in three decades of public opinion polling, Americans listed crime as the most serious national problem. At that time, crime rates were rising almost nine times as fast as was the population. Crime did not become an important political issue until the 1964 presidential campaign, although in 1960 the Democratic party platform had cursorily mentioned rising crime.[1] In 1965 Congress passed the Law Enforcement Assistance Act, and the President's Commission on Law Enforcement and Administration of Justice was established, which issued its volumes of reports in 1967. Since that time the National Advisory Commission on Criminal Justice Standards and Goals—appointed in 1971 and the first commission in this country formed for the purpose of formulating national criminal justice standards and goals for reducing and preventing crime—has also issued several reports, including one on disorders and terrorism, which reflects the growing concern with the increase in civil disorders and terrorism during the 1970s.

In the 1980s Americans have come to view inflation, the recession, and other domestic problems as more serious than the issue of crime, but considerable attention continues to be given to "law and order" issues. Increasing violence among juveniles as well as violence against the elderly has made many Americans fearful of being on the streets during the day as well as at night, and others are terrified even behind the locks and bars of their own homes. This fear of violent crime has led to a boom in the sales of locks, bars, and sophisticated crime-prevention alarm systems.

It will be the purpose of this chapter to look more carefully at the official and unofficial data on crime. The importance of this discussion cannot be overemphasized, and the reader should realize that in many respects all other discussions of crime hinge on such data. How we count crime and criminals greatly influences the theories we advance for "causation," and to a large extent it also influences the allocation of resources in the criminal justice system.

THE PERCEPTION OF CRIME

Popular articles on crime in America depict the country as being in a state of actual and perceptual crisis in regard to the incidence and fear of crime. According to a dramatic presentation by *Newsweek* in 1981, "Defying any cure [violent crime] overwhelms the police, the courts and the prisons—and warps U.S. life."[2] Criminologists have turned recently to analyses of public perceptions of crime, which has led them to examine media coverage and the public's reaction to that coverage. According to one study of television, there is an average of 1.7 crimes per television show, a much higher percentage of violence than is the case in real life. In addition, media misrepresent not only the incidences of crime but also the type and the persons involved. TV crime is much more violent than real crime, and the offenders are more often "brought to justice" than is the case in real life. By sensationalizing crime in this way, TV misses its opportunity to educate the audience about the actual dimensions of the crime problem in the United States.[3]

Sociologists know that perceptions are important in determining how the public will react. If we believe that crime is more extensive and more violent than it actually is, we may change our life-styles unnecessarily, and there is some evidence that this does occur. As the early sociologist W. I. Thomas said, "If men believe situations are real, they are real in their consequences." It is therefore important to have an accurate measure of crime and to convey that accuracy to the public. This raises two issues, measuring crime and altering the public perception of the extent of crime. We shall look at the latter first and then devote the remainder of the chapter to the topic of measuring crime and its impact.

Recent studies have revealed that the public agrees in their perceptions of the seriousness of crime,[4] but many researchers have concluded that the public's perceptions of crime are inaccurate[5] and that this inaccuracy is due to distorted presentations by the media. One investigator, after reviewing research by psychologists, political scientists, and sociologists, concluded that "in general, the available research shows that crime is a relatively staple topic in the media's news and entertainment presentations. The amount of crime depicted has little relationship to the amount of crime occurring, and violent crimes are highly overrepresented by the media." The research differs in its conclusions regarding the impact of this distortion. "On the other hand, the research strongly supports the notion that the viewing of violence increases the probability of behaving aggressively."[6]

Others have questioned the conclusion that the media present a distorted picture of crime, arguing that this conclusion is not based on empirical evidence, that there is no evidence that even if that is the case, the public bases its perceptions of crime totally on media presentations, or that, finally, the public accepts media presentations without critical analysis.[7] Empirical investigations have questioned these assumptions, finding, for example, that although the people who most often watch television tend to be the most afraid of crime, "when the effect of neighborhood is removed, the 'effect' of television is reduced to almost nothing."[8] Finally, there is some evidence, although tentative, that the public has fairly accurate perceptions of actual crime.[9] That, of course, assumes that actual crime can be measured, and it is to that issue that we shall devote the remainder of this chapter.

THE MEASUREMENT OF CRIME

In order for a science of criminal behavior to develop, it is necessary to have empirical data on criminals and to be able to analyze those data. First, however, we shall look briefly at the history of the scientific study of crime before we analyze the most recent crime data for this country.

THE EMERGENCE OF SCIENTIFIC CRIMINOLOGY: THE CARTOGRAPHIC SCHOOL

The **cartographic** school views crime as a necessary expression of social conditions, and indeed, even geographic phenomena are thought to influence criminal behavior. These phenomena include climate (temperature, humidity, barometric pressure, and so on), topography, natural resources, and geographic location.[10] Cartographic studies were made possible only when data became available on population distribution, births, and deaths. The systematic collection of such data did not begin, however, until the nineteenth century, in France with the work of André Michel Guerry and in Belgium with the work of Adolphe Quételet. Guerry's work is considered by many to be the "first work in 'scientific criminology'," and Quételet has been called "the first social criminologist."[11]

Guerry analyzed crime data by districts in France. He made charts, tables, and maps and studied the variables of age, sex, and education. He also classified crimes as those against property and persons. His purpose seemed to be to find those factors that predispose a person to criminal behavior rather than those factors that cause the behavior. He mapped not only regional variations in crime but also variations in per-capita rates of crime. In his analysis of the relationship between poverty and crime, he predated the modern sociologists, indicating that the important variable seemed to be the opportunity to commit crime. He rejected the simplistic explanation that increases in population density caused an increase in crime, as well as the belief that education would prevent criminal behavior.

Guerry's work appears to have been the first to use data on crime to test "armchair" assumptions about the relationship of certain variables to criminal behavior. He also questioned the belief that crime is the result of the offender's moral turpitude, by showing that there are objective facts associated with crime, and his cartographic method of presenting data was widely followed.

Like Guerry, Quételet was concerned with patterns and regularity found in the analysis of social data. A statistician, Quételet is sometimes called "the father of modern statistics," as he tried to measure social phenomena by means of statistics, and he published detailed analyses of crime and moral social conditions in Holland, Belgium, and France.[12]

Both Guerry and Quételet were important in influencing other researchers, particularly in England where researchers began to look at the relationship between crime and such factors as density of population, examining that density to see whether it produced or "**caused**" the crime or merely accumulated or attracted the types of people who were likely to engage in criminal activity.[13]

Although these early "researchers" are not often mentioned by sociologists and criminologists who are studying crime today, they were responsible for the beginning of scientific criminology, and their contributions should be accorded an important place in the development of criminological thought. Although they were naive about statistics and the principles of causation, their great value is that they did use quantitative techniques "with some skill" and that they categorically stated that "whatever the nature of individual motivation might be, the objective consequences of individual action, and the modes of its expressions are social phenomena par excellence, characteristic not of the individual, but of the collectivity of which he is but a part."[14] They thus paved the way not only for the measurement of crime but also for the analysis of crime according to relevant variables such as geography and climate,[15] as well as the more frequently used variables of age, sex, socioeconomic class, race, and ethnicity.

CURRENT SOURCES OF DATA ON CRIME

There are two basic sources for crime data in this country, official and unofficial. Official data come from governmental agencies and are collected for a variety of purposes. Unofficial data come from two sources: social science studies—which are of two types, self-report studies and survey studies of victimization—and private agency records.

OFFICIAL SOURCES OF DATA

Numerous governmental agencies collect data on crime for a variety of different purposes. The most common source is agency reports. At the state level, data on the criminal justice system are maintained routinely, but the systems differ in their scope, definitions of crime, and data quality. Consequently, comparing crime data obtained from the state level is difficult. The situation is not much better at the national or federal level. Many agencies have independent data systems, and again the usefulness of the data is reduced because of different definitions, reporting periods, and crime classification schemes.[16]

Partly as a response to this fragmentation, Congress in 1981 authorized the creation of the Bureau of Justice Statistics (BJS).[17] The main goal of BJS is to furnish an objective, independent, and competent source of policy-relevant data to both the government and criminal justice and academic communities.[18] But the bureau is not to be involved in policy decisions. The director stresses that unification of data is one main goal, as is the development of a program to follow an offender from the time of entering the criminal justice process until that person is finally released from the correctional system. Another goal for the bureau is providing services to states and local communities to aid in comprehensive data gathering.[19]

Although the BJS data are useful, the most comprehensive source of data on crime is still the *Uniform Crime Reports (UCR),* under the jurisdiction of the Federal Bureau of Investigation (FBI).

The Uniform Crime Reports

In 1870, Congress passed a law mandating that the attorney general report annually on the amount of crime in the United States, and in 1871, the International Association of Chiefs of Police passed a resolution that recommended the gathering of national crime data. Both of these efforts were ignored for years, but finally, in 1927 the International Association of Chiefs of Police appointed a Uniform Crime Records Committee to study the possibility of gathering national crime data. Two years later, the committee published *Uniform Crime Reporting: A Complete Manual for Police.* In 1930, the Federal Bureau of Investigation began issuing the *Uniform Crime Reports.* In the beginning, the reports were issued on a monthly basis and then were published quarterly until 1941. From 1942 until 1957, the reports were semiannual, and in 1958 the present format of one annual publication was started.

Standardized definitions of crime were developed for all offenses in order to provide national uniformity in the reporting of data. Local agencies compile and submit data through state UCR agencies.[20] Although the FBI has the responsibility for administering the UCR program, the organization has no authority to compel reporting by state and local jurisdictions. Even though the program is voluntary, the national UCR program currently covers 98 percent of the United States population.

UCR coverage.   Seven crimes were originally selected, because of their seriousness and frequency, to constitute the *Uniform Crime Reports* Crime Index. These are known as Part I Offenses and include murder and nonnegligent manslaughter, forcible rape, robbery, aggravated assault, burglary, larceny-theft, and motor vehicle theft. Congress added the crime of arson to the index in 1978. Each month, law enforcement agencies report the number of **crimes known to the police,** that is, the number of Part I Offenses verified as having been committed after police investigation of the complaint. The number of actual crimes in the index category is reported whether or not there is any further action in the case. A crime known to police is counted even if no suspect is arrested and no prosecution occurs.

If a criminal activity involves several different crimes, only the most serious is reported as an **index offense.** For example, if a victim is raped, robbed, and murdered, only the murder is counted in the UCR. Offenses known to police do not reveal how many persons were involved in a particular reported crime.

Table 2.1 illustrates two types of index crime information and shows the differences in the absolute numbers of index crimes reported to police each year from 1973 to 1982. The lower portion of the chart shows the **crime rate.** The national crime rate is calculated by dividing the number of reported crimes by the number of people in the country (data obtained from census reports), and then the result is expressed as a rate of crime per 100,000 people. To calculate the overall rate of index crimes, the reported numbers of the index crimes are added and then divided by the total population in the country. Therefore, the crime index rate for 1982 was 5,533.1 per 100,000 people.

Table 2.1 Index offenses, 1973–1982

Population[1]	Crime Index Total[2]	Violent Crime[4]	Property Crime[4]	Murder and Nonnegligent Manslaughter	Forcible Rape	Robbery	Aggravated Assault	Burglary	Larceny-Theft	Motor Vehicle Theft	Arson[3]	Modified Crime Index Total[3]
Number of offenses												
1973—209,851,000	8,718,100	875,910	7,842,200	19,640	51,400	384,220	420,650	2,565,500	4,347,900	928,800		
1974—211,392,000	10,253,400	974,720	9,278,700	20,710	55,400	442,400	456,210	3,039,200	5,262,500	977,100		
1975—213,124,000	11,256,600	1,026,280	10,230,300	20,510	56,090	464,970	484,710	3,252,100	5,977,700	1,000,500		
1976—214,659,000	11,304,800	986,580	10,318,200	18,780	56,730	420,210	490,850	3,089,800	6,270,800	957,600		
1977—216,332,000	10,935,800	1,009,500	9,926,300	19,120	63,020	404,850	522,510	3,052,200	5,905,700	968,400		
1978—218,059,000	11,141,300	1,061,830	10,079,500	19,560	67,130	417,040	558,100	3,104,500	5,983,400	991,600		
1979—220,099,000	12,152,700	1,178,540	10,974,200	21,460	75,990	466,880	614,210	3,299,500	6,577,500	1,097,200		
1980—225,349,264	13,295,400	1,308,900	11,986,500	23,040	82,090	548,810	654,960	3,759,200	7,112,700	1,114,700		
1981—229,146,000	13,290,300	1,321,900	11,968,400	22,520	81,540	574,130	643,720	3,739,800	7,154,500	1,074,000		
1982—231,534,000	12,857,200	1,285,710	11,571,500	21,010	77,760	536,890	650,040	3,415,500	7,107,700	1,048,300		
Rate per 100,000 inhabitants[5]												
1973	4,154.4	417.4	3,373.0	9.4	24.5	183.1	200.5	1,222.5	2,071.9	442.6		
1974	4,850.4	461.1	4,389.3	9.8	26.2	209.3	215.8	1,437.7	2,489.5	462.2		
1975	5,281.7	481.5	4,800.2	9.6	26.3	218.2	227.4	1,525.9	2,804.8	469.4		
1976	5,266.4	459.6	4,806.8	8.8	26.4	195.8	228.7	1,439.4	2,921.3	446.1		
1977	5,055.1	466.6	4,588.4	8.8	29.1	187.1	241.5	1,410.9	2,729.9	447.6		
1978	5,109.3	486.9	4,622.4	9.0	30.8	191.3	255.9	1,423.7	2,743.9	454.7		
1979	5,521.5	535.5	4,986.0	9.7	34.5	212.1	279.1	1,499.1	2,988.4	498.5		
1980	5,899.9	580.8	5,319.1	10.2	36.4	243.5	290.6	1,668.2	3,156.3	494.6		
1981	5,799.9	576.9	5,223.0	9.8	35.6	250.6	280.9	1,632.1	3,122.3	468.7		
1982	5,553.1	555.3	4,997.8	9.1	33.6	231.9	280.8	1,475.2	3,069.8	452.8		

[1]Populations are Bureau of the Census provisional estimates as of July 1, except April 1, 1980, preliminary census counts, and are subject to change.
[2]Due to rounding, the offenses may not add to totals.
[3]Although arson data are included in the trend and clearance tables, sufficient data are not available to estimate totals for this offense.
[4]Violent crimes are offenses of murder, forcible rape, robbery, and aggravated assault. Property crimes are offenses of burglary, larceny-theft, and motor vehicle theft. Data are not included for the property crime of arson.
[5]Crime rates calculated prior to rounding number of offenses.
Source: Federal Bureau of Investigation, *Uniform Crime Reports, 1982* (Washington, D.C.: Government Printing Office, 1983), p. 43.

Table 2.2 illustrates the way in which the UCR reports the percentage of change over time in the number of crimes known to the police and in the crime rate. For example, the crime rate of 5,553.1 crimes per 100,000 inhabitants in 1982 represents a decrease of 4.3 percent over the 1981 rate, an increase of 8.7 percent over 1978, and an increase of 33.7 percent over 1973. Such comparisons may also be made for each of the index offenses, as indicated in Table 2.2.

Each month, police also report the number of Part I Offenses that are "cleared." Offenses are cleared in two ways: first, by arrest when a suspect is arrested, charged, and turned over to the judicial system for prosecution and second, by circumstances beyond the control of the police. For example, a suspect may die, or the victim may refuse to press charges, which normally signals the end of police involvement. Crimes are considered cleared whether or not the person arrested is convicted of the crime.

Several persons may be arrested and one crime is cleared, or one person may be arrested and many crimes are cleared. The *clearance rate* is the number of crimes solved expressed as a precentage of the total number of crimes reported to the police. This rate is critical to policy decisions because it is one measure used to evaluate police departments. The higher the number of crimes solved by arrest, the better the police force will look in the eyes of the public. Figure 2.1 indicates the national percentage of crimes cleared by arrest in 1982. The figures added to the 1982 data indicate a slight increase in violent crimes cleared by arrest in 1982, compared with those of 1981. In **property crimes**, the clearance rate remained the same for motor vehicle

Table 2.2 *National Crime, Rate, and Percent Change*

Offense	Estimated Crime 1982		Percent Change over 1981		Percent Change over 1978		Percent Change over 1976	
	Number	Rate per 100,000 Inhabitants	Number	Rate per 100,000 Inhabitants	Number	Rate per 100,000 Inhabitants	Number	Rate per 100,000 Inhabitants
Crime Index total[1]	12,857,200	5,553.1	−3.3	−4.3	+15.4	+8.7	+47.5	+33.7
Modified Crime Index total								
Violent crime	1,285,710	555.3	−2.7	−3.7	+21.2	+14.0	+46.8	+33.0
Property crime	11,571,500	4,997.8	−3.3	−4.3	+14.8	+8.1	+47.6	+33.7
Murder	21,010	9.1	−6.7	−7.1	+7.4	+1.1	+7.0	−3.2
Forcible rape	77,760	33.6	−4.6	−5.6	+15.8	+9.1	+51.3	+37.1
Robbery	536,890	231.9	−6.5	−7.5	+28.7	+21.2	+39.7	+26.7
Aggravated assault	650,040	280.8	+1.0		+16.5	+9.7	+54.5	+40.0
Burglary	3,415,500	1,475.2	−8.7	−9.6	+10.0	+3.6	+33.1	20.7
Larceny-theft	7,107,700	3,069.8	−.7	−1.7	+18.8	+11.9	+63.5	+48.2
Motor vehicle theft	1,048,300	452.8	−2.4	−3.4	+5.7	−.4	+12.9	+2.3
Arson								

[1]Because of rounding, offenses may not add to totals.
Source: Federal Bureau of Investigation, *Uniform Crime Reports, 1982* (Washington, D.C.: Government Printing Office, 1983), p. 40.

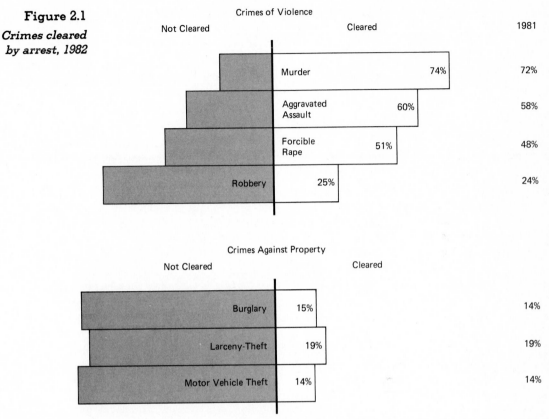

Figure 2.1

Crimes cleared by arrest, 1982

Source: *Federal Bureau of Investigation,* Uniform Crime Reports, 1982 *(Washington, D.C.: Government Printing Office, 1983),* p. 157.

theft and larceny theft and decreased from 15 percent to 14 percent in burglary.

In addition to crime and arrest data for Part I Offenses, agencies also report the number of arrests for the less serious offenses, listed as Part II Offenses, which cover a wide range of crimes and are listed in Table 2.3.

Arrest information in the UCR is presented in two forms. Table 2.3 lists the total estimated numbers of arrests by crime for each of the recorded offenses. The UCR also lists the number of arrests made during one year for each of the serious offenses per 100,000 population, but it does not report the numbers of persons arrested each year, because some individuals are arrested more than once during the year. The actual number of arrested persons, therefore, is likely to be smaller than the number of arrests.[21]

Limitations of the UCR.   It has been argued that the number of crimes known to the police seriously underestimates the actual crime in society[22]

Table 2.3

Total Estimated Arrests,[1] United States, 1982

Total[2]	12,136,400	Drug abuse violations	676,000
Murder and nonnegligent manslaughter	21,810	Opium or cocaine and their derivatives	112,900
Forcible rape	33,600	Marijuana	455,600
Robbery	157,630	Synthetic or manufactured drugs	24,800
Aggravated assault	313,150	Other dangerous nonnarcotic drugs	82,900
Burglary	527,100		
Larceny-theft	1,368,100		
Motor vehicle theft	129,100	Gambling	41,200
Arson	20,500		
		Bookmaking	3,400
Violent crime[3]	526,200	Numbers and lottery	7,100
Property crime[4]	2,044,800	All other gambling	30,600
Crime Index total[5]	2,571,000	Offenses against family and children	58,700
Other assaults	543,400	Driving under the influence	1,778,400
Forgery and counterfeiting	97,300	Liquor laws	501,200
Fraud	334,400	Drunkenness	1,262,100
Embezzlement	9,000	Disorderly conduct	895,500
Stolen property, buying, receiving, possessing	137,500	Vagrancy	36,800
		All other offenses (except traffic)	2,324,100
Vandalism	245,700	Suspicion (not included in totals)	11,200
Weapons; carrying, possessing, etc.	193,500	Curfew and loitering law violations	91,100
Prostitution and commercialized vice	121,200		
Sex offenses (except forcible rape and prostitution)	78,800	Runaways	139,400

[1]Arrest totals based on all reporting agencies and estimates for unreported areas.
[2]Because of rounding, items may not add to totals.
[3]Violent crimes are offenses of murder, forcible rape, robbery, and aggravated assault.
[4]Property crimes are offenses of burglary, larceny-theft, motor vehicle theft, and arson.
[5]Includes arson.
Source: Federal Bureau of Investigation, *Uniform Crime Reports, 1982* (Washington, D.C.: U.S. Government Printing Office, 1983), p. 167.

because there are so many variables that can affect crime data. We shall examine the most significant of these variables.

Police discretion

The police's **discretion** in deciding whether a complaint is actually a crime affects the number of crimes known to them. In Chicago, an internal investigation by the police department revealed that the police were throwing out fourteen times more crime reports than were other city police departments. At least 40 percent of these crimes were erroneously labeled *unfounded.* The Chicago police blamed part of the problem on poor guidelines to classify a complaint as unfounded and a belief that superior officers wanted the cases dropped. After the procedures for classifying crime reports were changed, Chicago's crime figures "rose" by 25 percent, a direct result, say the Chicago police, of paperwork changes.[23]

EXHIBIT

**VARIABLES IN POLICE–CITIZEN INTERACTION THAT AFFECT
WHETHER POLICE WILL TAKE OFFICIAL ACTION ON
COMPLAINT OF A CRIME**

1. Police–citizen encounters on crime result in official data much more often in cases of felonies than in cases of misdemeanors.
2. The wish of the complainant is associated with police action. In no cases in which the complainant wanted an informal disposition of the case did police write an official report. In most cases where the complainant wanted official disposition of the case, the police did so; the incidence was higher for the more serious offenses.
3. The greater the relational distance between the complainant and the alleged offender, the more likely the police are to file an official report. When friends of family are involved in an alleged offense, the police are less likely to record the crime.
4. The more deference the complainant showed to the police, the more likely an official report would be made.
5. There was no evidence that the race of the complainant was related to official reporting.
6. There was some evidence the socioeconomic status was related to official reporting. Police gave preferential treatment to white-collar complainants but only in felony situations. There appeared to be no relationship between social class and the reaction of the police to a complainant in cases of misdemeanors.

Source: Donald J. Black, "Production of Crime Rates," *American Sociological Review* 35 (August 1970): 733–748.

---

*Victims'
cooperation*   The reporting of crimes may also be affected by the climate surrounding those crimes and the belief that something will be done. Some individuals do not report crimes because they do not think the police will do anything. In the case of rape, the victim's feelings that nothing will be done and, in addition, that she will be suspected of encouraging the crime have probably led to the underreporting of this crime. Therefore, an "increase" in rape might not reflect an actual increase in the incidences of rape but, rather, an increase in the willingness of the victims to report the crime. Several cities have developed rape relief centers that provide counseling for victims of rape, and some jurisdictions have given their police special training in the handling of these cases; these and other changes may result in increased reporting by rape victims.[24]

Administrative and bureaucratic changes

An increase or decrease in the size or location of the police force may also affect data on crime. In addition, methods of reporting may be changed, resulting in a false "increase" or "decrease" in the crime rate. This may happen as the police force becomes more professionalized. In Chicago between 1928 and 1931, robberies "increased" from 1,263 to 14,544 and burglaries from 879 to 18,689. Before 1950, New York reported "crimes known to the police" on a precinct level, which resulted in gross underreporting, to the extent that by 1949 the FBI would no longer report the figures from New York because it did not believe them. But in 1950, New York changed its system of reporting, and in one year robberies "increased" 400 percent and burglaries, 1,300 percent.

A study of the crimes of larceny, burglary, and robbery in Washington, D.C., where such crimes constituted 73 percent of the index offenses in that city, revealed some of the ways in which the analysis of the act determines the number of crimes in a given category. For example, the criminal act of stealing might be classified as burglary or larceny, depending on the circumstances. Burglary requires an unlawful entry into premises for the purpose of stealing. The investigators found, however, that in some cases the police would ignore the unlawful entry, especially if the premises were not locked, and classify as larceny an act that had all of the elements of burglary. Police might also have an incentive to downgrade the classifications of crime, to make the police force look better.

A program of crime control was begun in Washington and included a significant increase in police staff, which gave the District of Columbia the largest number of police per resident in the country; more cars and other equipment; the use of a computer to provide quick information on arrests, stolen cars, and so on; younger, better-educated police; and more black police, many of whom had participated in police-community sensitivity programs. Although a cause-and-effect relationship cannot be assumed, because all the other variables that might affect crime rates could not be controlled, the data did indicate "a decline in crime in the District, roughly coincident with at least some features of the administration's program." It was also possible, however, that a change in administration "caused" the change in crime rates. In 1969, a new chief of police indicated that police who could not reduce crime in their jurisdictions would be replaced.

After examining the data on larcenies and burglaries, the investigators concluded that "the political importance of crime apparently caused pressures, subtle or otherwise, to be felt by those who record crime—pressures which have led to the downgrading of crimes." They also analyzed data for twenty-nine other cities and concluded that crime data are misleading because they are used as official data under pressures to have them show certain things, and so they can be and are manipulated to show higher or lower crime rates. "We conclude that the Uniform Crime Reporting System is useless as a tool for evaluation of social policy."[25]

Methods of counting crime

Data on crime will also be affected by decisions as to whether a series of criminal acts by one person will be counted as one crime or as several. For example, if a person appears before a group of people, pulls a gun, and asks each of the group for money, has the individual committed one act of armed robbery or several? If a person twice engages in sexual intercourse with force and without the consent of the woman, have two crimes of rape been committed or only one?

England and Wales follow the "one victim, one crime" rule, although the English rule with regard to property crime is not clear. The "one operation, one crime" rule is followed in America and Canada. Official reports thus record "crimes" as single events, but victim surveys may record each victim separately.[26]

Finally, the way in which crimes are counted for purposes of the *Uniform Crime Reports* does not take into account the differing degrees of seriousness of crimes that have the same legal label. "In other words, the UCR method provides no solution for the problem of how to deal statistically with a complex of offenses or with simple offenses that vary in seriousness but carry the same legal title." Two researchers devised an index for measuring delinquency, an index that takes into account "both the components and the aggravating factors of an event." For example, greater weight would be given in a rape case aggravated by use of a dangerous weapon, as contrasted with one in which no weapon was used. The index would thus be one of all of the "events" involved, not merely of the "crime" or "delinquency."[27]

Crimes not included in the official reports

Official reports have been severely criticized for excluding some crimes. The *Uniform Crime Reports,* for example, do not include federal offenses, and the index crimes, on which crime rates are based, do not include organized crime or **white-collar crime.** Most of these offenses, although they are violations of criminal law, are handled by administrative agencies rather than by criminal courts. Because these "crimes of the middle and upper classes" are not included in the crime index, by looking only at the official data on crime, it is easy to conclude that there is a high correlation between crime and socioeconomic status, with the greatest proportions of crimes being committed by the lower class.[28]

Finally, the UCR does not include crimes handled by administrative agencies rather than by criminal courts, and to help overcome this problem, other methods of counting crime have been developed. In the next section, we shall look briefly at victimization surveys that attempt to analyze the extent of crime in society instead of the number of crimes reported to law enforcement agencies.

UNOFFICIAL SOURCES OF DATA

The first source of unofficial data that we shall analyze is victimization surveys.

Victimization surveys

Victimization surveys were developed in response to criticisms of the underreporting of crimes by the FBI *Uniform Crime Reports.* For policy purposes of determining actual crime trends and ascertaining the true level of crime in society, the "dark figure" of crime is important. As this dark figure of crime rises when victims do not report crimes to law enforcement officials, one goal of victimization surveys is to determine why citizens do not bring crime to the attention of the police.

The surveys reveal that the most common reason for not reporting crimes is the belief that the police could not do anything or that there was no proof of the crime. Other victims stated that the event was not important enough to report; that the offenders would not be punished even if apprehended; that the crime was too personal, as in the case of rape; or that the matter was private or family and did not require police intervention.[29]

Despite some unwillingness to report crimes, the victims are still the most important link in the system. "In the overwhelming majority of cases, if the victim does not report the crime to the police, the event will not be dealt with by the criminal justice system." Those victims who do report crimes say that the decision involves a sense of obligation to society, the desire for retribution or revenge, or the fact that reporting the crime is the only means they have to deal with the crisis of a criminal incident. Some victims report crimes merely for financial reasons: the jurisdiction may have a victim's compensation program, a plan of restitution for offenders, or a requirement that insurance companies not pay claims unless the crime is officially reported. The more serious the crime, the more likely the victim will bring it to the attention of the authorities. Similarly, if a weapon is used or if the victim sustains serious physical or financial injury, the crime is more likely to be reported. In fact, the seriousness of the crime is the most important factor in the decision to report the crime.[30]

The measurement of criminal victimization has had a short history in the United States.[31] In 1965, the National Opinion Research Center (NORC) conducted its first victimization survey, of ten thousand households, under authority granted by the president's crime commission. The NORC found that only one-half of all crimes were being reported to law enforcement officials. Homicide and auto theft were the only two categories with a higher incidence of crime reported in the UCR, as compared with the NORC results. The NORC also found substantially more crimes of rape, robbery, aggravated assault, burglary, and larceny than had been reported to the police.[32]

The Law Enforcement Assistance Administration, in conjunction with the Bureau of Census, continued the studies, releasing a massive survey in 1974. This study involved 200,000 people and found that at least twice as many serious crimes had occurred as had been reported. These national crime panel surveys measured not only victimization rates, but also how many crimes were reported and why some victims did not contact the authorities after a criminal act.[33]

Currently, the National Crime Survey (NCS) is operated by the Bureau of Justice Statistics within the Department of Justice. The NCS measures six crimes: rape, robbery, assault, household burglary, personal and household larceny, and motor vehicle theft. Of the other two UCR index crimes, murder obviously cannot be measured by survey, as the victim is dead. In the case of arson, it is too difficult to determine whether the victim, the property owner, was also the perpetrator of the crime. The NCS is based on the results of interviews with about sixty thousand households every six months. A recent NCS revealed that only about 33 percent of crimes were reported to the police, although for violent crimes, nearly one-half were reported.

Comparison of UCR and NCS. Policymakers and social analysts realize that both official reported crimes and citizen-defined victimization incidents are imperfect measures of crime. Analyzed together, it is hoped that information about the actual level of crime in society, the limitations of each crime measurement method, or the possibility of a new way to count crime can be discovered.[34]

Discovering demographic characteristics of offenders is one goal of comparison studies. The NCS includes questions about the sex, age, and race of the offenders. When these data are compared with age-sex-race-specific counts on the general population, the NCS can give age-sex-race-specific estimates of rates of offending throughout the nation, something the UCR arrest data cannot do. There is one important drawback, however. NCS data are based entirely on the victim's description of the offender, and as often as the victim is wrong, the data will be wrong.

One limitation common to both the NCS and the UCR is that neither can estimate the extent to which a few offenders are responsible for large numbers of crimes. These reports tell us only how many crimes occurred (not how many of those crimes can be traced to the same offenders) and how many arrests were made (not how many times a particular person was arrested).

Another limitation in comparing these studies is the time period designated for each. The UCR reports events over a calendar year, and some victimization surveys also cover twelve months, but not necessarily January through December.

Perhaps the most serious problem in comparing NCS and UCR data is that the UCR crime definitions are *legal* in nature and that citizen reports often characterize crime by how they *feel* about the event. Of course, the legal elements may not always be present in the crimes reported by the UCR but certainly are more likely to be than in cases in which citizens are asked to report what happened. The result is that the elements of a legal assault and battery may not be present in an action reported in the NCS data to be an assault and battery.

Some of the methodological problems in comparing these sources of crime data can be resolved. Clearly, more research is needed to determine the precise relationship between reported crime and reported victimization. It may be that information from one crime data source can be used to test or predict the other, or further research may make it possible to ascertain criminal activity in areas not actually measured. Research is progressing rapidly in this area now that victimization surveys are conducted on a regular basis.[35]

Self-report surveys Official crime data report the number of crimes that come to the attention of law enforcement officials, and victimization surveys report the number of crimes that occur, regardless of whether they are reported to the police. Another way to measure the dark figure of crime is to survey people about their involvement in crime as lawbreakers or offenders.

Earlier self-report studies revealed that much criminal activity is not reported to officials. In 1947, two investigators reported the results of their sample of upper-income persons, 99 percent of whom answered that they had committed one or more acts for which they could have been arrested.[36] Such results were also reported in a study of college students and institutionalized delinquents. Similar types of delinquency were reported by the college students as by those youths who had been officially judged to be delinquent. Although probably with less frequency of commission, the college students admitted having committed delinquent and criminal acts as serious as those for which delinquents had been officially adjudicated. Some of these students were leaders of school organizations and honor students.[37] These studies were, however, somewhat unsystematic. The actual systematic use of the self-report method of measuring delinquency was introduced by James F. Short and F. Ivan Nye in 1957,[38] and since that time it has been improved and used extensively.

> Short and Nye were able to show that adolescents would report delinquent acts, that these reports were internally consistent, and that they were related both to differences in official delinquency status and to other differences predicted from research and theory—for example, the quality of family relations.

The Short/Nye studies revolutionized ideas about the feasibility of using survey procedures with a hitherto taboo topic. They also eventually led to a revolution in thinking about the substance of the phenomenon itself.[39]

Critique of self-report data.   Despite the widespread use of self-report data and the initial differences found between data secured by this method and official crime data, the method has come under criticism for several reasons.[40]

First is the problem of deliberate falsification. There is the danger that respondents, especially juveniles, will overreport their involvement in illegal activities. A second problem with these studies concerns inaccurate recall and raises the opposite difficulty of underreporting. One study found, in a limited sample, that 20 percent of those persons known to have reported crimes to the police did not report that information in a follow-up interview.[41]

Other criticisms of self-report studies indicate that the surveys include too many nonserious and trivial offenses and sometimes omit serious crimes such as burglary, robbery, and sexual assault. Furthermore, self-report studies include too few blacks. Taken together, these criticisms raise serious questions. White respondents tend to report greater involvement in less serious crimes that occur more frequently, and blacks tend to report illegal acts that are less frequent but more serious. One study revealed that black male offenders fail to report known offenses three times more often than do white male offenders.[42]

But self-report studies may yield more useful data in the future. A new program, the National Youth Survey (NYS), is using interviews with adolescents over a five year period to gather crime involvement data, and it has been structured to overcome many of the criticisms of the older self-report studies.[43]

The NYS includes all UCR offenses, except homicide, and crimes that are likely to be relevant to a "delinquent lifestyle or culture," such as gang fights, sexual activity, and misdemeanors. The NYS may be more useful for comparison, as it measures criminal activity "from Christmas a year ago to the Christmas just past." This period is close to the UCR calendar period and coincides with the more recent victimization surveys. The NYS also allows researchers to pinpoint more types and levels of delinquent behavior and shows promise for gathering more accurate data.

CRIME IN THE UNITED STATES IN 1982: AN OVERVIEW   We shall briefly examine the data on crime for 1982 as reported by the Bureau of Justice Statistics and the *Uniform Crime Reports.* The data on some specific crimes will be analyzed more carefully in later chapters when we discuss the nature and elements of those crimes.

NATIONAL CRIME
SURVEY (NCS)
DATA

In September 1983, the Bureau of Justice Statistics (BJS) issued a special report containing a brief analysis of the 1982 victimization data, the tenth in its annual series. The 1982 data, compared with those for 1981, with a general downturn of 1.7 million victimizations, represented "one of the most sweeping, single-direction changes to have taken place since the program's inception. Virtually all categories of crime contributed to the reduction, and there were no statistically significant increases."[44]

Figure 2.2 graphs the trends in victimization rates for selected crimes from 1973 to 1982 and clearly shows the 1982 downturn. In 1981, 4.1 percent fewer victimizations were reported, even though the population aged twelve and over increased by an estimated 1.2 percent. The bulk of this reduction in victimization, however, was accounted for by the decrease in property offenses, particularly household burglary, whose rate dropped to a ten-year low. But as Figure 2.2 indicates, the rates of victimization involving violent crimes show no significant change between 1981 and 1982 or, for that matter, between 1973 and 1982. The most prevalent of the NCS violent offenses, assault, occurred at a rate of 26.4 victimizations for every 1,000 individuals, for a total of 5 million offenses. Rape, the most serious NCS offense, was reported to have occurred in 1982 at the rate of 1.4 per 1,000 women.

Figure 2.2

Trends in victimization rates in the United States, 1973–1982

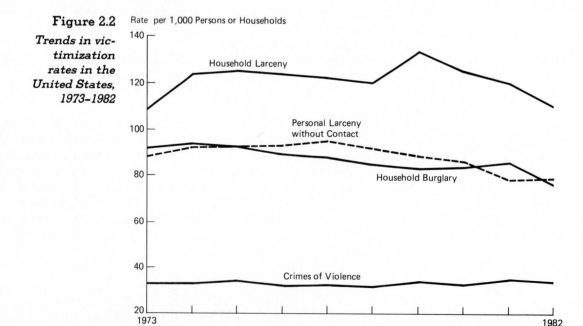

Source: "Criminal Victimization in the United States: 1973–82 Trends," Bureau of Justice Statistics Special Report, U.S. Department of Justice (September 1983), 1.

As Figure 2.2 indicates, the most common of the NCS offenses, personal larceny without contact between the victim and the offender, began a downward trend after 1978, with the sharpest decrease in 1980 but with a slight increase in 1981. The rates of victimization showed a slight decrease in 1982. The data also record victimizations of theft involving those in which the victim and the offender have some contact during the commission of the crime. This, however, is the least frequent of the NCS offenses, with a yearly rate of about 3 victimizations per 1,000 persons. The rate showed no significant change between 1981 and 1982.

The decrease in burglary victimizations, noted above as the largest decrease of the NCS crimes reported in 1982, represented a rate of 78.2 per 1,000 households. For the third consecutive year, there was also a downturn in residential larceny, with the latest rate of 113.9 crimes per 1,000 households, seven points lower than in 1981 and the lowest rate for this crime since 1973.

UNIFORM CRIME REPORTS (UCR) DATA

In the foreword to the 1982 *Uniform Crime Reports,* published in September 1983, the director of the FBI, with "cautious optimism," announced that the rate of serious, or index offenses, was down 3 percent from 1981. The cautiousness of his optimism stems from the fact that in the 1970s the crime rates also twice dropped, only to turn back upward shortly thereafter. The director also announced that a "multiyear, multiphase project" is underway to review and evaluate the UCR program.[45]

The UCR data can best be understood by using figures, graphs, and charts. Figure 2.3 graphs the changes in the number and rates of crime index offenses between 1978 and 1982, as reported by the UCR, indicating that both peaked in 1980 and have declined slightly since then. Table 2.2 charts the estimated number of crimes committed in 1982, compared with those in 1981, 1978, and 1973, and also includes the crime rates for those years for the serious, or index, offenses. The estimated 12.9 million crime index offenses of 1982, although up 47 percent from 1973 and 15 percent from the

Figure 2.3
Crime index rate

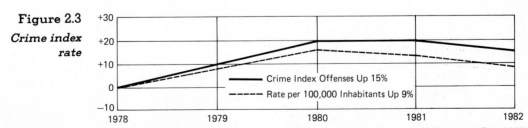

Crime Index Offenses Up 15%
Rate per 100,000 Inhabitants Up 9%

Source: Federal Bureau of Investigation, Uniform Crime Reports, 1982 *(Washington, D.C.: Government Printing Office, 1983), p. 39.*

1978 figure, were down 3 percent from the 1981 figure, representing the first significant decline in index offenses since 1977. The figures also were down in both violent and property crimes.

The number of murders in 1982, compared with that in 1981, decreased by 6.7 percent; forcible rape was down 4.6 percent; robbery was down 6.5 percent; but aggravated assault increased by 1 percent. Among property crimes, burglary decreased 8.7 percent, motor vehicle theft 2.4 percent, and larceny-theft 0.7 percent over the 1981 level. These decreases, however, must be viewed in the context of trends in property crimes. When the 1982 data are compared with the 1978 data for the crime of burglary, the rates are up in all categories, ranging from 1 percent for nonresidence burglary in the night to 12 percent for nonresidence burglary during the day. When the data on types of larceny-theft are compared for the same time period, larcenies show an increase in 1982, compared with 1978, in all categories except theft of bicycles, with the highest rise in thefts from motor vehicles, up 30 percent.

Thefts of motor vehicles decreased in 1982, compared with 1981, but the number increased by 5.7 percent between 1978 and 1982.[46] Finally, although the UCR data on arson were not complete in the 1982 report, the estimates were that during 1981 and 1982, there was a decrease of 12 percent.[47]

Figure 2.1 indicates that substantially more crimes against the person were cleared by arrest in 1982 than was the case for crimes against property. The highest clearance rate was 74 percent for the crime of murder, and the lowest rate was in the property crime of motor vehicle theft, with only 14 percent of the crimes cleared by arrest. A crime is listed as "cleared by arrest" when the police have enough evidence to take a suspect into custody and charge him or her with the crime committed. It is easier to clear crimes against the person than it is property crimes because of the more extensive investigation by the police, the greater willingness of the victim to cooperate, and the greater availability of witnesses.

CHARACTERISTICS OF OFFENDERS

It is also important to analyze the data in terms of the relevant variables that might be affecting the crime rates, and so we shall study age, race, and sex.

THE UCR AND SELF-REPORT DATA: A CONTRAST

Before the beginning of self-report studies in 1957, most criminological studies were based on official data, and those data, revealing that a higher percentage of the arrestees were black, from a lower social class, and young, led many to conclude that persons with these characteristics were more likely to commit crimes. Others concluded that the data represented discrimination against persons with these characteristics.

When looking at the data here, we should keep in mind that the differences between the crime rates of men and women, and blacks and whites, do not mean that those variables *cause* the criminal activity or the reaction to that activity. Indeed, there is evidence that it is not race or age or sex that influences the official reaction to the alleged offender but, rather, the seriousness of the offense committed and the degree of involvement in that offense.[48] There is also evidence that the differences in crime rates between the self-report data and the UCR data may be explained by factors such as a small number of blacks in the self-report studies. And the studies indicate that blacks and whites differ in their tendencies to report certain crimes.[49] On the other hand, there are those who believe that the differences in crime rates according to these variables are too great to be explained in any way other than discrimination.[50]

AGE   Of the 12.1 million arrests in this country in 1982, 53 percent were of persons under the age of twenty-five. When only the serious offenses are included, the figure rises to 64.4 percent. The percentage of arrestees under twenty-five was higher for serious property crimes, 67.3 percent, than for violent crimes, 53.4 percent.[51] A breakdown of the offenses reveals that in only two index offenses, murder and nonnegligent manslaughter and aggravated assault, were less than 50 percent of those arrested over twenty-five. Persons under twenty-five accounted for 77 percent of the arrests for burglary, 73.6 percent of motor vehicle theft, 69.3 percent of robbery, 62.2 percent of arson, 63 percent of larceny-theft, and 52 percent of forcible rape.[52]

Comparison of the 1982 crime data by age with those of previous years reveals, however, that the arrest rates for young people have changed in several areas. We have already noted that 1982 reflected a drop in the total crimes reported, as well as in arrests. The percentage of arrests for index crimes increased for only two crimes: up 2.5 percent for aggravated assault and 3.2 percent for larceny-theft. For persons under fifteen, an increase in arrests occurred in only one crime, in forcible rape, up .1% in 1982, compared with 1981. Among those under eighteen, the only increase was 0.4 percent in arrests for forcible rape. More encouraging were the decreases. Arrests for motor vehicle theft decreased 16.9 percent for those under fifteen and 16.4 percent for those under eighteen. Burglary arrests went down 6.4 percent for those under fifteen and 10.5 percent for those under eighteen but climbed slightly for those over eighteen.[53]

We are also experiencing more crime among the elderly, a situation that could become critical in view of their increasing numbers in the population. In 1982 the number of arrests of persons sixty-five and over was insignificant when compared with the total number of arrests, representing only 0.8 percent of the arrests for index offenses, with 0.7 percent for violent crimes and 0.9 percent for property crimes. When the index offenses are analyzed,

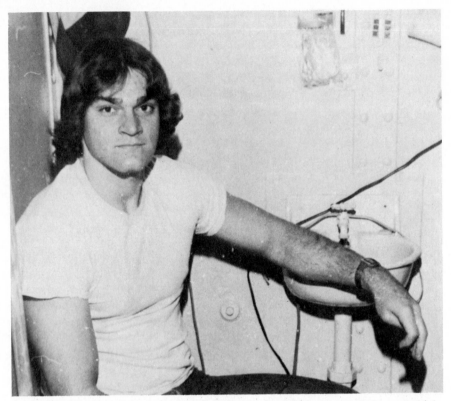

Youth and violent crime: Monte Lee Eddings at age 16 shot and killed a state high-way trooper when he was stopped for a routine traffic offense. Eddings was convicted and sentenced to death. In 1984, while Eddings waited on death row for the results of his second appeal to the Supreme Court on the issue of whether capital punishment is "cruel and unusual" when imposed for a murder committed by a juvenile, his sentence was reduced to life by a lower court.

however, it is obvious that by far the greatest number of arrests of the elderly are for larceny-theft, constituting 14,364 of the 18,269 arrests of persons in that age bracket. For less serious offenses, the elderly were most frequently arrested for drunkenness or driving under the influence.[54]

Although the numbers of arrests of elderly are insignificant compared with the total number of arrests in the population, their percentages are growing. During the 1970s the percentage of the population in the age bracket of fifty-five or older increased by 22 percent. During that decade, major-felony arrests for persons in that age bracket, however, increased by 148 percent. Between 1964 and 1979, the elderly arrest rate for murder increased by 200 percent, with arrests for rape and larceny each going up by more than 300 percent. The larceny-theft arrests of the elderly are mainly for shoplifting, a crime among the elderly that one criminologist describes as "alarming" and "reaching epidemic proportions."[55]

RACE   The National Commission on the Causes and Prevention of Violence reported in 1969[56] that black crime rates were four times higher than white crime rates for the four major violent crimes of homicide, rape, robbery, and aggravated assault. In 1967, the black arrest rate for homicide was about seventeen times higher than the rate for whites, and for forcible rape, twelve times higher. Among juveniles, the homicide rate for blacks was seventeen times higher than for whites. The commission also found that black rates for crimes of violence had increased more rapidly than had the rates for whites during the previous decade.

A study of ten thousand boys in Philadelphia measured their behavior from the age of ten until they were eighteen and found more crimes of violence among black youths, who had a robbery rate twenty-one times higher than that of white youths and an aggravated assault rate eleven times higher. During the study, one-half of the black youths, as compared with one-third of the whites, were in police custody. White youths also were less likely to follow an offense with an act of physical violence and were less often recidivists.[57]

Recent data on crime and race indicate that although 70.7 percent of all arrests in 1982 were of white persons, compared with 27.8 percent for blacks, the percentages were much closer in the serious crimes, with the greater differences occurring in arrests for less serious offenses. For example, 83.7 percent of arrests for "runaways" were white, and 87.7 percent of arrests for driving under the influence and 88.5 percent of arrests for violating liquor laws were white. Arrests for sex offenses (except forcible rape and prostitution) also more often involved whites than blacks, 77.7 percent compared with 20.7 percent. For serious violent crimes, 51.9 percent of all arrestees were white, compared with 46.7 percent black.[58]

In analyzing the above data, it is important to realize that even in cases in which the arrest rates are higher for whites than for blacks, they may still be disproportional, as blacks constitute only approximately 11 percent of the total population. Second, we must consider not only arrest data but also the fact that official and unofficial data on crime reveal differences between blacks and whites at all levels of the **criminal justice system.**[59]

SEX   Historically, the crime rates for males have been higher than those for females, with the exception of those crimes that are by definition predominantly female, such as prostitution. Although males constitute roughly 50 percent of the population in the United States, they account for approximately 90 percent of all arrests for serious crimes. However, when the arrests of males and females in this country were examined recently, some interesting trends were found.

Between 1967 and 1976, the total number of arrests increased more dramatically for females than for males, an increase of 64.3 percent, compared with 14.8 percent for males. During that period the percentages of arrests for females increased more rapidly than for males in all categories of offenses except for murder and nonnegligent manslaughter, narcotics, and prostitution and commercialized vice. During that period, the arrests of females increased most dramatically in narcotic drug laws, stolen property, fraud, robbery, larceny-theft, and forgery and counterfeiting, in that order. The percentages of arrests of females for these offenses also show an increase when the data for 1976 are compared with those for 1972.[60]

Between 1978 and 1982, the percentages of the total number of arrests of females increased by 3.8 percentage points more than for males, whereas a comparison of the 1982 data with the 1981 data indicates an increase of 1.9 percent in total arrests of males and an increase of 4.4 percent in total arrests of females. Between 1978 and 1982, the greatest increase of arrests of females was in the crime of driving under the influence, with the increase of females leading that of males by 62.8 percent to 25.0 percent.

When the index, or more serious, crimes are considered, the data reveal that between 1981 and 1982, arrests of women for violent crimes increased 4.1 percent, compared with only 0.1 percent for men. Women also led in increases in arrests for property offenses, with a 3.4 percent rise, compared with −0.5 percent for men.[61]

VICTIMS OF CRIME   Earlier we noted that surveys of victims have produced significant insights into the nature and extent of crime. Such studies have also given us information on the characteristics of victims, who for years were ignored by scholars and researchers in the field of criminology,[62] as well as by institutions that have been of assistance to them. But in the past decade or so, this situation has changed. Professional societies have been formed; workshops on victims have been held; journals have been established, and a national organization has been actively pursuing the rights of victims.

An analysis of data on victimization indicates that there are differences in the rates of victimization of specific groups in the population. As Figure 2.4 indicates, young people, males, blacks, Hispanics, divorced or separated, unemployed, and those with an income of less than $3,000 are the most common victims of violent crime.

RACE   Blacks are far more often the victims of crime than whites are and have only slightly higher rates than do members of other minority races. In 1980, the

Figure 2.4   *Selected characteristics of violent crime, 1980**

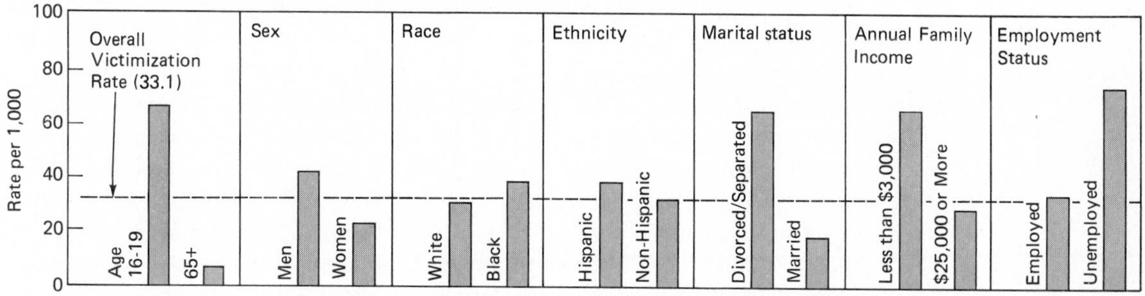

*Limited to persons age 16 and over. Note: The differences between rates within categories are statistically significant. Rate differences between categories may or may not be significant.

Source: Criminal Victimization in the United States, 1980. *A National Crime Survey Report. U.S. Department of Justice, Bureau of Justice Statistics (Washington, D.C.: Government Printing Office, 1982), p. 4.*

main difference in the victimization rates of whites and blacks was the robbery rate, 2.4 times higher for blacks than for whites. Blacks were more often the victims of personal larceny with contacts, but whites were more likely to be victimized by larceny without personal contact. When the variables of race as well as sex are compared, the highest rates of victimization for violent crimes were among black males, followed by white males, black females, and white females. Blacks, as compared with other minorities and with whites, are more often the victims of serious crimes, and they are most often victimized by other blacks. Black-on-black homicide, for example, is a major cause of death among black Americans, particularly among black males,[63] and black women may be particularly victimized by rape, both in terms of the crime itself as well as the way in which the criminal justice system reacts to the crime.[64]

Various explanations have been given for the high rates of violent crimes against blacks. One recent study of the impact of violent crime on blacks emphasized the importance of not only race but also social structural variables. For example, as urbanization increases, crime rates also increase. Violent crimes in particular are "committed in heavily populated areas which have larger proportions of blacks in the population. The view that crime is committed more frequently in the black community should be restricted to violent crime." [65] This might explain why the rates of victimization of blacks are higher for the crimes of homicide, robbery, and larceny with personal contact than, for example, for the crime of larceny without personal contact, for which the rates of victimization are higher among whites.

The rates of victimization are also higher among the unemployed and the poor than among the employed and the higher-income population, and blacks, compared with whites, represent a higher proportion of these groups.

A *New York Times Magazine* article focused on the problem of crime among blacks, noting that only recently has the disproportionate involvement of blacks in crime—"as both predators and prey"—received much attention in this country. According to this article, the high incidences of black-on-black crime is because "most street crimes are committed by poor people out of desperation, impulse and opportunity." These crimes are committed within one mile of the home of the victim and of the offender. "A very small percentage of the offenders are jumping in their cars and speeding to suburbia or traveling to white neighborhoods to commit their crimes. By and large, criminals operate in areas of opportunity and familiarity."

Many blacks believe that they are more often the victims of crime because of what they call *systemic racism,* the differential impact of unemployment, poor schools resulting in a lower quality of education, the greater likelihood of police to arrest blacks, and the other injustices of the criminal justice system:

> They contend that, despite society's clear reluctance, in economically troubled times, to support "massive solutions"—and its conviction that the ambitious programs of the 1960's and 70's failed—the best way to reduce crime is to provide jobs, educational opportunities and decent housing for the masses of poor black people.[66]

Finally, there is evidence that when blacks are victims of crimes, people are less likely to assist the victim,[67] and the offenders are more likely to receive harsher treatment than if the victims were white.[68]

SEX   In 1980 and in the preceding seven years, males were much more likely than females to be the victims of violent crime, with the rates of robbery and assault twice as high for men as for women. The rates of personal larceny without contact were also higher for men.

Even though males are more often the victims of violent crimes than females are, the fear of violent crime is perhaps greater among females, mainly because of the crime of forcible rape, whose victims are usually female. Female victims of violent crimes are further victimized by the reaction (or lack thereof) of the criminal justice system to the types of violent crimes that victimize women more often than men. In addition to rape, women are more often the victims of family violence, a crime that is gaining more attention and will be discussed in a later chapter.

AGE   Age is also an important variable in the study of victims. Although it is often suggested that the elderly are most often victimized by crime, the data do not support this position. A 1980 study of victimization revealed that for crimes of violence or theft, the elderly were least frequently the victims, and those persons aged twelve to twenty-four were most frequently the victims. The rates of victimization decrease with each age group after the age of twenty-four, and this pattern holds when sex is also considered as a variable. Males aged twelve to twenty-four were particularly vulnerable to the crimes of assault, robbery, or personal larceny.

Most of the crimes against the elderly are not violent. Assaults, robberies, or rapes account for only one-fourth of such crimes, with these crimes occurring at a rate of about eight per one thousand elderly persons. That rate is about one-fifth of the rate for similar crimes against younger persons.[69]

Once again, however, neither the UCR nor the NCS data reveal the total impact of crimes against the elderly. For example, violence against the elderly committed by members of their own families appears to be on the increase. **Granny bashing,** as it is often called, is becoming a serious problem and will be discussed in more detail in our chapter dealing with family violence.

The incidence of crimes against the elderly may not be as important, however, as their perception of the probability of such crimes. According to some authorities, the fear of crime is the number one fear among the elderly.[70] This fear may be unrealistic, but its impact on the elderly is dramatic. Many change their life-styles as a result, moving if possible. If that cannot be done, many will become "prisoners" in their dwellings, afraid to venture out even in the daylight hours.

For many elderly people, it is not the *probability* of becoming a victim that is crucial; it is the *possibility.* For the elderly, a purse snatching can have a far more serious effect than is the case with younger victims. The elderly are more likely to be seriously injured if there is any altercation between the assailant and the victim, and such direct contact may also be much more frightening to an elderly person. As well, the loss of money may be more severe to a person living on a fixed income.

Just as the elderly may be peculiarly susceptible to some kinds of crime because they are so defenseless, the very young may also be easy prey. Children as victims of sexual abuse, child abuse, and other forms of family violence, will also be discussed later in the text. Finally, the young are often victimized by the growing incidences of violence in our schools.[71]

RELATIONSHIP OF VICTIM AND OFFENDER

One final issue with regard to victims is the relationship between the victim and the offender. Violence in the form of assault or murder is usually preceded by social interaction of some kind, and physical violence is more likely if both the offender and the victim define the situation as one calling for such violence. If only one is prone toward physical violence, the altercation will probably not become a physical one. In this sense, the victim may contribute to his or her own injury or death. Often these social interactions have been preceded by numerous other interactions, some of these recent. In an earlier study of the victims of homicide, one social scientist

Figure 2.5

Percentage of violent crimes committed by strangers, by selected victim characteristics, 1980

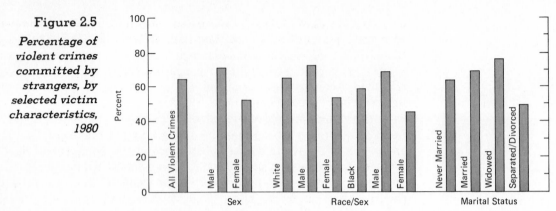

Source: Criminal Victimization in the United States, 1980. *A National Crime Report. U.S. Department of Justice, Bureau of Justice Statistics (Washington, D.C.: Government Printing Office, 1982), p. 10.*

found that one out of four of the victims of homicide precipitated the event that led to their deaths. The victim was the first to strike a blow, show force with a deadly weapon, or use that weapon.[72]

Such studies, as well as the *Uniform Crime Reports,* for years have provided us with data on the relationship between the victim and the offender in the crime of homicide, but with the beginning of the NCS, we have had an opportunity to analyze this relationship between offender and victim in other types of crimes. The 1980 data indicate that a majority of all violent crimes, 64 percent, are perpetrated by strangers. The *Report* indicates, however, that there is good reason to suspect that domestic violence is underreported because the victims do not wish to have their family members arrested.[73] If that is true, it is possible that a majority of all violent crimes are committed by friends, family members, or acquaintances (see Figure 2.5).

Males are much more likely than females to be attacked by strangers (71 versus 52 percent), and whites are more likely than blacks to be attacked by strangers (65 versus 59 percent), as shown in Figure 2.5. The differences are marked, however, when we look at the age of the victim. Approximately nine out of every ten violent crimes against the elderly (sixty-five and over) are committed by strangers, which is not the case with any of the younger age groups.[74]

SUMMARY AND CONCLUSION

In this chapter we examined the official and unofficial sources of data on criminal activity. After a brief look at Americans' perceptions of crime, we considered early attempts to measure crime. The cartographic school, despite its lack of sophistication in statistical analysis, at least began to emphasize the need for a scientific study of crime, which set the stage for the development of criminology.

The official source of official data on crime in this country, the *Uniform Crime Reports,* was examined in terms of its coverage and its limitations. Recognition of those limitations led to the use of other sources of data, and we studied victimization surveys and self-report surveys.

After the discussion of sources of data, we looked at the data to see what has been happening in crime in this country. This overview of the extent of crime and the demographic characteristics of criminals and their victims established the background for a later study of particular types of crime and particular types of criminals.

We saw that the data from official and unofficial sources do not always agree, and we considered the pros and cons for using the different methods of measuring crime. In the final analysis, the debate has been over which method is "most accurate"—that is, which most successfully minimizes the "dark figures" of unreported crime. Has the emphasis been misplaced?

One sociologist concluded that in trying to understand the data on crime, the important question is not the accuracy with which they describe the extent of criminal behavior or illuminate the dark figures of unreported crime but, rather, the way in which the data reflect the complex relationship between society and criminal behavior, with the result that they provide a barometer of society's attitudes toward its deviant members, rather than an objective measure of its social behavior.[75] Others emphasize that official crime data are the product of decisions to classify some behavior as criminal and that therefore crime rates "can be viewed as indices of organizational processes rather than as indices of the incidence of certain forms of behavior."[76] The official data represent decisions by those in authority, and the decision to detain is based on a whole network of social action.[77]

Such positions have led some to argue that new approaches should be taken toward official crime data. Instead of criticizing the data for not including all crimes, the data should be recognized for what they are—data concerning the social control of crime. The data should also be considered an end in themselves rather than as a means to an end. Crime rates are phenomena that are part of the natural world; they therefore cannot be evaluated as inaccurate or unreliable. As an aspect of **social organization**, they cannot, from a sociological point of view, be wrong.[78] Thus, official crime rates may be viewed as rates of socially recognized deviant behavior. Any **social system** has rates of deviance that are not socially or officially recognized, but deviance should be regarded in terms of the reaction of legal and social control systems.

It is sociologically relevant to determine from the official data what behavior is defined as deviant and how society organizes, classifies, and treats those forms of behavior. Official data do indicate that deviants are distinguished from nondeviants, and it is sociologically relevant to analyze the difference between a "convicted" person and a person whose crime stops at the crimes-known-to-the-police stage. That both persons may have committed the same deviant act is sociologically important, as is the fact that they have been officially treated differently. Thus, official crime data may be viewed as the sturctural response to crime rather than as indicators of the actual incidence of deviancy.[79] They also provide important information about the victims of crime. The data can be used to determine changing policies of the court (increases or decreases in the number of offenders placed on probation or fined) or trends in the length of sentencing and can be viewed as an *index of official* action.

Stanton Wheeler has suggested that the concept of crime data be reformulated and considered as the interrelationship of three elements: (1) the person who commits the crime, (2) the victim or other citizens who may report the crime, and (3) the official agents of the state who are charged with controlling crime. Wheeler recommends this reformulation because there is increasing recognition that deviance depends on a social definition. Therefore any analysis of crime data should recognize not only those who commit crimes but also those who define the behavior as criminal. He compares crime data to admission to and release from mental hospitals, arguing that neither can be understood by referring only to the characteristics of the subjects. Patients referred to child guidance clinics by doctors are more quickly admitted than those referred by members of their families; people with a higher socioeconomic status can more quickly get their family members into mental hospitals than can people from lower classes. In these cases the reaction of others is important in determining who is labeled deviant.

Wheeler found three practical consequences of this reformulation of the concept of crime data. First, police forces could be analyzed: perhaps the crime rates are high because the police are efficient. The police organizations of high-rate and low-rate areas could then be compared. The crime rates might, for example, reflect the relationship of the number of police cars to the number of people in an area. Differences among individual police could also be analyzed. According to Wheeler,

> the chief practical consequence of adopting a new rationale is that we would begin to understand the dynamics of police systems in relation to offenders . . . if we transform the degree of police efficiency into a variable to be explained, rather than one to be eliminated by the production of uniformity in procedure, we will enhance our understanding of crime.[80]

A second consequence of Wheeler's approach would be an improved understanding of citizens and social control. Citizens who observe crimes being committed, who are victims, or both frequently account for the crime rate by their decisions of whether to report the crimes. Wheeler cites one study that compared the delinquency rates of two communities, one with high and one with low rates, holding the factor of socioeconomic status constant when possible. The investigators found that the community with high cohesion had lower delinquency rates. Apparently the people living there pitched in and helped when they saw a child in trouble. It is therefore important to understand the ways in which different neighborhoods respond to deviant acts.

Third, Wheeler's approach to crime data would lead to the development of consumer-oriented crime data. Crime data indicate who commits the crimes by age, sex, race, and so on. But more relevant to consumers is the probability that a crime will be committed against them. It is important to know that the crime rate went up because of an increase of people in the age bracket that typically commits crimes, but it is more important to citizens to know the increase or decrease of their chances of being victimized. Empirical data could be used to describe the victims, not just the criminals. Wheeler concluded that the result of this approach would be an improved understanding of criminals and criminal acts. Currently, comparisons of crime rates of one community with another have little meaning because of all of the variables that make such comparisons of data unreliable. But within a community, by examining the relevant variables, crime could be better understood. Wheeler suggests that this new orientation toward crime data begin by collecting data on (1) the complaining witnesses, (2) the social characteristics of the community, (3) the reporting or arresting officer, and (4) the nature of the police system as a whole.

In addition to deciding how to collect data and what kind of data on crime should be collected, we have the problem of analyzing the data and explaining the meaning of the variables that appear to be related to crime. In the next chapter, we shall look at the emergence of the scientific analysis of data on crime and the subsequent developments of theories to explain criminal behavior.

PART II

EXPLANATIONS OF CRIMINAL BEHAVIOR

CHAPTER 3

Early explanations of criminal behavior and their modern counterparts

This chapter begins with a brief discussion of the nature and purpose of research in criminology and then analyzes the contributions of the classical, neoclassical, and positive schools to the development of a science of criminology. The impact of those schools on our modern punishment philosophies is examined in detail. The classical position of "letting the punishment fit the crime," with its emphasis on the belief that we are rational in our thoughts and that we rationally choose to seek pleasure and avoid pain, argued that sufficient punishment would be a deterrent to criminal behavior. If the punishment is a little worse than the pleasure of committing the crime, we just will not commit the crime! Empirical research on this issue is analyzed, with an emphasis on the recent contributions of the economists. This current emphasis on deterrence and retribution or, in the terms of the perhaps more palatable terms of today, "just deserts," is contrasted with the former emphasis on the need to reform or rehabilitate the criminal.

In the previous chapter we discussed the measurement of crime and its evaluation. We also considered some of the variables, such as age, sex, and race, that are related to crime data. Criminologists want to do more than count, however. Collecting data on crime is only a beginning step toward the eventual goal of controlling or preventing criminal behavior. In order to do that, we must develop ways to evaluate the data. Why do males have a higher crime rate than females? What are the reasons, the explanations? Just as physical scientists develop explanations to assist in ordering and understanding data in the physical world, social scientists develop explanations that aid in understanding criminal behavior. If we can understand why people engage in criminal behavior, we can then predict criminal behavior and eventually learn to control that behavior.

But simple explanations are not sufficient; for example, it is not very helpful to know only that the data reveal more arrests of males than of females for criminal behavior. We need to know what the patterns and the variables are that might explain these differences. To answer these questions, social scientists, like physical scientists, engage in research, developing and testing ideas. The research can be very complex, and we shall not go into a detailed analysis of research methods; rather, we shall look at the process of research with the view of understanding its overall purpose.

This chapter is an extremely important one, for it will set the stage for our discussions of theory: what happens in research will also influence the decisions that are made with regard to the processing of offenders. If we believe, for example, that stiff penalties are greater deterrents to criminal activity than are lighter sentences, in our efforts to control the crime rate, we probably will institute harsher penalties. Unfortunately, such "policy" decisions are often made on the basis of "intuition" or "common sense," without any reference to existing social science findings or an attempt to conduct research if such is needed.

RESEARCH IN CRIMINOLOGY

Research in criminology is conducted for the purpose of understanding criminal behavior. If we can understand the behavior, we will have a better chance of predicting when it will occur and then be able to take policy steps to control, eliminate, or prevent the behavior. All of these purposes are, however, controversial.

POLICY DECISIONS FOR CONTROLLING CRIMINAL BEHAVIOR

Although it might seem obvious to the casual observer that the purpose of research is to control, there has traditionally been a disagreement within the social sciences over the role of the social scientist in the decision-making process. In a provocative book entitled *Can Science Save Us?* one sociologist stated the problem succinctly: "If we want results in improved human relations we must direct our research to the solution of these problems."[1] But it

---

EXHIBIT

SOCIAL SCIENCE AND VALUES

"In all seriousness, then, and with careful weighing of my words, I register my belief that social science is the holiest sacrament open to men."

These words of Albion Small, one of the founding fathers of American sociology, show that early sociologists were full of moral vigor and ideas of reform. Many of them were ministers or the sons of ministers, although many lost their faith after embarking on a career in sociology, especially after being exposed to the works of Charles Darwin and Herbert Spencer (early sociologist influenced by Darwin).

"The first and second generation of American sociologists were very much part of the growing reform movement. Whether directly tied to the Social Gospel and related developments or not, they saw themselves as reformers and addressed themselves largely to an audience of reformers." This moralistic background may have been important, given the thought of that period, in getting sociology started and accepted.

Source: Adapted from Lewis A. Coser, "American Trends," in Tom Bottomore and Robert Nisbet, eds., *A History of Sociological Analysis* (New York: Basic Books, 1978), pp. 287–320. Quotations are on p. 289.

---

has also been argued that social scientists should not take positions on issues of value. That is, they should not be involved in decision making on the basis of the results of their research; they should be "value-free." They should conduct their research rigorously but leave the policymaking decisions to others. A 1949 pronouncement by a sociologist-demographer illustrates this position:

> Social science itself and the utilization of the products of social science research may both gain considerably, however, if it is recognized that it is not within the province of the social scientist as a social scientist to give "advice" or to participate in policy decision and action programs. The functions of conducting research and giving advice are, in my judgment, to be regarded as diverse functions to be achieved through a division of labor, the former by the social scientist and the latter by the social engineer.[2]

Others have taken the position that the whole process of the criminal justice system is political and, furthermore, that the system is used to discriminate against those people who are not in positions of power in the society, for example, minorities.

More recently, because of the widespread belief that "nothing works" in the criminal justice field, there is a tendency to avoid research findings and just use "common sense" in making policy decisions. In a recent review of the usefulness of crime-causation theories, sociologist Daniel Glaser contends that public officials and many criminologists have abandoned crime-causation theory. But, says Glaser,

> Causal explanation is evident, although often not explicit, even in the crime control efforts of practitioners who deride "theorists." Explanatory theory cannot disappear, for it is inherent in human thinking, even in that of persons who disavow it.

Glaser emphasizes that any time we explain, we theorize, "and we theorize scientifically whenever we offer explanations that observation could prove erroneous." It is therefore important to recognize these processes, for unless "it is made explicit, it cannot have cumulative growth and improvement." Most importantly, says Glaser,

> The foundations of any science are the basic statements of its theory—its principles. If evidence inspires increasing confidence in their validity and utility, they gradually acquire the status of scientific laws . . . causal theory is germane to public policy on crime.[3]

RESEARCH: THE SEARCH FOR EXPLANATIONS

The need for adequate research on criminal behavior has long been emphasized by social scientists and recently gained the attention of the President's Task Force on Violent Crime. When the task force made its preliminary report in 1981, it stated, "It is imperative that we discover what works—and what does not."[4] If we are to discover the answer to that question—what works—we must conduct scientific research. Such research is complicated, and an adequate understanding requires, at the minimum, a course in research methods. Accordingly, our discussion here will be limited to analyzing the pitfalls and problems that we need to keep in mind as we review the results of empirical research throughout this text.

Common errors in research

In scientific research, both in the physical and the social sciences, many different types of errors may occur. Some may be avoidable, and others may be due to the nature of the material being studied. Social scientists are studying human beings who are capable of thinking, reflecting, forgetting, misrepresenting, and even refusing to tell the truth. Given this practical reality, no research is without problems for the social scientist studying criminal behavior. In this discussion, we shall consider two basic areas of error; errors in selecting the research design, and errors in interpreting the data.

SELECTION OF A RESEARCH DESIGN

Social scientists have used a variety of research designs in their studies of crime. There are advantages and disadvantages of each type, and the researcher must, in each case, consider the kind of study that is to be conducted before choosing the research design and method. For example, although an in-depth study, or a case study, of a few inmates convicted of serial murders may give us detailed information on the history of those criminals, such information is not sufficient to allow us to generalize to the whole population of **serial murderers.** Such case studies are, however, very helpful in leading us to variables that we might study in larger populations. Early case studies of juvenile delinquents in the city of Chicago, for example, led investigators to study in depth the possible relationship between delinquency and the relationship of the delinquents with their families (many came from broken homes). These early studies, revealing that rates of delinquency were higher in certain areas of the city than in others, led to a broader analysis of the relationship of **ecology** to delinquency and crime.[5]

If a researcher wished to know the extent of involvement of juveniles in delinquent behavior at, for example, ages thirteen, fourteen, and fifteen, **samples** of juveniles from each of those age groups might be selected and studied for involvement in delinquency. The investigator would measure the delinquency of each age group at approximately the same point in time, thus trying to eliminate the influence that the passage of time might have on delinquency. For this purpose, the cross-sectional design is quite appropriate. On the other hand, if the researcher wanted to know what might happen to delinquent behavior over a period of time, a more appropriate method might be the longitudinal design. In this design, the researcher might begin the study with a sample of fourteen-year-old juvenile delinquents and study those same juveniles until they were, say, twenty years old.[6] At the end of that period, the researcher would be able to tell us to what extent the sample continued to be involved in delinquent activities over that six-year period, but the research would not tell us anything about delinquents who began their activities at earlier (or later) years.

The selection of a research design will depend not only on the nature of the study but also on the cost of the project. Following a sample over a period of years is expensive, and research funds are not always available for such studies. Likewise, selecting a large sample for an in-depth study would be costly in the short run, particularly if the subjects were located in different cities and numerous researchers had to be hired to conduct the research.

The selection of a research design might also be influenced by the fact that the activities the researcher wishes to study have already taken place and cannot be repeated. In that case, an *ex post facto* design would be appropriate. A sample of people already convicted of serial murders might be selected and studied to find out whether any past events or characteristics of these persons could explain why they became involved in crime. In contrast, when researchers want to study ongoing activities, they might go into the field to study behavior as it occurs. In this case, the researchers must be careful not to get so involved in the behavior under study that they lose their objectivity.[7]

ERRORS IN
INTERPRETING
DATA

Extreme care must be taken in analyzing empirical data, for the facts do not always speak for themselves. They must be interpreted. Researchers must also be careful not to go beyond the data—that is, to use the data to explain something that never was measured and not to generalize the findings beyond the scope of the study. For example, if all members of the sample are male, we cannot conclude that the research findings also apply to females, as the variable of sex might be important in explaining the delinquent or criminal behavior under study.

The dualistic
fallacy

One of the most common errors in interpreting data on crime is what we might call the **dualistic fallacy,** the assumption that there is a distinct dichotomy between two groups: (1) criminals or delinquents and (2) noncriminals or nondelinquents. The assumption is that these groups are homogeneous and that studies can therefore compare them on a given trait and conclude that the findings represent the differences between the two groups. The assumption is that criminals violate the law and noncriminals do not, but research indicates that this is not true. This dualistic fallacy is so serious that all empirical studies of delinquent and criminal behavior involving the error must be assumed to have limited scientific validity in distinguishing those who commit crimes from those who do not. But this does not mean that the studies are useless. The key question is whether the conclusions are limited to the subject matter that is actually being studied.

Science assumes that a phenomenon can be measured empirically with valid and reliable tools. Further, it assumes that this phenomenon can be clearly distinguished from something that is similar but not of the same classification. Even if the phenomenon cannot be measured with the senses, science presumes that it has consistent indicators of its existence and that those indicators can be measured empirically.

Applying these assumptions to the study of crime, the critical issue is what phenomenon is assumed to exist. Is there something called crime that is *sui generis,* that is, the only one of its own kind? Can it be distinguished from all other kinds of behavior? The answer to that question must be no. There is nothing intrinsically unique or distinguishable about crime. No form of behavior, not even **incest,** is universally considered to be criminal. A crime is defined not in terms of the properties or attributes of an act but in terms of the social situation in which it occurs. Sexual intercourse may be the lawful relationship between a husband and wife. That is a physical act that can be described. However, the same act may be incest, adultery, rape, statutory rape, or fornication, all of which are crimes in some jurisdictions. Finally, even though certain acts are defined as crimes, the violators often are not prosecuted, in which case people should not be considered criminals.

Crime, then, is clearly a definitional term. It exists because certain acts are defined as such. But those acts cannot be clearly distinguished from similar acts, or even from identical acts, except by social reaction. That is because intrinsically, crime is just like noncrime. The behavior in question is a crime when committed by some people in some situations and not a crime when committed by others in other situations. In trying to understand criminal behavior, then, it is important not only to understand why people commit acts that are defined as crimes, the approach taken by many sociological theorists, but also to understand the process by which some people are labeled criminal, whereas others who engage in the same behavior are not so labeled.

It would be possible to conclude that social science research is inherently suspect, that it will never be sufficiently free of methodological problems to answer our questions. But many of the problems can be resolved with adequate planning. As one noted methodologist observed, "Many of the fruits of science . . . can be used to advantage while still in the process of development. Science is at best a growth, not a sudden revelation." Research in the social sciences can be used "imperfectly and in part while it is developing."[8]

We have come a long way from the writings and thinking of the men whose ideas dominated the nineteenth century, but those ideas were critical in laying the foundation for our success today.

NINETEENTH-CENTURY EXPLANATIONS

The formal development of criminology as a discipline is very recent. Despite its recent development, the ideas of people who might be called early **criminologists** can be traced historically. Most of these people were lawyers, doctors, philosophers, or sociologists: all were reformers of the criminal law and not interested in creating a science of criminal behavior. Nevertheless, their contributions to criminology are immense, and for an adequate understanding of current criminological theories, some familiarity with these earlier approaches is important.

THE CLASSICAL BEGINNINGS

Ideas and philosophies do not exist within the vacuum of a human mind, and so they must be understood in the light of the social context in which they appear. Thus, to understand the classical writers and their contributions to criminology, it is necessary to know something about the social conditions that existed at the time they were writing.

The **classical** writers were rebelling against a very arbitrary and corrupt system of law, in which the judges held an absolute and almost tyrannical power over those who came before them. The law was applied unequally, and corruption was rampant. Confessions were obtained by means of torture, and the death penalty was used for many offenses.

Cesare Beccaria The leader of the classical school was Cesare Beccaria, born in Milan, Italy, on March 15, 1738. He published only one major book,[9] and his treatise was not entirely original, for many of the ideas were merely syntheses of ideas already expressed by others. But it was widely received "because it constituted the first successful attempt to present a consistent and logically constructed penological system—a system to be substituted for the confusing, uncertain, abusive and inhuman practices inherent in the criminal law and penal system of his world."[10] The work was also widely accepted because many people in Europe were ready to hear and to implement the kinds of changes Beccaria proposed.

Beccaria's work is extremely important today. "It is not an exaggeration to regard Beccaria's work as being of primary importance in paving the way for penal reform for approximately the last two centuries."[11] His short essay contains almost all of the modern penal reforms, but its greatest contribution, again, was "the foundation it laid for subsequent changes in criminal legislation."[12]

The underlying philosophy of Beccaria's position was that of **free will.** He maintained that behavior is purposive and is based on **hedonism,** the pleasure-pain principle: human beings choose those actions that will give pleasure and avoid those that will bring pain. Therefore punishment should be assigned to each crime in a degree that will result in more pain than pleasure for those who commit the forbidden acts. That is, the *punishment should fit the crime.* This hedonistic view of conduct implies that the laws must be clearly written and not open to interpretation by the judges. Only the legislature can specify punishment. The law must apply equally to all citizens; no defenses to criminal acts are permitted. The issue in court is whether a person committed the act; if so, the particular penalty prescribed by law for that act should be imposed. Judges are mere instruments of the law, allowed only to determine innocence or guilt and thereafter to prescribe the sentence of punishment. Under this system the law is rigid, structured, and impartial.

Influence on contemporary criminal law. The impact of Beccaria's arguments on modern American criminal law can be seen in this statement: "Our substantive criminal law is based upon a theory of punishing the vicious will. It postulates a free moral agent, confronted with a choice between doing right and doing wrong, and choosing freely to do wrong."[13]

But perhaps most important is Beccaria's contribution to making the law impartial. Contemporary America holds that all people should be equal under the law and that all cases must be weighed on an impartial, blind scale of justice. Although that ideal has never been fully implemented, Beccaria should be recognized for his contributions to the concept of justice.

The major weaknesses of Beccaria's ideas on crimes and punishments were the rigidity of his concepts and the lack of provision for justifiable criminal acts. These faults were acknowledged by the **neoclassical school.**

EXHIBIT

CLASSICAL INFLUENCE IN OTHER COUNTRIES

"Thinking about criminal sentencing has undergone a remarkable transformation in Scandinavia during the last decade. There has been a movement away from positivist sentencing ideology—that is, away from indeterminacy of sentence, and from rehabilitation and prediction of future criminality as the basis for sentencing. There has been growing support for a 'neoclassical' sentencing rationale, that would emphasize penalties proportionate to the gravity of the criminal conduct. This movement has had its greatest impact in Finland, where 'neoclassicism' has come to be official policy. Article 6 of the Finnish criminal code, as amended in 1976, declares that sentences should be in 'just proportion' to the harmfulness of the criminal conduct and the culpability of the offender."

Source: Andrew von Hirsch, "'Neoclassicism,' Proportionality, and the Rationale for Punishment: Thoughts on the Scandinavia Debate," *Crime & Delinquency,* January 1983, p. 52.

Jeremy Bentham Jeremy Bentham, born in 1748 and therefore a contemporary of Beccaria, was a British philosopher trained in law. His impact on legal thinking led one critic to admit that he was tempted to "proclaim Bentham the greatest legal philosopher and reformer the world has ever seen."[14]

Bentham's philosophy can be summed up in the phrase "let the punishment fit the crime," for Bentham believed that people act rationally. We choose certain acts because they bring us pleasure; likewise, we avoid acts that result in pain. Our choice is a rational one. Therefore, if we perceive that an act will bring pain—that is, the punishment for the crime is sufficiently severe—we will choose to avoid that act because engaging in it would result in pain that would outweigh any pleasure we might have in committing the crime.

Bentham referred to his philosophy of social control as that of **utilitarianism:** "An act is not to be judged by an irrational system of absolutes but by a supposedly verifiable principle . . . [which is] 'the greatest happiness for the greatest number' or simply 'the greatest happiness.'" Despite his belief in utilitarianism and the free will of individuals, Bentham also hinted at the theory of learned behavior as the explanation of criminal behavior. "He deserves considerable credit . . . for his adherence to a theory of social (i.e., pleasure pursuit) causation of crime rather than a concept of biological, climatic or other non-social causation."[15]

THE
NEOCLASSICAL
SCHOOL

The neoclassical school of criminology flourished during the nineteenth century. It had the same basis as the classical school—a belief in free will. But the neoclassical criminologists, who were mainly British, began complaining about the need for individualized reaction to offenders, as they believed the classical approach was far too harsh and, in reality, unjust.[16]

Perhaps the most shocking aspect of these harsh penal codes was that they did not provide for the separate treatment of children who committed crimes. One of the changes of the neoclassical period was that children under seven years of age were excepted from the law on the basis that they could not understand the difference between right and wrong. Mental disease also became a reason to except a would-be criminal from conviction under law. Mental disease was seen as a sufficient cause to impair responsibility; thus, defense by reason of insanity crept into the law. Indeed, any situation or circumstance that made it impossible to exercise free will was seen as reason to exempt the person involved from conviction. As such, the validity of mitigating circumstances, whether they be physical, environmental, or mental, was recognized by the neoclassicists.

Although the neoclassical school was not a scientific school of criminology, unlike the classical school it did begin to deal with the problem of causation. By making exceptions to the law, varied causation was implied, and the doctrine of free will could no longer stand alone as an explanation for criminal behavior. Even today, much modern law is still based on the neoclassical philosophy of free will mitigated by certain exceptions.

The classical and neoclassical schools were based on philosophy and "armchair" thinking. But before a science of criminal behavior could emerge, it was necessary to gather empirical data on criminals and to be able to analyze those data. The emphasis of the cartographic school on the collection and analysis of data was discussed in the previous chapter, and the use of data to explain criminal behavior can also be seen in the positive school of thought.

THE POSITIVE SCHOOL

The positive school of criminology was composed of several Italians[17] whose approaches differed to some extent, but they all agreed that the emphasis in the study of crime should be on the scientific treatment of the criminal, not on the penalties to be imposed on the criminal once he or she was convicted.

The classical school, defining crime in legal terms, emphasized the concept of free will and the position that punishment gauged to fit the crime would be a deterrent to crime. The **positivists** rejected the harsh legalism of the classical school and substituted the doctrine of **determinism** for that of free will. They focused on the **constitutional,** not the legal, aspect of crime, and they emphasized a philosophy of individualized, scientific treatment of criminals, based on the findings of the physical and social sciences. As Stephen Schafer said, "their emergence [in the late eighteenth century] symbolized clearly that the era of faith was over and the scientific age had begun."[18]

Cesare Lombroso   Cesare Lombroso (1835–1909) has often been called "the father of modern criminology."[19] Lombroso rejected the classical doctrine of free will, but he was strongly influenced by the contemporary writings on positivism by early influential sociologists. Lombroso was most famous for his biological theory of crime, which will be discussed in the next chapter.

Lombroso described himself as a "slave to facts." Indeed, he should be recognized for his emphasis on careful measurement in securing data, an approach that led him to confine his collection of data to organic factors. He believed that psychic factors were important but difficult, if not impossible, to measure. Despite his conscientiousness, Lombroso may be criticized for his failure to interpret his data in light of his theory. It was his belief that the data, even if they appeared unrelated at the moment, would subsequently evolve into a theory of universal applicability. In addition, his method was largely one of analogy and anecdote, from which he drew his conclusions.

The reaction to Lombroso ranges from severe criticism to high praise. Edwin H. Sutherland and Donald R. Cressey, in an early edition of their text, *Criminology,* asserted that Lombroso and his school "delayed for fifty years the work which was in progress at the time of its origin and in addition made no lasting contribution of its own." In an edition published nineteen years later, the authors were milder in their criticism, stating only that the Lombrosian school "fell into disrepute."[20] Marvin Wolfgang's response to that criticism was:

> The fear of these critics that Lombroso diverted attention from social to individual phenomena reveals their basic misunderstanding of his work and its effect; . . . Lombroso served to redirect emphasis from the crime to the criminal, not from social to individual factors.[21]

After discussing the serious methodological problems in Lombroso's research, as evaluated by modern techniques and knowledge, Wolfgang concluded that Lombroso "also manifested imaginative insight, good intuitive judgment, intellectual honesty, awareness of some of his limitations, attempts to use control groups and a desire to have his theories tested impartially. Many researchers of today fare little better than this."[22]

But even if modern scholars disagreed with everything Lombroso said, he still deserves an important place in the development of criminological thought. As Thorsten Sellin suggested, "his ideas proved so challenging that they gave an unprecedented impetus to the study of the offender. Any scholar . . . whose ideas after half a century possess vitality, merits an honorable place in the history of thought."[23]

Contributions of   The contributions of the positive school to the development of a scientific
the positive school   approach to the study of criminal behavior and to the reform of criminal
of thought   law were extensive. The positivists emphasized the importance of empirical

research in their work. They believed that punishment should fit the criminal, not the crime, as recommended by the classical school. The positivists substituted the doctrine of determinism, some arguing that it was physical, others that it was psychic, social, or economic, thus introducing the concept of environment into the study of crime. The writers in the cartographic school had emphasized the empirical study of crime, but the positivists stressed the criminal.

The research of the positivists has been greatly criticized, but despite the criticisms, the positive school had an important impact on the emergence and development of criminology:

> Few today can fail to appreciate that Lombroso, together with Ferri and Garofalo, the "holy three of criminology," revolutionized the way of looking at the criminal and excited the world toward the scientific study of crime. The works of these three Italians may well last as long as criminology itself.[24]

The classical and positive schools compared   The basic differences between the classical and positive schools of thought are listed in the chart below. This visual summary will facilitate our discussion of the impact that the two schools have had on modern criminology. In fact, the basic premises on which our policies of punishment, treatment, and sentencing have been based for the past quarter of a century can be traced to these schools of thought.

THE CLASSICAL AND POSITIVE SCHOOLS AND PUNISHMENT PHILOSOPHY

The writings of the classical and positive schools illustrate all of the basic philosophies of punishment: retribution or revenge, deterrence of the individual and of others, and reform or rehabilitation.

RETRIBUTION OR REVENGE

Historically, victims (or their families) were permitted to take measures to "get even" with criminals. This practice is referred to as revenge, retaliation, or retribution. But the terms are not synonymous.[25] **Retribution,** which focuses on the conduct of the wrongdoer, is the concept in vogue today and will be discussed in detail below. **Revenge,** or retaliation, more accurately reflects the practices of earlier days when victims could, within the law,

Classical School	Positive School
1. legal definition of crime	1. rejected legal definition
2. let the punishment fit the crime	2. let the punishment fit the criminal
3. doctrine of free will	3. doctrine of determinism
4. death penalty for some offenses	4. abolition of the death penalty
5. anecdotal method—no empirical research	5. empirical research, inductive method
6. definite sentence	6. indeterminate sentence

inflict upon their attackers the same or similar kind of **offense** as that suffered by the crime victim. The practice is often traced back to the Bible as well as to the Code of Hammurabi and is referred to as the "eye for an eye, tooth for a tooth" doctrine.

The classical thinkers did not, however, accept this extreme philosophy of punishment. They rejected punishments that were too harsh and believed that the criminal law should not be used as vengeance against the criminal. The punishment should "fit the crime." Beccaria, for example, insisted that the state had no right to impose a punishment greater than was necessary: "The right of the state to impose punishment is therefore limited to the minimum restriction of freedom adequate to this end," referring to the belief that individuals have given to the state only "that portion of his liberty necessary to preserve the rest." But "in all other matters, individuals should suffer no other consequences beyond the natural results of their acts. Any law or punishment in excess of this limit is an abuse of power, not justice, and no unjust punishment may be tolerated, however useful it seems."[26]

DETERRENCE

In addition to emphasizing a philosophy of punishment based on what the criminal deserves, the classical thinkers believed that a major purpose of punishment was **deterrence.**[27] There are two types of deterrence, individual and general.

Individual deterrence refers to the effect of punishment in preventing a particular individual from committing additional crimes. In the past, this form of deterrence often took the form of **incapacitation,** making it impossible for a particular offender to commit again the crime for which he or she had been convicted. For example, the hands of the thief would be amputated; rapists would be castrated; prostitutes would be disfigured in ways that would repel potential customers; and so on.

The second type, **general deterrence,** is based on the assumption that punishing individuals who are convicted of crimes will set an example to potential violators who, being "rational" beings and wishing to avoid such pain, will not violate the law. Again, we can see the influence of the classical thinkers, with their emphasis on free will and rational choice. People will seek pleasure and avoid pain; thus, if the punishment is perceived as too painful, people will avoid the criminal activity that might result in that punishment.

REFORM OR REHABILITATION

Retribution and deterrence were the philosophies of the classical and neoclassical schools, with their emphasis on "let the punishment fit the crime." The positive school, on the other hand, emphasized the importance of the "punishment fitting the criminal." It was the individual criminal, not the crime, that was the focal point in positive thinking. This school emphasized that if we were to prevent crime, changes must be made in the social environment. They favored indeterminate sentences, tailored to meet the needs of individual criminals. They also set the stage for further developing the philosophy of rehabilitating the offender, a philosophy that dominated our criminal justice system until recently.

Rehabilitation—a
modern ideal?

An article in late 1982 in *Time* magazine phrased the key question and then answered it in the subtitle of the article: "'What Are Prisons For?' No longer rehabilitation, but to punish—and to lock the worst away."[28] The article referred briefly to the original purpose of prisons in this country, not only to punish, but also to transform criminals "from idlers and hooligans into good, industrious citizens." The article concluded, however, that "no other country was so seduced for so long by that ambitious charter. The language, ever malleable, conformed to the ideal: when a monkish salvation was expected of inmates, prisons became penitentiaries, then reformatories, correctional centers and rehabilitation facilities." The simple fact is that prisons did not work as intended.

The philosophy of rehabilitation nonetheless continued and even gained momentum during this century. The concept of rehabilitation became the "modern" philosophy of incarceration. It was described by one authority as the "rehabilitative ideal," characterized by the **juvenile court,** probation, **parole,** and the **indeterminate sentence.**[29] The ideal was based on the premise that human behavior is the result of antecedent causes that may be known by objective analysis and that permit scientific control of human behavior. The assumption was, therefore, that the offender should be *treated,* not punished.

Social scientists strongly endorsed the rehabilitative ideal and began developing treatment programs for institutionalized **inmates.** The ideal was even incorporated into some statutes as well as proclaimed by courts, and supported by the president's crime commission.[30]

The indeterminate
sentence

The backbone of the philosophy of **rehabilitation** was the indeterminate sentence. No longer would a court, at the time of sentencing, give an offender a definite term, as a judge could not possibly predict in advance how much time would be needed for the treatment and rehabilitation of that offender. Consequently, in most jurisdictions the legislature established minimum and maximum terms for each offense. In its purest form, the indeterminate sentence meant that a person would be sentenced to prison for "one day to life." Treatment personnel would then evaluate the person, recommend and implement treatment, and decide when that individual had been rehabilitated and could safely be released back into society. The punishment was

"This spot is reserved for the indeterminate prison sentence."
(Renault-Sacramento Bee, Rothco.)

fitted to the criminal, not to the crime. In short, then, the basic philosophy was that society should incarcerate people until they were "cured" or rehabilitated.[31]

The decline of the rehabilitative ideal   The philosophy of rehabilitation was based on a belief that we could indeed predict when offenders had been rehabilitated and were therefore ready for release. But prediction is not that accurate in the social sciences, although individuals trained in the behavioral sciences would be in a better position to make that decision after working with an offender than would a judge at the time of sentencing. But, it is alleged, treatment has not been very effective in prisons.

Perhaps an even greater problem has been the administrative abuse of the power to release. For example, under the indeterminate system in California, offenders served longer terms than they would serve under definite sentences, and there was no evidence that such was necessary for rehabilitation.[32]

Another criticism of the indeterminate sentence was that it caused feelings of frustration and even hostility toward the criminal justice system. Offenders never knew when their release would be; all they knew was the first date at which they could apply for parole. According to one report, inmates referred to the indeterminate sentence as the "never-knowing system," and it created psychological problems for them.[33]

Another serious problem with the indeterminate sentence was the lack of guidelines, rules, or standards for release. This, coupled with the general unwillingness of the appellate courts to review the trial judges' sentencing decisions, led to serious attacks on this form of sentencing. The problems were increased by the extensive discretion given to parole boards in most jurisdictions. Such boards, in effect, often had the power to determine how much of the judicially imposed sentence each offender would serve. Even in those jurisdictions in which the legislature specified a minimum percentage of time that must be served before an offender would be eligible for parole, the parole board still had considerable discretion in the final determination of how much time an offender would serve in prison. The abuses of such discretion were exacerbated by the tremendous overcrowding in prisons that occurred in the past decade, a situation that led judges and parole boards often to base their sentencing or parole decisions solely on this factor.

The increasing dissatisfaction with the rehabilitative ideal and the concern about the extent of crime, especially violent crime, led many Americans to favor a "get tough" policy in sentencing, demanding even more severe sentences than are actually imposed.[34] The argument is that treatment did not work; so let us try incarceration for longer periods of time. "Lock 'em up and throw away the key! Crudely put, that increasingly is the rallying cry in an America fed up with violent crime."[35]

The trend toward harsher punishments, including greater use of the death penalty, is "justified" today on the basis of two philosophies. First, harsh punishment is what the criminal "deserves," and second, by imposing harsh penalties on "deserving" individuals, they and others will be deterred from committing crimes; thus the two philosophies of justice and of deterrence. These two philosophies have virtually replaced the former emphasis on rehabilitation as a means for punishment by incarceration.

"Let the punishment fit the crime" has been heard once again, with the background of Beccaria and the classical school of thought ringing in the ears of those who follow cycles in history. This time, however, the philosophy of retribution carries a different name.[36] We now talk about **just deserts** or "justice," but the underlying philosophy of retribution remains. We shall now examine the modern use of that philosophy, as a prelude to our examination of the justice approach and its companion philosophy of deterrence.

MODERN PUNISHMENT PHILOSOPHY

The concept of retribution, severely criticized in much of the scholarly social science literature as well as in judicial opinions in the first two-thirds of this century, was recognized in 1972 by the United States Supreme Court as an appropriate reason for the use of capital punishment.[37] In a 1976 opinion, the Court again discussed retribution as a justification for capital punishment. It indicated that although retribution is no longer the dominant philosophy,

> neither is it a forbidden objective nor one inconsistent with our respect for the dignity of men. . . . Indeed, the decision that capital punishment may be the appropriate sanction in extreme cases is an expression of the community's belief that certain crimes are themselves so grievous an affront to humanity that the only adequate response may be the penalty of death.[38]

The Court noted that the instinct for retribution is a part of human nature and that if the courts do not handle these situations, private individuals might take the law into their own hands. With regard to retribution, the Court concluded,

> In part, capital punishment is an expression of society's moral outrage at particularly offensive conduct. This function may be unappealing to many, but it is essential in an ordered society that asks its citizens to rely on legal processes rather than self-help to vindicate their wrongs.[39]

It has been argued that the Supreme Court justices have lately given more support to the doctrine of retribution as a justification for capital punishment because they realize the evidence on deterrence is not strong and the public has become disillusioned with the doctrine of rehabilitation. Retribution is the only doctrine supporting punishment in general and the death penalty in particular in which there need be no question of effectiveness. Effectiveness is not an issue. The argument under retribution is that people are incarcerated because that is what they deserve. Retribution is not *utilitarian.* Because its goal is "'doing justice' rather than the prevention of crimes, it makes no instrumental claims" and that is its principal merit. Its central defect, however, is that it "leaves so many questions about legal punishment unanswered that it cannot serve as a basis for a penal policy."[40] As we shall see in our critique of the justice model, this approach does not answer the question of *how much* punishment is deserved.

Another justification given today for the philosophy of retribution is that the retributive view of punishment serves the important social function of legitimizing punishment. The argument is that society desires to see crime punished because "the criminal has pursued his interests, or gratified his desires, by means noncriminals have restrained themselves from using for the sake of the law and in fear of its punishments." Therefore, the offender's act must be punished to justify the self-restraint of noncriminals. Finally, it is argued that society punishes because it feels it wants to or it ought to; the sole purpose of retributionism is its importance "as an expression of moral feeling."[41]

THE JUSTICE MODEL OF PUNISHMENT

Retribution as a justification for punishment not only has been seen in recent cases on the issue of capital punishment, but in addition it constitutes the framework for what is today called the **justice model** of punishment and sentencing.

Andrew von Hirsch represented the position of the report of the Committee for the Study of Incarceration in his book *Doing Justice: The Choice of Punishments.*[42] Indicating their basic mistrust of the power of the state, the committee members rejected rehabilitation and the indeterminate sentence and turned to deterrence and "just deserts" as reasons for punishment. In their rejection of rehabilitation as a reason for punishment, the committee, however, advocated shorter sentences and a sparing use of incarceration.

The person most often cited as responsible for the current popularity of the justice model is David Fogel, who expressed his views in detail in his book, *. . . We Are the Living Proof . . . The Justice Model for Corrections.*[43] Fogel formulates twelve propositions on which he believes the justice model can be based.[44] Essentially he argues that punishment is necessary to implement the criminal law, a law based on the belief that people act as a result of their own free will and must be held responsible for their actions. Prisoners should be considered and treated as "responsible, volitional and aspiring human beings." All of the processes of the agencies of the criminal justice system should be carried out "in a milieu of justice." This precludes a correctional system that "becomes mired in the dismal swamp of preaching, exhorting, and treatment," a situation that, according to Fogel, results in a correctional system that is dysfunctional as an agency of justice. Discretion cannot be eliminated, but under the justice model it can be controlled, narrowed, and subject to review.[45]

In the justice model, the emphasis is shifted away from the processor (the public, the administration, and others) to the "consumer" of the criminal justice system, a shift from what Fogel calls the "imperial" or "official perspective" to the "consumer perspective" or "justice perspective." Justice for the offender must not stop with the process of sentencing but continue throughout the correctional process. "The justice perspective demands accountability from all processors, even the 'pure of heart.' *Properly understood, the justice perspective is not so much concerned with administration of justice as it is with the justice of administration.*"[46]

Under Fogel's justice model, a person sentenced to serve time in a correctional facility should retain all of the rights "accorded free citizens consistent with mass living and the execution of a sentence restricting the freedom of movement."[47] Thus inmates should be allowed to choose whether they wish to participate in rehabilitation programs. The purpose of the prison becomes solely to confine for a specified period of time, not to rehabilitate the criminal. Offenders receive only the sentences they deserve, and those sentences are implemented according to fair principles. "The entire case for a justice model rests upon the need to continue to engage the person in the quest for justice as he moves on the continuum from defendant to convict to free citizen."[48]

The influence of the classical school can be seen in this recent return to a theory of "just deserts" or retribution. Bentham and Beccaria argued that the punishment "should fit the crime." The "just" and "humane" approach is to punish the criminal for what he or she has done, not to follow the treatment-rehabilitation, or so-called humanitarian, approach.

Critique of the justice model   The retribution-justice model leaves many questions unanswered: How *much* punishment is deserved? Further, it has been argued that the new approach is characterized by "an absence of rationale of cement or framework. Most of the recommendations are 'reactions' to past abuses, not prescriptions for future successes."[49]

Finally, for those members of society who already see themselves as victims of the social structure of power held by the middle and upper classes, the retribution-justice model may not appear "just." Some scholars have concluded that this model has been perpetuated by the ruling class to justify their continued attempts to repress the lower class. "The new justice model dispenses justice (that is, punishment) to preserve the capitalist social order and according to what the offender deserves in pursuing rational action. This notion of justice is appropriate for the capitalist order; it assumes a hierarchy of rights and competitive social relations."[50]

"MODERN" DETERRENCE THEORY   The classical position that the punishment should fit the crime, not the criminal, and the belief in free will and rational thought led to the conclusion that appropriate punishments could deter criminal activity, as rational humans would not choose behavior that would bring more pain than pleasure. Again, we see the modern counterparts, illustrated by a *Time* magazine article on capital punishment, stating the position quite simply: *"If I know I will be punished so severely, I will not commit the crime."*[51] But the author quickly noted that capital punishment in this country is not swift or sure, thus reducing the deterrent effect. Nonetheless, the philosophy is clear: punishment will deter. Today's reaction to the criminal is based on this philosophy, and it is therefore important not only to see the connection between this emphasis today and the writings of the classical thinkers but also to examine whether the philosophy has merit.

Empirical evidence regarding deterrence
Pro and con reactions to the question of whether punishment deters are too often based on conjecture, faith, or emotion, with few or no empirical data. Advocates simply "know" that punishment does or does not deter, and this is particularly so in the death penalty debate.

Such dogmatic statements cloud the issues and "do a disservice to a complicated question."[52] It therefore is important to analyze the empirical evidence on this critical question.

HIGHLIGHT

CHINA USES CAPITAL PUNISHMENT—CLAIMS CRIME RATE DROPS DRAMATICALLY AS A RESULT

Belief in the effectiveness of capital punishment as a deterrent led the government of the People's Republic of China to announce in the spring of 1982 that corrupt government and Communist Party officials would be executed. According to the party newspaper *People's Daily,* "It is necessary to kill one to warn a hundred . . . the seriousness of a few economic offenses has reached such an extent that the death penalty may have to be employed to beat down the offenders' arrogance and to educate and save others."[1]

The current wave of executions began in August of 1983, with reports of thousands of people being executed for the crimes of murder, rape, arson, robbery as well as gangsterism and even less violent crimes. Some of those executed were driven through the streets, accompanied by placards proclaiming to the masses the crimes for which the offenders would be executed.

The list of capital crimes in China was expanded in 1983, and now included are gang leaders, organizers of prostitution, and embezzlers. Furthermore, there is no longer a requirement that capital sentences have to be reviewed by the Supreme People's Court. In cases of violent crimes, execution may be carried out swiftly after the sentence is imposed by a lower court. The processes of arrest, indictment, trial, sentence, and execution may take place in four days. In China, the usual method of execution is a single shot in the back of the head.[2]

In the spring of 1984, the Chinese claimed that as a result of increased executions (estimated by some to be as high as ten thousand since August of 1983), the crime rate had dropped 42 percent.[3]

Sources: (1) "Peking to Execute Corrupt Officials, Paper Indicates," *Los Angeles Times,* March 11, 1982, pt. I, p. 10, col. 1. (2) "China Suddenly Taking a Tougher Line on Crime," *New York Times,* September 13, 1983, p. 10Y, col. 1. (3) National news broadcast, spring 1984.

Jack P. Gibbs has addressed the issue of deterrence in an insightful and provocative book, *Crime, Punishment, and Deterrence,* in which he reviews the empirical findings on the issue of punishment and deterrence. Noting that much of the earlier sociological research on deterrence was concerned solely with the relationship of crime rates and the statutory existence of the death penalty, Gibbs points out that more recently, sociologists have turned to an "examination of the relation between actual legal punishments (imprisonment in particular) and crime rates."[53] According to Gibbs, the findings of the earlier studies cannot be generalized to other types of punishment. They are even limited in their application to our understanding of the deterrent effect of capital punishment, as most ignore the variable of certainty of actual execution. In addition, studies of the deterrent effect of punishment, argues Gibbs, must allow for the differences between general and individual deterrence and take into account properties of punishment such as the perceived certainty that one would actually suffer a punishment. Most importantly, "the very idea of testing the deterrence doctrine is dubious without first restating the doctrine as a systematic theory." Gibbs concluded, however, that until further exploratory research enables us to refine some of the properties of punishment, the development of a systematic theory would be premature.[54]

Other sociologists have agreed that we cannot actually test deterrence until we can refine our research models and specify the variables determining whether or not punishment deters.[55] There is, for example, some evidence that punishment may have a quick but not a long-term deterrent effect.[56]

Deterrence and capital punishment	Despite the lack of sophisticated theoretical development, there has been research on the deterrent effect of punishment, with most of the earlier research focused on capital punishment. This earlier research, dominated by the work of sociologist Thorsten Sellin, generally found no support for the deterrence theory.[57]

After analyzing Sellin's work and that of others in the same period, Professor Richard O. Lempert observed that the researchers in general realized the necessity of controlling for factors that might be important in measuring the deterrent effect of capital punishment but that they did not use "the techniques of modern mathematical social science to hold these factors constant."[58] Lempert then reviewed some of the work of more recent researchers who did use such techniques but still failed to find support for the deterrence theory.[59] He concluded:

The strength of the research reviewed thus far rests not in individual studies but on the work taken as a whole. Deterrent effects of capital punishment have been given many different kinds of chances to appear. If capital punishment has any strong deterrent effects, it is likely that some deterrence would have been evident. While it is impossible to prove a negative, this failure to find a deterrent effect provides reason to believe that none exists.[60]

Some of the earlier studies actually found higher homicide rates in states with capital punishment, as compared with those without the death penalty. On the basis of their analysis of homicide rates between 1930 and 1970, Daniel Glaser and Max S. Ziegler found that the existence of capital punishment on the statute books was not a significant deterrent to homicide and therefore "[a] state should express its abhorrence of homicides not through the coldblooded means of capital punishment but through severity and certainty in its confinement penalties for those who kill."[61] William C. Bailey, in his analysis of the Glaser and Zeigler study, decided that their methodology was questionable and that their conclusions were contradicted by other studies. Bailey asserted that other research contradicted their conclusion that abolition of the death penalty would result in a reduction of homicides. Empirical studies have not yet produced evidence to support that conclusion or that homicides would rise if capital punishment were abolished.[62] Further, in analyzing the effect of the death penalty as a deterrent, we must distinguish between the fact that the penalty is statutorily available and the actual use of the penalty.[63]

In responding to Bailey's reactions, Daniel Glaser, among other comments, said that he had not argued that eliminating the death penalty per se would decrease homicide rates but, rather, that "advocating the death penalty is not as expressive of outrage at murder as is opposition to the death penalty" and that one effective way the state could encourage alternatives to violence is by eliminating this form of violence.[64]

Isaac Ehrlich. Recent support for the death penalty as a deterrent has centered on the work of Isaac Ehrlich,[65] an economist. In 1975 Ehrlich "published in his profession's most prestigious journal what is probably the most important article on capital punishment to date. The article . . . is important for its timing, its methods, and its results."[66] This article formed the basis of the government position argued by the solicitor general in the *Furman* case, that capital punishment is not unconstitutional: "The use of Ehrlich's article by the Solicitor General guaranteed that it would attract substantial attention, perhaps more than it merited."[67] Lempert concluded that the 1975 article written by Ehrlich was important because it was used to support the belief that executions deter homicides, and it was published at a time when many were looking for that kind of support. Lempert quickly added his analysis that Ehrlich found no support for the deterrence theory and that his work "has stirred up the pond, but only to muddy the waters at a time when we need to see clearly."[68]

Deterrence of types
of crime and types
of people
The debate over deterrence should be narrowed to examining types of crime and types of people, which is often overlooked in the debate concerning punishment as a deterrent. Perhaps punishment (or the threat of punishment) is effective in deterring a woman from shoplifting but not necessarily from poisoning her husband. Perhaps certain types of people are deterred by laws, but others are not.[69]

In the case of murder and other violent crimes, offenders are often under the influence of drugs or alcohol or are consumed by passion, as in the case of domestic crimes. Thus most of these people are probably not thinking very rationally when they commit the crime.

Another area in which the type of crime is important to analyzing the potential deterrent effect of legal sanctions is crimes that are considered "moral." In Chapter 1, in our discussion of the use of law as a form of social control in regulating morality, one of the behaviors we considered was alcohol abuse. We noted that laws may not be effective in deterring people from drinking but that they may have significant deterrent effect on driving while intoxicated.

An expert on deterrence and traffic laws, sociologist H. Laurence Ross has studied this issue in other countries as well as in the United States. In a recent book he discussed the impact that drunk-driving laws have had on the incidence of drunk driving. Ross concludes that there is an immediate deterrent effect when such laws are passed or there is a crackdown on enforcement but that the deterrent effect is short-lived. Ross believes that social learning is the key variable; over time, individuals learn that despite the crackdown, their chances of being caught are slim; and if caught, the chances of significant punishment are also slim, and so the deterrent effect is low.[70]

What the Ross study does not show, however, is what the deterrent effect of severe punishment might be or what is considered severe punishment. For example, for an executive who must drive for business, entertainment of clients, and so on, the revocation of a driver's license and publication in the paper of the arrest and type of punishment might be sufficient to deter that person from again driving while intoxicated. It might also be sufficient to deter others of that type from this prohibited behavior. On the other hand, even if those sanctions are sufficient deterrents, their effect may also be short-lived. And the effect might be lost entirely if people perceive that (1) they will not be caught and/or (2) if caught, the probability of actually receiving these or other punishments is slim.

One final type of crime should be mentioned in relationship to the issue of whether the threat of legal sanctions deters criminal behavior, and that is **corporate crime.** Two prominent social scientists have argued that although the traditional reasons for punishment may not be effective with those who commit "traditional crimes," they will work on corporate criminals. Corporate crimes are not crimes of passion or emotion; rather, they are usually rationally calculated and consequently more amenable to deterrence: "incapacitation . . . can be a highly successful strategy in the control of corporate crime."[71] Other experts agree: "Punishment may work best with those individuals who are 'future oriented' and who are thus worried about the effect of punishment on their future plans and their social status rather than being concerned largely with the present and having little or no concern about their status."[72]

Perceived deterrence

What we are really talking about, say some researchers, is perceived deterrence—what people actually think will happen will determine whether they are deterred. Thus, the perception of the certainty and severity of punishment may be the key variable in explaining deterrence.

With regard to certainty, it is said that the *actual* certainty of punishment influences people's perceptions of certainty—if they believe that punishment is certain, they will be afraid to violate the law. This proposition has not, however, been examined explicity,[73] although the conclusions of two studies question its validity.[74]

The relationship between the actual certainty of punishment and the perceived certainty of punishment is difficult to test empirically, although there have been some suggestions of ways in which it might be done.[75] But until this relationship is measured empirically, it would be difficult, if not impossible, to measure the deterrent effect of certainty of punishment.[76]

Furthermore, perceptual deterrence may involve more variables than just perceived legal punishment. For example, two investigators studied the deterrent effect of three variables: moral commitment (internalization of legal norms), fear of social disapproval, and fear of legal punishment, and they found that all three forms of social control were important as inhibitors of illegal behavior.[77] They note that according to some deterrence theorists, many people who internalize norms behave in legal ways, not because they fear punishment, but because this is the "proper" way to behave. For those people, internalization of norms is thus a more effective form of social control than is fear of legal apprehension and punishment.[78] They conclude, however, that the perceived threat of punishment is effective to some extent at all levels of moral commitment and that "the accumulated research supports . . . [the] argument that the threat of physical and material deprivation should have a more central place in sociological theories of social control."[79]

In analyzing the above conclusions on the data concerning perceived deterrence, critics have argued that the findings might be explained by experience rather than by deterrence. Tentative conclusions drawn from recent studies suggest, for example, that the behavior is not explained by perceptions—that is, not the perceived threats of legal sanctions but, rather, the perceptions following the behavior deter criminal behavior. Thus, it is possible that it is the *experience* of criminal behavior and the subsequent processing that defines our perceptions of the threat of legal sanctions. The studies, however, are limited, and "future research should concentrate on replicating these findings on more representative samples involving different criminal acts."[80]

ECONOMIC
THEORY

Economics has been defined as "a discipline which studies the allocation of scarce means among alternative ends" and as "the science of human choice in a world in which resources are limited in relation to human wants."[81] Economists assume that individuals are the best judges of their own needs and that their actions, based on rationality, will be governed by their desires to maximize their own welfare. Economists do not deny that these choices may be socially conditioned, but they are not interested in explaining what causes or forms these choices. Rather, they view the individual in terms of that person's preferences, and they call these preferences, which may be either material or nonmaterial, *goods.* Some of these are free goods, defined as those that are so plentiful that a person may have any amount without depriving others of them. Others are scarce and are called *economic goods,* and for them people must compete. "Because economic goods are scarce, choices must be made in allocating their use. Since economics is the study of choice in a world of scarce resources, it is, by definition, interested only in economic goods."[82]

Economists believe that people are rational and that they look for ways to improve their welfare. In terms of criminal activity, the person weighs the benefits of crime against the cost of illegal behavior and chooses the latter; thus, in the words of Gary Becker, whose 1968 article began the current involvement of economists in explaining criminal behavior:

> A person commits an offense if the expected utility to him exceeds the utility he could get by using his time and other resources at other activities. Some persons become "criminals," therefore, not because their basic motivation differs from that of other persons, but because their benefits and costs differ.[83]

The criminal behavior is thus "explained" by a cost-benefit analysis, just as economists use this to explain other kinds of behavior. Some people may make an inaccurate judgment on a cost-benefit basis, but the explanation remains: they decide whether to abide by the law or to engage in illegal behavior on the basis of their own mental calculations of the costs and benefits of each. Deterrence comes into play in their theory in that adjustments in the incentives and disincentives can alter the behavior. Thus, if we increase the cost of crime, the "demand," or incidence, will decrease; but if we decrease the cost of crime and increase the benefits, the demand, or prevalence of crime, will increase.[84]

Once again, we see the influence of the classical thinkers. Becarria and his followers believed that people were rational and operated on a pleasure-pain principle; they engaged in behavior that brought pleasure and avoided behavior that brought pain. To "control" their behavior, all we need to do is adjust the costs and benefits—make the punishment just a little greater than the pleasure of committing the crime—and the rational person will not commit the crime.

Empirical research in economics   Economist Gary S. Becker, after his 1968 application of economic theory to an analysis of criminal behavior, tested his theory empirically by measuring the effect of a 50 percent increase in the New York City police force on the ratio of arrests to reported crimes. He found that the ratio of arrests went up. In other words, said Becker, the probability of arrest and the level of sanctions reduce the "supply of offenses"—that is, crime. People who think they will be arrested, convicted, and sentenced severely will decide not to take the risk. "Further," he noted, "whether increases in the probability of convictions or in sanction levels are relatively more effective in deterring offenses depends critically on the individual's attitude toward risk." Those who like to take risks will be more often deterred by increases in the probability of conviction, whereas those who do not like to take risks will be more deterred by increases in the level of the penalty.[85]

Becker's theory and findings were just what many people wanted to hear, and he set the stage for increased attention to the philosophy of deterrence. The immediate tests of his economic theory, for the most part, supported his position. Isaac Ehrlich, whose work on deterrence and capital punishment we examined earlier in this chapter, reported that his research indicated that in this country, we can reduce index offenses by 3 percent and correctional costs by 2.7 percent with a 1 percent increase in police and judicial expenditures.[86] In a later study, Ehrlich reported that he had found evidence that without exception, the rate of specific crimes went down with the estimate of the probability of apprehension, punishment by imprisonment, and average length of time served in state prisons.[87]

Other support for the theory comes from the test of an economic model of crime using data collected on the postrelease activities of a sample of men released from the prison system in North Carolina. The result:

> Both the expected certainty and severity of punishment are found to deter criminal activity in a number of instances and a 1 percent increase in certainty is generally found to have a greater effect than a similar increase in severity. Certainty of punishment is found to have a greater effect for relatively minor offenders and severity for persistent offenders.[88]

Analysis of economic theories and deterrence   In addition to the criticisms of the economic theory and the deterrence of the death penalty, critics have reported data that contradict the findings of econometrics. For example, a study of the relationship between the strength of the police force in Detroit and its crime rate led two sociologists to conclude:

> [P]olice strength and crime are not systematically related and . . . the tightly coordinated adjustments envisioned in economic theory are not characteristic of the real world. . . . Our findings indicate that the economic model is too simple to account for the relationships between crime and police strength.[89]

Critics have attacked the basis of the economic theory—that behavior is rational. That assumption has two major objectives, says one critic:

> (a) It implies that people who contemplate committing a crime have a realistic perception of the probabilities of being sanctioned and of the severity of the sanction. The little evidence we have on perceptions of legal sanctions by the general public indicates that these perceptions are incorrect and variable. . . .
> (b) It implies that people who commit crimes act after rational calculation rather than on impulse. We have much reason to believe that many crimes are committed on impulse, either under the influence of alcohol or simply as the result of opportunity and need intersecting.[90]

With respect to the belief that we are rational, the words of philosopher Bertrand Russell are pertinent:

> Throughout a long life, I have looked diligently for evidence in favor of this statement [that people are rational animals], but so far I have not had the good fortune to come across it, though I have searched in many countries spread over three continents.[91]

Critics have also attacked the economists' general methodology. Two investigators, after reviewing the works of Becker, Ehrlich, and others, concluded:

> We find serious flaws with the Becker-Ehrlich model, with the data used in its empirical implementation, and with Ehrlich's conclusions regarding evidence to support the deterrent effect of punishment on crime. Indeed, we can find no reliable empirical support in the existing economics literature either for or against the deterrence hypothesis.[92]

The criticisms of the economic model have, however, come mainly from sociologists and criminologists, and despite the intensity of some of these criticisms, the economists remain well received, both by scholars and by the public. As one political scientist pointed out, they talk in terms that most people like to hear—"dollars and cents"—whereas sociologists, in discussing causes of crime, talk about self-concepts, alienation, and other concepts that do not gain as much public recognition.[93]

One economic theorist has defended the position and the contributions of the economic theories:

> Economists studying criminal behavior have done two basic things: First, they have developed simple, but rigorous deductive models that are consistent with

---

EXHIBIT

IMPACT OF ECONOMIC THEORY

"Of all the social scientists, the economists have been most successful in selling the idea that they are the most scientific: their methods of model-building, their adaptations of mathematical and statistical analyses, and their procedures for hypothesis-testing more closely approximate those of the physical sciences, and where they do not, economists design analytic and predictive techniques that facilitate our understanding of how society works and of how government policies should be changed to achieve specific goals."

Source: Richard F. Sullivan, "The Economics of Crime: An Introduction to the Literature," *Crime & Delinquency* 19 (April 1973): 139, quoted in John E. Monzingo, "Economic Analysis of the Criminal Justice System," *Crime & Delinquency* 23 (July 1977): 261.

---

both the deterrence hypothesis and with the assumption that individual actions are affected by the relative gains available in legal and illegal activities. Second, economists have provided more sophisticated and systematic statistical tests of these hypotheses than were to be had prior to their reentry into the study of criminal behavior.[94]

Regardless of our position on economic theory, the contributions of these researchers and theorists cannot be ignored, as they set the stage for a return to deterrence as one of the basic philosophies behind punishment. Perhaps their greatest impact has been in the use of their findings to support the death penalty. The refusal of the United States Supreme Court to declare that penalty unconstitutional and the resulting increase of the imposition of that penalty may be to a great degree related to the economists' reported findings, often cited by the Court.

Finally, the economists force us to consider that rationality as an explanation of human behavior may not have lost its importance in the classical period and that we should give more thought to motivation as a factor in a person's choice of behavior. Despite the flaws of their research, their conclusions should not be discredited. "Given the simplicity of their deductions and the often unavoidable flaws in their empirical tests, the work of economists should be viewed as giving policy insights rather than guidance."[95]

It is thus important to be careful in making generalizations from the economists' findings on the issue of deterrence:

The appeal of this approach lies in the seeming generality of its empirical results. I believe there is a moral here: the quest for a single set of universally applicable estimates of deterrence effects is hopeless, given the nature of available data and the complexity of the underlying process which generates crime rates and sanction threats.

But this critic sees hope, as he concluded:

> It may pay deterrence researchers of the next decade to be modest. Sound generalizations will gradually emerge from the accumulation of carefully tested evidence on the deterrence process.[96]

PUNISHMENT THEORY: AN ANALYSIS
Where does this discussion leave us? The classical thinkers argued that punishment should fit the crime, and some modern thinkers have taken that to mean that criminals should get the punishment they deserve. Others have interpreted classical thinking in terms of its utilitarian principle of deterrence—that people behave rationally and will seek pleasure and avoid pain. Therefore, in order for the criminal law to deter, it must be swift and sure and provide penalites that are considered just a little worse than the pleasure that would be gained from engaging in the criminal behavior. What happens, however, when what a criminal deserves, if indeed we can define that, conflicts with utilitarian or deterrent principles? For example, under the just deserts approach, we cannot give a criminal more punishment than he or she deserves; that would be as unfair as too little treatment. But what if the just punishment is not sufficient for deterrence, either individual or general? The just punishment, as defined by law, may be a revoked license for drunk driving. But what if that punishment is not sufficient for deterrence? Suppose that the only effective general deterrent to rape is castration. Is that a just punishment, particularly if for a given criminal, a lesser penalty would be sufficient for individual deterrence? Or is the real issue that "the question is not what penalties are effective, but 'what in the name of decency can properly be inflicted?'"[97]

> In summary, the efficiency of punishment as deterrence is clear, [but] . . . it is important to emphasize that deterrence need not be inhumane; penal sentences can be made comparable by converting them into their monetary equivalent or worth. The task of the criminal justice system becomes clear: to produce justice as efficiently as possible given the scarce resources with which to operate.[98]

Finally, how do the principles of just deserts, utilitarianism, and deterrence apply to the punishment of corporate offenders? Should the corporation be punished, for example, by fine or by withdrawing its charter, or should its individual executives be punished, and, if so, how? Would it ever be just to punish the corporation for the criminal behavior of its employees? On the other hand, would it be just to punish the employees if they were acting as directed? And which would be the greater deterrent?[99]

SUMMARY AND CONCLUSION
We began this chapter with a brief overview of the importance of research as well as a glance at the methods of social science research and its problems.

This background was necessary for understanding the modern empirical studies on which the chapter focused, the relationship between the modern views of punishment and sentencing and the view of the thinkers of the classical, neoclassical, and positivist periods. We studied the debate over how much punishment we should have in order to deter criminal behavior. Despite the extensive research, two authorities have described that debate as having deteriorated since the writings of Beccaria: " ... Discussions of this ancient antinomy which have consumed gallons of jurisprudential ink turn out on examination to resemble nothing so much as boxing matches between blind-folded contestants."[100]

We briefly discussed retribution as a philosophy for punishment, noting that it was the dominant reasoning before the return of deterrence and just deserts. Unfortunately, when these philosophies of deterrence, retribution, and just deserts overtook rehabilitation as the dominant themes of our approach to criminals, the goal of rehabilitation was mostly abandoned. As one judge said, "The guiding faith of corrrections—rehabilitation—has been declared a false god."[101] The problem with rehabilitation as a justification for punishment was that it "should never have been sold on the promise that it would reduce crime. Recidivism rates cannot be the only measure of what is valuable in corrections. Simple decency must count too. It is amoral, if not immoral, to make cost-benefit equations a lodestar in corrections."[102]

Others, in recognizing and even approving of the demise of the rehabilitative ideal as the primary purpose of punishment, have emphasized the importance of maintaining the *opportunity* for treatment. David Fogel's justice model does not preclude treatment; it only precludes coercive treatment. As he said in 1975, "What I suggest we do is give up this nonsense [coerced treatment] and return to a very open system ... where we don't try to screw people's heads on right." In reporting those comments from his speech, the *Seattle Times* ran the headline "Ex-prison Director Mocks Rehabilitation."[103] But that is not correct. It is only the *coerced* treatment, the attempt to *force* rehabilitation, that is being shunned.

Norval Morris, a noted authority on criminal justice and a professor at the University of Chicago College of Law, also argues for salvaging something of the rehabilitative ideal: "Rehabilitative programs in prisons have been characterized more by false rhetoric than by solid achievement. They have been corrupted to punitive purposes. But it does not follow that they should be discarded." According to Morris, we should not send people to prison for *treatment*. We should keep treatment programs but distinguish between the purposes of incarceration and the opportunities that might be provided to the incarcerated person. "Rehabilitation can be given only to a volunteer." Morris is not arguing that treatment does not work and therefore should be abolished. Rather, he is saying that the treatment model should be liberated, should not be coercive, and is referring to the *"substitution of facilitated change for coerced cure."*[104]

The "rehabilitative ideal" retains some support, however, with the author of the terminology not only writing a history of the concept but also expressing his hope that it will still have a role in punishment,[105] and a recently published text, *Reaffirming Rehabilitation,* clearly indicates in the title the position of its authors.[106]

CHAPTER 4

Biological and psychological theories

This chapter brings together a wide variety of approaches to understanding criminal behavior, many of which were popular in the past, lost favor, and are now being revived, but with more sophisticated research. The current developments in biology and psychology are discussed against the background of the earlier contributions of the positive school, the constitutional approach, and the body-type theories. We also shall consider the importance of genetic background as well as the possible relationship of the nervous system, endocrinology and body chemistry, and criminal behavior. Closely related to these biological approaches and, in some cases actually overlapping, are the recent explanations of criminal behavior advanced by psychologists. We shall briefly look at the historical developments in both psychology and psychiatry, including Freud's contributions, before turning to more recent developments in personality theory, cognitive development theory, and behavior theory. Finally, we shall study the practical and legal implications of these developments in biology and psychology. Our focus will be on defenses to criminal law, particularly the insanity defense, successful and highly controversial in the case of John W. Hinckley, Jr., who attempted to assassinate the president of the United States, Ronald Reagan.

The fashions and fads in human thought are interesting, and the field of criminology is no exception. We have already seen that in the eighteenth century the major emphasis regarding criminals was a philosophy of punishment and sentencing that lost favor in the following century. During the nineteenth century, on the other hand, the influence of biology was strong, stemming from the theory of evolution of Charles Darwin, who in 1859 published his *Origin of the Species,* a work hailed by many as one of the most important books ever written, in its impact on our thought. The immense controversy that immediately surrounded the theory of evolution is still present today, as some people continue to debate whether the theory should be taught in our public schools.

BIOLOGICAL FACTORS AND CRIME

In the field of criminology, however, biological explanations of behavior have been "out of style" for some time. A glance through the criminology texts of the past two decades will reveal less and less attention being given to the subject, with the major emphasis instead on sociological theories of criminal behavior. But as we shall see in this chapter, there recently has been a resurgence of interest in biological and psychological theories of criminal behavior. The latter has received considerable attention in the context of the hotly debated insanity defense. Recent controversial defenses to criminal behavior have also involved biological explanations, such as the presence of an extra male chromosome in males, the **XYY chromosomal abnormality,** and the **premenstrual syndrome** (PMS) defense used by some female defendants.

Not only has the law given more recognition to biological explanations of behavior; so have scientists, and in this chapter we shall examine some of the most recent studies of the alleged relationship between our bodies and our behavior.

> Taken together, research into the relation between biology and crime leaves no doubt that social and biological variables, and their interactions, are important to our understanding of the origins of antisocial behavior.[1]

HISTORICAL BACKGROUND OF BIOLOGICAL EXPLANATIONS

Although the major biological theories of criminal behavior were developed in the nineteenth century, biological explanations can be found much earlier. One criminologist has traced back to Aristotle the belief that personality is determined by the shape of the skull. The relationship between criminal behavior and body type has been traced back to the 1500s, and the study of facial features and their relationships to crime, to the 1700s, when phrenology emerged as a discipline. **Phrenology** has been defined as "the study of the external conformation of the cranium."[2] Its development is associated mainly with the work of Franz Joseph Gall (1758–1828), who investigated the bumps and other irregularities of the skulls of inmates of penal institutions and asylums for the insane. He also studied the heads and head casts of persons who were not institutionalized and used these findings to compare with his data on criminals.

The theory of phrenology is based on the idea that the exterior of the skull corresponds to the interior and to the brain's conformation. The brain can be divided into functions that are related to the shape of the skull. "Corollaries to these propositions held that, in general, the brain was the organ of the mind, and that certain areas of the brain contained organs to which corresponded an equal number of psychological characters, or powers."[3]

Some studies in phrenology were conducted in European and American prisons, and for a few years we even had a professional journal, the *American Journal of Phrenology*. However, the issue of whether phrenology had an impact on the understanding of criminology or, for that matter, whether the theory that the brain is connected to behavior was ever really tested, is debatable. One sociologist concluded that phrenology, "in its 19th century meaning, was not substantiated; it has been rejected, and the modern experimental science of brain pathology has advanced far from the investigation of peculiar bumps and a mysterious 'intellect.'"[4]

Others have taken the position that Gall did conduct "scientific" experiments to the degree that such was possible during his time and that he "postulated a theory within his own acknowledged area of professional expertise. . . . The original theory was based on years of painstaking research followed by the continuing data collection of other . . . phrenologists, and it seems never to have been scientifically disproven." Furthermore, the most relevant phrenological organ, "destructiveness," is the same area of the brain, right over the ear, on which modern surgeons have operated in an effort to control violent and aggressive behavior. This surgery has met with only moderate success, but the conclusions of the early phrenologists, "with some slight modifications, [are] not patently absurd within the light of contemporary scientific knowledge."[5]

THE POSITIVE
SCHOOL

If the above evaluation of Gall's contributions and the study of phrenology is considered seriously, then we are placing the beginning of "scientific" criminology about seventy years before the contributions of Lombroso and the positivists. With historical perspective, this may become a more commonly accepted conclusion, but today, most scholars begin that study with Lombroso and his colleagues Garofalo and Ferri, the "holy three of criminology." The emergence of these three men, it is argued, "symbolized clearly that the era of faith was over and the scientific age had begun."[6]

Cesare Lombroso   Cesare Lombroso (1835–1909) is "rarely discussed in a neutral tone; he is either adulated or condemned. 'In the history of criminology probably no name has been eulogized or attacked so much as [his].'"[7] Yet he was the recognized leader of the positive school.

Lombroso developed several categories of criminals, but he was best known for his concept of the biological, or born, criminal. Lombroso believed that he saw in criminals some of the same characteristics of "savages."[8] He called this phenomenon an *atavism,* a "throwback," or a reversion to prehuman creatures.

Theories of evolution introduced during the time Lombroso was writing argued that as humans evolved, their physical constitution changed, becoming more complex as it developed to a "higher stage." Lombroso used these theories of evolution to support his belief that criminals were not only physically different from noncriminals; they were also physically inferior, as they had not evolved as far as noncriminals had. In addition to the characteristics that distinguished criminals from noncriminals, Lombroso said he found biological characteristics that distinguished criminals according to the kind of crime they committed. Despite the criticism of Lombroso for his overemphasis on the born or biological criminal, he has been praised for his part in redirecting our "emphasis from the crime to the criminal."[9] Finally, he set the stage for the development of scientific, biological theories of criminality.

Raffaele Garofalo   Baron Raffaele Garofalo was born in Naples, Italy, in 1852 and died in 1934. His major work in criminology was a book, *Criminology,* that appeared in 1885 in Italian. Garofalo, another positivist, rejected most of the philosophies of the classical school, seeing the need for empirical research to establish theories of criminal behavior. Although he was close to Lombroso in some of his ideas, Garofalo was critical of others.

Garofalo differs from Lombroso in his emphasis on the criminal's physical abnormality. Garofalo agreed that the criminal was abnormal, as he thought him or her to be lacking in the degree of "sentiments and certain repugnancies" held by others in society. But Garofalo thought that the question of whether or not this abnormality was caused by physiological factors must remain unanswered. He did note some physical differences between criminals and noncriminals, but he was cautious in his analysis of this phenomenon, as he did not think the scientific evidence existed to substantiate the theories. He thus rejected the basis of Lombroso's theories and substituted what he called "psychic anomaly."[10]

Garofalo argued that the absence of the "proper development of the altruistic sensibility"[11] in the true criminal was not due to environmental or economic factors but, rather, had an organic basis and was therefore inherited. He had difficulty, however, in specifying this organic basis. At times he used Lombroso's term "atavism," but at others he referred to "moral degeneracy." He admitted that environmental factors *might* play a role in some crime. But he felt strongly that there was in the instincts of the true criminal one element that was congenital, inherited, or somehow acquired early in infancy, which became inseparable from the criminal's psychic organism. He did not believe in the *casual* offender, "if by the use of this term we grant the possibility of a morally well-organized man committing a crime solely by the force of external circumstances."[12]

Like Lombroso, Garofalo also contributed to the empirical study of criminal behavior. Although he did not test all of his ideas empirically, he did at least recognize and articulate the need for a scientific approach to the study of criminal behavior. The purpose of his book, he said, was to introduce the experimental method into criminal law and behavior. In discussing this issue, he implied the importance of an interdisciplinary approach to the study of criminal behavior.[13] Finally, like Lombroso, Garofalo also contributed to our understanding of the impact of biology on our behavior.

Enrico Ferri   Enrico Ferri (1856–1929) was the son of a poor shopkeeper. In 1880, before he reached the age of twenty-five, he delivered a two-hour lecture on the new horizons in criminal law and procedure, a lecture that became the basis for his best-known book, *Criminal Sociology.*

Ferri, who studied with Lombroso for a year, had a strong influence on the latter's thinking. In fact, it was Ferri, not Lombroso, who coined the term *born criminal* to describe Lombroso's concept of the atavistic criminal. "While Ferri owed much of his system of ideas to the stimulation of Lombroso, he also became the catalyst who synthesized the latter's concepts with those of the sociologist and had no little influence on Lombroso's thinking."[14]

Ferri's contributions also include his differences with Lombroso. Ferri gave more attention to the impact of environment in his explanation of criminal behavior. Although he believed in the born criminal, he argued that the "criminal neurosis" that some people inherit is not in itself sufficient to cause crime. Rather, he saw born criminals as those born with characteristics that predispose them to engage in criminal activities.[15] Crime, however, was primarily produced by the type of society in which those people live. Ferri talked about his *law of criminal saturation,* which means that "in a given social environment with definite individual and physical conditions, a fixed number of [crimes], no more and no less, can be committed."[16] Crime, then, can be corrected only by making changes in society.

The positive school: a brief summary We have already looked at some of the criticisms of the positive school of thinkers, and those criticisms, especially of their methodology, are very important. Still, we must give these three men credit for the attention they brought to the need to study the criminal from a scientific point of view and the need to respond to each criminal as an individual. They laid the foundation for a scientific and biological analysis of criminal behavior but they also foresaw the need for changing the social structure and environment if crime prevention is to be effective. They also set the stage for psychological developments.

But despite their contributions to the background of a sociological and psychological approach to criminology, it was Lombroso's biological approach that dominated the thought of that period. His approach was bitterly attacked, but it was also highly praised, and even many of his critics were driven by their objections to conduct research on the biological aspects of criminal behavior. One authority, in emphasizing the importance of Lombroso's work, described the "last quarter of the nineteenth century and the beginning of the twentieth" as perhaps the "age of criminal biology." This emphasis on the biological abnormality of the criminal stems from Lombroso's emphasis on the atavistic criminal, the born criminal:

> The criminal is, partly or totally, an abnormal organism, and this determines or at least largely motivates his criminal behavior. Thus the criminal is a biological anomaly whose criminal conduct originates in his somatic or psychic abnormalities.[17]

In that respect, then, the positive school of thought established the framework for both the biological and psychological study of the relationship between human characteristics and human behavior:

> Each criminal characteristic has an anatomical, physiological, psychological, or psychiatric basis. As Ferri suggested, the criminal anthropologist studies the criminal in anatomical or physiological laboratories. The criminal's freedom of will is beaten by deterministic psychosomatic forces.[18]

In that last statement we see the critical difference between the classical school based on free will and the deterministic position of the positive school. We shall look briefly at some of the early developments of this deterministic perspective before concentrating on more recent thought and research in the biological understanding of criminal behavior.

CONSTITUTIONAL APPROACH

Constitutional or physical-type theories rest on the assumption that function is determined by structure. Applied to crime, this means that the behavior is determined by the body's build, which may be the body type, the endocrine system, some other physical characteristic, or the mind. The positivists classified criminals in order to show how their theories could be applied to actual cases, although they were not the first to use typologies. Many different methods of typing people have been used, and the only conclusion with which most would agree is that they do not agree. Even the three major figures of the positive school did not agree on how to type criminals. Furthermore, the early typologists did not develop typologies and then test cases; they fit the typologies to their observations, thus "proving" their "theories." Nevertheless, their contributions cannot be entirely dismissed, for again, the influence of their work can be seen in modern developments.

BODY-TYPE
THEORIES

The belief that criminal behavior is related to body type can be formally traced back to a 1926 book,[19] but the first real development of this approach began in the 1940s with the work of William Sheldon.

William H. Sheldon

William Sheldon began to measure physique and compare body type with temperament. He thus developed the concept of three body types: ectomorph, endomorph, and mesomorph. The ectomorph is the tall, skinny body; the endomorph, the short fat body; and the mesomorph, the athletic type. Sheldon also identified three types of temperament that he claimed were associated with body types.[20]

Sheldon's purpose was to lay a foundation that would be helpful for a systematic study of human behavior and human personality. He thought the basis for the study might be in the "solid flesh and bone of the individual," and then this information could "provide a frame of reference for the analysis of variables at other levels." Although he said that he found a high correlation between physique and temperament, he did not think it was in a one-to-one relationship. He believed that more research would be needed on the permanence of the somatotype, but he stated that his evidence indicated that it did not change, that even the adjustment of body fat did not change the basic bone structure of the skeleton and the shape of the head, with which he was concerned in somatotyping.[21]

Evaluation of Sheldon's work.   Sheldon has been strongly criticized for the selection of his samples, the implication being that he selected those that would best support his theory.[22] One critic attacked him for giving only a vague definition of delinquency and observed that the "varieties of delinquent" were scientifically meaningless, as the different types were not distinguished on somatotypal or psychiatric indexes. Nor did Sheldon actually distinguish criminals from noncriminals on physical or generic traits of personality. Finally, Sheldon's "argument for selective breeding is based on preconceptions, not on the data of his study."[23]

Sheldon has also been criticized as a determinist. In all fairness to him, however, it should be noted that in his writings he appears to suggest that constitutional physique is not deterministic. He asserted, for example, that somatotyping was only a first step, "a kind of temporary scaffolding, for the description of the individual."[24] He also answered the criticism that he over-emphasized the constitutional factors and underemphasized environment, pointing out that he was not trying to say that the environment was unimportant: "It means only that we are presenting here the neglected side of the picture, without which a general psychology seems fatuous or anomalous."[25] He thought that psychology needed a physical-anthropology base, one that could be expressed in variables that could be measured.

Sheldon and Eleanor Glueck   To Sheldon's three body types, the Gluecks added a fourth—balanced—and in measuring these four body types, they found that delinquents, as compared with nondelinquents, were significantly more often mesomorphic. The Gluecks were two of the most prolific and most controversial writers in the field of constitutional criminology.[26] They spent ten years researching and writing their widely acknowledged work, *Unraveling Juvenile Delinquency*. They claimed that their research was of high quality, skillfully utilizing the method of precision control of matched samples of five hundred delinquents and five hundred nondelinquents. The two groups were matched on age, general intelligence, ethnic-racial origins, and residence in underprivileged neighborhoods. There were four levels of inquiry: sociocultural, somatic, intellectual, and emotional-temperamental. Physicians, psychiatrists, anthropologists, and others were involved in gathering the data from the samples.

Evaluation of the Gluecks' work.   Some critics point out that the Gluecks' "finding" that delinquents are more often mesomorphic is not surprising, as many delinquent activities require a strong body build. Other critics, after examining the researchers' data, concluded that the information was complicated and not revealing, that there was no specific combination of character, physique, and temperament that would permit a prediction about whether or not a young person would become delinquent.[27]

Other critics pointed out that because the delinquent sample was taken from "persistently delinquent" boys, the data could not be generalized to the total population of delinquents. The Gluecks' concepts have also been described as vague, as have their methods of somatotyping.[28]

Two prominent sociologists, Edwin H. Sutherland and Donald R. Cressey, harshly criticized the Gluecks' work: "Like Sheldon, they have adopted a system characterized by a noted physical anthropologist as a 'new Phrenology in which the bumps of the buttocks take the place of the bumps on the skull.'"[29] We should point out, however, that the Gluecks were also highly critical of the work of Sutherland and Cressey (discussed in Chapter 6) and that the Gluecks verbally disclaimed a deterministic relationship between physique and behavior. They concluded that although "it is quite apparent that physique alone does not adequately explain delinquent behavior, it is nevertheless clear that, in conjunction with other forces, it does bear a relationship to delinquency."[30]

Biopsychosocial theory of Cortés

Concerned that theories of the relationship between constitutional variables such as body type and criminal behavior were too quickly dismissed by sociologists and others, Juan B. Cortés, after ten years of research and writing, published his major work in 1972.[31]

Cortés found an association between mesomorphy and delinquency as well as personality traits; but he warned that body build did not *cause* delinquency or personality, although the high correlation between the two might be useful for the prediction of future behavior.

Evaluation of Cortés's work. Cortés limited his sample of delinquents to institutionalized populations; thus his findings have limited application to the population of delinquents and nondelinquents. In addition, his samples were very small and not randomly selected. His use of self-evaluation techniques to determine temperament may be questioned, and there is also a problem with his imprecise definitions of variables such as aggressiveness, need for achievement, and impulsivity, all of which he found related to delinquency. Finally, although he recognized the importance of environmental factors, it is not clear how he thought he could separate them from the body-type analysis. He might have thought that the environmental factors were the important "causes" and that the body type was of no significance in an understanding of the causes of delinquency.

Cortés's work is important, however, in establishing the foundation for a return to some concern with the genetic factor in criminal behavior. He emphasized that constitution (which he said was a term used almost synonymously with "physique" and "body build") was not fixed and unalterable but was a result of genetics and environment: "It is not, therefore, and should not be, heredity or environment, nor heredity versus environment nor heredity under or over environment, but only and always heredity *and* environment."[32] It is therefore necessary to look at heredity and examine what, if any, role genetic factors play in human behavior.

GENETIC FACTORS

It was perhaps not too difficult for some of the early students of criminal behavior, upon seeing the differences between criminals and noncriminals, to conclude that these differences caused the criminal behavior and, furthermore, that those differences were inherited. As we have seen in our discussions of the positive thinkers, the deterministic nature of physiological factors, though at times denied, was often accepted. In essence, the criminal was seen by many as one who was predisposed or predetermined by biological factors to commit crimes. The next step was to look at the family background to see whether the family had a history of criminal behavior. If so, then criminality must be inherited.

Unfortunately, the early "criminologists" did not have sophisticated research tools; their studies were often based on small samples, and their analysis of data was unsophisticated. In this century, with the development of modern tools of analysis and the increased sophistication of the study of genetics, the conclusions of the early studies have been seriously questioned and, in many cases, rejected. For the past several decades, little attention has been paid to genetic explanations of criminal behavior, and many criminologists have thought it unnecessary to tell their students about these earlier approaches.

Recently, however, the study of genetics has again gained attention as a possible explanation of criminal behavior. The once-discredited approaches of studying family histories, the behavior of twins, and the behavior of adopted children, in order to gain insights into their behavior, are gaining respectability, combined, of course, with more sophisticated methodological approaches. Yet, some of the same problems remain—and the same skepticism. Genetics' increased popularity has, however, made it important for us to look once again at its historical background, in our realization that there are fads and fashions in the sciences as well as in clothing!

Family studies   Most of the early studies of family histories,[33] conducted in an effort to show the relationship between heredity and crime as well as other forms of deviant behavior, have been discredited as lacking sufficient methodological sophistication to permit significant conclusions.[34] Two exceptions, however, deserve brief attention.

First, the Gluecks, whose work we have already noted, included family histories in their comparisons of delinquents and nondelinquents. They found that delinquent boys, as compared with nondelinquent boys, more often came from families characterized by a history of delinquency and crime. Specifically, the criminality of the father was the best predictor.[35]

Second is the work of Charles Goring,[36] an English psychiatrist and philosopher who, in his pursuit of evidence to disprove Lombroso's theory of the born criminal type, used some of the newly developed statistical techniques to measure the degree of correlation, or resemblance, of members within a family line. He compared brothers as well as fathers and sons, attempting to show that the correlations for general criminality, as measured by imprisonment, were as high as for two other categories he measured: (1) ordinary physical traits and features and (2) inherited defects, insanity, and mental disease. He then attempted to show that the correlations were the result of heredity, not environment. He used several arguments to support his position; for example, the findings that boys who were taken out of the home early in life became criminals as frequently as did those who remained longer in the home with their fathers. Also, he found the correlations as high for sex crimes (in which the fathers would presumably try to conceal their activities) as for stealing (in which the fathers might set an example for their sons).

Goring's findings may be criticized on several grounds. First, he did not adequately measure environmental influences; indeed, it is questionable whether all environmental variables can be satisfactorily isolated. Second, he did not consider criminality among sisters. If criminality is inherited in the same way that eye color is, cannot criminality also apply to daughters as well as to sons? Third, Goring assumed that mental ability is inherited but offered no proof. Finally, he assumed that removing a boy from his criminal father's home and placing him in some other environment at an early age automatically was putting him in an environment that was noncriminal.

Impact of family studies.   Although the earlier studies of families have been strongly criticized, they were influential in terms of policy. The belief that criminality was inherited led to the passage of laws that permitted the compulsory sterilization of persons thought to be capable of passing on to their children "bad genes" that would result in criminal behavior.[37]

The basic problem, however, with these early family studies was that they could not control for environment. The parents who produced the children, thereby determining their genetic background, were also those who socialized them; thus, genetics and environment were inseparable. This problem led to two other methods of studying genetic factors and criminality: the study of twins and adopted persons.[38]

Twins studies   If behavior is inherited, then we would expect to find the same behavior among people with identical genes. Thus, identical twins, who have identical genes, should behave alike. Fraternal twins (nonidentical) of the same sex have about 50 percent identical genes; their behavior should therefore be quite similar.

Earlier studies of twins led researchers to conclude that heredity does play a major role in explaining their behavior, but these studies were usually based on very small samples.[39] Until recently, the most recognized studies of twins were those conducted by Karl O. Christiansen, who managed to solve most of the sampling problems of the earlier studies. Christiansen studied the incidences of criminal behavior among 3,586 twins in one region of Denmark between 1881 and 1910 and found support for the hypothesis that criminality is inherited. If one twin engaged in criminal behavior, the probability that his or her identical twin would also be a criminal was 35 percent, compared with only 12 percent if the twins were not identical.

Sarnoff A. Mednick and his associates have updated the Christiansen study to over five thousand twins and are now working on a study of over thirteen thousand: "This number should be sufficient for a more detailed analysis ... than has been possible before. Despite the limitations of the twin method, the results of these studies are compatible with the hypothesis that genetic factors account for some of the variables associated with anti-social behavior."[40]

Despite this conclusion, other investigators have emphasized that even when we control for genetic background, as in the case of twins, we still cannot isolate the factor of inheritance. Thus, in a study of eighty-five pairs of Norwegian twins—resulting in a higher percentage of criminal behavior found among twins who were indentical, as compared with those who were not identical—the investigators pointed out that these differences might be the result of environment. Parents are more likely to treat identical twins, as compared with nonidentical twins, alike. Identical twins thus not only have the same genes; they also have a more similar environment than other siblings do, nonidentical twins included.[41] Although this study has been criticized,[42] the point about the potential influence of environment must be considered seriously.

Adoption studies   Concern with the problem of separating the influence of environment and of heredity, even in the study of twins, has led some researchers to select samples of adoptees for study. Most adoptees are adopted at birth and do not know their biological parents. Indeed, many do not even know they are adopted, at least not during their formative years. Thus, it is possible to separate out the factor of genetic characteristics from the study of environmental influences.

Mednick and his associates have already completed some adoption studies on the basis of the adoption register in Denmark, recording information on all nonfamilial adoptions between 1924 and 1947, for a total of about 72,000 persons. These and other recent studies of adoptees, says Mednick, indicate that we cannot ignore the genetic factor in explaining criminal behavior.[43]

Mednick's studies have come under fire (see the following Highlight), and he and his associates have raised some pertinent questions about the research. In Denmark, where the studies were conducted, efforts are made to place adoptable children in "homogeneous" environments, and the evidence is that the efforts are successful. So, for example, babies born to lower-class parents are usually adopted by lower-class parents, and so on. It is also important to consider that Denmark is a rather homogeneous society. These

---

HIGHLIGHT

GENETICS AND CRIME—THE COMMENTATORS RESPOND

"Are some children born with the genetic bent to commit crime? . . . Is the discredited, old 'bad seed' theory going to be recycled again? . . .

What caused the latest born-to-crime flap was a report by Sarnoff A. Mednick . . . that genetic factors predispose some people to criminal behavior.

It's an old can of worms. But because it's labeled 'science' and was presented at the prestigious American Association for the Advancement of Science session, it needs to be looked at very carefully. . . .

But a few statistics and a theory don't add up to a 'gene for crime.'

. . . In evaluating research like Mednick's, several points are essential: Science is a process, a way of trying to piece together the truth—not necessarily truth itself. Science and pseudoscience have floated genetic theories of criminality many times before—most recently in the XYY supermale flap. None has stood up to further evaluation.

The interaction of genes, biology and environment is so complex they are [*sic*] almost impossible to untangle and relate to behavior. Science does much better when it deals with molecules and particles than with people. And statistical relationships don't necessarily prove cause-and-effect."

Source: Joan Beck, "Criminal Genes: Recycling the 'Bad Seed' Theory," *Chicago Tribune*, reprinted in *Tulsa World*, January 17, 1982, p. 15, col. 1.

---

and other factors that imply the impact of the environment have been studied by Mednick and his associates, who remain firm in their belief that there is some association between genetic factors and criminal behavior:

> The cumulative evidence of the family, twin, and adoption studies does not allow rejection of the hypothesis that some genetically transmitted factor increases the likelihood that an individual will behave in an officially noticed, antisocial manner. Rather, this hypothesis received support from such studies.[44]

Chromosomal abnormality   The possible relationship between chromosomal abnormality and criminal behavior has also been the subject of research. The most common area of investigation has been the XYY chromosome abnormality. The X chromosome is female; the Y, male. Males are XY and females, XX. The XYY theory is concerned with the male who has an extra Y chromosome, a "supermale" as some have called him. The abnormality was first discovered in 1961 but did not receive much attention until papers were published in the mid-1960s by Scottish researchers who studied 197 inmates and found that a significant number of them were XYY.[45]

Later studies[46] do not consistently find that XYY males are more likely

"You can't talk to that crowd—they've all got extra Y chromosomes."

Playboy, April 1979. Reproduced by special permission of Playboy Magazine; copyright © 1970 by Playboy.

to be criminals than are males without the chromosomal abnormality, but the studies were based on very small and nonrandom samples that prohibit generalization. They were usually conducted on institutionalized populations and did not have control groups from the noncriminal population. But they did indicate that the XYY male is more introverted and has more asocial attitudes than does the rest of the population and that he has a tendency toward homosexuality and aggressiveness.

What was needed, however, was a larger study using a **control sample** of noncriminals. In 1977, several investigators reported the results of that kind of study, conducted in Denmark, on all of the 31,436 men who were born in Copenhagen during a four-year period and who were over a certain height. Their blood was then checked for chromosome composition; only twelve XYY men were found:

> There was little or no recorded evidence of violent behavior by XYY men. They did, however, evidence significantly more criminal behavior than did the XY men of their age, height, intelligence, and social class. Their low intelligence did not fully explain this excess criminality.[47]

Evaluation of genetic studies and crime

The conclusion of some biologists and psychologists is that although genetics may play a role in the cause of crime, it may be that the main impact is in relationship to the autonomic and central nervous systems of the body:

> It is conceivable that part of the genetically transmitted predisposition to criminal behavior is biologically mediated by the nervous system. Genetic findings in criminal behavior may be significant chiefly in that they point to the importance of studying biological factors in the causation of crime.[48]

We shall turn, therefore, to a discussion of the central nervous system and criminal behavior.

NEUROLOGICAL FACTORS

All of the nervous systems enclosed within the bony portions of the skull and spine are part of the central nervous system (CNS). Complex sensory information is processed in the CNS, which also controls voluntary muscle movement. Two basic tests of the CNS's functioning are the electroencephalogram (EEG) and various forms of neuropsychological testing.[49] The EEG has been the most common form of research on the relationship between the functioning of the central nervous system and criminal behavior, with some findings that "incarcerated individuals tend to have higher proportions of abnormal EEGs than do individuals in the general population."[50] The relationship between epilepsy and criminal behavior has also been tested, but the results have not yet resolved the issue of whether epilepsy is significantly related to crime.[51]

The second way to examine the CNS's functioning is by means of tests such as X-rays, CAT scans, and spinal taps, which determine whether the brain has been damaged. The results may then be used to analyze the relationship between brain damage and criminal behavior. "Results of neuropsychological tests administered to criminals suggest that violent, impulsive individuals suffer from damage to specific brain areas."[52] Studies reveal that criminals suffer injury with resulting unconsciousness, earlier in life than noncriminals do. Brain injury can also occur during pregnancy or delivery, and recent research indicates that Danish delinquents convicted of more than one violent offense "were characterized by significantly worse neurological status than other delinquents immediately after birth and at one year of age. Recidivist violent offenders showed the most severe neurological problems at one year of age."[53]

Neuroendocrinology

Criminal behavior has also been attributed to an imbalance of the body's chemicals. The endocrine, or glandular, system and its relationship to criminal behavior were the focus of a 1928 book entitled *The New Criminology*. At that time, it was alleged that "the glandular theory of crime accounts for all the discrepancies, errors, oversights and inadequacies of the earlier explanation,"[54] a conclusion that in 1941 was seriously criticized by a well-known anthropologist.[55]

More recent research has revealed, in both animals and humans, a relationship between male hormones and behavior, with lower levels of certain hormones occurring in males who are more dominant, aggressive, and hostile than normal.[56] Research revealing a relationship between female hormones and the reduction of the male sex drive and potency has led to "chemical castration" as a method of treating sex offenders. Such findings should be considered tentative,[57] claim some researchers, pointing to other research that does not reveal a significant relationship between hormones and male behavior.[58]

Among women, premenstrual tension, which is common in about 25 percent of the female population, appears to be associated with the imbalance of the two female hormones, estrogen and progesterone. There also appears to be a relationship between the presence of premenstrual and menstrual tension and the number of suicides, suicide attempts, admissions for psychiatric illness or acute medical and surgical reasons, and criminal acts. "It would appear that, for a number of women, hormonal changes resulting in irritability, tension, nervousness, and related symptoms markedly increase the probability of committing crimes." The researchers are quick to point out, however, that a cause-and-effect relationship between endocrine factors and behavior cannot be assumed because endocrine factors do not work independently of other factors. One researcher found, for example, that women who complained that they were irritable during premenstrual and menstrual periods were more likely to be irritable at other times than were women who did not so complain.[59]

Neurochemistry   Changes in body chemistry have also been linked to criminal behavior, the most common example being perhaps the abuse of alcohol and drugs. Although both have been linked with crime, we do not have studies that indicate that they are the causes of criminal behavior. In the case of alcohol, for example, the fact of alcohol is based on reports of alcohol use rather than on actual tests of use (with the exception of driving under the influence, in which the alcohol level in the blood is usually tested by the police). Furthermore, they do not isolate how many others were drinking at the time the criminal behavior occurred; indeed, a large percentage of the population drinks but does not engage in criminal behavior, at least as far as the official data indicate. Thus, alcohol use or abuse "may be an effect of the same social or other environmental factors which cause the individual to engage in criminal activity. The question unanswered by the existing literature is whether alcohol ingestion accounts for a portion of variance of criminal behavior independently of environmental factors."[60]

The alteration of body chemistry through the abuse of drugs has also been linked to criminal behavior. "Drugs cause crime" is a popular belief, both in terms of the drug's impact on the person and the need to steal in order to finance the drug habit. Again, the evidence shows links but not causes. "Biochemical and pharmacological factors play a role in the development or expression of antisocial behavior, but no drugs or substances are intrinsically criminogenic."[61]

Finally, the alteration of body chemistry by food has been linked with crime. In October 1983, the National Conference on Nutrition and Behavior focused on an issue of growing recognition—the effect of nutrition (or the lack thereof) on human behavior. Some of the speeches at the conference discussed the relationship between chemicals or food additives or preservatives and criminal behavior. In 1981, the director of the American Institute for Biosocial Research in Tacoma, Washington, reported that a dietary deficiency of zinc might cause a teenager to desire salt and sugar and reduce the

---

HIGHLIGHT
JUNK DIET MAY ESTABLISH BIOCHEMISTRY FOR CRIME
William Raspberry, *Washington Post*

"Add one more theory to why criminals behave as they do . . . social disadvantage, economic hard times, televised violence. . . . Now add . . . junk food.

[After citing several studies, he continues] the evidence of these studies so convinced [a New York assemblyman] that he will shortly be reintroducing legislation designed to help determine whether improved nutrition might be an effective—and cheaper—way of reducing crime. Under his bill, prison inmates would be screened for hypoglycemia (too little blood sugar) and, where indicated, given special diets and up to six meals a day.

. . . It all sounds a little crazy—like the 'television intoxication' defense offered on behalf of the Florida kid who murdered an 83-year-old woman. . . . But suppose the theory proved to be correct. What do you do with a young man convicted of a violent offense if it later turns out that his behavior resulted from junk-food-induced chemical imbalance? Release him on condition that he eat his spinach and give up Sugaroos? And then what do you do with the thousands of others who throw themselves on the mercy of the courts as junk-food junkies? How could you hope to distinguish between the chemically confused and the merely rotten? And assuming it were possible to do so, what would you do about the people who manufacture and sell the crime-inducing junk? Force them to post a warning: 'Caution: the Surgeon General has determined that eating this product can lead to criminal behavior'?"

Reprinted in *Tulsa World,* January 4, 1983, p. A7, col. 1.

taste for vegetables, leading to more aggressive behavior, irritability, and oversensitivity to criticism. Deficiencies in diet may also lead to unhealthy desires for alcohol, marijuana, tobacco, and drugs. "Food can directly affect particular behavior patterns." He cited the example of a child who, only eight minutes after he ate two slices of citric fruit, became hyperactive and, within twenty minutes, became manic-depressive. He was allergic to oranges. Chronic incest offenders were found to be deficient in certain vitamins that help inhibit emotions. Finally, the director cited the example of a man who beat his wife: he agreed to undergo nutritional testing, and his behavioral problem was resolved after it was discovered that his body was being poisoned by such industrial metals as lead, mercury, and cadmium.[62] Findings in this area, however, are currently based more on "anecdote" than on "science."

Autonomic nervous system studies

One final area of biological studies involves the Autonomic Nervous System (ANS), which "mediates physiological activity associated with emotions. . . . Examples of peripheral manifestations of ANS activity include changes in heart rate, blood pressure, respiration, muscle tension, pupillary size, and electrical activity of the skin," with the last being the most frequently used measure of the psychophysiological characteristics of antisocial persons.[63]

Psychologists have for a long time studied criminals classified as psychopaths or, more recently, sociopaths, and the lack of emotion, the inability to feel guilt or to love, and the callousness of these diagnosed persons finally led psychophysiologists to experiment with measuring whether those personality or character traits were accompanied by changes in physiology.

Consider a simple example. In order to learn not to steal, a child must be taught—socialized—that it is wrong to take the property of others without their permission. This socialization usually occurs within the family, acting as a censuring agent. The appropriate fear response is developed—that is, children learn to fear punishment if they steal, and that fear enables them to inhibit their stealing impulses. Antisocial children, however, do not learn adequate initial fear responses; thus, they are not usually able to anticipate negative reactions if they steal, and the fear inhibitor does not work to repress their stealing impulses.

How does this relate to ANS? The ANS largely controls the fear response. If children have quick ANS responses, they will learn to react to stimuli with fear, and that fear will generally inhibit their desire to steal. Children who have slow ANS responses, however, will learn slowly to inhibit stealing, if at all. A number of research studies have indicated that those who exhibit criminal behavior do tend to have slower ANS responses.[64]

PSYCHOLOGICAL EXPLANATIONS OF CRIMINAL BEHAVIOR

Biologists and chemists were not the only professionals to link behavior with physical characteristics. Some early psychologists attempted to explain criminal behavior by means of the inherited trait we now call *intelligence.* The influence of the positivists can also be seen in these early attempts to link criminal and other forms of antisocial behavior with mental retardation. The family studies mentioned earlier were their sources of data, and as the researchers traced criminality through generations of the same family, they concluded that mental retardation was the cause of crime. It was not important to them what happened in the mind of the criminal: "It never occurred to positivists to ask *how* feeblemindedness could affect an individual, causing him to rob a stagecoach or habitually drink to excess."[65]

Nor did the early positivists consider why some people with the trait thought to be the "cause" of crime became criminals and others with the trait became law-abiding citizens. Thus, the *process* of becoming a criminal was not an issue, and it was not until the twentieth century that social scientists began researching the question of process.

THE MIND AND ITS RELATIONSHIP TO CRIME: THE BEGINNINGS

Today we often hear comments about the "criminal mind," and the literature devoted to explaining that concept is extensive. Attempts to explain the criminal mind are not new. The modern approach, based on an attempt to apply scientific methods to research in this area, was preceded by centuries of less scientific attempts to understand the mind.

Demonology

Before the development of more scientific theories of criminal behavior or mental illness, one of the most popular explanations was *demonology.* When persons became "possessed" by spirits, they were considered to be unclean. They also were often banished from society to protect others from their actions and to placate the gods who were thought to have caused the possession. Writings of the Chinese, Egyptians, Hebrews, and Greeks indicate widespread belief in demonism. Individuals were possessed by good or evil spirits, and the decision as to which usually depended on the type of symptoms.

The earliest example of the practice of "psychiatry" was during the Stone Age when cave dwellers would use a crude stone to cut a hole in the skull of a person thought to by possessed by devils. The process, called *trephining,* was thought to permit the evil spirit to escape; there is evidence that some people survived the surgery. But the usual treatment for evil spirits was exorcism, which included drinking horrible concoctions, praying, making strange noises, and other methods. Medicine men, or shamans, often performed the ritual. Later, exorcism became the function of priests; during medieval times, when the priests were in charge of the mentally ill, they were treated rather kindly. Later during that period a theory developed that the only way to drive out the devils was to insult them or to make the body an unpleasant place for them to inhabit. Thus flogging and other forms of corporal punishment were used to treat persons considered to be possessed by evil spirits. During the latter part of the fifteenth century the belief arose that some possessed people were actively and deliberately working with the devil of their own free will. This led society to react to this alleged witchcraft by severe methods, such as burning the so-called witches at the stake. Because the possessed person was acting of his or her own free will, he or she deserved to be punished for this sin of working with the devil.

In the eighteenth century, people began accumulating knowledge about human anatomy, physiology, neurology, general medicine, and chemistry. The discovery of an organic basis of many illnesses led to the discovery of an organic basis for some mental illnesses. This organic view of mental illness in turn replaced the demonological theory of causation and dominated the fields of psychology and psychiatry until 1915. But by the turn of the twentieth century, it began to be argued that psychological problems could cause mental illness, and a new viewpoint in psychiatry was created.

It is difficult to categorize as psychological or psychiatric all of the research that we shall discuss in this section as some of the studies embrace both. Today, in criminology, the major emphasis is on psychology, not psychiatry, and we shall therefore focus on the most recent contributions in psychology. First, though, we shall briefly consider psychiatry.

PSYCHIATRIC APPROACH

Psychiatry is a field of medicine that specializes in the understanding, diagnosis, treatment, and prevention of mental problems. **Psychoanalysis** is a special branch of psychiatry, based on the theories of Sigmund Freud and employing a particular personality theory and a particular method of treatment. The approach mainly utilizes the method of individual case study. Psychiatry holds that each person is a unique personality and that the only way that person can be understood is by means of a thorough case study.

The case study: a shift in emphasis

William Healy, a psychiatrist who was head of the Juvenile Psychopathic Institute in Chicago, is credited with shifting the positivists' emphasis in studying the criminal's anatomical characteristics to an emphasis on the psychological and social elements. According to one analysis, Healy, "like Lombroso more than a half century before, closed one era of criminology to open the next. . . . Healy's work was a continuation of that same Lombrosian spirit, fortunately implemented with twentieth century tools."[66] The basic tool used by Healy and his colleagues was the case study. They thought that the only way to find the roots or causes of delinquent behavior was to delve deeply into the individual person's background, especially his or her mental and emotional development. But they also measured personality dis-orders and environmental pathologies, theorizing that delinquency was pur-posive behavior resulting when children were frustrated in their attempts to fulfill some of their basic drives, such as the need for secure social relations both inside and outside the family, for new experiences, for recognition, and for freedom from adult supervision. Indeed, they studied samples of young people and reported that delinquents had a higher frequency of personality defects and disorders than did nondelinquents.

Evaluation of Healy's work. Despite his impact of the study of the indi-vidual case, Healy has been criticized for basing his studies on vaguely defined terms and giving little information on how he measured the con-cepts. Furthermore, his samples were too small to permit generalization to the total population of delinquents. Finally, his work did not attempt to explain the process of criminality; it was, like its predecessors, basically a trait-oriented approach. Healy told us which mental and personality char-acteristics distinguished delinquents from nondelinquents but added noth-ing to our understanding of *why*. Why did some siblings, for example, with the personality traits in question become delinquents, whereas others did not? Despite these deficiencies, however, Healy's emphasis on the case study and his influence in shifting the study of the criminal from biology to psy-chology were outstanding contributions.

Contributions of Sigmund Freud Sigmund Freud (1856–1939), who is credited with having made the greatest contribution to the development of psychoanalytic theory, did not advance a theory of criminality per se. His theories attempted to explain all behavior and, in so doing, have implications for criminological theory. The psycho-analytic theories of Freud and his colleagues introduced the concept of the *unconscious,* along with techniques for probing that element of the person-ality, and emphasized that all human behavior is motivated and purposive.

According to Freud, humans experience mental conflict because of desires and energies that are repressed into the unconscious. These urges, ideas, desires, and instincts are basic, but they are repressed because of society's morality. People are constantly trying, however, to express these "natural" drives in some way, often indirect, to avoid the reactions of others. Dreams are one example of indirect expression.

Freud saw original human nature as assertive and aggressive. It is not learned but is deeply rooted in early childhood experiences. We all have criminalistic tendencies, but during the socialization process, most of us learn to control them, by developing strong and effective inner controls. But the improperly socialized child does not develop an ability to control impulses and acts them out or projects them inward. In the case of the latter, the child may become neurotic; in the case of the former, delinquent.[67]

Evaluation of the psychiatric approach

The psychiatric approach has been criticized on several bases. First, the terms are vague, so vague that they may be described as "the unknown." No operational definitions for most concepts are given. Second, projective techniques are open to the analyst's subjective interpretation. Third, the research has been based on samples that are too small, and that have usually been selected from psychiatric patients and often from institutionalized patients, and the use of control groups has not been adequate. Fourth, the individual is the focus of the psychiatric approach, and that focus permits no patterns of behavior and prevents generalization. Thus "there will be as many explanations of criminal behavior as there are individuals behaving in a manner called criminal. This has little in common with the accepted idea of science as a body of generalizations going beyond the individual, particular case."[68]

The emphasis on early childhood experiences as deterministic has also been seriously questioned lately by social scientists who de-emphasize the deterministic nature of such experiences. "It is little debated that long-forgotten early events can have lasting influence. However, these events are now seen as having produced behavior that can be unlearned at any time with the proper application of the principles of learning."[69]

Despite these criticisms, the impact of Freud and his followers must be recognized. "It is possible that never before has so much constructive work been done in reaction to—or in argument with—the master."[70]

PERSONALITY THEORY

Emotional conflict and personality deviation obviously exist in a great number of criminals and delinquents, especially habitual offenders. But the critical questions are whether these factors distinguish delinquents and criminals from law-abiding persons and, if so, whether the traits cause the illegal behavior. A number of earlier researchers[71] found such differences, but others found evidence that questioned the relationship between certain personality traits and criminal behavior,[72] with one criminologist concluding that "personality diagnosis on the basis of objective tests or scales has not yet developed to such a degree of specificity that differences established as statistically significant for particular groups may then be extended to correspondingly significant theoretical formulations about personality deviation and delinquency."[73]

Personality traits and treatment of criminals and delinquents

Recently, with the increasing attention paid to the "treatment does not work" approach, attempts have been made to refine treatment by dividing delinquents and criminals into types and applying particular treatment methods to particular types. The most extensive effort has been the California Treatment Project, which classified juvenile offenders on the basis of a test that measured their interpersonal maturity,[74] although many questions have been raised about this and other efforts to apply differential treatments to juveniles.[75]

A recent study of the self-esteem and interpersonal behavior patterns of 150 adult male offenders with alcohol and drug problems utilized a control group in an attempt to find the effect of treatment on different types of offenders. The investigators found that offenders who scored high in self-esteem had fewer reconvictions and lower reconvicted offense severity than those who had low self-esteem, suggesting that the typing of offenders by personality characteristics may be helpful in designing programs.[76]

COGNITIVE DEVELOPMENT THEORY

Another type of psychological theory that has been used to explain criminal behavior is that of **cognitive development.** This approach is based on the belief that people organize their thoughts about rules and laws, and the way in which those thoughts are organized results in either delinquent (or criminal) or nondelinquent behavior. Psychologists refer to this organization of thoughts as *moral reasoning,* and when that reasoning is applied to law, it is termed *legal reasoning,* although that term has quite a different meaning to persons trained in law. The approach stems from the earlier works of Jean Piaget, who believed that there are two basic steps in moral reasoning: (1) the belief that rules are sacred and immutable and (2) the belief that rules are the products of humans. According to Piaget, we leave the first stage at about the age of thirteen, and the second stage leads to more moral behavior than the first does.[77]

In 1958, Lawrence Kohlberg made some changes in Piaget's position. He called the first stage *preconventional* and the second *conventional* and added a third and higher stage, *postconventional reasoning.* According to Kohlberg, between the ages of ten and thirteen, a person usually moves from preconventional to conventional reasoning or thinking; those who do not make this transition may be considered arrested in their development of moral reasoning, and they may become delinquents.[78] He and others later refined this position, with a final development of six stages of moral judgment, as indicated in the Exhibit on page 120. The stages of moral judgment are applicable to all kinds of behavior, and the investigators sought to determine where offenders would fall along the continuum. They placed the majority of adult offenders at Stages 3 or 4 and the majority of adolescent offenders at Stages 1 or 2. The progression to higher stages should preclude criminal behavior.[79]

A recent analysis of the research on cognitive development theory evaluated the work in terms of its impact on treatment, noting that one of its advantages is that it "may provide an attractive alternative to more traditional forms of corrections." It might provide a "rationale for a course of action that stands midway between continued use of questionable forms of psychological treatment and outright rejection of all rehabilitation efforts."

EXHIBIT

KOHLBERG'S SIX STAGES OF MORAL JUDGMENT

Stage 1. Right is obedience to power and avoidance of punishment.

Stage 2. Right means to take responsibility for oneself, to meet one's own needs and leave to others the responsibility for themselves.

Stage 3. Right is being good in the sense of having good motives, having concern for others and "putting yourself in the other person's shoes."

Stage 4. Right means to maintain the rules of a society and to serve the welfare of the group or society.

Stage 5. Right is based on recognized individual rights within a society with agreed-upon rules, a social contract.

Stage 6. Right is an assumed obligation to principles applying to all humankind, principles of respect for human personality and justice and equality.

Source: Lawrence Kohlberg et al., *The Just Community Approach to Corrections: A Manual* (Niantic: Connecticut Department of Corrections, 1973).

But the researcher concluded that "studies of reasoning and lawbreaking are inconclusive."[80]

BEHAVIOR THEORY

Another psychological theory that has been used to explain criminal acts is **behavior theory.** This theory originated in the late 1800s but gained more attention in this century through the work of B. F. Skinner. Behavior theory is the basis for behavior modification, the approach used in institutionalized and noninstitutionalized settings for changing behavior. The primary thesis is that all behavior is learned and can be unlearned. The approach is concerned with observable behavior, in contrast with the traditional psychoanalytic emphasis on deep, underlying personality problems that must be uncovered and treated. Behavior theory holds that it is not the unconscious that is important but, rather, the behavior, which can be observed and manipulated. It is assumed that neurotic symptoms and some types of deviant behavior are acquired through an unfortunate quirk of learning and are in some way rewarding to the patient. The significant aspect of this approach is the belief that deviant behaviors are learned just as all other behavior is learned. The undesirable behavior can be eliminated, modified, or replaced by taking away the reward value or by replacing the behavior by rewarding a more appropriate one that is incompatible with the deviant behavior. Behavior, it is argued, is controlled by its consequences. In dealing directly with behaviors that are undesirable, behavioral therapy attempts to change the person's long-established patterns of response to himself or herself and to others. It was described in 1973 by one expert on jails and prisons as the "in" treatment technique among avant-garde correctional personnel in the United States.[81]

SOCIAL-LEARNING
THEORY

Another important psychological theory is social-learning theory, defined by Albert Bandura, the leading theorist in the field of social learning today, as follows:

> In the social learning view, people are endowed with neurophysiological mechanisms that enable them to behave aggressively, but the activation of these mechanisms depends on appropriate stimulation and is subject to cognitive control. Therefore, the specific forms that the aggressive behavior takes, the frequency with which it is expressed, the situation in which it is displayed, and the specific targets selected for attack are largely determined by social learning factors.[82]

Social-learning theory may be contrasted with behavior theory in that the latter emphasizes performance and reinforcement, whereas social-learning theory emphasizes that learning may be accomplished by using other people as models; it is not necessary to engage in all the behavior that we learn. We engage in the behavior only if we have incentives and motivations to do so. Motivations may come from biological factors or from mental factors, with the latter giving us the ability to imagine the behavior's consequences.

Under social-learning theory, behavior is seen as maintained by consequences, of which there are three types: (1) external reinforcement, such as goods, money, social status, and punishment[83] (effective in restraining behavior); (2) vicarious reinforcement (for example, observing the status of others whom you observe being reinforced for their behavior; and (3) self-regulatory mechanisms (people respond to their own actions in ways that bring self-rewards or self-punishment). Social-learning theorists emphasize the importance of the family,[84] the subculture, and the media. Social-learning theory has also been compared with similar theories in other diciplines:

> The social contexts that appear to be criminogenic have been extensively studied from other points of view and by disciplines other than psychology. What social-learning theory offers is an understanding of the mechanisms by which these contexts exert, or fail to exert, their predicted influences.[85]

Conditioning and crime

Social-learning theories have been combined with biological approaches to explain criminal behavior. An English scholar and psychologist, H. J. Eysenck, in his work *Crime and Personality,* emphasizes the interrelationship between psychology and biology in explaining how humans learn to behave. Unlike most psychologists, he relates his approach directly to criminal behavior.[86]

Eysenck's approach is based on the principle of conditioning. We learn appropriate and inappropriate behavior through a process of training that involves rewards for appropriate behavior, punishment for inappropriate behavior, and the establishment of models of appropriate behavior. Through these processes, we learn moral preferences as well as behavior. The process is slow and subtle, and we often do not realize how we obtained our moral preferences, but in the process of learning, most of us develop a conscience. This conscience provides us with feelings of responsibility and duty, shame and guilt, of the need to do the "right" thing. If we do the wrong thing, we will feel guilty, assuming of course, that our conscience incorporates the moral preferences that define that activity as wrong.[87]

The process of training uses three tools: classical conditioning, operant conditioning, and modeling. Most of us have heard about classical conditioning in terms of Pavlov's dogs, who were trained to salivate when a bell rang, as they knew from conditioning that they would be fed. Classical conditioning, then, is a learned response to a stimulus.

Operant conditioning is based on a reaction after we have acted, and it is argued that this is the most powerful form of training. We are rewarded, or reinforced, when we behave appropriately, and we are punished when we misbehave. Finally, we also learn by models; social learning occurs through the observation of others and from the media. In many languages, the verb "to teach" is synonymous with the verb "to show."[88]

Eysenck's approach was based almost entirely on classical conditioning, and took the position that "both neurosis and criminality can be understood in terms of conditioning principles." Neurotics condition anxiety and fear responses too quickly to stimuli that were previously neutral, and criminals do not condition adequately to stimuli that society deems should be incorporated in a conscience.[89] Eysenck believed that conditioning depends on the sensitivity of the autonomic nervous system that we inherit, as well as the quality of conditioning that we receive during the process of socialization in our social environment.

In the third edition of his book, Eysenck emphasized that his original plan in 1964 was to outline a theory of antisocial behavior, relate that theory to personality, "and indicate some of the biological factors underlying both personality and criminality." Biological and psychological approaches were not given much credit at the time, but by 1977, Eysenck argued that we had much more evidence of the relationship between genetic factors and criminality, more evidence that personality traits of delinquents are strongly determined by genetic factors, and much more empirical work "on the biological causes of personality differences, and by implication of psychopathic and criminal conduct." Eysenck also took the position that some of the sociological theories that had previously overshadowed biological and psychological theories were now less acceptable in explaining criminal behavior. He cited particularly the variables of poverty, poor housing, and social inequality. In fact, "even that universal catalyst of social disaster in the Marxist textbooks, the capitalist system, has been exonerated from blame."

In short, Eysenck concluded that the research since his first edition in 1964 had surpassed even his expectations in its support for this theory. Perhaps more importantly, he pointed out, his original suggestion "that both neurosis and criminality can be understood in terms of conditioning principles" has had an impact on the treatment of neurotics and criminals. Eysenck has been criticized for his overemphasis on classical conditioning to the exclusion of operant conditioning and modeling.[90]

In subsequent discussions of theories of criminal behavior, we shall continue to see the influence of psychology on the understanding of such behavior, as we note the overlap between the sociological and psychological approaches.

IMPLICATIONS OF BIOLOGICAL AND PSYCHOLOGICAL RESEARCH

The first implication of what we have discussed thus far is the possibility of integrating the social and physical sciences and psychological sciences in our attempt to understand criminal behavior. As recently as 1967 we were warned that we should not ignore biology and psychology: "Contrary to the beliefs of many American criminologists, the constitutional school is not dead. Research continues in this area, and it behooves the skeptic whether he be sociologist, psychiatrist or psychologist to at least keep an open mind toward it."[91] That declaration had little effect; among criminologists, the biological or constitutional school of thought lost its importance as a reasonable explanation for criminal behavior. More recently, psychologists and biologists have gained more attention in the areas of biology discussed in this chapter. Much of the work has been done by Sarnoff A. Mednick and his associates. His conclusion, therefore, seems warranted:

> A half century of research and common sense leaves no doubt that social and cultural factors play a considerable role in the etiology of crime. The biological factors . . . must be seen as another set of variables involved in the etiology of crime. Both social and biological variables *and their interactions* are important for our complete understanding of the origins of antisocial behavior.[92]

The key in the above statement is *interaction.* Many scholars today argue that the issue is no longer nature *or* nurture but nature *and* nurture. It is not a question of whether human behavior is the result of biology *or* environment, but what effect each has on the other.

SOCIOBIOLOGY

One of the manifestations of using both the physical and social sciences to explain behavior is seen in the work of sociobiologists. Edward O. Wilson,[93] who introduced the concept of *sociobiology,* defines the term as "the systematic study of the biological basis of all social behavior."[94] The concept has been denounced by some as just another deterministic approach to explaining criminal behavior,[95] but others view the work of Wilson and his colleagues as "the catalyst of a paradigm shift that could some day unify the social sciences and the natural sciences."[96]

That claim may not be accurate, but there are important policy implications of integrating the social and physical sciences in explaining criminal behavior. One implication has been analyzed by criminologist C. Ray Jeffery, who has written extensively about the use of "environmental" design to prevent criminal behavior. The progress of the sciences, he believes "will be developed to the point where the major behavioral disorders can be brought under control." According to Jeffery, we must explain criminal behavior "directly in terms of the consequences of the behavior, and not indirectly in terms of noncriminal variables such as poverty, race, or social class." If we are to change criminal behavior, we must work directly on the factors in our environment that reinforce that kind of behavior.[97]

REACTION OF CRIMINOLOGISTS

A second important implication of the recent attention given to biology and psychology is that it has created some tension among criminologists. Some of the approaches discussed in this chapter have been and still are unpopular with some criminologists. It has been suggested that one of the reasons may be the fear that "in the wrong hands positive biological findings could be misused politically as a pretext for not ameliorating the racial, social, and cultural disadvantages associated with high crime rates."[98] It may also be feared that less attention will be given to the sociological concepts, theories, and empirical findings relevant to understanding criminal behavior.

Other sociologists and criminologists welcome the current research in biology and psychology, proclaiming that it is "apolitical and based on the best canons of science. Sociological criminology welcomes these multi- and interdisciplinary researches that embrace our understanding of criminality and criminals."[99]

LEGAL IMPLICATIONS

The final implication of the emphasis on biological and psychological research is a legal one and concerns the use of such research in the insanity defense in criminal cases. The most controversial defense is the insanity defense, and the current movement is away from its use. The public was apparently incensed at the successful application of the insanity defense in the case of John W. Hinckley, Jr., who on March 30, 1980, attempted to assassinate President Ronald Reagan. That case appeared to be an easy one for the prosecutor to win, for many of us watched on television as Hinckley fired shots at the president and his party, wounding the president, his press secretary James Brady, and a policeman. When he was apprehended by the United States Secret Service agents, Hinckley was still holding his smoking gun.

HIGHLIGHT
THE INSANITY DEFENSE AND ME

Not Guilty by Reason of Insanity

I don't feel guilty for being found not guilty by reason of insanity. It was the proper verdict and, although I was surprised by it, my fragile conscience is clear of useless guilt. The American people are angry with me, my parents' money and my fame. They are jealous and just drooled at the thought of me spending the rest of my life in some wretched prison in the backwoods of North Carolina.

Those people who wish to abolish the insanity defense are a little nuts themselves. I wish they would move to Iran or Turkey, where defendants are shot in record time. America has the insanity defense because it is a compassionate and fair country. The passions of the mind separate the mental case from the criminal, and thank God we make such a distinction in this country.

Let's leave the insanity defense alone and accept the fact that, every once in a while, someone is going to use this "defense of last resort" and win with it. I was acquited not because of my parents' money, or my attorneys, or the black jury; I was found not guilty by reason of insanity because I shot the president and three other people in order to impress a girl.

"I was not responsible for my actions."

Source: Statement by John W. Hinckley, Jr., acquitted of the attempted assassination of President Ronald Reagan. Reprinted from *Newsweek,* September 20, 1982, p. 30.

Because it was obvious that Hinckley had pulled the trigger, his attorneys indicated that they would have him plead not guilty by reason of insanity.

Hinckley was then ordered to undergo nearly four months of psychiatric testing.[100] Nearly fourteen months after the shooting, Hinckley's trial finally began.

To show that Hinckley had deliberately planned and executed the attempted assassination of the president, the prosecution presented evidence showing that Hinckley had been only six feet away from President Jimmy Carter in October of 1980; that he had chosen deadly exploding bullets for his gun; that he had practiced at a rifle-target range as least two separate times; that his room contained postcards with pictures of President and Mrs. Reagan along with notes to actress Jodie Foster; and that he had a collection of books about mass murderers and assassins, specifically that he possessed a book about a master criminal who feigned insanity to escape punishment for his crimes.[101]

The prosecution then called on expert witnesses—psychiatrists—to testify that Hinckley was sane the day he fired the shots. The first doctor stated Hinckley suffered from four minor and quite common mental disorders that involved extensive sadness, narcissistic self-centeredness, feelings of the absence of friendship, and indifference to the feelings of others, and that none of these illnesses was serious. Testimony also indicated that Hinckley was in control of his behavior and was proceeding according to his plans on the day of the shootings. Another prosecution psychiatrist testified that Hinckley functioned too well to be mentally ill and that the shooting was his way to get even with the world. According to the doctor, Hinckley decided that "if he wanted to make a powerful statement, you make an attempt on a powerful figure."[102]

Ironically, the defense relied on the same evidence as the prosecution did to prove that Hinckley was insane. The letter that Hinckley had left in his hotel room addressed to actress Jodie Foster was used by the defense to show Hinckley's obsession with her. During the trial, the jury watched the movie *Taxi Driver*. Defense attorneys argued that Hinckley was so affected by this film that he tried to live out the story of the lonely, bitter taxi driver who wants a liaison with a prostitute (played by Jodie Foster) and resorts to violent fantasies, finally stalking a presidential candidate with a gun. At the end of the film, the driver is acclaimed as a hero. Hinckley had apparently viewed the film numerous times and become obsessed with Foster, attempting to contact her many times in writing and by telephone and even traveling to Yale University, where she was a student, in the hopes of meeting her. Foster told Hinckley over the telephone that he should stop bothering her, and so Hinckley then plotted to become famous by committing a great crime to show her that he was important enough to be noticed.

The defense psychiatrists contradicted the prosecution's testimony by saying that Hinckley was psychotic, was consumed by paradoxical thoughts, was severely depressed, had hypochondriacal tendencies, hated himself, suffered from schizophrenia spectrum disorder, had a totally abnormal thought process, thought of himself as a little boy who had done something terrible, and was torn between childish love and dependence on his father and subconscious fantasies about killing him.[103]

During the closing arguments, the prosecution contended that Hinckley was completely rational when he shot the president and emphasized the months of planning that went into his scheme to attract Jodie Foster's attention. The defense attorney reviewed Hinckley's life from childhood to adulthood and tried to convince the jury that anyone who thinks that he or she can shoot the president in order to gain attention from a woman has to be suffering from delusions.[104]

The jury deliberated for twenty-five hours over four days and found Hinckley not guilty by reason of insanity. The public's reaction was immediate outrage. A Texas district attorney commented, "Only in the U.S. can a man try to assassinate the leader of the country in front of 125 million people and be found not guilty." The next day's headline in the *Indianapolis News* stated: "Hinckley Insane, Public Mad."[105]

In defense of insanity   The defense of insanity is allowed in our legal system because, like other defenses, it is assumed to remove the requisite culpability or guilt. Under our system, only persons who are responsible for their actions may be held criminally liable. A person who was "insane" at the time he or she committed a crime is considered to have been legally incapable of having had the requisite intent. Therefore, if the defense of insanity is substantiated at trial, the appropriate verdict will be "not guilty by reason of insanity." But what is the meaning of the term?

Insanity is a legal, not a medical, term, and there is no agreement on its meaning. It is a legal conclusion that the defendant was not responsible for his or her actions, and the basic test for determining whether a defendant was insane at the time the crime was committed is called the **M'Naghten rule.** This test arose from the celebrated case of Daniel M'Naghten, who committed a murder in 1843. M'Naghten intended to kill British Prime Minister Robert Peel, because he was under the delusion that Peel was persecuting him, but shot Edward Drummond instead, believing that Drummond was Peel. At his trial, M'Naghten claimed that he was insane and that he should not be held responsible for his actions as his delusions caused him to murder Drummond.[106]

The M'Naghten rule became the majority rule in most of the United States, and it provides that a mental disability must produce one of two conditions to be valid as a defense. First, the accused must have suffered from a defect of reason, from a disease of the mind: *and* consequently, at the time of the act, the accused did not know the nature and quality of the act or that the act was wrong.

Some states use the M'Naghten test plus the "irresistible impulse test," which allows a defendant to use the insanity defense if a mental disease has rendered the defendant incapable of choosing between right and wrong, even though he or she can recognize the difference. This is sometimes called *temporary insanity* and means that a defendant cannot control his or her behavior and conform it to the law.[107]

Public attacks on the insanity defense

The results of the Hinckley trial created intense public reaction to the use of the insanity plea. An ABC news poll in 1982 showed that 75 percent disapproved of laws allowing defendants to be found not guilty by reason of insanity. An Associated Press/NBC poll revealed that 87 percent of the public believed too many killers were using the insanity defense to avoid incarceration.[108] These conclusions are, however, factually inaccurate. Although it is difficult to gather accurate data on the frequency of insanity pleas nationwide, the estimates range from 1 to 2 percent. In other words, only 1 to 2 percent of defendants plead insanity, and only one in four of them is successful in obtaining a verdict of not guilty by reason of insanity.[109]

Despite the relative infrequency with which the insanity plea is used successfully, it is usually used in a highly publicized case, arousing great public indignation that heinous criminals are allowed, as a result of the defense, to "go free." That conclusion is also inaccurate in that the small percentage of persons found not guilty by reason of insanity is not necessarily turned loose in society. Hinckley, for example, is now confined in a mental hospital. The public fear, however, rests on the realization that Hinckley and others could be released. Apparently the public feels that a term of years is necessary to protect society from such persons.

Expansion of the insanity defense

There is also the concern that the defense of insanity will be expanded and used more frequently, and there is some evidence that this concern is correct. Some Vietnam veterans, for example, have argued successfully that **post-traumatic stress disorder** (P-TSD) is grounds for an acquittal under the insanity defense. P-TSD symptoms include nightmares, flashbacks, depression, and "survivor guilt."

Veterans afflicted with P-TSD often lose their orientation and believe that they are back in the jungles of Vietnam, taking action to protect themselves and their combat buddies by shooting, attacking, or maiming the people around them—people they believe are dangerous Viet Cong or North Vietnamese. Defense lawyers have argued that these trances or flashbacks are so severe that the veterans are not responsible for their acts and that reliving combat so intensely has destroyed their ability to distinguish right from wrong. The defense has been used to acquit not only veterans accused of murder but also veterans who have committed armed robberies and violated drug laws. P-TSD can manifest itself in the flashbacks mentioned above, can be responsible for veterans committing crimes in the hope they will be caught or shot in order to relieve the guilt of surviving Vietnam combat while good friends died, and can also be responsible for the "action junkie" syndrome in which veterans deliberately put themselves into dangerous situations in order to relive the emotional thrill of their experiences of Vietnam.[110]

Premenstrual tension defense

Another area related to the insanity defense is **premenstrual tension** (PMT) in women. PMT is characterized by both physical symptoms and pyschological symptoms: abdominal bloating, backaches, weight gain, tenderness in the breasts, headaches, skin disorders, cravings for sweet or salty food, irritability, fatigue, insomnia, tension, depression, lethargy, and clumsiness. "In its most extreme form [PMT] can spark uncontrollable rages that vent in violent acts."[111]

PMT is recognized as a form of legal insanity in France and has been used to mitigate or reduce sentences in England. The English debate over PMT began when Sandie Smith, a barmaid with thirty previous offenses, was put on probation for threatening to kill a police officer and for carrying a knife. Her attorney argued that PMT had turned her into "a raging animal each month" and had forced her to act out of character. The second English case involved a woman charged with murder: Christine English had run over her lover with a car. She was given twelve months of jail-free supervision after a medical expert witness testified that she suffered from "an extremely aggravated form of premenstrual physical condition."[112]

PMT was used in America for the first time by a Brooklyn woman who had been accused of child abuse, assaulting her four-year-old daughter. The lawyers in this case, however, believe that the mother will lose custody of her children and that the legal issue of PMT will not be reached. The case, however, has sparked a medical and legal debate about the appropriateness of PMT as an issue in criminal cases.

The concern over the extension of the insanity defense is the fear that P-TSD will become a way to excuse all the violent acts of Vietnam veterans and that PMT will become an "all-purpose excuse for female violence."[113]

The XYY chromosome defense

A final attempt to expand the basis for the insanity defense is the use of the **XYY chromosome** abnormality, discussed earlier in this chapter. The defense has been used somewhat successfully in other countries; for example, the French case of Daniel Hugon, who in 1968 was accused of murdering a sixty-five-year-old prostitute. But the XYY chromosome defense has not yet become an acceptable extension of the insanity plea in this country. For example, when it was raised in a criminal case in Los Angeles in 1969, the judge ruled that there was "no clear link between the chromosomal abnormality and behavior." He stated that the "field of genetics is 30 years behind the point where it can be used in the courts."[114] A 1975 case in New

York raised some of the issues and outlined the reasons that American judges have been reluctant to permit this extension of the insanity defense. In *People v. Yukl,*[115] the defense attorney requested the court to order the appointment of a qualified cytogeneticist to examine, at the county's expense, the chromosomal characteristics of the defendant's blood. That would not have been very expensive, and the procedure is not mechanically complex. But the court's refusal to grant this motion was based on the fact that the information would then be introduced as "evidence" of the defendant's insanity.

The court first articulated the basic principle used in determining whether to admit scientific evidence: "is the scientific theory, instrument, or test sufficiently established to have gained general acceptance in the particular field to which it belongs?" The court's answer to that question is excerpted in *People v. Yukl,* below.[116]

The insanity defense: an analysis

The insanity defense illustrates the basic conflict in our system of law today—the conflict between the rights of the defendant and the rights of the victim and society. On the one hand, the defendant in our system of criminal justice may not be held legally accountable for acts committed without the requisite intent and ability. On the other hand, society has a right to be

People v. Yukl

[I]n New York an insanity defense based on chromosome abnormality should be possible only if one establishes with a high degree of medical certainty an etiological relationship between the defendant's mental capacity and the genetic syndrome. Further, the genetic imbalance must have so affected the thought processes as to interfere substantially with the defendant's cognitive capacity or with his ability to understand or appreciate the basic moral code of his society.

While there is strong evidence which indicates a relationship between genetic composition and deviant behavior, the exact biological mechanism has yet to be determined. Moreover, studies have failed to indicate why only some XYY individuals appear to have a propensity for violence and aggression and not others. The answers to these problems are currently being sought by scientists and their solution will assist immeasurably in providing a firmer footing for the incorporation of chromosome abnormality under the defense of insanity. . . .

[I]t appears on the whole that the genetic imbalance theory of crime causation has not been satisfactorily established and accepted in either the scientific or legal communities to warrant its admission in criminal trials.

Accordingly, the motion for the appointment of a cytogeneticist is denied.

protected from the criminal acts of its members. The defense also demonstrates the principal conflict between law and the social sciences. If we are to recognize defenses regarding the lack of intent and the lack of ability, we must be able to measure those characteristics. The current debate over the insanity plea calls into question the ability of psychologists and psychiatrists to diagnose and predict. But the main problem is not that we are dealing with the human mind, as some people argue. The problem of measuring cause-and-effect relationships is also acute when we are dealing with some physical characteristics and their alleged relationship to criminal behavior, as the discussion of the XYY chromosome defense illustrates.

SUMMARY AND CONCLUSION

In this chapter we have continued our inquiry into the explanations of criminal behavior by concentrating on the contributions, both historical and recent, of biologists and psychologists. Once again, we saw the impact of the positive school, how its constitutional approach to explaining criminal behavior influenced the body-type theories of Sheldon and the Gluecks. But these researchers, along with Cortés, also saw the importance of environmental factors.

From a discussion of genetic factors, including family studies, studies of twins and adoptees, and chromosomal abnormalities, we considered the importance of the central nervous system, neuroendocrinology and neurochemistry, and the autonomic nervous system.

After our examination of these biological approaches, we turned to psychiatry and psychology, beginning with a brief glance at demonology before exploring the psychiatric approach and personality theory. We also studied cognitive development theory, behavior theory, social-learning theory, and the relationship between psychological conditioning and biology. We considered the implications of the current research in biology and psychology as well as the impact of these findings on criminology in understanding criminal behavior.

Finally, we looked at the legal implications, particularly the insanity defense, as well as related defenses based on biology.

Sociological theories of criminal behavior
I. The social-structural approach

In this chapter we shall begin analyzing sociological theories of criminal behavior, especially structural theories, theories that look to society's social structure or organization in an attempt to explain criminal behavior. There are two basic approaches, consensus and conflict. In the first, folkways, mores, and laws are seen as reflecting the society's values. Some crime is seen as inevitable, even functional. In the conflict approach, however, criminal behavior is seen as emerging as the result of conflicts within society. The first position, consensus, is illustrated by the ecological school, the contributions of Durkheim and Merton, and the subculture theories. After discussing these earlier theories, we shall look at some of the "modern" counterparts. Our examination of the conflict approach will distinguish the pluralist model, which sees conflict as emerging from multiple sources, from the critical view, which is based on the Marxist position of conflict created by capitalism.

Most of the explanations of criminal behavior that we have examined thus far have been centered on the characteristics of the individuals classified as criminals. How they differ from "noncriminals" has been the main issue. They have been distinguished on the basis of their psychological and biological makeup. Although these analyses may consider some other factors, such as economic conditions in the case of the economists' explanations, the emphasis has been on the individual. Even the economists attempt to explain criminal behavior in terms of the individual's rational thinking, as that thinking relates to behavior. There are some exceptions, however. For example, the cartographic school attempted to relate crime to characteristics outside the individual. Geographic phenomena, such as climate, topography, natural resources, and geographic location were studied in relation to criminal behavior, and that school of thought, although a very early one, was a forerunner of the approaches we shall discuss in this chapter.

Contemporary sociologists have approached the study of the etiology of crime from two perspectives: structure and process. The first views crime in relation to the social organization or structure of society and asks how crime is related to the social system. What are the characteristics of the situation or structure in which crime takes place? More importantly, do crime rates vary as these situations or structures change? The second approach looks at the process by which criminals are produced, but it is not an individualistic approach. Sociologists look for *patterns* of variables and relationships that might explain how a law-abiding citizen changes into a criminal.

Although for analysis, sociological contributions to the study of crime may be classified abstractly as structural or process theories, these approaches or theories do not fall exclusively into either category. Likewise, it is not possible to isolate sociology from biology, psychology, and economics. "The empirical world rarely comes organized into neat cubbyholes of sociological phenomena, economic phenomena, sociological phenomena and the like."[1] But again, for analysis, some categorizations may be made, and in these two chapters, we shall examine those explanations and theories that illustrate the sociological approach to criminal behavior.

THE CONSENSUS APPROACH

According to the **consensus** perspective, in order to prevent the disruption of society, it is necessary to define some forms of behavior as deviant. "Because therefore it is in everyone's interest to control these kinds of behavior, there is considerable agreement throughout society on norms regulating behavior in a way that is *functional* for the whole society."[2]

Several social-structural theories may be categorized under the consensus approach. We shall begin with the ecological approach that resulted in several empirical studies in this country earlier in the century. The impact of the ecological school will be seen later in the chapter in our discussion of recent developments in consensus theories.

ECOLOGICAL
THEORIES

The study of **ecology** is concerned with the distribution of certain phenomena and their relationship to their environment. The ecologists attempt to explain crime as a function of social change that occurs along with environmental change. Such studies were abundant at the University of Chicago during the 1920s and 1930s, but in our earlier discussion of the cartographic school in Europe in the nineteenth century, we noted the early works of Guerry in France and Qúetelet in Belgium and the influence they had on the works of Mayhew and Fletcher in England. All of these men were concerned with the geographic and spatial distribution of crime: "Although present day criminologists who adopt the ecological approach do not refer to their English predecessors for guidance and corroboration, it is surprising to find that the emphasis which is being placed upon social factors in the causation of crime is closely paralleled in these earlier studies."[3]

*The Chicago
School*

The early ecological school in the United States was centered at the University of Chicago, where it was strongly influenced by the works of Ernest Burgess and Robert Park. Burgess and Park developed their ecological approach in an attempt to describe the growth of the city of Chicago. They saw the city as a living, growing, organic whole—the various areas of the city were "organs" that served different "functions."

Studies of the city's areas of high crime rates and other forms of deviance indicated to researchers that even the deviant's world was characterized by differentiated social roles that were both ordered and stratified and that had rules that were enforced. In addition, the deviant worlds "possessed their own peculiar satisfaction or *rewards* that were by no means limited aspects of the deviant enterprise."[4] Some researchers found evidence of this approach in, for example, their studies of deviants such as hobos and homeless men, who were found to have a stratified society consisting of five groups or classes, as well as defined social roles, regulations, and traditions.[5]

The city's characteristics, social change, and distribution of people were studied by means of the **concentric circle,** an approach developed to study the city of Chicago but thought to be equally applicable to other cities. The concentric circle theory divided the city into five major zones. At the center of the city was Zone 1, the central business district. This zone, according to Burgess, is characterized by light manufacturing, retail trade, and commercialized recreation. Zone 2, surrounding the central business district, is the zone of transition, which is in the "immediate path of business and industrial expansion and has an ephemeral character." This zone is heavily populated by low-income people, although it also typically has an area of high-cost luxury housing—for example, the "Gold Coast" in Chicago's zone of transition. Zone 3 is the zone of workingmen's homes, which is less deteriorated than the zone of transition and populated largely by "workers whose economic status enables them to have many of the comforts and even some of the luxuries the city has to offer." Next comes Zone 4, the area of middle-class dwellers, populated largely by homes of professional people, clerical forces, owners of small businesses, and the managerial class. Finally, on the outer edge of the city is Zone 5, the commuters' zone. This zone includes satellite towns and suburbs. Many of the occupants vacate the area during the day and commute to the city for their employment.[6]

To explain crime, delinquency, and other vices, the key zone in Burgess's theory was Zone 2, transition. Because of the movement of business functions into this zone, the area, which previously claimed some of the most desirable housing in the city, becomes an undesirable place in which to live. Houses, already old, deteriorate. Zoning laws change; people who can afford to move out do so, and there is no prospect of improving the housing in the area without public subsidy. "The general effect of this process has been the gradual evacuation of the central areas in all large American cities, leading to the expression frequently heard: The city is dying at its heart."[7]

The population in the city is segregated by economic and occupational forces; the poor live in Zone 2, and they represent mainly unskilled workers. This economic and occupational segregation often leads to racial and ethnic segregation. The area in Zone 2 is characterized by warehouses, pawn shops, cheap theaters, restaurants, and a breakdown in the usual institutional methods of social control. The investigators hypothesized that crime and vice would flourish there.

Clifford Shaw, often with other associates, conducted several research projects in an effort to determine the relationship between crime (and especially juvenile delinquency) and the zones of the city in Chicago. Shaw and Henry McKay plotted the residences of delinquent youths on transparent maps. They marked the city off in square-mile areas and computed a delinquency rate for each area.[8] They then looked at the distribution of other community problems in Chicago—rates of school truants, young adult offenders, infant mortality, tuberculosis, and mental disorder—and compared them with rates of delinquency and adult crime. "It will be noted that there is not a single instance in which they do not vary together. . . . On the basis of the facts presented, it is clear that delinquency is not an isolated phenomenon."[9]

Evaluation of the Chicago Ecological School. Numerous criticisms have been hurled at the ecological studies, but these must be analyzed in light of what the investigators actually claimed for their studies. They did not argue that "the area causes the crime," as some have suggested. In fact, Shaw and McKay specifically warned that high correlations between variables may not be taken as cause-and-effect relationships. Rather, the "cause" may be a third factor in each case. Another criticism is that the rates of crime and delinquency may be higher in Zone 2 because of differential law enforcement. Shaw and McKay were aware of this problem. The authors say that they are not stating that geographical areas produce the delinquency and crime but that "rates of delinquents reflect the effectiveness of the operation

---

EXHIBIT

CONCLUSIONS OF THE ECOLOGICAL SCHOOL

1. "There are marked variations in the rate of school truants, juvenile delinquents, and adult criminals between areas in Chicago. Some areas are characterized by very high rates, while others show very low rates. . . .
2. Rates of truancy, delinquency, and adult crime tend to vary inversely in proportion to the distance from the center of the city. In general the nearer to the center of the city a given locality is, the higher will be its rates of delinquency and crime. . . .
3. Another striking finding in this study is the marked similarity in the distribution of truants, juvenile delinquents, and adult criminals in the city. Those communities which show the highest rates of juvenile delinquency also show, as a rule, the highest rates of truancy and adult crime. . . .
4. The difference in rates of truancy, delinquency, and crime reflect differences in community backgrounds. High rates occur in the areas which are characterized by physical deterioration and declining populations. . . . In this study . . . we have indicated in a general way that there are characteristic social conditions which accompany crime and delinquency. . . .
5. The main high rate areas of the city—those near the Loop, around the Stock Yards and the South Chicago steel mills—have been characterized by high rates over a long period. . . . Relatively high rates have persisted in certain areas notwithstanding the fact that the composition of population has changed markedly. . . .
6. The rate of recidivism varies directly with the rate of individual delinquents and inversely with the distance from the center of the city. . . . Delinquents living in areas of high delinquent rates are more likely to become recidivists, and . . . the recidivists from these areas are more likely to appear in court three or more times than are recidivists from areas with low rates of delinquents."

Source: Clifford R. Shaw et al., *Delinquency Areas* (Chicago: University of Chicago Press, 1929), pp. 198–204, footnotes deleted.

---

of processes through which socialization takes place and the problems of life are encountered and dealt with."[10]

The ecologists have been criticized on the grounds that the theory does not explain all types of deviant behavior. Their response is that it was never intended to do so, that it was intended to explain mainly those offenses involving groups and social organizations that are usually crimes against property. Those crimes account for a large proportion of crimes committed by young boys.

Areas with high rates and those with low rates of crime and delinquency are distinguished on the basis of physical status, economic status, and population composition, as well as social values. Data were secured from Philadelphia, Greater Boston, Cincinnati, Greater Cleveland, and Richmond,

Virginia. In all of these cities, support was found for the Chicago findings. Shaw and McKay noted that despite changes in the population, rates remained highest in the zone of transition. They concluded that "the delinquency-producing factors are inherent in the community." But they described these as social as well as economic factors, with delinquency seen as a normal reaction to living in a disorganized area.[11]

In contrast with children who live in the zone of transition are those who live in the zones with better physical and economic conditions. These children are not exposed to contrasting values, for values are relatively consistent. In most of their social contacts they find support for the same types of values, and there are few cases of delinquency in the areas in which they live. The community's agencies of social control are effective in keeping the young free from delinquent activities. Shaw and McKay concluded that there was obviously a high correlation between social and economic status and rates of delinquency.

In the revised edition of Shaw and McKay's *Juvenile Delinquency and Urban Areas,* an introduction by contemporary sociologist James F. Short, Jr., pointed out that although much has been learned about delinquency in the thirty years since the original publication, the book was a foundation that has not only stood the test of time but also remains a stimulus for research and for programs of delinquency control. In addition, the revised edition presents new data that substantiate the claim that rates of delinquency and crime are highest in the zone of transition.

More recently several sociologists have written critical analyses of Shaw's and McKay's theory and research.[12] One of those critics concluded that "in view of the limitations of the data and the questionable methodology, and the internal inconsistencies, and the lack of logical consistency, it seems clear that the works . . . have not demonstrated that all nationality groups evidence the same rate of juvenile delinquency in the same urban areas and that nationality is not vitally related to juvenile delinquency." Although it is possible that Shaw's and McKay's position is still valid "and that it might be demonstrated by different data and methodology, the critic thought that improbable and concluded that we should look at conclusions "with some reservation and that, from the point of view of further research, there might be a number of other tenable propositions worthy of investigation which might yield results significant both for sociological theory and human engineering."[13]

CONTRIBUTIONS
OF
ÉMILE DURKHEIM

Émile Durkheim (1858–1917), an outstanding sociologist, made significant contributions to the study of all human behavior. But his greatest contribution to the study of crime was his idea that crime is both normal and **functional** and that no society can be completely exempt from it: "There is . . . no phenomenon that presents more indisputably all the symptoms of normality, since it appears closely connected with the conditions of all collective life."[14]

According to Durkheim, it is impossible for all people to be alike and to hold the same moral consciousness that would prevent any dissent. Because there will always be some individuals who differ from the collective type, it is inevitable that some of these divergences will include criminal characters. That is not because there is some intrinsic quality of their acts that is criminal but because the collectivity will define their acts as criminal. Crime is therefore "bound up with the fundamental conditions of all social life, and by that very fact is useful, because these conditions of which it is a part are themselves indispensable to the normal evolution of morality and law."[15]

Durkheim saw crime as the product of the very existence of norms. The concept of "wrong" is necessary to give meaning to "right" and is inherent in that concept. Even a community of saints will create sinners.

According to Durkheim, crime is also functional and is a necessary prerequisite for social change. In order for the collective sentiment to be flexible enough to permit positive deviation, it must also permit negative deviation. If no deviation is permitted, society will become stagnant. Consequently,

> nothing is good indefinitely and to an unlimited extent. . . . To make progress, individual originality must be able to express itself. In order that the originality of the idealist whose dreams transcend his century may find expression, it is necessary that the originality of the criminal, who is below the level of his time, shall also be possible. One does not occur without the other.[16]

Crime helps prepare society for such changes. The criminal, says Durkheim, should no longer be viewed as a completely unacceptable human being. "On the contrary, he plays a definite role in social life. Crime, for its part, must no longer be conceived as an evil that cannot be too much suppressed." Crime is one of the prices we pay for freedom.[17]

In 1893 Durkheim published *The Division of Labour in Society* and introduced his version of the concept of **anomie,** which derives from a Greek word meaning "lawlessness." Durkheim was not the first to use the term, nor did he develop the concept as extensively as did the American sociologist Robert Merton. But Durkheim was responsible for making the concept an integral part of sociology and, to some extent, criminology.

Durkheim believed that one of a society's most important elements is its social cohesion, or *social solidarity,* which represents a *collective conscience.* In explaining this phenomenon, he defined two types of solidarity, mechanical and organic. Primitive societies are characterized by *mechanical solidarity,* which is dominated by the collective conscience. The type of law manifests this dominance—the reason for law is to repress individuals from acting in a way that would threaten the collective conscience. As societies become larger and more complex, the emphasis in law shifts from the collective conscience to the individual wronged, and law thus becomes *resti-*

tutive. This shift from mechanical to *organic solidarity* is characterized by an increased need for a division of labor, a division that is often forced and therefore abnormal, leading to the creation of unnatural class and status differences among people. People are then less homogeneous, and the traditional forms of social control, appropriate to a simple homogeneous society, are no longer very effective in controlling behavior. Greater loneliness, more social isolation, and a loss of identity result, with a consequent state of anomie, or "normlessness," replacing the former state of solidarity and providing an atmosphere in which crimes and other antisocial acts may develop and flourish.[18]

Impact of Durkheim

As we shall see, Durkheim had an impact on Merton's ideas as well as those of the early subculture theorists. Durkheim's theory of the relation between social integration or anomie and suicide is still important today, with a recent study of suicide and other causes of death finding support for his approach. Events such as presidential elections result in increased social integration in the society, and during those periods, rates of suicide and other causes of death decrease. Such findings "suggest the importance of increasing the social integration of societies and of encouraging social participation by individual members of those societies."[19]

ROBERT MERTON'S THEORY OF ANOMIE

Durkheim's belief that crime is normal and his theory of anomie form the basis of Robert Merton's contributions toward an understanding of criminal behavior. Whereas Durkheim's theory of anomie is very abstract, Merton, a contemporary sociologist, develops a paradigm and relates the theory to real cases in American life.[20]

Merton was reacting against biological theories—which suggested that behavior is the result of inherited traits—and psychiatric, especially Freudian, theories—which state that humans are characterized by the inevitable struggle between biological desires and social restraints. The problem, said Merton, is to answer the question of "why it is that the frequency of deviant behavior varies within different social structures and how it happens that the deviations have different shapes and patterns in different social structures.[21] Merton's thesis is that *social structures* exert pressures on some persons to behave in nonconforming rather than conforming ways. His approach is therefore sociological, with the emphasis on the social structure. If evidence is found for this thesis, then it will follow that nonconforming behavior is as normal as conforming behavior.

Merton begins by suggesting that all social and cultural structures are characterized by two elements that are not always separable in reality but that may be categorized that way for analysis. First are the goals, which are to be the aspirations of all individuals in the society. These goals are those things that are "worth striving for." Second are the means by which those goals may be obtained. The means are socially approved methods, and that involves the element of norms, which are culturally defined. In other words, a society's norms define not only the goals but also the methods by which those goals may be obtained. According to Merton, when there is a focus on the goals to the virtual exclusion of the norms and when the socially approved means for obtaining those goals are not equally available to all, many will turn to unapproved and unacceptable means in order to achieve those goals. For example, if there is a great emphasis on winning a football game, with no significant emphasis that this goal must be accomplished by means of the game's acceptable rules, the players may resort to slugging one another or even bribing other players. "The technically most effective procedure, whether culturally legitimate or not, becomes typically preferred to institutionally prescribed conduct. As this process of attenuation continues, the society becomes unstable and there develops what Durkheim called 'anomie.'"[22]

Merton suggests that in contemporary American culture, the emphasis is primarily on goals, not means, and that the main goal is a monetary one. Noting that money is "well adapted to become a symbol of prestige," Merton argues that to a large extent, money is a value in itself. Americans are also faced with the pressure to be highly ambitious. It is assumed that high goals are open to all and that all should aspire to those goals, that what may appear to be failure now is but a stepping-stone to success, and that real failure consists only in quitting or lessening one's ambition.[23]

Modes of adaptation

After examining these American cultural patterns, Merton designed a typology to describe the methods, or *modes,* of adaptation that were available to those who react to society's goals and means. He identified five modes: conformity, innovation, ritualism, retreatism, and rebellion. Table 5.1 summarizes Merton's typology. It is important to remember that these are *modes of adaptation,* not personality types. Merton is not suggesting that individuals may be categorized as personalities that fit any of the typologies but that in a given situation, one of the modes of adapting to the social

Table 5.1

*A Typology of modes of individual adaptation**

Modes of Adaptation	Culture Goals	Institutionalized Means
Conformity	+	+
Innovation	+	−
Ritualism	−	+
Retreatism	−	−
Rebellion	±	±

*+ signifies "acceptance"; − signifies "rejection of prevailing values and substitution of new values."
Source: Reprinted with permission of Macmillian Publishing Co., Inc., from Social Theory and Social Structure by Robert K. Merton. Copyright 1968 by Robert K. Merton.

structure may be adopted. Merton is talking about socially or culturally *approved* means and goals, and he argues that the modes of adaptation are means of adapting to the tensions of goal attainment in a competitive society.

Conformity. Conformity describes the acceptance of a society's goals and also of its means. It is the most frequently used adaptation.

Innovation. Innovation represents acceptance of the goals but rejection of the means for obtaining those goals. For example, assuming that obtaining a college degree is the goal, the student who adopts that goal but who chooses to reject the acceptable means for attaining it may cheat.

Merton illustrates the innovative adaptation as it leads to deviant and criminal behavior. He draws attention to the criminal behavior that is engaged in by most people but that is not reacted to officially by society and notes studies in which the investigators have concluded that criminal behavior is a common type of behavior. Merton refers to studies that indicate that the social class structure, which imposes the goals, also prevents some from attaining them by the socially approved means. The low status and low income of unskilled labor and the basic occupational opportunities open to members of the lower class do not often permit them to achieve high status in terms of power and income, and they may therefore turn to deviant behavior.

Merton says that the social-structural pressure to attain the goals, along with the social-structural limitations of the availability of legitimate means, produces the pressure toward deviant behavior. The social structure places incompatible demands on persons of the lower socioeconomic class. The key to widespread deviant behavior is that the social structure is proclaiming that *all* should achieve these goals but is blocking the legitimate efforts of large numbers of persons to do so: "In this setting, a cardinal American virtue, 'ambition,' promotes a cardinal American vice 'deviant behavior.'"[24]

This situation helps explain the high rate of crime in poverty areas. Merton is quick to point out that poverty does not cause crime but "when poverty and associated disadvantages in competing for the culture values approved for *all* members of the society are linked with a cultural emphasis on pecuniary success as a dominant goal, high rates of criminal behavior are the normal outcome."[25]

Ritualism. Ritualism is rejection of the goals but acceptance of the means. People may lose sight of the reasons for doing things, such as going to church, but continue the socially approved methods, thus making a ritual out of the method. Merton says this adaptation is more characteristic of the lower-middle class than of any other in American society, whereas innovation is more characteristic of the lower class. The middle class stresses the socially approved means of obtaining goals, thus making it more difficult for its members to deviate from those means. Often this adaptation is characteristic of the person who lowers his or her ambition to avoid the frustration that comes with failure: "I'm not sticking my neck out," "Don't aim high and you won't be disappointed," and so on.

Retreatism.   Retreatism, the least common of the five adaptations, pertains to the type of person who is a true alien from society. This person rejects both the goals and the means of society. Merton suggests that this occurs after a person has accepted both the goals and means but has repeatedly failed to achieve the goals by legitimate means. At the same time, because of prior socialization, the individual is not able to adopt illegitimate means. Thus, in terms of the social structure, he or she is cut off from both legitimate and illegitimate methods of obtaining the society's goals. The method of adaptation is to reject both the goals and the means. "The escape is complete, the conflict is eliminated and the individual is asocialized."[26] This type of adaptor is criticized more by conventional society than is the innovator, who is at least "smart"; the conformist, who keeps society running as it was intended; and the ritualist, who at least accepts the means. The retreatist mode of adaptation, on the other hand, represents a nonproductive liability to the conventional society and is characterized by psychotics, autists, outcasts, tramps, chronic drunkards, drug addicts, vagrants, and vagabonds. People who follow this form of adaptation do so mainly as isolates, although they may gravitate toward other similar deviants. But it is not a collective form of adaptation.

Rebellion.   Rebellion is characterized by a rejection of the goals and means of society and an attempt to establish a new social order. Merton says this adaptation is clearly different from the others, as it represents an attempt to change the social structure rather than to make an individual adaptation within that structure. It is therefore an attempt to *institutionalize new goals and means* for the rest of society.

Evaluation of Merton's theory   Merton has raised some criticisms of his own theory. For example, the theory does not take into account social-psychological variables that might explain the adoption of one adaptation over the other; it only briefly examines rebellious behavior; and it does not consider the social-structural elements that might predispose an individual toward one adaptation over another. Merton also acknowledges that at least at this stage of the development of knowledge, it might not be possible to explain all types of behavior; middle-range theories might be necessary. In concluding his development of anomie, Merton said, "This essay on the structural sources of deviant behavior remains but a prelude."[27]

Others have argued that Merton's theory of anomie does not explain the nonutilitarian element of much juvenile delinquency, which appears to be engaged in for fun and not in order to meet the society's specific goals. It has also been argued that the theory does not explain the destructive nature of some delinquent and criminal acts, that it does not explain crime in societies that do not assert that "esteem goals" are available to everyone, and that it has not been empirically tested. Merton is most severely criticized for his "image of a society in which there is a consensus of values and goals that is inculcated into almost everyone. Rather, the critics say, the world is pluralistic, with culture conflict and with many diverse reference groups from which people obtain a variety of conflicting guideposts and values."[28]

But even those who have tested Merton's theory and not found full support for his conclusions have emphasized the practical aspects of his approach. For example, in a study of anomie among juveniles we find this conclusion: "[M]ore attention should be paid to the strain of failing students as a motive force for delinquency ... identification of types of delinquents in terms of typologies [like those developed by Merton] ... could be conducive to specifying methods of intervention that capitalize either on the norm or on the goal commitment of the youth in question and their success drive or lack of it."[29] Merton's theory has gained wide support, and its influence can be seen in some of the subcultural theories.

SUBCULTURE THEORIES

The theory of anomie, as developed by Durkheim and Merton, established a framework for the development of **subculture** theories of delinquent and criminal behavior. Modern subculture theories were preceded by the classic study of Frederic M. Thrasher, who saw the juvenile gang developing in Chicago as a result of social disorganization in the zone of transition.[30] Although Thrasher did not specifically talk about subcultures, his work is a forerunner to these theories. The subculture theorists do not agree on why certain norms exist within the subcultures, but all their studies may be characterized by their attempt to understand delinquent behavior as sanctioned by the subculture and influenced by the status requirements of the gang or subculture.

Cohen's middle-class measuring rod

The publication in 1955 of Albert Cohen's *Delinquent Boys* set the stage for a new look at delinquency and the development of subculture theories to explain the phenomenon.[31] Cohen says the lower-class child is constantly measured by a middle-class measuring rod, suggesting that the lower-class boy accepts the goals of the middle class but is unable to meet those goals by the socially approved means. The lower-class boy must function within institutions that are run by middle-class people who judge him according to their standards. All are expected to strive for accomplishments, and all are expected to succeed. The lower-class boy, however, does not have the prior socialization that the middle-class boy has and is therefore unprepared for middle-class goals. He has been socialized to live for today and to place more value on physical aggression than does the middle class. In addition, he is less likely to have been able to play with educational toys, and he has restricted aspirations. He thus finds himself deprived of status, as compared with middle-class norms. His problem is further complicated because he accepts the middle-class standards. He learns this acceptance from his parents, who want him to achieve at a higher level than they did; from the mass media; from the realization that some people do move up in the social hierarchy; and from the cultural emphasis on competition. The lower-class boy learns that the way to status and success is to adopt middle-class values, but he is not able to do so. The result is low self-esteem and major adjustment problems. To meet these problems, says Cohen, lower-class boys develop a subculture that inverts middle-class values.

The basic difference between Merton's adaptations and Cohen's subculture theory lies in Cohen's explanation of the subculture's emergence. According to Cohen, the "crucial condition for the emergence of new cultural forms is the existence, *in effective interaction with one another, of a number of actors with similar problems of adjustment.*" The emphasis is on *interaction.* If one boy "finds" a new solution to a problem, that will be "adjustive and adequately motivated provided that he could anticipate a

---

EXHIBIT
CHARACTERISTICS OF THE ADOLESCENT SUBCULTURE

1. *Nonutilitarian.*   The delinquents do not steal things for which they have a need or a desire. They steal "for the hell of it."
2. *Malicious.*   Delinquent activities are characterized by "an enjoyment in the discomfiture of others, a delight in the defiance of taboos itself."
3. *Negativistic.*   The norms of the delinquent subculture appear to be the polar opposites of those of adult society.
3. *Versatility.*   They steal a variety of different things.
4. *Short-run hedonism.*   The boys are interested in momentary pleasures, giving no thought to planning activities or budgeting time and money for the future. The gang usually congregates with no specific activity in mind.
5. *Group autonomy.*   The gang is intolerant of restraint except from the informal pressures within the group itself. The members resist efforts of social institutions, such as the family, school, or church, to regulate their lives.

Source: Albert K. Cohen, *Delinquent Boys: The Culture of the Gang* (New York: Free Press, 1955).

simultaneous and corresponding transformation in the frames of reference of his fellows." The boys look for "signs" or "gestures" of agreement from their peers. As those signs gradually appear, the boys as a group become progressively committed to the new behavior, a process Cohen calls *mutual conversion*. Again, the process of interaction is crucial . . . "we do not first convert ourselves and then others. The acceptability of an idea to oneself depends upon its acceptability to others." As these new "group standards" emerge, the new subculture is formed.[32]

Evaluation of Cohen's theory. The reviews of Cohen's book have been generally positive,[33] and his theory has been given considerable recognition in texts on juvenile delinquency and criminology. Nevertheless, specific issues have been criticized by several sociologists.

Cohen's statement that the working-class boy measures himself by middle-class norms has been questioned.[34] Cohen himself was ambivalent about this point: "It may be argued that the working-class boy does not care what middle-class people think of him." Although Cohen recognizes that this is an empirical question, he assumes that "there is, however, reason to believe that most children are sensitive to some degree about the attitudes of any person with whom they are thrown into more than the most superficial kind of contact."[35] Critics have responded that Cohen is not convincing in his rejecting the argument that lower-class boys may not care what middle-class people think. On the contrary, if there are class differences in socialization, "surely they may be expected to insulate the working-class boy from the responses of middle-class people."[36]

Cohen's use of the psychological concept of *reaction formation* to describe the culture of the delinquent gang has also been questioned. Cohen's development of this concept is based on the assumption that the lower-class boy wants to improve himself in terms of middle-class status. But Cohen also suggests that the lower-class boy is constantly confronted by middle-class standards, by the people who are in charge of the agencies within his community, "which he does not share. . . . [In order] to win favor of the people in charge he must change his habits, his values, his ambitions, his speech and his associates. . . . Having sampled what they have to offer, he turns to the street or to his 'clubhouse' in a cellar where 'facilities' are meager but human relations more satisfying."[37] Critics argue that this statement does not support the concept of reaction formation as Cohen wanted but, on the contrary, suggests that the lower-class boy does not want to strive for middle-class standards and resents the intrusion into his community of those who hold such values and try to impose them on him.

Cohen's description of the delinquent subculture as nonutilitarian, malicious, and negativistic has also been criticized. Some of the activities attributed to the lower-class gang are not characteristic of those gangs today but do characterize some middle-class delinquent activities, which are excluded from Cohen's theories. In contrast, many of the lower-class gangs' activities are much more serious than Cohen indicates. The critics thus question what Cohen considers to be the "facts" supporting his theory.

Finally, Cohen's theory is also debated from a theoretical and methodological point of view. The first problem is that the theory depends on a historical method of research; that is, it attempts to explain why the subculture developed. In order to do so, it must analyze the psychological motivations of past populations, an impossible task empirically. But the critics suggest that it may be reasonable to approach the theory from a functional point of view, attempting to ascertain what conditions are necessary to maintain the delinquent subculture. More importantly, "what are the consequences of participation in the delinquent subculture for the motivational structure of the participants?" This question "places the theory of the delinquent subculture in its proper relation to the value-transmission theories of delinquency, and directs us to examine the heuristic value of Cohen's theory."[38]

Sykes's and Matza's techniques of neutralization

The theory of *techniques of neutralization,* developed by Gresham Sykes and David Matza, and Matza's theory of delinquency and drift are in one sense social-process theories. But we shall consider them here because of their relationship to the subculture theories, which do involve an analysis of the social structure.

In developing their theory, Sykes and Matza attack Cohen's assumption that delinquents are responding to values that differ from those of the adult society as a reaction to the failures they experienced in their initial acceptance of those values. First, they argue, if delinquents had established a subculture with different norms and had accepted those norms in place of the society's norms, they would not exhibit shame or guilt when violating them. Such feelings are, however, evident. Second, the juvenile delinquent often admires the law-abiding citizen. He often resents the attribution of criminal or immoral behavior to those who are important to him, for example, his mother. He therefore appears to be recognizing the "moral validity of the dominant normative system in many instances." Third, juvenile delinquents distinguish appropriate victims and consider other persons or groups to be inappropriate targets for their activities. Finally, the delinquent has already internalized some of the society's norms. He is not "totally immune from the demands for conformity made by the dominant social order." For these reasons, Sykes and Matza argue that the delinquent is "at least partially committed to the dominant social order."[39]

Sykes and Matza theorize that the delinquent may become committed to the dominant norms but permit excuses or rationalize actions for his deviance from those norms. "It is our argument that much delinquency is based on what is essentially an unrecognized extension of defenses to crimes, in the form of justifications for deviance that are seen as valid by the delinquent but not by the legal system or society at large." They describe the delinquent's reaction not as a rejection of society's values, as Cohen indicates, but as an "apologetic failure. . . . We call these justifications of deviant behavior techniques of neutralization." They list five major types of neutralization: (1) denial of responsibility, (2) denial of injury, (3) denial of the victim (the delinquents choose a person who deserves to be a victim), (4) condemnation of the condemners, and (5) appeal to higher loyalties. Sykes and Matza argue that these techniques of neutralization may not be strong enough to shield the individual from his own values and those of others, but they help reduce the impact of social-control forces. These techniques "lie behind a large share of delinquent behavior."[40]

Evaluation of techniques of neutralization.   Support for the neutralization theory has been found by two sociologists who developed a scale for measuring the concept of neutralization as articulated by Sykes and Matza,[41] but others have questioned it. For example, Sykes and Matza proposed that certain types of offenders would favor certain types of neutralizing excuses. Researchers who tested that proposition did not find a significant relationship between the type of offense and the types of neutralization excuse.[42]

Cohen responded to Sykes and Matza in an article with James F. Short, Jr. Cohen and Short agree that the failure of Cohen's theory to consider techniques of neutralization was a serious omission. They then try to incorporate it into their theory, suggesting that their discussion of reaction formation is really a technique of neutralization in which the subculture itself is a neutralizing factor.[43]

Matza's theory of delinquency and drift   A theory similar to neutralization theory is David Matza's theory of delinquency and drift. Matza's studies of delinquency adopted an approach that he called *soft determinism*. It was a middle-of-the-road position between the extremes of the classicists—who believed that crime was the product of free will—and the positivists—who argued that crime was the result of forces beyond the perpetrator's control. Matza argued that although modern-day criminologists' theories incorporate different elements of determinism, compared with those of the positivists of Lombroso's day, they had gone to an extreme. Although Matza did not adopt the doctrine of free will, he did argue that some movement should be made back in that direction; hence his "soft determinism." Orienting his theory toward delinquents, he suggested that the delinquent *drifts* into delinquency. He saw the delinquent as an

> actor neither compelled nor committed to deeds nor freely choosing them; neither different in any simple or fundamental sense from the law abiding; nor the same; conforming to certain traditions in American life while partially

unreceptive to other more conventional traditions; and finally, an actor whose motivational system may be explored along lines explicitly commended by classical criminology—his peculiar relation to legal institutions.

According to Matza, the delinquent drifts between conventional and criminal behavior "responding in turn to the demands of each, flirting now with one, now with the other, but postponing commitment, evading decision."[44]

Cloward's and Ohlin's theory of differential opportunity

When Richard Cloward and Lloyd Ohlin introduced their theory of **differential opportunity,** they said that their work was influenced by two schools of thought: Durkheim's and Merton's concepts of anomie—whose "focus is largely upon the sources of pressure that can lead to deviance"—and Sutherland's differential association theory. The purpose behind Cloward's and Ohlin's work was to try to bring together these two schools of thought in a theory of differential opportunity.[45]

Cloward and Ohlin maintain that sociological and psychological factors limit a person's access to both illegitimate and legitimate roles. The theory of anomie looks at the person from the legitimate opportunity structure and it asks questions about the differentials in access to legitimate means to success goals. It assumes that either illegitimate routes to success goals are freely available or "differentials in their availability are of little significance." Sutherland's theory of **differential association** (discussed in detail in Chapter 6) "assumes that access to illegitimate means is variable, but it does not recognize the significance of comparable differentials in access to legitimate means." Cloward's and Ohlin's theory of differential opportunity structures unites the theories of anomie and differential association and considers the individual, not in terms of either the legitimate or the illegitimate systems, but in terms of both. If the legitimate opportunity structures are readily available and the illegitimate are not, adolescents cannot be expected to solve their problems through illegitimate means. "Given limited access to success-goals by legitimate means, the nature of the delinquent response that may result will vary according to the availability of various illegitimate means."[46] The theory of differential opportunity contains three types of subcultures, defined in the Exhibit on page 150.

Evaluation of Cloward's and Ohlin's theory. One of the problems of differential opportunity theory is the lack of precise, measurable definitions of the relevant concepts. In addition, Cloward and Ohlin do not specify what degree of organization is required in order for a gang to fall within their theoretical framework.[47] It has also been pointed out that some of the theory's claims do not correspond to empirical reality. For example, in their discussion of the three types of subcultures, Cloward and Ohlin suggest that a particular type of subculture will accompany a certain type of social struc-

EXHIBIT
BASIC TYPES OF SUBCULTURE

Criminal Subculture

The criminal subculture develops mainly in lower-class neighborhoods where the successful criminal is not only visible to juveniles but often willing to associate with them. The juveniles in this social class do not have the conventional role models of successful people who have achieved their success through legitimate channels. But they do have access to criminal success models. Consequently, they have an opportunity structure that permits and facilitates illegitimate instead of legitimate activities.

Conflict Subculture

The conflict subculture features a manipulation of violence as a method of getting status. Although slums are not always disorganized, some are characterized by disorganization resulting from transiency and instability. Such unorganized communities cannot provide the criminal subculture that is based on an integration of different age levels and on an integration of conventional and criminal values. The youth are thus left without access to legitimate or illegitimate opportunities, and social controls are weak. The area is populated by failures from conventional society as well as failures from the criminal world. With no organized way in which to solve their frustrations, the youth in these areas "seize upon the manipulation of violence as a route to status not only because it provides a way of expressing pent-up angers and frustrations but also because they are not cut off from access to violent means by vicissitudes of birth."

Retreatist Subculture

Finally, youths who fail in both the criminal and the conflict subcultures tend to retreatism, which is manifested by the use of drugs. Again, the social-structural emphasis can be seen. Cloward and Ohlin contend that "whether the sequence of adaptations is from criminal to retreatist or from conflict to retreatist. . . . limitations on legitimate and illegitimate opportunity combine to produce intense pressures toward retreatist behavior."

Source: Richard A. Cloward and Lloyd E. Ohlin, *Delinquency and Opportunity: A Theory of Delinquent Gangs* (New York: Free Press, 1960), pp. 161–171, 175, 186.

ture. But some neighborhoods that have high delinquency rates are characterized not by one type of subculture but by several.

Another criticism is that the proposition that retreatism is the result of double failure is questionable empirically. Despite these criticisms, it has been concluded that the theory's real merit is that it identifies an important element in the development of deviant behavior that up until now has largely been ignored:

Delinquents clearly perceive limited opportunities in the legitimate system, they are sensitive to artificial barriers against achievement, and they estimate their prospects for success as being better in illegitimate or semi-legitimate occupations. . . . Consequently, the theory of opportunity . . . appears to be on solid ground in attempting to explain delinquent organizations in terms of variations in perceived accessibility of legitimate and illegitimate opportunity systems.[48]

Others have emphasized the impact that differential opportunity theory has had on social science research and on attempts to control crime and delinquency, as illustrated by the following quotation and exhibit on the use of differential opportunity principles in the Chicago area.

Not since the advent of psychoanalysis has a theory had such impact on institutionalized delinquency control as the theory, explicit or implied, in *Delinquency and Opportunity*. Given the impetus of major foundation and federal support, the theory has been extensively adopted as a rationale for action programs in many areas of the country.[49]

Finally, in a study of delinquency and school dropout, investigators attempted to modify and elaborate on the formulations set forth by Cloward and Ohlin in *Delinquency and Opportunity*.[50] The study was not a test of

---

EXHIBIT

PRACTICAL APPLICATIONS OF OPPORTUNITY THEORY

In a study of gang behavior in the city of Chicago, researchers tested the differential opportunity theory and concluded that the Cloward and Ohlin theory needed some modification. These researchers found that the adolescent boys "were neither as isolated from adults nor as antagonistic toward them as some theorists would have us believe." It was found that the black gang boys, who lived in an area "where criminal and conventional elements are 'integrated,'" all had regular contact with the community's older persons. But the researchers concluded that the most important finding of the study was probably "its beginning attempt to specify the manner in which adult-adolescent relations operate to guide (or fail to guide) the passage of youngsters through conventional structures of opportunity. Within the *same* urban communities there are profound gang-nongang differences in the *types* of intergenerational contacts that occur. Nongang boys are given guidelines and advice that are likely to enhance their life changes; gang-dominated adults may live in the same community but they do little to prepare the boys they know to live, as adults, in a better world."

Source: James F. Short, Jr. and Fred L. Strodtbeck. *Group Process and Gang Delinquency* (Chicago: University of Chicago Press, 1965) describes the research in full. The quotations are from Ramon J. Rivera and James F. Short, Jr., eds., *Gang Delinquency and Delinquent Subcultures* (New York: Harper & Row, 1968) pp. 242–243.

their differential opportunity formulation, which was limited to gang delinquency among lower-class urban males. Rather, it was extended to males and females of all social classes. Nevertheless, it was essentially an attempt to modify and extend Cloward's and Ohlin's efforts to integrate the theories of anomie and differential association.

The guiding principle for this extension of opportunity theory was that "both delinquent behavior and dropping out are alternative responses to failure, alienation, and selective exposure to these forms of behavior" and that of the three contexts in which the investigators studied delinquency and dropout—the home, the school, and the community—the school would be the most important. With regard to delinquent behavior, the research revealed that "the school is the critical social context," and that for dropouts, the strongest predictors are "academic failure, school normlessness and social isolation, exposure to dropout in the home, and commitment to peers," with no significant sex differences in these variables. School "dropout is related to class while delinquency is not," and "a strong commitment to one's peers was conducive to delinquency, regardless of the extent of delinquency in that group." The investigators concluded that "peer culture itself is conducive to delinquency."[51]

The relevance of the study to subculture studies of delinquency is important, for the results challenge some of the usual conclusions. First, there appears to be no relationship between delinquent behavior and social class or ethnic origins, although there is a relationship between those variables and status deprivation ("the perception that others have nicer clothes and homes").

Second, the degree to which students participated in extracurricular activities was not predictive of delinquency, and "delinquency among males is less of a response to rejection and alienation from the home than female delinquency." The school is "the most critical social context for males and females but more so for males." Finally, the study revealed that "the relationships between failure, normlessness, association with delinquent peers, and delinquent behavior are mutually reinforcing. Failure, normlessness, and association with delinquent friends are both causes and consequences of involvement in delinquent behavior. Delinquency increases the likelihood that youth will do poorly in school and perceive themselves as rejected by their parents. Involvement in delinquent behavior has a particularly strong influence on feelings of normlessness in school as well as friendship choices."[52]

Miller's lower-class boy and lower-class culture
Walter Miller developed his class theory of delinquent subcultures around the thesis that lower-class delinquents are, in several ways, responding to a distinct lower-class subculture. First, the lower class has a *female-based household;* the family is organized around a woman, not a man. Men may be present, but not in the stable form of marriage known in the middle and

Subculture theories of criminal behavior focus on the influence of peer groups on the behavior of young people. Early sociologists often studied "the gang" as a factor in delinquent behavior.

upper classes. When present, the male in the lower class does not participate as fully in the rearing of children and in the economic support of the family, as is characteristic of other social classes. In addition, "it is the *one-sex peer unit* rather than the two-parent family unit which represents the most significant relational unit for both sexes in lower class communities."[53]

The lower class is characterized by six *focal concerns,* which Miller defines as "areas or issues which command widespread and persistent attention and a high degree of emotional involvement." He labels them *trouble, toughness, smartness, excitement, fate,* and *autonomy,* resulting in a *cultural system* that distinguishes the lower class from the middle and upper classes. He contends that there is an indication that this cultural system is growing more distinctive and that the size of the group that shares the tradition is also growing larger.

In contrast with Cohen's theory that the lower-class boy is engaging in reaction formation against the middle-class values that he cannot attain, Miller is suggesting that the lower-class values come from the inherent characteristics of the lower class itself. When lower-class males act according to the focal concerns that dominate the socialization within their social class, they conflict with middle-class values.

Evaluation of Miller's theory.   An ecological study in Portland, Oregon, revealed that "the type of area described by Miller is virtually nonexistent except in lower class, Negro areas.... Any attempt to 'test' Miller's hypothesis regarding class and delinquency in terms of a single, overall, summary correlation coefficient is doomed to failure."[54]

More recently, a study conducted in three high schools in Seattle, Washington, reported "no firm evidence that social class, no matter how it is measured, is a salient factor in generating delinquent involvement."[55]

Evaluation of the earlier subculture theories.   The subculture theories of Cohen, Cloward and Ohlin, and Miller seek to explain the high crime rates of delinquency in the lower class. Despite their focus on delinquency rather than crime, we included them in this text because of their importance to criminological theory in general and their emphasis on social class in particular. These researchers and their critics have assumed a significant place in criminology, and they cannot be ignored. On the other hand, their approaches do have limitations. Tests of these theories, which have often been based on samples from institutionalized populations, have been questioned by studies based on noninstitutionalized populations, such as questionnaires administered anonymously to the general population.[56] These studies have revealed that most people commit acts for which they could be adjudicated delinquent or criminal and that social class is not a significant factor in these findings among the general population. Such findings appear to contradict the findings that delinquent behavior, as contrasted with adjudicated delinquency, is more frequently a phenomenon of the lower class than of the middle or upper classes.

Other researchers have suggested that the differences between the findings of the earlier and those of the later studies may be due to differences in the types of communities from which the samples were taken. The subculture studies usually select samples from metropolitan areas, and the anonymous questionnaries given to the general population of young people have usually been administered in rural areas and small urban but not metropolitan cities.

In a study of samples from diverse communities in the northern half of Illinois, two investigators found that "when the rates of juvenile misconduct are compared on individual offenses among communities, it appears that as one moves from rural farm to upper urban to industrial city and lower urban, the incidence of most offenses becomes greater, especially in the more serious offenses and in those offenses usually associated with social structures with considerable tolerance for illegal behavior."[57]

This study raises the possibility that social class per se may not be the important element that some researchers have concluded. It is therefore important to look more closely at social class and delinquent and criminal behavior. The variable of social class, however, is in many cases inseparable from other relevant variables such as race, socioeconomic class, and distribution in space of people and their institutions. It is therefore necessary to examine more recent studies of these variables, studies of both delinquency and criminology.

RECENT DEVELOPMENTS IN THE CONSENSUS APPROACH

The theme of our discussion thus far is that the environment's structure is related to behavior, specifically criminal behavior. The early ecologists were concerned with the distribution in space of people and their institutions; Durkheim and Merton studied social integration or anomie; and the subculture approach examined the norms that groups, usually adolescents, developed in response to the social structure. Although the primary emphasis is on the social structure, the approaches in this chapter also provide a basis by which process theories, sociological or otherwise, may be considered. For example, an environmental explanation of criminal behavior might include not only the ecology of the area in which the criminal behavior occurs but also the impact that the environment has on a person's decision to engage in criminal behavior. Thus, the process of becoming a criminal might be intertwined with the structure in which the behavior takes place. These social-structural explanations are therefore important not only for their own merit in explaining criminal behavior but also for the framework they establish for process theories.

Location of crime

Recall that the Chicago ecologists found that crimes are most frequently committed in the "zone of transition." A recent study of land use in Washington, D.C., confirmed this finding. The investigators computed the "commuting distance" of criminals and found that in general, criminals victimized people who lived in transitional areas—areas with a high proportion of construction, demolition, and temporary lodgings, with the correlation highest for robbery and burglary but also significant for rape. Business areas (Zone 1 of Burgess's approach) were also heavily hit by criminal activity. The areas of high crime rates were also characterized by multiple-family dwellings, as contrasted with single-family homes. Finally, the offender most often lived in the area in which the crime was committed:

> For the most part, offenders commit their crimes in the vicinity of their domiciles. But when they do travel, they seem to commit their crimes in areas that are public in nature, a pattern consistent with the theory that the offender formulates a cognate map of the areas he visits and commits his offenses within those areas.[58]

That does not mean, of course, that offenders never travel to commit their crimes. Indeed, some commuting does take place, but when it does, it appears to be related to the characteristics of the offender, where he or she lives, the type of crime he or she intends to commit, the attractiveness of the area, and the location of potential targets. Commuting to commit a crime is an investment; it takes time and expense and will probably increase the risk. By traveling outside their own environments to commit the crime, the offenders may be indicating that they view the crime as worth the increased risk.[59] If that is the case, opportunity theory and economic theory may be combined. That is, the economic motivation to commit a crime, as pointed out in Chapter 3, may be related to the existing opportunities or the need to expand the opportunities for successful criminal behavior.

Density and crime   In 1972 Oscar Newman published a book called *Defensible Space.*[60] Other writers had recently introduced the concept of environmental impact[61] on crime, and although Newman does not give his predecessors much credit,

> he must be credited with succeeding, where others failed, in firing the public imagination and in bringing about an unusual dialogue between criminologists and members of the architectural and planning professions. His ideas, expressed in a readable if polemical style, have fascinated researchers and newspaper reporters alike, and a substantial body of published research testifies to this fascination.[62]

Newman introduced the concept of *defensible space.* He believed that crime could be reduced by modifying the environment's physical features, and he described his approach as

> a model for residential environments which inhibits crime by creating the physical expression of a social fabric that defends itself. . . . "Defensible space" is a surrogate term for the range of mechanisms—real and symbolic barriers, strongly defined areas of influence, and improved opportunities for surveillance—that combine to bring an environment under the control of its residents.[63]

The approach may be illustrated by a simple example. Assume that a potential burglar makes decisions concerning the probability of successfully getting into and out of the place to be burglarized. Any increase in the probability of no success will increase the probability that the person will not commit the crime. The judgment involves a particular street, a particular house site or lot, and a residence. A series of cues are used by the potential offender in making the decisions regarding potential success or failure, and the potential for intrusion will be greater if the person perceives the area to be public rather than private, the assumption being that private areas, such as houses, are more likely to be occupied for longer periods of time than are public places. The latter, therefore, are more accessible and risk-free.

Environmental factors may also affect the defensible space of houses. For example, houses in certain neighborhoods may be considered too risky in the summer because people are often outside, and neighbors might have a better watch on the potential target. On the other hand, people go on vacation during the summer, and that can make the house more attractive as a target. Lighting is also important—a well-lighted area is less likely to become a target because of the increased possibility of detection.[64]

Analysis of the defensible space approach. C. Ray Jeffery has criticized Newman's approach as follows:

> Unfortunately, most of Newman's discussion involves hardware: floor materials, fire doors, window materials, window bars and grills . . . and other hardening of the target techniques. This is not a very imaginative approach to environment-behavior interaction, though it represents the thinking of today on crime prevention.[65]

Newman's approach has also been criticized as difficult to test empirically because many of his concepts are not clearly articulated and defined. Yet, numerous researchers, many in Great Britain, have conducted research on his concepts, with strong support for his position coming from studies of burglary revealing that the "border blocks in city housing areas are much more vulnerable to burglary offenses than the interior blocks."[66] Another criticism is that changing the environment does not reduce crime; it just displaces it—the potential criminals go elsewhere: "Creating ramparts, battlements, parapets and walls in high-crime areas may deter criminal attacks in a specific area, but it leaves untouched the real social causes of criminal behavior and may . . . disperse bad actors into secret nooks and crannies elsewhere."[67] If this is the case, it raises serious problems for research, for it will be difficult, if not impossible, to measure this process of displacement.

Physical environment and social integration It is quite possible that it is not the physical environment itself that is relevant in explaining criminal behavior, but the social integration or anomie that the physical environment facilitates or perhaps produces. Recall that in Durkheim's analysis of suicide, he spoke of anomie, the feeling of normlessness, of a lack of integration within society, which is characteristic of people who commit this crime.

Similarly, the design of a building—or its location—may affect the social integration of the people who live in that area and in turn affect the potential for crime. The physical environment, according to both Jeffrey and Newman, may impair the informal social controls that help inhibit criminal behavior. Others have suggested that the physical environment might also influence formal controls, such as the police who, according to research, are more likely to expect to find criminal activity in high-density areas. Thus, it is possible that the research does not accurately indicate a higher crime rate in dense areas but, rather, a higher rate of apprehension.[68] Finally, density alone might not be the important variable, for there is some evidence that "a decrease in the density of the population in physical locations that are normally sites of primary groups should lead to an increase in criminal opportunities and hence in property crime rates."[69]

Anomie and environment

What this suggests, then, is that we must look at not only the characteristics of the area but also the reaction of the police and the characteristics of the people who live there. Thus, it may be argued that "crime will be highest where the characteristics of the residents and of the environment increase the opportunities for crime." Density and overcrowding are not the only relevant variables; the "complex interactions among the social and environmental variables" must also be considered. Low levels of interaction among residents will result in low levels of knowledge about the area and increase the anonymity of the people, thus increasing the opportunities for successful criminal activity. In a neighborhood characterized by a lack of social integration, or anomie, residents are not as likely to be concerned about what is happening in other homes.[70]

This anomie may be increased where there are high rates of mobility[71] or fast rates of industralization.[72] On the other hand, urbanism itself may not create alienation and anomie in general. There is some indication that we need to distinguish between public and private life when examining the effects of urbanization on social integration, for it has been found that "urbanism does not produce estrangement from close associates, or from familiar groups such as neighbors. It does seem to produce estrangement from, and even conflict with, the unknown, socially dissimilar, and potentially threatening people and subcultures who make up the city—the inhabitants of the 'world of strangers'"[73]

Routine activity: a convergence of theories

Lawrence Cohen and Marcus Felson have taken the position that crime may be explained as the convergence of three elements: (1) likely offenders (people who are motivated to commit crimes), (2) suitable targets (presence of things that are valued and that can be transported fairly easily, and (3) absence of capable guardians (people to prevent the criminal activity). This combination of motivation theory, opportunity theory, and social-control theory is not new. "The most original aspect of Cohen and Felson's work is not their recognition of the need for all three and for their convergence at the same time and place, but rather their demonstration that this convergence is produced by the patterning of **routine activity patterns** [boldface added]."[74]

According to Cohen and Felson, human ecology may be used to explain

The concept of space is becoming increasingly important as a variable that is related to criminal activity. In a crowd like this, for example, picking pockets might be done quickly, easily, and without detection.

how legal activities increase the probability of illegal activities. For example, the movement of women into the work force reduces the number at home during the day. That increases the "absence of capable guardians." The family's larger income as a result of the woman's working may also increase the number of desirable goods, or suitable targets. If these two elements converge in time and space with likely offenders, the crime rate will increase. But "the lack of any of these elements is sufficient to prevent the occurrence of a successful direct-contact predatory crime." Furthermore, "the convergence in time and space of suitable targets and the absence of capable guardians can lead to large increases in crime rates without any increase of change in the structural conditions that motivate individuals to engage in crime."[75]

The routine activity approach was tested in Sweden with the result that it was found to be as effective in explaining increasing crime rates there as in this country: "This is true despite the considerable difference in welfare expenditures and the resulting income redistribution between the two nations." The researcher emphasized that this is not the finding we would expect from a theory emphasizing that income redistribution would be an effective crime preventive, as some have suggested.[76] He concluded: "The results suggest that opportunity factors may be more important in generating blue-collar crime than the presence of social welfare institutions."[77]

Evaluation of routine activity theory

The routine activity theory, however, has been questioned by sociologists in this country. Leo Carroll and Pamela Irving Jackson raise the possibility that the dispersal of routine activities away from the home does not have a direct effect on the crime rate, as is suggested by the routine activity explanation. Rather, it "is itself a process influencing the structural factors that motivate offenders to commit direct contact predatory crimes." It influences income inequality at both ends of the income distribution. As more married women enter the work force, there are more two-income families with a higher total income than before. On the other hand, as the number of families headed by females increases, the number of families at the lower-income level also rises, as the incomes of working women remain considerably lower, on the average, than those of working men. And this income inequality is directly related to crime rates.

Carroll and Jackson stress, however, that their study is limited and is not an exact test of the routine activity explanation. They emphasize the need for additional research to consider the impact of income inequality on crime, particularly considering the passage-of-time factor. "Indeed, the whole question of the impact of income inequality on crime seems to be a central one that for some unknown reason has been largely overlooked by criminologists."[78]

SOCIAL-STRUCTURAL THEORIES AND VICTIMIZATION

These theories have also been used to explain victimization. For example, women are warned not to leave their purses in shopping carts at the grocery store and not to walk in crowds with their purses open and easily accessible to others. Someone might steal the purse "because she presents them with the opportunity to do so easily and quickly and probably with little likelihood of apprehension." Women are told not to walk alone at night in isolated areas or to leave a bar with someone they do not know. To do so is to provide a male with an opportunity to rape; indeed, some have argued that such actions "encourage" rapists, in which case the woman is seen as having "asked for it."

An analysis of burglaries also indicates the importance of considering the victims' characteristics. One study revealed that the types of people who are most likely to be burglarized are central city residents,[79] the young, persons with incomes higher or lower than average, nonwhites, and persons whose homes are relatively often unoccupied. "[T]hese data suggest that the key to a reduction in burglary rates may be tighter social organization of neighborhoods, whereby residents pool their resources to increase guardianship of their own property and that of their neighbors."[80]

The opportunity or life-style concept theory suggests that if we understand offenders, we may also understand victims, and vice versa:

One of the central building blocks of the lifestyle concept has been the discovery that the factors most closely associated with victimization are factors which have also been found to be associated with offending. . . . In control theory terms, the processes that reduce the restraints to offend are similar to the processes in lifestyle terms that affect the probability that persons will be in places at times and around people where the risk of victimization is high.[81]

SOCIAL-STRUCTURAL THEORIES AND FEMALE CRIMINALITY

Social-structural theories, especially opportunity theory, have been utilized to "explain" not only the victimization of women but also the criminal behavior among women. This approach has been rejected, however, as an explanation of why women engage in criminal behavior. In fact, scholars do not even agree on the nature of female criminality, and like other issues, the data are questionable in terms of giving us an accurate picture of the behavior's extent. Is is therefore important to examine the various approaches to female criminality.

THE STUDY OF FEMALE CRIMINALITY

Until recently females were seldom studied either as offenders or as victims in the system of criminal justice. Various "reasons" have been given for this neglect. As offenders, women have constituted a much smaller percentage of total offenders than of their proportion of the population. Their crimes have generally been kinds that do not seriously threaten society, except perhaps its moral fiber, as in the case of prostitution, and women arrested for violations of the law are usually first offenders. In general, women offenders have not been seen as a serious social problem and have not presented the serious problems of violence in prison that have been characteristic of men's prisons. As inmates they have been considered easier to manage than male inmates, resulting in less security in institutions for women. It has generally been considered that they have been better treated, exemplified by the comments that correctional facilities for women are "country clubs" compared with those for men.

Some of these widely held beliefs, however, have been challenged, as scholars within the past few years have begun to take a serious look at the female in the criminal justice system.

The extent and nature of female criminality

A 1975 article in a popular news magazine indicates the position of some on the issue of female criminality: that it is increasing and that women are becoming more violent in their criminal activity. In effect, they are becoming more like male criminals. The headline was "Crimes by women are on the rise all over the world" and the subhead, "In one country after another the story is the same: Female criminals are growing in numbers—and becoming more violent, as well. Why?"[82] In the past decade, especially in the past five years, scholars have debated that conclusion.

In 1975, in her *Sisters in Crime,* criminologist Freda Adler set the stage for the debate on the amount and nature of female criminality. According to Adler, the data indicated that crime among women was not only increasing but that women were more frequently engaging in crimes considered to be "male" rather than "female" crimes. Women, she said, are becoming murderers, muggers, bank robbers, and even penetrating organized crime[83] (although they have not attained much success).[84]

Others have supported Adler's position that female crime is increasing and becoming more violent,[85] although not all agree on why this is occurring. On the other hand, some scholars take the position that the "differences" in the extent and nature of female, as compared with male criminality, may be due to the source of data used, with official data generally revealing that males are more involved in property and violent offenses and females in sex and home-related offenses. But studies based on self-report data more often reveal similarities than differences in male and female criminality.[86] Finally, it is argued that female crimes today are quite similar to the crimes women have always committed and that these crimes are closely associated with sex roles and opportunities.

Opportunity theory and female criminality

Sociologist Rita Simon has taken the position that female crime rates have been increasing only in certain property crimes, such as larceny/theft and fraud/embezzlement and that the increase in these crimes can be explained by opportunity theory. According to this position, "women are committing those types of crimes that their participation in the labor force provide them with greater opportunities to commit than they had in the past." The propensities of men and women to commit crimes are not basically different; the difference has been in opportunities. "As women's opportunities to commit crimes increase, so will their criminal behavior; and the types of crimes they commit will resemble much more closely those committed by men."[87]

Simon's position is that women are more involved in economic crimes because they have more opportunities to commit such crimes and they are less involved in violent crimes because the frustrations that lead to the latter are decreased as women become liberated:

> Case histories of women who kill, reveal one pattern that dominates all others. When women can no longer contain their frustrations and their anger, they express themselves by doing away with the cause of their condition, which most often is a man and sometimes a child or an unborn baby. Thus, the thesis is that as women's employment and education opportunities expand, their feelings of being victimized and exploited decrease and their motivation to kill becomes muted.[88]

Darrell J. Steffensmeier, who has written extensively on female criminality, agrees that there has been an increase in some kinds of crime among females, but he takes the position that women are still basically involved in "female" types of crimes. Shoplifting, for example, is a crime for which traditionally the most arrests have been of women. Increases in shoplifting are reflected in the higher rates of larceny. Such crimes are tied to the traditional female roles "in the legal and illegal marketplaces; they move from shopper to shoplifter, from cashing good checks to passing bad ones, from taking aspirins to popping bennies and barbs, from being a welfare mother to being accused of welfare fraud, and so on."[89] According to Steffensmeier, "Women may be a little more active in the kinds of crime thay have always committed," but they are "still typically nonviolent, petty property offenders."[90]

Steffensmeier argues that "American women are not catching up with males in the commission of violent, masculine, serious, or white-collar crimes."[91] This is particularly true in the exclusion of women in the underworld of organized crime.[92]

With regard to female criminality, Steffensmeier concludes that women are still principally regarded as sex objects as well as wives and mothers. Finally, Steffensmeier argues that the evidence suggests that female delinquency also continues to reflect traditional female sex roles; the women's movement has had little effect on this phenomenon.[93]

HIGHLIGHT

OPPORTUNITY THEORY AS AN EXPLANATION FOR FEMALE CRIMINALITY

In applying Cloward's opportunity theory to an explanation of the limited role women play in organized criminal activity, as well as to explain the role of women in other types of crime, Darrell J. Steffensmeier stated:

> . . . no study of sex differences in crime can be considered complete which ignores the special roles, positions, and constraints affecting women in organized crime activities, as well as the men who have traditionally peopled crime organizations. Compared to their male counterparts, potential female offenders are at a disadvantage in selection and recruitment into criminal groups, in the range of career paths, and access to them, opened by way of participation in these groups, and in opportunities for tutelage, increased skills, and rewards.
>
> The availability of concrete opportunities, in turn, helps explain why among their supposed options, women select criminal behaviors congruent with sex roles. . . . Like male offenders, female offenders gravitate to those activities which are easily available, are within their skills, provide a satisfactory return, and carry the fewest risks. . . . Thus, if women are less into crime and are relatively less successful at it, this is less a result of singlemindedness in the rational pursuit of crime than because they lack access to organizations and social contacts that would enable them to pursue criminal enterprise more safely and profitably.

Source: Darrell J. Steffensmeier, "Organization Properties and Sex-Segregation in the Underworld: Building a Sociological Theory of Sex differences in Crime," *Social Forces* 61 (June 1983): 1024–1025.

Other scholars have supported Steffensmeier's argument that women are still engaging in traditional female sex roles even when they commit crimes generally considered to be "masculine." For example, Lee H. Bowker, in his provocative book on female criminality, raised this issue. He referred to one study that found that

> The criminal roles played by female robbers and burglars were more consistent with general female sex-role behavior than with the behavior of male robbers and burglars. In the majority of cases, the women were partners rather than sole perpetrators of the acts, and there were also a number of cases in which they were only accessories (who played secondary roles) or conspirators (who did not participate at all in the criminal acts). In only one case out of every seven did a woman carry out a robbery or burglary on her own.[94]

Finally, Joseph W. Weis has taken the position that the "new female criminal" is a myth based on "pop" criminology and too much reliance on official crime data. After studying self-reports of middle-class delinquency, he concluded that these data reflect sex-role opportunities, and that the alleged relationship between female liberation and the emergence of a new type of female criminal is a social invention, not reality: "Women are no more violent today than a decade ago and the increase in property offenses suggests that the sexism which still pervades the straight world also functions in the illegal marketplace."[95]

These statements about the nature of female criminality were, however, made before the 1982 data that show some increase in the percentage of female arrests for violent crime. On the other hand, the higher percentages of women arrested, as compared with men arrested, are much greater in property than in violent crimes. Higher percentages of arrests for larceny/theft and forgery, higher in both cases for women than for men when the 1982 data are compared with those for earlier years, may indeed illustrate that women are "still typically nonviolent, petty property offenders."

Conclusions: the need for research and analysis on female criminality

After examining the studies and analyses of female criminality, as compared and contrasted with those of males, one investigator concluded:

> Reports of steadily accelerating increases in female relative to male crime across all types of crime or particularly in property crime, along with reports of decreases in female crime relative to males, provide a confusing picture of the changing nature of sex differences.[96]

Some of the differences clearly stem from the differences in the data base used for analysis, as we noted in our discussions in Chapter 2 of the differences between official and self-report data. Part of the problem also comes from a too-narrow focus in some studies; it is entirely possible that if there are significant differences between actual male and female delinquency and criminality, those differences cannot be explained by one variable, such as women's liberation, or one theory, such as opportunity theory.

After considering the studies of female criminality, Stephen Norland and Neal Shover warned against premature conclusions, arguing that "no clear-cut pattern of change in the criminality of women can be observed. . . . The inconsistent picture presented by these different types of data appears to require a more complex explanation than the relatively simple one suggested in the argument that crime is a function of aggressiveness or masculinity."[97] They also pointed out, however, that significant progress in understanding female criminality could not be made until scholars systematically analyzed the "sexist assumptions" on which the studies have been conducted: "Until these ideas are critically examined and subjected to empirical scrutiny, progress will not be made in understanding female criminality and the allegation that it is on the increase."[98]

THE CONFLICT APPROACH

In the beginning of this chapter, we noted that the consensus approach sees the emerging norms and laws of society as representative of the common feeling about what is right and proper; that is, they represent a consensus of views. They also represent a mechanism for maintaining social order, but that order is maintained through consensus.

In the **conflict perspective,**[99] on the other hand, values, norms, and laws are viewed as creating dissension, clash, conflict. Conflict thinkers do not agree on the nature of this process; in fact, they do not agree on what to call this approach. Nor have the thinkers in this field agreed with one another over time; for some, the process has been an evolving one, and their positions today differ from their earlier ones. It is therefore quite difficult for the student who wants a quick perspective of this area of thinking in criminology to get an accurate view. We shall not be able to go into great detail on any one approach, but we shall compare and contrast the ideas of the most frequently cited authorities in the field.

THE PLURALIST MODEL

The pluralist approach was briefly described by a sociologist in his analysis of the critical perspective: "Until recently . . . conflict theory has gone beyond class conflict to interest-group conflict of all kinds and has had more similarity to political-interest-group theory, or a *pluralistic* model of society."[100] Unlike Marxism, with its focus only on the class struggle, the pluralistic approach sees conflict emerging from several sources.

Culture and group conflict

Conflict may exist between cultures, between subcultures within cultures, and between interest groups. The first, **culture conflict theory,** is illustrated by the work of sociologist Thorsten Sellin, whose work on capital punishment we examined in an earlier chapter. Sellin argued that crime must be analyzed as conflicts among *norms*. For every person, he said, there is a right (normal) and wrong (abnormal) way of acting in specific situations, and these "conduct norms" are defined by the groups to which the individual belongs. In the normal process of social differentiation, these norms clash with other norms; *culture conflict* is thus the inevitable result of conflict between conduct norms.

Sellin distinguished between *primary conflict*—which refers to the conflict of culture norms when two different cultures clash—and *secondary conflict*—which occurs within the evolution of a single culture. The first is exemplified by the man from Sicily who, while living in New Jersey, killed the man who seduced his sixteen-year-old daughter. The father was surprised to be arrested for committing a crime. In his country, such an act by a father would be expected behavior for defending the family's honor. But in the United States it was a crime. Here is a clear case of conflict between the norms of two different cultures. But, said Sellin, because the volume of crime is higher among the native born than among the foreign born, it is the secondary conflict that is most important in explaining crime in the United States. Such conflicts "grow out of the process of social differentiation which characterizes the evolution of our own culture."[101] In the normal growth of cultures from homogeneous to heterogeneous, social differentiation occurs. This in turn produces different social groupings, each with its own values and its lack of understanding of the values of other groups. The result is an increase in social conflict.

Sellin's theory has been attacked by those who disagree with his thesis that criminals and delinquents are responding to different norms. They argue that such people are responding to the same norms but that there is a scarcity of rewards associated with them. In support of culture conflict theory, it has been pointed out that the data do indicate that in areas having high rates of delinquency, there is more often a duality of conduct norms than a dominance of conventional or criminal norms.[102]

Perhaps the way to resolve these differences is to recognize that culture conflicts may account for some types of crime, especially among subculture groups, such as gangs, and among the foreign born, but that they do not explain all types of crime. An example of this approach is Miller's subculture analysis, discussed earlier in the chapter. Miller's approach focuses on subcultures but is also a conflict theory in that he sees the lower class's values as conflicting with the middle class's values and laws.

Conflict may also exist between interest groups within the same society, an approach developed by George Vold.[103] Vold did not believe that the conflict between groups was caused by any abnormality. Rather, he thought that these conflicts were "normal, natural responses" made by "natural human beings struggling in understandably normal and natural situations for the maintenance of the way of life to which they stand committed."[104] Vold's examples are racial conflicts that involve violence between interest groups, violent behavior accompanying conflict between the interest groups of management and labor, and so on. The focus is on conflicts between interest groups, not subcultures or cultures.

Austin Turk views society's social structure as organized into weak and powerful groups, with the powerful dictating the norms that are proper for all and establishing the sanctions if those norms are violated. But Turk then begins to sound like a labeling theorist (**labeling theory** is discussed in the next chapter), thereby taking a social-process approach, for he suggests that the persons most likely to be designated criminal because of their law violations are members of the least powerful groups in society.[105] His is also a social-structural approach, in that he sees the structure of social institutions as relevant to the labeling process.[106]

Turk emphasizes that criminology must study the differences between the status and role of legal *authorities* and *subjects.* He argues that these two statuses will be differentiated in all societies and that authority-subject relationships are accepted because it is felt that they are necessary for the preservation of a social order that permits "individuals" to coexist. He speaks, then, of the *norms of domination* and the *norms of deference,* which he says exist in all social arrangements: "*Lawbreaking* is taken to be an indicator of the failure or lack of authority; it is a measure of the extent to which rulers and ruled, decision-makers and decision-acceptors, are not bound together in a stable authority relationship."[107] Turk thus does not view conflict over social norms in the traditional sense that some have internalized the norms and others have not. Instead, he contends that people relate differently to different norms, according to "their own individual bio-social experience—some of which norms are institutionalized as norms of domination, others of which are assigned the status of deference. Conflict, and the assignation of a criminal status to various kinds of behaviour, will depend on the congruence or lack of congruence between social norms and the cultural evaluation of the norms."[108]

Turk, then, is a modern conflict theorist who views political organization as the result of, and characterized by, conflicts. Those in power have some control over the goods and services that might be available to people in social relationships. That control is exercised through the use of power, and Turk isolated five forms of power, based on the resources controlled by each:

1. police or war power—control of the means of direct physical violence
2. economic power—control of material resources
3. political power—control of decision-making processes
4. ideological power—control of definitions, beliefs, and values
5. diversionary power—control of human attention and living times[109]

Turk's conflict theory has been criticized for dismissing, as do most conflict theorists, "the new voluminous body of research findings . . . that there is considerable normative consensus in society cutting across class, sex, race, and age divisions on the undesirability and seriousness of certain criminal acts." On the other hand, Turk's approach—viewing crime as a status that is conferred on those who do not follow the laws of society—indicates the conflict between those in power and those not in power. "As such, this perspective may be applied to a wide range of 'criminal behavior' occurring in various types of social structures and diverse political and economic systems."[110]

CRITICAL CRIMINOLOGY

The second model of conflict theory, quite different from the pluralist types, is called by many names: radical criminology, the "new conflict approach," the "new criminology," "Marxist" criminology, "materialist" criminology, "socialist" criminology, and "critical" criminology.

The important point about critical criminology is that there is considerable divergence among these "new" theorists. Furthermore, it is not possible to show precisely how their approaches differ from the traditional approaches. "What seemingly unifies much of radical criminological thought while at the same time separating it from mainstream criminology is the greatest emphasis on the notion that crime control cannot be ultimately realized within the prevailing socioeconomic order of modern society."[111] For most of the thinkers in this field, the focus is on the economic system, more specifically, capitalism. They are often referred to as Marxist criminologists, deriving their positions from the developmental thinking of Karl Marx. We shall therefore look briefly at the **economic determinism** approach of Marx and some of his followers.

Historical approaches

For centuries, criminal behavior has been explained in terms of economic conditions. Some of these explanations have been concerned with the influence of economics on rational thought, and others have argued that economic situations facilitate criminal behavior. This approach is illustrated by the writings of Frank Tannenbaum and William Bonger. But it was the deterministic position of Karl Marx,[112] that provided the framework for many of today's radical criminologists. Marx believed that private ownership of property results in poverty, which distinguishes those who own the means of production from those whom they exploit for economic benefit. The latter turn to crime as a result of this poverty. Marx believed that the economic system was the sole determinant of crime. Although he did not develop a specific theory of criminal causation, he saw the mode of production as the causative element in all social, political, religious, ethical, psychological, and material life. Because crime is, as are all other social phenomena, the result of the economic system, the only way to prevent crime is, therefore, to change that system. Marx saw social revolution as the only way to bring about the necessary changes in the economic system.

Other historical contributions that are important to an understanding of recent developments in critical criminology are the works of Frank Tannenbaum and William Bonger. Tannenbaum felt that criminals are as much a part of the community as are scholars, investors, scientists, and business people, and that the community must provide a facilitating environment for their behavior to exist. "The United States has as much crime as it generates. . . . If we would change the amount of crime in the community, we must change the community. The criminal is not a symptom . . . he is a product . . . of the community.[113] The community gives the criminal his or her methods as well as ideals and goals.

Finally, Bonger, a Dutch criminologist, examined the lives of primitive peoples and noted that they are characterized by altruism. Such people are very social; they help one another. This altruistic way of life, based on mutual help, he pointed out, can only be explained by the social environment that is determined by the mode of production. Among these people, production is for personal consumption and not for exchange. Furthermore, neither property nor wealth exists. When there is abundance, all are fed; when food is scarce, all are hungry. Finally, people are subordinate to nature. As a result of these three characteristics, said Bonger, people are not egotistic. Society is characterized by social solidarity, which is the result of the economic system.[114]

In a capitalistic system, added Bonger, people concentrate only on themselves, and this leads to selfishness. They are interested only in producing for themselves, especially in producing a surplus that can be exchanged for profit. They are not concerned with the needs of others. Capitalism thus breeds social irresponsibility and leads to crime. For example, the economy prevents some from marrying when they desire; that leads to rape, illegitimacy, and infanticide. Bonger did not argue that capitalism creates an egotistic tendency that forces people to become criminal, but he did say that it makes them more capable of becoming criminals. The economic system thus provides a "climate of motivation" for criminal behavior. At times, however, Bonger sounds like a determinist. "Upon the basis of what has gone before, we have a right to say that the part played by economic conditions in criminality is preponderant, even decisive."[115]

The development of modern critical criminology

The most prolific writer in the development of modern critical criminology has been Richard Quinney. A conflict theorist in his early thinking, Richard Quinney came to view both the theory and practice of criminology as "a form of cultural production" or "cultural politics," whose purpose should be to move us from the acceptance of a capitalist to a socialist society. Quinney tried to develop a social theory that supports socialist rather than capitalist development and that "provides the knowledge and politics for the working class, rather than knowledge for the survival of the capitalist class."

The necessary basis for the development of this theory, says Quinney, is Marxist theory and practice.[116]

In earlier developments of his perspective, Quinney examined and rejected the traditional criminological approaches.[117] He then developed his approach: *critical philosophy*. Quinney's critical philosophy is a radically different approach, one that permits us to question everything, and to develop a new form of life. But according to Quinney, negative thinking is not sufficient. There must be something to replace what is rejected.[118]

Quinney argues that traditional criminology has not critically questioned the legal order. His thesis is that the state is a political organization that serves to maintain the interests of the ruling class over and against those of the ruled.

Quinney proposes a socialist society in which the "goal is a world that is free from the oppressions produced by capitalism." In a socialist society, all will be equal, and all will share equally in the society's material benefits. A new human nature will arise, one that is totally liberated from acquisitive individualism and "no longer suffers the alienation otherwise inherent in the relations of capitalism." There will be no need for the state once classes, bureaucracy, and centralized authority are abolished. Law as it is now known will exist only in history.[119]

According to Quinney, the traditional notion of causality in criminology should be abandoned, and the attempt to discover "what is" should be replaced by an approach that would try to understand "what is in terms of what *could* be." His purpose in developing what he calls a theory of the "social reality of crime" is to "provide the ideas for correct thought and action. Only with a critical theory are we able to adequately understand crime in American society." Quinney developed six propositions:

1. *The official definition of crime:* Crime as a legal definition of human conduct is created by agents of the dominant class in a politically organized society.
2. *Formulating definitions of crime:* Definitions of crime are composed of behaviors that conflict with the class interests of the dominant class.
3. *Applying definitions of crime:* Definitions of crime are applied by the class that has the power to shape the enforcement and administration of criminal law.
4. *How behavior patterns develop in relation to definitions of crime:* Behavior patterns are structured in relation to definitions of crime, and within this context people engage in actions that have relative probabilities of being defined as criminal.
5. *Constructing an ideology of crime:* An ideology of crime is constructed and diffused by the dominant class to secure its hegemony.
6. *Constructing the social reality of crime:* The social reality of crime is constructed by the formulation and application of definitions of crime,

the development of behavior patterns in relation to these definitions, and the construction of an ideology of crime.[120]

The body of Quinney's theory consists of the middle four propositions.

> These form a model of crime's social reality. The model . . . relates the proposition units into a theoretical system. Each unit is related to the others. The theory is thus a system of interacting developmental propositions. The phenomena denoted in the propositions and their interrelations culminate in what is regarded as the amount of character of crime at any time—that is, the social reality of crime.[121]

Like many critical criminologists, Quinney's position has changed over time. His most radical work was written during the late 1960s and early 1970s, but during the middle 1970s, he became even more closely identified with the Marxist position, arguing that the real conflict is between the ruling class and those who are victimized by that class. The solution, Quinney stated, is the establishment of a socialist system.[122] In more recent years, Quinney has been comparing the spiritualism of Christianity with the moral position of the Marxist philosophy.[123]

Evaluation of critical criminology The most serious criticism of critical criminology is that it is not a theory of empirically tested propositions but, rather, a "viewpoint, a perspective, or an orientation."[124] The terms that are crucial to the theory, such as social class, are not clearly defined in terminology that enables empirical testing. Consequently, the Marxists have done little testing. For example, Marxists take the position that social class determines our treatment by the police, the courts, and other institutions and that the ruling power discriminates on the basis of race, ethnic origin, and sex. According to Quinney, law is used as "the tool of the ruling class. Criminal law, in particular, is a device made and used by the ruling class to preserve the existing order."[125] Differentials in rates of arrest as well as convictions and sentences may be "explained" by this process. Yet, what appears to be discrimination in arrests, convictions, sentencing, and so on, must be examined more closely. This is not to suggest that discrimination does not exist, but merely that empirical studies in which relevant variables such as the previous offense record and the seriousness of the current crime must be considered before conclusions are drawn. In the words of a noted criminologist, Gresham M. Sykes,

> if critical criminology is to make a significant contribution to a sociology of crime, it will need to avoid the error of believing that because the legal stigma of crimes does not match the occurrence of crime-in-general in the population, the stigma is necessarily based on irrelevant factors such as income and race. Certain patterns of criminal behavior may still have much to do with the matter.[126]

Finally, critical criminology has produced a large body of literature in criminology,[127] not all of which is Marxist. But it is the Marxist, or radical approach, that has drawn the greatest criticism. In a review and critique of a series of original papers written by conflict criminologists, some of whom were Marxists, Ronald L. Akers, a sociologist and criminologist, commented on Marxist criminology. Akers, who first acknowledged that he was personally and professionally acquainted with all of the authors whose papers he reviewed, indicated that he found little empirical support for Marxist theory in criminology and that he disagreed with Marxism, thus rejecting Quinney's argument for the need for a socialist society:

> The whole tenor of Quinney's appeal is that of a mystical, true-believing apostle. Capitalism is evil. Socialism is good. The ideal society is a communist society. . . . Because of this faith in the righteousness of his cause, Quinney does not ask questions or search for answers; rather, he starts with conclusions assumed to be true and plays out the implications of these . . . I sometimes get the impression that Quinney and I are not living in the same society.

According to Akers, even if we do not like the society in which we live, that is no reason to establish a socialist country. "Marx the social theorist left an abundant intellectual heritage; Marx the coffee-house revolutionary left a legacy of human suffering. We should welcome the first Marx and totally reject the second."[128]

Despite these criticisms, Akers concludes that "however much I disagree with Marxist criminology, I believe we should continue to hear about it and respond to it."[129] Others have pointed out that critical criminology "holds out the promise of having a profound impact on our thinking about crime and society." Conflict or critical criminology forces a reexamination of notions of equality before the law and a consideration of whether such really exists, or whether "there is ample evidence that our ideals of equality before the law are being compromised by the facts of income and race in an industrial, highly bureaucratized social order. If a 'critical criminology' can help us solve that issue, while still confronting the need to control crime, it will contribute a great deal."[130]

What is needed now in regard to both types of conflict theory is the "careful derivation of propositions concerning the legal process from the concepts and propositions of more general conflict sociologists" and the "wider accumulation of empirical evidence relative to existing conflict propositions than has heretofore been accomplished."[131]

On the other hand, a professor of criminal justice has taken the position that the Marxist school of criminology is not likely ever to have as much influence on our thinking as did the positive school. Acknowledging that much of the positive school's influence was on others trying to prove that the advocates' ideas were wrong, Richard Sparks concluded that "Marxists would presumably prefer not to achieve immortality in quite the same way.

But at least the Italian positivists had a theory, which *could* be proved wrong; nobody ever accused them of having a mere 'perspective.'"[132]

SUMMARY AND ANALYSIS OF SOCIAL-STRUCTURAL THEORIES

In the previous two chapters we studied explanations of criminal behavior that focused on the individual and his or her characteristics. In this chapter we have examined explanations that focus on crime as a function of the social structure. During the past several decades, this approach has been the most popular one of liberals, many of whom concentrated on unemployment and other forms of economic deprivation characteristic of the social structure and not the individual criminal. They viewed the entire society as being to blame for crime. Even violent crime was seen as the result of the social structure—the depressed will kill and steal in order to get even with a society that has wronged them.

Juvenile delinquency in particular was seen as caused by the social structure: Although some saw delinquency and crime as a reflection of the family and other social institutions, and some even offered psychological and psychiatric causes, the consensus of the liberal writings was that whatever or whoever was blamed, severe punishment based on a concept of personal evil and wickedness was not appropriate. The principal problem in dealing with crime was to curb poverty and racism. Conflict and critical criminology explanations particularly stressed the role of poverty in explaining crime rates.[133]

The social-structural emphasis has lost popularity in this country. As we saw in our discussion of deterrence theory, the swing now is away from seeking the causes of crime outside the criminal and is toward the criminal who is presumed to think rationally and who, it is assumed, can be deterred from criminal activity if the correct disincentives are imposed.

The contributions of social-structural theories must not however, be overlooked. In identifying social institutions and political institutions as possible causes of crime, we have made some significant changes, some that may be questioned and some that have obviously been functional for individuals as well as for society. One hopes that we have also learned that "neither the patterns of criminal areas nor the putative causes for them will yield to simplistic explanations. The motivations to crime are not just economic, nor social nor yet psychological but a complex and ever-changing amalgam."[134] Thus it is important to consider crime from many perspectives.

Consider, for example, the reactions of a former street gang leader in Chicago in the early 1970s, who was the subject of a case study on criminal behavior. The young man talked about motivation theory and the influence of peers on young people, but he said that he basically believed that he and his peers committed crimes because it was economically feasible and the opportunities were available. He emphasized that crime was not a "good bargain" but that to them it appeared to be the best way to get what they wanted. The advantages of legitimate work were not obvious to them. His conclusion was to show young people the advantages and disadvantages of crime, and you will change their behavior. He believed that "young people from his background will respond rationally to clearly attractive employment opportunities, and to information from a trusted source about the costs of crime."[135]

Such explanations combine motivation theory, with its emphasis on the individual, and social-structural theory, with its emphasis on social institutions. And there are practical implications, even if these theories do not explain all criminal behavior. We know that the location of goods and services, housing density, and certain population characteristics are related to crime. That knowledge should lead us to redistribute justice resources and work on urban renewal and to encourage people in high-crime areas to decrease the opportunities for crime.

Developing an understanding of crime that will reduce the motivation of crime has been discussed with regard to economic theory, but we also need to assess sociological theories that are concerned with the process of becoming a criminal. The contributions of sociologists in this area are significant, and to those developments we shall devote the next chapter.

CHAPTER 6

Sociological theories of criminal behavior

II. Social-process theories

In this chapter we shall be concerned with the process by which people become criminals. Do they learn this behavior and, if so, how and under what types of circumstances? The chapter will begin with a discussion of the social-learning theory approach called *differential association*. The impact of that theory will be assessed in light of the recent "reformulations" of social-learning theory by sociologists and criminologists. The second part of the chapter will examine social-control theories, based on the assumption that criminal behavior occurs when society's normal methods of controlling people break down. Finally, we shall look at labeling theory, which focuses on the process by which people who engage in certain acts come to be called (or labeled) criminal, whereas others who engage in those same kinds of behavior are not labeled criminal.

In Chapter 5 we discussed sociological theories that emphasized the relationship of criminal behavior to the social structure or organization of society. How crime is related to the social system was the basic question. Whether the environment was seen as a determining factor in the causation of crime—as in Marx's economic theory—or a facilitating factor—as in Bonger's climate of motivation theory—the emphasis was on the structure of the environment, not on characteristics of the individual, as in the constitutional theories. The social-structural theories, however, give no attention to how individuals become criminal. This chapter, therefore, will focus on an analysis of *social-process theories,* which attempt to explain how people become criminals. Is criminal behavior acquired in the same way as noncriminal behavior? The approach seeks to explain the *process* of becoming a criminal rather than the characteristics of the criminal or of the crime-conducive environment.

It is, of course, not possible to separate all sociological theories neatly into the two categories of social structure and social process. Some could easily be considered in both categories. For example, Bonger's theory was discussed in the previous chapter as a social-structural theory because of his concentration on the relation of the economic environment to crime. But because he stressed that that environment created a "climate of motivation," his theory might also be analyzed as a social-process theory that considers the process by which the motivation necessary for criminalization occurs. Similarly, the "techniques-of-neutralization" theory of Sykes and Matza might also be considered a social-process theory because of its emphasis on the motivation of the youth who are committing delinquent acts. That theory explains the process by which a person neutralizes any inhibitions he or she might have against violating laws. On the other hand, the theory is related to subcultures, an aspect of the social structure. In this chapter, we shall study labeling theory. It may be considered a process theory, in that it explains the process by which a person becomes a criminal: the person is labeled by those in a position to make that determination. Labeling theory has also been characterized as a social-structural theory, with some similarities to conflict theory,[1] although it can also be seen as the *process* by which the *structure* of conflict is applied.

These theories developed as sociologists began to analyze the obvious fact that not all people exposed to the same social-structural conditions respond in the same way. Some become law-abiding citizens, and others become criminals. Not all criminals always respond in criminal ways; likewise, not all "noncriminals" always respond by observing the law. Thus there must be some process that explains the differential reaction to the environment. In addition, sociologists began to hypothesize that human behavior is learned and that criminal behavior may be acquired in the same way that we acquire noncriminal behavior. This approach has also been taken by other disciplines, as we have seen in previous chapters.

DIFFERENTIAL ASSOCIATION

Differential association theory as an explanation of criminal behavior is based on the premise that criminal behavior is learned in the same way that any other behavior is learned. The key figure in the development of differential association was Edwin H. Sutherland.

SUTHERLAND'S CONTRIBUTIONS

Sometimes referred to as the "dean of American criminology," Edwin H. Sutherland has had a tremendous impact on sociologists and criminologists in the United States. He is best known in criminology for his theory of differential association, a theory of crime causation he introduced in 1939. It was at that time intended to be a theory to explain systematic criminal behavior. In 1947, he extended the theory to apply to all criminal behavior.

When Sutherland was asked to write a text on criminology in 1921, his primary interest was in the controversy that was raging between theories of environment and theories of heredity. Sutherland wanted to analyze criminal behavior utilizing some of the prevailing sociological concepts and was also interested in finding concrete causes of crime. But as he examined the concepts, he decided that no concrete explanation could explain crime. For example, the concrete condition most frequently associated with crime is sex, and most people apprehended for crimes were male. But Sutherland said that it was obvious that sex was not the cause of crime. So he turned to abstract explanations and finally decided that a learning process involving communication and interaction must be the principle that would explain all types of crime.[2]

In the 1939 edition of his book, Sutherland introduced the concept of differential association, although he was reluctant to do so. His concern about the hypothesis was expressed in his reference to it as "an hypothesis which might quickly be murdered or commit suicide."[3] The hypothesis was, however, developed into a theory. The 1947 version of the theory, containing nine statements, was Sutherland's final version:

1. Criminal behavior is learned.
2. Criminal behavior is learned in interaction with other persons in a process of communication.
3. The principal part of the learning of criminal behavior occurs within intimate personal groups.
4. When criminal behavior is learned, the learning includes (a) techniques of committing the crime, which are sometimes very complicated, sometimes very simple; (b) the specific direction of motives, drives, rationalizations, and attitudes.
5. The specific direction of motives and drives is learned from definitions of the legal codes as favorable or unfavorable.
6. A person becomes delinquent because of an excess of definitions favorable to violation of law over definitions unfavorable to violation of law.

7. Differential associations may vary in frequency, duration, priority, and intensity.

8. The process of learning criminal behavior by association with criminal and anticriminal patterns involves all the mechanisms that are involved in any other learning.

9. While criminal behavior is an explanation of general needs and values, it is not explained by those general needs and values, since noncriminal behavior is an expression of the same needs and values.[4]

Evaluation of Sutherland's differential association

In one of his efforts to test a portion of Sutherland's theory, James F. Short, Jr., called the theory "the most truly sociological of all theories which have been advanced to explain criminal and delinquent behavior."[5] Short, however, also pointed out some of the problems with the theory, which he said was not testable in its general terms; some reformulations were necessary for testing it. Short did attempt to measure the theory's frequency, duration, priority, and intensity dimensions. Within the limitations of his study he found strong support for the theory, although in a later study he again concluded that a reformulation might be necessary before the terms of the theory could be used for precise measure.[6]

Others have attempted to test the theory of differential association by measuring actual delinquency as reported by best friends. Their conclusions: "We are led to question the postulate that differential association is a necessary and sufficient condition explaining delinquency."[7] Sutherland considered this and other criticisms in a paper that was not published until after his death: "The Swan Song of Differential Association," written in 1944. He acknowledged that some of the criticisms were valid, and he concluded that criminal associations alone do not explain criminal behavior. Rather, it is those

associations plus tendencies toward alternate ways of satisfying whatever needs happen to be involved in a particular situation. Consequently, it is improper to view criminal behavior as a closed system, and participation in criminal behavior is not to be regarded as something that is determined exclusively by association with criminal patterns. . . . For the reasons that I have outlined and doubtless for additional reasons differential association as a sufficient explanation of criminal behavior is invalid.[8]

In that article, Sutherland considered returning to multiple causation and abandoning the attempt to explain all criminal behavior by means of one theory. But in the 1947 edition of his text, he did not try to incorporate these ideas, and the theory of differential association has remained as he stated it in that edition.

*Cressey's defense
of differential
association*

Donald Cressey, who wrote the editions of the Sutherland text since Sutherland's death in 1950, acknowledged the criticisms. He agreed with some. The theory of differential association "is neither precise nor clear. . . . Most significantly, the published statement gives the incorrect impression that there is little concern for accounting for variations in crime and delinquent rates. This is a serious error in communication on Sutherland's part."[9] Cressy believed that the theory needed reformulation, but he made no attempt to do so in subsequent editions of the text. He stated his reasons: "The theory is presently in a period of great popularity. . . . It would be inappropriate to modify the statement in such a way that research work now in progress would be undermined."[10]

Cressey did, however, analyze the criticisms and defend the theory against some of the attacks. He stated that one result of the ambiguity of the theory and the critics' failure to read the theory carefully was the assumption that people become criminals because of their association with either criminals or criminal patterns of behavior and attitudes. But, observed Cressey, the theory was that people become criminals because of an *overabundance* of associations with criminal, as compared with anticriminal, behavior patterns.[11]

Some argued that an individual can become a criminal without associating with criminals and that therefore, differential association does not apply. That, said Cressey, was not the point. One may be exposed to criminal attitudes and behavior without being exposed to criminals. For example, a mother who teaches her child not to steal may indicate that it is permissible to steal a loaf of bread if one is starving. "One can learn criminal behavior patterns from persons who are not criminals, and one can learn anti-criminal behavior from hoods, professional crooks, habitual offenders, and gangsters."[12]

Critics have reasoned that certain types of criminal behavior are not covered by the theory of differential association. Cressey's reaction to this criticism was that in all but five of the cases, no research was conducted. Thus the criticisms are research proposals, not valid criticisms. He did agree that if research was done testing the theory and it was found that a type of crime was not covered, the theory should be revised.

According to Cressey, Sutherland was aware of the criticisms of his theory by social psychologists, who believed that the theory did not explain why some people responded to opportunities for crime by committing crimes, and other people responded to such opportunities by engaging in law-abiding behavior. But differential association was perceived by Sutherland to account for such "differential response patterns." Whether or not a person took money from an open cash register would be related to his or her previous associations. "The differential in 'response pattern,' or the difference in 'receptivity' to the criminal behavior pattern . . . is accounted for by differential association itself."[13]

More damaging criticisms, asserted Cressey, are those that point out the difficulties of operationalizing some of the theory's terms, which make it impossible to measure the precise mechanism by which people learn criminal behavior. Cressey believed that this problem would not affect "the value of the theory as a general principle which organizes and makes good sense of the data on crime rates."[14]

The theory of differential association was developed by Sutherland primarily to interpret the data of crime. Sutherland was probably not trying to devise a theory that would explain individual criminal behavior but, rather, to develop a theory that would bring some order to the understanding of crime rates. Cressey cites other sociological "theories" that are analogous. Durkheim did not develop a theory of suicide that produced hypotheses he empirically tested. Rather, he had a "principle of group integration" that made sense out of the data on suicide. Likewise, Sutherland developed a theory of differential association, which is a "principle of normative conflict." Cressey feels that the theory is really a "principle," not a "precise statement of the process by which one becomes a criminal."[15]

Even after Cressey's defense, criticisms of the theory remained, and have led to modifications of the theory.

DIFFERENTIAL ASSOCIATION AND SET THEORY

Melvin L. DeFleur and Richard Quinney attempted to express differential association in the language of set theory. They developed a formal model of differential association theory and formulated a "limited number of underlying postulates from which the Sutherland assertions are then deduced. By this means, it can be shown, with some reformulation, that the Sutherland scheme (as developed in set theory terms) appears to be internally consistent and consistent with more general behavioral theory." DeFleur and Quinney also devised a strategy for empirically testing the theory.[16] Cressey's reaction was that "their English translation of set theory language states the theory of differential association more beautifully and more efficiently than it has ever been stated before. It goes 'beyond Sutherland' by displaying relationships which have been hidden."[17]

DIFFERENTIAL ASSOCIATION REINFORCEMENT

In an effort to provide a "more adequate specification of the learning process" required in the theory of differential association, Robert L. Burgess and Ronald L. Akers created what they called **differential association-reinforcement theory.** Their purpose was to integrate Sutherland's theory with the more general behavior theory associated with the work of B. F. Skinner. Their assumption was that in so doing the theory would be made more testable while at the same time the learning processes would be indicated more clearly.[18]

The social-learning theory is based on the assumption that the "primary learning mechanism in social behavior is operant (instrumental) conditioning in which behavior is shaped by the stimuli which follow, or are consequences of the behavior." Direct conditioning and imitation of others are important in determining this behavior. Rewards, or positive reinforcement, as well as avoidance of punishment, or negative reinforcement, strengthen this behavior. The behavior may be weakened by aversive stimuli, or positive punishment, as well as by loss of reward, or negative punishment. The determination of whether the behavior is deviant or conforming depends on *differential reinforcement,* defined as "past and present rewards or punishments for the behavior and the rewards and punishments attached to alternative behavior." Furthermore, from others who are important to them, people learn norms, attitudes, and orientations that define certain behaviors as good or bad. Such definitions help reinforce behavior and serve as cues for behavior. The more positive definitions people have of the behavior, the more likely they will be to engage in that behavior. These definitions are learned from peer grops as well as from family but also may come from schools, churches, and other groups. The definitions lead to deviant behavior when "on balance, the positive and neutralizing definitions of the behavior offset negative definitions of it. Therefore, deviant behavior can be expected to the extent that it has been differentially reinforced over alternative behavior (conforming or other deviant behavior) and is defined as desirable or justified."[19]

This social learning first occurs in a process of differential association. The person interacts and identifies with groups that provide "the social environments in which exposure to definitions, imitation of models, and social reinforcement for use of or abstinence from any particular substance takes place." The person first learns the definitions through imitation within these groups; the definitions are then reinforced by the group and eventually serve as "discriminative stimuli for use or abstinence." They thus become reinforcers for the person's behavior.[20]

Akers and his colleagues tested this social-learning theory, using adolescents and the behavior of drug and alcohol use and abuse. They administered self-report questionnaires to 3,065 adolescents, both male and female, who were enrolled in grades 7 through 12 in seven communities in three midwestern states. The researchers emphasized that previous research, as well as their own analysis, indicated the reliability and validity of using the self-report method to measure the involvement of young people in drug and alcohol use and abuse.

Akers and his colleagues found support for the theory of differential association, with the theory explaining 55 percent of the variance in drinking behavior and 68 percent of the variance in the use of marijuana. Although they found all of the dependent variables "strongly related to the social learning variables of differential association, definitions, differential reinforcement, and imitation," they found that the most "powerful of these independent variables is differential association."[21]

The social-learning theory of Burgess and Akers has been widely cited. Cressey, the major proponent of Sutherland's theory of differential association, included the work of Burgess and Akers with a group of works he described as "the major theories of criminologists."[22] But the theory has also been criticized. One critic reviewed the application of operant conditioning principles to criminology in general and looked at Burgess's and Akers's application of such principles to the theory of differential association in particular. He concluded that the Burgess and Akers effort contained major oversights and that these might have misled sociologists and criminologists who were not familiar with the principles of operant conditioning.[23]

DIFFERENTIAL ASSOCIATION AND PEER GROUP INFLUENCE

Many of the empirical tests of differential association theory have found strong relationships between the variables of delinquent associations and delinquent definitions and delinquent behavior.[24] Many of the studies do not, however, examine the complete causal structure that the theory implies. What is the order of cause? Do the delinquent associations cause the delinquent definitions which in turn lead to delinquent behavior? Or does the delinquent behavior occur for some other reason, followed by a need to develop delinquent associations and then delinquent definitions? Is it possible that adolescents who have delinquent friends "are more likely to experience short-run, situationally induced pressures to deviate?"[25] That is, the adolescent is pressured into deviate acts before he or she develops "an excess of definitions favorable to violation of the law." "If this finding is replicated in other studies, differential association theory will have to account for the direct effect of peer group behavior on individual behavior."[26] This conclusion, however, is based on a simplistic view of "excess of definitions" and fails to consider the concepts of frequency, priority, duration, and intensity that are also important to Sutherland's theory of differential association.

Finally, recent research also raised the issue of needing to consider the type of primary group influences on behavior when testing differential association. Thus, it may very well be that during adolescence, peer groups have a very strong influence on the development of attitudes favorable or unfavorable to violating the law but that the impact decreases significantly with age, whereas other primary groups, such as the family or work groups, take on a greater significance. It may also be that the impact of any of these groups will differ according to type of delinquent or criminal behavior.[27]

DIFFERENTIAL IDENTIFICATION AND DIFFERENTIAL ANTICIPATION

Daniel Glaser studied differential association theory and the empirical tests of that theory in relation to other theories of criminal behavior. He outlined all of the facts that such a theory must explain, for example, why the frequency, duration, and intensity of criminal or delinquent associations is predictive of criminal behavior. Glaser concluded that differential association theory is more successful than other sociological theories as an explanation of such predictors but that the theory is deficient in other predictors. Glaser therefore developed his own approach, first with the theory of **differential identification** and later with **differential anticipation** theory.

In his earlier development of differential identification, Glaser related his approach to role theory. Criminal behavior is seen basically as role playing, and the theorist must explain why criminal roles are selected. Glaser defined identification as "the choice of another, from whose perspective we view our own behavior." The selected choices may come from direct association with criminals, through identification with persons heard or viewed through the mass media or "as a negative reaction to forces opposed to crime." In essence, according to Glaser, the theory of differential identification is that "a person pursues criminal behavior to the extent that he identifies himself with real or imaginary persons from whose perspective his criminal behavior seems acceptable." It focuses on persons' interactions with the situation or environment as well as persons' interactions with themselves in rationalizing their conduct. In this sense, the theory, Glaser stated, is an integrative one, for it permits us to analyze the relevance, in each case of criminality, of "economic conditions, prior frustrations, learned moral creeds, group participation, or other features of an individual's life." Any or all of these may be important in that they may affect the person's choice of behavior. Glaser recognized, however, that the one objection to the theory of differential association that is not solved by differential identification is the area of "accidental" crimes.

Later, in an attempt to account for the successes and failures of inmates after they are released from prison, Glaser created the theory of differential anticipation. This theory relies on differential association but also on differential opportunity theory. The theory postulates that when people consider the legitimate and illegitimate behaviors available, they select the alternative that is perceived or anticipated to be the best alternative. Thus, it makes no difference which actually is the best alternative; the anticipation of what is best is what counts. "While a theory of differential opportunity permits deduction of some successful criminological prediction hypotheses, opportunities affect voluntary actions only when the opportunities are perceived. Perhaps the most adequate criminological theory of extreme generality which can be formulated from our present knowledge is a theory of *differential anticipation.*"[28]

Glaser, who is concerned with the practical implications of sociological theory for the correctional system, stresses that a theory of differential anticipation recognizes that our perception of opportunities will to some extent depend on our self-concept, how we perceive ourselves in relationship to others and their reactions. Self-concepts are developed through the process of differential association, and they are influenced by the reinforcement we get from others. Thus, if we define people as successful when they are economically successful, then it is important to provide sufficient economic opportunities for released inmates. In short, Glaser believed that "the correctional treatments of maximum reformative effect are those that enhance a prisoner's opportunities in legitimate economic pursuits and those that improve his conception of himself when he identifies with anti-criminal persons."[29]

Glaser's theory of differential anticipation draws on opportunity, differential association, social-learning, and self-concept theories. This approach, along with differential association in general, also has implications for the impact of the mass media on criminal behavior.

DIFFERENTIAL ASSOCIATION AND THE MASS MEDIA

The importance of differential association in explaining criminal behavior can also be seen in the recent studies of the mass media's impact on behavior. Recall that Glaser stressed that identification with criminal behavior may be the result of contact with the media and is therefore not dependent on association with actual criminals. Whether the process is one of identification or imitation, the result is the same: what the media portray may influence how the viewers behave. Some of that impact can be seen in the current concern over whether television has an effect on behavior, a concern that raises the possibility of both psychological and sociological explanations of the process by which a person becomes deviant or, for that matter, law abiding.

In Chapter 4, in our examination of psychological learning theories, we mentioned the work of Albert Bandura. According to him, research has revealed that television, the most influential of the media for adolescents, has four types of effects on their social behavior:

1. the teaching of aggressive styles of conduct;
2. the lessening of restraints on aggression;
3. desensitization and habituation to violence; and
4. the shaping of images of reality upon which people base their actions.[30]

According to Bandura, research has shown that television can distort people's perceptions of the real world. "Heavy viewers see the society at large as more dangerous regardless of their educational level, sex, age, and amount of newspaper reading."[31]

The research to which Bandura referred was conducted by George Gerbner and his colleagues. In his earlier research, Gerbner found that young viewers of television were more likely to think it is "almost always all right" to hit someone if you have a good reason for it. They also found that 80 percent of the prime-time television shows and weekend day shows and 60 percent of the major characters on those shows are involved with some kind of violence and that the percentage of violence has not changed very much in ten years. But they warn that although most studies of individual reaction to television violence pertain to behavior after a specific show of violence, the effects of watching the show cannot be assumed. Watching television does not occur in a vacuum.

HIGHLIGHT
VIOLENCE AND TELEVISION

A study conducted by the Media Institute has found that there is little relationship between real life and life as portrayed on TV. Among the major findings are:

- Crime pervades television entertainment, with an average of 1.7 crimes per show.
- Television crime is far more violent than real life and over 100 times more likely to involve murder.
- Most crime is punished on television, but police officers are rarely the heroes.

According to the President of The Media Institute, "The findings of this study are very unsettling because they suggest the American public is receiving a grossly distorted picture of what crime and law enforcement are all about."

Source: *Justice Assistance News* 4 (March 1983): 9. Copies of the study are available at a cost of $5.95 from the Publications Dept., The Media Institute, 3017 M St., N.W., Washington, D.C., 20007.

The consequences of living in a symbolic world ruled largely by violence may be much more far-reaching. Television violence is a dramatic demonstration of power which communicates much about social norms and relationships, about goals and means, about winners and losers, about the risks of life and the price for transgressions of society's rules.[32]

Gerbner and his associates concluded that it might be fear, rather than imitation, that is produced by television violence:

The violence scenario thus serves a double function. By demonstrating the realities of social power, it generates fear, insecurity, and dependence, and thus serves as an instrument of social control. The objective is achieved at a great human price. The price is the incitation of the few to destructive violence, the cultivation of aggressive tendencies among some children and adults, and the generation of a sense of danger and risk in a mean and selfish world in many of our children.[33]

This conclusion indicates the necessity of avoiding simplistic explanations of behavior—for example, imitation or identification based on television viewing—and examining that behavior in the total context in which it occurs. Again, we are back to the importance of process. By what process do some people react to television viewing with fear, some with deviant behavior and some with no negative reactions? This study also illustrates the importance of considering both psychological and sociological theories of behavior. For example, in addition to the learning process that may help explain reactions to television viewing, the social-structural concept of a subculture of violence, discussed in Chapter 7, may also be important.

"*But we're not watching any of those violent shows . . . we're just watching the hockey game.*"

Tulsa World, May 12, 1982.

The simplistic approach continues, however, and is given even greater strength by the mass media reports. For example, in April 1984, a twelve-year-old boy was charged with the sexual assault of a ten-year-old girl whom he forced to perform oral sex on him and then forced her onto a pool table and further assaulted her while other children watched. Officials claim that he might have gotten the idea from watching the television account of the rape trial in New Bedford, Massachusetts, in which several defendants were tried for raping a woman on a pool table in a bar while other people watched and did nothing to prevent the attack. That case, discussed in the next chapter, resulted in two acquittals and two convictions.[34]

These and other claims of the influence of television viewing on behavior have led to a greater emphasis on research in this area. One of the most extensive studies of the effects of television violence on childhood and adolescent aggression involved a panel study of 3,200 youngsters between 1970 and 1973. The study examined the effects of watching television on such behaviors as mugging, knifing, and participating in gang fights. In the introduction to the preliminary report of this study, issued in 1982, the following conclusion was drawn:

[T]he full report . . . will be carefully scrutinized because of its rich data and important implications. The conclusion . . . is likely to provide a new argument about the relationship between televised violence and viewer aggression.[35]

This recent return to an interest in the impact of television on behavior, especially criminal behavior, may result in even greater attention being paid by social scientists to the theory of differential association. Furthermore, a study of television's impact might also be important to our continued development of theories in the second major category of social-process theories, social control.

SOCIAL-CONTROL THEORY

In our earlier discussions of the classical approach and modern deterrence theory, we examined the proposition that criminal behavior is rational, that it is the response of people who have decided what they want and calculated the costs: crime is more attractive than achieving the goods or services by legitimate means. If that is the case, goes the economic approach, the way to control such behavior is to increase the cost or the punishment.

Sociologists and psychologists have developed other explanations of how behavior can be controlled. According to control theorists, deviance results when social controls are either weakened or break down. When controls are strong, deviance does not occur.[36] The problem, therefore, is to try to explain what can be done in a positive way to elicit appropriate behavior. That is, the question is not how to prevent criminal behavior but, rather, how to train people to engage in law-abiding behavior. This is done through control theory, which begins with the assumption that we all have to be trained to behave properly.

Like many other explanations of criminal behavior, social-control theory is really not a theory in the sense of rigorous scientific procedures of developing and testing hypotheses. Rather, it is an approach or an explanation, and there are several types. In one, training is basically a psychological approach, which we considered in Chapter 4. In this section we shall examine the other two types: containment, illustrated by the work of Reckless, and attachment and commitment, illustrated by the work of Hirschi. It is important, however, to begin by pointing out that all of these approaches have some common assumptions, articulated by one sociologist as follows:

1. That the human animal requires nurturing.
2. That differences in nurturing account for variations in attachment to others and commitment to an ordered way of living.
3. That attachment and commitment may be described as "internal controls," commonly called "conscience" and recognized in *guilt,* and "external controls," usually tested by the production of *shame.*
4. That evidence from experimental studies, longitudinal research, comparative studies, and cross-cultural investigation tells us *how* attach-

ment and commitment are developed. Conversely, such evidence describes the situations that loosen the moral bond with others and that are, therefore, productive of crime.[37]

CONTAINMENT THEORY

According to Walter Reckless and Simon Dinitz, "we live in a society of alternates, where the self has more and more opportunities for acceptance or rejection of available confrontations."[38] Clearly not everyone chooses the illegal opportunities; thus social-structural theories that stress the availability of illegal and legal opportunitites, the existence of a subculture, the location of goods and services within the city, density, and so on, cannot adequately explain criminal behavior. What we need to know is why those phenomena affect some people and not others. Why are some of us apparently "immune" to such influences, in that our exposure is not followed by criminal behavior? Reckless suggests that the answer lies in **containment theory,** which he defines as follows:

> The assumption is that there is a containing external social structure which holds individuals in line and that there is also an internal buffer which protects people against deviation of the social and legal norms. The two containments act as a defense against deviation from the legal and social norms, as an insulation against pressures and pulls, as a protection against demoralization and seduction. If there are "causes" which lead to deviant behavior, they are negated, neutralized, rendered impotent, or are paired by the two containing buffers.[39]

There are two types of containment: outer containment and inner containment. Outer containment might also be called social pressure, and in simple societies, this kind of social control works quite well. The community's social norms are taught to new members, who internalize those norms but who are also restrained by the community's reaction to violation of those norms. Social ostracism may be the most effective social control in such societies or communities, but as we have seen in earlier discussions, as societies become more complex, such outer containment is not so effective. It is therefore important that people develop inner containment mechanisms by which they can control their own behavior.

Inner containment refers to our ability to direct ourselves, which is related to our self-concept. "One of the components of capability of self is a favorable self-image, self-concept, self-perception. The person who conceives of himself as a responsible person is apt to act responsibly." A high goal level, especially regarding societal goals, and a high aspiration level geared to society's expectations are also essential components of the self. Frustration tolerance and identification with the society's values and laws are important. The opposite of this is alienation—the release of inner containment.[40]

Reckless emphasizes that the components of external and internal containment are buffers, not causes. They operate to help the individual refrain from succumbing to the pressures of violating the law. If the buffers are strong, the person will be law abiding. But if they are weak, he or she will commit a crime.

One way that these buffers operate is in aiding the delinquent in neutralizing the norms. In the previous chapter we discussed Sykes's and Matza's techniques-of-neutralization approach, which opposed the subculture theory that delinquents are responding to different norms. Rather, said Sykes and Matza, they may be responding to the same norms as does the rest of society, but they have developed ways to reject or neutralize the impact of those norms. We also noted that neutralization theory is a social-process theory in one sense but that it also pertains to the social-structural approach of the subculture theories. Here we are concerned with the *process* of neutralization as it relates to the social-control theory of containment.

Recent research on self-concept has given us more insight into the process of neutralization. A sample of white, working-class males were examined when sixth graders and then again when ninth graders. The study revealed that when the boys were in the sixth grade, their behavior appeared to be more strongly controlled by the norms they attributed to their peers than by their own internalized norms. But by the time they were in the ninth grade, internalized norms were a stronger factor. This suggests that inner containment theory does not have the same influence at all stages of adolescent development. The study also found that the youngsters' self-concept "is especially important as an explanation of such behavior and as an intervening variable that affects the relationship between other attitudes and possible behavioral outcomes."[41]

Analysis of containment theory

Despite the claims of Reckless and his associates that containment theory can explain most delinquency and crime, that the theory might bring psychologists and sociologists together in the study of crime because it involves both disciplines, and that the theory, unlike many others, can be used in the individual case history,[42] the theory has also been severely criticized. The theory cannot explain why people who do the same things are differentially labeled; it is limited in its predictive ability,[43] and its measure of self-concept has been questioned, along with the lack of control groups in some of the early works. The difficulty of measuring the strength or weakness of external and internal containment indeed is a problem. Finally, the theory does not show why youngsters with bad self-concepts are not delinquent.[44]

Containment theory may be most useful when combined with other approaches. In a comparison of containment theory with differential association theory, one sociologist concluded that they are similar, with the exception that differential association emphasizes the process of differential association, whereas containment theory emphasizes the product of social-ization—the self-concept. Both of these theories can account for delinquency more fully than either can separately.[45]

Finally, it has been argued that containment theory, "like other explanations of crime, describes some true things," but it is too general. Its concepts are too vague and its theory too broad to produce testable hypotheses for rigorous empirical research.[46] One attempt to eliminate these criticisms by refining the elements of control theory is the work of Travis Hirschi.[22]

HIRSCHI'S
SOCIAL-CONTROL
THEORY

Travis Hirschi emphasizes that it is not deviance that we need to explain but, rather, conforming behavior. "Why do men obey the rules of society?"[47] he asks.

> The question "Why do they do it?" is simply not the question the theory is designed to answer. The question is "Why don't we do it?" There is much evidence that we would if we dared.[48]

In formulating his social-control theory, Hirschi first analyzed other theories of crime, delinquency, and deviance, using Durkheim's statement as a starting point. According to Durkheim,

> The more weakened the groups to which [the individual] belongs, the less he depends on them, the more he consequently depends only on himself and recognizes no other rules of conduct than what are founded on his private interest.[49]

The basic concept of control theory, asserts Hirschi, is "the bond of the individual to society." That bond consists of four components: attachment, commitment, involvement, and belief, which are defined in the Exhibit on page 193. Hirschi believes that delinquency becomes more likely as this social bond is weakened:[50]

> In every case, the conclusion is the same: the absence of control increases the likelihood of delinquency regardless of the presence of group traditions of delinquency. Although social support increases the likelihood that delinquent acts will be committed, the view that the child must somehow be taught crime in intimate, personal groups greatly overstates the case.[51]

Hirschi tested his theory on a sample of California youth, using the self-report method of collecting data. The four thousand junior and senior high school students were given questionnaires designed to measure their attitudes toward friends, neighborhood, parents, school, teachers, and human relations. They were asked to respond to the following six questions, indicating whether they had (1) never committed the offense, (2) committed the offense more than one year ago, (3) had committed the offense during the

---

EXHIBIT

HIRSCHI'S SOCIAL-CONTROL THEORY: ELEMENTS OF THE SOCIAL BOND

1. *Attachment* refers to our affective ties to people who are important to us and to our sensitivity to their opinions. Our feelings of obligations to others help control our behavior.

2. *Commitment* refers to the time and energy that we invest in our way of living. According to Hirschi, commitment "is the rational component in conformity." Youngsters who are involved in smoking, drinking, and wasting time, for example, are not investing time and energy in conventional behavior. They are therefore risking the chances of attaining sufficient education and a high-paying job. Without this commitment to conventional values, they are more likely to become delinquent.

3. *Involvement* refers to engrossment or immersion in conventional values. Involvement is a consequence of commitment. The person who chooses to pursue nonconventional behavior because of a lack of commitment will thereby exclude some opportunities, as will the person who chooses involvement in conventional behavior. Thus, the student who is committed to and involved in academic work excludes some possibilities for "fun and games." Likewise, the person who is committed to and involved mainly in living the "good life" will thereby exclude some opportunities for development in the academic world.

4. *Belief* means that a person attributes moral validity to conventional norms. The laws and rules of society are seen as "right" and "moral." Youngsters with intense belief are less likely to become delinquent.

Source: Paraphrased from Travis Hirschi, *Causes of Delinquency* (Berkeley and Los Angeles: University of California Press, 1969), pp. 16–34.

---

past year, or (4) had committed the offense during the past year as well as more than a year ago. The questions were

1. Have you ever taken little things (worth less than $2) that did not belong to you?
2. Have you ever taken things of some value (between $2 and $50) that did not belong to you?
3. Have you ever taken things of large value (worth over $50) that did not belong to you?
4. Have you ever taken a car for a ride without the owner's permission?
5. Have you ever banged up something that did not belong to you on purpose?
6. Not counting fights you may have had with a brother or sister, have you ever beaten up on anyone or hurt anyone on purpose?[52]

The responses to these questions were used as an index of self-reported delinquency. In addition, questions were asked about work, money, expectations, aspirations, participation in school activities, and use of leisure time. School records, including grades, and police records were also utilized as sources of data for the study.

The high association between low socioeconomic class and crime, found in the earlier studies using "official" crime data, was questioned by self-report studies. Hirschi found strong evidence that this "traditional association" does not exist. Indeed, he found very little association between social class as measured by father's occupation and admitted or official delinquency, with the exception of low incidences, by both measures, of delinquency among the sons of professionals. He did find, however, that boys "whose fathers have been unemployed and/or whose families are on welfare are more likely than children from fully employed, self-sufficient families to commit delinquent acts."[53]

The study also revealed that positive attitudes toward teachers and school were related to nondelinquent behavior. "Academic ability and school performance influence many, if not most, of the variables that turn out to be important predictors of delinquency. The causal chain runs from academic incompetence to poor school performance to disliking of school to rejection of the school's authority to the commission of delinquent acts."[54]

Finally, Hirschi found that the closer the ties to the parents, the less likely it was that the youths would engage in delinquent acts. It was not the parent's status that was important but, rather, the child's *attachment* to the parent: ". . . the child attached to a low-status parent is no more likely to be delinquent than the child attached to a high-status parent."[55]

Hirschi concluded that young people who are not very attached to their parents and to school are more likely to be delinquent than are those with these kinds of attachments. He also found that youths who have positive attitudes toward their own accomplishments are more likely to believe in the validity and appropriateness of conventional laws and moral rules of society than are youths who have negative feelings about their own accomplishments.

Criticism of Hirschi's theory   Although Hirschi's study in California was based on a sample of urban respondents, a study of a rural sample in New York State, conducted by Michael Hindelang,[56] found support for Hirschi's social-control theory. However, Hindelang "failed to replicate a positive relationship between attachment to parents and attachment to friends . . . he failed to show that attachment to friends increases the likelihood of delinquent behavior." In fact, claimed a critic, Hindelang "found a slight positive relationship between identification with peers and delinquency which is unexplainable in terms of control theory."[57] This does not mean, however, that the theory is incorrect—only that it is incomplete. We need to go beyond attachment to peers and discover the type of peer to whom the individual is attached before the analysis has validity for prediciton of delinquent behavior: ". . . no real predictions can be made until the type of peer is taken into account."[58]

Others have found that the type of peer does not matter or that the likelihood of delinquent behavior seems to be decreased by attachment to conventional peers but increased by attachment to delinquent peers.[60]

Hirschi recognized that his theory of social control "does not escape unscathed." In the first place, his theory "underestimated the importance of delinquent friends; it overestimated the significance of involvement in conventional activities." He also decided that one should probably look at the relationship between delinquent activities and the person's self-concept or self-esteem. That relationship might be important in explaining "the potency of the adult-status items, such as smoking, drinking, dating, and driving a car." Although social-control theory can help us understand these relations, Hirschi noted, it leaves a lot unexplained. However, he concludes on an optimistic note with regard to his theory: "I am confident that when the processes through which these variables affect delinquency are spelled out, they will supplement rather than seriously modify the control theory, but that remains to be seen."[61]

Impact of Hirschi's theory

Hirschi's 1969 work, *Causes of Delinquency,* in which he stated his theory, has been described as "a benchmark for theory construction and research in the delinquency field."[62] The theory has generated considerable research, some of which was mentioned in Chapter 2 in regard to the self-report method of acquiring data on delinquent and criminal behavior. Here we shall examine some recent attempts to test his theory, which have suggested modification or extension of the theory.

According to some critics, Hirschi's social-control theory is more complete than subcultural or differential association theory, but it does not give a complete explanation. The theory does not show how the four elements of attachment, commitment, involvement, and belief might operate simultaneously to affect delinquent behavior. Furthermore, Hirschi does not empirically test the relationships among the social bond's four elements. Consequently, the theory raises three questions. First, are the four elements "empirically distinct components of socialization"? Second, why are only four elements identified? Third, although Hirschi talks about educational and occupational aspirations, he does not incorporate into the theory elements such as family socioeconomic level, ability, and the influence of significant others, and research has found that all of them are important.[63]

Investigators who attempted to replicate Hirschi's theory and incorporate these additional elements found general support for the social-bond theory's four elements but found that the theory needed reformulation and expansion. They concluded:

> In the context of statistical controls for ability, social class, and grades in school, the bond elements which emerge as important explanatory variables are attachment to parents, dating, attachment to school, belief, and involvement. A model incorporating these bond elements appears more isomorphic with theories of adolescent socialization which treat education as important in the integration of the youth into adult social life.[64]

Rural-urban differences and social-control theory

A study of the reported delinquencies of rural and urban youth was also based on the Hirschi model, especially the element of commitment. The degree of commitment to five institutions was measured: family, school, church, conventional peers, and legal authority. "The combined influence of these institutional orders and of the individual's perception of his relationship to them comprises the social bond which insulates the youth from delinquency." The combined commitment of young people to these institutions represents their stake in conformity. "Among the sample of rural and urban juvenile offenders, a strong inverse relationship is found between the composite commitment scores and delinquency. Viewed separately, only commitment to family does not prove to be statistically significant," but the authors explained that that could be because only about one-third of the sample lived with both parents. The elements most strongly associated with delinquent behavior were commitment to school and to legal authority.[65]

EXHIBIT

SOCIAL-CONTROL THEORY—AN EVALUATION

"The theme of [social-control] theory is that human beings may be domestic animals, but they need domestication. Human creatures may be civic organisms, but they need civilization. And this means steeping in a culture.

The trouble with this theme is that it gives no political handle for planned change.

Explanation, particularly correct ones, need not promise cures. Knowing the causes of earthquakes does not prevent them, although such knowledge may promote better defense against them.

A difficulty with control theory is that it gives politicians and others who would 'solve social problems' no lever with which to manipulate change according to plan. For people who want promising answers, control theory is unsatisfactory."

Source: Gwynn Nettler, *Explaining Crime,* 3rd ed. (New York: McGraw-Hill, 1984), p. 314.

SOCIAL CONTROL:
A CONCLUSION

Social-control theory has produced extensive and significant research that is helpful in understanding and explaining delinquent and criminal behavior. It has the advantage of an individualized approach in that it recognizes that we all do not respond in the same way to the same environments. For that reason, the theory may be popular with the public, but it does not give us blueprints for the kinds of changes that can be implemented by politicians. In that sense, it may be less attractive, despite its empirical basis, than social-structural approaches that do give a basis for political change. If unemployment is seen as the cause of crime, plans can be implemented to change employment opportunities. But if commitment to and involvement with family are significant elements, change will be more difficult. As one expert concluded, "The truth sometimes tells us more clearly what we can-*not* have and what will *not* work."[66]

LABELING
THEORY

A final type of approach to explaining crime is quite different from the others we have discussed. Most theories and explanations of criminal behavior look for the *cause* of the behavior. Why did the individual commit the crime, and what can be done to prevent such actions in the future? The "answer" may be individual phsique, body build, chemical imbalance, hormones, chromosomes, or it may be found in the environment, or it may be the result of some type of social process. The emphasis is on finding out why the person engaged in the behavior.

Labeling theory, in contrast, asks, Why was the person *designated* deviant? The perspective thus applies to all kinds of deviant behavior or, for that matter, to nondeviant behavior. The critical issue is not the behavior but why the behavior is labeled deviant. We are not interested in what was done but, rather, in how people reacted to what was done. Not all who engage in certain kinds of behavior are labeled deviant, but some are. What is the reason for this distinction? One sociologist has described this approach as follows:

> Some men who drink heavily are called alcoholics and others are not, some men who behave oddly are committed to hospitals and others are not . . . and the difference between those who earn a deviant title in society and those who go their own way in peace is largely determined by the way in which the community filters out and codes the many details of behavior which come to its attention.[67]

If criminal behavior is to be explained according to the response of others rather than the characteristics of the offender, the appropriate subject matter will be the *audience,* not the individual, for it is the existence of the behavior not why it occurred that is significant. Only the audience's response determines whether that behavior will be defined as deviant.

In this final section of the chapters on theory, we shall consider the history and development of the labeling perspective, along with a critique of this approach. In some respects it, like conflict theory, is a social-structural approach, but it is primarily a social-process theory in that it attempts to explain labeling as a process by which some people who commit deviant acts come to be known as deviants, whereas others are not so designated.

EMERGENCE AND DEVELOPMENT OF LABELING THEORY

A 1983 statement by Frank Tannenbaum, reprinted in the following exhibit, describes what has become known as labeling theory. This was further developed by Edwin Lemert, whose 1951 book outlined the labeling perspective in detail. One of Lemert's earlier contributions was a distinction central to labeling theory: the distinction between primary and secondary deviance, explained as follows:

> Primary deviation is assumed to arise in a wide variety of social, cultural, and psychological contexts, and at best has only marginal implication for the psychic structure of the individual; it does not lead to symbolic reorganization at the level of self-regarding attitudes and social roles. Secondary deviation is deviant behavior or social roles based upon it, which becomes a means of defense, attack or adaptation to the overt and covert problems created by the societal reaction to primary deviation.[69]

EXHIBIT

THE PROCESS OF LABELING BEHAVIOR

"The process of making the criminal is a process of tagging, defining, identifying, segregating, describing, emphasizing, making conscious and self-conscious; it becomes a way of stimulating, suggesting, emphasizing, and evoking the very traits that are complained of.

The person becomes the thing he is described as being. Nor does it seem to matter whether the valuation is made by those who would punish or by those who would reform. In either case the emphasis is upon conduct that is disapproved of. The parents or the policeman, the older brother or the court, the probation officer or the juvenile institution, insofar as they rest on the thing complained of, rest upon a false ground. Their very enthusiasm defeats their aim. The harder they work to reform the evil, the greater the evil grows under their hands. The persistent suggestion, with whatever good intentions, works mischief, because it leads to bring out the bad behavior it would suppress. The way out is through a refusal to dramatize the evil. The less said about it the better."

Source: Frank Tannenbaum, *Crime and the Community* (Boston: Ginn, 1938), pp. 19–20.

EXHIBIT

THE "CREATION" OF DEVIANT BEHAVIOR

"Social groups create deviance by making rules whose infractions constitute deviance, and by applying those rules to particular people and labelling them as outsiders. From this point of view, deviance is not a quality of the act a person commits, but rather a consequence of the application by others of rules and sanctions to an 'offender.' The deviant is one to whom the label has successfully been applied; deviant behavior is behavior that people so label."

Source: Howard S. Becker, *Outsiders: Studies in the Sociology of Deviance* (New York: Free Press, 1963), p. 9.

To labeling theorists, primary deviance is relatively unimportant; it is secondary deviance that is most important, for it is the *interaction* between the person labeled deviant and the labeler that is important, and this approach is often called *interaction theory*.

Another contributor to the early development of labeling theory was Howard S. Becker. Becker pointed out that because many people who break rules are not considered deviant, that is, labeled delinquent or criminal, whereas others are, we must distinguish between rule breaking and deviance. Rule breaking describes the behavior, but deviance describes the reaction of others to that behavior; rule breaking is thus defined as deviant when engaged in by some people. Then it becomes important to find out who is and is not labeled deviant. According to labeling theorists, the people who will most often be labeled deviant for their rule-breaking behavior are those on the margin of society. They are the "underdogs." Furthermore, once they are labeled deviant, they usually cannot escape the designation. "An important feature of these ceremonies [of labeling people deviant] in our culture is that they are almost irreversible."[70]

The impact of the deviant label also extends to the self-concept of the person who, according to labeling theory, has experienced a socialization process that is virtually irreversible, not only from the point of view of the labeler, but also from that of the person labeled. That person develops a self-concept consistent with the label of deviant and acquires the knowledge and skills of the labeled status as well.[71]

Finally, whether or not labeling occurs depends on (1) the time when the act is committed, (2) who commits the act and who is the victim, and (3) society's perception of the consequences of the act. "Whether a given act is deviant or not depends in part on the nature of the act (that is, whether or not it violates some rule) and in part on what other people do about it."[72]

Empirical evidence   Attempts have been made to test labeling theory empirically. Richard Schwartz and Jerome Skolnick designed a study to measure the reaction of employers to a potential employee with a criminal record. The one hundred employers were divided into four groups, and each group was shown a different folder on the prospective employee. Stated simply, the conclusion was that employers would not offer a job to a person with a criminal record. One folder described the individual as not having a criminal record; the second, as having been acquitted with a letter of explanation; the third, acquittal without a letter; and the fourth, conviction. As the responses move from the group receiving the first folder through those receiving the second, third, and fourth, the positive responses of the employers declined. "Of the twenty-five employers approached with the 'convict' folder, only one expressed interest in the applicant." The investigators further concluded that "the individual accused but acquitted has almost as much trouble finding even an unskilled job as the one who was not only accused of the same offense, but also convicted."[73] The prospective employee had a better chance of being employed when the folder contained a statement of acquittal and a letter of explanation of the presumption of innocent until proven guilty.

In the second phase of this study, Schwartz and Skolnick studied doctors who had been sued for malpractice in Connecticut. They had a sample of fifty-eight physicians. They were interviewed by phone, personally, or asked to complete a mailed questionnaire. "The malpractice survey did not reveal widespread occupational harm to the physicians involved. Of the fifty-eight respondents, fifty-two reported no negative effects of the suit on their practice, and five of the remaining six, all specialists, reported that their practice *improved* after the suit. The heaviest loser in court (a radiologist) reported the largest gain. . . . Only one doctor reported adverse consequences to his practice."[74]

Schwartz and Skolnick warn of the problems of comparing these two phases of their study. The doctors had a *protective institutional environment* that did not exist for the prospective employee in the first phase of the study. The doctors were permitted to continue using the facilities of the hospital and had no difficulty getting malpractice insurance, although often at a higher rate. This protective institutional environment perhaps eliminated the negative labeling process that normally occurs after one loses in a court battle. Possibly another reason is that physicians are in short supply, and unskilled laborers are not. But most probably the difference in reaction was due to the doctors' occupational status and the protection they get from their profession. An interesting question unanswered by this study, however, is how the doctor would be labeled if he or she had been acquitted of a charge of assault and battery.[75]

Another example of the effect of labeling gained national attention in the 1970s. Eight persons of varied backgrounds but all "sane" sought admission to the psychiatric wards of twelve hospitals in various parts of the United

States. The hospitals were also of different types, some with excellent treatment facilities and others with poor ones. The researchers called the hospitals for appointments, and upon their arrival for the initial interview, they each feigned mental illness, all stating that they heard voices. When asked about the significant events in their backgrounds, all related the events accurately; none had a history of pathological experiences. After admission to the hospital, all of the pseudopatients acted like sane persons. All except one had been labeled schizophrenic, and none of the hospitals suspected the researchers' pseudopatient status. All the participants had the responsibility of gaining their own release by convincing the staff that they were actually sane. The point of the research was that although they were released, with a diagnosis of schizophrenia "in remission," the label of schizophrenia stuck with them during their confinement.[76] Once labeled insane, they were presumed insane by the staff who interacted with them daily. Their behavior did not identify them as insane; the identity came from a label given to them upon admission. Thus they differed from "sane" persons only in the label.

Another study involved the simulation of prison life, with student volunteers assigned to the role of guards and others to the role of prisoners. The experiment had to be terminated because of the serious problems that developed. In short, "conferring of differential power on the status of 'guard' and 'prisoner' constituted, in effect, the institutional validation of those roles. . . . Within a surprisingly short period of time, we witnessed a sample of normal, healthy American college students fractionate into a group of prison guards who seemed to derive pleasure from insulting, threatening, humiliating and dehumanizing their peers—those who by chance selection had been assigned to the 'prisoner' role. The typical prisoner syndrome was one of passivity, dependency, depression, helplessness and self-deprecation."[77]

Finally, there are some empirical studies on the effects of labeling juveniles. In analyzing these studies, Anne Rankin Mahoney has categorized them as those that measure (1) the effect of labeling on subsequent delinquent behavior, (2) the effect of the family's and community's reaction to a youth who has contact with the juvenile justice system, and (3) the effect that labeling a youngster juvenile has on his or her self-concept. In summary, the studies report some evidence that white youths are more affected than minority youths are by the juvenile delinquency label, that the community's reaction to the labeled youth is negative, but that the little evidence available on family reaction indicates that the labeled youths found little change in their parents' perceived attitudes toward them after the label had been attached. Juveniles do not feel the experience is highly stigmatizing, although there is some evidence that some youths, especially whites, do change their self-definitions after a juvenile court experience. But "there is a hint in two of the studies . . . that the labeling effects of court contact may erode over time. In summary, we don't know much about the effects of court labeling on juveniles." The research raises interesting questions but reveals few answers.[78]

CRITICISMS OF
LABELING THEORY

One of the most serious criticisms of labeling theory is that it is not a theory—it is a perspective. No systematic theory has been developed. The empirical assessment of a theory requires that the theory produce testable propositions. Not only is that difficult with labeling theory, but some of the theorists "unashamedly claim to eschew precise propositional statements in favor of 'sensitizing observations' which 'jostle the imagination,' to create a crisis of consciousness which will lead to new visions of reality." From this perspective, "empirical tests of labeling theory are both impossible and ridiculous."[79]

A systematic theory cannot be created unless it has precisely defined terms that can be measured. Characteristic of the empirical research on labeling is the assumption "that the imposition of any sanction or any official act of negative classification constitutes labeling," without systematically defining that term. Critics have contended that the theory's major propositions have not been supported empirically but that that is no reason for rejecting it. The methodological problems of the empirical efforts are "crippling," and the data are poor. The research therefore cannot be used to support the theory, but neither can it be used to reject it. For adequate testing, it is imperative that specific hypotheses be derived and tested after precise, operational definitions have been articulated.

> The lessons are clear. Labelists must get down to serious theoretical business. Evasiveness, eluding of ambiguity, and hiding behind a facade of sensitizing concepts will no longer suffice. Researchers, on the other hand, must apply themselves with more facility and care. The meagerness and sloppiness of research on a question of this importance is embarrassing.[80]

One of the common criticisms of labeling theory is that it avoids the question of causation. Even if labeling is the key to continued criminal behavior, it is still important to know why a person committed the first criminal act, especially when the act is a serious violation of the law.

Another criticism of labeling theory is that it views the actor, or labelee, as too passive[81] and that greater acknowledgment should be given to the reciprocal relationship between the actor and the reactor. Thus, most labeling theorists overemphasize the action of society and de-emphasize the place of the action of the subject being labeled.[82] Social interaction should receive greater attention.

Labeling theory has also been criticized for its lack of attention to the personality characteristics of those who engage in deviant behavior. To the labeling theorists, characteristics of the individual, such as personality traits, are just not important to explaining behavior. It is the reaction to the person that is critical. Yet, labeling theory does not really explain differential law enforcement.

In an analysis of the basic assumptions of labeling theory, Charles Wellford pointed out that although there is evidence that those who are labeled deviant or criminal are often characterized in terms of age, socioeconomic class, and race, differential law enforcement is not *explained* by such variables. For example, in the case of those labeled juvenile, there is evidence that the complainant and the type of offense committed by the youth are more important than race and sex in explaining why the youth is labeled delinquent. There are some studies that report support for the labeling perspective on these assumptions, but, observes Wellford, those "represent studies of questionable rigor which do not control for offense seriousness and focus on non-citizen initiated police behavior, a minor portion of formal sanctioning."[83]

A final category of criticisms of labeling theory is the assumption that labeling produces negative results. It is argued that labeling might have both positive and negative effects. Labeling a person deviant might deter that person from further deviant behavior rather than plunge him or her into further deviance. Labeling theorists may be overemphasizing the impact of the label

"You are charged with getting caught stealing."

Drawing by Handelsman. © 1974 The New Yorker Magazine, Inc.

The same acts that entitle some people to receive society's label of criminal are committed by numerous other persons who never receive that label.

on the person. "One sometimes gets the impression from reading this literature that people go about minding their own business and then 'wham'— bad society comes along and slaps them with a stigmatized label. Forced into the role of a deviant the individual has little choice but to be deviant."[84] It is suggested that whether or not the labeling process produces negative or positive results depends on a number of factors that have been overlooked by labeling theorists.[85]

First, it seems that labeling has different effects on the "deviant" at various stages in his or her "career." Labeling thus might thrust a delinquent into a career but deter a female shoplifter. For example, one investigator found that the female shoplifter does not think of herself as a thief and has no peer support for that role; thus it is abandoned once she is apprehended.[86] Perhaps the key element is peer support, not labeling. On the other hand, labeling may create a subculture, thereby establishing the peer support.

A second factor concerns the confidentiality of the labeling. It is hypothesized that if the label is confidential and given to a nonprofessional deviant, that person will be more likely to abandon his or her deviant behavior than if the label is public and the individual is a professional. Third, the result is more often positive than negative when the subject has some commitment and is sensitive to the person who is doing the labeling. For example, there is some evidence that former alcoholics and drug addicts are more successful than are nonpeers, counselors, or psychiatrists in the rehabilitation of fellow deviants through Alcoholics Anonymous and Synanon. Fourth, a person is more likely to abandon deviant behavior if the label of deviant, once given, can easily be removed. The study of Schwartz and Skolnick discussed above is an example of this proposition.

Fifth, the reaction of friends and society is important to whether the label results in positive or negative behavior. If friends and others are supportive in assisting the individual to improve, the results are more likely to be positive. Finally, the labeling theorists have generally overlooked the possibility that positive labeling can increase positive behavior. In one study, public school teachers were told that certain students, based on tests given at the end of the previous school year, could be expected to be fast learners. At the end of the school year, these students scored considerably higher scholastically than other students did. And they were described by their teachers as happier, more affectionate, more interesting, more appealing, better adjusted, and having less need for social approval.[87]

SUMMARY AND EVALUATION OF SOCIAL-PROCESS THEORIES

In this chapter we examined theories that emphasize the process by which a person becomes a criminal. The social-process theories have been instrumental in achieving a better understanding of criminal behavior. As a group, social-process theories are probably more acceptable to sociologists and criminologists today than are any other approaches. The theories attempt to explain differential reaction to the social structure, and they are based on the sociological proposition that behavior of humans is acquired through the process of social interaction, just as noncriminal behavior is acquired. In addition, the research faces fewer methodological problems than do any of the other approaches. Some theorists—for example, Sutherland—tried to avoid the class bias in criminological studies created by selecting samples of convicted criminals who are mainly lower-class individuals and also to analyze the crimes of the upper classes. The use of random samples has helped in this. The studies of self-concept involved follow-up studies, although more research on that procedure is needed.

Despite these factors, the social-process theories still face some methodological problems, most of which have already been noted. In summary, the concepts are often not precisely defined, and the samples used in empirical research are often not properly selected to avoid bias. Finally, some of the theoretical approaches do not go beyond theory to empirical research.

CONCLUSION TO THEORIES OF CRIMINALITY

We have now completed our discussion of the various theories of criminal behavior. We looked at economic, biological, physiological, psychological, psychiatric, and sociological approaches. All have been faced with methodological problems: crime is difficult to define in operational terms; samples are often limited; and follow-up studies are expensive and time-consuming. All of the research today is plagued with an increasing lack of public interest in what caused the behavior; rather, the hue and cry is "Let the punishment fit the crime." Thus understanding the reasons for the behavior does not command a high priority in research funding.

These problems do not, however, mean that the theories of causation should be abandoned. But it does mean that we must be careful in our interpretations of such studies. As we saw in earlier chapters, conclusions must be analyzed according to the type of sample and the source of data; thus, "official" data must be compared with the self-report survey data collected from large samples of crime victims.

We need more extensive research, watching and controlling for as many methodological problems as possible and integrating the approaches of the various disciplines. Most importantly, we should not conclude that research on criminal behavior is hopeless:

> Many of the fruits of science ... can be used to advantage while still in the process of development. Science is at best a growth, not a sudden revelation. ... We do not abandon cancer research because the patients of today may not be saved by it.

Research in the social and physical sciences can be used "imperfectly and in part while it is developing."[88]

PART III

TYPOLOGIES OF CRIMINAL BEHAVIOR

CHAPTER 7

Crimes of violence

This is the first of three chapters on criminal typologies. After explaining the typology approach, we shall begin discussing the nature and impact of violence in our society. We shall look at violence historically, noting that it has some positive aspects, before focusing the chapter on its negative aspect: crime. We then shall turn to the violent crimes of murder, nonnegligent manslaughter, aggravated assault, robbery, and rape, including a brief history of each, an analysis of the data, and sociological studies of criminals of those categories. The approach called the subculture of violence is analyzed. Finally, we shall examine the impact of violence on our society. The fear of violent crimes leads many people to change their life-styles so as to avoid being a victim. Likewise, people buy protective devices for their homes; neighbors become involved in crime prevention; and many people move to other, perhaps safer areas.

Criminologists use typologies to study criminal behavior in order to determine whether there are characteristics that distinguish, for example, rapists and robbers. This is not a new approach. Lombroso, for example, wrote about the "born" criminal, a person whom he saw as inferior in terms of physique. Later he expanded his typologies to include the insane criminal and the criminal by passion. Lombroso also spoke of the occasional criminal, the person who has certain criminal characteristics but who needs, in addition, the appropriate environment in which to commit crime.

More recently, sociologists and criminologists have developed many new typologies of criminal behavior, but they do not agree on them. Indeed, there are probably as many different typologies as there are typologists. Some of these types are supported by empirical evidence, and others are merely descriptive.

CRIMINAL TYPOLOGIES

Some sociologists take the position that if crime is to be studied as a social phenomenon, it will be necessary to categorize criminals by the crimes they commit.[1] But this approach has been criticized by criminologist Don C. Gibbons, who argues that we should not focus on the specific crime for which a person is convicted but, rather, on the progression of that person's career in crime.[2] Gibbons is critical even of his own approach, however. After reviewing the research on the use of his typologies, he concludes: "To begin with, the research . . . indicates that no fully comprehensive offender typology which subsumes most criminality within it yet exists."[3]

Despite these criticisms, we do need some basis for categorizing criminals if we are to determine which variables are related to different kinds of criminal behavior. The legal approach will be used to define each crime discussed in this and the following two chapters. The official data on crime are based on the legal definition, and many of the sociological studies of criminals are based on samples of inmates who have been categorized as robbers, rapists, murderers, and so on, because those are the appropriate legal labels to categorize the behavior for which they have been incarcerated. This is not to suggest that other perspectives are not important. In fact, we also shall look at data secured from victims and based on their perceptions of which crimes describe the actions of their assailants.

The use of legal definitions of crime should not be taken to imply that, for example, attaching the label of aggravated assault to a person means that that was the crime actually committed. For a variety of reasons, discussed in later chapters, defendants might not be charged with the precise crime they are thought to have committed, or they may be charged with that crime but allowed to plead guilty to a lesser crime. For example, a man who rapes may be permitted to plead guilty to aggravated assault. In official data, therefore, he would be classified by the latter, not the former, category.

SERIOUS CRIMES The official crime data, the FBI *Uniform Crime Reports,* originally selected seven crimes, because of their seriousness and frequency, as the index crimes. These are known as Part I offenses and are murder and nonnegligent manslaughter, forcible rape, robbery, aggravated assault, burglary, larceny-theft, and motor vehicle theft. In 1978, Congress added arson. Murder and nonnegligent manslaughter, forcible rape, robbery, and aggravated assault are considered by the FBI to be violent crimes, and they will be discussed in this chapter. The rest are property crimes and will be discussed in Chapter 9. These eight serious crimes are listed on Table 7.1, with a brief statement of facts about each. All are serious crimes, but the category of violent crime is used to designate those that might result in injury to a person. Thus robbery, although it means the taking of property and thus could be considered a property crime, is a violent crime because it means the taking of property by force. Such force might, and sometimes does, result in personal injury or even death. Property crimes, on the other hand, "are unlawful acts with the intent of gaining property but which do not involve the use or threat of force against the individual."[4]

A comparison of property and crime rates in 1981 is shown in Figure 7.1, indicating that property crimes outnumbered violent crimes by nine to one. It is the possibility of violent crimes, however, that seems to engender the most fear.

VIOLENCE IN AMERICA In 1980, America's homicide rate was the highest in this century,[5] and *Newsweek* labeled 1981 as the "year that mainstream America rediscovered violent crime." Referring to the traditionally high rates of violent crime among the blacks in the ghetto, *Newsweek* cited several cases of "random Mayhem"—acts of violence against strangers—and concluded: "Defying any cure, it overwhelms the police, the courts and the prisons—and warps U.S. life."[6]

Violence is not new to our society. President John F. Kennedy and later his brother Robert Kennedy, as well as civil rights leader Dr. Martin Luther King, Jr., all were assassinated. The urban violence of the 1960s also is part of our history. But the 1979 National Commission on Violence, an updated version of the 1968 President's Commission on Violence, concluded that although our cities were no longer burning and our campuses exploding, "the dark side of American tradition in which some find a rationale for violence still broods on the edge of memory." The direction may have changed, but the violence has continued.[7]

As we consider violence in our society today, it is indeed important to consider its historical context: "Our nation was conceived and born in violence." The violence that led to and characterized the activities of the American Revolution involved "the meanest and most squalid sort of violence,"

Table 7.1

Characteristics of the most common serious crimes

Crime	Definition	Facts
Homicide	Causing the death of another person without legal justification or excuse.	Homicide is the least frequent violent crime. 93% of the victims were slain in single-victim situations. At least 55% of the murderers were relatives or acquaintances of the victim. 24% of all murders occurred or were suspected to have occurred as the result of some felonious activity.
Rape	Unlawful sexual intercourse with a female by force or without legal or factual consent.	Most rapes involved a lone offender and a lone victim. About 36% of the rapes were committed in the victim's home. 58% of the rapes occurred at night, between 6 p.m. and 6 a.m.
Robbery	Unlawful taking or attempted taking of property that is in the immediate possession of another by force or threat of force.	Robbery is the violent crime that typically involves more than one offender (in about half of all cases). Slightly less than half of all robberies involved the use of a weapon. Less than 2% of the robberies reported to the police were bank robberies.
Assault	Unlawful intentional inflicting or attempted inflicting of injury upon the person of another. *Aggravated assault* is the unlawful intentional inflicting of serious bodily injury or unlawful threat or attempt to inflict bodily injury or death by means of a deadly or dangerous weapon with or without actual infliction of injury. *Simple assault* is the unlawful intentional inflicting of less than serious bodily injury without a deadly or dangerous weapon or an attempt or threat to inflict bodily injury without a deadly or dangerous weapon.	Simple assault occurs more frequently than aggravated assault. Assault is the most common type of violent crime.

Crime	Definition	Facts
Burglary	Unlawful entry of any fixed structure, vehicle or vessel used for regular residence, industry or business with or without force, with the intent to commit a felony or larceny.	42% of all household burglaries occurred without *forced* entry. In the burglary of more than 3 million American households, the offenders entered through an unlocked window or door or used a key (for example, a key hidden under a doormat). About 34% of the no-force household burglaries were known to have occurred between 6 a.m. and 6 p.m. Residential property was targeted in 67% of reported burglaries, non-residential property accounted for the remaining 33%. Three-quarters of the nonresidential burglaries for which the time of occurrence was known took place at night.
Larceny (theft)	Unlawful taking or attempted taking of property other than a motor vehicle from the possession of another by stealth, without force and without deceit, with intent to permanently deprive the owner of the property.	Pocket picking and purse snatching most frequently occur inside nonresidential buildings or on street locations. Unlike most other crimes, pocket picking and purse snatching affect the elderly as much as other age groups. Most personal larcenies with contact occur during the daytime, but most household larcenies occur at night.
Motor vehicle theft	Unlawful taking or attempted taking of a self-propelled road vehicle owned by another, with the intent of depriving the owner of it permanently or temporarily.	Motor vehicle theft is relatively well reported to the police because reporting is required for insurance claims and vehicles are more likely than other stolen property to be recovered. About three-fifths of all motor vehicle thefts occurred at night.
Arson	Intentional damaging or destruction or attempted damaging or destruction by means of fire or explosion of the property without the consent of the owner, or of one's own property or that of another by fire or explosives with or without the intent to defraud.	Single-family residences were the most frequent targets of arson. More than 17% of all structures where arson occurred were not in use.

Source: Bureau of Justice Statistics, *Report to the Nation on Crime and Justice: The Data* (Washington, D.C.: U.S. Government Printing Office, 1983), pp. 3–4.

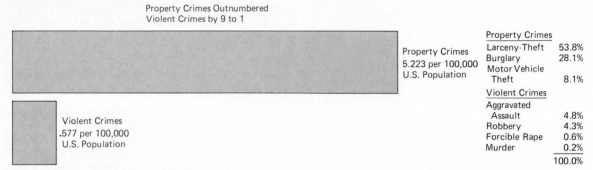

Figure 7.1 *Comparison of property and crime rates, 1981.*

Source: Report to the Nation on Crime and Justice: The Data. *Bureau of Justice Statistics (Washington, D.C.: Government Printing Office, 1983), p. 7.*

operating on the philosophy that the end justifies the means. "Thus, given sanctification by the Revolution, Americans have never been loath to employ the most unremitting violence in the interest of any cause deemed a good one."[8]

It is thus essential, in our discussion of criminal activity, to keep in mind that atrocious forms of violence have historically also accompanied activities considered by most Americans to have been "positive"—for example, the violence accompanying the revolutionary attainment of political independence, the violence in the Civil War in order to emancipate the slaves and preserve the Union, "the occupation of the land (Indian wars), the stabilization of frontier society (vigilante violence), the elevation of the farmer and the laborer (agrarian and labor violence)," and the police violence committed in the preservation of law and order. "We have resorted so often to violence that we have long since become a trigger-happy people. Violence is clearly rejected by us as a part of the American value system, but so great has been our involvement with violence over the long sweep of our history that violence has truly become part of our unacknowledged (or underground) value structure."[9]

THE FUNCTION OF VIOLENCE

Sociologists refer to **functional** results as those that contribute to the harmony or positive elements of society. For example, Émile Durkheim believed that crime was functional and that no society could be completely free of crime. He thus saw crime as a necessary prerequisite for social change. In order for the collective sentiment to be flexible enough to permit positive deviation, it must also permit negative deviation. If no deviation is permitted, society will become stagnant. "In order that the originality of the idealist whose dreams transcend his century may find expression, it is necessary that the originality of the criminal, who is below the level of his time, shall also be possible. One does not occur without the other."[10]

The usefulness of violence and its place in our society have also been examined by more recent social scientists. They point out that, first, we use violence for retribution, to get even with those who have offended us, as a form of punishment or retaliation. And in this society, retribution is an acceptable reason for the use of capital punishment. Second, we use violence, even killing, as a means to an end. For example, we not only permit but also expect police and prison officials to use violence when necessary to secure the release of hostages. In fact, violence is an expected part of the life of a police officer as well as of those who fight in the armed services and in certain other professions—and indeed, it may be one of the main attractions of those professions.

Violence is an institutionalized part of sports such as boxing, hockey, and football. Parents, teachers, and others are allowed, in some circumstances, to use forms of violence to assert their authority. Finally, we not only permit but also appear to enjoy the media presentations of violence that permeate many of our television shows, despite the evidence that viewing such vio-

On March 23, 1981, two national news magazines dramatized the nation's growing concern with violent crime.

Reprinted by permission from TIME, the Weekly Newsmagazine; copyright Time Inc. 1981. Copyright 1981 by Newsweek, Inc.; all rights reserved; reprinted by permission.

lence is often related to violent behavior. In short, "violence is pervasive in society, socially approved in many instances, and has many uses in human affairs. While it is aberrant and pathological at times, it is more often normal and commonplace."[11]

DATA ON
VIOLENT CRIME

The rates of violent crime in this country recently have declined. But it is important to consider those declines in light of the historical trend. We had high crime rates in the 1920s, before a downswing during the Depression and World War II. The rates of violent crime then began climbing again in the 1960s. Between 1960 and 1976, the chances that a person would become the victim of a major violent crime such as robbery, rape, murder, or aggravated assault increased threefold. Violent crime increased more than 16 percent each year between 1965 and 1970, although during this period the rates of increase were much lower, only 6 percent a year. In 1976 and 1977 the rate of violent crime decreased for the first time since 1961, but by 1978 the rates began climbing again. By the time the 1980 data were analyzed, the Department of Justice proclaimed, "Since the early 1960s, the United States has been in the grip of a crime wave of epic proportions."[12]

In 1982, the volume of violent crime dropped 2.7 percent over that of the previous year, the first significant decline since 1977, with the greatest decrease occurring in murder, down 6.7 percent, followed by robbery, down 6.5 percent, and forcible rape, down 4.6 percent. The overall rate of violent crime dropped 3.7 percent. When the 1982 data are compared with the 1978 data, however, the result is an increase of 21.2 percent in the volume of violent crime and 14 percent in the overall rate of violent crime.[13]

The preliminary reports of the 1983 data analysis reveal an overall 7 percent decrease (over 1982) in the number of serious crimes, the largest decrease since 1960. All of the serious violent crimes showed decreases, although the decrease in violent crimes was only 5 percent, compared with 7 percent for property crimes. In 1983, the decline was 9 percent in murder, 1 percent in rape, 9 percent in robbery, and 3 percent in aggravated assault.[14]

Data secured from victims of crime also revealed decreases in serious crimes. Although the data collected by the National Crime Survey showed an increase in victimization in 1981, compared with 1982, the 1983 data revealed a reported decline of 4.1 percent, representing the "largest one-year decline since the Government began its National Crime Survey 10 years ago."[15]

TYPES OF
VIOLENT CRIME
AGGRAVATED
ASSAULT

Officially, **aggravated assault** is an unlawful attack by one person upon another for the purpose of inflicting severe or aggravated bodily injury. This type of assault is usually accompanied by the use of a weapon or by means likely to produce death or great bodily harm. Attempts are included, as it is not necessary that an injury result when a gun, knife, or other weapon is used that could and probably would result in serious personal injury if the crime were carried out.[16]

Data on aggravated assault   Aggravated assault constitutes the most common type of violent crime in this country, in 1982 accounting for 51 percent of the violent crimes. For each 100,000 people in this country in 1982, an average of 281 persons were victims of aggravated assault, with the number as high as 315 in some metropolitan areas and as low as 131 per 100,000 in some rural areas. The region with the largest percentage of the crimes was the southern states, with 39 percent, followed by the western states with 23 percent, the northeastern states with 20 percent, and the north central states with 19 percent.

Aggravated assault not only constitutes the most frequently reported violent crime, but it also has the largest percentage of arrests for violent crime, constituting 58 percent of all arrests for violent crime. Sixty percent of the arrestees were white, and 39 percent were black.[17] There are few empirical studies of persons convicted of aggravated assault. The main reason is probably the expected similarity between these offenders and those convicted of murder.

MURDER AND NONNEGLIGENT MANSLAUGHTER

The *Uniform Crime Reports* combines **murder** and **nonnegligent manslaughter** and defines the crime as "the willful (nonnegligent) killing of one human being by another."[18] This definition may appear simple, but not all willful killings are included. For example, the killing of another person might be *justifiable homicide,* as when a police officer kills in the line of duty. It therefore is not murder or nonnegligent manslaughter. A homicide may also be excusable. For example, if a small child discharges a firearm and kills another, the child, because of his or her "tender years," will usually not be held criminally responsible. There are other kinds of excusable and justifiable homicides, and as with distinguishing any crimes, the definitional lines are often very thin.

Some statutes separate murder and nonnegligent (or voluntary) manslaughter and provide different penalties. The definitional problem remains, however, as the English case of *Bedder v. Director of Public Prosecutions,*[19] excerpted below, illustrates. The defendant, convicted of murder, argued on appeal that the circumstances of his case required the trial judge to instruct the jury that he could be convicted of a lesser offense, **voluntary manslaughter.**

Voluntary manslaughter usually means an intentional killing that takes place while the defendant is in the "heat of passion," provoked by the victim, a situation that mitigates but does not excuse the killing. The nature of the "heat of passion" and the surrounding circumstances must be examined, however, to determine whether the crime is a form of murder or manslaughter. In general, the provocation must be such that it would cause a reasonable person to kill.

The judge in the *Bedder* case obviously did not agree with the defendant, and the conviction for murder was upheld. The court refused to rule that the jury should have been instructed to judge the defendant's conduct by a standard of the reasonable impotent male rather than the reasonable man. Had the jury been so instructed, the act that resulted in the killing of another human being might have been considered manslaughter rather than murder. This case is only one of many in which the categorization of murder or manslaughter may rest on a very fine line.

Bedder v. Director of Public Prosecutions

... The relevant facts as far as they bear on the question of provocation can be shortly stated. The appellant has the misfortune to be sexually impotent, a fact which he naturally well knew and, according to his own evidence, had allowed to prey upon his mind. On the night of the crime he saw the prostitute ... and spoke to her and was led by her to a quiet court off a street in Leicester. There he attempted in vain to have intercourse with her, whereupon ... she jeered at him and attempted to get away. He tried still to hold her, and then she slapped him in the face and punched him in the stomach: he grabbed her shoulders and pushed her back from him whereupon (I use his words), "She kicked me in the privates. Whether it was her knee or her foot, I do not know. After that I do not know what happened till she fell." She fell, because he had taken a knife from his pocket and stabbed her with it twice, the second blow inflicting a mortal injury.

It was in these circumstances that the appellant pleaded that there had been such provocation by the deceased as to reduce the crime from murder to manslaughter.... [The appellate judge then indicated his belief that the instruction to the jury on the issue of reasonableness had been proper.] "Provocation would arise if the conduct ... of the deceased woman ... was such as would cause a reasonable person, and actually caused the person, to lose his self-control suddenly and to drive him into such passion and lack of self-control that he might use violence of the degree and nature which the prisoner used here. The provocation must be such as would reasonably justify the violence used, the use of a knife ... an unusually excitable or pugnacious individual, or a drunken one or a man who is sexually impotent is not entitled to rely on provocation which would not have led an ordinary person to have acted in the way which was in fact carried out."

A final, crucial term in the definition is "human being." The victim must be a viable human being in order for the offender to be charged with murder. In a recent case in which a husband forced his hand up his estranged wife's vagina and killed a fetus, later delivered by abdominal incision, the Kentucky Supreme Court ruled the husband could not be convicted of criminal homicide because the fetus did not meet the statute's "person" requirement.[20]

Data on murder and nonnegligent manslaughter

In 1982, the FBI reported 21,021 murders, down 6.7 percent from 1981, representing a rate of 9.1 deaths per 100,000 people in this country. As Figure 7.2 indicates, when the 1982 data are compared with the 1978 data, the number of offenses shows a 7 percent increase, but the rate per 100,000 inhabitants increased only 1 percent.

Arrests for murder are higher than for any other crime. In 1982, 74 percent of the murders were cleared by arrest. Of those arrested, 43 percent were under the age of twenty-five, and 9 percent were seventeen or younger. The greatest involvement by age group was the eighteen- to twenty-four-year-olds, accounting for 34 percent of the total arrests for murder. Fifty percent of those arrested were black, and 49 percent were white.[21]

Types of murderers

The typical murderer. According to some psychiatrists, most murders are committed by the type of person categorized as the "normal murderer," meaning that the offender is not characterized by marked psychopathology.[22] Most of the earlier studies of murderers were based on this type of offender. Marvin Wolfgang, a noted criminologist who has conducted extensive research on murder as well as other forms of violence, summarized his findings on the "typical" murderer:

> The typical criminal slayer is a young man in his 20s who kills another man only slightly older. Both are of the same race; if Negro, the slaying is commonly

Figure 7.2

Trends in murder.

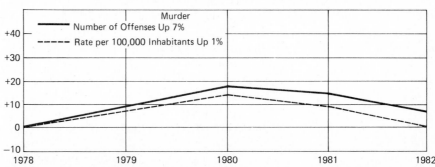

Source: Federal Bureau of Investigation, Uniform Crime Reports, 1982 *(Washington, D.C.: Government Printing Office, 1983), p. 7.*

with a knife, if white it is a beating with fists and feet on a public street. Men kill and are killed between four and five times more frequently than women, but when a woman kills she most likely has a man as her victim and does it with a butcher knife in the kitchen. A woman killing a woman is extremely rare, for she is most commonly slain by her husband or other close friend by a beating in the bedroom.[23]

This typical murderer is often a friend or relative of the victim. Fifty-five percent of the murders committed in 1982 involved either relatives or persons acquainted with the victim, leading the UCR to state: "It has long been recognized that murder is primarily a societal problem over which law enforcement has little or no control." Of those murders involving "intimate persons," 17 percent involved family members, and one-half of those victims were spouses killing spouses. The largest percentage of these murders were preceded by arguments between the family members or friends.[24]

The interaction patterns in situations that lead to violence in the typical murder were examined by one investigator who found that such transactions took a sequential form. First, the victim did something that was considered a defensive move by the offender, who then responded with a verbal or physical challenge. The victim's response indicated that the use of violence would be favored, and the victim and offender then have a "working agreement" that violence is the way to resolve the problem or just to "save face." Violence then ensues, leaving the victim dead or dying.[25]

The hit man or professional murderer. Perhaps the most serious of all deviants is the professional murderer—the person who can be hired to murder. Although we might understand the process by which someone "drifts" into a career of crime, kills during a fit of passion, or associates with deviants and learns to accept their way of life, is it possible for us to accept murder as a profession? One theory, the neutralization theory of Sykes and Matza discussed in Chapter 5, is appropriate to explain the professional murderer. The stigma in the early stages of his career is neutralized by his social organization. He learns to negate his feelings about the act; these feelings are then neutralized, and he adopts a "framework" appropriate to the crime of murder. This is a process called *reframing,* by which the person entering the new profession—murder—must reframe his experiences. By so doing, he is able to become a professional murderer without seriously damaging his own self-concept, which probably has been socialized earlier to think murder is wrong.[26]

The mass and serial murderers. These final types of murderers are the atypical types, but they are the most feared. Recently, the media and social scientists have focused on the **serial murderer,** highlighted in January 1984, by the attendance of police from twenty states at a conference called specifically to discuss the serial murderer, often a "drifter," who roams the country and kills at random. In contrast, the mass murderer kills several people at once.

The conferences came about mainly because of the slayings by two men, Henry Lee Lucas and Otis Elwood Toole, described by police as drifters. These two men claimed they had murdered over two hundred people, mostly women and children, in the United States during the past thirty-five years. Such numbers far surpass those of previous attention-getting murderers, such as the Boston Strangler, who killed thirteen people, and the "Son of Sam," David Berkowitz, who killed six. Officials estimate that there are as many as thirty-five "drifters" who kill twenty to thirty people but that they do not just kill; they also torture and mutilate their victims. According to one official, "Something's going on out there. . . . It's an epidemic. Yet, if you look at these people, they look normal, you couldn't pick them out of a crowd."[27]

What do serial murderers have in common? Authorities say sex is a shared element. Many of the violent, torture-type murders have involved homosexual males. John Wayne Gacy, convicted in Illinois of the slaying of thirty-three young men, apparently had sexually molested most of the victims before they were strangled. Their bodies were found in the crawl space of Gacy's home in Des Plaines, Illinois. Gacy awaits execution for those murders.

Henry Lee Lucas, a serial murderer, a drifter who claims he has murdered 165 women since he was thirteen, said the reason was sex. He said he killed them because they refused to have sexual relations with him; he then had sex with the deceased victims—a practice known as necrophilia. Said Lucas, "I keep asking for help. . . . I know it ain't normal for a person just to go out and kill a girl that won't have sex with them. They turned me loose and told me to go back home. They said 'you are all right'" (referring to the fact that each time he was jailed, he asked for psychiatric help but it was never given).[28]

In contrast, James Oliver Huberty, who opened fire in a McDonald's restaurant on July 18, 1984, killing twenty-one people and injuring twenty others, had been earning $25,000–$30,000 as a security guard until he was fired the previous week. Seven months before the mass murders, he had lost his job as a welder after the closing of the plant where he worked in Massillon, Ohio. Workers say that at that time, he vowed to kill people if he could not work to support his family. July 18 is believed to be the worst one-day massacre by one person in U.S. history.

ROBBERY | **Robbery,** a form of theft, is usually distinguished from the crime of **larceny.** It is also considered more serious than larceny, because of the threat of violence involved. However, distinctions between the two crimes have not always existed. In ancient times, although robbery and larceny were considered as two different offenses, larceny was considered the more serious because it usually took place secretly. Because the robber acted openly, he was not considered as low as the larcenist. Despite this view, the common law came to regard robbery "amongst the most heinous felonies."[29] Robbery became a felony and at one time, in early English law, was punishable by death or mutilation.

Robbery is distinguishable from larceny (theft), discussed in Chapter 9, by means of two elements. In robbery, possessions are taken from a person by the use or threat of force. The FBI defines robbery as "the taking or attempting to take anything of value from the care, custody, or control of a person or persons by force or threat of force or violence and/or by putting the victim in fear."[30]

Robbery is thus not just a property crime but is also a crime against the person, a crime that might result in personal violence. The use or threat of force is a critical element in defining robbery, as the force must be such that it would make a reasonable person fearful. In that sense, the line between theft and robbery is sometimes thin. For example, if an offender grabs a purse, billfold, or other piece of property from the victim so quickly that he or she cannot offer any resistance, in some jurisdictions the crime will be classified as larceny, not robbery. But in others it will be robbery because of the possibility of force. However, if there is a struggle between the victim and the offender, it will more likely be a crime of robbery than of larceny. The crime of robbery may be further classified according to the degree of force used or threatened; thus, a state might consider armed robbery a more serious crime than robbery, aggravated robbery a more serious crime than simple robbery, and so on.

The requirement of the use or threat of force to distinguish robbery from other types of theft is not, however, without problems of interpretation. The Illinois case of *People v. Stewart* illustrates one of the problems—the time at which the intimidation or threat of force took place. It is clear that in order for the elements of robbery to be established, the threats must precede or accompany the taking of property; it is not sufficient if the threats occur after the property has been taken, although another crime may result (for example, the crime of intimidation.)[31]

In *People v. Stewart,* the defendants argued that the elements of armed robbery or robbery had not been met, as the force they used preceded the actual taking of property by two to three hours. In this case, defendants entered the Winters' store about 1:00 P.M and sought out Mr. Winters, who was lying down in the back room. Two of the defendants carried guns; the other had a paper bag. Mr. Winters was told not to get up; a gun was placed to each side of his head; and he was cursed and threatened. The defendant with the paper bag removed a jar from the bag, threw a portion of the white liquid from the jar onto some pieces of metal, struck a match, and as the metal burned, told the victim that the jar contained acid that would be used to disfigure his face if he did not cooperate. Mr. Winters said he would do anything, whereupon he was told to have $1,000 ready for the defendants by 4:00 P.M. that day and, when they called, to bring the money to a specified location. The defendants left, after spending about fifteen minutes in the above situation. Mr. Winters then told his wife about the threats, and together they proceeded to gather $1,000 from his two stores and her funds. At about 3:00 P.M., one of the defendants came back, asked Mr. Winters if he had the money, and was told he had. The defendant and Mr. Winters then left the store together and went to the specified location, where the envelope of money was turned over to the other defendants. On appeal, the defendants argued that because no force or threat of force took place at this second meeting when the money was delivered, they could not be found guilty of robbery. The court disagreed, as the following excerpt from the opinion indicates:[32]

People v. Stewart

It is well established that the requisite force which induces a victim of robbery or armed robbery to part with his property must be of such a character as to temporarily suspend the power to exercise his will. The cause which gives rise to the fear need not be contemporaneous with the taking, but rather may precede it.

In the case at bar, Winters testified that he was subjected to violent threats in the back room of his store for about 15 minutes between 1:00 and 1:30 p.m., during which time the defendants held guns and acid to his head and ordered him to give them a thousand dollars by 4 p.m. They also threatened to harm his family and burn down his stores. . . . After Winters gathered the money, he saw Stewart "casing" his store before he entered. He gave Stewart the money at the named location upon demand. Stewart had put a gun to his head about two hours earlier. He was told that Newbern was nearby. Newbern too had earlier threatened him with a gun.

Under these circumstances the time span between the defendants' use of deadly force and threats of future use of deadly force, and the taking of Winters' money, was not so long, given the imminent nature of the threats, as to preclude these events from constituting a single uninterrupted and inseparable incident of terror to satisfy a conviction for armed robbery. Moreover, Winters could have reasonably believed that the gun Stewart had held to his head at 1:30 p.m. was still in his possession at the later time. The use of a dangerous weapon at any point in a robbery, so long as it can reasonably be said to be a part of a single occurrence or incident, may constitute armed robbery.

We find that defendants were proved guilty beyond a reasonable doubt of armed robbery.

Another reason for considering robbery a serious violent crime, as compared with larceny—a serious property crime—is illustrated by the cases in which crimes that apparently were intended to be robberies actually become homicides as well. In 1982, a report by the New York City Police Department revealed that a growing number of robberies were ending in homicides, rising by 36 percent between 1976 and 1980. The report indicated that more offenders were carrying guns during robberies; in the past they had used force but not guns, and more guns mean more deaths.[33] Finally, in 1983, in the east Texas town of Kilgore, a robbery at the Kentucky Fried Chicken outlet ended in the death of five people. The victims were apparently ordered to walk down the road, lie down, and then were executed, gangland style.[34]

These examples of deaths during robbery may be misleading in regard to its extent and trends. According to the *Uniform Crime Reports,* the percentage of murders that have occurred during the course of robberies has not changed significantly in the past five years: in 1982, 10.7 percent fell into that category, compared with 10.2 percent in 1978.[35]

Data on robbery   Between 1981 and 1982, the number of robberies in this country decreased by 6 percent. In 1982 the rate also decreased, by 7 percent or 773 per 100,000 inhabitants, ranging from 299 robberies per 100,000 in cities with over 250,000 in population to a low of 19 per 100,000 in rural areas. These robberies represented 4 percent of all index crimes and 42 percent of all crimes of violence.[36] Nearly half of the robberies occurred on streets or highways, but the highest average loss occurred in bank robberies, which also represented the greatest increase in robbery rates, as Figure 7.3 indicates.

Although we generally think of armed robbery as involving a gun or a knife, other weapons may also qualify a theft crime for the more serious offense of armed robbery. For example, one court held that a stapler was a "dangerous weapon," as defined by that state's statute. It is not the intended use that qualifies the alleged weapon, said the court, but the actual use. In this case the victim had been badly beaten with a stapler during the robbery.[37] In fact, one study of victims of armed robbery in Washington, D.C., and Atlanta found that robbery victims were more likely to be injured if their assailants carried a weapon other than a gun, although the probability of being killed during an armed robbery was five times greater for victims whose assailants carried guns rather than other weapons.[38]

Nationwide, the most recent data reveal that firearms were the most frequently used weapons in 1982, with 40 percent of robberies being committed with guns. The use of guns was highest in the southern states, 47 percent, and lowest in the northeastern states, where 33 percent of the robberies involved the use of guns. The second most frequently used "weapon" is "strong-arm tactics," representing 37 percent of robberies nationwide.[39]

Figure 7.3

Trends in robbery.

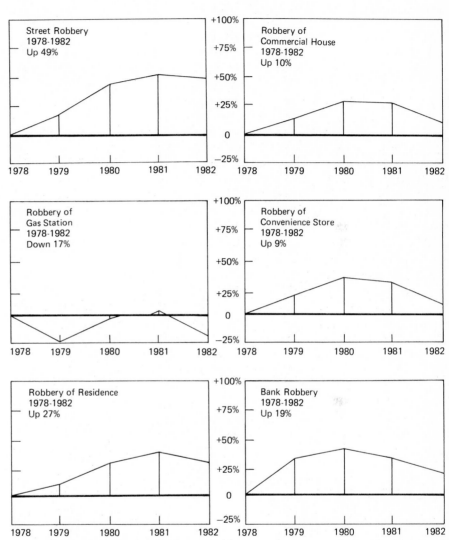

Source: Federal Bureau of Investigation, Uniform Crime Reports, 1982 *(Washington, D.C.: Government Printing Office, 1983), p. 19.*

Empirical research on robbery

An in-depth study of forty-nine inmates serving time for armed robbery in a medium-security facility in California revealed some interesting data on those who are convicted for this particular crime. All of these men had served at least one prison term before the one being served at the time of the study. The inmates indicated that they had committed a total of 10,500 crimes, ranging from 6 rapes to the largest number of offenses, drug sales, at 3,620. They averaged 20 crimes per person per year. The level of criminal activity diminshed with age. Most of the inmates had started their criminal careers with auto theft in their juvenile years, then moved to burglary, and, as they got older, to robbery. They shifted to robbery because they could do it alone and therefore did not run the risk of being implicated by a partner. Robbery has the additional advantage of requiring few tools; there are unlimited targets, and usually the crime does not require the offender to hurt anyone. Most of the robbers did not "become substantially more sophisticated" in their crimes over time, despite their persistence.

Most of the career robbers did not earn much money from their crimes. Drugs and alcohol were frequently involved. The investigators had expected the data to reveal a consistent pattern from juvenile delinquency to career criminal, but they found that the presumed pattern was too simplistic. The major overall finding was diversity, both in personality and in the career offenders' conduct. The investigators concluded that "many of the traditional assumptions about the development of criminal careers need to be reconsidered." Finally, they decided that rehabilitative efforts had not been successful. The best approach probably would be to help the offenders decrease their dependence on drugs and alcohol and to provide more help in finding employment upon release. Most inmates indicated that the possibility of long prison terms was not a deterrent to armed robbery. In fact, most said that nothing would deter them from additional crimes once they got out of prison. "For those who said they could have been deterred, the certainty of apprehension would have influenced them more than such other factors as the possibility of a long prison sentence or stricter parole supervision."[40]

Empirical studies of robberies have been conducted to test some of the sociological theories we discussed in the two previous chapters. Analyses of robberies supported the "routine activity" theory, as the data led researchers to conclude that "robbery victimization is far from a random event." People do differ significantly in the probability that they will be victimized by this crime. The most likely to be victimized are people who fall into the category "young (16–29), unemployed, low income, black, living alone," as compared with the least likely category, "older (50 +), home centered, high income, white, not living alone." Our chances of becoming a robbery victim decrease, not increase, with age and substantially increase with unemployment. As our income increases, our chances of being victimized by robbery decrease, but our chances increase if we live alone. The evidence suggests "that individuals with the highest probability of noncommercial robbery victimization are those whose lifestyles increase their exposure to risk, not only by placing them in proximity to likely offenders, but also by increasing their attractiveness as targets to potential robbers."[41]

Such findings have significant practical implications, as they are relevant to "public education, police patrol strategies and environmental engineering procedures designed to reduce the incidence of crime such as robbery, which have generated a good deal of fear and suspicion among the American population."[42]

FORCIBLE RAPE   Although the act of rape probably dates back to the earliest times, for centuries, rape was not illegal, as women were considered to be the property of men, who had unlimited sexual access to them. In exchange, the women were to be given protection and economic support. As men created laws to protect their property, they also created some to protect their women, but these laws were not viewed as protecting the women themselves, but the man's property. "Rape was a crime, to be sure, but not against the woman: only against the woman's father or husband since it was his property that had been damaged." Women were even punished for being the "victims" of rape. The Hebrews, for example, stoned to death the rape victim, along with her assailant, at the gates of the city. The Assyrians even punished the wife of the rapist. If her husband raped a virgin, the father of that virgin was entitled to take the rapist's wife.[43]

In the Middle Ages in England, rape became a crime against the woman herself, and it was not until the second half of this century that laws protecting women as rape victims began to emerge. Some have attributed that emergence to the women's movement,[44] with its emphasis on abolishing laws discriminating against women and developing institutional services to meet the particular needs of women, for example, as rape victims.[45]

In common law, **rape** was defined as unlawful sexual intercourse with a woman against her will and by force or threat of force. The term *unlawful* exempted husbands from the charge of rape, for they had "lawful" sexual access to their wives, even if the wife did not consent to the act. Further, in common law the victim had to be a woman; homosexual rape was not included. Finally, sexual intercourse had to take place. Even the slightest penetration would be sufficient, but the contact had to involve the male and female sexual organs.

All of these elements have resulted in considerable litigation. Other legal problems pertain to evidence. How could one "prove" that the act was rape, not consensual sexual conduct? In some jurisdictions, the female's testimony was not sufficient to establish the issue of force; that testimony had to be corroborated by other evidence, which of course makes it very difficult to establish proof, as the crime is normally committed in secret. The victim also had to show that she resisted the male's advances. If the woman had agreed to meet with the defendant, her chances of convincing a jury that she did not consent to the sexual acts were considerably fewer. Many of these elements remain today, as shown in the case of *People v. Reed.*[46]

People v. Reed

Defendant Edward S. Reed, was found guilty of rape, three counts of deviate sexual assault and one count of unlawful restraint. . . .

The complainant testified at the time of the incident she was 19 years old, a student at the Art Institute of Chicago, and was living with her aunt in Hyde Park. On April 23, 1976, she received a telephone call from defendant, who identified himself as Dr. Reed and told her he was an acquaintance of her best friend, whom she knew in high school in North Carolina and was at that time attending art school in Atlanta. Defendant told her he was a doctor in Atlanta, was divorced and had come to Chicago to visit his children.

On April 25, 1976, defendant telephoned again and made arrangements to take her to dinner. . . .

Defendant told her he was a psychologist and that her friend had mentioned the complainant had sex problems. The complainant thought it unusual her friend would make such a remark and told defendant she had no problems. She explained to defendant that she had high priorities and she would want to love and respect someone before giving herself sexually. At trial she stated she had not had sexual relations prior to that time.

They then talked about her school and about the fact that she was tired and tense trying to finish her work. Defendant told her he knew about a method of massage which would relieve tension and make her feel better. He stated the massage required that both of them be nude. She inquiried if there were any sex involved, and defendant said no. . . .

When they got to his apartment, they walked up the back stairs to the third floor, and she saw lights on in other apartments. Upon arriving in the defendant's apartment, she asked him to tell her about the massage technique, but he declined and said they would just go ahead and do it. She went into the bedroom and voluntarily took off her clothes and put a blanket around herself. When she look up she noticed that defendant had also disrobed.

Defendant told her to lie on the bed and he would give her the massage. He started at her head and massaged the entire front of her body including her breasts. She thought he knew what he was doing because she felt relaxed. He then told her to massage him, that it was part of the relaxation technique. She massaged his back, but he told her she was not doing it right, and he began to show her again how it was done, with her lying on her stomach. She stated he became rough, slapped her on the buttocks, and told her to turn over and close her eyes.

[Defendant engaged in sexual relations with the complainant and then fell asleep. Complainant testified that she fought his advances during the attack and that she] twice tried to get away, but defendant awoke each time and prevented her from leaving. She then fell asleep for a period of 15 minutes or longer. Upon waking she dressed and left the apartment at 4 A.M. without disturbing defendant.

She tried to get a taxi but there were none available. However, two men stopped in a car and asked if she was in trouble. After a conversation they took her to Henrotin Hospital. . . .

[Defendant was later arrested in his apartment.] Defendant said that complainant had gone with him to the lounge and they had a conversation during which he deduced she had a problem, and she agreed to come to his apartment for the purpose of his administering sex therapy. He admitted engaging in acts of sexual intercourse and cunnilingus, but stated the sexual acts were part of his therapy which he knew complainant needed because of his experience as a doctor. He stated he had used the method before on many occasions, and the complainant had consented to the acts. . . .

The degree of force exerted by defendant and the amount of resistance on the part of the complainant are matters that depend upon the facts of the particular case; resistance is not necessary under circumstances where it would be futile or would endanger the life of the complainant, as where defendant is armed with a deadly weapon. Proof of physical force is unnecessary if the complainant was paralyzed by fear or overcome by the superior strength of her attacker; but it is fundamental that in order to prove the charge of rape, there must be evidence to show the act was committed by force against the will of the female. If the victim had the use of her faculties and physical powers, the evidence must show such resistance as will demonstrate that the act was against her will.

. . . In rape prosecutions it has also been held that although the testimony of the complaining witness is uncorroborated by other witnesses, it is sufficient to justify a conviction if her testimony is clear and convincing. . . .

Defendant contends there was insufficient evidence to establish forcible rape, and he is characterized in the brief as being "a rather frail man, 49 years old." However the record discloses he was 7 inches taller and 50 pounds heavier than the complainant.

The complainant's testimony, which was unrebutted and apparently believed by the trial court, was that she struggled with defendant, screamed out the window, was struck and was finally overpowered by defendant. She also stated she feared for her life. Her testimony established that she consented to a nude massage but to nothing more, and that testimony was corroborated either by medical findings or by other witnesses. The doctor testified there was a significant and painful laceration in the complainant's vaginal area which he had not seen in any woman but those giving birth, and it was usually accompanied by a significant stretching of the skin. It is difficult to believe that the complainant would consent to an act that resulted in such an injury. . . .

It may be concluded with some justification that complainant's voluntary consent to a nude massage with no apprehension of sexual involvement was remarkably naive, but it is more understandable in the context of her art school background where nudity does not always elicit sexual responses. Complainant's actions might also be reasonably explained from the facts that defendant, who is 30 years older than she, introduced himself as an acquaintance of her best friend and indicated that he was a doctor and psychologist. These considerations apparently caused her to believe he could be trusted to respect the moral beliefs she had related to him during their conversation. . . .

The testimony of the complainant in this case was forthright, and the court apparently found her to be a credible witness. . . . After carefully reviewing the record in this case, we find no reason to disturb the determination of the trial court.

Modern rape statutes. Recently, several jurisdictions have revised their rape statutes. Some of these statutes are now sexually neutral, meaning that females as well as males may be charged with the crime of rape. Some also extend the crime to sexual assaults that do not involve penetration with the sexual organ. One of the most common changes, however, involves the admissibility at trial of evidence of a woman's previous sexual experience. The Michigan statute, for example, excludes evidence of the victim's previous sexual conduct as well as opinion and reputation evidence of the victim's sexual conduct. It does, however, allow evidence of the victim's previous sexual conduct with the defendant and evidence of "specific instances of sexual activity showing the source or origin of semen, pregnancy, or disease."[47] In 1978 the Supreme Court of Colorado upheld a similar statute, referred to as a "rape shield" statute, which prohibited introduction of the victim's past sexual experience in a rape trial, except in limited circumstances.[48]

Data on forcible rape Despite the modern rape statutes in some jurisdictions in analyzing the official data on forcible rape, it is important to keep in mind the FBI definition: "Forcible rape . . . is the carnal knowledge of a female forcibly and against her will. Assaults or attempts to commit rape by force or threat of force are

Figure 7.4

Trends in forcible rape.

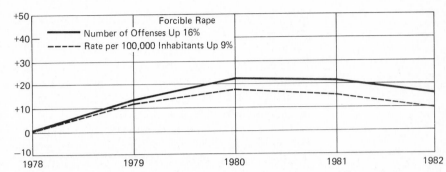

Source: Federal Bureau of Investigation, Uniform Crime Reports, 1982 *(Washington, D.C.: Government Printing Office, 1983), p. 14.*

also included; however, statutory rape (without force) and other sex offenses are not included in this category."[49]

In 1982, the FBI recorded 77,763 incidences of forcible rape, down 4.6 percent from 1981, with the rate per 100,000 inhabitants of 33.6, down 5.6 percent from 1981. Figure 7.4 shows the trend in number and rate of rapes per 100,000. Both reached a peak in 1980, declined slightly in 1981, and declined again in 1982. However, the 1982 data represent a 9 percent increase over 1978.

Of the incidences of forcible rape reported in 1982, 76 percent involved rape by force, with the remainder composed of attempts or assaults to commit forcible rape. Fifty-one percent of the rapes were cleared by arrest. The number of arrests in 1982 dropped 2 percent from 1981, and of those arrested, 52 percent were males under the age of twenty-five, with 27 percent of the arrestees falling into the eighteen- to twenty-two-year-old age group. Forty-nine percent of the arrestees were white, and 50 percent were black.[50]

Empirical research on rape

Empirical research on violent sex offenders and on the victims of such crimes is not limited to the FBI's definition of forcible rape, and it is important sociologically to consider such studies.[51] Some of them have been conducted on the victim in addition to or in place of the rapist. Some of the research has included self-reports, which can increase our insights into the actual extent of crime. Consider, for example, the phenomenon referred to as *acquaintance rape,* or rape that occurs in social situations in which the victim and the assailant are known to each other. Women may be less likely to report these rapes than those in which a stranger is the assailant; thus, the rape never becomes official. There is also evidence that some people do not consider these "actual rapes." Yet the studies also indicate that college women, ranging from 11 percent to 25 percent, depending on the study, reported they had been in situations in which their "boyfriends" forced them to have sexual intercourse; other studies have found that as many as

23 percent of male college students reported they became so sexually aroused that they forced themselves on unwilling females.[52] In another study, 35 percent of male college students responded that they believed they were capable of rape.[53] But it is not likely that these males will ever be subjects in a study of "rapists," and, with the exception of surveys of college students, the females involved in "situation rape" are not likely to be subjects in studies of rape victims.

Research based on data on rapists and rape victims must, therefore, be analyzed carefully. Furthermore, the development of theory in this field of study has been sparse. In short, "criminal justice research related to rape has suffered from insufficient theoretical development, inadequate data, and poorly developed methodology."[54] With these reservations in mind, let us consider some of the empirical studies of rapists.

Characteristics of rapists   Most studies of rapists do not separate out the violent rapist. Thus, it is not surprising that these studies indicate that those convicted of rape are not generally psychologically deviant. In fact, one study showed that those who rape adult women are generally not distinguishable except for their sexual conduct, although those who are convicted of statutory rape are rather impulsive individuals.[55] Further insight into rapists has come from the work of Menachem Amir, who studied a sample of 646 forcible rape cases in Philadelphia in 1958 and in 1960.[56] He studied the victims as well as the offenders and found that the rapes were primarily intraracial, with the rate much higher among blacks than among whites; the offenders and victims were young, usually under twenty-five; and they were unmarried. Most of the offenders were unemployed and from the lower socioeconomic class. Like murder, most of the rapes occurred on weekends, although unlike murder, Amir did not find an involvement of alcohol in more than one-third of the cases. There were no significant seasonal variations in rates. Most of the victims and offenders were from the same geographic area, and the act took place within that area. About one-half of the victims had had a previous relationship with the offenders, and that was often a primary relationship. The majority of the victims were found to be submissive (although that could be because of fear), and the majority of the incidences did not involve repeated intercourse, fellatio, cunnilingus, or brutality.[57]

Myths about rapists were discussed by A. Nicholas Groth, who conducted clinical studies of five hundred rapists. According to Groth, rape is more often an expression of nonsexual than of sexual needs. One-third of his sample were married men who had an active sex life with their wives, and the majority of the unmarried offenders had an active sex life with a consenting woman. According to Groth, rape is not the result of a sexual arousal "that has no other opportunity for gratification. . . . Rape is always a symptom of some psychological dysfunction, either temporary and transient or chronic and repetitive. It is usually a desperate act which results from an emotionally weak and insecure individual's inability to handle the stresses and demands of his life." Most rapists are not "insane," but neither are they "simply healthy and aggressive young men" who are "sowing their wild oats." They are persons who lack secure and close emotional relationships with others, male or female.[58]

Motives for rape   Sex is a motivating factor in some rapes, usually those occurring between persons who have a previous acquaintance, but sex is not the primary motivation for rape, and in many cases, sex is not even a relevant variable. Motivation for rape has been analyzed according to three categories: anger, power, and sadism.

Anger rape.   The anger rapist is expressing hostility, anger, rage, contempt, hatred, and other negative emotions, usually toward a significant woman in his life. But the rape victim is insignificant; she could be any woman. The rape is often impulsive, not planned, and the victim is brutalized far beyond what is necessary to cause her submission.

Power rape.   In the power rape, the perpetrator uses his power to force a woman into submission. This control is necessary in order for the male to cope with his own feelings of insecurity and inadequacy. For him, the act is full of anxiety, excitement, and anticipation. It is planned and preceded by sexual fantasies, though the crime is repeated and compulsive. The power rapists may even think the victim has "asked for it," but he experiences little sexual satisfaction during the attack. Rather, his gratification comes from the power that he feels from the act.

Sadistic rape.   The sadistic rapists stalks his victims; he plans carefully and waits for the right moment to attack. He then brutalizes and tortures his victims. He may not have sexual intercourse with the victim; rather, the "rape" occurs with the use of an instrument such as a stick or a bottle. The victim suffers severe injury and may die. This type of rape is usually committed by a person who is mentally ill or under the influence of drugs.[59]

Victims of rape   Recent studies of rape have also focused on the crime's impact on the victim, which may be illustrated by the case of Connie Francis. In 1961, at the age of twenty-two, she was an internationally known pop singer who, when asked about her success, said she had a "guardian angel" who did not let anything bad happen to her. But in 1974, after a successful performance in Westbury, Long Island, she awoke in her hotel room to find a man standing over her with a knife. She was raped, tied to a chair, and then covered with a mattress and a suitcase. The rapist, who fled with her mink coat and some jewelry, was never apprehended. Her engagements were canceled; she spent a long time in bed, was afraid to go out alone, and could not read the papers or watch the news. She sued the hotel for negligence in not maintaining proper security and won a settlement of $1.5 million. The jury awarded her $2.5 million; the settlement was reached to avoid an appeal. Although there were other tragedies in her life in the seven years before Ms. Francis went back to her career (including the shooting death of her brother and the end of her third marriage), her difficulty in overcoming the traumatic effects of rape was a major factor. Finally, in 1982 she began working again, but in the fall of 1983, Connie Francis was involuntarily committed to a hospital for psychiatric care.

Empirical studies of rape victims. The reaction of the victim to rape may vary according to the type of experience during the rape. In earlier, clinical studies, a psychiatric nurse and a sociologist, who opened a counseling center for rape victims in Boston, found that 79 percent of the victims could be classified as having "rape trauma," defined as a "crisis reaction to a life-threatening situation and including an acute phase of disorganization to the victim's life-style." Another 5 percent, mainly children, were categorized as an "accessory to sex." These victims were pressured into having sex by a person having authority over them. A final 16 percent were diagnosed as being in a "sex-stress situation," meaning that the experience was initially based on consent by both parties but that the one for whom the situation created a great deal of anxiety brought the experience to the attention of authorities. The investigators found that most victims were able to cope again within a relatively short period of time. Not all could go back to their former jobs, but most of those did work elsewhere. Children, however, had more trouble coping. "Their resiliency to cope and adapt was not, on the surface, as successful as adults who had the freedom to move or to change to another setting." Finally, those victims who had supportive families adjusted more quickly.[60]

Other studies indicate that women raped by an acquaintance have more difficulty coping than do women raped by a stranger. In the former situation, the woman tends to blame herself either for getting into the situation or not preventing the attack. She may also blame herself more if the attack, regardless of her relationship with the assailant, took place at her home. She may argue to herself that she was negligent in protecting herself in her own dwelling. If she was injured in the attack, she may be less likely to blame herself, for it is then obvious to everyone that she was really raped and could not defend herself. Another common reaction is the fear of being raped again, and there is evidence that women who have been raped more than once have more difficulty coping with its effects than do women who have been victimized only once. In many of those cases, the woman did not report the first rape and then had to deal again with that problem—one that was never really resolved.[61]

There is also empirical evidence that rape may have long-term effects. In a study of twenty victims of rape and twenty nonvictims matched to the victim sample on relevant variables, interviews were conducted one month, six months, and one year after the victim's rape experience. The results indicated that even after a year, the rape victims were more anxious, suspicious, fearful, and confused than were their nonvictim counterparts.[62]

The Philadelphia study. The Center for Rape Concern in Philadelphia was the setting for a study, claimed by the investigators to be "the largest investigation of rape victims ever conducted." The sample consisted of 1,401 women who reported a rape or sexual assault to the police in Philadelphia. Attempted rape and statutory rape victims were also included.[63] Interviews were conducted with the victims, usually within forty-eight hours of the rape, with a follow-up a year later. Data were also secured from other sources such as the police, court reports, and hospital records.

The study revealed that the victims had eating problems, with some nervously overeating and others not eating at all. Over one-half suffered prolonged problems that may have indicated their lack of a feeling of self-worth. Almost one-half had sleeping problems. "As was the case with changed eating habits, whether one's difficulties take the form of undersleeping or oversleeping will depend on the individual and the way in which she views the assault. . . . The data indicate that 1 year after the rape there is a decrease in the number of victims unable to sleep and an increase in the number of victims sleeping excessively."[64]

Some of the victims had nightmares—at first of the rape but later of how they might have liked for the event to take place. In those dreams, the victim was in control and may even have killed the offender. The victims also feared being alone on the street as well as at home. In the case of the latter, more had the fear if they had been raped at home (72.2 percent versus 34.4 percent). One-half had problems with social activities, with their normal social activities altered after the rape. Many had problems with their general feelings toward known men. "[A] fear of known men following a rape may be indicative of the victim's general loss of trust in herself and in others. If she has been raped in the offender's home or car, she may no longer trust her judgment. In addition, the motives of others, even those who have been close to her, may become suspect in the face of what she perceives as misplaced trust."[65]

Over one-half of the victims experienced more negative feelings toward unknown men after the rape, with many questioning their ability to deal with people they do not know. Two-fifths had more trouble with sex, and one in four had trouble with their husbands or boyfriends, mainly because of communication problems, such as "he thinks she seduced the rapist" or his feelings of inadequacy in not protecting her.

> For many victims being raped is equated with committing adultery. Although the victim recognizes that she did not consent to sexual relations with her attacker, she is unable to escape the fact that she has had sexual relations with another man.[66]

This is especially true if the victim felt sexually aroused in any way during the attack, or if her husband or boyfriend questioned her role in the act. Some men (as well as women) believe that rape is a sexual act, not an act of violence. Although legally it is an act of violence, cultural attitudes still view rape as sexual, which makes it difficult for family and others to view the female rape victim as the victim of violence. "Perhaps the most crucial underlying and typically unstated issue is whether the husband or boyfriend sees the rape primarily as sex or primarily as violence."[67]

The Philadelphia study revealed that the greatest adjustment problems were among adult victims, then adolescents, and then children. Those living with family other than the husband adjusted better than those living with a husband.[68]

The San Antonio study. One other study of rape victims should be mentioned. Rape victims in San Antonio were studied according to their own reactions, and residents of the community were studied for their reactions to the crime.[69] The investigators found that the impact of the rape experience differed in terms of certain variables, such as race and ethnicity. "In effect, we found degrees of change in victims' usual style of functioning, all significantly related to the race-ethnicity of the victim." In comparing the reactions of Anglos, blacks, and Mexican-Americans, the authors emphasized that each of these groups has a long history of sex-role relationships that may be expected to influence how they react to rape. For Anglos, with the possible exception of the very poor, sex-role interaction patterns are described as *sexual bargaining*; women and men engage in competitive and reward-seeking behavior. For blacks, sex roles are mainly a matter of *sexual survival;* the relationships between males and females are mainly adaptive and secondary to the problems of survival in a white-dominated society. Mexican-Americans, however, are characterized by sharply dichotomized male-female role complements that together form the nuclear family as an institution—a pattern called *sexual differentiation.*

> To be Black, Mexican-American, or Anglo in America is a compendium of historical experience and contemporary racial and sexual inequality. This thesis is fundamental and essential to the empirical study of rape, for rape is a manifestation of power, of inequality. Consequently, rape risks are unequally distributed in terms of powerlessness, sex and/or racial-ethnicity. Therefore, it is reasonable to assume that how one deals with the experience of rape, that

the kinds of attitudes about rape manifested by racial-ethnic communities, are largely determined by the differential statuses (power) roles, and related attitudes that are a part of being Black, Mexican-American, or Anglo, and male or female.[70]

This study revealed that not only did the attitudes of rape victims differ by race and ethnicity, but so did the attitudes of the community. The most conservative and narrow definitions of rape were held by the Mexican-American respondents, and the most legalistic or feminist conceptions were held by the Anglos, who would even include in the legal definition of rape, the rape of a spouse. Finally, in contrast with some earlier studies, the San Antonio sample of rape victims suffered long-term effects of rape, not just a quick "crisis" reaction.

SUBCULTURE OF VIOLENCE

In late 1983, in a frantic effort to acquire a Cabbage Patch Kid, five thousand shoppers in Charleston, West Virginia, knocked over tables, fought with one another, and in general created a dangerous situation for everyone. In Wilkes-Barre, Pennsylvania, five people were injured, one suffering a broken leg, when one thousand people, some of whom had been waiting for eight hours, rushed into the department store as the doors were opened, eager to buy the few remaining Cabbage Patch Kids. The store manager, armed with a baseball bat, said, "This is my life that's in danger."

Why the craze over homely dolls described by some as dolls that "only a mother could love"? Unlike the Barbie doll, beautiful and well dressed, the Cabbage Patch Kid is one about which any child can say, "Hey, this could be me."[71]

What does this mean? Are we all prone to violence in some situations? Have we produced a culture that encourages violence? After the arrest of John Hinckley, Jr., a popular news magazine alluded to a subculture of violence with this statement:

> Hinckley, like most of his forebears in the American past, was the agent of no discernible cause larger than his own dementia—a Valium-dulled stew of rock songs, Nazi scriptures and an unrequited passion for the teenage movie star Jodie Foster. But he is as well the child of the bloodiest generation in the history of America's public life and popular culture. JFK fell into the bulls eye when Hinckley was 8, Malcolm X when he was 9, King when he was 12, Bobby when he was 13, George Wallace when he was 16, Gerald Ford when he was 20, Vernon Jordan and John Lennon when he was 25. He saved cuttings on some of them, and on their assailants, and read them to mean that murdering Reagan would be regarded—even honored—as a "historical deed."

The article went on to proclaim that "the disturbing lesson of the attempt on Reagan was not that Americans condone or encourage public violence but that they have grown numb to it."[72]

HIGHLIGHT

DEEP INSIDE, WE'RE ALL CABBAGE PATCH KIDS

"What mature adult would risk snapped ribs and peptic ulcers in pursuit of a bit of misshapen rubber? [Cabbage Patch Kid]

I thought of this recently as I passed a newly trendy restaurant in my neighborhood in New York—one of those eating establishments that, through some secret communications system, becomes sanctified as The Place To Be Seen This Week.

Well past 11 o'clock at night, stretch limousines clog the narrow street; inside, men in $700 suits and $500 leather jackets, women in $800 suede ensembles, besiege the head waiter with threats, imprecations, pleadings and bills of large denominations.

At the bar, ladies and gentlemen with six-figure incomes and five-figure face-lifts crush against each other for the privilege of paying $4 for foreign water, while waiting an hour in a smoke-filled room for the further privilege of paying $75 apiece for dinner.

I wondered how many of them, once they finally obtained a table, might chatter about the Cabbage Patch Kids craze and pronounce it a sign of Middle American hysteria. . . .

So the next time you see a story about the insanity of the Cabbage Patch Kids, do yourself a favor. Check to see whether you paid double the price of a good pair of jeans to put somebody's name on your backside. Check to see whether you spent $200 or $1,000 on a home computer so that you could file your recipes and balance your checkbook—which a pencil and index cards would have done for a fraction of the cost.

. . . Deep in our hearts, friends, we all lust for a Cabbage Patch Kid.

Source: Jeff Greenfield, Universal Press Syndicate, 1983, reprinted in *Tulsa World*, October 6, 1983, p. A19, col. 1.

More specifically, some have argued that although violence pervades our entire culture, there still are areas in which the social structure is more conducive to violence than in others. Sociologists speak of these areas as characterized by a "subculture of violence."

Some have explored this subcultre in terms of social class differences. In Chapter 5 we discussed Miller's subculture theory of delinquency, in which he talked about the "focal concerns" of the lower class, which included, among others, "trouble," defined as the suspicion of others, especially law enforcement agencies from whom one anticipates trouble, and "excitement." Both of these concerns can be seen as part of a subculture of violence.[73]

After analyzing his data on homicide, Marvin Wolfgang concluded that homicides were mainly crimes of passion "or violent slayings that are not premeditated or psychotic manifestations." He argued that the conflict between middle-class values and the values of the class to which most of the homicide offenders belong was significant. He referred to the latter class as having a "subculture of violence," and he observed that "the greater the degree of integration of the individual into this subculture the higher the likelihood that his behavior will often be violent; or we may assert that there is a direct relationship between rates of homicide and the degree of integration of the subculture of violence to which the individual belongs."[74]

Others have analyzed the subculture of violence in terms of geographical location. The southern states had the highest murder rates in 1982, with 12 per 100,000, compared with 9 per 100,000 in the western states and 7 per 100,000 each in the northeastern and the north central states. The decline from the 1981 murder rate was less in the southern states than in any of the other areas.

In 1982, the southern states also had the highest volume of rapes, with 37 percent of the total. The South is, however, the most populated of the regions, as categorized by the FBI data, and the rate of rape was actually higher in the West. Aggravated assaults were highest in the southern states, accounting for 39 percent of the total. The next highest was only 23 percent in the western states. When 1982 data are compared with the 1981 data, the changes in the volume of aggravated assault (recall that this was the only serious violent crime that showed an increase during this period) ranged from a 4 percent decrease in the western states to a 5 percent increase in the southern states.[75]

Still others have argued that the crucial factor characterizing the subculture of violence is the availability and use of handguns, and they refer to a "gun-carrying" subculture, more characteristic of the South than of any other region.[76] A brochure for a recent publication on guns and violence in this country began with this statement:

> The United States today houses probably the most heavily armed private population in world history. Half of the households in the country own at least one firearm, bringing the total number of such weapons in private hands to substantially over one hundred million. Criminal violence in America has reached record proportions, making it among the highest in the world.[77]

The critical question is not whether guns are available but whether that availability increases the incidences of violent crime.[78] As the following Exhibit indicates, the evidence on this issue is not clear. The greater availability of guns may not be the relevant variable in explaining the higher rates of violence in the southern states. Rather, argue some authorities, those higher rates are the result of economic inequalities, especially when they are associated with ascribed status such as race. But when the factor of poverty is controlled, the "relationship" between poverty and violence is not so clear, leading researchers to believe that "aggressive acts of violence seem

---

EXHIBIT

THE LIKELY EFFECTS OF GUN AVAILABILITY ON VIOLENT CRIME*

- Gun availability does not have much effect on the rates of robbery and aggravated assault, but it does have a direct effect on the fractions of such crimes that involve guns.
- Since gun attacks are intrinsically more deadly than attacks with other weapons, gun availability is directly related to the homicide rate.
- Increased gun availability promotes a relative increase in robberies and homicidal attacks on relatively invulnerable targets.

UNDER THE GUN**

- There is little evidence to show that gun ownership is an important cause of criminal violence.
- Over a quarter of a million guns are stolen each year, but there is no reason to believe that a very large percentage go into permanent criminal circulation.
- There is no hard evidence to support or refute the theory that private gun ownership reduces crime by deterring offenders who fear getting shot.
- There is no persuasive evidence that people are buying guns out of fear of violent crime.
- About seven percent of the nation's gun-owning adults say they carry handguns with them for protection outside the home.

*Source: Philip J. Cook, "The Influence of Gun Availability on Violent Crime Patterns," in Michael Tonry and Norval Morris, eds., *Crime and Justice: An Annual Review of Research,* vol. 4 (Chicago: University of Chicago Press, 1983), p. 84.
**Source: Brochure advertising James D. Wright, Peter H. Rossi, and Kathleen Daly, *Under the Gun: Weapons, Crime, and Violence in America* (Hawthorne, N.Y.: Aldine, 1983).

---

to result not so much from lack of advantages as from being taken advantage of, not from absolute but from relative deprivation. Southern cities have higher rates of criminal violence not as the result of the historical experience of the South that produced a tradition of violence but owing to the greater economic inequality there."[79]

ANALYSIS OF THE SUBCULTURE APPROACH

The subculture of violence approach has been questioned by an investigator who conducted two independent studies of violence, one on the values and attitudes associated with interpersonal violence and the other on value differences among men incarcerated for various violent and nonviolent felonies. These data did not support the subculture of violence thesis. The investigator concluded that one interpretation of the findings "is that values and attitudes are relatively unrelated to violent behavior because violence is primarily interpersonal rather than intrapersonal."[80]

In response, another investigator argued that because of serious methodological problems in the study, it could not be concluded that the subculture of violence theory had been rejected. The concept of a subculture of violence has not been adequately tested, but the available evidence suggests that the concept is questionable.[81]

Finally, a recent analysis of the subculture approach, based on homicide data, determined that "both the southern region and the relative size of the black population exhibit significant partial effects on the homicide rate even with controls for theoretically important socioeconomic and demographic variables." The researcher found that in the South the proportion of blacks in the population had a strong positive effect on the homicide rate but that this was not the case in other regions. He stated, "Perhaps racial differences in value orientations toward violence are greater in nonsouthern regions than in the South. This would be consistent with the argument that violent values permeate all elements of southern society but in other areas are more restricted to special segments of the population, especially those likely to contain individuals of southern origin."[82]

REACTIONS TO VIOLENCE

Using the concept of a subculture of violence to "explain" crime may be a mistake, however, as that subculture may be a reaction to crime. We cannot be sure, but we do know that many people believe it is necessary to change their life-styles because of their fear of crime. The use of weapons may be one type of reaction. Table 7.2 shows the types of immediate reactions of people who are being victimized by violent crimes.

FEAR OF CRIME AND CHANGING LIFE-STYLES

In May 1982, six gunmen burst into the Sea Crest Diner in Old Westbury, New York. The diner was crowded with people ranging in age from sixteen to the early sixties: people who had come for dinner and people who had come for coffee and dessert after attending other functions. Approximately eighty people were robbed of their jewelery and cash, forced to undress, and then told to engage in sexual acts. Women who did not have male companions were told to engage in sex with other women; couples were singled out and commanded to perform specific sexual acts; one woman was raped; and two people were shot. One victim said, "The degradation and humiliation seemed to transcend the robbery." Victims reacted with disbelief, hysteria, reality, and then anger. Men as well as women responded like victims of rape. According to one counselor, "They are afraid to be out alone, they experience a loss of independence and I would say the guilt feelings. They

Table 7.2

How do victims of violent crime protect themselves?

Rape victims are more likely than other violent crime victims to use force, try a verbal response, or attract attention, and they are less likely than the others to do nothing to protect themselves.

Robbery victims are the least likely to try to talk themselves out of being vicitmized and the most likely to do nothing.

Assault victims are the least likely to attract attention and the most likely to attempt some form of nonviolent evasion.

Compared with simple assault victims, aggravated assault victims are more likely to use a weapon, less likely to try to talk themselves out of the incident, and less likely to do nothing to defend themselves. The fact that weapons are used more frequently by victims of aggravated assault than by victims of any other violent crime leads to the suspicion that some of these victims may have played a part in causing the incident.

		Percent of Victims Who Used Response by Type of Crime*		
*Victim Response**		*Rape*	*Robbery*	*Assault*
Weapons use Used or brandished gun or knife		1%	2%	2%
Physical force Used or tried physical force		33	23	23
Verbal response Threatened, argued, reasoned, etc., with offender		17	8	13
Attracting attention Tried to get help, attract attention, scare offender away		15	7	6
Nonviolent evasion Resisted without force, used evasive action		10	11	19
Other		5	4	7
No self-protective actions		19	45	30
Total		100% (873)	100% (5,868)	100% (24,876)

Source: Bureau of Justice Statistics, *Report to the Nation on Crime and Justice: The Data* (Washington, D.C.: U.S. Government Printing Office, 1983), p. 23.
*Victim self-protective responses are listed in the table in order of assertiveness. If victims indicated that they took more than one type of action, only the most assertive action was used in the analysis.

feel like there was something they could do." Five men pleaded guilty to terrorizing the people at the Sea Crest and at another dinner at a private home. They were sentenced to fifteen to thirty years in prison.[83]

As he sentenced the five defendants, the judge observed, "These men are guilty of the most gross, base, horrendous crimes conceived by man. . . .

They should serve every single last possible day that is consistent with the law." The district attorney argued that we are all victims "of these rampaging thugs." "Of course, the most obvious victims of these five spineless parasites . . . are the unfortunate individuals who fell prey to their self-indulgent, immoral, inhumane and antisocial crime spree, which provoked the largest indictment in Nassau County history."[84]

These incidences of violence illustrate what is probably Americans' greatest fear of violent crime—its randomness. *Newsweek* described the year 1981 as "the year that mainstream America rediscovered violent crime . . . confirmation that random mayhem has spilled out of bounds and that a sanctuary can become a killing ground almost at whim."[85] This fear of violent crime by strangers who often pick their victims randomly led Supreme Court Chief Justice Warren E. Burger to refer to the "reign of terror in American cities" and one privately funded study of crime to conclude, "The fear of crime is slowly paralyzing American society."[86]

The fear of crime has changed our lives in many ways. We must have exact change for buses, and taxi drivers will not change large bills. We lock our doors and bar our windows, thus increasing the cost of security. Many

The New Yorker, *November 1, 1976; Drawing by C. E. Martin;* © *1976 The New Yorker Magazine, Inc.*

of us refuse to go out alone at night, and there are even reports that some elderly people have suffered or even died from heat strokes in their apartments, not leaving their homes during hot weather for fear they would be burglarized or attacked while they were out. On Halloween, we must be careful where our children "trick or treat"—they might be given candy or other treats that have been laced with poison or injected with razor blades.

Data and research on fear

The fear of crime has been a significant research focus for only the past decade or so, but the amount of research has increased, and the fear of crime is today one of the most important topics in the study of crime. Such studies indicate that "the relationship between crime and its consequences is neither obvious nor simple."[87]

Who is affected by the fear of crime. Research reveals that many people are affected by the fear of crime, including many who have never been victims of crime. The chance of being a victim of violent crime, with or without injury, is greater than the chance of being hurt in a traffic accident, being affected by divorce, or dying from cancer or injury or from a fire, as Table 7.3 indicates. But we are more likely to die from natural causes than from victimization by a violent crime.

Research indicates that we are particularly afraid of being victimized by strangers. In 1967, the President's Commission on Law Enforcement and the Administration of Justice concluded that "the fear of crimes of violence is not a simple fear of injury or death or even of all crimes of violence, but at bottom, a fear of strangers."[88] This fear of crime by strangers is a realistic one for most violent crimes, as Figure 7.5 indicates, although it is not realitstic for murder, as we saw earlier in the chapter.

Women and the elderly. What is not realistic, however, is the fear by women and the elderly. Research indicates that these are the two groups who most fear violent crime but that they are also less likely than the young and males to be victims of violent crime.[89] These facts raise the issue of the relationship between actual victimization rates and the fear of crime. Earlier research indicated that victimization rates could not explain the extent of fear of crime. "While victims are more fearful than those who have not fallen prey, most of the fearful have not recently been attacked."[90] More recent research, however, has emphasized the *indirect* effect of actual victimization on creating fear of crime, resulting in even greater fear by the elderly and minorities than had previously been reported.[91]

Crime and the media. We have already seen that the media influence perceptions of crime and that public perceptions of crime, as a result of the

Table 7.3

How do crime rates compare with the rates of other life events?

Events	Rate per 1,000 Adults per Year*
Accidental injury, all circumstances	290
Accidental injury at home	105
Personal theft	82
Accidental injury at work	68
Violent victimization	33
Assault (aggravated and simple)	25
Injury in motor vehicle accident	23
Divorce	23
Death, all causes	11
Serious (aggravated) assault	9
Death of spouse	9
Robbery	7
Heart disease death	4
Cancer death	2
Rape (women only)	2
Accidental death, all circumstances	0.5
Motor vehicle accident death	0.3
Pneumonia/influenza death	0.3
Suicide*	0.2
Injury from fire	0.1
Homicide/legal intervention death	0.1
Death from fire	0.03

These rates are an approximate assessment of your chances of becoming a victim of these events. More precise estimates can be derived by taking account of such factors as age, sex, race, place of residence, and lifestyle. Findings are based on 1979–81 data, but there is little variation in rates from year to year.

*These rates have been standardized to exclude children (those under ages 15 to 17, depending on the series). Fire injury/death data are based on the total population because no age-specific data are available in this series.

Source: Bureau of Justice Statistics, *Report to the Nation on Crime and Justice: The Data* (Washington, D.C.: U.S. Government Printing Office, 1983), p. 18.

inaccuracies of many media presentations, are not always accurate.[92] For example, a recent study revealed that the fear of crime is increased, particularly among well-educated whites, by reading about crime in the newspaper. Among members of minorities and the less educated, however, the lack of confidence in the police outweighed their fear of "crime waves." "Individuals who ordinarily are not fearful become fearful when they perceive rising crime rates," but among the elderly,[93] there is generally fear, although with the elderly, as with women, it may be the *content* of the media presentations, rather than the *extent* of crime, that is crucial in producing fear of crime. As one study found, "such communications emphasize stories about old and female victims. These stories may become reference points for women and the elderly to judge the seriousness of their own condition."[94] Let us look more closely at the problems of women and the elderly as potential crime victims.

Figure 7.5

*Strangers commit
most violent crimes,
especially robbery.*

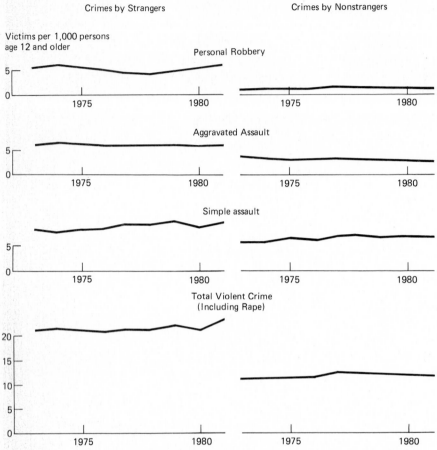

Crimes by Strangers   Crimes by Nonstrangers

Victims per 1,000 persons
age 12 and older

Source: Bureau of Justice Statistics, Report to the Nation on Crime and Justice: The Data
(Washington, D.C.: Government Printing Office, 1983), p. 15

Increased vulnerability. Both women and the elderly perceive that they are
more vulnerable to crime and that they are less able to protect themselves
from violent predators than are men and the young. Research indicates that
compared with men, women take far more precautions to protect themselves. They are more likely to avoid being on the streets at night and, if on
the streets, to use what has been called "street savvy," meaning the use of
"tactics intended to reduce risks when exposed to danger, such as wearing
shoes that permit one to run, or choosing a seat on a bus with an eye to who
is sitting nearby." They are also less likely to go to a laundromat alone at
night, and so on.[95]

The nature of crimes against women is also important in understanding
their fear of violent crime. Men are rarely raped outside prison. Although

rape is, according to the official data, not a common crime, women are almost always the victims. Furthermore, as we have seen, there is evidence that many rapes are not reported. Rape usually takes longer to commit than other crimes, and so there is increased contact with the offender as well as an increased probability of personal injury. Studies of the effects of rape indicate that it is one of the most traumatic of all personal crimes. In our brief description of the gunmen who burst into the diner in Old Westbury, New York, even the men who were not raped but who were forced to engage in (or, according to some reports, simulate) sex in front of others reacted with the same kinds of problems as do victims of rape. Further, the rape victim is often blamed for the crime. Finally, rape may be greatly feared because of the inaccurate belief that it is usually coupled with violence beyond that of the rape itself.[96]

The elderly are also more vulnerable to crime and thus to fear, for they are less likely to be able to move to protect themselves, to be able to afford locks and other protective measures for their homes, and to be able to defend themselves should they be attacked on the streets.[97]

PROTECTIVE DEVICES FOR THE HOME

The following excerpt from *Time* magazine indicates the financial extent to which we as a nation have gone to protect our homes from intruders, a process called *target hardening*.[98]

HIGHLIGHT

THE NEW FORTRESS AMERICA: FEAR OF CRIME TRANSFORMS HOME PROTECTION INTO A RUNAWAY GROWTH INDUSTRY

"In Phoenix, metal lawn signs in front of homes warn burglars that gun-wielding-guards will greet them if they enter. In Cleveland, a school for canines turns tail-wagging family pooches into snarling guard dogs. In Los Angeles, uniformed attendants at a bunker-like command post study screens and consoles day and night. When an alarm goes off, they lift a red telephone to summon police, or bark out a microphone command that dispatches members of their own gun-toting security force.

Across the U.S., the rising fear of crime has turned the once sluggish home-security business into a runaway growth industry. Sales of burglar alarms and other residential safeguards have zoomed to nearly $900 million a year, up from $500 million in 1979, and are expanding at the dazzling annual rate of about 30%."

Source: *Time,* September 12, 1983, pp. 50–51.

This reaction to crime has produced its own problems. One of the biggest is the increase in police time devoted to false alarms, with the Los Angeles police reporting that in 1980, 98.4 percent of the alarm calls to which they responded were alarms set off by cats or other pets, wind, or "even the mid-day sun." A second problem is the false sense of security that might be gained by having such devices, leading us to be careless with our home environment, leaving papers out, the lawn unmowed, and other signs of not being home. "Let your newspapers pile up on the sidewalk and you'll get hit, no matter how good a system you've got," declared the San Jose, California, police chief. The best protection, say the experts, is good locks and good common sense.[99] In that respect, recall our earlier discussions of opportunity theory and the relationship between placing yourself (or your home) in a victimizing situation and your chances of actually being victimized.

PERSONAL PRECAUTIONS   We have already noted that women and the elderly take more personal precautions than men and the young and that one of their precautions is to restrict activity. They may be afraid to go out alone at night and, lacking companions, just stay home. But this reaction is not limited to women and the elderly. "Surveys tell us that close to 50 percent of the adult urban population are afraid to be out at night in their own neighborhoods."[100] Others have argued that people do not isolate themselves in reaction to their fear of crime, but they may alter their behavior. Thus, women and the elderly may shop during the day rather than at night.[101]

One study of reaction to fear of crime reported these findings:

> Women, the elderly, and Black residents ... all reported more circumspect behavior with regard to crime. Those who knew victims from their neighborhoods seemed to translate that knowledge into action, and people were more cautious in exposing themselves to possible attack when they believed that people in their social categories are likely victims.[102]

NEIGHBORHOOD INVOLVEMENT   Responses such as becoming involved with neighborhood activities and developing crime prevention measures vary according to research findings. Thus in one study, "collective responses to crime include positive youth oriented activities, programs aimed at improving the local environment, personal and property protection behaviors, formal and informal surveillance, and criminal justice oriented activities such as court watching." But the authors warned that the relationship between such involvement and attitudes and perceptions regarding crime is not a simple one and that other studies have reported different findings.[103]

Rather than joining with others to prevent crime, some people develop a distrust of others and an unwillingness to participate in crime prevention measures. "Although we lack conclusive evidence, crime also seems to reduce social interaction as fear and suspicion drive people apart. This produces a disorganized community that is unable to exercise informal social control over deviant behavior."[104] This position disagrees with Durkheim's "crime-is-functional" position.[105]

FLIGHT TO THE SUBURBS

Moving to the suburbs to avoid the high crime rates of the cities was highlighted in a 1981 survey of the residents of several large cities. In contrast with surveys in the 1970s, when people listed as their reasons for flight, crowding, schools, pollution, high taxes, and crime, in the 1981 survey, they named crime as the main reason for moving out of the city. Furthermore, "the fear of crime . . . has become so pronounced that it is threatening the . . . renewal of some of the older cities as a hospitable environment for the middle class."[106] Other studies have shown, however, that although "crime seems to shape decisions about where" to move, it does not shape the decision *when* to do so. "It is the well-to-do from lower crime central city areas who more often actually flee."[107]

SUMMARY AND CONCLUSION

Official data indicate that the rates of violent crime have fallen in the past two years; yet there is evidence the fear of violent crime remains high and in many cases is unfounded.

In this chapter we examined violent crimes individually, beginning with aggravated assault, the most common type of violent personal crime. Murder and nonnegligent manslaughter, rape, and robbery were also considered. They all were placed in the context of the history and function of violence in this country, as well as in the concept of the subculture of violence. Finally, we discussed our reaction to violence—our fear of violent crime and the changes we make in our life-styles as a result of that fear.

It may be that the fear of crime and the reactions to that fear are more important than the prevalence of crime, reminding us once again of the often-quoted statement by the early sociologist W. I. Thomas: "If men believe situations are real, they are real in their consequences." But the fears appear to be out of proportion to the data, especially in the case of women and the elderly. If our fears of being victimized by crime are unrealistic, then we should concentrate on programs for reducing that fear, and some efforts are being made in this direction.[108] We also need to conduct more research on how people respond to their fears of violent crime; much of the current "evidence" on this issue is anecdotal, not empirical.[109] Lastly, we need to continue to assess more accurately the extent and nature of crime in this country and to try to prevent crime.

CHAPTER 8

Domestic violence

This chapter focuses on a "new" area of interest in criminology: violence within the family. Such violence has existed for centuries. In fact, historically some forms of violence (for example, husbands "disciplining" their wives) were not only acceptable—but expected and socially and legally sanctioned! This historical acceptance of family violence, or at least a tolerance of such violence, has led many people to deny that we have a problem. But today, at many levels, the problem is "out in the open." These are the crimes that previously "no one mentioned." Sexual abuse of children, along with other types of child abuse, child stealing by parents who have lost custody battles, and abuse of elderly parents will be discussed along with spouse battering. Finally, we shall examine recent legislative attempts to control domestic violence.

Deborah's first memory of her father was when she was four years old, and he crushed her dollhouse and threw her around the room, punching and choking her. Her brother Richard recalled that when he was seven, his father began beating him after finding that a friend had broken one of Richard's toys. When Richard's mother protested, the father began beating her, and she later reported that she lived in fear of being killed by her husband, an Internal Revenue Service criminal investigator who kept knives and guns in the home where he attempted to keep his family isolated from other people. According to his wife, he did not even go to the bathroom without taking a knife with him.

The expensively furnished and immaculately kept house gave no clues to the outside world that it was filled with child and spouse abuse at the hands of a "respectable professional" who was apparently obsessed with cleanliness. The father, who thought his children did not pay enough attention to personal hygiene, would, according to the teenagers, brush their teeth for them—until their gums bled. When Deborah had pimples, he would scrub her face until it bled, telling her that she was dirty. When she showered, he would watch, and at times he entered her bedroom and fondled her. She said, "I just kept my eyes closed and wondered when it would be over." The mother, when asked whether she knew about the alleged sexual molestation, replied that she knew he touched the daughter intimately but that she thought he was just showing affection. "I saw it as affection since I rarely saw him show affection." Why did the mother allow these abuses to continue? "I was afraid to try to stop him. I was afraid he would kill the children." Finally, the teenage son told a teacher who then took him to the sheriff's office. The father, called to the office, put on his best behavior, showed his IRS badge, and convinced the officer that there was no problem. A social worker who visited the home reported that he saw no problem. When asked why he did not talk with the children in private, he replied that he usually left his phone number for the children to call if they wished to speak privately with him, but he apparently forgot to follow that procedure in this case.

A physician who is the director of the National Center for Child Abuse in Denver, told the interviewer on "60 Minutes"[1] that all of the classic signs of a situation in which someone could get killed were present in this case. In a damning indictment of our general response to such problems, the doctor said, "If anyone had seen paint peeling off the house, the diagnosis would have been easier."

The violence in this family came to a climax one evening when Richard decided that his father would never beat him again. As his parents were going out for dinner, the father, according to Richard, said, "We will find a way to get rid of you." It was then that Richard resolved to kill his father. He armed himself with a revolver, shotgun, and knife and waited in the garage. He said he was afraid. "What I really wanted to do when he got home was to hug him and tell him I love him, but I knew nothing would change. When he returned home, I opened fire. Those shots hurt me so much. . . . I felt like I was shot with him."

Each of the teenagers was tried separately. Richard was found guilty of voluntary manslaughter and given a five- to fifteen-year sentence, but the governor later commuted the sentence to three years. Deborah was convicted of aiding and was given a three- to seven-year sentence. Deborah is in a school for emotionally disturbed women, and her case is being appealed.

The killing shocked the small town in Wyoming, but the jury obviously did not believe the self-defense argument of the defendants, whose attorney took the position that they had been "killed for years."

DOMESTIC VIOLENCE

Domestic violence occurs within the setting where people can and should expect warmth, reinforcement, support, trust, and love. But our study of public violence left us with the fact that most murders as well as other violent crimes are perpetrated against friends or at least acquaintances and, in many instances, family members. Domestic violence, on the other hand, is thought to be seriously underreported, leaving us with the possibility that if all acts were reported, violence between friends or family would be found to exceed violence between strangers. Furthermore, an assault by a spouse is more likely to require medical attention or hospitalization than is an assault by a stranger.[2] Despite the seriousness of domestic violence, it has only recently become recognized as a type of violent crime.

HISTORY OF DOMESTIC VIOLENCE

"Granny bashing" and "male spouse battering" are relatively new to our vocabulary, but certain forms of domestic violence have been talked about for years, even centuries—for example, **infanticide.** And although the first recorded discussion of juvenile problems dates back some 3,700 years,[3] the Bible was the first "juvenile code," clearly providing for actions that today would be considered both "child abuse" and criminal according to the statutes of all jurisdictions. For example, the Bible provided that a stubborn and rebellious child could be taken by the parents into the city and there stoned to death by the elders. Other provisions allowed the death sentence for children who cursed or killed their fathers or mothers. Parents were the recognized authorities for disciplining their children, and the children were admonished to "Honor thy Father and Mother, that thy days may be long upon this earth." Roman law and English common law also recognized the almost-exclusive rights of parents to discipline their children.[4]

Like children, wives were historically the "property" of their fathers and then their husbands, and they were also supposed to "honor and obey" them. Husbands were allowed to "discipline" their wives virtually without penalty. Child and spouse abuse as we recognize it today must be understood against this background, for these beliefs are still held by some people.

Even after the abuse of family members was no longer sanctioned as "proper," little attention was paid to such actions. They were, after all, considered to be domestic matters and of little or no concern to the rest of society. Thus, although we have known about family violence for a long time, it has been only recently that these long-known facts about family violence have been pulled together into a general analysis of violence in the home. "What formerly was thought of as an individual's aberrations or pathologies, is now seen as a pattern of family relations in millions of American families,"[5] and data indicate that family violence is also a problem in other countries.

The seriousness of domestic violence in this country was emphasized by the Task Force on Victims in its 1982 report to President Ronald Reagan. Domestic violence, the commission reported, is far more complex than is violence against strangers. The entire family is more intimately victimized by the crime and the guilt that the immediate victim displays in deciding to report the crime. The very nature of the family relationship makes it difficult for many victims to complain to the police, and knowing that the police might minimize the incident increases the likelihood of not reporting it. Finally, the risk of retaliation by the offender is greater. Because of the phenomenon's complexity, the task force could not study the problem in the same depth as it could other types of crime and therefore recommended that the government appoint a new task force specifically to study the problem of family violence. The new task force was to be commissioned to "study the serious problem of violence within the family, including violence against children, spouse abuse, and abuse of the elderly, and to review and evaluate national, state, and local efforts to address this problem."[6]

On September 19, 1983, the attorney general of the United States announced the formation of the Task Force on Family Violence. He stated, "The incalculable costs of these crimes in physical and emotional suffering, ruined lives and future crimes, are intolerable in our civilized society. . . . Yet, this problem has for too long been viewed as a private matter best resolved by the parties themselves."[7]

DEFINITION
OF DOMESTIC
VIOLENCE

The seriousness of domestic violence is beyond question, but its definition is difficult. In this chapter, we shall use the broad concept of domestic violence in the recently enacted statute in the state of Oklahoma.

Protection from domestic abuse act

§ 60.1 Definitions

As used in this act:

1. "Domestic abuse" means the occurrence of one or more of the following acts between family or household members:
   a. causing or attempting to cause serious physical harm, or
   b. threatening another with imminent serious physical harm; and
2. "Family or household members" means spouses, ex-spouses, parents, children, persons otherwise related by blood or marriage, or persons living in the same household or who formerly lived in the same household. This shall include the elderly and handicapped.[8]

This definition incorporates all of the victims of domestic violence that we shall study: children, elderly parents, spouses, ex-spouses, and people who live together but who are not related by blood or marriage. Even so, the definition is ambiguous, and the courts will still have to determine the meaning of such terms as "serious physical harm" and "threatening another with imminent serious physical harm." Finally, this definition excludes an important type of domestic violence, verbal abuse that may lead to serious problems.

DATA ON DOMESTIC VIOLENCE

There are several reasons that the data on domestic violence vary according to the source of collection. The first is the lack of a clear definition of what constitutes domestic violence. Second, most of the surveys on domestic violence have utilized small samples, have been highly localized, and are thus not representative of the total population. Third, funds for research in this area have been limited. Finally and perhaps most importantly, many people are still reluctant to report incidences of family violence, and it is agreed that these crimes are underreported. "Because of underreporting, intrafamily conflict and abuse no doubt constitutes the most obscure of intimate violence."[9] After making that statement, the Bureau of Justice Statistics study of intimate crime estimated the amount of such crimes in 1980 as 3.8 million. A sociologist who has studied family violence for many years, however, estimated that at least 6 million men, women, and children each year are "victims of severe physical attacks at the hands of their spouses or parents."[10]

TYPES OF FAMILY VIOLENCE

The different types of domestic violence are not mutually exclusive and are often, if not always, interrelated. Nevertheless, for purposes of study, it is important to look at the separate categories of child abuse, abuse of the elderly, and spouse abuse.

CHILD ABUSE   Recent media attention to specific incidences of child abuse has shocked and startled the nation, leading one policeman to conclude that "child abuse is the ultimate crime, the ultimate betrayal."[11] Child abuse includes not only child battering but also the exploitation of children through pornography and coercion into "voluntary" sexual relations. Such actions may and do often occur outside the family. In fact, at the Third National Conference on Sexual Victimization of Children, held in the spring of 1984, the focus was on sexual abuse of children in schools, highlighted by the national attention given to a California nursery school in which the owner and six other members of the staff have been charged with 115 counts of sexual molestation of children. The molestation involved rape, sodomy, and the taking of pornographic pictures, with some of the victims as young as two years of age. The children were kept quiet for years because of threats from staff members, including the physical torture of animals in the presence of the children, who were told, "This will happen to you if you tell."[12]

The current focus on sexual and other types of abuse of children is, of course, not limited to what occurs within the domestic unit. Although our concentration will be on the family and we shall look at specific types of abuse that, by definition, occur within the family (for example, incest), the data and much of the research do not isolate cases by family and nonfamily occurrences.

Definition of domestic child abuse   Although domestic child abuse is difficult to define, it is generally used to refer to actions by parents who deliberately or inadvertently inflict physical harm on their children, in contrast with cases of neglect in which the parent's action is passive. But the term *physical injury* may be interpreted broadly. For example, a family court judge ruled that the New York State's Family Court Act had been violated when a father continually called his fourteen-year-old son a homosexual and told him that he should have been a girl. According to the judge, the "physical injury" need not have been inflicted by actual force but could, as in this case, include the stomach pain the boy experienced when his father repeatedly challenged his sexuality.[13]

A quick look at earlier studies of the sexual abuse of children also reveals the problems of definition. The studies simply are not comparable because they do not use comparable definitions. For example, sexual abuse may be defined so broadly that it includes the perhaps-common "sexual experimentation" of little children with each other, as contrasted with "sexual abuse" by an older person.[14] More recently, attempts have been made to implement the definition of sexual abuse, for example, by clearly defining a "spectrum" of sexually abusive behaviors.[15] But even such attempts will not be sufficient unless various reporting agencies actually use the definitions so that the data from different areas will be comparable.

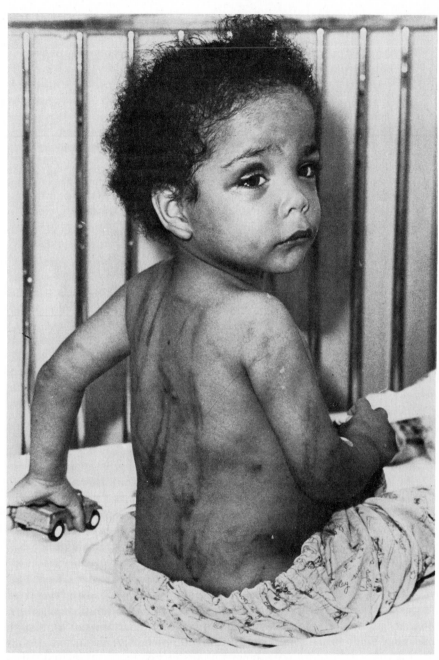

Abuse of children is currently an issue of great national concern, with reports of an increase in the number of cases both within and outside the family, including psychological and emotional abuse as well as sexual and other forms of physical abuse.

Finally, it is important to consider psychological and emotional abuse as well as physical abuse. Although these kinds of abuse are more difficult to measure, they are no less severe in their repercussions. Furthermore, emotional abuse may be more pervasive than physical abuse. A 1978 survey in Texas found that in 98 percent of the cases of reported physical abuse and 93 percent of the cases of reported sexual abuse, emotional abuse was also present.[16]

Those data on child abuse are, as noted, based on *reported* cases, and we know that many cases are never reported. It is therefore important to take a closer look at the data on child abuse, particularly sexual abuse.

Data on child abuse In 1982, the reported incidence of child abuse in the United States increased by 10 percent, according to a survey of the fifty states conducted by the National Committee for Prevention of Child Abuse. The survey also revealed that deaths resulting from such child abuse increased by over 40 percent in many states and by 100 percent in New Jersey.[17]

Particular attention has been given to what are thought to be rising rates of the sexual abuse of children. "Sexual abuse is emerging as one of the major forms of child abuse. As recently as a decade ago it was regarded as a rather uncommon problem. But starting in the late 1970s, official reports of sexual abuse began to mushroom at a much more rapid rate than reports of other forms of abuse." It is also thought that the incidences of sexual abuse of children are rising in other countries.[18] Nor is the sexual abuse of children "passive," as was previously thought, rather about 50 percent of the cases involve violence. The largest group of offenders are "caretakers—parents, baby sitters and those to whom we entrust children."[19]

The director of the Child Sexual Abuse Diagnostic and Treatment Center of the Children's Institute International, who is interviewing the child victims of sexual abuse in the California nursery school currently under investigation, reported that not only have they found sexual abuse among very young children but that also some children have been "so sexualized that we must wean them away from sex—they go through withdrawal when they lose that stimulation. We also see children who become offenders themselves, among them three 7 year-olds."[20]

Earlier estimates, conducted by researchers studying the sexual abuse of children, were quite varied. A 1979 national estimate put the figure at 336,200,[21] although an earlier estimation, based on a study that is considered a "classic" in the field, put the figure at 500,000 annual cases of sexual exploitation of females under fourteen.[22] The difference may be in the method used. In the higher figure, the estimate was based on interviews with a sample of 4,400 female adults, 24 percent of whom indicated that during their childhood they were sexually abused. That finding was then projected to the total population. By using this method, a small bias in the original data could be magnified in the projection nationwide. On the other hand, the 336,200 figure is based on the reported incidences of sexual abuse in four metropolitan areas in the Northeast multiplied by 3.5, because it is estimated that the number of actual incidences of sexual abuse is three to four times higher than the reported incidences. But even this figure may be too small, as the number of unreported incidences may be much higher than three or four times.

There also may be other problems with the data; for example, reporting agencies may have different definitions of sexual abuse. Thus rape and incest may be combined, though they represent two different behavioral problems according to our analysis. It is quite possible that the reasons for having a sexual relationship with one's own child, incest, are quite different from the motivations of a nonfamily member who rapes that child. Another problem is that serious sexual assault, such as rape or incest, might be recorded as "taking indecent liberties with a child," an offense that is easier to prove in court and therefore more likely to result in a conviction.[23] It has also been suggested that the rate of reporting sexual abuse may be much higher for female than for male victims.[24]

Finally, we must analyze the method by which the samples of cases are selected for the respective studies. Some are based on cases brought to the attention of psychiatrists or others who work with sexually abused children, but most come "from the files of a special purpose agency," and therefore generalization is limited. "It would be precarious indeed, to draw conclusions about child sexual abuse generally based on the reported findings of an agency that primarily handles cases of intrafamilial abuse."[25]

One of the ways researchers have attempted to alleviate these problems is to select a sample from the general public and ask them about sexual abuse during their childhood. One advantage of this method is that we may find out about unreported cases, much in the same way as with general victimization surveys. A problem, however, is the difficulty of recall; earlier incidences of sexual abuse may be either exaggerated or minimized. Furthermore, these surveys do not give us a picture of current sexual abuse.[26]

Others have tried to solve this sampling problem by taking cases from agencies that handle primarily intrafamily abuse as well as those that handle extrafamily abuse, recognizing that the results tell us only about *reported* cases and give no information on the actual *prevalence* of the sexual abuse of children. Still, such studies are important in that they do reveal the characteristics of victims and perpetrators of reported cases.[27]

The only firm fact is that we do not have accurate data and that we must be extremely careful in our interpretation of published reports. The lack of accurate data has also hindered the development and testing of theories of causation.

Finally, in considering the data on child abuse, especially sexual abuse, we must consider that the reports indicating that incidences of abuse are rising may reflect a growing awareness of the problem and the consequent willingness to report, rather than an actual increase.

Empirical studies of child abuse   With the problems of data collection in mind, we shall take a cautious look at some of the studies of child abuse and see what they reveal about the characteristics of the victims and the offenders, as well as the incidences of abuse.

One study that did not focus on sexual abuse found that parents abuse their male children as frequently as they abuse their female children and that in approximately 60 percent of these cases, the mother is the perpetrator of the crime. This study, conducted by the American Human Association (AHA), also found that although there are more cases of child abuse among low-income families,[28] there were also cases of child abuse among high-income families. The higher reporting of incidences among lower-income families may reflect their greater visibility to social welfare agencies, whose personnel might report the crimes. Children of all ages are affected, but half of the reports in the AHA study were of children under age six, a particularly important finding "because the younger the child the more serious the physical consequences of abuse and neglect." Of those who die from child abuse, 60 percent are under the age two.[29]

A recent survey of 521 parents in Boston revealed some interesting information on the problem of sexual abuse. First, most parents think that the perpetrators of such crimes are strangers, a myth that may indicate why most parents do not warn their children about the possibility of sexual abuse by friends, siblings, parents, or other relatives. These parents did, however, indicate knowledge of the existence of sexual abuse of children and their support for educational programs in schools to help children avoid or deal with the problem. Nearly one person in ten indicated that his or her own child had been the victim of sexual abuse or attempted abuse, and nearly one-half of the parents indicated that they knew a child who had been victimized sexually. Of those children, 37 percent were six or younger. Fifteen percent of the mothers and six percent of the fathers indicated that they had been sexually abused as children, and in one-third of those cases, the abuse occurred before the child was nine years old. A higher percentage of the cases of child abuse occurred in families in which one or both parents had remarried. Children of both sexes were abused, but the abuser was most often male.[30]

A study of sexual abuse in Texas found that the average age of all victims was 10.82 years; 19.5 percent of the abused children were under the age of seven. Females constituted 83.5 percent of the victims. Fifty percent of the cases involved family members as perpetrators, although males were much more likely than females to be victims of sexual abuse by persons who were not members of the family. The racial and ethnic background of the victims was similar to that of the general population, and the race of the perpetrator and the victim were almost always the same. The mean age of perpetrators was 33.98 years, but they ranged in age from five to ninety-nine! Most of the perpetrators were male, 86.8 percent of the total. When women were the perpetrators, they most often were family members of the victim. Like the victims, the racial and ethnic composition of the perpetrators was similar to that of the general population. About 50 percent of the male perpetrators were married, but most of the females were single, separated, or divorced. The Texas study found all kinds of sexual abuse, although fondling and heterosexual intercourse were the most common forms of behavior reported.

In interpreting their data, the authors emphasized that we still need to know how these data from agencies compare with victimization studies of sexual abuse that has not been reported. We also know very little about the sexual victimization of children by more than one perpetrator and how those perpetrators and offenses compare with cases in which only one perpetrator is involved. "The fact that such information is not readily available speaks to the still elementary state of our knowledge in this area."[31]

INCEST   The increased attention given nationally to the sexual abuse of children has created a greater awareness of the "crime no one talked about" for years—the crime of **incest**. Incest means sexual relations between members of the immediate family other than the husband and wife.

HIGHLIGHT

CHILD ABUSE, RAPE AMONG FAMILY VIOLENCE ISSUES AIRED

A child abuse intake worker for the Oklahoma State Department of Human Services spoke about the eighteen hundred allegations in 1982 investigated by the department. About one in seven involved the sexual abuse of children.

"We're getting more sexual abuse cases than anything else right now," she said, emphasizing that not all sexual abuse cases come from "deprived" or "wrong-side-of-the track" homes. "We've seen people beat the heck out of a kid on Saturday nights and take him to Sunday school the next morning."

Blame for the abuse of children should be placed on society as well as on the parents, claimed the intake worker.

"Societal expectations of parents are incredible . . . children are portrayed as 'Gerber babies,' cooing, contented and sweet-smelling. In real life, they bite, scream and, sometimes, smell the opposite of sweet. They're little stinkers."

"When we have children, who are not parenting-trained, having children, sometimes I wonder what else we can expect."

Source: Paraphrased from an article by the same title, in the *Tulsa World,* November 9, 1983, p. D12, col. 4.

Children, eager to please their parents or siblings and not understanding what is involved, often cooperate with the abusing parent in the physical acts. Children also usually cooperate in the warning "not to tell anyone" about the sexual behavior. "Daddy's little girl is locked into a conspiracy of silence, torn between shame and a need to keep the family together, nurturing her father's adult needs while shrouding the behavior in secrecy."[32]

Data on incest Because many cases of incest are not reported, the data on this crime are not accurate, but approximately 50,000 cases of father-daughter incest are reported each year. A 1979 study indicated that 360,000 cases of the sexual abuse of children were reported annually and that 40 percent of those abusers were parents, stepparents, or surrogate parents. Retrospective studies of adult women, responding to questions about their childhood, reveal that one out of ten of the women were sexually abused by a member of their families.[33]

Characteristics of the act and the participants. Incest usually involves father and daughter; cases of incest between mother and son are rare.[34] The relationship usually does not begin with sexual intercourse; other forms of activity may take place for years before penetration. The activity usually begins with exhibitionism, then masturbation, mutual masturbation and other fondling, digital penetration of the vagina and/or anus, and finally sexual intercourse. Daughters who are involved usually have poor relationships with their mothers and therefore do not feel they can turn to them when their fathers initiate sexual activity. Fathers who have sexual relations with their daughters are usually having problems, often sexual, with their wives, and they see their wives as threatening and rejecting. "Incest begins when both father and daughter feel abandoned. Incest is really the story of a distorted search by each family member for caring and warmth."[35]

This "compassion" approach to understanding the father involved in incest has been criticized by some authorities. Referred to as a "startling new piece of analysis," the compassion approach is attacked as follows:

> We are now to understand that these men are emotionally troubled and incest is not something that happens *to* a victim but rather something that happens between *two* victims, circling back to the suggestion that these men have been victimized by poor parenting (read 'mothering'). . . . Once again, our work, our images as women, our reality is being defined by males.[36]

Fathers usually deny the incestuous relationship or, if it is admitted, attribute the activity to overindulgence in alcohol or drugs. The father often begins the relationship with his daughter when she is quite young. When confronted, the father rationalizes the behavior in terms of "teaching his daughter the facts of life" or "she seduced me." The mother is often passive

---

EXHIBIT

SUFFERING IN SILENCE: THE MALE INCEST VICTIM

"Male incest victims have been virtually ignored by most investigations of incest. . . .

The writer found in the boys a consistent pattern of extreme resistance to discussing their molestation experiences. Most of the boys wanted 'just to forget it ever happened.' Though repeatedly assured that they had done nothing to feel ashamed of, most boys refused to discuss their feelings. When referred for individual therapy, the majority also refused to deal with their sexual abuse experiences. . . .

What does it indicate about our society that male children tell us they cannot look for protection because they have been taught that they are responsible for protecting themselves? The writer submits that there is a real need to reexamine society's role expectations of male children. Unrealistic demands and emotional restrictions on boys create a climate conducive to their victimization, and in turn their victimization of others."

Source: Maria Nasjleti, "Suffering in Silence: The Male Incest Victim," *Child Welfare* 59 (May 1980): 269, 270, 275.

---

and possesses other traits characteristic of battered wives: extreme dependence on her husband, poor self-image, hostility, and jealousy of her spouse. "By exploiting her jealousy, her husband conditions her to accept the incest." In some cases, the mother even becomes an accomplice.[37]

Brother-sister incest is thought to be the least damaging of all types of incest and is usually transitory. Very little has been written about brother-brother incest. Mother-son sexual relationships are rarely reported. "Masters and Johnson state that the most traumatic form of incest is mother-son contact. The boy's social relationships with peers of both sexes are badly damaged."[38]

Sociological theories of child abuse

The literature on theories of family violence and child abuse is extensive,[39] but the approach has moved from an emphasis on the individual offender's pathology to sociological analyses such as the social organization of the family and an analysis of the culture in which family violence occurs.[40]

Both social-process and social-structure theories are used to explain child abuse. For example, the lack of social integration is used to explain why the mother is the most frequent family child abuser in those situations not involving sexual abuse. The female offender in child abuse cases is generally a socially isolated person who probably came from a background of inadequate nurturing. "More often than not, the abusing parent has had a wretched childhood. The axiom about not being able to love when you have

Known as the "candy man," Ronald Clark O'Bryan was sentenced to death in 1982 and was executed on March 31, 1984. He was convicted of lacing his 8-year-old son's Halloween candy with cyanide.

not known love yourself is painfully borne out in their histories." These are mothers who are not able to sublimate or redirect their anger; yet they constantly face strains and stresses that contribute to feelings of anger. Such parents have a low threshold for children's typical activities, such as crying, soiling, and periodically rejecting food. One study found that battering parents "yearned for a mature response from their babies, for a show of love that would bolster their sagging egos and a lack of self esteem."[41]

The lack-of-self-esteem approach was seen frequently in the earlier attempts to explain the abuse of children. In times of crisis, we all need some reassurances from others, but with the parent who abuses his or her children, this need is severe, and it is suggested that the reason mothers are more often involved in nonsexual child abuse than are fathers is that the child interferes to a greater extent with the self-esteem of the mother than that of the father.[42]

Social-structural variables were the focus of a national study of family violence, including child abuse, conducted by sociologist Richard Gelles. Gelles emphasized that the causes of child abuse are complex. Clearly they are not solely attributed to mental illness or psychiatric disorder. A number of variables are involved, including "stress, unemployment and underemployment, number of children, and social isolation." Gelles examined the social characteristics of the abusing parents, the social characteristics of the abused children, and finally the situational or contextual properties of the child abuse itself.[43] Gelles concluded that if we are to treat and prevent the abuse of children, we must stop thinking of the abuser as a "sick" person who can be "cured" and begin working on social-structural variables, such as unemployment and child-rearing techniques.[44]

Consequences of violence against children

"Violence against children breeds violence.... Clinical experience shows many abusive parents were themselves battered as children."[45] Victims of child abuse not only often become child abusers when they have children, but they also often become violent against other children and other adults while they are children. Studies of juvenile offenders reveal that many were victims of child abuse or witnessed the abuse of other children.[46]

A second consequence of violence against children is that the children's reactions may also be violent, not only toward outsiders, but also toward their own families. The violence of children against their parents is reportedly on the increase. Finally, abused and neglected children also suffer physical reactions. Twenty to 50 percent have significant impairment of neurological function, retardation, or impairment of intelligence, and many have personality disorders. And even when the child does not manifest problems, sexual abuse may be considered a time bomb that will go off later in the victim's adult sexual experiences.[47]

Preventing child abuse

The most effective way to reduce child abuse is to prevent it, but we still know very little about how to do that. Recently, however, in addition to more research on the subject, organizations have been formed to focus on the effects of child abuse and the need for preventive action. For example, in September 1982, the International Congress on Child Abuse and Neglect held its fourth annual meeting in Paris, celebrating its fifth year of existence.

HIGHLIGHT
FAMILY BACKGROUND AND CHILD ABUSE OF INCARCERATED OFFENDERS: A REPORT

A High Number of Offenders Come from Unstable Homes

"Research shows a higher incidence of unstable homes among delinquents than among nondelinquents. State prison inmates were more likely than not to have grown up in a home with only one parent present or to have been raised by relatives. Forty-seven percent of all inmates grew up in a two-parent household; in contrast, 77% of all children under age 18 in 1979 were living with two-parent families.

Because criminal careers typically begin at a young age, the identification of characteristics that distinguish delinquents from nondelinquents has been given considerable attention and has focused largely on what researchers term "under the roof culture"—the interactions of love, discipline, and supervision that occur between parents and children in the home.

Violent Behavior Is Linked to Abuse as Children and to Neurological Abnormalities

Violent behavior and physical and psychological abnormalities often appear among children and adolescents subjected to extreme abuse and violence in their families. Lewis and others in a study comparing an extremely violent group of delinquent boys with a group of less violent delinquent boys found striking psychological and neurological differences between the two groups. The more violent groups exhibited a wide range of neurological abnormalities, were significantly more likely to have paranoid symptoms, and were more likely to have suffered and to have witnessed physical abuse. They also had far more severe verbal deficiencies.

Prison Inmates Were Likely to Have Relatives Who Served Time

Forty percent of prison inmates had an immediate family member (father, mother, brother, or sister) who had served time in jail or prison. Similar data are not available for noncriminals, but it is highly unlikely that the proportion is as high."

Source: Bureau of Justice Statistics, *Report to the Nation on Crime and Justice: The Data* (Washington, D.C.: U.S. Government Printing Office, 1983), p. 37, footnotes omitted.

Particular efforts are being made to alert children to the possibilities of sexual abuse and to train them both how to deal with the problem effectively and how to avoid such encounters. Telephone "hot lines," and films and books made and written especially for children are being used.

Increasing the public's awareness of child abuse is also an important step currently being taken. In January 1984, a television movie entitled *Something About Amelia* focused on the problem of father-daughter incest. The movie attracted the second-highest television audience of the season, with an estimated 60 million viewers. Support groups for victims of incest have also been formed. "The silence that has enveloped incest is being broken. Treatment and research programs are being organized all over the country. . . . Incest is one of the primary topics at hearings being conducted in six cities by the United States Attorney General's Task Force on Family Violence."[48]

PARENTAL CHILD STEALING

One final form of abuse of children that occurs by definition within the family is **child stealing.** Recently, considerable attention has been given to parental child stealing, highlighted in 1983 by the appearance of a father on the Phil Donahue television show. The father had taken his son, in violation of the court's custody provisions, and moved to Tulsa, Oklahoma. When he appeared on the Phil Donahue show, his ex-wife recognized him, despite the attempts to disguise his identity. She then asked Donahue's staff to help her find her son, but they refused, saying they did not know where he was, and even if they did, they would not violate their promise of anonymity made to his father who would agree to appear on the show only if he could not be recognized by anyone who might know him and his son. The ex-wife sued and won a judgment of $1.7 million in actual damages and $4.2 million in punitive damages. The child was later found, three and a half years after he was abducted by his father, when a Tulsa resident saw the child's picture on television and recognized him as a youngster attending school in that city.

Data on child stealing and characteristics of the parental abductor

Child stealing has been defined as "the abduction of a child by a parent in violation of a custody order."[49]

The accuracy of data on child stealing is questionable, but it is estimated that between 25,000 and 100,000 children are "stolen" each year by one of their parents. In a study of the problem in Los Angeles, a sociologist found that "the offender and custodial parent are generally young, usually Caucasian, and employed. Fathers overwhelmingly abduct children from the care of their mothers." In 64 percent of the cases, only one child was involved in the abduction, with most victims between the ages of three and eleven. Only about one-half of the abducted children were returned to the custodial parent. Despite the belief that a parent steals a child in order to "get even" with the ex-spouse, the study revealed that love for the child and desire to maintain a continued relationship with him or her was the main reason.[50]

Legislation for the prevention of child abuse

In 1974 Congress passed the Child Abuse Prevention and Treatment Act,[51] which provides that in order to obtain assistance under the act, a state must have child abuse and neglect laws that meet requirements specified by the act. Among other provisions, those laws must provide for a *guardian ad litem* (attorney for the child) in court cases involving the child in neglect or abuse proceedings. The state must require reporting of suspected cases of child abuse and make provisions for informing the public about problems of child abuse, provision of services for abused children, and so on.

The passage by Congress of the "Missing Children Act" in 1982[52] should also help reduce the problems of sexual exploitation of children, as many of the children who become involved in these cases are either runaways or have been kidnapped or coerced away from home. Under this statute, the federal government is required to assist states in the acquisition and exchange of information that will help in the identification of missing persons. The statute will be facilitated by the trend toward fingerprinting children to help future identification in cases of missing children.

ABUSE OF THE
ELDERLY

One type of violence against the elderly that has just recently gained our attention is the abuse of elderly parents by members of their own families. "Elderly and dependent, these long-silent victims are being physically assaulted and psychologically degraded by their own resentful children or even grandchildren."[53]

This form of violence has been referred to as the "King Lear syndrome" (after the aging character in Shakespeare's play who was mistreated by his two daughters), **granny bashing,** "gram slamming," and the simple but descriptive "parental abuse." According to the chairman of a subcommittee of the House Select Committee on Aging, "domestic violence against the elderly is a burgeoning national scandal." Witnesses before that committee in 1980 testified that such abuse includes not only violent attacks upon the elderly person but also such acts as withholding food, stealing their savings and social security checks, and verbal abuse and threats of sending the elderly family member to a nursing home.

Accurate data on domestic abuse of the elderly are not available. Some victims will not report the abuse because of fear of losing financial support—or of being placed in a nursing home. This type of abuse is also difficult to prove even when reported. Elderly people bruise easily, and they fall often, accounting for three-fourths of all home accidents. And doctors are not trained to detect abuse, perhaps do not even think in those terms. Consequently, many incidences of domestic abuse of the elderly do not come to the attention of those who collect data on the problem. Thus, despite the estimates that range from 500,000 to 1 million incidences of such abuse annually,[54] we really have no idea of the extent of the problem.

*Causes of abuse of
elderly parents*

Because social scientists have only recently begun to study the family abuse of the elderly, we do not know much about its causes. It has been suggested, however, that the roots of the problem may lie in child abuse, "for there is considerable evidence of intergenerational transmission of family violence. We know that individuals exposed to a high degree of physical punishment as children are more likely to resort to family violence as adults. Children reared in an environment of violence batter their children and spouses and in turn may find themselves exposed to violence in their latter years from their own children, who in turn were brought up by violent parents."[55]

Abuse of elderly family members may also be the result of an attempt to do the right thing but an inability to cope with the problems of an aging parent or grandparent, coupled with the inability, because of guilt, to place that parent in a nursing home. Transferring the responsibility for that person is difficult. "You can't divorce your parents."[56]

Prevention of domestic abuse of the elderly

Some attempts have been made to detect family abuse of the elderly. For example, since 1978 Connecticut has had a statute providing that anyone who has regular contact with an elderly person must report suspicious occurrences or risk assessment of a $500 fine. About one-third of the reported cases during the first year the statute was in effect involved physical abuse.[57]

Elderly people have themselves taken steps to prevent crimes against them, including abuse by their own children. They have formed groups like the American Association of Retired Persons, lobbying for such services as day-care centers for the elderly. The director of one organization that specializes in problems of family abuse stressed the need for such protection. "Even a battered child is more protected." He pointed out that most elderly people do not come into daily contact with people who can help them when they are abused, thus the need for social service organizations. "About the only place many of the elderly can call for help is the police department, and few will sign an arrest warrant for their own son or daughter."[58]

FEMALE BATTERING

Despite the seriousness of child abuse and the apparently growing incidences of abuse of elderly parents by their children, it is the wife who is most often the victim of domestic violence. Two researchers described the problem:

> It is still true that for a woman to be brutally or systematically assaulted she must usually enter our most sacred institution, the family. It is within marriage that a woman is most likely to be slapped and shoved about, severely assaulted, killed, or raped.[59]

Recall however, that in our definition of domestic violence, physical violence against a woman who lives with but is not married to the male batterer is also a type of domestic violence. Thus, we include former spouses, estranged spouses, and persons who are not married to each other but who live together. One study, for example, found that instances of violence are greater among cohabiting couples than among married couples, although it was also found that cohabitation without marriage is not the only critical variable. For example, persons over thirty, divorced women, people with high incomes, and couples who had cohabited for over ten years had very low rates of domestic violence in their relationships. In short, this study found that the same variables related to low (or high) rates of violence among married couples are also related to low (or high) rates of violence among the unmarried who live together. There was one exception, however, in that "the married couples . . . seem to be ahead in coping with their problems, as they are less violent than cohabitors with the same characteristics. The greater social support and integration in the kin network of the married couple may explain this difference."[60]

It is also important in an analysis of intimate violence to consider psychological as well as physical beating or battering, for this kind of "verbal abuse" may have an even greater negative effect on the victim than physical abuse does.

History of female battering   The battering of wives may be documented from early times. Historically husbands have been viewed, by the law as well as by social convention, as having the authority to control their wives, considered to be their property, and wives have been expected to submit to that control.

Much of our law comes from English common law, which gave men the authority to chastise their wives. The "rule-of-thumb" measure apparently refers to the specification that a husband could discipline his wife by beating her as long as he used a stick "no thicker than his thumb."[61] The following excerpt from a 1896 case illustrates the legal position of wives under the English common law.[62]

Culmer v. Wilson

The wife, by entering into the marriage relation, was, at common law, entirely deprived of the use and disposal of her property, and could acquire none by her industry. Her time and personal labor belonged to her husband. Under the common law, he could inflict punishment on her, for he was answerable for her misconduct, and the law left him with this power of restraint and correction, the same as he could correct his children or his apprentices. At common law, the husband had almost absolute control over the person of the wife, as well as her property, and he became the arbiter of her fortune. She was in a condition of complete dependence. She could not contract in her own name, was bound to obey him, and her legal existence was merged into that of her husband; so that they were termed and considered one in law. As a consequence, he was made liable for her debts contracted before marriage, and for her torts and frauds committed during coverture.

Other scholars have traced wife beating to before biblical times, with medieval practices permitting the beating, even the killing, of a wife or a serf if done for the purpose of "disciplining."

> Women were burned at the stake for many reasons, including scolding and nagging, talking back, refusing to have intercourse, *miscarrying* (even though the miscarriage was caused by a kick or blow from the husband), and permitting sodomy (even though the husband who committed it was forgiven). These inhuman practices and attitudes toward women were incorporated into the dominant culture by law, allowing men to avoid responsibility for their own behavior.[63]

In this country, wife beating was permitted by statute, and even today some people react to wife beating with the question, "What did she do to deserve it?" Indeed, even some of the victims of wife battering take that position: "I deserved it."[64]

This historical recognition of a husband's legal right to "discipline" his wife, even to the point of physical brutality, has changed as the excerpt below illustrates.[65]

Data on female battering   The data on abuse of female companions are probably less accurate than the data on any other crime, including rape.[66] The most recent data, based on the Justice Department's National Crime Survey for the last six months of 1983, reported that there were an average of 456,000 cases of family violence each year, with the most common type of violence being that between

Bailey v. People

This assertion of the right of a husband to control the acts and will of his wife by physical force cannot be tolerated. . . .

In Fulgham v. State, the rule is stated as follows: "But in person the wife is entitled to the same protection of the law that the husband can invoke for himself. She is a citizen of the state, and is entitled, in person and in property, to the fullest protection of the laws. Her sex does not degrade her below the rank of the highest in the commonwealth."

In State v. Oliver, it is said: "We may assume that the old doctrine that a husband had a right to whip his wife, provided he used a switch no larger than his thumb, is not law in North Carolina. Indeed, the courts have advanced from that barbarism until they have reached the position that the husband has no right to chastise his wife under any circumstances."

To say that a court of law will recognize in the husband the power to compel his wife to obey his wishes, by force if necessary, is a relic of barbarism that has no place in an enlightened civilization.

spouses or former spouses. Such violence accounted for 57 percent of the total cases of family violence, and of those, 91 percent involved attacks on females by males. Of the violent crimes, 88 percent were assaults, 10 percent were robberies, and 2 percent were rapes. The Justice Department, however, emphasized in its report that the number reported, 456,000, seriously underestimated the extent of domestic violence. The attorney general, in his appearance before the Task Force on Domestic Violence in the spring of 1984, estimated "conservatively" that 2 million wives are beaten each year by their husbands.[67]

Popular magazines report that as many as 6 million women are physically abused each year by their spouses or other males with whom they currently have (or have had) an intimate relationship.[68] Sociologists have reported that one out of every six couples in this country engages in at least one incidence of violence each year and that during the years of their marriages the chances are greater than one in four (28 percent) that a couple will engage in physical violence.[69]

Approximately two thousand to four thousand women are beaten to death

---

HIGHLIGHT
WOMEN YOU KNOW MAY BE VICTIMS

Domestic violence is a problem shared by women of every age, religion, ethnic background, income and educational level. Battered women may be 17 or 85. They are housewives, secretaries, teachers, sales clerks, and lawyers. They live in large cities, small towns, and rural areas. As different as their backgrounds may be, battered women have much in common. They are all victims of physical, verbal, or emotional abuse.

- According to the Federal Bureau of Investigation, every 18 seconds, somewhere in America, a woman is beaten.
- 50% of all American wives are beaten by their husbands at least once during their married life.
- 25% of all reported victims of domestic violence are pregnant women.
- Over 40% of women who are murdered die at the hands of their husbands or lovers.
- 73% of all abusive males came from homes where they watched their father beat their mother.
- 63% of boys, ages 11–20, who commit homicide, murder the men who are beating their mothers.
- In one-half of spouse abusing families, the children are battered as well.
- 80% of all men in America's prisons were abused as children.

Source: Statement from a brochure, "Violence: Could It Strike You?" Domestic Violence Intervention Services, Inc., 1331 East 15th, Tulsa, Oklahoma 74105.

each year by their spouses, and battery is the "single major cause of injury to women, more significant than auto accidents, rapes, or muggings."[70] Finally, according to a study in a major metropolitan hospital, completed in 1983, "25% of all women's suicide attempts are preceded by a prior history of battering."[71]

The male batterer   Despite the stereotype of a low-class, pathological male, researchers have found that "the practice of wife beating crosses all boundaries of economic class, race, national origin, or educational background." Statistically, it may "occur" more often in the lower than in the upper classes, but that may be due to variations in reporting. The incidences among lower-class people, more often in contact with social service agencies, may more frequently come to the attention of authorities, whereas middle- and upper-class women may more often have other options than to call the police.[72]

We are not dealing with a "sick" or "pathological" man in most cases. Rather, we are dealing with an "average" man under severe stress, who has a "low level of self-esteem, a learned response of violence to stress, and very traditional concepts of acceptable masculine and feminine behavior." According to this point of view, there appear to be three major variables associated with wife beating: frustration or stress, sex roles or learned behavior, and alcohol.[73]

Frustration or stress.   Stress in the male spouse may occur for many reasons. Frustration and stress may occur from the man's deep sense of inadequacy as a male, as a provider, and as a father or a husband. Insecurities may result from his extreme dependency on his wife, coupled with his fear of losing her. As one clinical psychologist who runs a program for wife abusers in Georgia said, "The husband is trying to make her be closer to him by controlling her physically—and he doesn't realize that he's driving her away." These kinds of men will often engage in very loving acts after the battering, such as sending flowers and telling his wife he loves her, but not so much out of love as a desire to regain control of her.[74]

Sex roles and socialization.   Sex roles, learned through the process of socialization, may be related to wife battering. Men learn to be aggressive and dominant and to expect women to be feminine and passive. Any show of power in the favor of the wife—for example, she is employed and he is unemployed,[75] or both are employed and she earns more money—may trigger a violent response. Of course, many men and women adjust to changing sex roles without violence; the point is that those who continue to hold traditional sex-role differentiations, who expect those of themselves and of their spouses, may be more likely to explode when the situation gets out of hand, by their own definitions. This desire to maintain traditional sex-role stereotypes may also explain the willingness of the female spouse to tolerate the physical abuse—she views her husband's role as that of the dominant spouse and upon seeing that she has gained control is willing to permit him to exert physical control in the form of abuse.[76] After the abuse, the males may feel guilty or ashamed and deny their behavior, or they may feel that the behavior was necessary in order to "control" their wives.[77]

The entire socialization process may trigger a violent reaction in the male. If he comes from a home in which his mother was battered, a characteristic of many batterers, he may have accepted that form of behavior. That is, he has accepted violence as a method for solving the problems between men and women. If he himself was a battered child, he may have decided that it is acceptable for the one who loves you to beat you as a method of control.[78]

The role of alcohol in abusive behavior. Because of the frequent association of alcohol with violence, many battered wives have assumed that it is drinking that causes the violence, but the relationship is much more complex. In some situations, both spouses are under the influence of alcohol when the act occurs. In others, the husband is drunk but the wife is sober; in still others, neither party has been drinking. There is a tendency of both the abuser and the abused to "blame" alcohol. The abuser uses it as an excuse for his behavior, and the wife assumes that if she can get her husband to stop drinking, the physical abuse will end.[79]

Battered women: myths, stereotypes, and a research profile

Investigators have examined the prevalent public attitudes toward victims of wife battering. Such women are thought to be weak, "sick," at fault (she nagged him until he beat her), from a lower class, and willing to take physical abuse for a "meal ticket."[80] All of these characteristics are "proved" by the woman's refusal to press charges.

Although research on the battered woman is just as limited in scope and depth as is research on the battering male spouse, the results available do indicate similarities between them. One writer has described the battered woman in these terms:

> The profile of the battered woman looks almost identical to that of her batterer: she is all ages, all ethnicities, from all socioeconomic groups, has a low level of self-esteem, and for the most part has very traditional notions of male and female behavior. She may feel that her husband is supposed to be in charge of the family, even if that means beating her; she must be supportive of him, even if that means allowing herself to be abused repeatedly. Her role as a woman includes marriage, even a bad marriage and to leave the home would be to admit that she is a failure as a woman.[81]

The process of socialization is apparent in the above statement and, indeed, does place the battered woman in the same category as the battering male, in that she is basically an insecure person who has internalized the concept of the traditional role of a woman in this society. Like her husband, she often blames herself for her husband's battering. It is not until she rejects the rationalizations that she caused the battering and sees herself as a victim of abuse that she is able to ask for intervention.[82]

Perhaps the battered woman is best understood by analyzing the reasons that she remains in the marriage. The pioneer work on this approach was done by Richard Gelles, who in 1974 published one of the first empirical studies on the subject of wife battering in violent families.[83] In a later article, Gelles explored the three main reasons that battered women do not leave their husbands.

> Three major factors influence the actions of abused wives. The less severe and less frequent the violence, the more a wife remains with her husband. Secondly, the more a wife was struck as a child by her parents, the more likely she is to remain with her abusive husband. Lastly, the fewer resources a wife has and the less power she has, the more likely she is to stay with her violent husband. In addition, external constraint influences the actions of abused wives.[84]

Severity and frequency of violence. Gelles found in his interviews with members of eighty families that both the frequency and the type of violence were related to a woman's decision to take action to terminate the marriage or call the police. Those women who were hit infrequently were more inclined to get a legal separation or divorce than were those hit more frequently, who were more likely to call the police. According to Gelles, these differences might indicate that women who are struck frequently by their husbands want immediate protection and perceive that they can obtain that protection only by calling the police. It may also indicate their fear of a "radical and possibly lethal reaction from an already violent husband" if they seek divorce or separation.[85]

Other researchers have found data contradicting Gelles's findings. One found, for example, that "severity and frequency cannot predict length of stay" and, indeed, that some women who are severely abused by their husbands are more likely to remain in the marriage than are those who are only slightly abused. Although most of the differences were not statistically significant, the direction of the relationship of variables indicated "that the longer the cohabitation in a violent relationship, the more severe the injuries, the more intense the pain, the more frequent the attacks, and both frequency and severity tend to increase over time."[86]

Experience with an exposure to violence as a child. We have already seen that violent persons often have a history of violence toward them as children. Gelles points out that just as one may learn to accept violence as an appropriate method of behavior for himself or herself, one might also learn from violent situations that being a victim of violence is appropriate too.

He found that women "who observe spousal violence in their family of orientation were more likely to be victims of conjugal violence in their family of procreation. . . . In addition, the more frequently a woman was struck by her parents, the more likely she was to grow up and be struck by her husband." He suggests two explanations for these findings. The more violence a woman sees, the more likely she is to think of such violence as appropriate behavior and may indeed even grow up with an expectation of spousal violence. Second, women who grow up watching violence may be more likely to marry persons prone to the use of violence.[87]

Again, Gelles's findings have been challenged. The argument is made that we should separate the categories of violence in a child's home. In the first, the child is the victim of physical abuse, and in the second category, the child observes but is not a victim of physical abuse. One study, although not primarily testing the relationship between being a victim of spouse abuse and having observed spouse abuse as a child, found some evidence that male batterers are likely to have observed spousal battering in their childhood but that female victims of spouse battering did not generally have that experience. The investigator concluded that her data did not adequately prove or disprove the Gelles position on this issue. "Without obtaining a representative sample of battered and nonbattered women, it cannot be established that observation of parental violence either propels women into violent relationships or stimulates them to get out any sooner than other women."[88]

The victim's resources and her decision to remain in the marriage.   Gelles found that one of the main factors in a woman's decision to leave her battering spouse was her perception of her alternatives. He found that "the variable that best distinguishes wives who obtain assistance from those who remain with their husbands is holding a job. The less dependent a wife is on her husband, the more likely she is to call for help in instances of violence." In addition to giving a woman more alternatives, Gelles found, a job gave her another view of the world, a view that enabled her to realize the seriousness of spouse battering.[89]

Gelles emphasized, however, that these three factors related to a woman's decision to seek intervention when she was a victim of spouse battering were complex and must be considered in relation to one another and to the total situation in which the violence occurred. Perhaps most discouraging, however, was his conclusion that even when women did seek outside help in cases of spouse battering, the help was not easily and readily available.

MARITAL RAPE   Wife beating may indeed be considered the "silent crime," but another form of wife abuse, marital rape, has received even less attention. Like wife beating, historically there simply has been no such concept. A husband had "unlimited" sexual access to his wife; she was expected, and in most cases she herself expected, to comply with his sexual desires. He could be charged with rape only if he forced her to have sexual intercourse with a third person. No amount of force on his part would classify his sexual intercourse with his wife as rape, and this was true even if the couple had legally separated.[90] This common law provision became a part of most of our states' rape statutes. The Texas statute is an example of the definition of rape: "A person commits an offense if he has sexual intercourse with a female not his wife without the female's consent."[91]

In 1979, the Texas legislature considered but rejected a proposal to include spousal rape within the rape statute. One commentator, in discussing the arguments against recognizing rape of a wife by a husband, emphasized the continued impact of the 1736 statement that became the "authority" for immunity for interspousal rape in England and in this country:

> The husband cannot be guilty of a rape commited by himself upon his lawful wife, for by their mutual matrimonial consent and contract the wife hath given up herself in this unto her husband, which she cannot retract.[92]

Research and data on marital rape

One authority on women as both offenders and victims marked the beginning of scholarly interest in marital rape in 1975, with a chapter entitled "Fathers, Husbands, and Other Rapists," in her book *The Politics of Rape: The Victim's Perspective.*[93] But she notes that as late as 1983, most of the "research on marital rape is so new that it is not yet in print, but is contained in papers presented at recent professional meetings,"[94] with the exception of two books, one on marital rape in general and one on wife beating.[95] These research papers indicate that the incidences of marital rape are much higher than previously thought and probably exceed all other kinds of rape, with possibly as many as one of every eight wives victimized. The investigators of a recent report on interviews with victims of marital rape found

> There is increasing evidence that forced sex in marriage is a widespread social problem ... such incidents seem to occur both in generally violent and in violence-free relationships, often near their end. The offender's goal in many instances, appears to be to humiliate and retaliate against his wife and the abuse may often include anal intercourse. It is time for a serious investigation of this problem by researchers and clinicians.[96]

It is suggested, on the basis of preliminary research, that marital rape is a "common form of family violence" and that "the effect on these women is profound." The forms of abuse are serious, with many women reporting repeated rapes by their husbands over a period of years. The women, however, did not realize "that the rape label could apply to something in their marriage. Women have the stereotype of rape as an assault in an alley by a stranger, but frequently it's by people you know."[97] Another study revealed that women reported being raped by their husbands twice as often as they reported rape by strangers. Twelve percent of a sample of 644 married women over eighteen reported being raped by their husbands.[98]

One word of caution is in order in analyzing the studies of marital rape. The concept is new, as are the statutory provisions, and the research to date has been based on very small samples. Projections to the general population are therefore risky. The research is valuable, however, in giving us more insight into family problems and into the abusive behavior of spouses. One hopes that the publicity given to the research, as well as to the actual prosecutions of spousal rape, will encourage more victims to report this form of violence and seek assistance.

Changes in spousal rape statutes

In 1977, Oregon became the first state to repeal the marital rape exemption.[99] The state of Oregon, upon complaint by Greta Rideout, filed criminal charges against her husband, John, and he was tried under this statute. This was the first trial on marital rape in the country, but on December 27, 1979, John Rideout was acquitted.[100] Shortly thereafter, the Rideouts were reconciled, although the reconciliation did not last very long.

Several other states have also repealed the marital rape exemption, and in 1979, a defendant in Massachusetts, convicted of raping his estranged wife, was believed to be the first person in this country to be convicted of that offense. On appeal, his conviction was upheld, and he was sentenced to three to five years in prison and to three years on probation after release.[101]

HUSBAND ABUSE

Most victims of spousal abuse, and certainly of spousal rape, who come to the attention of authorities are women. But in the past few years, an increasing number of husband-battering cases have also come to our attention. Sociologist Murray Straus, one of the pioneers in the study of spouse abuse, estimates that each year 282,000 men are physically beaten by their wives.[102] The victims of such offenders are frequently either the spouse of a current or a former boyfriend, and the violent act most often occurs in the home. Women have for centuries been murdering their husbands, and according to Gelles, "it was inevitable that battered husbands would be discovered."[103]

The female batterer and murderer

In his national study, Gelles found that although women kill their husbands about as frequently as men kill their wives, the reasons are quite different. Women are seven times more likely to commit this violent act in self-defense, either to avoid physical attacks in general or physical violence in the form of rape.

In 1980 a Kansas woman, after years of alleged sexual abuse and torture, shot and killed her husband. At her trial for murder, she testified that he repeatedly mentally and sexually tortured her and stuck pins in her breasts, shocked her with a cattle prod, and shackled her in a rusty underground tank. When he told her that he was planning to build a plywood coffin, wrap her in adhesive tape like a mummy, and keep her under the bed, she decided to kill him. She was acquitted of murder. The shocked prosecutor, arguing that the murder was "in cold blood," said the jury "perceived the defendant as the victim and the victim as the aggressor."

The self-defense argument was also argued in an Oklahoma case in which a woman admitted murdering her husband, placing his body in a wooden box, and using that box for a dining room table for over a month before the death was reported. Her attorney admitted that she was an "abysmal alcoholic, a psychotic alcoholic" but argued that she shot her husband in self-defense after the man, who allegedly terrorized and brutalized her frequently, said on the night of the murder, "One of us will die tonight." She shot him, said her attorney, to preserve her own life and not out of anger. She "loved her husband and preserved the body as a way to avoid dealing with his death."[104]

CONTROL OF DOMESTIC VIOLENCE

We have already looked at legislation aimed at preventing abuse of the elderly and children. Legislative changes have also been made in the area of spouse abuse.

CIVIL ACTIONS AGAINST A SPOUSE BATTERER

When a person has been harmed by the intentional assault and battery of another person, the victim usually brings a civil action for damages against the offender. When the victim is a spouse, however, the civil action may be prohibited by common law or by statute. Under common law, because husband and wife were considered to be one person—at least in **civil law**—"and that one person was the husband," such civil legal actions were not permitted.[105] More recently, though, most states have changed this doctrine either judicially or legislatively and now permit spouses to sue each other for some torts, such as assault and battery, although some of the states limit such civil actions to cases in which, for example, the parties are already divorced at the time the civil action is filed.[106]

In many cases, however, suing the assaulting spouse is not a reasonable solution to the problem, as the spouse may not have any money. More importantly, the victim spouse may be more concerned about safety, and what is really needed is either a shelter where the victim may stay or a protective order to get the offending spouse out of the house.

LEGISLATIVE RESPONSE

Although legislative attempts to control domestic violence at the national level have had limited success, some states have enacted statutes in this area. Ohio is an example. Ohio's legislation was in response to the 1978 Report from the Attorney General's Task Force on Domestic Violence. In the forward to that report, the attorney general of the state of Ohio declared,

> It is . . . disturbing to learn that the majority of these domestic violence victims suffer silently, virtually ignored by society. So the vicious cycle of abuse continues: parents (who probably were abused as children) beat their own children, who then grow up to abuse their spouses or their children or their abusive parents.
>
> We must find ways to stop this cycle of abuse and provide services to both the abuser and the abused.[107]

The Ohio task force report included recommendations concerning the police's inadequate response in situations involving domestic violence, revision of the criminal code and provision of civil injunctive relief, resulting in legislation passed in 1981.[108] In this statute, spouse battering is defined as a separate criminal offense, providing that anyone who knowingly causes, attempts to cause, or recklessly causes physical harm to a family or a household member will be guilty of domestic violence, which is a first-degree misdemeanor. A family or household member includes a spouse, a former spouse, or a person living as a spouse, parent, child, or other person related by consanguinity or affinity who resides or has resided with the offender.[109]

Perhaps the most important provision of the Ohio criminal code is that the municipal courts may issue temporary protective orders. That order will generally prohibit the battering spouse from entering the residence of the victim spouse and may include other provisions designed to ensure the protection of the victim.[110]

Because many victims do not want criminal charges to be filed against the offending spouse, Ohio has provided civil remedies for domestic violence, which are broader in scope than are the criminal remedies.[111]

COMMUNITY RESOURCES

Domestic abuse is an area in which the best "solution" to the problem may not be legal action. The victim may need counseling or a temporary shelter but may not be ready for legal action. It is therefore important that other services be made available. A victim's decision to seek intervention in a case of domestic violence may be related to the existence or her perception of the availability of medical and social welfare services or the type of reaction she will receive from personnel who provide those services.

Women who do turn to social welfare or other types of agencies for help with their domestic problems often find that those agencies are not equipped to handle the problems effectively. Personnel may not be properly trained, and shelters to provide food and housing for women who fear retaliation from their husbands may not be available, may be overcrowded, or may just be inadequate.

One of the problems women must face in seeking help is the lack of a sympathetic and understanding attitude toward the victim—the myth that she "is getting what she deserves" is still held by many people.[112] Two researchers, after studying family violence, concluded, for example, that the medical profession and social agencies "are an essential part of the battered syndrome. They treat the women like they are crazy." Signs of domestic abuse are ignored in many cases, and in others, women are labeled as psychotic or hypochondriacal, are given prescriptions for tranquilizers, and are told to go home.[113]

Those personnel who are understanding and sympathetic may have difficulty continuing that understanding when the battered woman returns to her spouse. As one said, "Battered women have a history of leaving their marriages and later returning to their mates. Those of us who witness this pattern become discouraged and are often tempted to withdraw our support of these women. . . . It is important that we continue reaching out to the abused instead of falling into the trap of further victimizing her."[114]

Another problem is the lack of services and facilities,[115] although some progress has been made. The first shelter for battered women opened in 1964 in a private home in Pasadena, California, and in 1983, eight hundred shelters were available in this country, but all had waiting lists.[116] Such facilities also often face problems of continued funding, staff burnout, public awareness, and interagency communication and referral.[117]

RESOURCES OF
THE CRIMINAL
JUSTICE SYSTEM

The problem of domestic violence cannot be controlled without the cooperation of both the police and the entire criminal justice system. But there is evidence that police see domestic violence as domestic problems, not as acts of violence,[118] and that they do not respond as quickly to domestic violence calls as to other calls involving violence.[119] There is also evidence that prosecutors are reluctant to prosecute, juries to convict, and judges to sentence to incarceration in cases involving domestic violence.

On the other hand, female victims of domestic abuse often refuse to cooperate with police and prosecutors, some because of fear—some because they do not want to live without the assailant.[120] Personnel are being specially trained to interview and counsel victims of rape, child abuse, and spouse abuse. Police are being trained to answer to domestic calls quickly and to respond with an increased sensitivity as well as an eagerness to communicate to the victim what options are available. For example, in one police department, when the police respond to a domestic dispute call, they give the victim a card that, along with the phone numbers of the domestic violence shelter and the rape line in that city, contains information on the "rights" of the victim, including the right to request that charges be pressed against the assailant, the right to request protection from any harm or threat of harm arising out of the victim's cooperation with law enforcement and prosecution efforts, the right to be informed of financial assistance and other social services available, and the right to a free medical examination for the procurement of evidence to aid in the prosecution of assailants who rape their victims.

Finally, in some cities, police are making more arrests in cases of domestic violence. Preliminary results indicate that this process does in fact reduce the number of cases of domestic violence, but researchers quickly point out that many variables are involved, that the samples are small, and that we still do not know the most effective way to handle domestic violence.[121]

SUMMARY AND CONCLUSION

In this chapter we have examined the various areas of domestic violence. After a brief look at the historical reaction to these kinds of behaviors, we analyzed specific types of domestic violence, including child abuse, with particular emphasis on sexual abuse, an issue that is currently receiving considerable attention nationwide. Of course, not all sexual exploitation of children occurs within the family, but in many cases, it does, a fact brought out in spring 1984 after Senator Paula Hawkins testified before a Senate committee on the sexual abuse of children. She also revealed that she herself had been sexually abused as a child. Shortly after that testimony, she received hundreds of letters and telephone calls, many from people who said that they too had been sexually abused as children. The senator said, "I'm simply astounded. I'm particularly amazed at the extent of in-family sexual abuse by uncles, fathers, brothers, grandfathers. It's just mind-boggling."[122]

We also discussed the crime of incest, especially the problems of assessing the nature and extent of the crime and the characteristics of the victims and their assailants. Then we explored theories of child abuse, child stealing, and legislative and other attempts to prevent child abuse.

Abuse of elderly parents was also considered. Once again, we saw the difficulty of obtaining accurate data, the problems of research, and the reluctance of victims to complain about the actions of their family members. All of these problems have been recognized for years in the last topic, spouse abuse. We have known that the problem existed, but we have not given serious attention to it until recently. Sociologists have, however, been conducting research in this area of domestic violence for longer than in some of the other areas, and we do have more empirical findings on the nature of spouse abuse.

We discussed female battering by looking at the issue historically as well as currently, the latter in terms of the assailant, the victim, and the circumstances of the crime. Martial rape, only recently recognized as a crime in a few jurisdictions, was studied in the context of empirical research. Attention was given to violence perpetrated by women against their domestic partners, also a behavior that has only recently received much attention. Finally, we covered some of the attempts to control and prevent domestic violence.

In conclusion, our discussion has indicated that although we do not know the extent of the problem of domestic violence, we do know that it is a serious problem that is currently receiving extensive national attention. We also know that domestic violence is not an isolated phenomenon, with recent research indicating that one out of four victims of domestic violence suffers from repeated acts. We have evidence that those who engage in domestic violence do not confine their violent behavior to the home; they are also often violent in other contexts.[123] We know that violence appears to follow violence, that children who are abused at home or who see their parents abused are frequently involved in the abuse of their own spouses and/or children in the future. This information clearly indicates a need for action to prevent domestic violence. The problem, however, is that most of the research in the area is quite recent and that funds are lacking for more extensive research and theoretical development. We are making progress, but we still have few answers. We can only hope that the current national emphasis on the problems of domestic violence will continue.

CHAPTER 9

Property crimes

In this chapter we shall discuss major property crimes. We shall begin with the "serious" crimes of larceny-theft and burglary, two of the index crimes in the FBI's *Uniform Crime Reports*. After looking at some of the historical approaches to property crimes, we shall turn to more "recent" property crimes such as white-collar and corporate crimes. Some of these business activities, defined today as criminal, were in earlier days not considered to be criminal. Rather, they were seen as "shrewd" business transactions. But times have changed and business has become more complex. We are no longer able to protect ourselves in all business transactions, and governmental regulations and statutes have been designed to provide that protection for us. Sometimes, however, we ignore those regulations; either we do not enforce statutes and regulations, or if they are enforced, we do not consider the activity as really "criminal" or even "serious." We may be changing our minds, however, as we become more familiar with the impact that the illegal manipulation of a computer can have on our lives—and our bank accounts! The chapter will close with a discussion of organized crime, including two approaches to that concept and a comparison of organized crime with "legitimate" business transactions and white-collar crime.

"Law is never a mere abstraction. It is a very practical . . . matter. It represents the sum total of the rules by which the game of life is played . . . but this is quite a different game in different lands and in different times."[1] With those words, a noted law professor began his commentary on the development of the law of property, a development that to some extent applies to all of the crimes we shall discuss in this chapter.

It is the emphasis on "different times" that is significant, for in this chapter we shall be considering crimes that are quite different from those of the previous two chapters. Violent and property crimes differ not only in the personal threat of violent crime but also in that some property crimes were historically not considered criminal. Indeed, taking something from another by fraud or deceit or by what we would today call embezzlement used to be considered by many to be clever, not criminal.

During the time when business deals took place between people who had access to each other—indeed, in many cases knew each other well—it was considered the responsibility of both parties to the business deal to ensure that they were being treated fairly. Thus, if you wanted to buy ten chickens from your friend, it was your responsibility to make sure that you actually got ten chickens. If your friend managed to trick you, deceive you, or mislead you, he was just smarter than you!

Times changed, however, and business relationships became more complex. With those changes in social and business conditions, we also needed changes in laws governing business life. "The original rules of the English common law of crimes are hopelessly inadequate for the protection of property at the present day, and they have been generously supplemented by legislation."[2]

This is not to suggest, however, that today we have solved the problems, statutorily or otherwise, of such crimes. Rather, we are just beginning to cope with some of them, such as computer crime and other forms of corporate crime. And although we have been concerned for decades with organized crime, we still do not know how to control or prevent the serious types of crimes, both violent and economic, included in that broad category.

Nor do we know how to deal with the *people* who are involved in these crimes, as many of them are "just like us." That may also be true with some offenders involved in family violence, as we have seen, though most of us do not condone physical violence. On the other hand, some offenders' crimes are similar to what we consider, in other contexts, to be "good business practice."

At the other extreme, however, is organized crime which, although it may also encompass some of the same kinds of crimes involved in white-collar crime, still offends our sense of what is right and what is wrong and what definitely ought to be included in the criminal law, in contrast with practices that may be considered not so nice, but not so "criminal" either.

It is important to emphasize once again that the different types of crimes are not easily distinguished from one another. Violent crimes and property crimes are not distinct categories. As we saw, robbery contains an economic motive as well as a threat of violence. Likewise, violence may be involved in some cases of burglary when the victim who owns the property is encountered, and violence is often a part of organized crime.

TRADITIONAL PROPERTY CRIMES

Two property crimes that historically have been considered serious and are categorized as serious by the *Uniform Crime Reports* are **larceny-theft** and **burglary.**

LARCENY-THEFT

The category of larceny-theft, as used in the FBI's *Uniform Crime Reports,* is a broad category. Before defining this category, however, we shall look at theft historically, in order to see its evolution. This is also important to understanding the types of business crimes, not categorized as serious crimes, that we shall discuss later in the chapter.

Historical development of the crime of theft

Larceny, the first theft crime in English history, was a common law crime, meaning that it was "created" by judges in deciding cases, not by Parliament in passing statutes. Larceny was defined as a crime committed when a person misappropriated the property of another by taking that property from the possession and without the consent of the owner. The crime did not include the misappropriation of property that one already had; for example, if your boss asked you to take a sheep to a customer and you decided to keep the sheep, that act was not larceny because you already had the sheep in your possession. Under that definition, of course, the crime of **embezzlement** as well as other modern business crimes would not be considered as larceny.

One of the reasons for requiring for the crime of larceny that the property be taken from the possession of another was that the seriousness of the "stealing" was not so much taking possession of the property but doing so under circumstances that might cause the owner to retaliate. Then there might be an act of violence or, as they called it in England, a "breach of the king's peace." Another reason that taking possession by deceit, fraud, embezzlement, or similar ways was not considered as larceny was that such methods simply indicated that you were smarter than the owner of the property, and that was not a crime! Rather, it was the responsibility of the property owner to watch his business dealings more carefully.

Another feature of the early English common law of theft is important to understanding how theft laws evolved. Larceny was a felony—a more serious crime than a misdemeanor—and at one time, all felonies were punishable by death. Early statutes provided, however, that if the amount stolen did not exceed a specified amount, the punishment might be imprisonment rather than death, but the amount was relatively small, equivalent to about the price of a sheep. In today's market, that would be worth less than a dime.

As money depreciated in value over the years and the statutes remained unchanged, the amount required for grand larceny, as compared with petit larceny, was very small. Many judges were reluctant to impose the death penalty in cases of grand larceny, and they began looking for technical ways to avoid finding the defendant guilty. One of those ways was to find something peculiar about the way in which the property was taken. The result was that many loopholes opened in the law of theft, with statutes being passed to fill the gaps in the law, resulting in a patchwork of laws pertaining to theft that are interesting as a matter of history but embarrassing as a matter of law enforcement.[3]

Modern types of theft

Because of the loopholes created in the common law and the belief that other types of "taking" or "stealing" should be included in the crime of theft, modern statutes are quite different from the English common law. The California statute is an example:

> Every person who shall feloniously steal, take, carry, lead, or drive away the personal property of another, or who shall fraudulently appropriate property which has been entrusted to him, or who shall knowingly and designedly, by any false or fraudulent representation or pretense, defraud any other person of money, labor or real or personal property . . . is guilty of theft.[4]

A statute as broadly worded as the California statute might include some of the "new" kinds of theft that have come to our attention in recent years. Let us look at a few examples that have occurred as technology has improved and life-styles have changed.

With the advent of modular telephones that can be plugged into almost any telephone connection has come the theft of telephones. Modular telephones are particularly susceptible to theft. Such phones allow the guest in a hotel to dial out without having to go through the hotel operator, a savings in time and cost. These phones do not have to be wired into the walls, a costly procedure. Some hotels, after several thefts of telephones, have spent additional money to secure the phones by wiring through the walls, buying devices that secure the phone in place, or replacing the phones with ones that are not modular.

Credit card thefts have become our fastest-growing crime, according to some experts. The estimated loss per year from credit card theft and fraud is $1 billion.[5] One credit card ring in the East charged $2 million each week in fourteen different states.[6] Credit card thefts thus indicate the relationship between what is often just theft and organized crime. Muggers, prostitutes, and burglars often steal credit cards and then sell them to credit card rings for $15 to $50 per card.

Cable television has also been the target of thefts. In Oklahoma, Tulsa Cable TV decided to spend $80,000 in advertising about cable TV theft and to offer $10 to anyone who returned an illegal cable TV box by a certain date, no questions asked. A rather effective ad on television and in the papers pictures "Larry" behind prison bars and carries the large caption, "Larry hooked himself up to Tulsa Cable. He got HBO, Cinemax . . . and Six Months. Stealing cable television service is a serious crime—a crime which could lead to a fine and imprisonment in the county jail." By the deadline, over eight thousand illegal boxes had been returned. Tulsa Cable warned that it would then begin gathering evidence and asking the state to prosecute violators who "stole" cable TV by illegally hooking up their sets. The number of sets returned under threat of prosecution may indicate that many people either see no wrong in this type of theft or think they will not get caught until pressure is put upon them through the media.

Like many other types of theft, stealing cable television has become "organized" and moved into "big business." In 1983, a man who called himself the "HBO Kid" was named as the mastermind of the largest known cable television piracy ring. This organization cost five legitimate firms up to $2.5 million over a five-year period. The men were so businesslike in their activities that they even made service calls. Their scheme involved selling cable television to customers for a one-time fee of between $100 and $125; the customer would thus have a lifetime service without paying the usual monthly fee required for legal access to cable television. The twenty-three-year-old mastermind was directly involved with the manufacture and sale of eleven hundred illegal converters between 1978 and 1983, when he was arrested and charged with one count of conspiracy and two counts of theft. His customers could also face criminal charges, but they were given a thirty-day grace period during which they could turn in the converters and not be prosecuted.

Finally, theft by computer is a modern way of stealing, but it is so extensive that it will be considered separately in the section on business crimes.

Larceny-theft: uniform crime reports definition

The exclusion of some types of theft from larceny-theft is made clear in the UCR's definition:

> Larceny-theft is the unlawful taking, carrying, leading, or riding away of property from the possession or constructive possession of another. It includes crimes such as shoplifting, pocket-picking, purse-snatching, thefts from motor vehicles, thefts of motor vehicle parts and accessories, bicycle thefts, etc., in which no use of force, violence, or fraud occurs. In the Uniform Crime Reporting Program, this crime category does not include embezzlement, "con" games, forgery, and worthless checks. Motor vehicle theft is also excluded from this category inasmuch as it is a separate Crime Index offense.[7]

UCR data   Combining so many different kinds of behavior into one category of theft may solve some legal technical problems, but it creates a heterogeneous category of behavior, as Figure 9.1 indicates. Thus, if we wish to study "thieves" by selecting persons who have been convicted of "larceny-theft," we shall find a wide range of people. But we shall exclude others who are in a real sense, thieves, such as people who steal computer time or who use their positions in banks to embezzle.

Larceny-theft offenses constitute the bulk of the crime index offenses recorded by the FBI. In 1982, over 7.1 million such offenses were recorded, constituting 55 percent of the index crimes and 61 percent of all property crimes. The crime rate for this offense decreased 1 percent from 1981, but the rate was twelve times higher than the rate in 1978.

The estimated loss nationally from this crime was $2.4 billion, with the average crime resulting in a $340 loss. "This estimated dollar loss is considered conservative since other studies have indicated that many offenses in the larceny category, particularly if the value of the stolen goods is small, never come to law enforcement attention."[8]

Finally, the arrest rate should be mentioned. Only 19 percent of larceny-thefts were cleared by arrest in 1982, but the number of persons arrested for this category of crimes rose 20 percent between 1978 and 1982. That increase represented a 41 percent increase in the arrest of adults and an 8 percent decrease in the arrest of persons under eighteen years of age. Of those arrested for larceny-theft violations, 29 percent were females, constituting the offense for which females were most frequently arrested in 1979.[9]

One word of caution in interpreting these data. Recall that in our discussion of robbery, we noted that one of the differences between theft and robbery was the use or threat of violence in robbery. We used the example of

Figure 9.1

Larceny analysis, 1982.

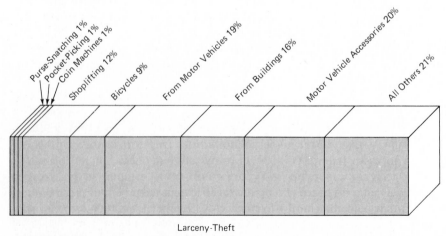

Larceny-Theft

Source: Federal Bureau of Investigation, Uniform Crime Reports, 1982 *(Washington, D.C.: Government Printing Office, 1983), p. 31.*

purse snatching. According to the UCR, this is a property crime of larceny-theft. But if sufficient force or the threat of force is used, the crime will be classified as robbery. It is these kinds of fine distinctions that make it necessary for us to realize that when we compare "robbers" with "thieves," we may not always be talking about different kinds of criminals.

Forgery

Forgery involves falsely making or altering a negotiable instrument, such as a check, that is legally enforceable, but this must be done with the intent to defraud. The most common type of forgery involves checks, and many of those who engage in check forgery are not professionals. Rather, they are what sociologists call *naive check forgers*. In an earlier study of check forgers, Edwin Lemert applied what he called his **closure theory** of behavior. The kind of person to whom this pertains is socially isolated and faces problems that tend to create even more isolation, such as divorce, unemployment, or alcoholism. The individual also has unresolved problems that usually require money. Check forging is seen as a way to clear up those problems or, in Lemert's words, to "get closure."[10]

Lemert found that check forgers did not associate with other criminals or engage in other types of crime. They were generally nonviolent and likable persons, older and more intelligent than most other criminals. He concluded that "naive check forgery arises at a critical point in a process of social isolation, out of certain types of social situations, and is made possible by the closure or constriction of behavior alternatives subjectively held as available to the forger."[11]

Shoplifting

Shoplifting, the illegal removal of merchandise from stores by persons posing as customers, has been steadily rising in recent years. According to the UCR, the volume of this type of larceny-theft increased 27 percent between 1978 and 1982. The National Coalition to Prevent Shoplifting estimates that the dollar loss to merchants from shoplifting is $26 billion a year.

Sociologists have studied shoplifters as types of people in addition to focusing on the merchants' reaction to shoplifting. We shall examine some of this research, beginning with the earlier study of Mary Owen Cameron.

A classic study: the "booster" and the "snitch." In 1964, Mary Owen Cameron published what has come to be a "classic" in the study of theft. After distinguishing the "snitch" (the pilferer) from the "booster" (the commercial shoplifter), Cameron concluded that "most shoplifting, including pilfering, appears to be chronic, habitual or systematic behavior."[12] In addition to the booster and the snitch, says Cameron, there might be a group of shoplifters who commit the offense because of an "unexpected urge to steal" or who are overcome "by an unpremeditated desire for a particular object."

Cameron's data indicated that most shoplifters are not associated with a criminal subculture. Most are females, and over 90 percent of them have probably never been convicted of another offense. Most are "respectable" women, many of whom are not employed outside the home. The value of the articles taken is small enough to lead to the conclusion that they were not stealing for "fences."[13] The items are usually taken for the shoplifter's personal use. Most of the women appear not to have thought about the possibility of being *arrested,* although they had considered that they might be caught. When apprehended, they often use the types of excuses and rationalizations characteristic of juveniles caught in a delinquent act. They do not manifest psychotic symptoms, and they are seldom recidivists. They probably have had childhood experiences with groups in which older children taught them the techniques of successful pilfering. Most of the women shoplifters are from families with modest budgets. They do not steal items they usually buy, but they steal "luxury" items that cannot come out of the family budget without sacrificing other family needs. The women rationalize that it is better to steal from the department store than from the family budget.

Pilferers, in contrast with other thieves, do not think of themselves as thieves and even when arrested will often resist defining their behavior as theft. The arrest procedure, however, including searching for the items in their possession, forces them to realize that their behavior is not just "bad"; it is illegal. The pilferer at this stage will often become quite upset, even hysterical. In contrast, the professional shoplifter, upon finding it impossible to talk her way out of an arrest, will accept the inevitable. The pilferer fears the reaction of family and expects no "in-group" support for the behavior in question. She does not know what to do or to whom to turn; the professional, in contrast, "either already knows what to do or knows precisely where and how to find out."

Finally, Cameron points out that the act of apprehension is usually sufficient to deter most pilferers from further illegal activity of this kind.[14] "Crime prevention would seem best achieved by helping the law violators retain their self-image of respectability while making it clear to them that a second offense will really mean disgrace."[15]

Shoplifting: a recent analysis. The extensive problem of shoplifting in England in recent years has led to studies of the crime, indicating that shoplifting is an enduring crime, highly resistant to efforts to control.[16] The offense gained wide publicity in England in late 1980, when Lady Isobel Barnett, widow of the lord mayor of Leicester, was arrested for shoplifting a can of tuna and a carton of cream, worth about $2.00. She admitted taking the items but said it was an oversight and that the cloth bag pinned inside her coat, where the items were placed, was normally used for the flashlight she carried for protection against muggers. Lady Barnett was convicted and finded $650 and court costs. Her comment was, "I have only myself to live with and I can live with myself." Four days later she was found dead, electrocuted in her bath, apparently a case of suicide. Newspapers in England carried front page headlines of these events, with one columnist reporting interviews with dozens of alleged female shoplifters, who were widowed or emotionally neglected by their husbands. They felt no guilt about the crime, and said that they did it for thrills and excitement. One woman indicated that shoplifting was sexually arousing. "I got an orgasm every time I slipped something into my handbag."[17]

BURGLARY

The second major type of property crime is burglary. The evolution of laws concerning burglary, like those involving larceny, indicates the problems the common law courts had in interpreting the elements of the crime. Because some of these elements have survived until recent legislation, it is important to look at the history of burglary.

The English common law—a historical development

Under the early English common law, burglary was defined as breaking and entering into the dwelling of another, in the nighttime, and with the intent to commit a felony, but it was punishable as a separate offense from that of the felony committed. The reason for the common law definition of burglary as a separate offense probably lies in the attempt to plug the loopholes in laws regarding attempted crimes. Attempted crimes are difficult to prove, and burglary is in effect defined as an attempt to commit another crime. Furthermore, the penalties for attempted crimes were usually less than for the completed crimes, a situation that also was changed by the categorization of burglary as a separate punishable crime. The result was that if the state could not prove all of the elements of the larceny or other crime that took place after the burglary, it might still be possible to convict on the crime of burglary.

Numerous problems arose with the common law definition of burglary. For example, what was meant by "breaking and entering"? The cases are fascinating and, in some instances, absurd. Early cases held that if the owner of a home left it unsecured, for example, did not close the door, he was not entitled to protection. Thus a person who entered the home through that door, even without permission, could not be convicted of burglary. Likewise, entering through an open door did not constitute breaking and entering. If the door or window was partly opened, opening it further to enter also would not meet the breaking-and-entering element of burglary. It was not, however, necessary that the door or windows be locked, only that they be closed.

The requirement of entering also presented problems. If an instrument were used to open the building and the instrument "entered" the building, that would not constitute entering unless that instrument was used in the commission of the felony for which the premises were entered. However, the entry of any part of the offender could constitute an "entry." The offender could also be held to have met this element of the crime by sending in a child or another person who could not be held legally responsible for the crime. In that situation, the offender was held to have "entered constructively."

The requirement of the "dwelling of another" also raised interesting legal problems. A person's home was his castle, and it was believed that breaking and entering that dwelling was a heinous crime, punishable by death. The occupant did not have to be present; indeed, he could have been absent for a long time, but it had to be his dwelling place. An unfinished house would not count even if the workmen slept there. In some circumstances, the term *dwelling* also included barns, stables, and other outhouses.

The burglary, under common law, must have been committed in the nighttime. The difference between night and day was defined as "whether the countenance of a man could be discerned by natural light even though the sun may have set. Artificial light or moonlight, regardless of their intensity, would not suffice." Finally, the offender, to be convicted of burglary, had to intend to commit a felony while in the dwelling. Passing through the home to commit a felony elsewhere would not suffice.[18]

Modern definitions and data on burglary

Over the years the meaning of burglary has been changed to the extent that statutes today bear little resemblance to the common law definition. Modern statutes are much broader; most do not require breaking; and they cover entry at all times of all kinds of structures. Illustrative of this approach is the *Uniform Crime Reports* definition of burglary: " . . . the unlawful entry of a structure to commit a felony or theft. The use of force to gain entry is not required to classify an offense as burglary. Burglary in this Program is categorized into three subclassifications: forcible entry, unlawful entry where no force is used, and attempted forcible entry."[19]

The 1982 volume of reported data on burglary represented an 8.7 percent drop from the volume in 1981. The rate of burglaries per 100,000 inhabitants also decreased by 9.6 percent during that period. But when burglaries for 1982 are compared with those for 1978, the volume is up in all categories by time, ranging from an increase of 12 percent in nonresidence burglary during the daytime to a low of 1 percent in nonresidence burglary during the nighttime. In 1982, burglaries accounted for 27 percent of the crime index total and 30 percent of the property crimes.

Seventy-three percent of the burglaries recorded by the UCR involved forcible entry. Victims of the crime of burglary suffered an estimated total loss of $3 billion, with the average loss per burglary set at $880. Only 15 percent of the crimes were cleared by arrest. Most of the people arrested for burglary were males, with females constituting only six out of every one hundred arrests.[20]

THE CAREER CRIMINAL Sociologists have approached the study of types of thieves in several different ways. Some have studied the people convicted of theft or burglary and attempted to discover whether these "types" of criminals have any distinguishable characteristics.[21] Others have looked at the circumstances surrounding the crime itself, for example, the type of establishment burglarized, the value of the loss, the type of entry (forced or nonforced), and the hour of the day or night.[22] Still others have looked at characteristics of the area in which the crime took place.[23] Finally, some researchers have concentrated on the characteristics of the victims of the crime.[24] The most extensive work, however, has been in the area of professional, or **career criminals.**

The earlier studies of career criminals focused on those who specialized,

Most major cities of the world have a serious problem with professional thieves who successfully pick pockets while victims are distracted.

for example, in professional theft; later studies have examined repeat offenders who may not be "professional" in their skills and attitudes.

PROFESSIONAL CRIMINAL BEHAVIOR: THE EARLY APPROACH

Numerous writers on professional crime have pointed out that over a long period of time there has been little change in conceptual categories of professional crime. In general, the professional criminal, such as the professional thief, manifests highly developed criminal career behavior characterized by nonviolence, a high degree of skill, loyalty toward the loosely organized group rather than toward individuals, association with other professionals as opposed to amateur criminals, long careers characterized by few arrests, and an attitude toward society that sees noncriminals as people who deserve to be victimized. Professional criminals have a status hierarchy that is related to a combination of the use of great skill and the expectation of high profits. They are not from the extremes of poverty; they start crime later in life than other criminals; and their peer group becomes important to reinforcing their deviant self-concepts and attitudes.[25]

The professional thief: Sutherland's study

The classic study of professional criminals was made by Edwin Sutherland, who talked extensively with a thief who had been in that profession for more than twenty years. He had the thief write on several topics and then submitted the manuscript to other professional thieves and talked with still others. He said that none disagreed with the account.[26]

Sutherland described the profession of theft as a group way of life that had all the characteristics of other groups—techniques, codes, status, traditions, consensus, and organization. He pointed out that these characteristics were not pathological. In addition, apprenticeship and tutelage by professional thieves were prerequisites for becoming a professional, and an individual had to be recognized by professional thieves in order to become one.

Contemporary conceptualizations of professional thieves

Traditional conceptions of professional criminals have been criticized, as most were based mainly on anecdotes and case studies[27] and were not systematic sociological approaches.[28] Few attempts were made to test propositions, and professional crime was often confused with full-time crime, the latter characterizing individuals who did not have the skills and other characteristics of professional criminals. More recent studies have tried to resolve these problems.

CAREER CRIMINALS: THE MODERN APPROACH

The skills, knowledge, attitudes, and values of "professional criminals" that were emphasized by earlier researchers may not be as important to the public today as are the "full-time" criminals. Today the stress is on the repeat offender, especially when he or she is violent. Most people are not terribly concerned with whether the offender is "professional," as a very unprofessional job in violent crime is still feared—nor is there a great concern for the attitudes and group affiliations of the person who burglarizes your home! This modern approach includes studies of what one sociologist called "semi-professional property offenders."[29]

Semiprofessional property offenders are distinguished from professional criminals in their lack of skill and the absence of a complex interactional pattern that is found among professional criminals. These criminals see themselves as "victims" of society and as a result have no guilt feelings about their behavior. In comparison with professional criminals, they are more hostile toward law enforcement officials as well as toward society, their parents, and occupational roles. Most remain in crime through middle age, at which point some change to noncriminal activities. Several studies indicate that an increasing number of amateurs are involved in bank robberies and car thefts,[30] and other studies show that these offenders have a rather stable criminal career.[31] It has also been found that semiprofessional burglars are predominantly nonwhite, male, and young and that the victims of burglary are also mainly from the lower class.[32] Finally, a study of black armed robbers found that they are generally older than other felons are, with predominantly lower-class urban backgrounds, a history of criminal activity as teenagers, and an unstable family background.[33]

The Rand Corporation studies In 1975, the Rand Corporation first received funding from the National Institute of Justice to study habitual offenders, and their final report was published in 1982.[34] These studies concentrated on **selective incapacitation** as a method for coping with increasing crime rates and overcrowded prisons. "Selective incapacitation is a strategy that attempts to use objective actuarial evidence to improve the ability of the current system to identify and confine offenders who represent the most serious risk to the community."[35] By studying repeat offenders, a formula can be developed by which predictions can be made with regard to how much crime is prevented by the incarceration of certain kinds of offenders. It is therefore necessary to know something about repeat offenders.

Methodology and sample. The Rand studies are based on data collected through self-reporting. Previous studies of the self-reporting of crime have indicated that most people have at some time committed a crime, although most have not been caught. However, most people do not commit the serious crimes of assault, homicide, robbery, rape, or burglary,[36] and only a small percentage who do commit them do so over a long period of time. For example, in a follow-up analysis of ten thousand boys, investigators found that 65 percent had no contact with the police. Those who did were categorized as "one-time offenders," "multiple offenders," and "chronic offenders." It was found that 46 percent of the delinquents stopped after the first offense, and of those who committed more than one offense, 35 percent had no more than three offenses.[37]

The Rand studies focused on the small percentage of offenders who do commit many offenses. The first Rand sample consisted of 49 prison inmates in California. The interviewers administered self-report question-naires face-to-face and asked questions about the offender's entire criminal career, in contrast with most of the earlier studies that administered anonymous questionnaires to students or other groups from the general population.[38] The next study used a sample of 624 inmates from five California prisons, selected to represent all male prisoners in that state in terms of custody level, age, offense, and race. The questionnaires were administered anonymously and focused on the inmates' criminal activities during the three years before their current incarceration.[39] Finally, a sample of 2,190 prison and jail inmates in three states, California, Michigan, and Texas, was gathered.[40]

Findings of the Rand studies. The first Rand study found that most offenders were not specialized in their criminal activity. At any given time, they engaged in a variety of criminal activities. Too, few criminals committed crimes at a high rate; most did so at a fairly low rate, and the rate of violent crime among these inmates was very low.[41] These findings were confirmed in the study of 624 male inmates in California. Most of the inmates reported having committed several other kinds of crime during the three years before their current incarceration. Of those who reported having committed any other type of crime than the one for which he was committed, 49 percent listed more than four other crimes. Again, as in the earlier study, only a few inmates committed most of the reported crimes.

The investigators also found that age was not strongly associated with offense rates nor was having served a previous prison term. What was significant however, was self-concept: "High-rate offenders tended to share a set of beliefs that were consistent with their criminal lifestyle—e.g., that they could beat the odds, that they were better than the average criminal, that crime was exciting, and that regular work was boring."[42]

The larger sample of 2,190 prison and jail inmates from three states was selected for study in order to check on possible problems in the first two samples and to include lesser offenses normally represented by jail populations. Analysis of self-report data from this study confirmed that most offenders report committing few crimes; only a few commit many crimes. Offenders were placed into categories, with the most serious being those who reported having committed robbery, assault, and drug deals during the period covered by the study. They were termed *violent predators* and usually reported having committed the crimes of robbery, assault, and drug deals at high rates and also numerous other property crimes.

Finally, an analysis of the study of 624 male inmates in California looked at the results in terms of three kinds of information, summarized as follows.

Personal characteristics—age, race, drug use. Younger offenders were more likely than older offenders to be heavily involved in crime. Although older offenders commit crimes in about the same numbers as younger ones do, they *reduce* the type of criminal involvement, although they continue to engage in different types of crime. "Younger offenders were more likely than older offenders to have extensive juvenile records, to use drugs, and to have criminal attitudes and self-identities," each of which is associated with high levels of criminal activity.

The self-report data indicated that on the average, white offenders were more violent and dangerous than were black offenders, although a disproportionate number of offenders in the sample were black. Blacks reported committing lower rates of crime and fewer types of crime. "The effects of race remain when the analyses are adjusted for other characteristics . . . such as prior record, age, drug use, or psychological characteristics."

Drug use was high, especially for those who reported property crimes. Drug use was not significantly related to violent crimes when the offenders' age and psychological characteristics were controlled.

Experience with the criminal justice system. There was no association between the number of prior prison terms and the reported commission of crimes; in fact, offenders who reported high criminal activity "were more likely to have been placed repeatedly on probation."

Analysis of reported criminal activity compared with the offense for which the offenders were committed at the time of the survey revealed how misleading it was to categorize offenders by the offense for which they were committed. The report gave three reasons: First, most offenders who had committed a particular type of crime had not been convicted of that crime. Second, a substantial number of respondents reported that they had only infrequently committed the crime for which they had been convicted. Third, relying on a single principal conviction offense label obscured the differences among offenders convicted of the same offense. The report estimated that "a typical group of 100 persons convicted of robbery would have committed 490 armed robberies, 310 assaults, 720 burglaries, 70 auto thefts, 100 forgeries, and 3400 drug sales in the previous year of street time."

Finally, offenders who reported that they started criminal activity at a very young age and engaged in serious criminal activity while young were more likely to report repeated offenses, both violent and property crime. "Indeed, respondents who became involved in crime before they were 13 reported the most crime." For them it was, in their words, "just a way of life."

Social-psychological characteristics. Respondents who did not work and those who moved from city to city reported more criminal activity, but although these findings were significant, psychological characteristics and drug use were more significant variables in predicting adult criminal behavior. For example, the study found a strong association between criminal activity and self-concept. Offenders who reported high criminal activity thought of themselves as criminals, in contrast with others who thought of themselves as "straight."

When asked why they committed their crimes, the offenders gave three main reasons: (1) distressed economic conditions reported by 47 percent; (2) desire for high living and high times, 35 percent; and (3) temper, 14 percent. The greatest criminal activity was reported by those who listed high living as their reason, whereas those who cited economic reasons reported the least amount of criminal activity.

In conclusion, the offenders identified as career criminals saw themselves as criminals; they expected to return to crime after release from prison; they began their criminal careers early in their juvenile years; they were hedonistic, viewing crime as "a safe and enjoyable way to obtain the good life"; and they viewed themselves as proficient criminals. They represented only 25 percent of the sample, but they committed 58 percent of all reported armed robberies, 65 percent of burglaries, 60 percent of auto thefts, and 46 percent of assaults. The investigators wisely pointed out that the criminal justice system might benefit by directing its incarceration efforts at these types of offenders rather than at the majority of offenders who do not exhibit these characteristics. "Presumably these offenders pose less of a threat to society than do career criminals. Their confinement, lengthy or not, may provide society with far less protection than confinement of career criminals."

But one warning note: the study indicated that career property offenders can be identified, and some of them commit violent crimes, but "it provides no evidence of an identifiable group of career criminals who commit only violence."[43]

Career criminals: the Bureau of Justice Statistics Special Report
In June 1983, the Bureau of Justice Statistics (BJS) issued its Special Report on Career Criminals, the first in a series of reports on crime issues of national concern.[44] The report was based on available national data on crime.

The BJS report briefly reviewed other studies of criminal careers, noting that most are retrospective studies in which known offenders are questioned about their previous criminal activity, as in the case of the Rand studies. The second most common type of study is the prospective study of officially known offenders. In this type, offenders are tracked after their release from confinement, usually for a period of a few years. Official data on crime are used, but like the retrospective studies, the prospective studies also often rely on self-report data of criminal activity. An example of this type of study was the FBI analysis of the subsequent criminal activity of offenders paroled from prison in 1972. That study found that within two years, two-thirds of the parolees had been rearrested at least once, with a rate of 67 percent for young adult parolees and less than 50 percent for middle-aged parolees.[45]

A third type of study of career criminals analyzes prospective data on the general population. This type of study is rare, but one widely recognized and extensive example is the study of ten thousand young males born in Philadelphia in 1945. Their criminal activity (or the lack of such) was investigated from adolescence into young adulthood, revealing that those who engaged in criminal activity as adolescents were more likely to do so as adults than were those who as adolescents did not commit criminal acts.[46]

Most of these studies are based on samples of the population from one area or only a few areas. The BJS study, on the other hand, used data on offenders from across the country. A random sample of 11,397 men and women offenders were personally interviewed during October and November 1979 and questioned extensively about their criminal careers.[47] Because the study's major purpose was to examine criminal careers, only those inmates who were at least forty at the date of last admission to prison were selected for intensive study. When statistically weighted, the 827 in that sample represented 24,398 inmates.

The data in the BJS study were analyzed as four types of offenders, all of whom were middle aged (forty or older) at the time of their last admission to prison. The typologies pertain to three of the major stages of life: adolescence (seven through seventeen), young adulthood (eighteen through thirty-nine), and middle age (forty and over). The sample was divided into the following:

> Type 1—offenders who engaged in criminal activity in all three stages.
> Type 2—offenders who engaged in criminal activity in all but young adulthood.
> Type 3—offenders who engaged in criminal activity in all but adolescence.
> Type 4—offenders who engaged in criminal activity in middle age only.

Table 9.1 indicates the number and percentage of inmates in each category. Of these category types, Types 1 and 2 offenders engaged in some criminal activity during adolescence, and combining those types in Table 9.1 reveals that 15.2 percent of the middle-aged inmates reported criminal activity during adolescence. But Type 2 inmates did not engage in criminal activity during young adulthood; rather, they were law abiding during that time and then returned to criminal activity in middle age. They represent an insignificant percentage of the inmate population, but it is significant that 92 percent of those offenders who reported criminal activity during adolescence continued it during young adulthood and into middle age. These are Type 1 offenders.

Perhaps the most surprising finding of this study is that the Type 4

Table 9.1

Number and percent distribution of middle-aged inmates by type of criminal career

Career Type	Number of Inmates (Unweighted)	Estimated Number of Inmates (Weighted)	% of Inmates
1	116	3,419	14.0
2	10	299*	1.2*
3	318	9,316	38.2
4	383	11,362	46.6
Total	827	24,398	100.0

Note: Detail may not add to total shown because of rounding.
*Estimate based on 10 or fewer cases is statistically unreliable.
Source: "Career Patterns in Crime," Bureau of Justice Statistics Special Report, U.S. Department of Justice (Washington, D.C.: U.S. Government Printing Office, June 1983), p. 2.

offenders, those middle-aged offenders who did not engage in criminal activity as adolescents or as young adults, represented almost half of all the inmates who entered prison in middle age. The BJS report explains this finding in terms of the reasons for incarceration. Persons arrested for property offenses often are incarcerated for those offenses only if they have prior criminal records. But those who commit violent personal crimes are likely to be incarcerated even without a prior criminal record. In this study, 66.4 percent of Type 4 offenders were currently in prison for violent crimes, compared with 46.6 percent of Type 1 offenders, the least likely to be currently imprisoned for a violent crime. Type 1 offenders, who represented only 14 percent of the total sample, accounted for 23.2 percent of the robberies, 32.9 percent of the burglaries, 26.8 percent of the larceny-thefts, 18.4 percent of other property offenses, 16.4 percent of the drug-trafficking crimes, and 20 percent of the drug possession crimes. But Type 4 offenders, representing 47 percent of the sample, were responsible for 64.7 percent of the murders, 54.7 percent of the manslaughters, and 57.9 percent of rapes and sexual assaults. Analysis of the data, however, indicated that although not currently as frequently confined for a violent crime as Type 4 offenders were, Types 1 and 3 offenders were just as likely to have been convicted and served time for violent crimes at some point in their criminal career.

It is therefore critical in an analysis of the crimes for which offenders are currently incarcerated to consider their prior records. Thus, the fact that 40 percent of the inmates in the above study were serving time for property offenses, not violent crimes, does not necessarily mean that too many people are being incarcerated for nonviolent crimes; rather, violence has been a part of the past record of many of these "property offenders." Finally, the report suggested that although the study did not investigate the issue, it is likely that the high rates of incarceration for violent crimes of the over-forty offenders represent domestic violence.

MODERN PROPERTY CRIMES

We began this chapter with a brief historical account of the evolution of the regulation of property crimes, noting that English common law distinguished between the clever acts of deceit and fraud to acquire the property of another and the direct, immediate taking of that property. It is perhaps the willingness not only to tolerate but even admire some of those early business deals, considered to be "shrewd," that underlies our reaction to the "shady" and in many cases illegal activities of the business world today. Our discussion of "modern" crimes will begin with the concept of white-collar crime.

WHITE-COLLAR CRIME

The term **white-collar crime** was coined by Edwin H. Sutherland in 1939 in his presidential address to the American Sociological Society and was later developed in a published work.[48] The concept, however, was not new, having appeared under the phrase "criminals of the upperworld" in a 1935 textbook.

By white-collar crime, Sutherland meant "a crime committed by a person of respectability and high social status in the course of his occupation." Embezzlement by a banker, illegal sales of alcohol and narcotics or price fixing by physicians, or frauds of a client's securities by a lawyer would be examples. Sutherland stated his thesis of white-collar crime:

> Persons of the upper socio-economic class engage in much criminal behavior; that this criminal behavior differs from the criminal behavior of the lower socio-economic class principally in the administrative procedures which are used in dealing with the offenders; and that variations in administrative procedures are not significant from the point of view of causation of crime.[49]

Sutherland was not trying to redefine those white-collar crimes, nor was he saying that the law should consider offenders of such crimes as criminals and handle them in the criminal courts, as opposed to administrative agencies. His concern was "for reforming criminology and nothing else." Sutherland was saying that if we want to know why crimes are committed, it is just as important to study white-collar crimes as it is the crimes of those who are processed through the criminal courts and incarcerated in penal institutions. Sutherland's criterion, then, is "punishability," not whether a person was actually sentenced to punishment by the criminal courts.

Analysis of the concept of white-collar crime

Not all recent scholars have accepted Sutherland's inclusion in white-collar crime of those actions that are violations of federal regulatory statutes or regulations of administrative agencies.[50] One suggestion is to replace the concept of white-collar crime with that of "occupation crime." The two concepts would in some cases be synonymous, but "the crucial point is that the behavior to be included in the concept must be directly related to occupations that are regarded as legitimate in the society. Thus, occupational crime can be defined as violation of the legal codes in the course of activity in a legitimate occupation,"[51] in contrast with "corporate criminal behavior," which includes such offenses as restraint of trade, false advertising, fraudulent sales, misuse of trademarks, and manufacture of unsafe foods and drugs.[52]

Sutherland's limitation of white-collar crimes to the upper-class's occupational crimes is also rejected by most authorities today. In defense of Sutherland's limitation, it has been emphasized that he was reacting to the social and economic situation of the 1930s. "In his time, and in his environment, only the wealthier classes had access to the requisite machinery necessary for the enactment of many of the crimes included in his concept of white-collar crime. . . . Technology and mass communications would ultimately open those areas of criminal endeavor to all strata of society."[53] One of the most dramatic and potentially far-reaching crimes made possible by this development of technology is computer crime, discussed later in this chapter.

The definition of white-collar crime adopted by the Congress's Subcommittee on Crime, Committee on the Judiciary, is as follows: "an illegal act or series of illegal acts committed by non-physical means and by concealment or guile, to obtain money or property, to avoid the payment or loss of money or property, or to obtain personal or business advantage," including corporate crime. This definition was adopted by Congress in 1979 in the Justice System Administration Improvement Act.[54] The other kinds of crime that might be included in this definition of white-collar crimes are extensive, and categorization is difficult. Herbert Edelhertz, a noted authority on the subject, has examined some of the ways in which white-collar crimes might be categorized, and he concluded that the best one would be to classify the various crimes "by the general environment and motivation of the perpetrator," and for that purpose he suggests:

1. Crimes by persons operating on an individual, ad hoc basis, for personal gain in a nonbusiness context. . . .
2. Crimes in the course of their occupations by those operating inside businesses, Government, or other establishments, or in a professional capacity, in violation of their duty of loyalty and fidelity to employer or client. . . .
3. Crimes incidental to and in furtherance of business operations, but not the central purpose of such business operations. . . .
4. White-collar crimes as a business, or as the central activity of the business. . . . [55]

Table 9.2 lists the various kinds of criminal activity that might be included under each of these categories. It is included here, despite its length, to show the wide variety of crimes that might fall under the rubric of white-collar crime.

White-collar law breaking. One final definition incorporates more than white-collar crime. The term *white-collar law breaking* includes those types of actions that are processed in civil courts or through administrative processes and thus technically are not "crimes." After extensively studying the sources of data on white-collar crime, Albert J. Reiss, Jr., and Albert D. Biderman decided that a new definition was needed:

> Our investigations quickly convinced us that the distinctions between civil, criminal, and administrative law and their definitions of violations and penalties are artifacts of these bodies of law and their administration, and that these distinctions are applied in practice more often than not in arbitrary and highly variable ways. They do not afford a satisfactory basis for defining for social descriptive purposes a set of events usefully treated as "white collar," as distinct from other kinds of violations of law.[56]

Reiss and Biderman also rejected the "social-status" connotation of the term *white collar* but decided that given the impact of the term *white collar* on our thinking, it would be useless to substitute a new term. They therefore decided on the term *white-collar law breaking* or *violations* defined as follows:

> White-collar violations are those violations of law to which penalties are attached and that involve the use of a violator's position of significant power, influence, or trust in the legitimate economic or political institutional order for the purpose of illegal gain, or to commit an illegal act for personal or organizational gain.[57]

Data on white-collar crime   Reiss and Biderman, whose purpose in studying white-collar violations was to examine and explore all of the sources of data, concluded that "vast amounts [of] data exist on white-collar law violations, but that problems in conceptualization, classification, and counting are barriers to the merging of information into statistical series."[58]

There are, however, estimates of the extent of white-collar crime, although we can never be sure how accurate they are or, for that matter, what types of crimes (or violations) are included. The federal government has estimated the cost to society of upperworld crimes to be more than $40 billion annually; others have estimated the figure to be as high as $100 billion, not including the cost of apprehension and adjudication.[59]

Other sources claim that the financial loss to the American public is higher than the government estimates. In a 1979 report, *Newsweek* ran the headline "Crime in the Suites," in which it claimed, "An explosion of white-collar crime that costs the nation 'staggering billions' of dollars every

Table 9.2

Categories of white-collar crimes (excluding organized crime)

A. Crimes by persons operating on an individual ad hoc basis
1. Purchases on credit with no intention to pay, or purchases by mail in the name of another.
2. Individual income tax violations.
3. Credit card frauds.
4. Bankruptcy frauds.
5. Title II home improvement loan frauds.
6. Frauds with respect to social security, unemployment insurance, or welfare.
7. Unorganized or occasional frauds on insurance companies (theft, casualty, health, etc.).
8. Violations of Federal Reserve regulations by pledging stock for further purchases, flouting margin requirements.
9. Unorganized "lonely hearts" appeal by mail.

B. Crimes in the course of their occupations by those operating inside business. Government, or other establishments, in violation of their duty of loyalty and fidelity to employer or client
1. Commercial bribery and kickbacks, i.e., by and to buyers, insurance adjusters, contracting officers, quality inspectors, government inspectors and auditors, etc.
2. Bank violations by bank officers, employees, and directors.
3. Embezzlement or self-dealing by business or union officers and employees.
4. Securities fraud by insiders trading to their advantage by the use of special knowledge, or causing their firms to take positions in the market to benefit themselves.
5. Employee petty larceny and expense account frauds.
6. Frauds by computer, causing unauthorized payouts.
7. "Sweetheart contracts" entered into by union officers.
8. Embezzlement or self-dealing by attorneys, trustees, and fiduciaries.
9. Fraud against the Government.
   (a) Padding of payrolls.
   (b) Conflicts of interest.
   (c) False travel, expense, or per diem claims.

C. Crimes incidental to and in furtherance of business operations, but not the central purpose of the business
1. Tax violations.
2. Antitrust violations.
3. Commercial bribery of another's employee, officer or fiduciary (including union officers).
4. Food and drug violations.
5. False weights and measures by retailers.
6. Violations of Truth-in-Lending Act by misrepresentation of credit terms and prices.
7. Submission or publication of false financial statements to obtain credit.
8. Use of fictitious or over-valued collateral.
9. Check-kiting to obtain operating capital on short term financing.
10. Securities Act violations, i.e., sale of non-registered securities, to obtain operating capital, false proxy statements, manipulation of market to support corporate credit or access to capital markets, etc.
11. Collusion between physicians and pharmacists to cause the writing of unnecessary prescriptions.
12. Dispensing by pharmacists in violation of law, excluding narcotics traffic.
13. Immigration fraud in support of employment agency operations to provide domestics.
14. Housing code violations by landlords.
15. Deceptive advertising.
16. Fraud against the Government.
    (a) False claims.
    (b) False statements:
        (1) to induce contracts
        (2) AID frauds

(3) Housing frauds

(4) SBA frauds, such as SBIC bootstrapping, selfdealing, cross-dealing, etc., or obtaining direct loans by use of false financial statements.

(c) Moving contracts in urban renewal.

17. Labor violations (Davis-Bacon Act).

18. Commercial espionage.

D. White-collar crime as a business, or as the central activity

1. Medical or health frauds.

2. Advance fee swindles.

3. Phony contests.

4. Bankruptcy fraud, including schemes devised as salvage operation after insolvency of otherwise legitimate businesses.

5. Securities fraud and commodities fraud.

6. Chain referral schemes.

7. Home improvement schemes.

8. Debt consolidation schemes.

9. Mortgage milking.

10. Merchandise swindles:

(a) Gun and coin swindles

(b) General merchandise

(c) Buying or pyramid clubs.

11. Land frauds.

12. Directory advertising schemes.

13. Charity and religious frauds.

14. Personal improvement schemes.

(a) Diploma Mills

(b) Correspondence Schools

(c) Modeling Schools

15. Fraudulent application for, use and/or sale of credit cards, airline tickets, etc.

16. Insurance frauds

(a) Phony accident rings.

(b) Looting of companies by purchase of over-valued assets, phony management contracts, self-dealing with agents, inter-company transfers, etc.

(c) Frauds by agents writing false policies to obtain advance commissions.

(d) Issuance of annuities or paidup life insurance, with no consideration, so that they can be used as collateral for loans.

(e) Sales by misrepresentations to military personnel or those otherwise uninsurable.

17. Vanity and song publishing schemes.

18. Ponzi schemes.

19. False security frauds, i.e., Billy Sol Estes or De Angelis type schemes.

20. Purchase of banks or control thereof, with deliberate intention to loot them.

21. Fraudulent establishing and operation of banks or savings and loan associations.

22. Fraud against the Government

(a) Organized income tax refund swindles, sometimes operated by income tax "counselors."

(b) AID frauds, i.e., where totally worthless goods shipped.

(c) F.H.A. frauds.

(1) Obtaining guarantees of mortgages on multiple family housing far in excess of value of property with foreseeable inevitable foreclosure.

(2) Home improvement frauds.

23. Executive placement and employment agency frauds.

24. Coupon redemption frauds.

25. Money order swindles.

Source: Herbert Edelhertz, *The Nature, Impact and Prosecution of White-Collar Crime,* National Institute of Law Enforcement and Criminal Justice (Washington, D.C.: U.S. Government Printing Office, 1970), pp. 73–75.

HIGHLIGHT
What Are White-Collar Crimes?

There is much debate over the proper definition of "white-collar" crime. Reiss and Biderman define it as violations of law "that involve the use of a violator's position of significant power, influence or trust . . . for the purpose of illegal gain, or to commit an illegal act for personal or organizational gain."[1]

White-collar crimes include such traditional illegalities as embezzlement, bribery, fraud, theft of services, theft of trade secrets, forgery, smuggling, tax evasion, obstruction of justice, and others, where the violator's position of fiduciary trust, power, or influence has provided the opportunity to abuse lawful institutions for unlawful purposes. White-collar offenses frequently involve deception.

New forms of white-collar crime involving political and corporate institutions have emerged in the past decade. For example, the dramatic growth in high technology has brought with it sensational accounts of computerized "heists" by sophisticated felons seated safely behind computer terminals. The specter of electronic penetration of the Nation's financial assets has spurred widespread interest in computer security by business and government alike.

In the area of political crime, exposés of illegal campaign contributions and the ability of powerful financial elements to influence government have gravely disturbed the public.

Some Organized Crime Is White-Collar Crime

"Organized crime" refers to those self-perpetuating, structured, and disciplined associations of individuals, or groups, combined together for the purpose of obtaining monetary or commercial gains or profits, wholly or in part by illegal means, while protecting their activities through a pattern of graft and corruption.

Organized crime groups possess certain characteristics that include but are not limited to the following:

- Their illegal activities are conspiratorial.
- In at least part of their activities, they commit or threaten to commit acts of violence or other acts that are likely to intimidate.
- They conduct their activities in a methodical, systematic, or highly disciplined and secret fashion.
- They insulate their leadership from direct involvement in illegal activities by their intricate organizational structure.
- They attempt to gain influence in government, politics, and commerce through corruption, graft, and legitimate means.
- They have economic gain as their primary goal, not only from patently illegal enterprises such as drugs, gambling, and loansharking, but also from such activities as laundering illegal money through and investment in legitimate business.

[1]Albert J. Reiss, Jr., and Albert D. Biderman, *Data Sources on White-Collar Lawbreaking,* National Institute of Justice (Washington, D.C.: Government Printing Office, September 1980), p.1.Source: Bureau of Justice Statistics, *Report to the Nation on Crime and Justice: The Data* (Washington, D.C.: Government Printing Office, 1983), p. 3.

year."[60] A study of illegal corporate behavior pointed out that the cost of corporate crime, one type of white-collar crime, does not begin to indicate the full cost of such crimes to the American public. That report mentioned the "injuries and health hazards to workers and consumers . . . the incalculable costs of the damages done to the physical environment and the great social costs of the erosion of the moral base of our society. They destroy public confidence in business and our capitalist system as a whole, and they inflict serious damages on the corporations themselves and on their competitors." Indeed, the report went further in referring to the statements of Ralph Nader that even in the matter of death, corporate crimes have a greater impact than do "street crimes" on the American public. "Far more persons are killed through corporate criminal activities than by individual criminal homicides; even if death is an indirect result the person still died."[61]

Reaction to white-collar crime

Sutherland felt that the public reaction to white-collar crimes was not severe, that most people just accepted the crimes.[62] More recently, however, studies have revealed that public reaction varies according to the crime's perceived impact. For example, in a study of two hundred people asked to give their reaction to types of crime, including white-collar as well as some of the more conventional crimes, physical impact crimes were considered more serious than those with only economic impact.[63]

In a recent replication of an earlier study of public reaction to white-collar crime, investigators concluded that the public perception of its seriousness had increased more than its perceptions of other crimes. It is, however, important to realize that white-collar crime is not a unitary concept and that the public reaction differs according to the specific crime. Finally, it is a mistake to believe that just because most of us do not consider white-collar crime to be as serious as other crimes, for example, crimes of violence, we therefore do not consider this type of crime to be at all serious.[64]

CORPORATE CRIME

Earlier studies of white-collar crime focused on individuals committing their crimes in secret, such as embezzlement.[65] The lack of attention to **corporate crime** may have been due to the complexity not only of the crimes but also of the corporate structure. A thorough understanding of corporate crime requires expertise in areas that traditionally have not been a part of criminologists' training. Then, the regulation of corporate crime is often carried out in administrative agencies rather than in courts. Sociologists and criminologists have generally not been as familiar with such agencies as with the judicial court process. Finally, research funds have been more readily available for the study of conventional crime than for corporate crime.[66]

Today, however, the primary emphasis is on corporate crime, the crimes of organizations, and thus the term *corporate crime* is more frequently used than *white-collar crime.*

Corporate crime is a form of white-collar crime, but unlike the latter, which often involves individuals or small groups of individuals acting within their professional or occupational capacity, corporate crime is "organizational crime," which occurs "in the context of extremely complex interrelationships. . . . Here it is the organization, not the occupation, that is of prime importance."[67] A more precise distinction between the two is

> if a policymaking corporate executive is acting in the name of the corporation and the individual's decision to violate the law is for the benefit of the corporation, as in price-fixing violations, the violation would constitute corporate crime.
>
> If, on the other hand, the corporate official acts against the corporation, as in the case of embezzlement, and financing benefits in a personal way from his official connections with the corporation, his acts would constitute white collar or occupational crime.[68]

Why change the emphasis from individual white-collar crime (and the more conventional crimes) to corporate crime? First, in this century, we have "witnessed a tremendous explosion in the number and size of corporations, to the point that virtually all economic and much social and political activity is greatly influenced by corporate behavior. During this same period, and partly as a response, there has been a dramatic increase in the efforts of the federal government to regulate that activity through the creation of multitudinous administrative agencies and volume upon volume of regulatory laws."[69]

Second, even though the media gave little publicity to the prosecution of corporate crimes during Sutherland's studies, that is not the case today. Third, the efforts of consumer advocate Ralph Nader have had a tremendous impact on public concern with corporate crime as well as on the legislative efforts to curb such crime. Fourth, greater concern with the environment, coupled with the realization that many corporations contribute to the pollution of the environment, led to the creation of the federal Environmental Protection Agency and other legislation in this area.

Fifth, the lack of success in curbing crime during the emphasis in the 1960s on the eradication of poverty, thought to be the best way to attack the crime problem, led to the realization that in concentrating crime control efforts on the poor, not only was the crime problem not being solved, but crimes committed by middle- and upper-class persons and corporations were being ignored. Similarly, the black revolution and the prison reform movement of the 1960s and 1970s, as well as the short sentences imposed on Watergate offenders, again focused attention on differential treatment in the criminal justice system. Finally, the influence of the Marxist or neo-Marxist writings in criminology has been on this differential treatment.

"Although their positions have often been overstated, they have had a salutary effort in making criminologists question whether they have been class-biased in their research and other work. Criminologists have become aware that they have perhaps contributed to the public image of 'the criminal' as a lower class person who commits the conventional crimes of larceny and burglary rather than the crimes of the corporate suites."[70]

Recent studies of corporate crime   In October 1979, the results of the "first large-scale comprehensive investigation of corporations directly related to their violations of law" was published.[71] This project, conducted by Marshall Clinard, included a thorough explanation of the types of crime included in corporate crime, attempted predictions of corporate crime violations, and analyzed methodological problems of studying corporate crime and statutory efforts to control the phenomenon. This study revealed that two-thirds of the sample's corporations were found to have violated criminal laws, and some corporations had done so repeatedly.

The two-thirds figure cited by Clinard is much higher than data reported by the media,[72] though his study has been severely criticized. The reasons are its methodology and its faulty conclusions, resulting from a study based on an imprecise definition of crime that encompassed any governmental act of punishment, regardless of whether the act fell under administrative, civil, or criminal law. For example, one critic points to consent decrees, considered by Clinard to indicate corporate crime. But in the context of corporate actions, consent decrees are an agreement or a contract between a federal regulatory agency and a corporation. Although a consent decree is made under the court's sanction, it binds only the parties and not the court. Many consent decrees, as well as other enforcement actions that Clinard tabulated, do not involve criminal behavior as it is commonly understood by the general public.

In conclusion, said the critic, Clinard actually studied the "federal administrative regulation of large corporations. The Clinard tabulation of violations is nothing more than a collection of discretionary decisions to initiate formal or informal noncriminal agency procedures against a particular corporation for a particular event; it appears that less than 1 percent of these 'violations' involve accusations of crime as Congress, lawyers, and courts have defined crime."[73]

Other crticis applaud the extension by Clinard and his colleagues of the concept of crime to include civil as well as administrative actions but criticize the study for failing to consider the relationships of such concepts as class, class struggle, and capitalism to corporate crime. Furthermore, the report did not answer many of the questions that are critical to a study of corporate crime, such as how well the American corporation is policed, the extent of corporate crime, and the rates of recidivism among corporate criminals.[74]

Control of
corporate conduct   The main issue in the study of corporate crime appears to be how to control it. Clinard suggested three ways to control corporate crime: improved ethics among those in corporate power;[75] strong intervention of state and federal legal agencies, including not only changes in corporate structure but also sanctions aimed at deterring illegal behavior; and, finally, pressure from the public.[76]

With regard to using corporate ethics to resolve the problem, it might be appropriate to quote a former lord chancellor of England who quipped, "Did you ever expect a corporation to have a conscience, when it has no soul to be damned, and no body to be kicked?"[77] Pressures from the public have not been great either, and so that leaves us with the criminal law.

The principal problem with deciding to use the criminal law to control corporate conduct is that we really do not know how effective it is. We have many who speculate about the deterrent effect of the criminal law but little empirical support for their conclusions. In fact, earlier studies on white-collar crime questioned the alleged deterrent effect of criminal sanctions on these types of criminals, concluding that "a large number of successful white-collar crime prosecutions serve no more than a symbolic purpose."[78]

Others have argued that sanctions do have a deterrent effect on white-collar criminals and that the problem has been that in the past "there appears to have been no appropriate research design for assessing the impact of sanctions applied to corporations." Using a research procedure based on the way in which corporations are organized and applying the procedure to evaluate the impact of prosecutions of corporate crime under Australia's Trade Practices Act, one investigator found that the sanctions were effective in reducing corporate recidivism and suggested the reasons for their effectiveness. In some cases, there was fear of revocation of a license to trade. Second, the fines might have been a deterrent. Third, company officials may have feared negative consumer reaction, although the evidence did not justify their unease. The evidence indicated that the main deterrent was "concern about loss of reputation, both that of the company and, more particularly, that of individual managers. This concern stemmed not from any fear that loss of reputation would lead to a consumer reaction, but because top management felt personally stigmatized by any imputation that the company had acted unethically or illegally."[79]

Note, however, that the study was conducted in another country and that it involved fines, not incarceration. It has been argued that in this country, for prison to be an effective deterrent for corporate criminals, sentences would have to be lengthened, and incarceration in hard-core prison facilities would have to become routine. It is doubtful, however, that Americans will go that far. Furthermore, it is quite possible that alternative forms of punishment will also be effective deterrents, particularly if they are applied consistently and fairly.[80]

Two final comments on punishing corporate criminals through the criminal law. Recall our discussion in Chapter 3 of the purposes of punishment.

It is alleged that even if we cannot prove that the criminal law deters, it does have an important function in that it serves society's need for retribution and helps preserve confidence in the system of rule by law.[81]

Finally, recall our discussion in Chapter 1 on the issue of what type of behavior should be covered by the criminal, as opposed to the civil, law. We looked at the criminal charge of homicide brought against the Ford Motor Company in the case of the teenagers who died when the Ford Pinto they were driving was hit from the rear, causing a fire. Ford was acquitted of the criminal charge, although the teenagers' families did receive civil damages as a result of their tort suit. The issue of negligence in design of the automobile (poor location of the gas tank leading to increased danger of fire), a civil problem, must be distinguished from the criminal charge of reckless homicide. Corporate "misconduct" may be severe and may, as in this case, result in death. The issue, however, is whether we should attempt to control that conduct through the criminal law or through the civil law. Deciding that the civil law is the best response does not mean that the misconduct is considered less serious; it simply means that the civil law is perceived as the best method of control. Criminal charges are hard to prove, and the Pinto case is a good illustration. But negligence is easier to prove. Of course, the Pinto case also illustrates that the civil and criminal law are not mutually exclusive, but we must consider too the cost in time, attorneys' fees, court personnel, and so on, that are involved in an unsuccessful criminal prosecution. Finally, it is important to understand that with regard to some types of corporate conduct that we wish to control, administrative regulation may be more effective than either the civil or the criminal law. For example, if corporations are mislabeling products such as dangerous drugs, a "cease-and-desist" order will probably be the quickest way to stop them. That administrative order might, of course, be backed up by a court order involving fines or even threats of criminal prosecution.

COMPUTER CRIME   A third type of modern property crime is **computer crime.** A widely published cartoon of a police line-up featuring four men and a computer with the caption "The computer did it" highlights this type of crime, described by a *Chicago Tribune* editorial as follows:

> Computer crime is already an international problem of formidable dimensions and is expected to increase with the growth of electronic data processing. The question is whether legal and technological means of combating it can at least stay apace of the problem. . . .
> As the paperless, totally wired society of the future moves from science fiction toward reality, high-tech crooks are bound to proliferate. And they won't be easy to outwit.[82]

Computers have revolutionized not only the way we do business but in many respects the way we think and act. Computers fascinate and challenge

Computers have not only revolutionized the way we do business but have also had an impact on criminal behavior. Some have argued that cracking computers has become a "rite of passage" of teenagers and college students. Rather than stealing and hot wiring cars, they steal information from computers.

many; others are so frightened that according to some reports, people not only develop an intense fear of computers, called *cyberphobia,* but they even become violent, attacking the computer.[83]

Cracking computers has become a "rite of passage" for some teenagers and college students. Rather than stealing and hot wiring cars, they steal information from computers. Encouraged by the popular movie of 1983,

War Games, in which illegal access to computer data leads to the brink of World War III, they turn their intellectual talents to their home computers and attempt to discover what information they can obtain. According to the 414s, the Milwaukee youths who named themselves after their area code, they are not trying to steal; they are just having fun. The 414s said their project was easy, and once they found a likely target, they tried various passwords until they broke into more than sixty business and government computer systems in Canada and the United States. Said one of the youths, "It was like climbing a mountain: you have the goal of reaching the top or accessing a computer, and once you reach the peak, you make a map of the way and give it to everybody else."[84]

The actions of the 414s illustrate more than the possibility of using computers to steal information from other systems; their reaction also reveals the common attitude that such actions are all right if you do not mean to commit a crime. The blame is also placed on those who have unsecured computers, as the following comment from one of the 414s illustrates: "It got out of hand . . . but it's not all our fault either. There is no security in it or nothing."[85]

Data on computer crimes

Data indicate that every year in this country the "computer thief" steals more than $100 million, but experts think that is only the "tip of the iceberg" and that losses may run as high as $40 billion a year.[86] Furthermore, only 1 percent of computer crimes are ever detected. Only 1 in 22,000 of the detected computer crimes will be successfully prosecuted, according to the president of Advanced Information Management, Inc. "We are placing enormous faith in increasingly sophisticated and pervasive computer systems that are neither secure nor trustworthy."[87]

The average loss per incident of computer crime theft is estimated to be $621,000.[88] That average seems quite distorted, however, when we read about the $21.3 million embezzled from the Wells Fargo Bank in 1981, the largest known electronic bank fraud in this country.

A further cost of computer crime that must be considered in analyzing the overall cost of computer crime is the rising cost of security to prevent computer fraud. For example, a Dallas-based oil, mineral, and chemical producer recently spent almost $500,000 for improvements on its computer security plan. Special software is being developed to eliminate outside access to computers, but even those devices cannot prevent computer thefts by company employees who are hired to run the computer.[89]

Types of computer crimes

Computer crimes may involve the same kinds of crimes already discussed in this chapter, with the exception that the computer is used in the perpetration of the crime. "Computer crime may also take the form of threats of force directed against the computer itself. These crimes are usually 'sabotage' or 'ransom' cases. Computer crime cases have one commonality: the computer is either the tool or the target of the felon."[90]

A special jargon has been developed to describe computer crimes, such as the following:

1. *Data Diddling,* the most common, the easiest, and the safest technique, involves changing the data that will be put into the computer or that is in the computer.
2. *The Trojan Horse* method involves instructing the computer to perform unauthorized functions as well as its intended functions.
3. *The Salami Technique* refers to taking small amounts of assets from a larger source without significantly reducing the whole. For example, one might, in a banking account situation, instruct the computer to reduce specified accounts by 1 percent and place those assets in another account.
4. *Superzapping.* Because computers at times malfunction, there is a need for what is sometimes called a "break glass in case of emergency" computer program. This program will "bypass all controls to modify or disclose any of the contents of the computer." In the hands of the wrong person, it can be an extremely powerful tool for crime.
5. *Data Leakage* involves removing information from the computer system or computer facility.[91]

Characteristics of computer criminals

Few studies have been conducted on computer criminals, but the little evidence we do have indicates that the criminals are usually young, very bright, and often see themselves as "pitted against the computer." A National Criminal Justice Information and Statistics Service Report of the Law Enforcement Assistance Administration suggests that in attempting to detect computer criminals, we should keep in mind the following characteristics, which are similar to those of the "modern-day, amateur, white-collar criminal." The median age is twenty-five years with a range of eighteen to forty-six years. Such younger people may not yet be as assimilated into the ethics and organization of their professions, and they have often been trained on college and university campuses where "attacking campus computer systems is not only condoned but often encouraged as an educational activity."

The second characteristic is that these people are highly trained and often overtrained for the jobs they occupy, and so they they may become bored by the routine computer work. Most will perform their criminal acts during the course of their job assignments, although that is not always the case. They are more likely than other white-collar criminals to need assistance in their criminal activity. They may have learned their acts from others in the same employ; thus, differential association cannot be ruled out. They demonstrate the "Robin Hood" syndrome—that is, they distinguish between victimizing individuals and victimizing organizations. "In addition, they rationalize that they are only harming a computer or the contents of the computer; therefore, doing no harm or causing no loss to people or organizations," a characteristic that is common to other kinds of white-collar criminals.

Some computer criminals rationalize that a computer that is not being used is "fair game" for their use, even though computer time is expensive and they are in essence "stealing" by not paying for it. It is common for computer criminals to rationalize that because they have the technical expertise, they are entitled to use computers for personal purposes, "for challenging intellectual exercise."[92]

Finally, as we mentioned, some people apparently try to crack computer systems "just for fun" and are examples of some of the theories we discussed in earlier chapters. They are succumbing to peer pressure; they are imitating television or movies; or they are just looking for new thrills and excitement.

Legislative control of computer crime

Computer crime has some of the same elements of common law theft, but the traditional theft statutes are not adequate for prosecution of computer crimes. For example, those statutes generally require the "taking of physical property," but does generating an electronic signal or executing a computer routine that changes an account balance constitute 'taking'? Do the contents of a computer memory constitute property?" Prosecution of computer crime under traditional fraud statutes is also difficult. Fraud requires the element of "willful misrepresentation to a person," and the issue is whether a computer is a person. Because of these difficulties, twenty-two states have passed statutes specifically aimed at computer crime. But as most of these statutes were enacted within the past five years, we do not know how effective they will be in curbing computer crime.[93]

It is quite possible, however, that passing statutes designed to prevent computer crime will not be as effective as some would like to think. First, many establishments might not want the public to know that their employees committed crimes with the company computers. In one case, in England, when an employee was confronted by management with his alleged use of the computer to steal money from the company over a period of years, he threatened "to expose the weaknesses of the company's computer system and ruin the company's reputation for efficient management of its affairs unless the company wrote him a letter of recommendation (so that he could get another job in the programming field). The company knuckled under, wrote him the letter, and the programmer went on to commit a similar theft against his new employer."[94]

A second problem, in addition to the lack of reporting and willingness to prosecute, is the difficulty of prosecuting these kinds of crimes. Police do not have the technical expertise to solve computer crimes, and cases that go to trial are usually highly technical, costly, and time-consuming.[95]

EXHIBIT

CALIFORNIA'S COMPUTER CRIME STATUTE

(a) Any person who intentionally accesses or causes to be accessed any computer system or computer network for the purpose of (1) devising or executing any scheme or artifice to defraud or extort or (2) obtaining money, property, or services with false or fraudulent intent, representations, or promises shall be guilty of a public offense.

(b) Any person who maliciously accesses, alters, deletes, damages, or destroys any computer system, computer network, computer program, or data shall be guilty of a public offense.

(c) Any person who violates the provisions of (a) or (b) is guilty of a felony and is punishable by a fine not exceeding five thousand dollars ($5,000), or by imprisonment in the state prison for 16 months, or two or three years, or by both such fine and imprisonment, or by a fine not exceeding two thousand five hundred dollars ($2,500), or by imprisonment in the county jail not exceeding one year, or by both such fine and imprisonment.

(d) This section shall not be construed to preclude the applicability of any other provision of the criminal law of this state which applies or may apply to any transaction.

Source: Cal. Penal Code § 502 (1981 Supp).

Ethics and the computer

What is needed, say some authorities, is not legislation but a code of ethics concerning computer use. The Privacy Act of 1974[96] was a legislative beginning in protecting all of us from the dissemination of information contained in computers. Perhaps we should also be able to bring civil suits against companies that, through their own negligence (for example, lack of adequate computer security), allow the records to be "stolen." The misuse of the computer by the 414s, mentioned earlier, raised this ethical question, especially when those involved argued that they were not trying to steal.

Actually, two ethical issues are involved—the abuse of individuals by institutions, for example, when private information held in the computer is disseminated to the improper sources, and the misuse by individuals of the computers of institutions. A professor of computer science says that the ethics issues are basic: "Don't do with computers what you would consider immoral without them. An act does not gain morality because the computer has made it easy to achieve. . . . If it is immoral for someone to rummage through your desk drawers, then it is unethical for someone to make a search of your computer files." His conclusion, however, perhaps illustrates our traditional attitude toward these kinds of criminals, as compared with "real criminals." "But because an electronic search is by definition somewhat ephemeral, many people don't see its ethical consequences."[97]

HIGHLIGHT

THE IMPACT OF COMPUTERS

"The positive impact of the computer has been immense and will continue to grow with time.

However, on the negative side of the ledger, the computer enables a small group of individuals to steal sums of money that would have made the gangsters of the 1920s blush. Computer technology has enabled small groups of political zealots or criminals to terrorize cities at the push of a button. A product of the electronic revolution, the computer criminal strikes anywhere and everywhere. He is not a product of our slums; his clothing is the best; his schooling the finest. He represents the criminal of the future. Our laws are challenged by him. Our jurists left stunned. What makes this criminal more dangerous than any before him is that should our system of laws fail to meet his threat, he may in fact ring the death knell of our entire system of justice. The stakes are high indeed."

Source: August Bequai, *Computer Crime* (Lexington, Mass.: Heath, 1978), p. xi.

Computer crimes of the future

Computer technology has already significantly decreased our reliance on "cash" and turned many of our financial transactions into a matter of pushing a button or making a call. Such technological "improvements" have and will continue to change the types of crime that are committed. "In a cashless society, armed robbery will have little meaning; muggings may become a thing of the past ... in this world the computer felon will emerge as the replacement for the common hoodlum. The world of EFTS [Electronic Funds Transfer System] ... is a world full of promise, and yet, one that holds serious challenges for our justice system."[98] Most importantly, such changes leave us vulnerable to invasions of privacy.

ORGANIZED CRIME

The crimes of the "underworld" have for a long time provided Americans with a source of mystery and excitement and have often captured our attention through movies and books. The successes of the underworld in eluding attempts at law enforcement are well known; in many cases, the activities of the underworld have given our society services and commodities such as prostitution, gambling, alcohol (during Prohibition), and drugs labeled illegal by statute but considered important by some to the enjoyment of their daily lives. We may thus see **organized crime** as a "necessary evil." In any case, we usually think of organized crime as a national, perhaps international, syndicate[99] that infiltrates at the local as well as the national level. This view is not accepted by many social scientists;[100] thus, it is important to distinguish the two major definitions of organized crime.

THE LAW
ENFORCEMENT
PERSPECTIVE OF
ORGANIZED
CRIME

The most common view of organized crime is what may be called the "law enforcement perspective." In its 1967 report, the President's Commission on Law Enforcement and Administration of Justice contributed to this view by defining organized crime as "a society that seeks to operate outside the control of the American people and their working government." Organized crime, according to that report, is an organization of thousands of criminals in this country, which operates in a complex organizational structure and has rules that are even more rigid and more strictly enforced than are those of legitimate government.[101] "Its actions are not impulsive but rather the result of intricate conspiracies, carried on over many years and aimed at gaining control over whole fields of activity in order to amass huge profits." Money and power are the goals, and organized crime infiltrates legitimate as well as illegitimate businesses.[102]

A few years later, the Task Force on Organized Crime of the National Advisory Committee on Criminal Justice Standards and Goals considered this definition of organized crime and refused to write a definition that would include all of the criminal activities covered by all state and federal statutes. Instead, the task force chose to delineate the major characteristics of organized crime, and those are enumerated in Table 9.3. A look at that list will reveal, however, some similarities to the concept as articulated by the earlier presidential commissions.

Table 9.3

Characteristics of organized crime

1. Organized crime is a type of conspiratorial crime, sometimes involving the hierarchical coordination of a number of persons in the planning and execution of illegal acts, or in the pursuit of a legitimate objective by unlawful means. Organized crime involves continuous commitment by key members, although some individuals with specialized skills may participate only briefly in the ongoing conspiracies. . . .
2. Organized crime has economic gain as its primary goal, though some of the participants in the conspiracy may have achievement of power or status as their objective. . . .
3. Organized crime is not limited to patently illegal enterprises or unlawful services such as gambling, prostitution, drugs, loansharking, or racketeering. It also includes such sophisticated activites as laundering of illegal money through a legitimate business, land fraud, and computer manipulation. . . .
4. Organized crime employs predatory tactics such as intimidation, violence, and corruption, and it appeals to greed to accomplish its objectives and preserve its gains. . . .
5. By experience, custom, and practice, organized crime's conspiratorial groups are usually very quick and effective in controlling and disciplining their members, associates, and victims. Therefore, organized crime participants are unlikely to disassociate themselves from the conspiracies and are in the main incorrigible. . . .
6. Organized crime is not synonymous with the Mafia or La Cosa Nostra, the most experienced, diversified, and possibly best disciplined of the conspiratorial groups. . . .
7. Organized crime does not include terrorists dedicated to political change, although organized criminals and terrorists have some characteristics in common, including types of crimes committed and strict organizational structures. . . .

Source: Organized Crime Report of the Task Force on Organized Crime, National Advisory Commission on Criminal Justice Standards and Goals (Washington, D.C.: U.S. Government Printing Office, 1976), pp.7–8.

SOCIAL AND
ECONOMIC
PERSPECTIVES

A second definition views organized crime as "an integral part of the nation's social, political, and economic life—as one of the major social ills, such as poverty or racism, that grew with urban living in America."[103] It is true that organized crime often involves ethnic and other minority groups, but that is seen by this second perspective as the process by which those groups begin to establish themselves and gain power in this society. As more acceptable avenues for this process become available, they may move on into legitimate enterprises, and other groups move into organized crime to begin their process of integration into the society.[104]

Another version of this functional perspective comes from other economists, who view organized crime as operating just as other economic enterprises do. Organized crime supplies goods and services to customers seeking them, and even when the supply is considered illegal by the government at a given time—for example, liquor during Prohibition—the economic process is the same as it would be if the enterprise were not defined as criminal. In organized crime, however, the proceeds from these illegal sales are used to engage in other illegal activites, such as corrupting public officials to protect against prosecution. "This theory of organized crime holds it to be a fundamental part of the American free-enterprise system, one end of a continuum whose other end is legitimate business."[105]

ANALYSIS OF
THE CONCEPT
OF ORGANIZED
CRIME

The two approaches to the concept of organized crime have some common elements. In both perspectives, the activity is organized and goes on beyond the life of any of its particular members. Both perspectives recognize the need for and the existence of some protection for organized crime, and this protection comes from corrupting public officials. Third, both perspectives view organized crime as providing illegal goods and services to a public that demands them. These similarities led two authorities to define organized crime "as a persisting form of criminal activity that brings together a client-public which demands a range of goods and services defined as illegal. It is a structure or network of individuals who produce or supply those goods and services, use the capital to expand into other legitimate or illegitimate activities, and corrupt public officials with the aim of gaining their protection."[106]

Despite this attempt at a definition of organized crime that is broad enough to include the two perspectives, the view of organized crime persists as being roughly synonymous with the national (or international) crime syndicate characterized by Italian membership. Taking this perspective of organized crime has obvious implications for the attempts to eradicate or control it. It leads to catching the "name" underworld criminals rather than to making changes in the social system. Finally, the lack of a generally accepted definition of organized crime results in a variety of definitions throughout all the states.[107]

THE EXTENT OF ORGANIZED CRIME

We do not know the extent of organized crime, for much of it eludes the criminal justice system, but we do know that it is not limited to the illegal businesses such as prostitution and drugs with which it is so often associated. Organized crime has infiltrated many legitimate businesses, such as the vending-machine industry and the solid-waste disposal industry.[108] In New York in 1983, officials reported that the illegal dumping of toxins was the responsibility of organized crime.[109]

Organized crime continues to move into new businesses. As one veteran investigator said, "These people are like cockroaches. . . . You step on them one place and they turn up somewhere else."[110] But the fight to control organized crime continues. President Reagan indicated his concern for combating organized crime in this country by naming the twenty-person Organized Crime Commission in July 1983. The commission is headed by Judge Irving R. Kaufman of the United States Court of Appeals for the Second Circuit. Under the leadership of Judge Kaufman, the commission will hold hearings throughout the country, with a report due on March 1, 1986.

ORGANIZED CRIME AND CORPORATE CRIME: A COMPARISON

In our discussion of organized crime, we have seen that legitimate businesses are infiltrated, that crime is not limited to "illegitimate" activities. In its infiltration of legitimate business, organized crime resembles corporate crime, and it is often involved in the same types of activities.[111] In some cases, the methods are similar or identical. But it is in the types of methods used that organized and corporate crime also differ. Violence will more often be found in organized crime,[112] although it may also occur among white-collar criminals. The use of force and threat is also more common in organized crime. Finally, "organized crime nullifies legitimate government more directly, and to a greater extent. . . ."[113]

SUMMARY AND CONCLUSION

This chapter has explored the more prevalent types of property crimes in this country. We began with the traditional property crimes of larceny-theft and burglary, both of which are defined by the *Uniform Crime Reports* as "serious" property crimes. In discussing larceny-theft, we looked at the historical types of thefts as well as the more modern versions. We examined forgery and shoplifting, including sociological studies of each. After discussing the crime of burglary, we examined the concept of career criminal. Many career criminals engage in some type of theft or burglary, and we studied early sociological approaches to the "professional" criminal before analyzing the more recent and much more extensive studies of the career criminal.

Then we talked about white-collar crime, including the contributions of Edwin H. Sutherland to the development of the concept and the more recent approaches to that concept, including corporate crime. Next, we looked at computer crime and the limited information we have on those who engage in this new criminal activity.

The final section of this chapter focused on organized crime, including the popular concept of organized crime as a type of nationally run syndicate that influences local as well as national and international businesses, both legitimate and illegitimate. We also looked at the approach of some social scientists who view organized crime as a collection of semiautonomous groups that both cooperate and compete and that may be seen as functional in the social and economic system.

This chapter completes our discussion of typologies and theories of criminal behavior. In analyzing the various typologies, it becomes clear that studying criminal behavior by means of such typologies demonstrates the position often taken by sociologists and criminologists—that in many respects, criminal behavior is like any other behavior. It manifests many of the same social processes and takes place within the same social structures. The difference often lies not in the behavior itself but in the reaction to that behavior. It is therefore appropriate that we turn our attention to the official reaction to criminal behavior, through an analysis of the criminal justice system in the United States.

PART IV

THE CRIMINAL JUSTICE SYSTEM

CHAPTER 10

The American system of criminal justice

This chapter begins our look into the criminal justice system by analyzing the philosophy on which that system rests. After examining the stages in the system, we shall consider the concept of due process and then analyze four of the basic constitutional rights of defendants: the right to be free of unreasonable search and seizure, the right not to be required to testify against oneself in a criminal proceeding, the right to counsel, and the right to trial by jury. These rights are illustrative of the constitutional provisions that were passed in order to give the accused in criminal trials an opportunity to match the powers of the prosecutor, the state. The rights are not recognized to "get the criminal off" but, rather, to make sure the state, in apprehending, charging, and trying people for alleged criminal activity, plays by the "rules of the game." Yet, in recognizing these rights, we run into conflicts with the needs of those who have been victimized by crime. Thus, we also shall study the recent attempts to provide for victims. Finally, we shall examine the tensions and conflicts between the rights of defendants and the needs of victims as well as of a society of people who not only wish but also deserve to be protected from criminal intrusion into their lives.

The philosophy on which the American system of criminal justice rests is embodied in the statement of ethics of the American Bar Association, "The continued existence of a free and democratic society depends upon recognition of the new concept that justice is based upon the rule of law grounded in respect for the dignity of the individual and his capacity through reason for enlightened self-government." In reality, however, what has come to be referred to as the "rule-of-law" or the "crime-control model" conflicts with the "due-process" or the "rights-of-defendants" model.[1] These models represent two extremes, with the crime-control model representing the need to curb and control crime and the due-process model emphasizing the importance of the **defendants'** rights. Many people today believe that the two are in serious conflict: crime cannot be controlled if the defendants' basic constitutional rights are recognized.[2] Some have argued that defendants already have too many rights, with the result being a failure to curb crime and to recognize the victims' rights.

The American **criminal justice system,** however, is based on the philosophy that the defendant's dignity must be recognized, that the defendant is innocent until proved guilty by the state, and that the state must play by the strict "rules of the game" in proving its case against the defendant. If the state violates those rules, it not only will impair the rights of the defendants involved, but it also will threaten the very foundation of our system of criminal justice.

STAGES IN THE CRIMINAL JUSTICE SYSTEM

The criminal justice system in the United States has four components: the **police,** the prosecution, the courts, and **corrections.** Figure 10.1 (pp. 330–331) illustrates these components, presenting a simple but comprehensive view of the movement of cases through the system.

INVESTIGATION PRIOR TO ARREST

When a complaint is received by the police department, or when the police are observers at the scene of a crime, an investigation may be made. Police may interview witnesses, and they may get information that will lead to an arrest. During this investigation, the police may briefly detain the suspect and often will search for weapons.

ARREST

Most police encounters do not result in **arrest**, and the police have great discretion at this stage. When a person is officially arrested, he or she is taken into custody (usually to the police station) in order to be charged with a crime.

BOOKING   When the police arrive at the police station with a suspect who has been arrested, the suspect is **booked,** that is, the name and when and where the arrest occurred (and for what purpose) will be entered in the police arrest book, or *log.* The suspect may be fingerprinted and photographed and may be released after booking if it is determined that either a crime was not committed or there is not sufficient evidence to hold him or her for the crime.

PRESENTMENT   Most states have a statutory requirement that after arrest, the suspect must be taken quickly before a magistrate for an initial appearance, or **presentment.** The **magistrate,** presumed to be a neutral party, must tell the suspect his or her rights and the charge filed. Such rules apply to federal magistrates through the Federal Rules of Criminal Procedure.

PRELIMINARY HEARING   The defendant may waive the **preliminary hearing,** in which the evidence against the accused is considered. If it is not waived, the government's evidence will be examined. The magistrate will decide whether there is **probable cause** that a crime has been committed and, if so, whether it was committed by the suspect. The magistrate may at this stage dismiss the charges or bind the suspect over to the grand jury for an indictment or to the prosecuting attorney for an information. The magistrate may also set bail.

INFORMATION   If a grand jury is not used, the prosecutor may return an information, based on the evidence available from police officers or private citizens. This **information,** which is really an accusation by the prosecutor, is a formal legal document that is sufficient to send the suspect to trial.

GRAND JURY INDICTMENT   In some jurisdictions the prosecutor must have the approval of the grand jury, which, after examining the evidence, returns an **indictment,** or a "true bill." The indictment serves the same purpose as the information—it requires the suspect to appear before a court that has **jurisdiction** to hear the charges. The **grand jury,** consisting of a specified number of private citizens chosen randomly, meets at periodic intervals.

The Fifth Amendment to the United States Consitution provides that in federal cases, felonies must go through the process of indictment by a grand jury. Some state laws also require this process, but the U.S. Supreme Court has held that states are not required to use the grand jury indictment.

Figure 10.1

A general view of the criminal system.

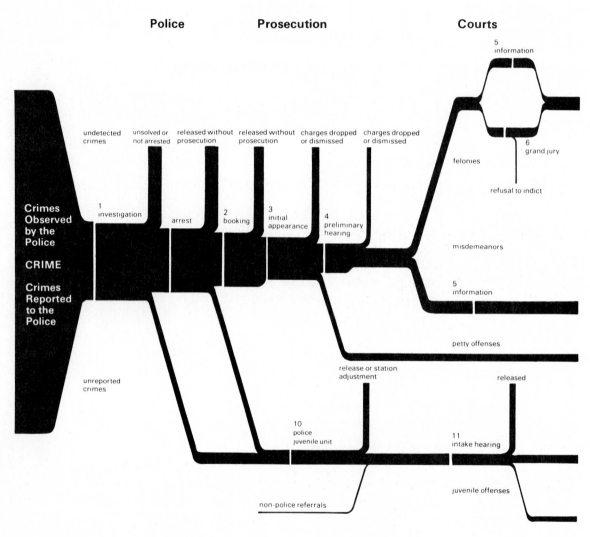

Police **Prosecution** **Courts**

5
information

undetected crimes

unsolved or not arrested

released without prosecution

released without prosecution

charges dropped or dismissed

charges dropped or dismissed

6
grand jury

felonies

refusal to indict

Crimes Observed by the Police

CRIME

Crimes Reported to the Police

1
investigation

arrest

2
booking

3
initial appearance

4
preliminary hearing

misdemeanors

5
information

petty offenses

unreported crimes

release or station adjustment

released

10
police juvenile unit

11
intake hearing

juvenile offenses

non-police referrals

---

1. May continue until trial.
2. Administrative record of arrest. First step at which temporary release on bail may be available.

3. Before magistrate, commissioner, or justice of peace. Formal notice of charge, advice of rights. Bail set. Summary trials for petty offenses usually conducted here without further processing.
4. Preliminary testing of evidence against defendant. Charge may be reduced. No separate preliminary hearing for misdemeanors in some systems.

5. Charge filed by prosecutor on basis of information submitted by police or citizens. Alternative to grand jury indictment; often used in felonies, almost always in misdemeanors.
6. Reviews whether or not government evidence sufficient to justify trial. Some states have no grand jury system; others seldom use it.

Procedures in individual jurisdictions may vary from the pattern shown here. The differing weights of line indicate the relative volume of cases disposed of at various points in the system. But this is only suggestive since no nationwide data of this sort exist.

Corrections

charge dimissed acquitted

probation

7 arraignment   trial   sentencing

out of system

guilty pleas

revocation

penitentiary

8 reduction of charge

appeal

parole

revocation

9 habeas corpus

charge dismissed acquitted

probation

7 arraignment   trial   sentencing

out of system

guilty pleas

revocation

fine   jail

nonpayment

released

probation

adjudicatory hearing

revocation

out of system

juvenile institution

12 nonadjudicatory disposition

parole

revocation

7. Appearance for plea; defendant elects trial by judge or jury (if available); counsel for indigent usually appointed here in felonies. Often not at all in other cases.
8. Charge may be reduced at any time prior to trial in return for plea of guilty or for other reasons.

9. Challenge on constitutional grounds to legality of detention. May be sought at any point in process.
10. Police often hold informal hearings, dismiss or adjust many cases without further processing.

11. Probation officer decides desirability of further court action.
12. Welfare agency, social services, counseling, medical care, and so on, for cases where adjudicatory handling is not required.

ARRAIGNMENT

After an information or indictment is secured, the suspect must appear before a court. At this stage—the **arraignment**—for the first time after hearing the formal charges and again being informed of his or her rights, the defendant may plead. If the defendant pleads guilty, the case will not go to trial. If the plea is not guilty, the **trial** will be set. If the defendant has a choice of a trial by judge or by **jury,** that decision will be made at this stage. Certain pretrial motions may also be made, such as a motion to change the venue (place where the trial will be held) or to suppress the evidence against the accused.

REDUCTION OF CHARGE

As a result of **plea bargaining** or for other reasons, the charge against the defendant may be reduced; that is, the defendant may agree to plead guilty to lesser charges rather than stand trial on the original charge. The defense and prosecution attorneys may also have a pretrial conference in the judge's chambers to discuss specific aspects of the case.

After all those proceedings, the defendant is ready for trial. Because most defendants plead guilty, trials occur in only a small percentage of cases. If the defendant is acquitted, he or she will be dismissed. If found guilty, the defendant then must face **sentencing,** a very important stage in the process of criminal justice.

The defendant may file a writ of **habeas corpus,** which, as Figure 10.1 indicates, is a "challenge on constitutional grounds to legality of detention." It may be sought at any stage in the judicial proceedings. After the sentence is pronounced, the defendant may have legal grounds on which to **appeal** the case to a higher court.

SYSTEM AND PROCESS

This process of proceeding through the various stages is only one aspect of the system, for the criminal justice system in the United States is both a system and a process. The system aspect is important but is often overlooked. Nonetheless, what happens at one stage may have a tremendous impact on what happens at another stage or in another component.

One way in which the system interrelates can be seen in the use of **probation** and **parole.** If the judges, who grant probation, begin to do so in significantly fewer cases and to substitute prison sentences, the **prisons** will be confronted with increasing populations, which may create serious problems for financing and staffing. If **parole boards** significantly decrease the number of people to whom they grant parole, thus increasing the amount of time the **inmates** will spend in prison, the prison population will increase. Prisons may also suffer staffing and other problems if the granting of probation and parole significantly increases, thereby decreasing the prison population.

In this chapter we shall see some of the effects that changes in one part of the criminal justice system have on other parts of the system, especially one of the most dramatic—the effect that observing the defendants' rights has on enforcing the law. Clearly, if we allowed police to search and seize without restrictions and if we tortured or tricked defendants to the point that they would confess, we could have more arrests and more convictions. If we did not allow trial by jury and many of the other rights we recognize in our system, we could speed up the process and decrease the congestion in courts. Of course, we might not realize until later that these processes also have such effects as enlarging the size of prison populations, and thereby increasing the cost of corrections.

CONCEPTS OF AMERICAN CRIMINAL JUSTICE

The American system of criminal justice is based on an adversarial model and is characterized by the concept of due process, which involves numerous rights of defendants who are on trial in criminal courts.

THE ADVERSARY VERSUS THE INQUISITORIAL SYSTEM

In the criminal justice system of the United States, unlike that of many countries, a person is innocent until proved guilty. Thus it is called an **adversary,** as opposed to an **inquisitorial,** system.[3]

The adversary system presumes that the best way to get the truth is to have a "contest" between the two sides—the state and the **prosecuting attorney** representing the side of society and the victim (in a criminal trial) versus the **defense attorney** and the defendant. In contrast with the adversary system is the inquisitorial system, under which the accused is presumed guilty and must prove his or her innocence. The basic difference between the two systems is in the presumption of guilt versus the presumption of innocence, which affects the **burden of proof.** Under the adversary system, the state has the burden of proving guilt; under the inquisitorial system, the defendant has the burden of proving innocence, and that is a very heavy burden.

The adversary system has aroused considerable criticism,[4] some of which is justified, but it is important to understand the *philosophy* of the system, a system that is based on the concept of due process for defendants.

THE CONCEPT OF DUE PROCESS

Due process is difficult to define, as a former Supreme Court justice explained in a frequently quoted statement:

> "Due Process," unlike some legal rules, is not a technical conception with a fixed content unrelated to time, place and circumstances. Expressing as it does in its ultimate analysis, respect enforced by law for that feeling of just treatment which has been evolved through centuries of Anglo-American constitutional history and civilization, "due process" cannot be imprisoned within the treacherous limits of any formula. Representing a profound attitude of fairness between man and man, and more particularly between the individual and gov-

ernment, "due process" is compounded of history, reason, the past course of decisions, and stout confidence in the strength of the democratic faith which we possess. Due process is not a mechanical instrument. It is not a yardstick. It is a process.[5]

The framers of the Constitution were concerned that the federal government might become too strong, and so to protect the citizens against it, the Bill of Rights was included. It is clear through early Supreme Court decisions that the Bill of Rights restricts only the federal government. But gradually the Court held that most of the provisions of those amendments apply to the states through the due process clause of the Fourteenth Amendment.

THE CONSTITUTIONAL RIGHTS OF DEFENDANTS

Because the battle would not be evenly matched in a criminal trial if all the powers of the government were thrown against the individual defendant, procedural safeguards have been instituted. The prosecution thus is required to prove its case beyond a reasonable doubt, which gives it a heavy burden. Defendants may not be forced to testify against themselves; their persons and possessions may not be searched unreasonably; they are entitled to be notified of the charges against them and to have impartial and public trials by juries of their peers; they are entitled to counsel, and if they cannot afford counsel, the state must provide attorneys; and defendants may be tried only once for the same offense and are presumed innocent until proved guilty.

It is important to understand that although a system based on the defendants' due process rights may, and indeed does, sometimes result in the release of a guilty person, it is also possible that an innocent person may be convicted. Our system is based on the concept that it would be better to allow ten guilty people to go free rather than have one innocent person convicted. According to the Supreme Court, speaking about the freedom not to testify against oneself when one is accused in a criminal court but applying to all of the rights of due process: "The basic purposes that lie behind our system of due process relate . . . to preserving the integrity of a judicial system in which even the guilty are not to be convicted unless the prosecution 'shoulders the entire load.'"[6]

THE RIGHT TO BE FREE FROM UNREASONABLE SEARCH AND SEIZURE

The Fourth Amendment prohibition against *unreasonable* searches and seizures has been tested in numerous cases, many of which have ultimately been decided by the United States Supreme Court. Unreasonable searches and seizures are prohibited because, according to the Supreme Court, the Constitution guarantees to all of us a "reasonable expectation of privacy." "The integrity of an individual's person is a cherished value of our society."[7] That integrity has also been extended to include some of our possessions, for example, our homes and cars. To assure that our privacy is protected,

---

EXHIBIT
SELECTED AMENDMENTS, UNITED STATES CONSTITUTION

Amendment IV (1791)

The right of the people to be secure in their persons, houses, papers, and effects, against unreasonable searches and seizures, shall not be violated, and no Warrants shall issue, but upon probable cause, supported by Oath or affirmation, and particularly describing the place to be searched, and the persons or things to be seized.

Amendment V (1791)

No person shall be held to answer for a capital, or otherwise infamous crime, unless on a presentment or indictment of a Grand Jury, except in cases arising in the land or naval forces, or in the Militia, when in actual service in time of War or public danger; nor shall any person be subject for the same offence to be twice put in jeopardy of life or limb; nor shall be compelled in any criminal case to be a witness against himself, nor be deprived of life, liberty, or property, without due process of law; nor shall private property be taken for public use, without just compensation.

Amendment VI (1791)

In all criminal prosecutions, the accused shall enjoy the right to a speedy and public trial, by an impartial jury of the State and district wherein the crime shall have been committed, which district shall have been previously ascertained by law, and to be informed of the nature and cause of the accusation; to be confronted with the witnesses against him; to have compulsory process for obtaining witnesses in his favor, and to have the Assistance of Counsel for his defence.

Amendment XIV (1868)

Section 1. All persons born or naturalized in the United States, and subject to the jurisdiction thereof, are citizens of the United States and of the State wherein they reside. No State shall make or enforce any law which shall abridge the privileges or immunities of citizens of the United States; nor shall any State deprive any person of life, liberty, or property, without due process of law; nor deny to any person within its jurisdiction the equal protection of the laws.

---

the Court generally holds that a search without a valid search warrant is a violation of the Fourth Amendment's right to be free of unreasonable searches and seizures. A 1948 decision indicated the reason. The Fourth Amendment, said the Court, does not prohibit searches, but it does require that "when the right of privacy must reasonably yield to the right of search," the decision should in most cases be "drawn by a neutral and detached magistrate instead of being judged by the officer engaged in the often competitive enterprise of ferreting out crime."[8]

The search warrant is to be issued by the neutral magistrate only after a finding of probable cause, which means that in light of the facts of the case, a reasonable person would think that the evidence sought exists and that it exists in the place to be searched. Despite its preference for warrants, the Supreme Court has allowed some exceptions to the requirement. The Court has, however, argued that these exceptions are "few," "specifically established," and "well-delineated."[9]

Automobile searches

The circumstances under which police may secure warrants to search automobiles resulted in a case generally considered to be the most important Fourth Amendment case decided by the Supreme Court during its 1982–1983 session. In *Illinois v. Gates,*[10] the Court considered what kinds of facts the police must produce in order to convince a magistrate that they have probable cause to obtain a search warrant.

In *Gates,* the Police Department of Bloomingdale, Illinois, received an anonymous letter indicating that two specified people, a husband and wife, were engaging in illegal drug sales and that on May 3 the wife would drive their car, loaded with drugs, to Florida. The husband, the letter indicated, would fly to Florida to drive the car back to Illinois with the trunk loaded with drugs. Finally, the letter indicated that the couple currently had about $100,000 worth of drugs in their basement in Illinois. After receiving this information, a police officer secured the address of the couple and also found out that the husband had made a May 5 reservation to fly to Florida. The flight was put under surveillance, revealing that the suspect took the flight, that he spent the night in a motel room registered to his wife, and that the next morning he left the motel in a car with a woman. The license plate of the car was registered to the husband. The couple were driving north on an interstate highway frequently used for traffic to Illinois. Based on these facts, the police secured a search warrant for the couple's house and automobile.

The police were waiting with the warrants for the couple when they returned to their home in Illinois. Upon searching the house and car, the police found drugs that the state attempted to use against the couple at trial. But the Gates's motion to have the evidence excluded was successful. In upholding the lower courts on this issue, the Illinois Supreme Court relied on two previous Supreme Court decisions regarding the use of informants to establish probable cause for warrants.[11] In those cases, the Supreme Court required information on the informant's veracity, integrity, and reliability before information from that source could be used to establish "probable cause." The Illinois court ruled that probable cause did not exist in the *Gates* case, as there was no information available on the informant's honesty or reliability, nor was there any indication of the basis on which the informant made the predictions regarding the Gateses.

Under some circumstances the police may make a reasonable search for weapons.

The Supreme Court agreed on that point but established a new test: the "totality of circumstances." In this case, said the Court, independent police verification of the allegations from the anonymous source provided sufficient information on which a magistrate could have probable cause to issue the warrants. Although neither the anonymous letter alone nor the police's conclusions concerning the reliability of the informer were sufficient for probable cause, the extensive corroborating evidence obtained by the police, coupled with the letter and the police's conclusions, provided a reliable basis for issuing the search warrant. The search warrant was therefore valid, and so the search of the house and automobile were valid.

Search of the person
The law of search and seizure has also changed in regard to the searching and seizing of persons. The "seizing" of persons will be discussed in the next chapter when we discuss the function of police in making an arrest. But unreasonable searches may occur even when the police have already conducted a lawful arrest as well as before an arrest.

In *Rochin v. California,*[12] the Supreme Court clearly states its position with regard to this serious intrusion of the body.

Rochin v. California

Having "some information that [the petitioner here] was selling narcotics," three deputy sheriffs of the County of Los Angeles, on the morning of July 1, 1949, made for the two-story dwelling house in which Rochin lived with his mother, common-law wife, brothers and sisters. Finding the outside door open, they entered and then forced open the door to Rochin's room on the second floor. Inside they found petitioner sitting partly dressed on the side of the bed, upon which his wife was lying. On a "night stand" beside the bed the deputies spied two capsules. When asked "Whose stuff is this?" Rochin seized the capsules and put them in his mouth. A struggle ensued, in the course of which three officers "jumped upon him" and attempted to extract the capsules. The force they applied proved unavailing against Rochin's resistance. He was handcuffed and taken to a hospital. At the direction of one of the officers a doctor forced an emetic solution through a tube into Rochin's stomach against his will. This "stomach pumping" produced vomiting. In the vomited matter were found two capsules which proved to contain morphine.

Rochin was brought to trial . . . on the charge of possessing "a preparation of morphine." . . . Rochin was convicted and sentenced to sixty days' imprisonment. The chief evidence against him was the two capsules.

. . . we are compelled to conclude that the proceedings by which this conviction was obtained do more than offend some fastidious squeamishness or private sentimentalism about combatting crime too energetically. This is conduct that shocks the conscience, illegally breaking into the privacy of the petitioner, the struggle to open his mouth and remove what was there, the forcible extraction of his stomach's contents—this course of proceedings by agents of government to obtain evidence is bound to offend even hardened sensibilities. They are methods too close to the rack and the screw to permit of constitutional differentiation.

In a later case, a federal court held that it was also an unreasonable search and seizure to require a defendant to undergo surgery in order to remove a bullet from his chest, especially when the surgery would require a general anesthesia and the bullet was in such a place that it could safely be left there forever. This type of intrusion, said the court, was a serious invasion of the body, as compared with taking a blood sample, a process held by the Supreme Court to be permissible.[13]

On the other hand, the Supreme Court refused to review, thus allowing the lower court's decision to stand, a case in which the police used a laxative on a suspect believed to have contraband in his rectum. Police introduced at trial the "evidence" of a crime that they retrieved from the defendant's excrement—balloons filled with marijuana. The court ruled that the evidence was admissible as abandoned property.[14]

Strip searches. In recent years, considerable attention has been focused on strip searches and searches of body cavities incident to arrest. In particular, several cases involving strip searches of women arrested for minor traffic violations or other less serious offenses have been reported. Such searches have gone on for a long time, but only in recent years have so many women complained.

Attention was focused on the practice in the city of Chicago when in 1979 a young woman, on her way to watch a television show at the home of a friend, was arrested for not carrying a driver's license. She was taken to the police station where a computer check revealed that she had a valid license. She sent a companion to her home to get it, but she was nevertheless taken by a matron to a room and ordered to remove her clothing. She asked the matron whether she was sure she had the right person. "I'm just here for a traffic ticket." She was told there was no mistake and ordered to "Pull down your pants, squat three times, and spread your vagina." When the woman refused, she was warned, "If you don't cooperate, six guys will come in and do it for me." The matron "first probed the girl's anus and then, without washing or using sanitary gloves, examined her vagina." She was extremely humiliated by this search as well as by the presence of video cameras in the room. These cameras, part of the security system, could be monitored by officers in another room, although the police said they were not on at the time of this examination. After the search, the woman was released on bond. Later, all charges against her were dismissed.[15]

Some of the women who were strip searched in Chicago settled out of court; others sued the city. In November 1983, a federal court held unconstitutional the practice of routinely strip searching women who were arrested for minor offenses and who were to be detained only briefly. In the excerpt on page 340, from *Mary Beth G. v. City of Chicago,*[16] the court also explained why the process of requiring female, but not male, defendants to be strip searched constituted unfair treatment of women. The court emphasized that the city had not shown an "exceedingly persuasive justification" for this difference in treatment. The city had argued that women, compared with men, were more capable of hiding drugs, weapons, or other contraband inside their body cavities.

The Supreme Court did, however, in *Bell v. Wolfish,*[17] allow the visual inspection of inmates' body cavities to continue when the issue was raised in a case involving persons who were detained in jail awaiting trial on serious charges. The court used a reasonableness test, emphasizing that security was important at the facility.

Mary Beth G. v. City of Chicago

The policy under which female arrestees are routinely subject to strip searches while similarly situated males were not establishes a significant disparity in treatment based on gender. . . .

The city argues that the strip searches used on women were no more intrusive than the thorough hand search used on men and that both sexes were therefore subjected to equal treatment. The assertion runs contrary to common experience, and this court finds the strip searches to be substantially more intrusive. Although the city's decision was based on the documented ability of women arrestees to secrete weapons and contraband in the vaginal cavity and the inability to discover such items by a thorough hand search, evidence also shows that weapons can be secreted on or within the bodies of males. The city failed to show why the presence of the vaginal cavity made it necessary to strip search only women and unnecessary to search the body cavities of men. The city has failed to show that men and women minor offenders are *not* similarly situated, and it cannot show a "substantial relation between the disparity and an important state purpose."

More recently, a federal court in Illinois upheld a routine jail practice of visual inspections of pretrial detainees' body cavities when the practice was applied to all inmates, "carried out (1) by same-sex personnel (2) in a separate room (3) without in any way touching the detainees."[18]

Search of the home   The U.S. Supreme Court has said that the "physical entry of the home is the chief evil against which the wording of the 4th Amendment is directed."[19] The Court recognizes a difference between searches and seizures within a home or office—a person's property and in other places. "It is accepted, at least as a matter of principle, that a search or seizure carried out on a suspect's premises without a warrant is *per se* unreasonable, unless the police can show that it falls within one of a carefully defined set of exceptions based on the presence of 'exigent circumstances.'"[20]

An example of an unreasonable entry into a home occurred in *Mapp v. Ohio.*[21] When police arrived at her home, Ms. Mapp, after calling her attorney, denied them entrance without a search warrant. They advised their headquarters of that response and put the house under surveillance. About three hours later, with more officers on the scene, they again attempted entry. When Ms. Mapp did not quickly come to the door, the officers forced their way in through one of the doors to the house. In the meantime, Mapp's attorney arrived, but the police would not let him enter the house or see Ms. Mapp. The following excerpt explains the subsequent events.[22]

Mapp v. Ohio

It appears that Miss Mapp was halfway down the stairs from the upper floor to the front door when the officers, in this highhanded manner, broke into the hall. She demanded to see the search warrant. A paper claimed to be a warrant, was held up by one of the officers. She grabbed the "warrant" and placed it in her bosom. A struggle ensued in which the officers recovered the piece of paper and as a result of which they handcuffed appellant because she had been "belligerent" in resisting their official rescue of the "warrant" from her person. Running roughshod over appellant, a policeman "grabbed" her, "twisted [her] hand," and she "yelled [and] pleaded with him" because "it was hurting." Appellant, in handcuffs, was then forcibly taken upstairs to her bedroom where the officers searched a dresser, a chest of drawers, a closet and some suitcases. They also looked into a photo album and through personal papers belonging to the appellant. The search spread into the rest of the second floor including the child's bedroom, the living room, the kitchen and a dinette. The basement of the building and a trunk found therein were also searched. The obscene materials for possession of which she was ultimately convicted were discovered in the course of that widespread search.

At the trial no search warrant was produced by the prosecution, nor was the failure to produce one explained or accounted for. At best, "There is, in the record, considerable doubt as to whether there ever was any warrant for the search of the defendant's home."

The seized evidence was used against her at trial, and Ms. Mapp was convicted of "knowingly have had in her possession and under her control certain lewd and lascivious books, pictures, and photographs." The U.S. Supreme Court reversed the conviction.

In the *Mapp* case, the police entered Ms. Mapp's home in search of contraband. Would it have made any difference if they had entered in order to arrest her? In 1980,[23] the Supreme Court considered that question, raised by a case involving a New York statute that permitted police to enter a home, without a warrant, and to use force if necessary to arrest a suspect. The Court said the distinction made by the lower court between entering a home to arrest a suspect and entering to search and seize property was one only of degree, with the basic premise remaining—that warrantless entries to a home are presumptively unreasonable:

The two intrusions share this fundamental characteristic: the breach of the entrance to an individual's home. The Fourth Amendment protects the individual's privacy in a variety of settings. In none is the zone of privacy more clearly defined than when bounded by the unambiguous physical dimensions of an individual's home—a zone that finds its roots in clear and specific consitutional terms. . . . In terms that apply equally to seizures of property and to seizures of persons, the Fourth Amendment has drawn a firm line at the entrance to the house. Absent exigent circumstances, that threshold may not reasonably be crossed without a warrant.[24]

Finally, in 1984 the Court held that the "warrantless, nighttime entry" of a suspect's home "to arrest him for a civil, nonjailable traffic offense, was prohibited by the special protection afforded the individual in his home by the Fourth Amendment."[25]

THE RIGHT NOT
TO BE REQUIRED
TO TESTITY
AGAINST ONESELF

The Fifth Amendment of our Consitution provides that in a criminal trial we cannot be compelled to testify against ourselves. Earlier in this chapter, in comparing the adversary systems with the inquisitorial system, we noted that in the latter, the guilt of defendants is assumed and that they must prove that they are innocent. That used to be very difficult to do, especially when the English star chamber courts subjected defendants to long hours of interrogation, assuming that if interrorgated long enough, they would confess. If they did not confess after such interrogations, they were often tortured physically until they did confess. Some of these methods were also used in our colonial courts.

Our Fifth Amendment was passed in reaction to such coercive measures. The idea behind the right has been expressed as follows: "We do not make even the most hardened criminal sign his own death warrant, or dig his own grave, or pull the lever that springs the trap on which he stands. We have through the course of history developed a considerable feeling of the dignity and intrinsic importance of the individual man. Even the evil man is a human being."[26]

There are some limitations on the Fifth Amendment right, but essentially it means that defendants may not be forced to give testimonial evidence that could help convict them. The interpretation of the privilege against self-incrimination has, however, presented the courts with some interesting challenges, resulting in decisions that are among the Supreme Court's most controversial.

The prohibitions against both physical and mental methods for extracting confessions will be illustrated by excerpts from two cases. The first case, *Brown v. Mississippi,*[27] gives an example of physical brutality used to elicit confessions from several black defendants. The only evidence on which the defendants could have been convicted was their involuntary confessions. Indeed, there was no question about the whippings they received. In fact, one deputy said, in reference to the whippings, "Not too much for a Negro: not as much as I would have done if it were left to me." The Supreme Court of the United States reversed the convictions of the defendants after the Supreme Court of Mississippi upheld the convictions of the young men, who were sentenced to death for their "crimes." After describing the beating of the first defendant, the Court continues:

Brown v. Mississippi

The other two defendants were also arrested and taken to the same jail. On Sunday night, April 1, 1934, the same deputy, accompanied by a number of white men, one of whom was also an officer, and by the jailer, came to the jail, and the two last named defendants were made to strip and they were laid over chairs and their backs were cut to pieces with a leather strap with buckles on it, and they were likewise made by the said deputy definitely to understand that the whipping would be continued unless and until they confessed, and not only confessed, but confessed in every matter of detail as demanded by those present; and in this manner the defendants confessed the crime, and as the whippings progressed and were repeated, they changed or adjusted their confession in all particulars of detail so as to conform to the demands of their torturers. When the confessions had been obtained in the exact form and contents as desired by the mob, they left with the parting admonition and warning that, if the defendants changed their story at any time in any respect from the last stated, the perpetrators of the outrage would administer the same or equally effective treatment. . . .

Because a State may dispense with a jury trial, it does not follow that it may substitute trial by ordeal. The rack and torture chamber may not be substituted for the witness stand.

. . . It would be difficult to conceive of methods more revolting to the sense of justice than those taken to procure the confessions of these petitioners, and the use of the confessions thus obtained as the basis for conviction and sentence was a clear denial of due process. . . .

Enforcement of the right: the Miranda warnings

With the prohibition against extracting confessions by means of physical brutality, some jurisdictions began to concentrate on psychological methods. Such methods are illustrated by the highly controversial **Miranda** case,[28] decided in 1966 by a five to four vote of the Court.

The *Miranda* decision actually involved questions that, according to Chief Justice Earl Warren who wrote the opinion for the majority, "go to the roots of our concepts of American criminal jurisprudence; the restraints society must observe consistent with the Federal Constitution in prosecuting individuals for crime."

Because of the importance of *Miranda,* we shall look at several portions of the decision. In the first excerpt, on page 344, we can see some examples of the psychological methods used by police to elicit confessions.[29]

The tactics utilized by many police departments to elicit confessions, and quoted in *Miranda,* indicate the immense advantage the police would have over the accused. Notice the emphasis on getting the accused out of his or

Miranda v. Arizona

In each of [the cases before the Supreme Court] the defendant was questioned by police officers, detectives, or a prosecuting attorney in a room in which he was cut off from the outside world. In none of these cases was the defendant given a full and effective warning of his rights at the outset of the interrogation process. In all the cases, the questioning elicited oral admissions, and in three of them, signed statements as well which were admitted at their trials. They all thus share salient features—incommunicado interrogation of individuals in a police-dominated atmosphere, resulting in self-incriminating statements without full warnings of constitutional rights. . . .

Again we stress that the modern practice of in-custody interrogation is psychologically rather than physically oriented. As we have stated before, this Court has recognized that coercion can be mental as well as physical, and that the blood of the accused is not the only hallmark of an unconstitutional inquisition.

Interrogation still takes place in privacy. Privacy results in secrecy and this in turn results in a gap in our knowledge as to what in fact goes on in the interrogation rooms. A valuable source of information about present police practices, however, may be found in various police manuals and texts which document procedures employed with success in the past, and which recommend various other effective tactics. These texts are used by law enforcement agencies themselves as guides. It should be noted that these texts professedly present the most enlightened and effective means presently used to obtain statements through custodial interrogation. By considering these texts and other data, it is possible to describe procedures observed and noted around the country.

The officers are told by the manuals that the "principal psychological factor contributing to a successful interrogation is privacy—being alone with the person under interrogation." The efficacy of this tactic has been explained as follows:

> If at all practicable, the interrogation should take place in the investigator's office or at least in a room of his own choice. The subject should be deprived of every psychological advantage. In his own home he may be confident, indignant, or recalcitrant. He is more keenly aware of his rights and more reluctant to tell of his indiscretions or criminal behaviors within the walls of his home. Moreover his family and other friends are nearby, their presence lending moral support. In his office, the investigator possesses all the advantages. The atmosphere suggests the invincibility of the forces of the law.

To highlight the isolation and unfamiliar surroundings, the manuals instruct the police to display an air of confidence in the suspect's guilt and from outward appearance to maintain only an interest in confirming certain details. The guilt of the subject is to be posited as a fact. The interrogator should direct his comments toward the reasons why the subject committed the act, rather than court failure by asking the subject whether he did it. Like other men, perhaps the subject has had a bad family life, had an unhappy childhood, had too much to drink, had an unrequited desire for women. The officers are instructed to minimize the moral seriousness of the offense, to cast blame on the victim or on society. These tactics are designed to put the subject in a psychological state where his story is but an elaboration of what the police purport to know already—that he is guilty. Explanations to the contrary are dismissed and discouraged.

her own environment into a strange environment and removing every other psychological advantage that the accused might have over the police.

After some of these interrogation techniques were used on Miranda, he confessed. When he appealed on the issue that he did not have an attorney when he was interrogated, the Arizona Supreme Court agreed with the state that none of Miranda's constitutional rights had been violated because he did not *ask* for an attorney. Miranda had signed a confession that indicated that his statement was "voluntary." On the basis of that testimony and other evidence, Miranda was convicted of kidnapping and rape and sentenced to twenty to thirty years in prison for each offense, with the sentences to run concurrently.

In deciding *Miranda,* the Supreme Court emphasized the possibility that under the kinds of psychological pressures used by police in the cases before the Court, innocent defendants might confess. In our system of law, said the Court, with the tremendous powers of the state in a criminal trial, it is necessary to give defendants procedural safeguards so as to avoid conviction of the innocent as well as coerced confessions from the guilty.

The Court then interpreted the Fifth Amendment right not to have to testify against oneself as requiring that the police must tell the accused of the specifics of that right. The procedures that the police must follow in the "*Miranda* rights" are explained by the Court in the second excerpt from the case, on page 346.

It is important to understand that the Court is not trying to "free" guilty people but, rather, to ensure that all accused are accorded their constitutional rights. In Miranda's case, at his second trial, he was found guilty and sentenced to prison.

Miranda v. Arizona

As for the procedural safeguards to be employed, unless other fully effective means are devised to inform accused persons of their right of silence and to assure a continuous opportunity to exercise it, the following measures are required. Prior to any questioning, the person must be warned that he has a right to remain silent, that any statement he does make may be used as evidence against him, and that he has a right to the presence of an attorney, either retained or appointed. The defendant may waive effectuation of these rights, provided the waiver is made voluntarily, knowingly and intelligently. If, however, he indicates in any manner and at any stage of the process that he wishes to consult with an attorney before speaking there can be no questioning. Likewise, if the individual is alone and indicates in any manner that he does not wish to be interrogated, the police may not question him. The mere fact that he may have answered some questions or volunteered some statements on his own does not deprive him of the right to refrain from answering any further inquiries until he has consulted with an attorney and thereafter consents to be questioned.

Reaction to Miranda

The *Miranda* decision immediately created a controversy. The intense negative reaction is illustrated by a comment made by a criminologist in 1968 in a speech before the Iowa State Police's Association. He referred to the Supreme Court as a "coterie of politicians forcing their views on the public. . . . The Supreme Court is not what it used to be. The rats are in the attic. The snakes are in the basement. The pigs are in the parlor. We ought to evict the occupants."[30]

Reactions have also ranged from the cry that we are licensing people to kill, rape, rob, and steal to the argument that all the decision did was to extend to all defendants, including the "poor, the naive, the ignorant, the uneducated, the insecure and frightened," the rights that the Constitution had always guaranteed and that the rich had always employed.[31]

Supreme Court interpretations of Miranda

Earlier we mentioned that the *Miranda* decision has led to considerable litigation,[32] with many of the cases going to the Supreme Court for final review. A few decisions will show the range of questions considered by the Court in recent years.

A 1977 case raised the issue of whether the *Miranda* warnings would have to be given to a person who went to the police station and confessed after an investigator had left a card at his home. The card "invited" the suspect, who was on parole, to go to the police station to talk. The police alleged that the suspect voluntarily went to the station to talk. He was told that he was under arrest after which he was questioned without an attorney. The *Miranda* warning was not given. The police told the defendant that his fingerprints were found at the scene of the crime. That was not true, but when the defendant heard that, he confessed. The Supreme Court held that the confession was not obtained in violation of the suspect's *Miranda* rights. According to the Court, "*Miranda* warnings are required only where there has been such a restriction on a person's freedom as to render him 'in custody.'"[33]

In one of its most recent interpretations of *Miranda,* the Supreme Court considered whether the *Miranda* warnings would have to be given by a probation officer when talking to a client about another crime. The probationer, upon being questioned by his probation officer, admitted to the officer that he had raped and murdered a teenage girl. This confession was used against the probationer when he was tried for the rape and murder, and he was convicted. His attorneys argued that his constitutional rights had been violated, because his probation officer had not given him the *Miranda* warning. The Court ruled, in a six to three decision, that the *Miranda* warnings were not required in such cases. In the majority opinion, the Court stated, "The nature of probation is such that probationers should expect to be questioned on a wide range of topics relating to their past criminality." Such probationers would be free to refuse to answer those questions, said the Court, but their rights would not be violated if they were not specifically told that they may invoke the Fifth Amendment and refuse to "testify against themselves."[34]

Finally, in 1984, the Court limited the impact of the exclusionary rule and the *Miranda* requirement. First, the Court held that "overriding considerations of public safety" may justify police questioning of a suspect without first giving the *Miranda* warning. Second, the Court ruled that illegally seized evidence is admissible if the police would later have found the evidence anyway, by legal methods. The Court calls this the "inevitable discovery" exception to the exclusionary rule. Finally, on the last day of the 1983–1984 term, the Court held that when police conduct a search in good faith, even though the technical search warrant is defective, the seized evidence will not be excluded from the trial.[35]

Extent of the Fifth Amendment   The police may take some evidence, such as hair and blood samples, without a search warrant. These may be used as evidence against the accused at trial, even though they might incriminate him or her. Thus, the Fifth Amendment prohibition against being forced to testify against oneself does not extend to certain types of physical evidence; rather, its purpose is to protect one's rights not to incriminate oneself through testimonial, communicative evidence.

THE RIGHT
TO COUNSEL

The Sixth Amendment, providing that in all criminal prosecutions the accused shall have "the Assistance of Counsel for his defense," became a part of our Bill of Rights in 1791. But it was not until 1963 and 1972, in two important cases, that the right to counsel became a reality for most defendants. We shall begin with the 1963 decision, *Gideon v. Wainwright.*

The case of Clarence Earl Gideon shows that it is possible (whether it is probable is quite another question!) for an indigent to attract the attention of the U.S. Supreme Court, resulting in a tremendous impact on the rights of defendants in the criminal justice system. Gideon was not a violent man, but he was often in trouble with the police for various violations of law. As a result, he had been in and out of prison.

At his trial for breaking and entering a poolroom with the intent to commit a misdemeanor, a felony under Florida law, Gideon, acting as his own attorney, argued that he needed a lawyer. Because he had no money, Gideon requested the court to appoint an attorney for him, but the judge replied that under Florida law, an indigent was not entitled to a court-appointed attorney except when charged with a crime that could result in a death sentence.

After telling the judge that "the United States Supreme Court says I am entitled to an attorney," Gideon conducted his own defense, "about as well as could be expected from a layman," according to the Court. Gideon was convicted and sentenced to five years in the state prison. On January 8, 1962, the Supreme Court of the United States received a large envelope from prisoner 003826 in Florida. Mr. Gideon, who had printed his request in pencil, was asking the highest court of this country to hear his case.

The Supreme Court agreed to hear Gideon's case and appointed an attorney from a prestigious Washington, D.C., law firm, to represent Gideon. Gideon's attorney convinced the Court that it should overrule a previous case in which the Court had held that the right to counsel applied only to capital cases. The Court reviewed that earlier decision[36] and other cases and then continued with an explanation of the reasons that counsel is important, as the excerpt on page 349 from Gideon's case illustrates.[37]

*The right to
effective counsel*

The right to counsel is of little value unless the attorney who represents the defendant provides an effective defense. Thus, the right to counsel means the right to *effective* assistance of counsel.[38] The problem, however, is that there is little consensus on the meaning of the effective assistance of counsel.

The Supreme Court has stated that the purpose of counsel is to "preserve the adversary process"[39] and that counsel is to serve as an "actual advocate on behalf of his client,"[40] but the Court has consistently refused to define what is meant by effective assistance of counsel. In fact, in 1970 the Court indicated that this is a function of the trial courts.[41]

Lower federal courts have attacked this issue, but their "answers" have

Gideon v. Wainwright

Not only these precedents but also reason and reflection require us to recognize that in our adversary system of criminal justice, any person haled into court, who is too poor to hire a lawyer, cannot be assured a fair trial unless counsel is provided for him. . . . The right of one charged with crime to counsel may not be deemed fundamental and essential to fair trials in some countries, but it is in ours. From the very beginning, our state and national constitutions and laws have laid great emphasis on procedure and substantive safeguards designed to assure fair trials before impartial tribunals in which every defendant stands equal before the law. This noble ideal cannot be realized if the poor man charged with crime has to face his accusers without a lawyer to assist him. A defendant's need for a lawyer is nowhere better stated than in the moving words of Mr. Justice Sutherland in Powell v. Alabama: "The right to be heard would be, in many cases, of little avail if it did not comprehend the right to be heard by counsel. Even the intelligent and educated layman has small and sometimes no skill in the science of law. If charged with crime, he is incapable, generally, of determining for himself whether the indictment is good or bad. He is unfamiliar with the rules of evidence. Left without aid of counsel he may be put on trial without a proper charge, and convicted upon incompetent evidence irrelevant to the issue or otherwise inadmissible. He lacks both the skill and knowledge adequately to prepare his defense, even though he may have a perfect one. He requires the guiding hand of counsel at every step in the proceedings against him. Without it, though he be not guilty, he faces the danger of conviction because he does not know how to establish his innocence." . . .

varied. A 1984 decision by the Ninth Judicial Circuit illustrates ineffective assistance of counsel. The defendant's attorney fell asleep during the trial, and the court ruled that this was inherently prejudicial; an unconscious or sleeping counsel is equivalent to no counsel at all! Actually, according to the court, this was not a case of "ineffective" assistance of counsel; this was a case of *no* counsel at all.[42]

Finally, in the spring of 1984, the Supreme Court did hear and decide two cases on effective assistance of counsel. The first case involved a defendant whose attorney specialized in real estate and had virtually no experience in criminal law and only twenty-five days to prepare a defense. The second involved a death row inmate who argued that he did not have effective assistance of counsel at the nonjury sentencing stage. The Supreme Court reinstated the convictions of both defendants, thus overruling the lower federal courts' rulings that the defendants did not have effective assistance of counsel. According to the Court's opinion, "The benchmark for judging any claim of ineffectiveness must be whether counsel's conduct so undermined the proper functioning of the adversarial process that the trial cannot be relied on as having produced a just result." Thus, in order to win on the issue of ineffective assistance of counsel, a defendant must be able to prove that his or her attorney's errors "were so serious as to deprive the defendant of a fair trial, a trial whose result is reliable."[43]

THE RIGHT TO TRIAL BY JURY

Among other rights, the Sixth Amendment to the United States Constitution guarantees the right to a speedy[44] and public trial by an impartial jury.[45] The Court has held that this also means the right to be tried by a jury that is drawn from a fair cross section of the community.[46]

Cases tried in federal courts are governed by a congressional statute that has, among other requirements, a statement that litigants who are being tried before a jury "shall have the right to grand and petit juries selected at random from a fair cross section of the community."[47]

The requirement of randomness does not, however, mean that the jury must be selected according to "statistical randomness."[48] Nor does it mean that the jury must "mirror" the community. "Defendants are not entitled to a jury of any particular composition."[49] What, then, does the requirement mean? Numerous issues have been raised, and the lower courts, as well as the Supreme Court of the United States, have heard relevant cases.

Jury selection

In England jurors are chosen randomly, but in the United States, although the list of potential jurors is usually selected randomly, actual jurors are selected after a procedure called **voir dire,** which literally means "to tell the truth." The defense attorney and the prosecuting attorney *voir dire* the jury; that is, they question each potential juror and then decide whether or not they will approve the selection of that person. In addition, the judge may question the potential jurors. Potential jurors may also be excused in two ways. If they are *excused for cause,* they are presumed to be biased in the case because of their association with or knowledge of the defendant or some other person involved in the trial, because of their personal financial interest in the case, or because of some particular background experience that might prejudice them. For example, a person whose spouse has been murdered might be presumed to be prejudiced against a defendant being tried for murder and therefore excused for cause. Other reasons for which a potential juror might be excused for cause are mental incompetence or the inability to speak English.

The second way in which a potential juror may be excused is by *peremptory challenge,* which means that the attorney may excuse without cause.

The defense and the prosecution are each given a specific number of these challenges.

Composition and size of juries

In a 1940 decision, the U.S. Supreme Court unanimously stated that "it is a part of the established tradition in the use of juries as intruments of public justice that the jury be a body truly representative of the community" and that to exclude racial groups from jury service was "at war with our basic concepts of a democratic society and a representative government."[50] It was therefore unconstitutional to exclude blacks systematically from jury duty. The Court has also held that rules that result in the systematic exclusion of women from juries are unconstitutional as well.[51]

The Court has also ruled on the required size of juries. A jury of less than twelve is permissible. For example, although there is evidence that smaller juries are less objective than larger ones,[52] a jury of six is permissible in non-capital cases,[53] but fewer than six is unconstitutional.[54] In a jury of six, however, the verdict must be unanimous,[55] although a unanimous verdict is not required in a twelve-person jury.[56]

The right to an impartial jury

An impartial jury means not only that it does not exclude classes of persons, like blacks (or other minorities) and women, but also that it does not bring to the trial people with such strong beliefs and convictions that it would be impossible for them to evaluate the facts objectively. The right to be tried by an impartial jury is particularly important in a capital case. The Supreme Court, in *Witherspoon v. State of Illinois,*[57] excerpted on page 352, emphasized the importance of an impartial jury when the imposition of the death penalty is a possibility upon conviction.

The right to an impartial jury also means that jurors have not been unduly influenced by the media. Defendants cannot have a fair trial if because of pretrial publicity, the jurors have already made up their minds about the case. Therefore, the Court has issued rulings concerning when pretrial publicity is prejudicial to the defendant. Perhaps the most publicized of those rulings was the Court's response to the trial of Dr. Sam Sheppard, accused and then convicted of the murder of his wife. Sheppard served ten years in prison before his case was overturned and sent back for retrial, at which he was acquitted of the murder charge.[58]

During Sheppard's trial the media were always present. Private telephones were installed to allow the press to get the reports to the papers with greater speed, and one station was permitted to set up broadcasting equipment in the room next to the jury deliberation room. "Newscasts were made from this room throughout the trial, and while the jury reached its verdict." Jurors and other participants in the trial were photographed as they entered and left the courtroom. With the crowd of media persons as well as the public, it was impossible for Sheppard to talk privately with his counsel during

Witherspoon v. State of Illinois

If the State had excluded only those prospective jurors who stated in advance of trial that they would not even consider returning a verdict of death, it could argue that the resulting jury was simply "neutral" with respect to penalty. But when it swept from the jury all who expressed conscientious or religious scruples against capital punishment and all who opposed it in principle, the State crossed the line of neutrality. In its quest for a jury capable of imposing the death penalty, the State produced a jury uncommonly willing to condemn a man to die.

It is, of course, settled that a State may not entrust the determination of whether a man is innocent or guilty to a tribunal "organized to convict." . . . It requires but a short step from that principle to hold, as we do today, that a State may not entrust the determination of whether a man should live or die to a tribunal organized to return a verdict of death. Specifically, we hold that a sentence of death cannot be carried out if the jury that imposed or recommended it was chosen by excluding veniremen for cause simply because they voiced general objections to the death penalty or expressed conscientious or religious scruples against its infliction. No defendant can consitutionally be put to death at the hands of a tribunal so selected.

Whatever else might be said of capital punishment, it is at least clear that its imposition by a hanging jury cannot be squared with the Constitution. The State of Illinois has stacked the deck against the petitioner. To execute this death sentence would deprive him of his life without due process of law.

Reversed.

the trial; for that purpose, they often had to leave the courtroom. Nor was it possible inside the courtroom for counsel to approach the judge out of the jury's hearing. The jurors were also exposed to the news media.

These and many other facts were considered by the Supreme Court before overruling Sheppard's conviction. Its opinion stressed the importance of the media's First Amendment rights but also the more important right of the defendant to be tried before a jury not biased by media reports. In conclusion, it declared, "With his life at stake, it is not requiring too much that petitioner be tried in an atmosphere undisturbed by so huge a wave of public passion. . . . The theory of our system is that the conclusions to be reached in a case will be induced only by evidence and argument in open court, and not by any outside influence, whether of private talk or public print." The Court referred to the trial as having a "Roman holiday" atmosphere, complete with murder, mystery, society, and sex.[59]

The influence of publicity on the jury was again considered in 1979 when the Court was faced with the issue of whether the press could be barred from a pretrial hearing.[60] The Court recognized the importance of open trials but refused to recognize a constitutional right of the public to be present at a trial. The decision reopened the power struggle between the press and the Court,[61] as well as between the "rights of the public" and the "rights of the defendant." Public and press reaction was predictably critical. The *New York Times* lead editorial was headlined "Private Justice, Public Injustice," adding "Now the Supreme Court has endorsed secrecy in language broad enough to justify its use not only in a pre-trial context but even at a formal trial. . . . The power to make public business private is a dangerous power, far in excess of the supposed benefit."[62] *Time* magazine referred to the decision as a "stunning shock" to the press. "It is also by far the court's sharpest blow to the press in a long string of such adverse rulings."[63]

Part of the controversy stems from the fact that the opinions in the case are unclear and go beyond the actual holding of the case. The case was based on a very narrow issue—whether the public can be excluded from a pretrial hearing on sensitive evidence issues when it can be shown that public access to such information might prejudice potential jurors. But Justice Potter Stewart, writing for the majority, asserted the public has "no constitutional right . . . to attend public trials." In a later decision, however, the Court ruled that the public and the press do have a constitutional right of access of criminal trials.[64] That right of access is, however, not unlimited.[65]

THE RIGHTS OF VICTIMS

Our discussion thus far has involved the due process rights of defendants who are tried in our criminal courts, though there are many other due process rights. The right to be free of unreasonable searches and seizures, the right not to be forced to testify against oneself, the right to counsel, and the right to trial by an impartial jury are at the heart of those rights but are only a sample of the efforts our system has made to give defendants a fair trial. Many people feel, however, that the pendulum has swung too far, that defendants have too many rights, that society is not protected, and that the victims are ignored. Recently we have heard demands for a "Bill of Rights for Victims." The movement in that direction is strong, but the demands for the victim's rights often conflict with the defendant's rights.

THE VICTIMS' PARTICIPATION IN THE CRIMINAL JUSTICE SYSTEM

Throughout most of our history, victims have been virtually ignored by the criminal justice system. They have been expected to testify when their alleged assailants were on trial, but they have not even been accorded the most simple courtesies concerning information on where, when, why, and how. In the past few years, however, many jurisdictions have tried to remedy this situation. The Victim/Witness Assistance Center in Tulsa, Oklahoma, exemplifies these changes.

OKLAHOMA CRIME VICTIM/WITNESS BILL OF RIGHTS

1. You, as a witness or victim, have the right to know the status of the case in which you are involved.

2. You have the right to know when property that might be held as evidence can be returned to you.

3. You have the right to receive a witness fee when you are subpoenaed to Court.

4. You have the right to be informed of existing Victim Compensation Laws and the right to ask for compensation under those laws.

5. You have a right to be informed of social services available in your area.

6. You, as a witness for the State of Oklahoma, have a right to receive protection from harm and/or intimidation.

7. You have the right to be informed, to appear and to be heard before the Pardon and Parole Board when the defendant in your criminal case is going to be reviewed. You have the right to be notified when the criminal is being released from prison.

8. You have the right to expect that criminals will not profit from their criminal actions for their past conduct or from any future recital of that conduct.

9. You have the right to sue in a civil court any person who commits a crime against you.

10. You have a right to participate in the criminal justice system designed to protect you.

NATIONAL VICTIM RIGHTS WEEK
APRIL 17 - 23, 1983

Sponsored By The Oklahoma District Attorney's Victim/Witness Coordinators Association

First, the Victim/Witness Assistance Center provides a clean, neat, and comfortable waiting area for victims who are called to testify in court. Professional assistance is available to answer any questions the victims might have about the trial, about their personal possessions taken for evidence at trial, and about financial compensation and other kinds of assistance available to crime victims. An "on-call" system is available for victims and witnesses who can reach the courthouse in thirty minutes. Previously, victims and witnesses were told to come to court on a certain day at a specific time and then had to wait for hours before they were needed, if ever. This was not done on purpose, as it is impossible for court clerks to know precisely when a witness will be needed. The result of this "on-call" system has been a tremendous increase in the attendance of witnesses at trials.

The Victim/Witness Center has a director, but trained volunteers are also an important part of its services. "Most victims are ordinary people, disoriented and anxious, who need to establish a sense of trust—it is a crisis time in their lives. A volunteer can offer empathy, concern and reassurance, helping to make a victim more relaxed, and a witness more effective."[66]

Its notification system is also essential to the Victim/Witness Center. If a defendant pleads guilty before trial, witnesses are often not notified and may consequently show up for a trial that will not occur, thus wasting their own

In many cities, the district attorney's office or other organization provides a victim/witness center that assists victims and relatives of victims of crimes.

time and money and increasing their disillusionment with the criminal justice system. The witnesses are also told when the trial has been postponed.

The victims may also need financial and other kinds of assistance before they can participate in the proceedings, including reimbursement for transportation to the court, parking, baby sitting, or other reasonable expenses.

The victims' actual participation in negotiation proceedings is also becoming a part of the Tulsa system. Volunteers will be trained to assist in negotiation meetings between victims and offenders, and victims will be allowed to express their concerns and opinions on issues such as sentencing or restitution.

The importance of victim participation in the criminal justice proceedings was emphasized on a national level in late 1983, when the National Institute of Justice (NIJ) provided funds for the National Judicial College in Reno, Nevada, to conduct a workshop on the subject. Two judges from each state, the District of Columbia, and Puerto Rico heard, among other speakers, the director of the National Institute of Justice report on research by the NIJ revealing that a majority of victims who had agreed to participate in sentencing conferences reported that they were satisfied with the results.

The judges who attended the conference were seen as "change agents" who would return to their home courts and encourage other judges, as well as other court personnel, to implement programs that would involve victims in the criminal proceedings of their assailants.[67]

VICTIM COMPENSATION PROGRAMS

In many cases, however, the victims' greatest need is for financial compensation for the property losses they have incurred as crime victims or for medical expenses or both. Many states have recently enacted **victim compensation** legislation,[68] but the federal program will be used to show some of the problems with the system of victim compensation.

Congress passed the Victim and Witness Protection Act of 1982,[69] applying to victims of offenders tried in federal courts. The act contains various provisions designed to prevent the harassment of victims and witnesses, establishes guidelines for the fair treatment of crime victims and witnesses in the criminal justice system, mandates the attorney general to report to Congress within a year from the statute's passage any laws necessary "to ensure that no Federal felon derives any profit from the sale of the recollections, thoughts, and feelings of such felon with regards to the offense committed by the felon until any victim of the offense receives restitution."[70]

Financial resources for victims may come from the federal government's compensation programs, but another source is the offender. The federal law, like many state laws, provides for restitution from offenders to victims. The federal requirement is almost mandatory. When offenders are convicted in federal courts, the sentencing judges must order them to make restitution to their victims or state the reasons for not ordering restitution.[71]

The federal statute's restitution provision was tested in a case in which three codefendants were convicted of kidnapping. One of the victims died, and another suffered sexual abuse and a laceration to her head for which she was hospitalized, suffering from psychological damage that was possibly severe and permanent. Another victim sustained damage to his automobile, which was used in the commission of the crime. The defendants, all of whom had some money, had been ordered to pay restitution, but after conviction and at the sentencing hearing, they filed a motion claiming that the restitution requirement was unconstitutional. The federal court that considered the defendants' appeals in this case agreed with the defendants that the restitution requirement was unconstitutional. In ordering defendants to pay an amount of money, without offering them the jury trial that is guaranteed by the Seventh Amendment ("the right of jury trial shall be preserved" in civil cases "where the value in controversy exceeds twenty dollars"), violated their constitutional rights. The court further chastised Congress for passing a statute illustrative of poor draftmanship and too few standards. In issuing its oral opinion in this case on July 20, 1983, the court said, "I don't expect to be the last court to speak on this question, but it looks like I'll be the first." The court's subsequent written opinion concluded with these words: "The Court knows that it is entering where angels fear to tread, but enter it must."[72]

Finally, the federal court indicated that Congress, in passing the Victim and Witness Protection Act of 1982, failed to consider the financial cost of implementing that act.

THE RIGHTS OF DEFENDANTS VERSUS THE RIGHTS OF VICTIMS

This brief discussion of victim's rights illustrates the tensions between the rights of defendants and the rights of victims. The federal statute providing restitution to victims was declared unconstitutional because it violates the defendant's right to a jury trial for the amount of restitution. The passage of victim's rights legislation in California also shows how attempts to protect victims may violate the defendant's constitutional rights. Proposition 8, known as the Victim's Bill of Rights,[73] limits plea bargaining, abolishes the right to bail in noncapital cases, restricts the use of the insanity defense, increases the sentences for repeat offenders, and limits the application of the exclusionary rule. On another issue, not relevant here, the constitutionality of Proposition 8 was upheld by a bitterly divided state supreme court in a five to four decision,[74] but other legal challenges are expected in the near future. Some of those challenges may be able to show that the victims' rights infringe on the defendants' rights.

Recognition of the rights of victims may also have other repercussions on the criminal justice system. For example, it is not at all clear that legislation such as Proposition 8 will achieve its goal of more convictions. Attorneys have argued that the result in some cases has been and will continue to be more acquittals and thus fewer convictions. The reason is that before the bill's passage, some defendants would plead guilty to a lesser charge offered through plea bargaining, even though the evidence against them was weak, because they did not want to take the chance of being convicted on a more serious charge. But juries often refuse to convict on the basis of the weak evidence, and the defendant is acquitted.

Finally, Proposition 8 has increased litigation, including whether the provisions are constitutional and whether many cases that would have been plea bargained now must go to trial.

SUMMARY AND CONCLUSION

This chapter has introduced the concept or philosophy that is the basis of our system of criminal justice and therefore has set the stage for a more thorough analysis of some of that system's elements: the police, jail and bail, the courts and attorneys, and finally, the process of punishment and sentencing. We examined the stages of the criminal justice system, the concept of due process in the adversary system, and then the four basic rights of defendants recognized by our system: the right to be free of unreasonable search and seizure, the right not to be required to testify against oneself, the right to counsel, and the right to trial by jury. We also discussed the need to recognize the victims' rights. Finally, we looked at the problems that arise when we attempt to recognize the rights of both the defendants and the victims.

This chapter showed some of the inevitable tensions and controversies in our system of criminal justice. On the one hand, we believe in individual rights; we do not think the police or any other governmental officials should be able to interfere in our personal lives without just cause. But we also want to walk the streets safely, and so we want adequate police protection from crime. When we are victimized, we want our property back and our medical bills paid, and we want the defendants "brought to justice." But all of these goals may be impossible to reach.

The tensions between the rights of the accused (or for that matter, those who are thought to be likely to commit a crime) and the rights of victims and of society have been brought into focus by the Federal Bureau of Investigation (FBI), which in March 1983 established new rules for FBI domestic security investigations. These rules were in part the result of a fear of terrorism at the Los Angeles Olympic games to be held in the summer of 1984.

These new rules no longer require that a crime be "imminent" before the FBI can investigate. Nor do they require an investigation into an organization to cease once its members have been prosecuted or the organization goes out of existence.

Just one month after the new rules were promulgated, the FBI began setting up files on persons considered by the Secret Service to be dangerous to any of the persons that the service protects. Thus these persons will be watched, even though they have not committed a crime.

The advisory board of the National Crime Information Center has proposed creating files on persons who are thought to be involved with terrorism, organized crime, or narcotics, even though there is no evidence to arrest those persons for actual crimes. Also included would be people "known to be, believed to be, likely to be or may be associated with" a drug dealer, even if there is no evidence that the person deals in drugs or, for that matter, even knows about the drug dealer's illegal activities.

Millions of people could be included under these proposals. Furthermore, with the continued development of computerized communications, the FBI can keep tabs on people all over the country and share that information with the local police in a matter of minutes, if not seconds. Such abilities, along with the broad scope of the "tracking" system proposed, leaves us all open to police surveillance and the invasion of our personal privacy and other individual rights.

It is this tremendous power of the government, a power that can—in the hands of the power hungry and ruthless—violate our constitutional rights even to the point of conviction for a crime we did not commit, that requires us to provide and maintain some protection for those accused of crime. In protecting their rights, we protect the rights of us all. This need was demonstrated in *A Man for All Seasons,* a play about the life, trial, and execution of the English humanist, author, and statesman, Sir Thomas More. More, who lived from 1478 to 1535 and in 1935 was canonized by the Roman Catholic Church, stated, "Yes, I'd give the Devil benefit of law, for my own safety's sake."[75]

But it is necessary for some to have the power of enforcement and the power of prevention. Nor can we eliminate discretion from that system, and much of that discretion is exercised daily by our local police. It is therefore essential that we have a professional police force.

CHAPTER 11

The police

A formal police system is relatively new in our society, and we shall begin this chapter with a brief overview of our current system. We shall then discuss police personnel, the type of training and education (or the lack thereof) that our officers have had historically and recent efforts to recruit more women and racial minorities into policing. We shall also consider the efforts to improve the education of police and the personal qualities necessary for effective policing. Our study of policing will focus on the three functions: law enforcement, order maintenance, and the provision of social services. We shall examine the way their time is allocated among these three functions and the role conflict and stresses that develop as the police try to fulfill all three functions. Police decision making will be analyzed, especially the decision whether to arrest or to use deadly force. That section will close with a look at police corruption. Finally, we shall consider how the courts, the legislature, the community, and the police departments can improve policing in our society.

The **police** occupy one of the most important positions in American society. To them is entrusted the right to protect the citizenry, even when that involves the use of violence. More is expected of the police than of most other professionals. They are expected to be brave in all situations and not to show the human emotions of fear, shock, surprise, and hurt, even in the face of the most serious tragedies of human life and death. The police are expected to make decisions quickly and with the calm, cool rationality that most people exhibit only in less traumatic situations. The police are expected to solve the problems in the ghetto that society has created but for which it has found no solutions. They are expected to treat the citizenry with respect, even when harassed, threatened, and verbally and physically abused.

The police also occupy one of the most controversial positions in contemporary society. At times the police are hated, but they are often essential in times of trouble. In short, the police are indispensable in a modern complex society, but most Americans do not know how to live with them. The police in turn fight back with their attitudes and their weapons and try to explain accusations of "police brutality."

THE POLICE SYSTEM

Although some countries have a centralized police system[1] the United States has a decentralized system having three levels: local, state, and federal, with the majority of law enforcement agencies located in counties, cities, towns, and villages. At the state level,[2] police are the main enforcers of the law. They patrol the highways and regulate traffic and have the primary responsibility for the enforcement of some state laws. They provide some services, such as a system of criminal identification, police training programs, and a communications system for local law officials. The sheriff is the main law enforcement officer at the county level of government. He or she is selected, usually for two to four years, to keep the peace, preserve order and enforce court orders, execute civil and criminal process, and patrol the area. The main law enforcers in suburban townships and municipalities are police officers. At all of these levels, jurisdiction is limited to the state, township, or municipality in which the person is a sworn officer of the law, unless the officer is in "hot pursuit" of a felon.

This highly decentralized system does have problems. **Jurisdictional** boundaries result in overlapping, communication problems, and difficulty in obtaining assistance from another law enforcement agency or agent. To some extent, the problems of decentralization may be met by the creation of agencies at local, state, and federal levels to supervise cooperation of the various agencies.

The United States does not have a national police system. But Congress does enact federal criminal laws, which govern the District of Columbia and all states when a "federal" offense has been committed—kidnapping, assas-

---

EXHIBIT

ORGANIZATION OF POLICE SYSTEMS IN THE UNITED STATES

Traditionally, the Police Function has Been Dominated by Local Governments

- More than 90% of all municipalities with a population of 2,500 or more have their own police forces. However, there is a trend toward consolidating law enforcement functions among local communities.
- In 1977, there were 11,475 municipal, 81 county, and 1,806 township general-purpose police agencies in the United States employing 488,832 full-time equivalent employees.
- There are 3,077 sheriffs' departments, nearly all of them at the county level. The responsibilities of the sheriffs cover a range of duties including standard police protection services, serving judicial process papers, and operating jails and detention facilities.
- Other participants in State and local law enforcement include State agencies such as the 52 State police and highway patrols and some 1,122 special police agencies including park rangers, harbor police, transit police, and campus security forces. In addition to their independent responsibilities, these agencies often provide valuable support to local law enforcement agencies in technical areas such as forensics and identification.

There Are More Than 50 Law Enforcement Agencies at the Federal Level

The Federal agencies that have the largest law enforcement workloads are the—

- Federal Bureau of Investigation (FBI) and the Drug Enforcement Administration (DEA) in the Department of Justice.
- Internal Revenue Service; the U.S. Customs Service; the Bureau of Alcohol, Tobacco and Firearms; and the Secret Service in the Department of the Treasury.
- Postal Inspection Service of the U.S. Postal Service.

Source: Bureau of Justice Statistics, *Report to the Nation on Crime and Justice: The Data* (Washington, D.C.: U.S. Government Printing Office, 1983), p. 47, footnote omitted.

---

sination of a president, mail fraud, bank robbery, skyjacking, and others. The Federal Bureau of Investigation (FBI) enforces these laws and also aids local and state law enforcement authorities in solving local crimes.[3] In the case of nonfederal crimes, the FBI may be asked by local or state authorities to assist in the investigation. If a particular offense is in violation of both state and federal law, state or local police often cooperate with the federal authorities in expediting the investigation without unnecessary duplication of effort.

POLICE PERSONNEL One of the most important aspects of a professional police force is the selection, education, and training of officers. Until recently, most police officers were young white males with a high school education or less.[4] They also lacked training and professionalism, but that now is changing. The urban riots of the 1960s, with television allowing us to see that the police were not really equipped to handle civil rights issues and problems, made us realize the need to educate police and professionalize police departments. Technological advances were no longer sufficient in the war against crime.

EDUCATION OF POLICE Despite some early attempts at general police education there was no real action until the 1967 report of the President's Commission on Law Enforcement and the Administration of Justice. That report recommended that the "ultimate aim of all police departments should be that personnel with general enforcement powers have baccalaureate degrees."[5] The government provided financial incentives and support for the development of programs of higher education for police, and by early 1980, it was estimated that approximately one-half of the police officers in this country had received some college education under the federally funded programs.[6]

Two criticisms of our efforts to educate the police must be considered. First, we have had good reasons for questioning the quality of the educational programs developed specifically for the police. Many of the curricula contain mainly technical courses and neglect the broad, liberal arts courses that might help officers develop more understanding of and a professional attitude toward the people they encounter. Many have also lacked a theoretical understanding of the criminal justice system: "At best, such programs constitute good training; at worst, they're lending status to an effort that serves only to re-enforce the most parochial concepts prevalent in the police field."[7]

Perhaps an even more serious criticism of higher education for police comes from those who question whether the goal of a college education for police officers is a reasonable one. Although supporters argue that the education would increase police tolerance and understanding of minorities in general and give some additional insights into some of the particular problems they face on duty, others contend that there is no evidence that higher education will produce more tolerant and understanding police officers.[8]

It is also possible that the routine work that occupies the greatest portion of a police officer's time will be less tolerable to the college-educated person. That is, the officer will be "overeducated" for the job, resulting in boredom with the little challenge of what is often a routine and dull experience and intolerance of people who have not shared in those same kinds of educational experiences.[9]

RECRUITMENT
OF POLICE

We have only recently acknowledged the importance of recruiting women and minorities to serve as police officers. The Commission on Civil Rights underscored this need by, first, pointing out the "serious underutilization of minorities and women in local law enforcement agencies" and, second, emphasizing the negative impact that it has on the police's ability to "function effectively in and earn the respect of predominantly minority neighborhoods." The result, said the commission, is increasing tension and a greater probability of violence in those areas. Its conclusion:

> Police department officials should develop and implement affirmative action plans so that ultimately the force reflects the composition of the community it serves.[10]

The need for women and minority police officers is particularly evident when we recognize that crime rates are high among minorities and that the degree of fear, as we saw in our discussions of violence, is high among women, many of whom are reluctant to report rapes. And they may be particularly reluctant if they know that there are no women police to investigate the crime or at least to interview the victims.

After over a year of investigation, in the summer of 1983, the Justice Department sued the tenth largest police department in the country, Suffolk County, New York, alleging that "the Long Island police department had refused to recruit, hire, assign and promote women, blacks and Hispanic people on an equal basis with white males."[11] The Justice Department has also initiated legal action in other cities. Some of the suits have been settled out of court, as police departments and the Justice Department have come to terms on reasonable affirmative action programs.

Recruitment of women and minorities may also be hindered by citizens' perceptions that local police departments are not seriously trying to recruit or that if they do recruit successfully, female and minority officers will not be welcome in the department. It is important that such images be changed, and one way of doing that has been affirmative action programs and educational efforts aimed at eliminating racism and sexism in police departments.

Minority police

As a result of affirmative action programs, we have been able to increase somewhat the number of minorities among local police. The Detroit Police Department, for example, instituted a plan that provided for two separate lists for promotion, one for black and one for white officers. Promotions would be made alternately from each list, resulting in a fifty-fifty plan for promoting blacks and whites, until 50 percent of the lieutenant corps were black. White police sergeants challenged the provisions, claiming that this system violated their legal rights, but a federal court upheld the plan. The

United States Supreme Court refused to hear the case, thus allowing the lower court decision to stand.[12]

Some minorities may even be found in the higher ranks of police departments. One example is the police chief in Houston, Texas. Lee Patrick Brown, a former public safety commissioner in Atlanta, Georgia, and leader of the investigation into the deaths of twenty-eight black youths in that city, is the first black to serve as police chief of a department alleged by some to be one of the most racist in the country.

Brown brought not only minority representation to the office and the prestige of the national recognition he had attained in the Atlanta investigation but higher education as well, as he has a Ph.D in criminology. Upon his appointment, Brown promised to make Houston "the showcase of policing in America."[13] Brown joins an increasing group of blacks in policing, including the commissioner of the nation's largest police department, in New York City, and the police chiefs in several other major American cities.

Female police   The recruitment of females as police officers has met even stronger resistance than the recruitment of minority males. Nevertheless, women have become a more significant part of policing in this country since they were first employed in 1854 as matrons in New York City's jail.[14]

The recruitment of women has been hampered by departmental policies that tend to eliminate them from consideration. For example, height and weight requirements have precluded many female applicants, and these and other issues have been litigated with some interesting results.[15] Height and weight requirements were struck down as discriminating against women as a class because women in general are not as tall as men.[16] However, a minimum height requirement for police officers was upheld when it was applied to an all-female applicant pool. One police department advertised for female applicants to fulfill positions in which police officers would work only with female prisoners. Men were not eligible to apply. But because the minimum height requirement applied only to women, the court held that it was not discriminatory when applied to a woman applicant who was not hired.[17]

Affirmative action programs, whether voluntary or under court orders do not, however, solve all of the problems. What happens to women after they become police officers? Can they do the job? Are they accepted by their male peers and by the community?[18] It is not easy for women to enter what has traditionally not only been considered a "male profession"[19] but also one in which the "male physique" has been considered by many to be a prerequisite to success in the job.

How do women officers compare with their male counterparts on those police activities that involve physical strength? One of the problems is that there is little agreement regarding the physical characteristics required for successful policing.[20] Physical differences between men and women do not in themselves mean that women do not possess sufficient physical abilities to police as well as men do. Although the research indicates that "women are not as efficient a working machine as are men" and that overall women have to work harder than men to perform certain physical tasks, such findings must be considered in perspective. "[W]hile males potentially have a higher plateau of fitness and strength than do women, this does not necessarily indicate that the physical jobs of policing are beyond the physical abilities of all women." Improved training programs "could prepare unfit individuals of each sex for police work. In fact, tests conducted on female athletes indicate that women can attain a degree of fitness well within the physical demands of policing." In addition, studies indicate that when police officers get into difficulties resulting in serious injury or death, the reasons are usually not the lack of physical fitness or strength, but circumstances beyond the officer's control or a mistake in judgment. Thus, it has been concluded that

> there is no evidence to suggest that women cannot successfully cope with the rigors of police work. In fact, even with the limited research on women in policing, differences noted between the sexes frequently favor the female officer.[21]

PERSONALITY CHARACTERISTICS OF POLICE

The police have often been described as a homogeneous group who differ from other groups on various personality traits and characteristics. Earlier studies reported that police as a group were "probably maladjusted" emotionally, extremely cynical and authoritarian, impulsive risk takers, more rigid, more punitive than others, more physically aggressive, more assertive, and more lacking in self-confidence, with a preference to being supervised.[22]

Investigators emphasize, however, the need to look beyond the results of these studies. For example, although some studies show that police are generally cynical, others indicate that they are not cynical toward all aspects of policing. Thus, we need to "recognize particular types of cynicism as they relate to specific individual or organizational characteristics."[23] More attention should be given to the variables associated with the cynical reactions of some police.[24]

Others have argued that cynicism is not a real trait of police; it is, rather, a label from society. The police are really a heterogeneous, not a homogeneous, group of people who become less, not more cynical as they grow older and as their length of service on the police force increases.[25] Still others have contended that whatever traits police officers have, such as authoritarianism or punitveness, they acquired them on the force, as recruits do not demonstrate these traits when they begin policing.[26]

In earlier studies of police, the emphasis was on the "police personality." The focus was on people and their qualities, with the assumption that if we could attract different types of people to policing, its quality would improve.

But the Commission on Civil Rights found that the standards used for selecting police recruits do not accurately reflect and measure the qualities needed for adequate job performance. The commission stressed the importance of psychological testing: "Psychological screening of all applicants should be an integral part of any selection process and should be performed by qualified experts."[27]

Psychological tests are important, but unless we know how they relate to the specific functions that police must perform, the results will be of little help. We need to focus on the requirements of policing and on training people to fulfill those requirements. We cannot analyze policing without looking at what police do and what conflicts and stresses they encounter. We need to know their priorities, and those priorities are not necessarily related to factors such as background or an authoritarian or nonauthoritarian personality.[28]

Qualities that contribute to good policing are high intelligence and an ability to think on one's own, to understand other cultures and subcultures, to switch functions, and to understand the importance of freedom and the dangers of abusing authority. "[O]fficers must have the self-discipline and maturity to enable them to deal with others in a clinical manner without outward display of emotion, that will equip them to tolerate stress in any number of different situations, and that will cause them to take an intense interest in incidents which, though routine for them, are crises in the lives of others."[29]

THE NATURE OF POLICING

Traditionally the police did not so much enforce the law as keep the peace. It was their function to find homes and shelter for the homeless; handle riots and civil disturbances; find jobs for girls who might be lured away from prostitution; regulate refuse disposal, street sanitation, explosives, health hazards, and so on; and inspect bakers, butchers, and other vendors.

Nor did police initially investigate criminal activities. That was the responsibility of the victim. But once the victim had identified the guilty person, the police would help apprehend him or her. People also would pay the police for helping them regain stolen property; the emphasis was on restitution. Thus, officers who became experts in finding stolen property could expect greater gain. This led to specialization in police forces, and the practice of paying police for their services made the police pay careful attention to those who had the means to pay. "This no doubt encouraged some of the symbiotic relationships that are today regarded as inimical to effective crime control."[30]

Today the function of the police differs in reality from the concept often held by the public and preferred by the police. "The policeman . . . considers the essence of his role to be the dangerous and heroic enterprise of crook-catching and the watchful prevention of crimes." The public wants to believe that it is what the police officer is doing; they see the dramatic and dangerous function. But in actuality most police time is spent in routine, boring, and nondangerous activities. But the system has developed a structure that gives the greatest awards for the dangerous activities of the stereotype and the fewest rewards for the routine behavior of the police.[31]

FUNCTIONS
OF POLICING

Police are empowered to apprehend and arrest people who violate the law. Their law enforcement function is not, however, mainly apprehending serious offenders. A considerable amount of their time is spent enforcing laws that regulate drinking, drugs, and sex. As we saw in Chapter 1, the attempt to legislate in these areas of activity that usually do not have complaining victims may result in dysfunctions such as police corruption and police violation of individual rights.

Law enforcement

It is also important to emphasize that the police's law enforcement function should not be confused with prevention of crime, and the 1967 report of the president's crime commission stressed that the police are limited in their ability to prevent crime. "They did not start and cannot stop the convulsive social changes that are taking place in America. They do not enact the laws that they are required to enforce, nor do they dispose of the criminals they arrest."[32] The police are only one element of the system of criminal justice. According to the commission, the role of the police in law enforcement is mainly apprehending people who commit crimes, not deterring crimes, but even in that role, they are dependent on citizens for assistance.

In a provocative and often cited work, Herbert L. Packer described what the role of the police should be in the area of law enforcement:

> Ideally, the police should be seen as the people who keep the law of the jungle from taking over. Their predominant role should be to enforce, by prevention of offenses and detection of offenders, those proscriptions that guarantee the first requisite of social living: that people be reasonably secure in their persons and possessions against the grosser forms of depredation.[33]

Order maintenance

A second police function is order maintenance, described by one authority as the "primary function of the police," taking precedence over fighting crime and enforcing the law or regulating public morals.[34]

Order maintenance has been described as the "management of conflict situations to bring about consensual resolution." It is similar to "situational management" and represents the police's real function.[35] By order is meant the "absence of disorder, and by disorder is meant behavior that either disturbs or threatens to disturb the public peace or that involves face-to-face conflict among two or more persons." The maintenance-of-order function is important because police encounter more problems in this area than in

EXHIBIT
MOST CRIMINAL CASES ARE INITIATED BY ARREST

**When a Crime Has Been Committed, a Suspect Must Be
Identified and Apprehended for the Case to Proceed through the
System**

Sometimes, a suspect is apprehended at the scene; however, often extensive investigations are required to identify a suspect, and, in many cases, no one is identified or apprehended. Law enforcement agencies have wide discretion in determining when to make an arrest, but to arrest a suspect properly, they must obtain an arrest warrant from the court prior to arrest or they must be able to show that they had probable cause that the suspect committed the crime at the time of arrest. A suspect who is arrested (taken into physical custody) must then be booked (official recording of the offenses alleged and the identity of the suspect). In some States, law enforcement agencies must fingerprint suspects at the time of arrest and booking.

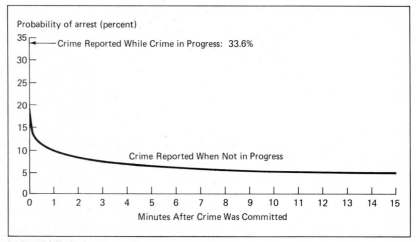

The probability of an arrest declines sharply if the incident is not reported to the police within seconds after a confrontational crime.

Source: Calling the Police: Citizen Reporting of Serious Crime. *Police Executive Research Forum, 1981.*

**Most Persons Enter the Criminal Justice System through the
Arrest Process, But Some Enter by Other Means**

For example, a person may be issued a citation by a police officer requiring a court appearance to answer a criminal charge. Generally, a citation creates a mandatory obligation to appear in court. However, in some jurisdictions, a payment of money can be made in lieu of a court appearance. The common example of such a provision is the minor traffic violation. In addition to citation, a person may be issued a summons (a written order by a judicial officer requiring an appearance in court to answer specific charges). A third means of entering the criminal justice system is through the issuance of an indictment by a grand jury. Grand jury indictments usually follow the referral of allegations and evidence by the prosecutor. Occasionally, a grand jury will issue an indictment following a criminal investigation intiated by the prosecutor. Such an indictment is commonly known as a grand jury original.

Several Factors Affect the Ability of Police to Make Arrests Which Result in Conviction

A principal factor relating to the criminal event and the arrest itself is the availability of tangible evidence and credible witnesses. The ability of the government to prosecute criminal cases successfully depends largely on evidence that establishes proof that a crime was committed and that an arrested person committed it. Evidence may be presented at the trial through witnesses, records, documents, and other concrete objects. The acquisition of criminal evidence is generally the task of the arresting police officer. Under the exclusionary rule, evidence obtained improperly may not be used in court.

A study of criminal conviction rates in the District of Columbia by the Institute for Law and Social Research demonstrated a strong relationship between the availability and strength of evidence and conviction of criminal defendants. For example, of all arrests for violent crimes brought before the District of Columbia Superior Court in 1974, the conviction rate in cases was 35% where tangible evidence was recovered, compared with only 24% where no tangible evidence was recovered. In addition, when at least two lay witnesses were available to testify about a crime, the conviction rate was 39%, compared with only 21% in cases when less than two witnesses were available.

Delay in Apprehension Affects the Ability of Police to Make Arrests That Result in Conviction

This is largely due to the fact that when delay is short, the ability of the police to recover tangible evidence from a "warm crime scene" is enhanced. For example, in the District of Columbia study cited above, conviction rates for robbery, larceny, and burglary declined significantly as time between offense and arrest increased.

Percent of arrests for robbery, larceny, and burglary that resulted in conviction by elapsed time from offense to arrest

Elapsed Time	Robbery	Larceny	Burglary
0–5 minutes	38%	34%	43%
6–30 minutes	36	30	45
30 minutes to 24 hours	30	29	40
More than 24 hours	26	26	38

Source: *What Happens After Arrest?* Institute for Law and Social Research, 1978.

Source: Bureau of Justice Statistics, *Report to the Nation on Crime and Justice: The Data* (Washington, D.C.: U.S. Government Printing Office, 1983), pp. 50, 51.

EXHIBIT
POLICE FUNCTIONS

Law Enforcement Is Only One of Several Roles of Police

Two main roles of police officers are—

- Law enforcement—applying legal sanctions (usually arrest) to behavior that violates a legal standard.
- Order maintenance—taking steps to control events and circumstances that disturb or threaten to disturb the peace. For example, a police officer may be called on to mediate a family dispute, to disperse an unruly crowd, or to quiet an overly boisterous party.

Two secondary roles of police officers are—

- Information gathering—asking routine questions at a crime scene, inspecting victimized premises, and filling out forms needed to register criminal complaints.
- Service-related duties—a broad range of activities, such as assisting injured persons, animal control, or fire calls.

Wilson's analysis of citizen complaints radioed to police on patrol showed that—

- Only 10% required enforcement of the law.
- More than 30% of the calls were appeals to maintain order.
- 22% were for information gathering.
- 38% were service-related duties.

Several Investigative Techniques Are Used by the Police

- Detection techniques are used when a crime has been committed, but the suspect has not been identified, or if identified, has not been apprehended.
- Undercover techniques are used when a person is suspected of participating in criminal activity, yet no specific crime has been committed. An example of undercover work would be when a person is supected of being involved with an organized drug-dealing operation and police investigators pose as drug buyers. The investigators hope to discover a drug sale that will implicate the suspect.
- Intelligence techniques are used when there is no identified crime or suspect. An investigator seeks only information; following hunches or tips, the investigator looks for relationships; the relationship sought may consist of finding similarities between a series of crimes committed in the area or simply of finding out that "something is up."

Source: Bureau of Justice Statistics, *Report to the Nation on Crime and Justice: The Data* (Washington, D.C.: U.S. Government Printing Office, 1983), p. 47, footnotes omitted.

any other area of law enforcement, with the exception of traffic laws. Further, problems in this area expose police to physical danger, which in turn might expose the citizen to danger. But most importantly, police have great discretion in the area of order maintenance, and this discretion occurs in an area that is characterized by intensive conflicts and often hostile participants.[36]

The disctinction between the police's order maintenance and social service functions may be illustrated by domestic disputes. Police receive many calls from spouses who are being threatened or physically abused within the home. It has been argued that police are not trained to intervene in such disturbances, and although the police are often not trained to serve as counselors, social workers, or legal advisers in such cases, it is true that these domestic disputes often result in violence. It is order maintenance, the prevention or control of violence, that is the police's function in such cases, and it is for that reason that responding to domestic calls should remain their function and not that of social work agencies.[37]

Provision of social services

Police spend a large portion of their time doing "other things," many of which are categorized as social services for the public. That is, people who do not know how else to solve a problem will often call the police department for help.

One "miscellaneous" call for a policeman in Fort Lauderdale, Florida, shows the types of services that the police may perform. A citizen called the police department to ask for help in capturing a rat in the bathroom. Policeman Steve Briggs's report on his response to this call indicated that his efforts resulted in a "frenzied chase after a cunning suspect who tried to elude him with a 'spectacular leap' and threatened to bite him. . . . However, during the course of this officer's action the animal, due to its size, was able to outmaneuver the undersigned." When the rat approached the officer, Briggs jumped up onto the bathroom sink cabinet. The rat jumped onto the towel rack at which point the officer "struck at the animal, and as a result broke his nightstick." The rat then "made a spectacular leap across the bathroom and landed on the mirror" which was on the wall next to the officer's face. In an attempt to keep the rat from jumping onto his face or shoulder, the officer leaned away from the rodent and began striking at it with what was left of his nightstick. The officer lost his balance, fell, received bruises to both elbows and a blow to his head which resulted in a broken tooth. At that point he called for help; another officer quickly arrived and captured the rodent.[38]

The police are also expected to perform such duties as taking censuses; reading schoolchildren's essays on the glories of the police department; issuing permits for pawnbrokers, guns, private detectives, dogs, itinerant musicians, and others; and filling out numerous forms.

Although arresting people who are suspected of committing crimes is an important function of police, many studies indicate that police spend more time in other activities, such as social services. Assisting young people's groups is one type of social service function that is very important.

Police do perform some social work functions, but their role has been questioned. Many calls to them for help in this area occur "after hours" when professionally trained people are not available, and some believe that the police should become "professionalized," which would include training in the behavioral sciences. However, it may be argued that social work and law enforcement are really conflicting value systems. Social work refers to helping, counseling, and facilitating, and law enforcement (as well as order maintenance) means controlling, restraining, and restricting. The effectiveness of the police in doing both has been questioned; furthermore, they have difficulty doing both while maintaining a congruent self-image. Studies indicate that most police resolve the conflict by thinking of themselves only as the crime fighter, the law enforcer. "Whenever this occurs, the ability of a police officer to resolve conflict situations without involving the criminal process, i.e., arrest, is greatly diminished."[39]

One solution would be to remove these essentially social work functions from the police, but to do so would raise the interesting question of what the police would be like if all their contacts were with criminals. Service calls offer the police their best opportunity to meet people they serve and to become acquainted with their habits and customs. And if the police did not make these calls, who would help the people?[40]

ALLOCATION OF POLICE TIME

There is obvious disagreement over which of the three functions, law enforcement, order maintenance, and social service, is the most important. There is also disagreement over how police time should be allocated among them. An earlier study reported that 38 percent of police time was spent in service-related duties, followed by 30 percent in order maintenance, 22 percent in information gathering, and only 10 percent in law enforcement.[41] Those figures were quite different from those from a study in Chicago conducted two years earlier, indicating that 58 percent of the calls to the police department were requests regarding criminal matters and 30 percent regarding noncriminal matters.[42]

Some of the more recent studies, based on observations of police on patrol rather than on analyses of calls to the police department, indicate that "the single most frequent type of activity overall was law enforcement . . . slightly less than a third of all the activities observed involved criminal incidents."[43]

The police contend that they spend more time in law enforcement than some of the studies indicate. In an analysis of the police's allocation of time, one investigator reported that the police in the inner cities may indeed spend most of their time on law enforcement activities. But another reason for the "differences" in the findings of the studies may be the various types of categorizations used. "Thus, in the breakdowns that have been used, dealing with disorderly drunks, abandoned cars, children playing in the street, shoplifters, soliciting street prostitutes, and motorists who run red lights would generally be classified as noncriminal activity. But because these incidents technically constitute violations of the law, the police and others classify them as part of the law enforcement/criminal responsibilities of the police."[44] Others might categorize such activities as "noncriminal" because the police frequently do not arrest in these situations.

Regardless of how these activities are categorized, it is clear that the police do not spend most of their time in the stereotypical police action: catching dangerous criminals. In fact, police spend very little time in actual crime detection. Their work is mainly **reactive,** not **proactive;** that is, police are dependent on the assistance of victims and other citizens for crime reporting and would detect very little crime without it. "Indeed, it is a rare event when a patrol officer proactively discovers a felony in progress and arrests a violator."[45] This is the case because crime is generally not visible to the police. Most crimes, for example, are against the household unit rather than the person, and so such crimes are almost always perpetrated out of view of police. Furthermore, many crimes against the person also take place within the home; indeed, many involve members of the family. Our constitutionally protected right of privacy thus would prevent the police, even if they had sufficient numbers to engage in such surveillance, from doing so.[46]

ROLE CONFLICTS　Our discussion has revealed that police have a variety of functions and that there is no consensus on how they do or should allocate their time or for that matter, whether all three of those functions should remain their responsibility. As a result, the police are often caught in a dilemma. They cannot effectively prevent crime, even with citizen support, and they often do not get that support. When they do prevent crime, there is really no adequate measure of what they have done. When they perform the roles of order maintenance and social services, they often face hostility in the former and unreasonable demands in the latter; that is, they are asked to solve problems for which they have no solutions.

In addition to expecting the impossible, society is often unclear as to what it expects the police to do in a given situation. Are they to enforce the law or ignore violations? The police may not always act legally because the community expects a different type of behavior. The reaction of Chicago police to the ambiguity of the expectations of the police on patrol made the point quite clear. The officers on the whole preferred not to have patrol duty. Among the many reasons they listed for preferring other duty assignments—more interesting work, higher pay, greater prestige, and greater freedom—the most important was "the officer has a better sense of what is expected of him."[47]

There are other conflicts the patrol officer faces with regard to community expectations. The community may be composed of persons whose life-styles include knifings, narcotics, and domestic quarrels, and that particular community may expect the officer to ignore the laws regulating such behaviors, and the officer who has worked in areas where such behaviors are not common may find great resistance when he or she tries to enforce these laws.

Police officers also face conflicts over human misery versus evil. When the officer arrives at the scene of an accident or other tragedy, he or she must control certain emotions. For example, an officer cannot punish the father who beat his child, nor can he or she get sick at the sight of a mangled body. Police must act with reason and perform their jobs as efficiently as possible.

The police also face conflicts between efficiency in their jobs and observation of the individual rights of citizens, as well as loyalty conflicts between their colleagues and honesty. For example, what should the police do if they know a colleague has done something dishonest? And they are probably subjected to more temptations—bribes, gifts, and so on—than any other professional.

They may have conflicts between fear and courage—the desire to do the courageous while realizing that in taking such action they risk their own health or lives. This is particularly the case when they are attempting to maintain order. That job

> exposes the patrolman to physical danger, and his reaction in turn may expose the disputants to danger.... the risk of danger in order maintenance patrol work, though statistically less than the danger involved in enforcing traffic laws or apprehending felons, has a disproportionate effect on the officer partly because its unexpected nature makes him more apprehensive and partly because he tends to communicate his apprehension to the citizen.[48]

Another problem is that maintaining order brings the officers into an environment that is often hostile, involving emotional and apprehensive people. The police are responding to what is an emergency and a crisis to the people who called. But because the officers have been involved in many similar situations, they have learned by experience that the victim's version of the incident is often not reliable. The police thus may not be as sympathetic as the victim desires, and the latter may become upset at this apparent lack of understanding. Further, because only 7 percent of all calls to police officers result in arrest, the client may feel that the police are doing nothing. The problem is that most crimes are property crimes with no clues or witnesses. Even if a suspect is found, officers must fulfill the requirements for making an arrest, and often those cannot be met.[49]

STRESS IN POLICING

The role conflicts in policing have created stress, a subject that has claimed considerable attention in recent years, as professionals have examined its impact in many professions. Formerly considered a personal problem, stress is now seen as a corporate problem because of the effect that reactions to stress have on employees. Some businesses now retain a professional person to assist employees who have difficulty handling stress. Stress causes physical illnesses, resulting in higher medical costs, lower productivity, absenteeism, and premature death, all of which may be extremely costly for business.

Although all people may encounter some stress in their jobs, there is evidence that it is particularly high among "air traffic controllers, lawyers, dentists, physicians, psychiatrists and law enforcement officers. Some studies place law enforcement as the most physically dangerous profession in the world; it is, by far, the most emotionally dangerous occupation."[50] Others identify police work as the "most psychologically dangerous job in the world."[51] And the impact goes beyond the individual officer: "Police work is a high stress occupation. It affects, shapes, and at times, scars the individuals and families involved."[52]

Stress in policing may account for the extremely high rate of divorce among police, a rate that is, according to some, higher than in most other professions (all others, according to some studies). Other contend that the divorce rate among police is not high and that those reports to the contrary are mainly anecdotal, not statistical.[53] But divorce is not the only measure of how stress may affect the personal lives of police officers. Spouses report that officers have difficulty shifting from the tough, hard, and sometimes cynical attitudes they display at work to the emotional and understanding needs of their spouses and children at home.[54] Night shifts, changes in shifts, and departmental policies also place stress on the family.[55] Some officers, experiencing problems at work, want to withdraw from the family when they come home at night, seeking peace, quiet, and an evening alone.[56] Suicide rates are also high.[57] But these problems are not unique to policing—they exist in many jobs and professions.

Are there any stressors that are unique to the police? There is one major difference between policing and most other professions. Police are trained to injure or kill, and if the situation requires, they are expected to use that ability; indeed, they may be sanctioned for not using their weapons. It is this requirement, say some officers, that is unique in creating stress in policing. It is distinguishable from fighting in war, claims one officer who spent time in Vietnam. "In a war, that's what you're there for—to wipe them out. Police work isn't like that. You're certainly not on a search-and-destroy mission." A psychologist notes that in a war, soldiers may cope by defining the opposition as bad—all of them. "The role is so well accepted and shared." But that is not true of police officers who, conversely, may also be highly criticized, even sanctioned, for *using* their weapons, for killing someone. Officers who kill may also be socially isolated from their colleagues; in fact, the routine procedure is to suspend officers pending investigation of a shooting.[58]

The impact of stress on police has led some departments to initiate stress reduction programs, a procedure recommended by the Commission on Civil Rights. The Los Angeles Police Department was cited by the commission as having an effective stress reduction program. This program not only includes counseling and other assistance in coping with stress but also puts officers into participative management in an effort to reduce job stress. A department psychologist is employed to assist officers in stress adjustment,[59] and the department also provides stress pensions for officers who are unable to continue working after a traumatic incident, such as a shooting resulting in death.[60] A few other cities, like Chicago and New York, have similar programs.

One of the ways that police officers attempt to cope with the stresses of policing, including the isolation and rejection from society they often feel, is to cut themselves off from others and associate only with "their own kind." One researcher described the police as a minority and found that they share many of the self-concepts characteristic of minorities. "Both suffer from a 'lack of respect,' both see the larger community as an enemy which does not understand them, both are aggressive in their response to those not in their community, both stay within their own group and both see the other as a threat and strike out at the other."[61]

Social solidarity may be the result of the danger that police face, thus the need to help one another. It may also be the result of their suspiciousness, resulting in a perceptual shorthand developed to help identify people who might commit an unlawful act. It may also be the result of the conflicting demands placed on the police. It is difficult for police to make friends among nonpolice.

Police isolation extends to professional isolation. Police argue that only those experienced in police work can train others to become police. They believe that police are professionals and can be trained only by other police professionals. They therefore have in many cases excluded all but police from teaching roles in their academies. They reward, promote, and reinforce those who uphold their norms and have organized quasi unions that exert considerable political power, which has often enabled them to "negotiate" practical autonomy. They thus are no longer under the democratic control of the communities in which they work but, rather, have become autonomous.[62]

Is the police's social isolation inevitable? It has been suggested that it is relative and that compared with the British police, "American police are more socially integrated." Furthermore, the isolation is to some extent functional. It allows the police to relate to the public without undue strain. "Without feelings of isolation a policeman's job would be untenable." If the police identify too closely with the public, they will often be placed in situations in which they would either have to alter their belief systems or suffer cognitive strain. "To protect himself from that eventuality he needs the belief that he is indeed the isolated if not alienated man."[63]

To the contrary, it is believed that "such self-enforced isolation was, and is, detrimental to the police and a disservice to the public. The police must open their organizational windows to let in fresh new ideas."[64] And there is some evidence that police are not as socially isolated as in the past. A 1979 study found that police did not have high social isolation scores. The investigator concluded that police are a "new breed of persons who desire to help the public and accomplish something worthwhile. Being less authoritarian and socially isolated, they desire involvement with their public in their communities."[65]

POLICE DECISIONS   The police are the only people that most citizens will encounter in the entire system of criminal justice. Most people never go before a judge, but most at some time have contact with a police officer. Their feelings of security on the streets and in their homes may in large part be determined by their attitudes toward the effectiveness or lack thereof of the police force. The police are among the most important administrators in America, and they have considerable decision-making discretion in the performance of their jobs.

INITIAL
APPREHENSION
AND DECISION TO
ARREST

The decision to interfere with the freedom, even if momentary, of another person is an extremely serious one. People do not like to be stopped by the police; it is a frightening situation for many, and they often do not know why they are being stopped. Some may perceive the action of the police as discriminatory, and indeed their perceptions may be correct. The police, however, reject this conclusion. "For the policeman these judgments are rooted in the reality of city life. He is not making a moral judgment . . . but is responding to what he sees daily on the street." Police resent the assumption that they stop people without cause. Even the most aggressive officers do not stop everyone. The police believe that when they have cause to believe a crime has been or is about to be committed, the questions they ask could and would be answered by honest people without difficulty and that they are therefore not imposing on a person who has a legitimate reason for being where he or she is. The only way the police can know whether the people they stop are law abiding or criminal is to stop them and ask.[66]

The issue is even more pronounced, however, when the possibility of an arrest exists. Here the police officer is not only momentarily interfering with freedom but is also setting in motion a process that may result in stigmatization and incarceration. What, then, are the factors that influence the decision to stop and then to arrest?

The decision to take a suspect into custody is governed by case and statutory law. This body of law is technical and complicated and, in general, is related to the *legal seriousness* of the suspected crime, although some studies have found that legal seriousness plays a small part in the decision to **arrest.**[67]

Remember that most of the problems that police are called upon to resolve are not of a legally serious nature. Rather, most are minor problems of the type in which arrests are not always made. Police must therefore base their decision on criteria other than the legal seriousness of the alleged crime. The question of what these other criteria are has been relatively well researched by social scientists, and we shall examine some of the results.

The right of the police to stop and question

In the previous chapter, we discussed the requirement that police must have probable cause in order to arrest, though probable cause is not required for the police to stop and question in some circumstances. For instance, it is permissible for police to stop a person who appears "suspicious" or "out of place" in a particular place. They may stop the person and ask for identification, but they may not detain him or her unreasonably, nor may they stop *classes* of people in order to harass them. The police, of course, contend that they are not harassing—they are trying to maintain order and enforce the law.

An example of the police's stop-and-question function came to our attention in 1982 through the national media as well as a Supreme Court decision. White police officers had on numerous occasions stopped a thirty-six-year-old tall, black muscular man who had long hair and frequently jogged in a predominantly white neighborhood. The police stopped him and asked him for identification, on about fifteen occasions between March 1975 and January 1977. When the jogger refused to identify himself or answer other questions, the police on several occasions arrested him. He was convicted once and served several weeks in jail.

According to the police, the jogger committed a misdemeanor when he violated a California statute that labeled as disorderly conduct the behavior of a person "who loiters or wanders upon the streets or from place to place without apparent reason or business or who refuses to identify himself and to account for his presence when requested by any peace officer to do so, if the surrounding circumstances are such as to indicate to a reasonable man that the public safety demands such identification."[68]

In deciding that the statute in question was void because it was too vague, the U.S. Supreme Court articulated the importance of individual freedoms. Recognizing that the police must be able to exercise some discretion in stop-and-question situations, the Court nevertheless struck down this statute because the legislature had not, in passing the statute, provided sufficient guidelines on that discretion. The statute, said the Court, leaves us free to walk the streets (or jog the streets) only at the "whim of any police officer."[69]

It is important to understand, however, that the problem with this statute is not that the police initially stop a person. Said the Court, "Although the initial detention is justified, the State fails to establish standards by which the officers may determine whether the suspect has complied with the subsequent identification requirement." Citing another case, the Court indicated that giving a police officer such discretion "confers on police a virtually unrestrained power to arrest and charge persons with a violation" and therefore "furnishes a convenient tool for 'harsh and discriminatory enforcement by local prosecuting officials, against particular groups deemed to merit their displeasure.'"[70]

The sociology of arrest   Although the police are legally permitted to stop and question people and to arrest them under certain circumstances, the Supreme Court has held that "it is not the function of the police to arrest, as it were, at large and to use an interrogating process at police headquarters in order to determine whom they should charge before a committing magistrate on 'probable cause.'"[71]

We have seen some of the *legal* reasons why the police may stop and question people, or even arrest them, but what do the studies indicate are the *real* reasons that the police apprehend people? Do they always observe legal restrictions, or do they stop to harass people who may be considered undesirable? For that matter, why did they so often stop the jogger in California? It is, of course, difficult—if not impossible—to answer those questions, for the police's stopping of people is not a public event and often never comes to our attention. There are, however, some studies on the sociology of arrest.

One variable that influences the decision to arrest is the police's perception of community standards and attitudes and the homogeneity between the police and the community. In a study of juvenile cases handled by the police in four communities in the Pittsburgh area, one investigator found patterns of enforcement indicating that they were related to the relationships the police had with the community, leading to the conclusion that the police were attempting to reflect community standards and attitudes.[72] Thus, it has been argued that the police decide whom to arrest not according to legal prescriptions or even departmental orders but according to their perceptions of community expectations, perhaps based on their desire to "get along" with the community.[73]

Community expectations may also influence the police's decision not to investigate or apprehend suspects in some areas. For example, police may not consider places like narrow alleys and abandoned buildings and cars to be areas that the community cares about being investigated, even though they are known to be used for illegal purposes. Buildings that have been condemned by the city and boarded up are still usable, and individuals break in to use the facilities for sexual activities, rapes, shooting drugs, and other illegal or illicit activities. But the police often simply ignore them. After they get to know an area, the officers know what behaviors to expect in particular areas and will permit or tolerate behavior in one area that would not be permitted in another.[74]

The serious problems arise, however, when discretionary decisions are made to harass, brutalize, or discriminate against persons because of their age, race, ethnic background, sex, political beliefs, or social class. For example, one study of police revealed their overall tendency to arrest more chronic drunks from the lower than from the middle or upper classes. Police also issued more traffic citations to lower-class than to middle-class individuals.[75]

Although there have been allegations concerning the police's misconduct in performing their function as law enforcers, an earlier but extensive study of police activity offered the following generalizations:

1. Most arrest situations arise through citizen rather than police initiative.
2. Arrest practices sharply reflect the preferences of citizen complainants.
3. The police are lenient in their routine arrest practices.
4. Evidence is an important factor in the arrest.

5. The probability of arrest is higher in legally serious crime situations than in those of a relatively minor nature.
6. The greater the relational distance between a complainant and a suspect, the greater is the likelihood of arrest.
7. The probability of arrest increases when a suspect is disrespectful toward the police.
8. No evidence exists to show that the police discriminate on the basis of race.[76]

THE USE OF
FORCE

Another area of police decision making involves the use of force. Laws regulating the police's use of force differ from jurisdiction to jurisdiction, but in general, officers may not use lethal force unless they or other persons are threatened with serious bodily harm or death. They may, however, use as much nonlethal force as is reasonably necessary to make an arrest, control a crowd, or engage in any other legitimate police function.

Generally, a police officer cannot use deadly force to apprehend a misdemeanant, but in some states the act of fleeing is a felony: if a person flees after an arrest, the officer may be permitted to use deadly force even if the original offense for which the arrest was made was a misdemeanor. Most jurisdictions permit officers to fire at a fleeing felon.

The historical background of the rules with regard to how much deadly force a police officer may use in the apprehension of a felon is very interesting. Historically, most felonies were punishable by death, and so it was assumed that the fleeing felon was merely getting his "due regard" sooner than usual.

Legal scholars, the National Commission on Reform of Federal Criminal Laws, the President's Commission on Law Enforcement and Administration of Justice, and others generally support the use of deadly force only when violence was used by the suspect in the commission of the felony or when the use of such force is necessary to protect human life and bodily security. The result is that there has been an erosion of the common law rule permitting the use of deadly force against any fleeing felon. Federal and many local and state law enforcement agencies prohibit the use of deadly force unless human life is threatened, and there is no evidence that the use of deadly force under other circumstances is a deterrent to further crime. "Instead, the use of deadly force often tends to increase hostility towards law enforcement and to exacerbate community tensions."[77]

*Recent challenge
to the fleeing felon
rule*

Even when a statute permits the police to fire a deadly weapon at a fleeing felon, the courts may rule that under some circumstances this action violates the felon's constitutional rights. In 1983 in Tennessee, an officer fired at a fifteen-year-old who had broken into an unoccupied residence in a suburban area. The young man was killed by the police officer, who had been taught that it was legal to fire at a fleeing felon. Furthermore, the Tennessee statute provided that "if . . . the defendant . . . either flees or forcibly resists, the officer may use all the necessary means to effect the arrest."[78]

But the court held that the law was too broad, that the state had shown no "compelling reason" that a police officer would need to shoot at any or all fleeing felons, and that the broad statute violated the suspect's rights. The court referred to the common law rule that permitted police to shoot any fleeing felon but observed that this rule came into existence when all felonies were capital offenses. In the excerpt below, the court explains why the statute is too broad.[79]

POLICE VIOLENCE
AND BRUTALITY

Police violence has probably existed as long as the police have, but it did not receive much public attention until the 1960s. Millions watched police violence on television in 1968 during the Democratic National Convention in Chicago, and in the late 1970s attention was turned to Philadelphia, where police brutality was allegedly so widespread that for the first time in history, the U.S. Department of Justice filed a lawsuit in federal court, charging that the police department fostered a pattern of brutality that violated the rights of all citizens in Philadelphia. The lawsuit was, however, dismissed by a U.S. district court judge in October 1979. The judge ruled that the Department of Justice did not have power to interfere in the operation of a local police department.[80]

Garner v. Memphis Police Department

A state statute or rule that makes no distinctions based on the type of offense or the risk of danger to the community is inherently suspect because it permits an unnecessarily severe and excessive police response that is out of proportion to the danger to the community. . . .

The Tennessee statute in question here is invalid because it does not put sufficient limits on the use of deadly force. It is "too disproportionate." It does not make distinctions based on "gravity and need" nor on "the magnitude of the offense." Before taking the drastic measure of using deadly force as a last resort against a fleeing suspect, officers should have probable cause to believe not simply that the suspect has committed some felony. They should have probable cause also to believe that the suspect poses a threat to the community if left at large. The officers may be justified in using deadly force if the suspect has committed a violent crime or if they have probable cause to believe that he is armed or that he will endanger the physical safety of others if not captured. A statute which allows officers to kill any unarmed fleeing felon does not meet this standard and is therefore invalid. . . .

In August 1983, the city of Philadelphia proposed to end the case by hiring 293 black officers and promoting 2 more over the next several years. The proposal needed approval of two federal judges. Said the mayor, "It is my hope that this agreement will be approved by the Federal courts and will close the books on a civil rights case that dates from a different era in the city's history."[81]

In recent years, the national news media have aired several programs on police brutality. On February 26, 1984, CBS's "60 Minutes" featured interviews with the "Guardians" and the "Cowboys," two groups of police officers in Richmond, California. When the citizens of that community filed charges of brutality against the police, some members of the Guardians admitted that as police officers, they had engaged in brutality but that they were no longer doing so. They testified against the police Cowboys, whom they claimed were administering "street justice" to the citizens of that community. At the civil trial, the families of two slain blacks were awarded $3 million in damages, the largest civil rights award in history. In 1984, another family was awarded a $1.2 million judgment for the death of their relative killed by a police officer, and many cases were still pending.[82]

Alleged police brutality in Miami and New Orleans, among other cities, has also been in the national news recently,[83] and alleged police brutality against blacks in New York City led to a congressional hearing on July 17, 1983. Mayor Edward Koch claimed that the hearing was politically motivated, and the meeting was continued until September, with the mayor saying that he would not attend because of the place chosen for the hearing— the state armory in Harlem. Koch claimed that the armory's "cavernous atmosphere" was an inappropriate setting for the hearing, and he did boycott the meeting, although he appeared to testify before the third hearing, held in a courtroom in Brooklyn in late November. Koch recounted a history of racism in this country, condemned such racism, and vowed that he would "stand behind police officers when they are right and condemn them when they are wrong."

The former chief of patrol, who is black, echoed Koch's comments, acknowledged that some police brutality existed, and testified that "unfortunately this nation has developed a racist society . . . [but] "police brutality, abuse of authority, discourtesy and ethnic slurs are not widespread, are not condoned and are not systemic. I am also certain . . . that a great deal of progress has been made by the department in the past decade in dealing with these problems."[84]

Effects of police brutality Even when the police are unjustfiably charged with brutality, there may be a significant impact on the whole community and not just on the individuals involved in the allegations. One reaction is that minorities feel the police are out "to get them." Indeed, approximately 50 percent of the victims killed by police officers are black. Studies indicate, however, that this high percentage for blacks might not necessarily represent a policy of discrimination against minorities. Two investigators concluded "that the high mortality rate of blacks in police shootings seems to result primarily from community characteristics, such as the high general rate of violence in the inner cities, rather than from a tendency among police to treat blacks and whites differently solely because of race. But, overall, the data available for decision making are slim, and the need for research is great." The authors concluded that there is evidence of some truth in the belief of blacks in many cities that the "police have one trigger finger for blacks and another for whites."[85]

Alleged police brutality has also led to riots. The President's commissions appointed to study urban riots have uniformly noted the impact of police brutality on such incidents. When the public perceives an act by a police officer to be unfair, unreasonable, unnecessary, or harassing, especially when minorities are the victims, that perception may provide the impetus for urban riots.[86]

This is not to suggest that police actions cause the riots. The police, of course, have no control over the root causes of civil disturbances, such as unemployment, lack of educational opportunities, poor housing, and inadequate health care facilities, but they can reduce violent confrontations by the policies they adopt.[87] According to the National Advisory Commission on Civil Disorder,

> Almost invariably the incident that ignites disorder arises from police action. . . . to many Negroes police have come to symbolize white power, white racism and white repression. And the fact is that many police do reflect and express these white attitudes.[88]

Police justification for violence and brutality **Violence against police.** The police's first response to charges of brutality is that their actions are not unreasonable but justifiable in reaction to the violence against them. Police maintain that they are facing more and more violence directed against them. This position was advanced by a 1980 article entitled "The War on the Cops," referring to a "new breed" of pathological killers in New York City. These killers were named "madmen" who engaged in random killings with no apparent motive. "The police have fallen victim not to the incorrigible, but to the uncontrollable." The new breed of killers has also been described as "a small but virulent strain of violent, conscience-free, 'Clockwork Orange' street criminals and mentally deranged men and women who have managed—admittedly, with little effort—to defeat the programs designed to constrain and heal them."[89]

Despite this "new form of violence" against the police in New York City, a systematic study of the killings of police officers in that city led to the following conclusion: "New York police are more likely to be killed by rational robbers fleeing the scene of a crime, who routinely use potentially lethal weapons as 'tools of the trade.'" Killing a police officer is in most cases, a functional act carried out to avoid arrest.[90]

It is unlikely that police officers find comfort in the data that indicate that although 1,109 law officers were killed in the past decade, the number of actual killings of police by citizens was only 91 in 1981 and again in 1982, the lowest figures during the twelve-year period that the FBI has kept such data.[91] Nor is it comforting to be told that violence against police is a relatively rare occurrence, given the frequency of police-citizen interaction.

The number of police officers killed by citizens does not, however, tell the whole story. The police have also encountered a growing hostility from the public that often has resulted in verbal abuse as well as physical abuse just short of murder. Although it is debatable which comes first and which causes which, there are indications that the violence against police officers is accompanied by violence by police officers. The Police Foundation, in its study published in 1977, focused only on the police's use of deadly force, but the authors indicated that they were "acutely aware of the interrelationship between acts committed *by* the police and acts committed *against* them."[92]

Demand for respect.   The demand for respect is another "justification" for police violence. An earlier study of police revealed that 37 percent of the sample thought it was permissible to use violence to coerce respect. Thus the "wise guy" who talks back to the police or who in some other way acts disrespectfully toward the police deserves brutality. "The police believe that certain groups of persons will respond only to fear and rough treatment. In the city studied they defined both Negroes and slum dwellers in this category."[93]

But the use of violence to command respect is self-defeating. Persons who are beaten by a police officer in an attempt to force respect become embittered and lose any respect they may have had. "The system within which the police work is evil, for the simplest of reasons: because it injures people and destroys their respect for the legal process."[94]

The use of violence to command respect may also lead to violence by citizens. "Much police violence comes about when either party to a confrontation engages the other in a test of respect. Violence becomes probable where issues of self-esteem are mobilized for both contenders; it becomes less probable where one party retreats from the threat he poses to the other's self-esteem."[95]

Street justice.   The final justification for brutality is often referred to as *street justice*. The police may become angered when they arrest a suspect whom they are certain committed a crime and then see the courts let that person go free because of a technicality. After several instances like this, police may decide to take matters into their own hands and "apply a little street justice." They may also take that action against suspects who they think should be punished but against whom they cannot get enough evidence for prosecution. Sexual offenders are a prime example. Because of the pressures to arrest in some cases and the difficulty of doing so in these and other circumstances, the police may begin to justify excessive violence. "They come to see it as good, as useful, as their own."[96]

POLICE CORRUPTION

Police corruption has also been a topic of concern and study. In response to an article charging widespread police corruption, in May 1970, the mayor of New York City established the Knapp Commission.[97] The commission found that police corruption was so pervasive within the New York City Police Department that rookies entering the force were subjected immediately to such strong pressures that many succumbed and became corrupt; others became cynical. This attitude was attributed to the departmental belief that corruption should not be exposed and to the code of silence with respect to the corrupt activities of one's peers.[98]

More recently, officials of the New York Police Department have reported that only a small percentage of the city's police officers have been corrupted. Undercover tests of integrity, whereby some officers are assigned to make secret reports on the behavior of other officers, have, they say, virtually eliminated organized corruption. The institutionalized, organized corruption found by the Knapp Commission has, however, been "replaced" by a new type of activity: cheating scams. "Where investigators once found evidence of widespread payoffs from narcotics dealers or other criminals, they are now more likely to uncover instances of an officer's stealing time, money or even gasoline from the department itself." The officers thus have "new areas" of abuse—sick leave, overtime, and military leave.[99]

Others advocate that corruption has not been replaced in the New York City or any other police department—that it is inevitable: "Corruption is endemic to policing. The very nature of the police function is bound to subject officers to tempting others. . . . Solutions, so far, seem inadequate and certainly are not likely to produce permanent results."[100]

Finally, even New York City police commanders have recently expressed concern about their police officers' use of drugs and the problems of corruption that go along with drug abuse. The seriousness of the problem was underscored by a recent report made by the city's Internal Affairs Division: "Narcotics is perceived as the department's No. 1 corruption hazard."[101]

Analysis of police corruption

According to sociologist Lawrence W. Sherman, "A public official is corrupt if he accepts money or moneys worth for doing something that he is under a duty to do anyway, that he is under a duty not to do, or to exercise a legitimate discretion for improper reasons."[102] From violators of traffic laws who offer an officer money not to write a ticket to organized criminals who in some cities have been able to gain extensive control over police activities, policing is rich in opportunities for corruption. In many cases such opportunities have not been overlooked by police, but the degree of corruption varies from jurisdiction to jurisdiction. In general, less corruption exists in rural police departments, with more extensive corruption being found in the older, more established departments in which more opportunities exist.

The opportunity for corruption is not the only important variable in explaining the degree of corruption. Variation in police corruption may also depend on the police department's type of organization. James Q. Wilson analyzed police departments according to what he termed *styles* of law enforcement: the Service Style, the Legalistic Style, and the Watchman Style. These styles were found to be related to the degree of police corruption, with the greatest degree being found among the Watchman Style.[103]

The *Watchman Style* emphasizes order maintenance over law enforcement. The law is used to maintain order rather than to regulate conduct. Juvenile offenses, unless they are serious, are ignored. Because blacks are thought to want and deserve less law enforcement, the police operating under this style of enforcement overlook crimes against blacks unless they are serious. They may also handle such crimes informally. In a department characterized by the Watchman Style, the police chief tries to limit the discretionary authority of the police on patrol, as one of the main concerns is that within the department no one "rocks the boat." The police are recruited locally, paid low salaries, given minimum training, not rewarded for higher education, and expected to have other jobs, any of which may make them more susceptible to opportunities for corruption.

The *Legalistic Style,* on the other hand, is characterized by an emphasis on specialization and promotional opportunities, on the higher education of police, and an attempt to recruit from the middle class. The law is seen as a means to an end; the police officer tries to be an impersonal agent of the law, uses formal rather than informal sanctions, issues traffic tickets at a high rate, and emphasizes law enforcement over peace or order maintenance or community services.

The *Service Style* combines law enforcement and order maintenance. The emphasis is on community relations; the police on patrol work out of specialized units; and the command is decentralized. The pace of work is more leisurely and more promotional opportunities are stressed, as is higher education. Corruption is not a serious problem, and the police are expected to live exemplary private lives.

Sherman has classified the type of corruption in police departments into three ideal types. Type 1, the *Rotten Apples* and the *Rotten Pockets,* describes a department in which only a few people are morally weak individuals who accept bribes. This is the type that most police administrators would pick to describe their particular departments, and it is the type predominant in northwestern Europe. The rotten apples are mainly the uniformed partrol. They are loners who, for example, accept bribes for not enforcing traffic laws. The rotten pockets are work groups involved in corruption. They accept money not to enforce the law and are found mainly among plainclothes police, especially those who rely on informants for information for enforcing the law. Sherman suggests that the very nature of vice squad work makes it susceptible to Type 1 corruption.[104]

Pervasive Unorganized Corruption, Type II, describes the police department in which corruption is widespread and pervasive but not organized. This type is characterized mainly by the "distortive," as compared with the "nondistortive," corruption, the latter referring to decisions that are made as they would have been otherwise but that are made more quickly, as opposed to the former, which involves decisions that would not have otherwise been made or made in that manner.

Pervasive Organized Corruption, Type III, describes the highly organized, hierarchical organization of the community's political processes, ranging beyond the police force to include even the media. There is no effective political opposition, and this form of corruption may even sanction murder.

The existence, type, and amount of corruption vary by police departments and also among individual police officers. The Knapp Commission found only a few police officers who used their positions and power for personal gain. The bulk of the problem was the officers who simply accepted the payoffs that came their way.[105]

Clearly, police corruption is a problem of opportunity *and* response and can be explained only by a close analysis of both variables.

External opportunities. Sherman[106] examined the external opportunities that might be conducive to police corruption and in so doing referred to numerous sociological theories, some of which have already been discussed in this book. First, he looked at Robert K. Merton's theories of community structure and anomie, indicating that the degree of anomie depends on the gap between the goals and the means to achieve these goals. Sherman emphasized that anomie can affect the corrupters and the corruptees and that an occupational group might suffer anomie not characteristic of the entire community. Police might have an occupational anomie and therefore be more susceptible to bribes. Another group, such as construction workers, might suffer occupational anomie owing to market changes and thus be more likely to attempt to bribe the police.

Second, Sherman distinguished between a political ethos, a type of community described as "public-regarding," as compared with one that is "private-regarding." In the first instance, those who participate in various governmental processes see themselves as mainly helping the general community; in the latter, they see their function as mainly helping themselves. There will be less police corruption in communities with a public-regarding ethos, as opposed to a private-regarding ethos, and, further, communities with less culture conflict will experience less police corruption. The conflict may be over conduct norms and which laws should be enforced or the unequal distribution of power.

Sherman then studied the organizational characteristics, referring to sociological analyses of patterns of bureaucracy. He postulated that police corruption would be less in a *punishment-centered* organization, in which neither management nor workers saw the rules of the other side as legitimate and rules enforced by the one were evaded by the other. Police corruption would be highest in the *mock* bureaucratic pattern (in which management did not enforce the rules and the workers did not obey), as both groups viewed the rules as imposed on them by an outside agency. The third type, between these two extremes in the degree of police corruption, was the *representative,* in which both workers and management saw the rules as legitimate because both sides could initiate them. In that type, management enforced the rules and workers obeyed.

Police corruption will be less in agencies characterized by leaders with a reputation of integrity. When leaders exhibit nonexemplary behavior, it is easier for police to become cynical and more susceptible to corruption. And exemplary behavior by the police leaders may create a charismatic effect that may lead to high status being placed by the police on integrity.

Next, Sherman looked to the police department's solidarity and determined that the less work group solidarity there was the less organized the police corruption would be. Solidarity may be affected by numerous factors, including work shifts and patterns, size of work group, ethnic mixtures, and other factors. The concept of self that permits the police officer to become corrupt is a gradual process. The less gradual it is, the less likely it is that the corruption will become serious.

Sherman referred to the opportunity structure of Cloward and Ohlin and argued that police were less likely to accept bribes if they perceived opportunities for advancement. Opportunities for corruption are also important to Sherman's analysis, and he stated that "a decrease in either the scope of morals laws or the demand for the services they proscribe, while holding the other constant, will reduce police corruption opportunities (also the converse)."[107]

Internal responses.   Many police who work in environments conducive to corruption do not become corrupt. Why not? Earlier explanations stressed the recruitment of persons prone to corruption. But more recently it has been argued that most recruits start out to do an honest job, that few intend to become corrupt. But they begin the road to corruption by accepting free meals, cigarettes, turkeys at Thanksgiving, and liquor at Christmas from the respectable people in their districts. This is forbidden by the rule book but is generally overlooked by police departments. The rookie's acceptance of such gifts makes him or her more tolerable to the police officers who have already moved further into corruption. This tolerance becomes increasingly important as the officer begins to believe that the community is hostile toward the police and that the only people who understand and accept them are other police.

According to Sherman, all of these and other experiences change the recruits' frame of reference, and they begin to feel that they are "outsiders" to the world of nonpolice. The recruits have radically redefined themselves in a relatively short period of time, and their almost-exclusive contacts with other police emphasize and reinforce that process. The process of accepting bribes then begins. The key factor here, Sherman observed, is the extent of such corruption in the work group to which the officer is assigned. The process goes by "stages," beginning with "police perks"—free coffee and meals—and then moves to a free drink after work, to money offered by a motorist. If the officer participates in these stages, he or she may be considered ready by colleagues to be cut in on gambling deals. That is hard to turn down, for it represents a chance to get into the social solidarity with the only "significant others" the officer now has. He or she may then move on to bribes from prostitutes, pimps, or brothel operators and finally into the field of narcotics. Police may stop anywhere along the ladder in terms of self-conception, but they will be greatly influenced in where they stop by the group definition of how far they can go.[108]

The police officer may then rationalize his or her behavior: "I am not hurting anyone. Everyone is doing the same thing. Most people are much worse. The public thinks a policeman is dishonest whether he is or not. Therefore, I am not doing wrong by taking a graft."[109] Because of the emphasis that police departments place on vice arrests, the police soon realize that the only way to get information needed for such arrests is to "get in and deal." And such officers learn that the only way to remain honest is to resign their positions on the police force.[110]

CONTROL OF POLICE ACTIVITIES

Quis custodiet ipsos custodes? Who guards the guardians? The question of controlling the police is an important one.

CONTROL BY THE COURTS: THE EXCLUSIONARY RULE

The main method exercised by courts to control police misconduct is the use of the **exclusionary rule.** As early as 1914, the Supreme Court held that the prohibition against unreasonable search and seizure would not be effective unless any illegally seized evidence was excluded from the trial against the defendant in federal cases,[111] and in 1961, the Court held that the exclusion also applied to cases tried in state courts.[112] But it was not until the 1960s that the rule gained much attention in the popular press. With the increasing recognition of the defendants' rights at trial, brought about by Supreme Court decisions in the 1960s, more attention has been given to what is perhaps the most controversial element of the criminal justice process.

Why is the exclusionary rule so controversial? It applies "after the fact." When the illegally seized evidence is excluded from the trial, we already know who the suspect is and often believe that the guilt is obvious. Thus, when the judge rules that the knife or gun allegedly used in the murder or the confession made by the suspect cannot be used against that person in court because the evidence was obtained illegally by the police, there is a strong public reaction—of disbelief and outrage.[113]

Arguments in favor of the exclusionary rule

First the exclusionary rule serves a symbolic purpose. In order to obtain evidence to convict alleged criminals, if the police violate the rights of those individuals, our government is, in a sense, supporting crime. According to the Supreme Court, when this occurs, the government becomes a lawbreaker, and "it breeds contempt for law; it invites . . . anarchy."[114]

The symbolic purpose is important, but the second reason for the exclusionary rule is a practical one: it is assumed that the existence of the rule will prevent police from engaging in illegal searches and seizures. According to the Supreme Court, the exclusionary rule "compel[s] respect for the constitutional guaranty in the only effectively available way—by removing the incentive to disregard it."[115] It is, of course, difficult to know whether that statement is true, as illegal searches may be conducted to harass or punish, generally take place in secret, and may not be reported. The research on the issue reports inconclusive evidence.[116] There is evidence, however, that the existence of the rule has led some police departments to increase the quantity and quality of police training, thus educating officers more in what they may and may not do in the area of search and seizure.[117]

Arguments for abolishing the exclusionary rule

In recent years the exclusionary rule has come under severe attack, with many people calling for its abolition or at least its modification. The arguments on this side of the issue are generally the reverse of the arguments in favor. First is the argument of the symbolism of abolition, based on the view that when people see "obviously guilty" persons going free because of a technicality, it undermines respect for law and order and therefore weakens the entire criminal justice system. It is the public's perception of letting "guilty" people free that is crucial. The classic statement on this issue was made by Benjamin Cardozo, then a state court judge and later a justice of the U.S. Supreme Court. Cardozo wrote the 1926 opinion in which the New York Court of Appeals refused to adopt the exclusionary rule for that jurisdiction: "The criminal is to go free because the constable has blundered."[118]

EXHIBIT

THE SUPREME COURT FOCUSES ON THE EXCLUSIONARY RULE

In January 1984, the Supreme Court heard arguments on whether the extremely controversial exclusionary rule should be abolished or modified. The major case argued before the Court involved evidence used to convict the defendant in the murder of a woman, age twenty-nine, whose body, badly beaten, bound in wire, and burned, was found in a vacant lot in Boston on May 5, 1979. Police investigation led them to the woman's boyfriend, Osborne Sheppard. He was brought to the police station, read his *Miranda* rights, and questioned about the night of the murder. He had an alibi, but the police found that to be a lie. They began to suspicion Sheppard in the murder and wanted to search his residence the next morning. Time was important, as the evidence could be destroyed.

The police officer on the case could not find a proper form for application for a search **warrant;** so he used the only one he could find. It was for drug cases, but he scratched out the words *controlled substances* and adapted the form to his case. On another sheet of paper, the officer described the place to be searched (the basement and second floor) and the evidence to be seized (wire, blood samples). He took the two pieces of paper to a magistrate and asked for a search warrant. The magistrate checked the forms but failed to scratch out another instance of *controlled substance,* signed the warrant, and gave it to the officer who then searched the residence and found the evidence. The blood samples matched the blood of the murdered woman, and the wire matched the wire on her body.

On the basis of this evidence, Sheppard was convicted and sentenced to life in prison. After the trial, his attorney made a motion for a new trial on the grounds that the search warrant was improper; therefore, defense argued, the evidence was not admissible. The search warrant, in addition to the changes, lack of changes, and improper form, was also not properly stapled. The Supreme Judicial Court of Massachusetts agreed with the defense and ordered a new trial. The Commonwealth of Massachusetts appealed the case to the Supreme Court. The Court praised the police search; it was proper in every respect. But, it declared, the Supreme Court of the United Stated had never recognized an exception to the exclusionary rule. If the evidence, although properly taken, was taken under an improperly secured search warrant, the evidence would not be admissible.

On the last day of its 1983–84 session, the U.S. Supreme Court reversed the Massachusetts Supreme Judicial Court and reinstated the conviction of Sheppard. In a 6–3 decision, the Court, for the first time since it adopted the exclusionary rule in 1914, narrowed the application of the rule. Writing for the majority, Justice Byron R. White said,

> The marginal or non-existent benefits produced by suppressing evidence obtained in objectively reasonable reliance on a subsequently invalidated search warrant cannot justify the substantial cost of exclusion . . . Even assuming the rule effectively deters some police misconduct and

provides incentives for the law enforcement profession as a whole to conduct itself in accord with the Fourth Amendment, it cannot be expected, and should not be applied, to deter objectively reasonable law enforcement activity.

When asked what he thought about the decision, President Ronald Reagan said, "I loved it." The Justice Department issued a statement: "Today's decision gives the American people a result we have sought for some time . . . It gives recognition to the principle that the ascertainment of truth is a priority in our criminal justice system."

Others were critical of the ruling. The Executive Director of the Civil Liberties Union of Massachusetts said he thinks the ruling sacrifices the rights of individuals by wiping out any remedy for those who are victims of governmental lawlessness. "I don't know how much of the Fourth Amendment we have left," he said.

In his dissenting opinion in the case, Supreme Court Justice William J. Brennan said, "It now appears the Court's victory over the Fourth Amendment is complete." Joined by Justices Thurgood Marshall and John Paul Stevens, Justice White's 32-page dissenting opinion proclaimed that the Court was trampling on individual rights and "strangulating the exclusionary rule."

Source: The information on reactions to this decision was taken from various news accounts on the day of the decision, July 5, 1984. The case is Massachusetts v. Sheppard, 441 N.E.2d 725 (Sup.Jud.Ct.Mass. 1982), *reversed U.S.Law Week* 52 (June 26, 1984); 5177.

Second, the abolitionists contend that the exclusionary rule should be eliminated because it results in the release of guilty people.[119] It makes no difference how many; one is too many, argue the abolitionists. Third, the possibility of having evidence excluded from a trial because it was not properly seized leads defendants to file numerous motions to suppress evidence, which takes up a lot of court time and contributes to their congestion. In criminal cases, objections to search and seizure are the most frequently raised issues.[120]

Legislative and judicial reaction: "good faith" exception

The most widely accepted proposal by legislatures and courts today appears to be a "good faith" exception to the exclusionary rule. Under this exception, illegally obtained evidence would not be excluded from trial if it could be shown that the officers secured the evidence in good faith, that is, if they reasonably believed that they were acting in accordance with the law. The good faith exception has been rejected by some states and adopted by others; it is opposed by the American Bar Association and the American Civil Liberties Union. But it has been adopted by some lower courts,[121] considered by the Supreme Court, sidestepped in 1982,[122] but adopted during the 1983–84 Court term.[123]

LEGISLATIVE CONTROL: DECRIMINALIZATION

Another method for curbing improper police behavior is to decriminalize the law. In Chapter 1 we examined the nature and purpose of the law and the problems that may arise when the police are expected to enforce laws aimed at regulating "morality." We suggested that decriminalization, or removing such behaviors from the criminal law, would decrease the police's problems in enforcing these laws. It is also believed that such decriminalization would decrease police corruption.

The Knapp Commission recommended the decriminalization of many laws. For example, in the area of gambling, the commission concluded that because of the "severe corruption hazard posed by gambling," it should not remain within the criminal law. If the legislature believes it must be controlled, it should be done by "civil rather than criminal process."[124]

In other areas in which regulation is necessary, the commission recommended revising the laws. It is not suggested that revising laws to decriminalize some activities would eliminate police corruption. Even the Knapp Commission admitted that it might just transfer the corruption to other agencies. But the commission concluded that though corruption anywhere is undesirable, it is preferable to have it in other agencies than in the police, for it would have "far less impact upon the body politic than corruption among the police."[125]

COMMUNITY CONTROL

"The police are the people, and the police powers are vested in them by the people," and in a democratic society the cooperation of the police and the public is essential.[126] Yet, as we have seen, many victims of crime do not call the police because they do not believe the police will be helpful. We have also seen that the police are dependent on the cooperation of citizens for effective control and prevention of crime.

Earlier suggestions included returning the control of police to the people by restructuring police forces along neighborhood lines.[127] This "neighborhood control" scheme would cover the variety of neighborhoods; for example, predominantly black areas would be policed and controlled by blacks; rural areas would be policed by a system appropriate to such areas; ethnic concentrations could be handled according to their needs; and perhaps even areas with heavy concentrations of youth could be aided by this system.

Police officers could be required to live in the areas they serviced and could thus become more familiar with the residents. The hostility that blacks have for the whites who control them might then be eliminated. Drunks in the ghetto could be taken home, as are drunks in upper-class areas, instead of being arrested. People living in areas that have limited playing space for children might decide that enforcing laws against playing games in alleys was less important than enforcing laws against inferior housing.

There are, of course, objections to this system. First, people would encounter different police systems as they moved from one neighborhood to another. A second criticism concerns the police's need to cross jurisdiction lines when in "hot pursuit" of a suspect.

Another method for community control over the police is the Civilian Review Board (CRB), a group of citizens whose function is to review cases of alleged police misconduct. One of the arguments against the CRB is that in some cases it has power only to recommend action on disciplinary cases or policy, with the final authority residing in the police department's internal review board, or that if the CRB did have final authority, it would constrain the police from doing their jobs aggressively. It is also thought that the members of such boards are not always trained for the positions they hold, the appointment of the board reflects on the inadequacy of police leadership, and citizens already have available remedies against the police, in the form of civil actions.[128]

Some improvements have been made in police-community relations, such as in Detroit. Detroit had a reputation for poor police-community relations, but after the 1967 riots, the city formed an organization, known as New Detroit, to improve black-white relations. In 1983, the president of New Detroit observed that "there is a greater sensitivity to the proper role

In the People's Republic of China, police tell us that they not only prevent crimes, direct traffic, intervene in domestic and other disputes, and assist people in social services, but they also believe it is their function to educate the people in the laws as well as in morality. "We cannot do anything without the people; we love the people; we cherish the people; we designate one month of the year as 'Love the people' month.' " (Conversation with police in a seminar in the People's Republic of China.)

of policing. . . . Blacks don't automatically assume brutality anymore when a police officer has to apply some force." A survey conducted by professors at Wayne State University in Detroit revealed that 82 percent of the sample felt that police brutality was not a problem. The professors concluded that the changes in police-community relationships in that city made Detroit "unique among large cities in the way its Police Department interacts with the community it serves." Between 1973 and 1983 the percentage of blacks on the Detroit police force increased from 18 to 32 percent, with more blacks occupying higher ranks than previously. With these and other changes, said the professors, the relationships between blacks and the police have significantly improved.

The importance of cooperation between the police and the community was emphasized by the police chief in Bismark, North Dakota. After twenty-two years on the force, he said, "We're going back to the public and saying, 'Look, folks, this is not our job alone. We're the professionals, but you've got to help.'"[129]

POLICE CONTROL
OF POLICE
ACTIVITIES:
PROFESSIONALISM

In the final analysis, however, only the police can effectively control police activities. Police discretion is necessary; the courts alone cannot control police activities; and even if legislation is changed and criminal codes no longer include laws that the public really does not want enforced, the police retain extensive opportunities for violating individual rights.[130] Thus, it has been argued that the only way the police can effectively be controlled is for them to control themselves. For these reasons professionalism has become *the* solution for police misconduct:

> The needed philosophy of professionalism must rest on a set of values conveying the idea that the police are as much an institution dedicated to the achievement of legality in society as they are an official social organization designed to control misconduct through the invocation of punitive sanctions. . . . What must occur is a significant alteration in the ideology of police, so that police "professionalization" rests on the values of a democratic legal order, rather than on technological proficiency.[131]

The importance of professionalism was dramatized by an earlier study revealing that police attitudes are not explained by social variables such as social class, ethnicity, age, rank, and authoritarianism but that "the impact of professionalism does play a major role in explaining variations in police attitudes and behavior." Police officers' attitudes toward racial and economic minorities, toward when it is appropriate to "rough a man up," and toward politics and the use of physical force differed according to their degree of professionalism.[132]

It is important, however, that the public is not misled; police professionalism must be real, not just illusory.[133] One scholar of police behavior contends that the police have adopted for themselves an impossible mandate "that claims to include the efficient, apolitical, and professional enforcement of the law." Because they cannot meet that mandate, they resort to "appearances of professionalism" that include creating a bureaucracy in police organization, as they see that as the best and most efficient way to run the organization; using technology to indicate a scientific perspective of crime; collecting official data and using them to show how "efficient" the police are; and devising styles of patrol that they see as part of bureaucratic efficiency. They also develop secrecy, one of their most effective sources of power, as it enables them to act without indicating what they are doing, such as cooperating with rather than fighting organized crime. Appearances are also important, as the police need convictions for their arrests. For a high rate of convictions, the police may cooperate with prosecutors in persuading people to plead guilty to lesser offenses, operating on the assumption that all the people they arrest are guilty and that if the police apply enough pressure, the suspects will plead guilty.[134]

Reorganization of police departments

One element of professionalism that has been suggested is to reorganize the police departments. As far back as 1967, the president's crime commission asserted that professionalism would be hindered if the police departments continued to refuse lateral entry.[135] In many departments, the police may enter the force only at the bottom and then work their way up. Such policies prevent the infusion of new ideas and deny the police the professional growth and development that can come through professional mobility.

The Knapp Commission also recommended lateral entry, concluding that if a department is tolerant of corruption, promotions only from within could carry that tolerance to supervisory levels.[136]

Specialization

Another aspect of professionalism that has been recommended for police departments is specialization. One suggestion is to have an organizational pattern that would have a "domestic unit . . . a juvenile unit, and a drunk unit with a detoxification center, all with a peace-keeping orientation and peacekeeping functions. Only a felony squad and perhaps a riot squad should be used to enforce the law."[137] Another suggestion is the creation of a social service academy sponsored by the federal government. It would be governed by an independent board composed of professionals, such as sociologists, psychologists, and criminologists, analogous to the board of scientists of the National Science Foundation. The social service academy would provide free higher education to those who wished to become police officers, social workers, or urban specialists. This approach, it is felt, would help in attracting a greater variety of people into police work.[138]

Still other supporters of professionalism have suggested that the police department be reorganized to involve "crisis intervention units," as the police receive so many family and friend disturbance calls that might erupt into violence. For example, one family crisis intervention experiment used a specially trained group of skilled officers to handle family disputes, with the result that the unit had a direct impact on violence. Eighteen patrolmen were given intensive training in on-the-spot crisis intervention and solution. Although family disturbance calls usually account for about 22 percent of the police killed and about 40 percent of those injured, after one year, the officers in the family crisis intervention unit had not sustained a single injury. Other benefits were that the community responded with unusual regard for the unit. The community was given readily available mental health workers, and the police were allowed to be compassionate within the traditional police role.[139]

Policies regarding the use of discretion

Another way that the police may "control themselves" is for departments to institute policies regarding the use of discretion. **Discretion** is an inevitable part of policing. It is impossible to eliminate it, and police will always have discretion in deciding when to stop a person and whether to detain, frisk, arrest, or whatever.

It is possible, however, to institute policies on the control of discretion. One method of controlling discretion is through administrative rule-making procedures. It is characteristic of administrative law that the government's legislative and executive branches delegate to adminstrative bodies the power to make rules and policies, and the police may be viewed as an administrative agency. The making of rules by administrative agencies is governed by statutes and administrative agencies are not free to make rules without following the specified procedures. The rules may be changed, but only according to specified procedures and then published. In contrast, the police are free to exercise their judgment, often even without guidelines. Therefore, it has been advocated that "rules" should be determined, not by the police on the beat, but by higher authorities within the system. A specified rule-making procedure should be established, and the public should be allowed to participate in it.[140]

The policies on discretion should include guidelines with regard to selec-

---

EXHIBIT

DISCRETION IN THE CRIMINAL JUSTICE SYSTEM

Discretion Is Exercised Throughout the Criminal Justice System

Discretion is "an authority conferred by law to act in certain conditions or situations in accordance with an official's or an official agency's own considered judgment and conscience." Traditionally, criminal and juvenile justice officials, in particular the police, prosecutors, judges, and paroling authorities, have been given a wide range of discretion.

Legislative bodies have recognized that they cannot foresee every possibility, anticipate local mores, and enact laws that clearly encompass all conduct that is criminal and all that is not. Therefore, those charged with the day-to-day response to crime are expected to exercise their own judgment within guidelines set by law.

Discretion is also necessary to permit the criminal and juvenile justice systems to function within available resources. The enforcement and procescution of all laws against all violators is beyond the financial resources available. Therefore, criminal and juvenile justice officials must have the authority to allocate resources in a way that meets the most compelling needs of their own communities.

The limits of discretion vary from State to State and locality to locality. For example, the range of options available to judges when they sentence offenders varies greatly. In recent years, some States have sought to limit the judges' discretion in sentencing by passing mandatory and determinate sentencing laws.

Who Exercises Discretion?

These Criminal Justice Officials . . .	*. . . Must Often Decide Whether or Not or How to—*
Police	Enforce specific laws
	Investigate specific crimes
	Search people, vicinities, buildings
	Arrest or detain people
Prosecutors	File charges or petitions for adjudication
	Seek indictments
	Drop cases
	Reduce charges
Judges or magistrates	Set bail or conditions for release
	Accept pleas
	Determine delinquency
	Dismiss charges
	Impose sentence
	Revoke probation
Correctional officials	Assign to type of correctional facility
	Award privileges
	Punish for disciplinary infractions
Paroling authority	Determine date and conditions of parole
	Revoke parole

Source: Bureau of Justice Statistics, *Report to the Nation on Crime and Justice: The Data* (Washington, D.C.: U.S. Government Printing Office, 1983), p. 44, footnotes omitted.

tive enforcement of the law. The police cannot enforce all laws, and therefore selective enforcement is not only necessary but legal. Police may not, however, enforce certain laws only against certain groups. Thus the adoption of proper rule-making procedures, although they refer only to general policy, would make it more difficult for the police to harass certain types of individuals with regard to certain laws. For example, if it is stated policy that the police will not arrest those who drink in public parks unless they become disorderly, the police would not be able to arrest an orderly drinking suspected homosexual so as to harass him.

Policies regarding the use of discretion should also include the use of force, especially deadly force. Some police departments do not have formal guidelines on the use of deadly force. Other departments have vague guidelines that leave too much discretion to individual police officers. For example, one department's policy on the use of a gun was, "Never take me out in anger; never put me back in disgrace." Such policies obviously leave great discretion to police officers.[141] Some police forces have guidelines that are clear but also clearly violated. Yet the police are rarely disciplined.[142]

HIGHLIGHT
POLICE USE OF DEADLY FORCE: THE IMPACT

On March 31, 1983, a police officer, responding to a call from a neighbor who had not seen five-year-old Patrick and his mother for two weeks, entered their apartment with a passkey provided by the building manager. Hearing noises coming from the bedroom, the officer opened the door that the mother had tied shut. The officer saw a silhouette holding what he thought was a gun, fired, and killed the little boy who was holding a toy while he watched television.

One year later, the news media reported that the mother, who had moved from that residence in Stanton, California, to Chicago, Illinois, could barely look at another child without thinking of her little boy whose life had been taken so quickly and, at least in her mind, unnecessarily. The officer, unemployed and receiving disability retirement pay, suffers from severe stress attacks. According to his father, "The memory of that awful event has intensely affected his life. It will be with him forever." He received a $32,000 cash settlement for the psychological damage he has suffered, and he filed a $25 million claim against the city, hoping that the courts will consider the city, not the officer, liable for any lawsuits in the case. The mother filed a $20 million claim against the officer and the city. A man who claims to be the father of the deceased boy has filed claims against the city, totaling $10 million. The city has rejected those claims, but he could be successful in a civil action should he choose that course of action.

The lawsuits in this case will probably not be decided for several years, and the pain, suffering, and stress for the immediate parties will perhaps never end.

Source: Summarized by the author from news media accounts.

SUMMARY AND CONCLUSION

This chapter has raised the relevant issues concerning the police in the system of criminal justice. After a brief overview of our system, we looked at a profile of the police and their various functions: law enforcement, order maintenance, and social services. Of those three, the police spend the greatest portion of their time in social services; yet that is the area in which they receive the least training.

We examined the attitudes and the hostility the police feel from the public. These and other conflicts and problems have led some police to withdraw into themselves, to develop a "code of secrecy," and to become socially isolated from society.

Understanding the police's insulation from society is necessary to understanding the police's abuse of their extensive discretion. Their decisions whether to apprehend and arrest may be made on improper grounds, and they may exceed the use of force to which they are legally entitled, leading to harassment, brutality, and sometimes violence. Examples of these were followed by a consideration of police corruption, the factors influencing that corruption, and a sociological analysis of police corruption. Finally, we discussed how the courts, the legislature, the community, and the police departments might exercise control over the police.

Experts on the police have concluded that our research on policing has not been adequate,[143] that we just do not know enough about the people who occupy one of the most important roles in our entire system of criminal justice. But we do know about the tremendous impact their behavior can have on us as individuals and as a society. We also need to understand that the behavior that so deeply touches our lives also has a tremendous impact on the police.

CHAPTER 12

Pretrial release or detention

A critical decision in the criminal justice process is the decision to release a defendant pending trial or detain that person in jail. In this chapter we shall discuss the implications of that decision. We begin with a brief look at the "right to bail" and the various methods by which a defendant can be released pending trial. Detention for "preventive" reasons—because the person is considered a threat to society—will be explored both in its practical implications and its legal issues. We shall also examine bail reform and jails both historically and currently. We shall consider the jail's physical facilities, programs, medical services, and problems of administration. Recent court decisions on jail conditions will be summarized. Finally, we shall study alternatives to jails.

One of the most critical periods of the criminal justice proceedings is the time between the arraignment and the trial. It is a time "when consultation, thoroughgoing investigation and preparation . . . [are] vitally important."[1] During this period the defendant either retains an attorney or is assigned counsel by the court. The defense counsel and the prosecutor negotiate and consider the possibility of plea bargaining. The defense may consider it important to a fair trial that the location of the trial be moved, and the judge must rule on the motion for a **change of venue.** Witnesses will be interviewed and other attempts will be made by both sides to secure evidence for the trial. The uncovering of additional evidence may change the nature of the case and can even result in the dropping or reduction of charges.

PRETRIAL RELEASE

The purpose of pretrial release is to enable the defendant to prepare for trial while avoiding the harmful effects of detention in jail. The problems faced by defendants who are incarcerated are enormous and extend beyond the most obvious one, deprivation of liberty. The United States Supreme Court recognized this problem in a 1975 decision in which the Court held that a person may not be detained for an extended period following arrest unless a neutral magistrate finds probable cause. The Court said, "The consequences of prolonged detention may be more serious than the interference occasioned by arrest. Pretrial confinement may imperil the suspect's job, interrupt his source of income, and impair his family relationships."[2]

Furthermore, detainees may lose their jobs permanently and acquire the stigma attached to a jail term, even though they are still *legally innocent of a crime.* They face days of loneliness and idleness, with limited opportunity to talk and visit with family and friends. They may develop psychological problems and even suffer physical problems as a result of incarceration.

Earlier studies revealed that defendants who are detained in jail before trial, as compared with those who are free during that period, are more likely to be convicted and to receive longer sentences.[3] More guilty pleas at trial are found among those who are refused bail than by those who are granted bail.[4] A recent study indicates that detention before trial increases the probability that the defendant will be convicted, even when the factor of privately retained versus court-appointed attorney is controlled.[5]

It is, of course, important to examine the various reasons that these findings occur. For example, perhaps the persons who are most likely to be convicted are those who are most likely to be denied bail. But it is also possible that the conditions of confinement are influential. The 1967 president's crime commission, noting that those detained in jail before trial often receive worse treatment than those who are convicted and sentenced to prisons or jails, accepted the conclusion of a report submitted to that commission:

> We doubt whether any innocent person (as all before trial are presumed to be) can remain unscarred by detention under such a degree of security. . . . The

indignities of repeated physical search, regimented living, crowded cells, utter isolation from the outside world, unsympathetic surveillance, outrageous visitors' facilities, Fort Knox-like security measures, are surely so searing that one unwarranted day in jail itself can be a major social injustice.[6]

METHODS OF
PRETRIAL RELEASE

There are several methods, both financial and nonfinancial, by which defendants may be released pending trial.[7] In any of these methods, the Court may impose restrictions on the accused—where they may live, with whom they may associate, conditions under which they may and may not travel—or they may be placed under the supervision of another person or agency.

EXHIBIT
TYPES OF PRETRIAL RELEASE

Both financial bonds and alternative release options are used today.

Financial Bond	Alternative Release Options
Fully secured bail—The defendant posts the full amount of bail with the court.	*Release on recognizance* (ROR)—The court releases the defendant on his promise that he will appear in court as required.
Privately secured bail—A bondsman signs a promissory note to the court for the bail amount and charges the defendant a fee for the service (usually 10% of the bail amount). If the defendant fails to appear, the bondsman must pay the court the full amount. Frequently, the bondsman requires the defendant to post collateral in addition to the fee.	*Conditional release*—The court releases the defendant subject to his following of specific conditions set by the court such as attendance at drug treatment therapy or staying away from the complaining witness.
Percentage bail—The courts allow the defendant to deposit a percentage (usually 10%) of the full bail with the court. The full amount of the bail is required if the defendant fails to appear. The percentage bail is returned after disposition of the case although the court often retains 1% for administrative costs.	*Third party custody*—The defendant is released into the custody of an individual or agency that promises to assure his appearance in court. No monetary transactions are involved in this type of release.
Unsecured bail—The defendant pays no money to the court but is liable for the full amount of bail should he fail to appear.	

Source: Bureau of Justice Statistics, *Report to the Nation on Crime and Justice: The Data* (Washington, D.C.: U.S. Government Printing Office, 1983), p. 58.

BAIL   More jurisdictions are using the nonmonetary forms of release, but it is the **bail** system that receives the greatest attention in discussions of pretrial release. When complaints are made about the harmful results (for example, the commission of additional crimes) that may occur when defendants are released before trial, those complaints focus on the use of bail. The assumption is that if bail either had been denied or had been set at a higher amount, the defendant would not have been released, and the additional crimes would not have occurred. This assumption involves a misconception of the purpose of bail as well as the obvious misconception that bail is the only form of pretrial release.

The purpose of bail   The bail system began in England[8] in order to ensure the presence of defendants at trials, which were held infrequently because the judges traveled from one jurisdiction to another. At that time, the facilities for holding people before trial were terrible, and it was expensive to maintain them. The sheriffs preferred to have someone else take care of the defendants while they were awaiting trial and would often relinquish them to other people, usually friends or relatives. These people would serve as *sureties*. When the system began, if the defendants did not appear for trial after they had been placed on bail, the surety would be tried. The party furnishing bail would be reminded that he or she had the powers of a jailer and was expected to produce the accused for trial. This policy of private sureties was also followed in America but was later replaced by a system of *posting bond* to guarantee a defendant's presence at trial.

The bail system in the United States also was used to ensure the defendant's presence at trial. Earlier court cases made it clear that bail was not to be used as "a means for punishing defendants nor for protecting public safety."[9] Furthermore, the Supreme Court has ruled that "bail set at a figure higher than the amount reasonably calculated to [ensure that the defendant will stand trial] is 'excessive' under the Eighth Amendment."[10]

According to federal rules and some state statutes, bail may be denied in capital cases. Bail may also be denied in noncapital cases in which the defendant has a history of fleeing to avoid prosecution. The reason in both cases is consistent with the purpose of bail, that is, to ensure the presence of the accused at trial. In capital cases, the rationale is that "no amount of money

---

EXHIBIT

AMENDMENT VIII (1791), UNITED STATES CONSTITUTION

Excessive Bail Shall Not Be Required . . .

will ensure the defendant's appearance at trial if, upon conviction, he risks loss of his life."[11]

The use of bail for preventive detention of the dangerous

Until recently, the *only* legitimate purpose of bail has been to secure the defendant's presence at trial. In 1970, however, with the passage of the District of Columbia Court Reform and Criminal Procedure Act, preventive **detention** was recognized as a legitimate purpose of bail.[12] This statute permits judges to deny bail to defendants charged with dangerous crimes if the government has clear evidence, including consideration of the accused's past and present pattern of behavior, that release would not "reasonably assure the safety of any other person or the community." Pretrial detention may also be ordered for persons who have been convicted of a crime of violence within the past ten years or charged with a crime of violence while on probation or parole from another violent crime or for those charged with an offense that threatens the safety of any prospective witness or juror.

A few other states have followed the example of Washington, D.C., and made provisions to deny bail for preventive detention. Perhaps the most publicized adoption of preventive detention occurred in California when the citizens of that state in June 1982 approved Proposition 8 to amend the state constitution to include the Victim's Bill of Rights. Among other things, Proposition 8 provides for preventive detention.[13]

The constitutional challenge to preventive detention

When defendants are denied bail because they are thought to be dangerous to the community, are their constitutional rights being violated? Remember that in our criminal justice system, persons accused of crimes are innocent until proved guilty, and the U.S. Supreme Court has ruled that any bail in excess of that necessary to ensure the presence of a person at trial is "excessive" and therefore a violation of the Eighth Amendment. It is clear that a system of preventive detention must be designed so that it does not violate the accused's constitutional rights.

There have been some challenges to the constitutionality of preventive detention laws. The District of Columbia statute has been upheld.[14] The Nebraska statute was declared unconstitutional by a federal court in that district, though the U.S. Supreme Court vacated that judgment on a technical issue; thus, the statute remains effective.[15]

But even when the denial of bail is permitted to detain persons thought to be dangerous, adequate procedural safeguards for the defendants' rights must be observed in making that judicial decision. For example, one federal court ruled against a trial judge who had denied bail to a defendant pending his appeal. The trial judge had stated that the defendant posed a danger to the three eyewitnesses who had testified against him at trial, and the defendant's motion for release on bail pending his trial had been denied without

EXHIBIT
MOST DEFENDANTS ARE ELIGIBLE FOR RELEASE PENDING TRIAL

The Traditional Objective of Bail or Other Pretrial Release Options Is to Assure Appearance at Trial

In medieval times, the accused was bailed to a third party who would be tried in place of the accused if the accused failed to appear. As the system evolved, the guarantee became the posting of a money bond that was forfeited if the accused failed to appear. In the United States, the Eighth Amendment states that bail shall not be excessive, but it does not grant the right to bail in all cases. The right to bail for many offenses was established by Federal and State laws early in our history.

The Modern Bail Reform Movement Resulted in New Release Options

The movement was based on the belief that detaining the poor because they could not afford bail violated the prohibition against excessive bail. In the early 1960's, seeking alternatives to the commercial bail bondsman, the Vera Institute created the Manhattan bail project, which showed that defendants with community ties could be released without bail and in most cases still return for trial.

The Pretrial Services Resource Center reports that more than 200 pretrial service programs currently operate throughout the Nation. Since the Federal Bail Reform Act of 1966, many States have passed laws that limit the role of bondsmen. Five States (Kentucky, Oregon, Wisconsin, Nebraska, and Illinois) have eliminated bail bonding for profit. Kentucky dealt with both bondsmen and release programs in 1976 when it banned bondsmen and set up a statewide system of pretrial services agencies.

Bail Reform and Other Factors Appear to Have Increased the Number of People Being Released Prior to Trial

A 1976 study in 20 cities found that the release rate had risen from 48% in 1962 to 67% in 1971. More recently, Toborg found that 85% of the defendants in her eight-site sample were released prior to trial.

Most Unconvicted Jail Inmates Have Had Bail Set

Of 66,936 unconvicted jail inmates surveyed in 1978—

- 81% had bail set.
- 46% could not afford the bond that had been set.
- 17% had not had bail set.
- 6% were held on nonbailable offenses such as murder.
- 3% had not yet had a bail hearing
- 2% were held on detainers or warrants.

Most Defendants Are Not Detained Prior to Trial

In Toborg's study, 85% of the defendants in her eight-site sample were released before trial. Some jurisdictions are much less likely than others to release defendants on nonfinancial conditions, but the overall rate of release is similar. Some jurisdictions detain a high proportion of defendants at the time of arraignment, but eventually release most of them before trial. According to Brosi, the detention rate in Salt Lake City dropped from 41% at arraignment to between 10% and 12% before trial.

How Many Released Defendants Fail to Appear in Court?

Pryor and Smith found that—

- Upwards of 85% of all defendants released pending trial appeared for all court sessions.
- People charged with the more serious offenses were more likely to appear.
- Willful failure to appear where the defendant absconds or is returned by force did not exceed 4% of all released defendants.

How Many of Those Released Are Rearrested Prior to Trial?

In Toborg's study of eight jurisdictions—

- 16% of all released defendants were rearrested; rates for individual jurisdictions ranged from 8% to 22%.
- 30% of those rearrested were rearrested more than once.
- About half of those rearrested were later convicted.

This is consistent with Pryor and Smith's analysis of release research that found rearrest rates between 10% and 20% with about half of those rearrested being convicted.

Many States Have Shown Concern About the Effect of Pretrial Release on Community Safety

Gaynes has noted that at the State level most changes in pretrial release practices prompted by concern over community safety have been enacted within the past decade, many since 1979. During 1982, voters in five States (Arizona, California, Colorado, Florida, and Illinois) approved constitutional amendments limiting the right to bail to assure community safety in pretrial release.

Source: Bureau of Justice Statistics, *Report to the Nation on Crime and Justice: The Data* (Washington, D.C.: U.S. Government Printing Office, 1983), pp. 58, 59, footnotes omitted.

a hearing. The federal court of appeals noted that although the federal statute permits denial of bail when a defendant poses a danger to others, there is a strong presumption of a defendant's right to bail pending trial. The defendant had presented strong evidence that he was not a threat to the eyewitnesses, and so the appellate court ruled that under those circumstances, the trial court was required to have a hearing on the evidence before bail could be legally denied.[16]

Finally, it should not be assumed that the use of preventive detention is limited to those jurisdictions in which it is permitted by statute or by constitutional amendment to the state constitution. Studies by sociologists have revealed that *protection of the community and society* is the reason used by judges for denying bail or for setting it so high that it is in effect a denial of bail.[17]

Making bail   Once the judge has decided to grant bail[18] and has set the amount, the defendant must "make bail." It is not usually required that he or she pay the entire amount. For example, under the ten percent plan, the defendant may be released on a bail bond by posting 10 percent of the amount. If the defendant appears at trial, 90 percent of the money posted is returned, and the rest is kept for administrative costs.

In jurisdictions that do not have the 10 percent or similar plans, such as allowing the defendant to post securities with the court, the defendant must either raise the entire amount of bail or hire a **bail bondsman.** In return for a fee, the bondsman will post the bond for the accused. Theoretically, if the accused does not appear for trial, the bondsman is required to forfeit the money. In practice, forfeitures of bonds are usually not enforced. Furthermore, some bondsmen are "straw" men, in that they do not have the necessary money to produce in cases of forfeiture. To avoid this situation, some jurisdictions require the bondsmen to prove their ability to pay in case of forfeiture.

The professional bondsman system has been criticized.[19] The bondsman may require a larger premium from an offender whom he or she does not know—a "poor business risk"—and thereby have considerable control over the accused. Professional criminals, on the other hand, may be considered by a bondsman to be better "risks" and not be required to post as much money. As one judge said,

> The effect of such a system is that the professional bondsmen hold the keys to the jail in their pockets. They determine for whom they will act as surety— who in their judgment is a good risk. The bad risks, in the bondsmen's judgment, *and the ones who are unable to pay the bondsmen's fees,* remain in jail. The court and the commissioner are relegated to the relatively unimportant chore of fixing the amount of bail.[20]

Criticism of the bail-bondsman system has led some states to place legislative restrictions on it or to eliminate it entirely. In 1976 in Kentucky, for example, a statute was passed that states that "it shall be unlawful for any person to engage in the business of bail bondsman." The system was replaced by a network of pretrial service agencies that offer other forms of pretrial release procedures, including unsecured bail bonds, 10-percent cash deposits, third-party custody, and "restricted" liberty.[21] Oregon, on the other hand, did not make the bail-bond system illegal but adopted procedures that have made it very difficult for the business to continue profitably. The Oregon statute provides that the judges "shall impose the least onerous condition" necessary to ensure that the defendant will appear at trial. The judge may also empower others, such as officers or jail wardens, to release defendants in minor cases.[22]

Bail reform   As a result of the increasing dissatisfaction with the bail-bond system, some bail reform programs have been established.[23] These reforms came after the Manhattan Bail Project, an extensive research project that investigated the results of releasing people on their own recognizance after careful evaluation of their cases.

Manhattan bail project: blueprint for change. In the 1960s a New York industrialist became concerned about the poor youths who could not make bail and were therefore detained while awaiting trial. He therefore established the Vera Foundation, which, along with the New York University School of Law and the Institute of Judicial Administration, conducted an experiment on bail. The experiment was based on the hypothesis that "more persons can successfully be released . . . if verified information concerning their character and roots in the community is available to the court at the time of bail determination."[24]

The project was begun in 1961 and early reports indicated a high success rate. Most defendants showed up for trial. This high success rate has, however, been questioned recently in New York where, in late 1983, officials began releasing more people on bail in order to alleviate overcrowding in the jails. A follow-up study of 613 of those releasees revealed that 75 of them, or 12 percent, did not appear in court for trial at the appointed time and date. Fifty-five of those 75 have been arrested again, and 35 of those arrested were charged with felonies, primarily burglary, larceny, and violations of drug laws.[25]

Pretrial services. The success or failure of pretrial release programs must be judged according to the pretrial services offered to the releasees, particularly when they are released on their own recognizance. To answer this need, Congress appropriated money for pretrial services agencies in ten representative federal districts,[26] and because of the success of these pilot projects and the District of Columbia Pretrial Services Agency, Congress legislated the Pretrial Services Act, which became law on September 27, 1982.[27]

Bail reform at the federal level. In 1966, Congress passed the Bail Reform Act[28] to ensure that in the federal system "all persons, regardless of their financial status, shall not needlessly be detained . . . when detention serves neither the ends of justice nor the public interest." The act requires a specific procedure for analysis. Judges are to consider alternatives to bail and base their decisions on specific information. The act established a preference for release without security.

If the judge decides that the defendant may not appear at trial if unconditionally released, he or she must follow a designated procedure for imposing conditions on the accused's liberty. The judge must consider the following factors, and in this order of priority: custody of a specified person or organization for supervision; restriction of travel; restriction on where the accused can live and with whom he or she may associate; requirement of bond of a specified amount, with 10 percent of that to be paid by the accused and returned if he or she does not violate the conditions of release; "execution of a bail bond with sufficient solvent sureties, or the deposit of cash in lieu thereof; or . . . any other condition deemed reasonably necessary to assure appearance as required, including a condition requiring that the person return to custody after specified hours." The judge may impose any combination of these conditions. The drafters of this bill said they were deferring until later the subject of preventive detention. But some of the conditions that the judge may impose are forms of preventive detention.[29]

Future of bail reform.   The debate over whether to release defendants before trial rages on, as evidenced by the following reactions to bail. In his annual "state of the judiciary" address to the American Bar Association in February 1979, Chief Justice Warren E. Burger of the U.S. Supreme Court called for a "fresh examination" of the conditions of bail release for those charged with serious crimes. Burger referred to what he called the "startling increase" in the number of crimes committed by persons on bail while awaiting trial.[30] The chief justice has subsequently repeated his concerns about the bail system.

Many unsuccessful attempts have been made to change the federal bail system. As this book went to press, Congress passed and President Reagan signed, a comprehensive revision of the federal criminal code. The 635-page statute includes a provision for denying bail, after a hearing, to persons judged to be dangerous to society if released.

PRETRIAL DETENTION   Defendants who are not released pending trial are usually detained in jails. In the number of persons confined, jails have a far greater impact on defendants than prisons do. The number of people who pass through jails in this country in a given year is at least four times higher than the number of people who are incarcerated in a given year in state and federal prisons.[31] The jail is a "major intake center not only for the entire criminal justice system, but also a place of first or last resort for a host of disguised health, welfare, and social problem cases."[32]

JAILS: AN
OVERVIEW

Definitions of the term "jail" are not consistent. The Latin root of the term is *cavea*, meaning "cavity," "cage," or "coop," and it has been suggested that jails should be defined as "public cages or coops."[33]

Generally the term **jail** is used to refer to those facilities used to detain persons awaiting trial and to incarcerate persons who have been convicted of minor offenses and received short-term sentences, usually less than a year, in contrast with **prisons,** which are used to incarcerate persons who have received longer sentences after being convicted of more serious offenses. That general definition includes police lockups, in which people are detained for only a few hours or at the most a few days, and detention facilities for juveniles and women, state farms, and road camps. Some experts exclude such facilities from the definition of jail. Also excluded are facilities administered by states, mainly because the "central evil of the 'jail problem,' and, therefore, the natural focus for study and reform, is the fact of local administration."[34]

History of jails

Ironically, although the jail is the oldest of the American penal institutions, less is known about it than about any of the other institutions. Except for an occasional scathing commentary, jails have been tolerated but have received little attention. It was not until 1970 that some systematic data on jails became available. At that time the first national jail census was conducted for the Law Enforcement Assistance Administration (LEAA) by the U.S. Bureau of the Census.

Jails can be traced far back into history, when they made their debut "in the form of murky dungeons, abysmal pits, unscalable precipices, strong poles or trees, and suspended cages in which hapless prisoners were kept."[35] The main purpose of those jails was to detain people awaiting trial, transportation, the death penalty, or corporal punishment. The old jails were not particularly escape-proof, and the persons in charge often received additional fees for shackling prisoners. Inmates were not separated according to classification; the physical conditions were terrible; the food was inadequate; and no treatment or rehabilitation programs existed. John Howard, the great prison reformer, asserted in 1773 after his tour of European institutions that more prisoners died of jail fever than were executed.[36]

In the 1600s, to replace the severe corporal punishments used on those who violated the law, the Quakers in Pennsylvania devised what they considered to be a more humane form of treatment. Later in 1790 in Philadelphia, the Walnut Street Jail (which was really a prison, not a jail) and other jails of that period were created as a "humane replacement" for corporal punishment. In reality, however, jails are not usually humane places. For example, in 1974 a federal court, examining the facilities of a jail in Boston, ordered that it be closed because its conditions imposed unconstitutional conditions on the inmates. The court concluded after studying these modern prisons that a serious argument could be made for returning to the system of corporal punishment which at least ended at some point.[37] There is serious doubt whether the harmful effects of prisons and jails ever can be erased from the lives of those who have been forced to endure this "modern, humane treatment."

The conditions of American jails have worsened over the years. In 1923 Joseph Fishman, a federal prison inspector, investigator, and consultant in the United States, published a book, *Crucible of Crime*, in which he described American jails, basing his descriptions and evaluations on visits to fifteen hundred jails. He said that some of the convicted would ask for a year in prison in preference to six months in jail because of their horrible conditions.[38] Typical of most jails were no space, inadequate meals, no bathing facilities, no hospital, and no separate facilities for juveniles. Although Fishman believed that jail conditions were terrible nationwide, they were the worst in the South: "The quarters of the white prisoners are as bad as can be imagined. It is needless therefore to attempt to describe those occupied by the Negroes."[39]

Fishman's conclusion might be summarized by his definition of jail as

an unbelievably filthy institution in which are confined men and women serving sentences for misdemeanors and crimes, and men and women not under sentence who are simply awaiting trial. With few exceptions, having no segregation of the unconvicted from the convicted, the well from the diseased, the youngest and most impressionable from the most degraded and hardened. Usually swarming with bedbugs, roaches, lice, and other vermin; has an odor of disinfectant and filth which is appalling; supports in complete idleness thousands of able-bodied men and women, and generally affords ample time and opportunity to assure inmates a complete course in every kind of viciousness and crime. A melting pot in which the worst elements of the raw material in the criminal world are brought forth blended and turned out in absolute perfection.[40]

In 1931, the American jail was described by the National Commission on Law Observance and Enforcement as the "most notorious correctional institution in the world."[41] More recently, the American jail has been described by noted authorities as "the worst blight in American corrections"[42] and a place where "anyone not a criminal when he goes in, will be when he comes out."[43] And therefore the courts are beginning to define jail facilities and programs (or the lack thereof) as "unconstitutional."

Purpose of jail   In the United States, offenders and alleged offenders are confined in one of three types of institutions: jails, prisons, and **community-based facilities.**

Jails are for detaining persons pending trial and for short-term punishment, usually for less serious offenses. The jail is in many respects the most important of all of our correctional facilities. First, more people come into contact with jails than with the other facilities, although on any given day, prison populations are considerably higher than jail populations. Second, many of those people are "pretrial detainees" who have not been found guilty of a crime. Some may have been arrested for minor traffic offenses or "suspicion."

Third, some of those detained in jail are not even suspected of having committed a crime but are witnesses to crimes and are being held to ensure their presence at trial.[44] Finally, all of these categories of people are held in facilities that are generally inferior to prisons and community-based facilities.

Data on jail populations

During the year ending June 30, 1982, according to the Bureau of Justice Statistics, more than 7 million people were in jail at some time, and many of them were jailed more than once. On June 30, U.S. jails held 210,000 people, about one-third more than the 1978 figure. Forty percent of these people were confined in the one hundred largest jails, constituting only 3 percent of all jails. The average length of stay was eleven days, but some inmates were incarcerated for over a year; others were released within hours.[45]

Figure 12.1 graphs the data regarding the 1978 jail population. The 1978 survey was conducted to improve and expand on the baseline data provided by the 1970 and 1972 surveys of local jails. As Figure 12.1 indicates, the typical jail inmate in 1978 was white, male, adult, and convicted. He was single, relatively young, and had an average annual income of $3,700.[46]

Some of this information should be clarified. Although a majority of the inmates were white, blacks were disproportionately represented according to their percentage of the total population. Four out of every ten male and five out of every ten female inmates were black. Women were far more likely than men to have been heroin addicts—one-fourth of the women. About one-fifth of the *convicted* inmates were under the influence of drugs at the time of their offense; about one-fourth had been drinking heavily just before the offense was committed, "and the proportion of whites who had was more than twice that of blacks."[47]

Organization and administration of jails

The typical jail in the United States is small and was built between 1880 and 1920. There has been little renovation of its physical facilities. It is located in a small town, which is often the county seat of a predominantly rural county. These small rural jails constitute the majority of jails but house only a minority of the jail population. Some of these jails are seldom used, and most are not crowded. Over one-half of the jail population is confined in

Figure 12.1

Profile of jail inmates.

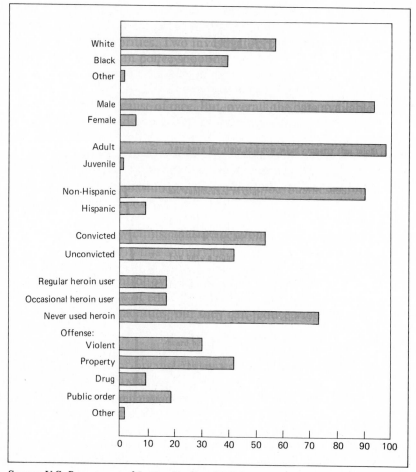

Source: U.S. Department of Justice, Profile of Jail Inmates: Sociodemographic Findings from the 1978 Survey of Inmates of Local Jails *(Washington, D.C.: Government Printing Office, 1980), front cover.*

large urban jails, which have most frequently been the targets of court suits on jail conditions.[48]

The typical jail is locally financed and administered, which inevitably involves in local politics the jail's administration. Historically, American jails have been under the direction and supervision of the sheriff, usually an elected official. In general, such administrators have shown little interest in jail inspections or improvements. Recently some states have assumed control of their jails, but in most jails, the standards remain low, and rehabilitative programs are practically nonexistent.

Lack of money is one of the serious problems with jail management today, leading some people to believe that private enterprise should be drawn into the jails. Some prisons already contract with private firms for food and medical services. A Nashville attorney established the Corrections Corporation of America, a private company composed of business people who are interested in contracting services for jails and prisons throughout the country. In late 1983, after two years of planning, this corporation was in the final stages of negotiation with administrators in several states and was preparing to sign its first contract to manage a jail facility. Its owners have already raised $1 million from investors, and the corporation will begin with minimum facilities, "develop a track record, then go into other possibilities. . . . We're on the cutting edge of a new industry."[49]

Finally, the advisory board of the National Institute of Corrections has endorsed the concept of the "new generation jail model." This model calls for smaller living units for inmates and increased supervision. The integrated architectural and management approach is already in operation at county and federal detention facilities around the country, as well as at several federal correctional institutions. The NIC's board is encouraging states and localities to explore the concept before building or renovating correctional facilities. According to the NIC's director, this jail model provides both greater security for the inmates and a more humane environment. And it is also more cost effective than the traditional models.[50]

Staffing problems   Staffing jails is a serious problem. The staff receive low pay and usually have no training for working with the incarcerated. Jails have low budgets because local governments have less money to spend than state or federal governments do, and jails usually have the lowest priority for local funds. They are usually administered by law enforcement officials, not correctional personnel, and those persons are often no more than custodial help. Jails are generally understaffed, and this absence of adequate supervision gives the inmates little protection from homosexual and other attacks. The lack of staff also increases the probability that inmates will be successful in suicide attempts. Suicide is the predominant cause of death among jail inmates and generally occurs within the first day that the inmate is incarcerated.[51]

But this is not the only problem. Most jails also do not have sufficient treatment personnel. Roughly one-half of all jail personnel are custodial, with only 7 to 9 percent treatment personnel and approximately one-fourth administrative.[52]

Cost of jails   The average cost per year of keeping an adult in a local jail is $8,000, which is the same as the average cost of a local community-based facility. That figure, however, compares favorably to an average cost of $13,000 in a federal prison and between $5,000 and $23,000 in a state prison. The average cost of keeping one offender on probation or parole ranges from $220 to $1,700.[53]

Table 12.1

Justice dollars also are used for buildings and equipment

Average construction cost per bed in a—	
maximum security State prison	$58,000
medium security State prison	$46,000
minimum security State prison	$26,000
"constitutional" jail	$43,000

Source: Bureau of Justice Statistics, *Report to the Nation on Crime and Justice: The Data* (Washington, D.C.: U.S. Government Printing Office, 1983), p. 93.

In figuring the cost of keeping people in jail, we have to consider not only the $8,000 that includes the daily costs for food, medical care and other services as well as maintaining the jail facility. It is also important to consider the cost of construction of new jails. Table 12.1 shows the cost of capital construction for correctional expenses. Notice that the average cost of building a new "constitutional" jail is $43,000 per bed, compared with only $26,000 per bed for a minimum security state prison.

We seem to think that jail (or prison) is necessary for our protection, and in some cases that is true. But for those offenders who are not a threat to public security while on probation, parole, or in some type of less-expensive community facility, cost should be an important consideration in our determination of how that offender should be punished. The cost of keeping an offender for one year in a New York City jail is an example. For the same cost, the inmate "could see a psychoanalyst three times a week, enroll full time at Columbia, buy season tickets to all of New York's professional sports teams, take an annual cruise to Europe, live on Park Avenue—and still return $10,000 to the City."[54] This is not to suggest that that is the way to process offenders, but it does put the cost into perspective!

Services to inmates

In both the historic and recent literature, there are many statements indicating that generally jails warehouse inmates, providing few if any services. For the most part, the statements are based on generalized observations rather than empirical data systematically gathered and analyzed. It has been suggested that this might be because of the perceived political control of jails and because criminologists prefer to research prisons, which are larger social systems whose turnover is not so high. The result is that "published research on jails and their relationship to service delivery systems is . . . in its infancy."[55]

The 1972 LEAA survey of jails found some progressive programs, but even in them, inmate participation was limited.[56] More recently, the work of Charles L. Newman and Barbara R. Price,[57] has provided significant information regarding jail services in general, and their conclusions are particularly relevant.

In analyzing drug treatment services for jailed inmates, Newman and Price developed a typology that depicts "the organizational arrangement for service delivery of drug treatment resources in local jails." In the first, the *internal system,* all of the services are provided for and administered by the jail. In the *intersection system(s),* the services are provided by and administered by community-based agencies outside the jail, which work independently of the jail but in cooperation with the jail administrators. In the *linkage system,* the jail inmates are screened in order to place them in appropriate community treatment facilities once they are released. "Basically, the linkage agency is an inmate case finding and referral system for the human services community." Finally, when two or more of the above systems are mixed, the result is a *combination system:* "Combination is generally found in very large urban jails, and frequently evolves ad hoc, due to a multiplicity of factors—outside funding support, court mandate, pressure from inmates, interests of community organizations and staff-recognized needs of inmates."[58]

Newman and Price noted that one of the major findings of their nation-wide study of jail resources "is that drug treatment needs of inmates and the associated pressures for service have provided a strong impetus for the development of new and innovative organizational arrangements between jails and community human service organizations and government."[59] In addition to these four organizational interaction systems, Newman and Price found that "jail orientations toward rehabilitative service provision vary significantly depending on the administrative arrangement (law enforcement or department of corrections) under which the jail operates."[60] They concluded that one rational approach to jail services was to view the jail as a place for screening and referral, with actual services being offered to the inmates in community facilities. Under this model, the purpose of the jail, in their words, would be to

1. develop comprehensive intake screening to deal with immediate inmate problems and identify other inmate needs
2. become conduits for treatment and motivate inmates to seek help by offering crisis assistance and by having an array of services in the jail conducted by outside agencies
3. provide information and assistance for continuing service and enrollment in rehabilitative programs upon release.[61]

MODERN JAILS:
AN ANALYSIS

The truth is, however, that jails are not viewed as a place for screening[62] and referral. Rather, they serve as places of incarceration for those awaiting trial, for witnesses who will be needed at trial, and for persons convicted and given short sentences. The condition of these "modern" facilities was recently described by a popular news magazine as "the scandalous U.S. jails."[63]

Jails have inadequate physical facilities and thus extreme overcrowding. An analysis of the 1978 National Jail Survey indicated that overcrowding is common in many jails throughout the country.[64] This overcrowding is often caused by federal court orders to reduce prison populations; thus, the defendants sentenced to prisons are often held in jails until the prison populations are reduced.

Overcrowding leads to many problems. An environmental psychologist observed that overcrowding may actually cause inmates and guards to become physically ill as well as irritable and aggressive. This, in turn, exacerbates the already-strained medical facilities that, according to an American Medical Association study, are inadequate in 99 percent of the jails in this country.[65] Overcrowding is related to aggressive attacks in jails and con-

---

HIGHLIGHT
SOME JAIL FACTS

- 6,200,000 commitments to jail are made each year.
- 40 percent of the people in jail are awaiting trial—they have not been convicted of a crime.
- 80 percent of those awaiting trial remain in jail because they are too poor to pay for bail.
- As many as 25 to 40 percent of the people in jail in some communities are there just for being drunk in public.
- 600,000 mentally ill people go through our jails each year.
- 500,000 youngsters under age 18 go through adult jails and lockups each year.
- the suicide rate for adults in jail is 16 times greater than for the general public.
- 70 percent of jail inmates are incarcerated for non-violent crimes.
- 45 percent of jail inmates are in 130 large jails in metropolitan areas, while the rest are housed in rural jails.
- 35 percent of our jails are more than 50 years old.
- 77 percent of our jails have no medical facilities.
- 75 percent have no rehabilitation or treatment facilities.
- 81 percent of jail inmates are housed in less than 60 square feet each (the accepted minimum standard), about the size of two regular mattresses.
- at least 10 percent of our jails are under court order and many others have litigation pending against them for overcrowding, lack of treatment facilities and other problems.
- jails are expensive and you, the taxpayer, pay for them: it costs an average of $12,000 to house one person in jail for one year; an average of $50,000 to build one new jail bed. New jail construction begun today will ultimately cost two to three times today's estimate due to spiraling user fees, interest rates and inflation.

Source: National Coalition for Jail Reform, pamphlet, "Look at Your Jail," 1828 L Street, N.W., Suite 1200, Washington, D.C. 20036.

tributes to other forms of violence, including riots and self-inflicted violence.

Self-inflicted violence, particularly suicide in jail, is receiving more attention. A new study based on 1979 data reveals that most of the jail suicides are committed within twenty-four hours after the inmate is admitted to jail and are white inmates who have no previous record and who are detained on suspicion of a nonviolent offense, usually public drunkenness or driving under the influence. "Ninety-two percent of the inmates who killed themselves had not even faced trial."[66] Another study reveals that the jail suicide rate is much higher than the suicide rate in prisons, 47 per 100,000, compared with 16 per 100,000. The rate for those not in prison is 11 per 100,000.[67]

One final problem of overcrowding is the risk of death to inmates confined in jails that are fire hazards. In 1977, within a fifteen-day period, sixty-eight people died in jail fires in this country. On November 8, 1982, in a ten-minute fire in the Harrison County Second District Jail in Biloxi, Mississippi, thirty-nine people died. A study of jail fires indicates that most are started by inmates with matches in their cells, not during a riot, and that inmates die from smoke inhalation, not burns. The buildings do not sustain much damage; the deaths are the result of the administrators' inability to get the inmates out of the building fast enough. "You look at a jail fire in hindsight, and you will usually see a jail administration that was not in control," claims an official of the National Institute of Corrections.[68]

Court findings on jail conditions

The brief excerpts on page 424 indicate some of the courts' findings in the 1970s when they began hearing numerous law suits on jail conditions.[69]

These court decisions were unusual for their time. Only recently have federal courts become involved in litigation concerning conditions in jails, although in the 1970s the courts began to abandon their hands-off policy toward prisons. Until then, most federal judges asserted that they were not in a position to handle the day-to-day supervision of correctional facilities, that that was the job of prison and jail administrators. The judges might not agree with the policies implemented in those institutions, but they did not interfere. The only function of federal court judges was to determine whether the jail or prison conditions violated the inmates' federal constitutional rights. It is this function that has led federal court judges in recent years to hear cases brought by inmates of local and state prisons and jails and to issue orders requiring changes in the conditions under which those inmates are incarcerated.

The limitations of federal court action in this area must be understood. Although litigation concerning the rights of inmates of jails and prisons has been extensive, in hearing similar cases, federal courts do not always reach identical conclusions. It is therefore impossible to discuss "the law" with

Miller v. Carson

All inmates, if kept overnight, were required to sleep in their own clothes, without benefit of a mattress, blanket, sheet, pillow or towel. . . . Inmates were kept under these conditions from one to eight days. There were no means for brushing their teeth or showering. . . . There were drunks, mental cases, homosexuals, first offenders, and recidivists. There was sometimes vomitus, urine and feces on the floor. Attempts were made to mop regularly, but conditions were so bad that acceptable sanitation was impossible. Syphilis, gonorrhea, body lice, hepatitis, and broken bones were admitted in the holding cell mix. Lighting in the cells was and is still very poor. Meals were served at regular times, but conditions were so bad that food had to be eaten while standing because of lack of sitting space. . . . The whole situation could only be classified as "depraved" and as "animal-like."

Cockroaches, mice and rats were in abundance, and despite some attempt through the use of a contract pest control company to eradicate these nuisances, they are still present. The problem was found by the Court to be so severe that inmates sometimes passed their idle time trapping mice and rats. There was evidence of rat and cockroach excreta in the kitchen and officer dining room areas. . . .

In summary, the overall environment of the inmate housing areas of the Duval County Jail gave one the psychological feeling of being trapped in a dungeon.

Lowery v. Metropolitan Dade County

The Dade County Jail is greatly overcrowded. . . . Inmates, who have not yet been tried or convicted of any offense are burned, sexually assaulted, beaten, abused and mistreated by fellow inmates. . . . The rule of the jungle exists in the cells where might is right, resulting in many prisoners being denied the food necessary to sustain life.

regard to the constitutional rights of jail inmates. The decision of a federal court in one district does not apply to jails in other federal court districts. Only a decision of the U.S. Supreme Court will apply to all jurisdictions, and it has heard few cases on the constitutional rights of jail inmates.

Physical and sanitary conditions of jails.   Courts have found jail cells with inadequate ventilation, lighting, and heating and cells that are cold in winter and hot in summer. Leaking pipes create water problems on the floor, where some inmates have to sleep because of overcrowding. Cell doors, originally intended to be locked and opened all at once by a central system, are often in need of repair. In case of fire each cell door would have to be unlocked individually by a guard, obviously impossible to accomplish quickly with a limited staff. Window screens are rarely provided so that when windows are open, flies and mosquitoes are free to move in and out of the jail. Plumbing systems are inadequate. Some have no flush toilets; in others that do have modern plumbing facilities, the plumbing is often in need of repair. Some toilets flush only from outside the cell. Although that may be a security measure to keep inmates from trying to drown themselves in the toilet, it is also a humiliating and degrading practice. Cells are small, but because of overcrowding, cells designed for one person often must accommodate two or more. The result, said one court, is that "it is impossible for two men to occupy one of these cells without regular, inadvertent physical contact, inevitably exacerbating tension and creating interpersonal friction."[70]

Prisons usually furnish clothing for inmates, but jails rarely do. Inmates who do not have adequate clothing of their own remain deprived. When clothing is issued, the inmates are frequently denied access to adequate laundry facilities. Sleeping is difficult because of the noise level. As one inmate states, "All night the jail sounds like a nuthouse. All the junkies are screaming their guts out going through cold turkey." A federal judge who spent the night in a Boston jail reported that after midnight the noise "approached a virtual bedlam which lasted until dawn."[71]

Many jails do not have dieticians and do not require health certificates from the staff who work in the kitchen. In some, the nutritional level of food is inadequate, and often the food is tasteless and cold. Too often, inmates do not get enough food for their daily needs. In small jails the cook is often the sheriff's wife, and in some cases the sheriff receives an allotment for food for the inmates. The sheriff may keep any of the allotment that is not used, and so the temptation not to feed the prisoners adequately may be overwhelming.

Visitation privileges. Generally, visitation privileges for jail inmates are inferior to those for state and federal prison inmates. Jail administrators usually claim that such restricted privileges are necessary for security, but the courts have often found the contrary. Time and frequency of visits to inmates are limited, and only certain visitors are allowed. Courts have recognized the need for security but have generally found that jails are too restrictive in their visitation rights. Therefore, the courts have forced the expansion of facilities and have required increased opportunities for inmates to have contact with the outside world. This especially has been the case for attorneys' visits. In addition, some jails have been ordered to provide untapped pay phones for the inmates' use. In the spring of 1984, the U.S. Supreme Court heard arguments on the issue of visitation in jails, and ruled that inmates have no constitutional right to contact visits.[72]

In many jails, contact visits are not allowed. Here, the inmate talks by phone with his visitor, who can be seen through the glass.

Staff. Untrained staff and a high staff–inmate ratio are generally found in jails. The result is that guards mistreat inmates, often brutalizing them. In other cases, they ignore the inmates' needs, such as for medical services or protection from other inmates. There is also evidence of discrimination against women in jail-hiring practices. In 1984, the U.S. Justice Department filed suit against the city of Lincoln and Lancaster County, Nebraska, alleging that they violated the Civil Rights Act of 1964 "by refusing to hire or promote women into any correctional officer position involving work at the male cell blocks of the Intake and Detention Facility."[73]

Health facilities. In general, health facilities are inadequate. Many jails do not have a doctor quickly available to provide medical care for the jailed inmates.[74] The Supreme Court has held that failure to provide adequate medical care is a violation of the Eighth Amendment prohibition against cruel and unusual punishment when the action of officials results from "deliberate indifference to a prisoner's serious injury or illness."[75]

Programs.   Jails usually do not offer educational, recreational, and vocational opportunities. Jobs are rarely available for inmates who must spend hours in idleness in their overcrowded cells. Many jails offer no library services, so reading opportunities are also limited.

The Justice Department responds   These kinds of conditions have led the Justice Department to file suit in federal court against some jails, asking for injunctions to prohibit the detention of persons in jails considered to subject inmates to "life-threatening and health-threatening conditions" that amount to "cruel and unusual punishment." Most recently the department filed suit against the city of Newark, New Jersey, the third filed by the department under the Civil Rights of Institutionalized Persons Act of 1980. This act gives the U.S. attorney general the right to file suit in order to remedy unconstitutional conditions at local and state prisons and health facilities. It also provides that a negotiated settlement must be attempted before a law suit is filed, but the Justice Department and the city of Newark were not able to agree on an appropriate settlement.

Newark claims that its jail facilities are overcrowded because the state facilities, also overcrowded, are refusing to accept inmates sentenced to prison. They are therefore being held in jails and lockups, thus overcrowding those facilities.

In addition to overcrowding, the Justice Department's suit also asserts that the officials at these five facilities

fail to provide minimally adequate bedding, furnishings, and hygienic materials.

hold prisoners in severely overcrowded quarters for indefinite periods of time without minimally adequate opportunities for physical exercise.

fail to provide minimally adequate plumbing, water supplies, waste disposal, and sanitation.

fail to provide access to bathing or shower facilities.

fail to provide minimally adequate staffing, supervision, facilities, and equipment to safeguard and protect prisoners from harm inflicted by other prisoners.

In addition, the suit claims that all of the facilities are "without a minimally adequate program, staff, and facilities for the treatment of serious physical and mental illnesses, amounting to deliberate indifference to the serious medical needs of persons confined."[76]

Besides this suit, the Justice Department has filed actions against the

The Metropolitan Correctional Center, New York City.

states of Michigan and Hawaii. In early 1984, the department had thirty-one active investigations pending in twenty-two states.

The Supreme Court rules: **Bell v. Wolfish**

In 1979 the U.S. Supreme Court decided an important case involving alleged violations of the constitutional rights of pretrial inmates held in jail awaiting trial. *Bell v. Wolfish*[77] pertained to inmates at New York City's Metropolitan Correctional Center (MCC), a federally operated facility for short-term custody. The facility was designed to detain those awaiting trial and was constructed in 1975 to replace a converted waterfront garage that had served as the federal jail in the city since 1828. The case is particularly interesting because of the type of facility involved: not the dungeon-type structure with unsanitary facilities characteristic of many of our jails, but a modern facility, which, according to the court of appeals, "represented the architectural embodiment of the best and most progressive penological planning." The facility was overcrowded, however, shortly after it was opened. Rooms designed for one were used for two, and some inmates had to sleep on cots in the common areas.

Less than four months after the MCC was opened, several inmates filed a petition that resulted in this appeal to the Supreme Court. Numerous charges were filed, including inadequate phone service, strip searches, searching of inmates' rooms in their absence, interference with and monitoring of mail, inadequate classification system, inadequate and arbitrary disciplinary and grievance procedures, restrictions on religious freedom, excessive confinement, overcrowded conditions, inadequate facilities for education and recreation and employment opportunities, insufficient staff, and excessive restrictions on the purchase and receipt of books and personal items. The lower court **enjoined** many of these practices, noting that pretrial detainees were "presumed to be innocent and held only to ensure their presence at trial." Consequently, a compelling necessity must be shown if they are deprived of any rights beyond those necessary for confinement alone. Most of the district court's rulings were affirmed by the court of appeals. Not all the issues were on appeal to the Supreme Court, but we shall discuss the four that it did consider.

"Double bunking."   The first major issue on appeal to the Supreme Court was the use of **double bunking**—the housing of two inmates in a room

Federal court orders to reduce prison population, as well as increased enforcement of some statutes such as driving under the influence, have resulted in severe overcrowding in most of our urban jails.

designed for one. The lower courts held that a compelling necessity must be shown before this practice would be acceptable. The Supreme Court rejected that test and considered whether double bunking constituted "punishment." The Supreme Court noted that although punishment is permitted in the case of convicted persons (although cruel and unusual punishment is unconstitutional), punishment is not permissible for those not yet convicted. The latter may be detained for trial but not punished. The Court held, however, that double bunking does not constitute punishment. Unless it can be shown that in engaging in a particular practice the jail officials *intend to punish* pretrial detainees, a practice will not be considered punishment if the restriction is reasonably related to a legitimate government purpose. The government has a legitimate purpose not only in ensuring the accused's presence at trial but also in managing the jail and keeping the facilities secure. "Restraints that are reasonably related to the institution's interest in maintaining jail security do not, without more, constitute unconstitutional punishment, even if they are discomforting and are restrictions that the detainee would not have experienced had he been released while awaiting trial."

The "publisher-only" rule.   Under the **publisher-only** rule, inmates could receive hardback books only from publishers. The assumption was that publishers could be trusted not to include drugs, weapons, and other contraband items with the shipment. Such books would presumably therefore not have to be inspected. The Bureau of Prisons amended that rule before this hearing to allow inmates to receive books and magazines from bookstores as well as from publishers and book clubs. The bureau had also already announced plans to allow the receipt from any source of paperbacks, magazines, and other soft-covered materials. The bureau argued that hardback books were the "more dangerous source of risk to institutional security." The Court agreed that prohibiting inmates from receiving hardback books from sources other than publishers, bookstores, and book clubs did not violate their constitutional rights.

Receipt of packages.   The Court also agreed with the institution officials that the receipt of packages from outside the institution (except one per inmate at Christmas) was a security problem and therefore upheld the regulation prohibiting it. It was argued that the probability of such packages containing contraband is high, thus requiring extensive searches, a time-consuming and expensive process.

Searches.   The Court agreed with officials that it was reasonable, in light of security needs, to search inmates' rooms when they were absent. The most controversial issue, however, was body searches, which involved visual inspection of body cavities after each contact visit of inmates. Although the

Court had difficulty with this practice, it held that such was reasonable in light of security problems.

Justice Lewis Powell concurred with part of the majority opinion but dissented on the holding on body cavity searches, which he called a "serious intrusion on one's privacy." Powell advocated some "level of cause, such as a reasonable suspicion, should be required to justify the anal and genital searches described in this case."[78]

Justice Thurgood Marshall, in his dissent, argued that the Court's emphasis on the issue of punishment was misplaced. The issue, Marshall asserted, is what effect the acts have on the pretrial detainees who are presumptively innocent. "By its terms, the Due Process Clause focuses on the nature of deprivations, not on the persons inflicting them. If this concern is to be vindicated, it is the effect of conditions of confinement, not the intent behind them, that must be the focal point of constitutional analysis." He suggested requiring "that a restriction is substantially necessary to jail administration. Where the imposition is of particular gravity, that is, where it implicates interests of fundamental importance or inflicts significant harms, the Government should demonstrate that the restriction serves a compelling necessity of jail administration."[79] With regard to the visual inspection of body cavities, Marshall said:[80]

Bell v. Wolfish
Justice Marshall, dissenting

In my view, the body cavity searches of MCC inmates represent one of the most grievous offenses against personal dignity and common decency. After every contact visit with someone from outside the facility, including defense attorneys, an inmate must remove all of his or her clothing, bend over, spread the buttocks, and display the anal cavity for inspection by a correctional officer. Women inmates must assume a suitable posture for vaginal inspection while men must raise their genitals. And, as the Court neglects to note, because of time pressures, this humiliating spectacle is frequently conducted in the presence of other inmates.

The District Court found that the stripping was "unpleasant, embarrassing, and humiliating." A psychiatrist testified that the practice placed inmates in the most degrading position possible, a conclusion amply corroborated by the testimony of the inmates themselves. There was evidence, moreover, that these searches engendered among detainees fears of sexual assault, were the occasion for actual threats of physical abuse by guards, and caused some inmates to forego personal visits.

Not surprisingly, the Government asserts a security justification for such inspections. These searches are necessary, it argues, to prevent inmates from smuggling contraband into the facility. In crediting this justification, despite the contrary findings of the two courts below, the Court overlooks the critical facts. As respondents point out, inmates are required to wear one-piece jumpsuits with zippers in the front. To insert an object into the vaginal or anal cavity, an inmate would have to remove the jumpsuit, at least from the upper torso. Since contact visits occur in a glass-enclosed room and are continuously monitored by corrections officers, such a feat would seem extraordinarily difficult. There was medical testimony, moreover, that inserting an object into the rectum is painful and "would require time and opportunity which is not available in the visiting areas," and that visual inspection would probably not detect an object once inserted. Additionally, before entering the visiting room, visitors and their packages are searched thoroughly by a metal detector, fluoroscope, and by hand. Correction officers may require that visitors leave packages or handbags with guards until the visit is over. Only by blinding itself to the facts presented on this record can the Court accept the Government's security rationale.

Without question, these searches are an imposition of sufficient gravity to invoke the compelling necessity standard. It is equally indisputable that they cannot meet the standard. Indeed, the procedure is so unnecessarily degrading that it "shocks the conscience."

Importance of Bell v. Wolfish

The Supreme Court decision in *Bell v. Wolfish* must be limited to the facts of the case. The inmates in this case were pretrial detainees in a modern facility for a short time and were not required to spend most of the day in their cells.

Subsequent federal court cases have interpreted *Bell v. Wolfish*.[81] In 1982 a federal court ruled that a county sheriff violated the constitutional rights of jail inmates when he instituted a policy that barred all hardcover books and pictorial magazines from his jail. The sheriff claimed that inmates would cut pictures from such magazines as *Sports Illustrated,* stick them on the wall, and thus damage the jail walls! Newspapers were not allowed because they could be used to start fires and jam toilets. Hardbound books were not allowed because they could be used as "lethal propellants." The federal court pointed out that toilets could be jammed or fires started with the *Readers Digest* or a soft-cover edition of the Bible, both of which were allowed. "Maintenance of security and discipline do not justify the wholesale prohibition of pictural magazines, hardbound books or newspapers."[82]

There is some evidence of progress in improving jail conditions as a result of court orders. For example, nine years after the Manhattan House of Detention—also known as the Tombs—was closed by federal court order, it was scheduled to reopen. New York City spent $42 million "in transforming the Tombs into what officials say is one of the most humane and efficient jails anywhere." The warden claims, "It's now a state-of-the-art jail." The inside of the jail was completely rennovated; the cells were enlarged to twice their original capacity; and new windows, lighting fixtures, and air-conditioning systems were installed. Classrooms and indoor gyms were added, and walls and cell doors were painted bright colors.[83]

Civil suits against jail officials

Another method of enforcing jail inmates' constitutional rights is to allow them to sue jail officials for damages. Jail officials owe a duty of reasonable care to inmates under their supervision. In determining whether that duty has been breached, courts look to all the circumstances and use a reasonableness test. For example, some courts have held that officials should expect that an inmate who is incarcerated while intoxicated will be in no position to exercise the care reasonably expected of an individual to protect himself or herself. In such cases, if the drunken inmate commits suicide, the estate may be able to sue jail officials for wrongful death.

Jail officials must also use reasonable care to protect inmates from bodily harm or death inflicted by other inmates, and if they do not, a civil suit may be allowed.[84] For example, the mother of a young man who committed suicide while in jail was awarded $122,422 plus funeral expenses. After her son had attempted suicide while in jail, the mother had requested that he be released to her custody or that additional security be provided. The officials refused, and he hanged himself. In this case, a statute provided that when minors in custody show symptoms of mental illness, they must be released to the custody of their families or transferred to a medical facility.[85]

One final note on the duty of jail officials toward inmates. One inmate whose sentence was extended when he was captured after his escape from jail sued the sheriff for $1 million for his negligence, which, alleged the inmate, caused the escape![86]

ALTERNATIVES TO JAIL

It has been suggested that the daily population of jails could be cut by 50 percent without endangering society. Some possibilities are

1. Release more detainees on their own recognizance if they cannot post bond awaiting trial.
2. Courts should give preference in scheduling trials to those in jails.
3. Use citations rather than jail terms for some offenses.
4. Allow individuals who cannot pay fines immediately to pay on an installment plan rather than take a jail sentence.
5. Use work-release and parole programs.
6. Provide detoxification and rehabilitation centers for alcoholics and drug abusers.[87]

Others have suggested that jails should be abolished and replaced with a "network of newly designed, differently conceived metropolitan (in the big cities) and regional (in rural areas) detention centers." Convicted persons

HIGHLIGHT
THE PUBLIC INEBRIATE: JAIL IS NOT THE ANSWER
What Is the Problem?

- One out of every three arrests in the United States is for public inebriation—a total of more than 1,000,000 such arrests every year. In some rural areas, 60 percent of arrests are for public drunkenness.
- 25 to 40 percent of the people in jail today are there for public intoxication.
- The costs of arresting, booking, jailing and trying public inebriates are well over $300 million per year. This is a major drain on the scarce resources available to our already overcrowded jails. The public inebriate takes up space needed for those charged with serious crimes.
- In states where public intoxication has been decriminalized, drunken people are still being arrested—only now they are charged with disorderly conduct, loitering or disturbing the peace. They are placed in cells which cost anywhere from $25,000 to $60,000 each to build and are held at a yearly cost of from $7,000 to $26,000 per person.
- Many persons arrested for public inebriation have been arrested hundreds of times before, on this or related charges. The majority are in desperate need of health and rehabilitation services. In one study, some 85 percent of those who committed suicide in jail were intoxicated at the time of death and more than half the suicides occurred in the first 12 hours of confinement.
- Half the nation's jails have no medical services; three-fourths have no rehabilitation services; only 10 percent have education and job training programs.
- In a sample study of more than 3,000 public inebriates in New York, 20 percent had bone fractures, 50 percent had wounds, cuts or burns, 20 percent had hallucinations, 20 percent suffered from severe brain damage, 20 percent had severe gastrointestinal bleeding, 15 percent had cardiopulmonary problems, and 25 percent had indications of seizure disorder.

Source: National Coalition for Jail Reform, pamphlet, "The Public Inebriate: Jail Is Not the Answer," 1828 L Street, N.W., Suite 1200, Washington, D.C. 20036.

would not serve time in these facilities but rather would be placed in prisons or community correctional programs. These detention centers would keep only those awaiting trial who presented a clear danger of flight before trial "or whose personal dangerousness warrants limited pretrial detention." The facilities would also serve as **diagnostic classification** and referral institutions for those arrested who should receive other types of services: alcoholics, addicts, and youth. The Human Resources Development or its counterpart agency, not the police, would administer the facility. The centers would have three wings, one for a pretrial detention of defendants to prevent flight or crime, to be supervised by a court or police official; the second for diagnostic and referral services, to be supervised by a medical official; and the third, a wing serving as a dormitory for people working in the community under supervision of correctional personnel, to be supervised by a social welfare or correctional department official. A noted authority on jails has concluded that this change from "awful correctional institutions to useful, helpful social services agencies makes sense. There is ample evidence that the new detention centers would be cheaper, safer and sounder than the present haphazard, onerous, counter-productive network of jails." The goals of such centers would be "the assurance of liberty and justice for all: even for those people who inhabit the ultimate ghetto."[88]

A program of services for pretrial defendants, designed to help them with personal, occupational, family, legal, medical, and psychiatric problems, would be of much greater value to them than sitting in a jail with nothing to do but be corrupted. The use of probation, **furloughs, halfway houses,** and other community resources could also be extended. Obviously, implementing such programs to convert "the jail into an effective local correctional center cannot be accomplished without some cost to the taxpayer." But until that is accomplished, the jail will continue to serve as a warehouse for the poor.

DIVERSION These programs, in lieu of jail, have been referred to as "diversion prior to adjudication," and **diversion** was one of the recommendations of the president's crime commission. The commission suggested that in many cases, incarceration may contribute to the problems of delinquency and criminals. For example, in cases of drunkenness, the individual may be better handled with detoxification treatment than with incarceration. If an individual needs education, that may be better obtained in local schools than in detention facilities. The field of corrections should be concerned with diverting some offenders into programs other than correctional facilities.

Alternative programs for persons incarcerated for violating drinking laws are being emphasized in many parts of the country. Weekend jail terms for drunk drivers is an example. In Los Angeles County, drunks are housed in a skid-row hotel, renovated at a cost of $7 million. The executive director of the National Coalition for Jail Reform in Washington proclaimed, "It's a waste of all our money" to place drunks, minors, and nonviolent offenders in jail.[89] Providing alternatives to jail for persons arrested for such nonviolent offenses should be given careful attention in light of the evidence we saw earlier, that jail suicides are most frequently committed by these kinds of nonviolent offenders.

WEEKEND OR NIGHT JAIL In some jurisdictions, defendants are sentenced to spend only weekends or nights in jail. In one Indiana town, those sentenced to weekend jail have to pay a daily rate of $21.75. That includes $18 for the cell and $1.25 each for three meals. The chief jailer said, "It's not only saving the county some money. . . . It's done to be an added punishment. A lot of these inmates sent here on the weekends thought this was a lot of fun. They got away from the wife and kids and played cards with the other guys for a couple of days. We wanted them to remember they were in jail."[90]

It may be difficult to believe that some people would consider going to jail for a weekend to be fun. It also seems likely, however, that most of us would consider weekend jail to be preferable to continuous jailing. But there is some evidence that weekend jail is not so desirable. Inmates who have served both straight time and weekend time prefer the former, indicating that it is too difficult to leave family and friends for jail on weekends. Said one inmate, "It's like going to jail twenty different times."[91]

"HOME" JAIL　Weekend and night jail do not relieve all of the problems of overcrowding, but another alternative to jail, however, does reduce that problem. In some areas, defendants are sentenced to "serve time" in their own homes. A Spider-Man cartoon reportedly provided the idea for the use of electronic "ankle bracelets" that are worn by the "inmate" while at home. The bracelet, which is waterproof, two inches wide, and crammed with thirty-two tiny wires, beams an electronic signal when the wearer strays more than two hundred feet from his or her home. The proponents call this use of home jail as a "jail without bars."

In late 1983, Florida became the third state to institute a "house arrest" program for adults sentenced to jail. The plan was instituted mainly to relieve overcrowding in the jails. An analysis of a similar program in Illinois revealed that house arrest can be successful and save money. It is, however, essential that members of the "inmate's" family cooperate with the arrangements, that the staff develop a "helper" and not a "hunter" attitude (hunting for violators), that offenders be classified (the program works best for first offenders), and that offenders are clearly notified of the rules and regulations concerning checking in by phone, and so on. Problems do exist when phones are unavailable or out of order, offenders need special care or programs (such as alcohol counseling; in fact, alcoholics are poor risks in this program), and there is little public support for the program.[92]

SUMMARY AND CONCLUSION　This chapter has focused on the handling of the accused after arrest and before trial, probably the most critical period in the entire system of criminal justice. A defendant detained in jail will be adversely affected by the experience. But if he or she is released, society may be endangered. The chapter therefore considered the two issues that arise during this period: pretrial release and pretrial detention.

Our discussion of pretrial release began with a look at the potentially harmful effects to the defendant who is incarcerated while awaiting trial. We then examined methods of release from pretrial incarceration, including the system of bail and bail reform. The section on pretrial detention considered jails, ranging from a brief history to recent court decisions regarding the rights of pretrial detainees.

Federal courts have made it clear that unconstitutional conditions will not be tolerated in local and county jails and that lack of funding will not be an acceptable reason for such conditions. The reform will be costly, but not as costly as the detrimental effects to inmates and to society if facilities that can be considered no better than "warehouses" for human beings continue to be operated.

Jail reform should, however, be viewed in the context of the total criminal justice system as well as of society. What happens in jails is related to these other systems. Inmates take with them to jail their subculture from the outside and when they leave, they take back to society some of the subculture of the jail.[93] What happens during that period of incarceration is therefore important to inmates, their families, and to society. A former administrator of the former LEAA (Law Enforcement Assistance Administration) emphasized the need for society to give more attention to the problems of jails: "The result is what you would expect, only worse. Jails are, without question, brutal, filthy, cesspools of crime—institutions which serve to brutalize and embitter men to prevent them from returning to a useful role in society."[94]

CHAPTER 13

The court system

This chapter will analyze the criminal court system, beginning with a brief look at the effects of congestion in our courts. After an overview of the criminal court system, we shall examine the roles of lawyers, judges, and juries. Our discussion of lawyers will include the prosecutor, the defense, and then the process of plea bargaining, the method, in contrast to trial, by which most cases are handled. In those cases that do go to trial, the issue of the guilt or innocence of the defendant will be decided by a judge or a jury, and we shall consider the function of each in that process. Decisions at the trial level may be appealed in some cases, and we shall study the last court of appeal: the United States Supreme Court. The final section will analyze the problem of court congestion and make suggestions as to how that problem might be eliminated or at least reduced.

**THE CRISIS
IN OUR COURTS**

Although the Sixth Amendment to our Constitution provides for the right to a speedy trial, the late U.S. Supreme Court Chief Justice Earl Warren declared that "the delay and the choking congestion in federal courts . . . have created a crucial problem for constitutional government in the United States . . . it is compromising the quantity and quality of justice available to the individual citizen, and, in so doing, it leaves vulnerable throughout the world the reputation of the United States."[1]

Chief Justice Warren's statement refers to the federal courts, in which the number of cases filed tripled between 1960 and 1980 and increased fivefold between 1940 and 1981. But the situation is far worse in the state courts, in which over five million cases are filed annually.[2]

Court congestion also exists at the appellate levels, both state and federal, with appellate filings in state courts increasing far more rapidly than the growth in population. The federal appellate courts between 1950 and 1981 experienced an increase in filings that was sixteen times as rapid as the growth in population.[3]

**EFFECTS OF
COURT
CONGESTION**

Court congestion results in delayed trials. For the accused who are not released before trial, court congestion may mean a long jail term in already overcrowded jail facilities. Because their court-appointed attorneys are so busy with trial cases, defendants may not see them during that period. The accused are left with many questions, no answers, and a long wait, often under inhumane conditions in local jails. Those who are incarcerated before trial face more obstacles in preparation for trial as well as in the reactions of the juries to them at trial.

The injustices created by an overworked court that must decide cases quickly and with little individualized attention are obvious, as is the lack of preparation time available to overworked prosecutors and defense attorneys. Finally, the inefficiency and injustice that the crowded court dockets and delayed trials project to the public colors their image of the entire legal system.[4]

**THE CRIMINAL
COURT SYSTEM**

The framers of the Constitution of the United States established three branches of government—legislative, executive, and judicial. They envisioned a separation of the powers of these three branches, although clearly there is some overlap. For example, the federal judges and justices of the U.S. Supreme Court are appointed by the president, from the executive branch, and must be confirmed by the Senate, from the legislative branch. In addition, the Constitution provides that with the exception of those few cases in which the Constitution specifically gives the Supreme Court **original jurisdiction,** the Court's **jurisdiction** is **appellate** but "with such exceptions and under such regulations as Congress shall make." Congress could therefore keep some issues from the Court by changing its jurisdiction. Finally, the Court is without power of enforcement; rather, the executive branch of the government must enforce the Court's decisions. "Bereft of coercive power, the Court must rely upon moral suasion. Thus it must tread softly, aiming for voluntary compliance. Its only weapon is the tradition of respect for the law; on emotionally explosive issues law and order may break down. . . . In such circumstances, the executive branch may step in. . . . But if it does not, the Court stands helpless."[5] It is said that President Andrew Jackson, in withholding enforcement of a Court decision, said, "John Marshall [then Chief Justice of the Supreme Court] has made his decision—*now let him enforce it!*"[6]

The U.S. Supreme Court hears **civil** as well as **criminal cases.** Some courts hear only civil cases; others hear only criminal cases. This chapter will be concerned only with the courts that hear criminal cases.

JUDICIAL REVIEW

The courts are responsible for deciding whether acts of the legislature and executive branches infringe upon the freedoms and liberties guaranteed by the state constitutions and the U.S. Constitution. This **judicial review** represents the courts' great authority. The Supreme Court, for example, has the power to declare acts of the president or Congress as unconstitutional.

The highest court of each state determines the constitutionality of that state's laws in relation to its constitution. The Supreme Court is the final decision maker in the process of judicial review of the U.S. Constitution, as indicated by Chief Justice John Marshall, writing for the majority of the Supreme Court in an 1803 decision, *Marbury v. Madison*, excerpted below.[7]

THE DUAL COURT SYSTEM

The United States has a **dual court system,** consisting of state and federal courts. State crimes are prosecuted in state courts, and federal crimes, in federal courts. The crimes of the former are defined by state statutes and of the latter, by acts of Congress. Some acts may violate both federal and state statutes, though most criminal cases are tried in state courts.

Marbury v. Madison

It is emphatically the province and duty of the judicial department to say what the law is. . . . So if a law be in opposition to the Constitution; if both the law and the Constitution apply to a particular case, so that the court must either decide the case conformably to the law disregarding the Constitution, or conformably to the Constitution, disregarding the law; the court must determine which of these conflict rules governs the case. This is the very essence of judicial duty.

EXHIBIT
THE COURTS ARE PARTICIPANTS IN AND SUPERVISORS OF THE JUDICIAL PROCESS

The Courts Have Several Functions in Addition to Deciding About Violations of the Law

The courts are responsible for—

- Settling disputes between legal entities (persons, corporations, etc.).
- Invoking sanctions against violations of law.
- Deciding whether acts of the legislative and executive branches are constitutional.

In making decisions about violations of the law, the courts must apply the law to the facts in individual cases. The courts have an impact on policy, while deciding individual cases, by handing down decisions about how the laws should be interpreted and carried out. Decisions of the appellate courts are the decisions most likely to have policy impact.

The Use of an Arm of the State in Settling Disputes Is a Relatively New Concept

Until the Middle Ages, disputes between individuals, clans, and families, including criminal acts, were handled privately. Over time, some acts such as murder, rape, robbery, larceny, and fraud were determined to be crimes against the entire community, and the state intervened on its behalf. Today in the United States, the courts handle both civil actions (disputes between individuals or legal organizations) and criminal actions.

An Independent Judiciary Is a Basic Concept of the U.S. System of Government

To establish its independence and impartiality, the judiciary was created as a separate branch of government equal to the executive and legislative branches. Insulation of the courts from political pressure is attempted through the separation of powers doctrine, established tenure for judges, legislative safeguards, and the canons of ethics of the legal profession.

Courts are without the power of enforcement. The executive branch must enforce their decisions. Furthermore, the courts must request that the legislature provide them with the resources needed to conduct their business.

Each State Has Established a System of Trial and Appeals Courts

Generally, State court systems are organized according to three basic levels of jurisdiction:

- Courts of limited and special jurisdiction are authorized to hear only less serious cases (criminal misdemeanors and/or civil suits that involve small amounts of money) or to hear special types of cases such as divorce

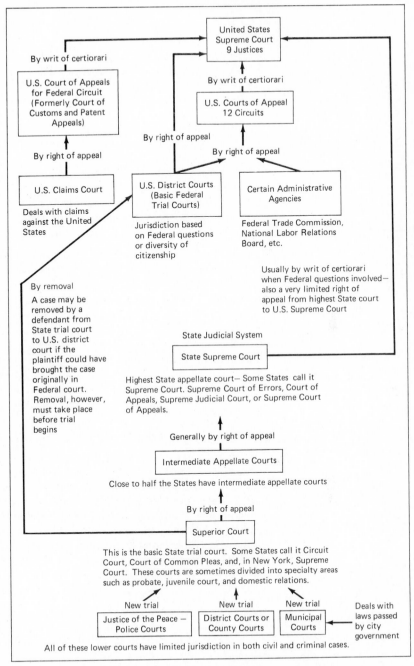

The flow chart contains the following labeled elements:

United States Supreme Court — 9 Justices

By writ of certiorari

U.S. Court of Appeals for Federal Circuit (Formerly Court of Customs and Patent Appeals)

By writ of certiorari

U.S. Courts of Appeal — 12 Circuits

By right of appeal

By right of appeal

By right of appeal

U.S. Claims Court

Deals with claims against the United States

U.S. District Courts (Basic Federal Trial Courts)

Jurisdiction based on Federal questions or diversity of citizenship

Certain Administrative Agencies

Federal Trade Commission, National Labor Relations Board, etc.

Usually by writ of certiorari when Federal questions involved— also a very limited right of appeal from highest State court to U.S. Supreme Court

By removal

A case may be removed by a defendant from State trial court to U.S. district court if the plaintiff could have brought the case originally in Federal court. Removal, however, must take place before trial begins

State Judicial System

State Supreme Court

Highest State appellate court— Some States call it Supreme Court. Supreme Court of Errors, Court of Appeals, Supreme Judicial Court, or Supreme Court of Appeals.

Generally by right of appeal

Intermediate Appellate Courts

Close to half the States have intermediate appellate courts

By right of appeal

Superior Court

This is the basic State trial court. Some States call it Circuit Court, Court of Common Pleas, and, in New York, Supreme Court. These courts are sometimes divided into specialty areas such as probate, juvenile court, and domestic relations.

New trial

New trial

New trial

Justice of the Peace — Police Courts

District Courts or County Courts

Municipal Courts

Deals with laws passed by city government

All of these lower courts have limited jurisdiction in both civil and criminal cases.

Courts at various levels of government interact in many ways.

Source: Updated and reprinted by permission from The American Legal Environment *by William T. Schantz. Copyright © 1976 by West Publishing Company. All rights reserved.*

or probate suits. Such courts include traffic courts, municipal courts, family courts, small claims courts, magistrate courts, and probate courts.

- Courts of general jurisdiction, also called major trial courts, are unlimited in the civil or criminal cases they are authorized to hear. Almost all cases originate in the courts of limited or special jurisdiction or in courts of general jurisdiction. Most serious criminal cases are handled by courts of general jurisdiction. In 1977, there were 3,588 courts of general jurisdiction.

- Appellate courts are divided into two groups, intermediate appeals courts, which have limited jurisdiction, and courts of last resort, which have jurisdiction over final appeals from courts of original jurisdiction or intermediate appeals courts. As of 1983, 32 States had intermediate appellate courts, but all States had courts of last resort.

The U.S. Constitution Created the Supreme Court and Authorized the Congress to Establish Lower Courts as Needed

Currently, the Federal court system consists of various special courts, U.S. district courts (general jurisdiction courts), U.S. courts of appeals (intermediate from the district courts and Federal administrative agencies), and the U.S. Supreme Court (the court of last resort). Organized on a regional basis, there are U.S. courts of appeals for each of 11 [now 12] circuits and the District of Columbia. In the trial courts for the Federal system (the 94 U.S. district courts), approximately a quarter of a million cases were filed in 1982; there was one criminal case for every six civil cases. In 1982, more than half of the criminal cases filed in district courts were for embezzlement, fraud, forgery and counterfeiting, traffic, or drug offenses.

Court Organization Varies Greatly Among the States

State courts of general jurisdiction are organized by districts, counties, dual districts, or a combination of counties and districts. In some States, the courts, while established by the State, are funded and controlled locally. In others, the court of last resort may have some budgetary or administrative oversight over the entire State court system. Even within States, there is a considerable lack of uniformity in the roles, organization, and procedures of the courts. This has led to considerable momentum among States to form "unified" court systems to provide in varying degrees for uniform administration of the courts, and, in many cases, for the consolidation of diverse courts of limited and special jurisdiction.

Most Felony Cases Are Brought in State and Local Courts

The traditional criminal offenses established under the English common law have been adopted, in one form or another, in the criminal laws of each of the States. Most cases involving "common law" crimes are brought to trial in State or local courts. Persons charged with misdemeanors are usually tried in the lower courts. Those charged with felonies (more serious crimes) are tried in courts of general jurisdiction.

In all States, criminal defendants may appeal most decisions of lower criminal courts; the avenue of appeal usually ends with the State supreme court. However, the Supreme Court of the United States may elect to hear the case, if the appeal is based on an alleged violation of the Constitutional rights of the defendant.

State Courts Process a Large Volume of Cases, Many of Them Minor

In 1981, more than 82 million cases were filed in State and local courts. About 67% were traffic-related cases, 16% were civil cases (torts, contracts, small claims, etc.), 15% were criminal cases, and 2% were juvenile cases.

Civil and criminal cases both appear to be increasing. Of 40 States that reported for 1977 and 1981, 36 reported increases in the volume of criminal filings, and 38 reported increases of civil filings.

Judges Are Selected by Popular Election, by Appointment, or by the Merit Plan

Thirty-two States use elections to select some judges; 19 States elect intermediate appeals court judges. Most judicial elections are nonpartisan, a method of selection designed to keep the judiciary insulated from partisan politics. In 37 States, some judges are appointed. Under the merit system, independent judicial commissions, which select nominees based on merit, operate in 22 States for initial selection although many other States also use the merit system to fill vacancies. In some States that use the merit system, voters may approve or disapprove of reappointments after the judge's initial term.

The Separate System of Justice for Juveniles Often Operates Within the Existing Court Organization

Jurisdiction over juvenile delinquency, dependent or neglected children, and related matters is vested in various types of courts. In many States, the juvenile court is a division of the court of general jurisdiction. A few States have statewide systems of juvenile or family courts. Juvenile jurisdiction is vested in the courts of general jurisdiction in some counties and in separate juvenile courts or courts of limited jurisdiction in others. However the juvenile courts are organized, they process juveniles under a separate system based on the concepts of nonculpability and rehabilitation.

Source: Bureau of Justice Statistics, *Report to the Nation on Crime and Justice: The Data* (Washington, D.C.: U.S. Government Printing Office, 1983), pp. 63–64.

State courts   The state criminal court system differs from state to state, but all have trial courts and appellate courts. In some states the trial courts may hear the serious cases (felonies) as well as the less-serious ones (misdemeanors). In other jurisdictions the trial court level is divided, with one level of courts hearing felony and the other hearing misdemeanor cases. All states have appeal courts, and some states have an intermediate appeal court. Others have only one court of appeals, which is often called the *state supreme court.*

Federal courts The federal court system has three levels, excluding special courts such as the U.S. Court of Military Appeals. The United States *district courts* are the trial courts. Cases may be appealed from those courts to the *appellate courts.* There are twelve courts at this level, and they are called *circuit courts.*[8] Finally, the highest court is the *Supreme Court,* which is basically an appeal court, although it has original jurisdiction in a few cases.

The lower federal courts and the state courts are separate systems, and so a state court is not bound by the decision of a lower federal court in its district. Cases may not be appealed from a state court to a lower federal court, but they may be appealed to the U.S. Supreme Court if a federal statutory or constitutional right is involved.[9]

TRIAL AND APPELLATE COURTS Trial and appellate courts should be distinguished. Trial courts hear the factual evidence of a case and decide the issues of fact.[10] These decisions may be made by a **jury** or by a **judge** if the case is tried without a jury. Appellate courts do not try the facts, such as the defendant's guilt or innocence, but, in essence, try the lower court. The **appellant**—the defendant at trial—alleges "errors" in the trial court proceeding (for example, hearsay evidence admitted, illegal confession admitted, minority groups excluded from the jury) and asks for a new trial. The **appellee**—the prosecution at trial—argues that errors either did not exist or, if they did, did not constitute "reversible errors"—that is, they did not prejudice the appellant—and therefore a new trial should not be granted.

When a trial court has ruled against a defendant, he or she has a right of **appeal,** both in the state and in the federal court system, although the defendant does not (except in a few specific types of cases) have the right to appeal to the highest court. For example, the Supreme Court hears only a small percentage of the cases for which appeal is requested.

On appeal, the case is heard by judges, not by a jury, and the issues are confined to matters of law, not fact. The appellate court looks at the trial court record and hears oral arguments from counsel for the defense and the prosecution. It then determines whether any errors of law have been committed.

The appellate court may affirm or reverse the lower court's decision. Usually when a lower court is reversed, the case is sent back for another trial—that is, the case is "reversed and remanded." In the controversial *Miranda* case, for example, Miranda's conviction was reversed and remanded. Miranda was, however, convicted again in the new trial, which excluded the confession ruled inadmissible by the Supreme Court.

Prosecutors may also appeal on points of law, but the defendant may not be retried because of the constitutional provision against **double jeopardy.** However, if he or she wins on appeal, the prosecutor has a decision that may be of benefit in future trials.

THE ROLE OF LAWYERS IN THE CRIMINAL COURT SYSTEM

Historically there have been two extremes of reaction to lawyers in America. One is exemplified by Alexis de Tocqueville, who came to America in the nineteenth century to study prison reform. "Lawyers," he said, "belong to the people by birth and interest, and to the aristocracy by habit and taste; they may be looked upon as the connecting link between the two great classes of society."[11] He believed that their special knowledge guaranteed them a separate status in society. In de Tocqueville's view, lawyers were, in effect, the American aristocracy.[12]

At the other extreme is the criticism of lawyers. In the early days of our country, lawyers were not considered necessary and were distrusted and scorned.[13] Later, as legal matters became more complicated, people began to recognize the need for them, and in the fifty years before the American Revolution, the legal profession flourished.

Gradually, the image of lawyers in this country improved, and by the early 1900s, public opinion polls revealed that lawyers were generally accorded high prestige.[14] In recent times, however, that has changed. A 1975 public opinion poll found that "the public had more confidence in garbage collectors than in lawyers, or doctors or teachers." State bar studies have found similar declines in the status of lawyers, and one even found that people who had retained lawyers had less confidence in the legal profession than those who had not.[15]

A 1978 Harris poll revealed that when asked to rate their confidence in sixteen institutions and professions in this country, the public placed attorneys at the bottom, along with members of Congress, organized labor, and advertising agencies.[16] In 1981, in a Harris poll on public confidence in various institutions and professions in America, lawyers were ranked last.[17]

THE PROSECUTOR

The **prosecutor**[18] plays a key role in the criminal justice system, to "seek justice." This function is clearly stated in the legal profession's Code of Professional Responsibility: "The responsibility of a public prosecutor differs from that of the usual advocate; his duty is to seek justice, not merely convict." The prosecutor must make timely disclosure to the defense attorney of evidence that might point to the innocence of the defendant or to a mitigation of the degree of the offense for which the defendant is accused or that might suggest reduction in punishment. In addition, the prosecutor should not intentionally avoid pursuing evidence because he or she thinks

EXHIBIT
THE PROSECUTOR'S DUTY IS TO SEEK JUSTICE

The American Prosecuter is Unique in the World

First, the American prosecutor is a public prosecutor representing the people in matters of criminal law. Traditionally, European societies viewed crimes as wrongs against an individual whose claims could be pressed through private prosecution. Second, the American prosecutor is usually a local official, reflecting the development of autonomous local governments in the colonies. Finally, as an elected official, the local American prosecutor is responsible only to the voters.

Prosecution Is the Function of Representing the Government in Criminal Cases

After the police arrest a suspect, the prosecutor coordinates the government's response to crime—from the initial screening, when the prosecutor decides whether or not to press charges, through trial and, in some instances, at the time of sentencing, by the presentation of sentencing recommendations.

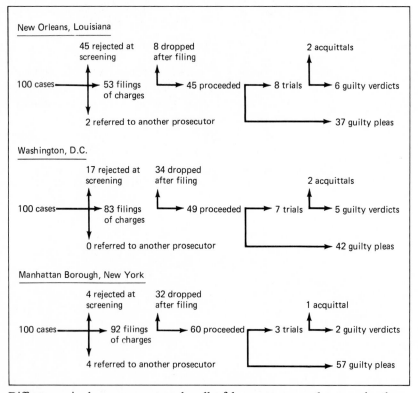

Differences in how prosecutors handle felony cases can be seen in three jurisdictions.

Source: B. Boland, INSLAW, Inc., The Prosecution of Felony Arrests. Bureau of Justice Statistics, 1983.

Prosecutors have been accorded much discretion in carrying out their responsibilities in that they make many of the decisions that determine whether or not a case will proceed through the criminal justice process.

Prosecuting Officials Include Local Prosecutors and District Attorneys, State Attorneys General, and U.S. Attorneys

Prosecution is predominantly a State and local function carried out by more than 8,000 State, county, municipal, and township prosecution agencies. In all but five States, local prosecutors are elected officials. Many small jurisdictions engage a part-time prosecutor who also maintains a private law practice. Prosecutors in urban jurisdictions often have offices staffed by many fulltime assistants. Federal prosecution is the responsibility of 94 U.S. attorneys who are appointed by the President.

The Decision to Charge Is Solely at the Prosecutor's Discretion

Once an arrest is made and the case is referred to the prosecutor, most prosecutors screen cases to determine whether the cases merit prosecution. The prosecutor can refuse to prosecute, for example, because of insufficient evidence. The decision to charge is not usually reviewable by any other branch of government. Some prosecutors accept almost all cases for prosecution; others screen out many cases.

The Official Accusation in Felony Cases Is Either a Grand Jury Indictment or a Prosecutor's Bill of Information

According to Jacoby, the accusatory process in a jurisdiction usually follows one of four paths:

- Arrest to preliminary hearing for bindover to grand jury for indictment
- Arrest to grand jury for indictment
- Arrest to preliminary hearing to a bill of information
- A combination of the above at the prosecutor's discretion.

Whatever the method of accusation, the State must demonstrate at this stage that there is probable cause to support the charge.

Nineteen States require indictments in felony prosecutions unless waived by the accused. Five States require indictments only in cases that involve capital offenses.

The Grand Jury Emerged from the American Revolution as the People's Protection Against Oppressive Prosecution by the State

Today, the grand jury is a group of ordinary citizens, usually no more than 23, which has both accusatory and investigative functions. The jury's proceedings are secret and not adversarial so that most rules of evidence for trials do not apply. Usually, evidence is presented by the prosecutor who brings a case to the grand jury's attention. However, in some States, the grand jury is used primarily to investigate issues of public corruption and organized crime.

Source: Bureau of Justice Statistics, *Report to the Nation on Crime and Justice: The Data* (Washington, D.C.: U.S. Government Printing Office, 1983), p. 55.

it will damage the case of the state against the accused. But the system does not always work that way. Because of the extensive discretionary powers of prosecutors, abuses may occur.

Discretionary power

Prosecuting attorneys possess great **discretionary power**. They may decide not to prosecute some cases and enter a **nolle prosequi,** which means "I refuse to prosecute." If they do decide to prosecute, they normally can do so even in cases that demand a **grand jury indictment**, for the grand jury usually follows the prosecutor's recommendations.

Prosecuting attorneys also have the power to discontinue prosecution. They may argue that the state has insufficient evidence to win the case or that other cases demand the time that would be involved in the case in question. If the defendant is found guilty, the prosecuting attorney may recommend leniency in the sentence or the most severe sentence. Here again, the prosecutor's recommendations are often followed.

Prosecutorial discretion is necessary in the criminal justice system. No system can state in advance which cases to prosecute and which to dismiss. Decisions must be made in light of the offense, the offender, and the resources of the system.[19] It would be a foolish waste of resources for a prosecutor to insist on taking to trial a case in which the evidence is so weak that there is no chance of conviction. On the other hand, it would be an abuse of discretion to dismiss that case because the defendant is from a particular race, religion, sex or because of any other extralegal reason.[20]

Allowing prosecutors considerable discretion, however, leaves open the possibility that that discretion will be abused. In other areas of the criminal justice system, we have tried to curb such abuses by placing checks on the system. Thus, as we saw in our discussion of the police, if the police abuse search-and-seizure rules in securing evidence, that evidence may not be admitted against the defendant at trial, unless it falls within the "good faith" or "inevitable discovery" exceptions. The discretion of prosecutors has, however, been subjected to few restraints, and some authorities have argued that abuse of prosecutorial discretion has increased significantly in the past decade.[21]

The main problem with curbing prosecutorial discretion is that the decisions take place out of the public view. There is little public knowledge of the workings of the prosecutor's office, in the first place, and although a victim of a crime may follow the details of a case from the initial investigation through **charging** and disposition, there are few data available about dismissals, charging decisions, and **plea bargains.** Thus, it is difficult to determine how suspects are being prosecuted and what disparities exist among prosecutors' offices.[22]

Not only is prosecutorial discretion more secret than are other potential abuses in the system, but the remedies that citizens have when other officials in the criminal justice system violate their rights are not available. For example, we mentioned the possibility of civil suits against police officers who violate a person's civil rights. Prosecutors, however, are not subject to civil suit while they are initiating and pursuing a criminal prosecution. In legal terminology, they have **immunity** from suit.[23]

There are, however, some instances in which prosecutors will have only a qualified immunity, meaning that they may be sued for actions that are not carried out in good faith.[24]

THE DEFENSE ATTORNEY	The Sixth Amendment of the Constitution provides that persons accused of committing a crime have a right to counsel. The attorney representing the defendant in a criminal trial is the **defense attorney.**
Function of the defense attorney	The function of a defense attorney is to protect the legal rights of the accused. The defendant, even if guilty, is entitled to a fair trial in which the state must prove guilt "beyond a reasonable doubt" and in accordance with the "rules of the game." That is, the proper procedure must be observed. The Supreme Court noted, "Procedure is to law what the 'scientific method' is to science." The defendant therefore is not legally guilty until the prosecution has proved its case within the rules of proper procedure and the question of guilt has been decided by a judge or a jury.

It is not the function of the defense attorney to decide the defendant's guilt or innocence. Attorneys are just as bound by the ethics of their profession in the defense of persons they think are guilty as in the defense of innocent persons. The function of defense attorneys is to give their clients the best advice they can within the law and the ethics of the legal profession. Once this function of defense attorneys is recognized, defending a "guilty" person becomes comprehensible. Defense attorneys are thus extremely important to the system of criminal justice. They should not be seen as individuals who are trying to "get criminals off" but as persons who are protecting that entire system. "If lawyers refuse to represent defendants who they believe are guilty, the right of a defendant to be represented by counsel is eliminated and with it the entire traditional criminal trial."[25]

This discussion is not meant to suggest that defense attorneys do not abuse the adversary system; indeed, that does occur, but that abuse must be distinguished from the *philosophy* of the system. That philosophy is one of the strongest points of our criminal justice process—that all persons are presumed innocent until proved guilty and that they may be punished only after the state proves beyond a reasonable doubt to the satisfaction of a jury (or a judge if the case is not tried before a jury) that the defendant is guilty. Furthermore, the state must prove its case without violating the accused's constitutional rights. It is, however, this commitment to preserve certain fundamental rights of defendants that has raised the most controversial arguments about defense attorneys.

Types of defense attorneys Defense attorneys may be in private practice or in public defender systems, with the latter providing most of the defense work.[26]

A small percentage of defendants are able to retain private attorneys. Most private attorneys who practice criminal law either are solo practitioners or are associated with small firms. Numerous studies earlier indicated that such attorneys have less prestige[27] and earn less money[28] than do attorneys who practice with large law firms or with corporations. They are usually not the leading members of the local or state bars or of the American Bar Association, and they are less likely to have been educated in the prestigious law schools, more likely to come from the working class, and less likely to have contact with the upper classes who can afford expensive legal services.[29]

An earlier, now-classic study of private attorneys who spent 10 percent or more of their time in criminal law work revealed that criminal lawyers, as compared with civil lawyers, were more often from families in which the fathers had low-status occupations. Twice as many criminal as civil lawyers reported that they had difficulty getting started in the practice of law, and three-fourths of the criminal lawyers indicated that their law school training was not adequate. In only one of the five cities studied were criminal lawyers getting higher salaries than those of other lawyers. Perhaps the most revealing finding of the study was that 71 percent of those practicing criminal law said that they had not planned to enter criminal law but had gotten there by default; that is, they failed to get established in other branches of law.[30]

More recent studies of the private defense bar are no more encouraging. "The picture which emerges is not likely to stir the hearts and minds of impressionistic first-year law students. Nor is it likely to cause Chief Justice [Warren] Burger to issue an immediate retraction [of his frequent comments regarding the defense bar's lack of trial skills]. . . . This once romantic breed of lawyers seems to face extinction. . . ."[31]

Most of the criminal defense work in this country is for poor clients who cannot afford private attorneys.[32] They are represented by **public defenders** who may be associated with a public defender system, a system operated with public funds, or by an attorney appointed by the court for a specific case. That attorney will be paid at a fixed rate from court funds. This latter method is most common in rural areas that do not have public defender systems. Assigned counsel will also be used in cases in which the public defender office would have a conflict of interest in representing a particular defendant.

Most indigent defendants are represented by an attorney associated with a public defender system. The growth of public defender systems has, however, encountered mixed reactions. Indigent defendants often see the system as ineffective, as illustrated by the defendant who, when asked whether he had a lawyer when he went to court responded, "No, I had a public defender."[33] Others have indicated that "all too frequently, . . . public defenders have been viewed as cheap, efficient labor by the jurisdictions they serve."[34]

At the other extreme, Chief Justice Burger wrote in 1971 that although one of the great weaknesses of the legal profession was the unavailability of attorneys for the poor, especially in criminal cases, "the half century of private development of legal aid and public defender programs is a tribute to the legal profession as the trail blazer for the recent developments of the legal right to counsel."[35]

Despite this rare laudatory comment, the best efforts thus far to recruit capable and bright young attorneys into legal services for the poor have not produced the desired results. A court-appointed attorney with a large case load, low compensation, low status, and inadequate resources cannot be expected to defend his or her clients adequately. Thus the burden of improving this situation clearly rests in two places. The legal profession should be challenged to discover ways to attract more qualified attorneys into criminal defense work, including greater prestige and reward for such work and better preparation in law school for criminal trial work.[36] Society must also provide the money and resources necessary to make the system work as conceptualized.

PLEA BARGAINING

With the emphasis on defendant's rights at trial, it would be easy to lose perspective in terms of the frequency of trials. Over 90 percent of persons convicted of crime do not go to trial;[37] rather, their cases are decided by a plea bargain between the prosecution and the defense.[38] **Plea bargaining**, despite its frequent use, is one of the most controversial processes in the entire criminal justice system.

Plea bargaining has been defined as a negotiation process between the prosecutor and the defendant in which the defendant agrees to submit a plea of guilty to the court in exchange for a reduction of charges or a recommendation of sentence from the prosecutor. One writer describes this as an "exchange of concessions for a defendant's act of self-conviction."[39] Others are careful to point out that plea bargaining includes a specific forfeiture of the right to trial.[40]

CONSTITUTIONAL ISSUES IN PLEA BARGAINING

The process of plea bargaining received the recognition of the Supreme Court in 1971, when it was approved as a means of managing overloaded criminal dockets. Indeed, the Court declared it to be "an essential component" of the criminal process, which "properly administered . . . is to be encouraged."[41] In addition, the state may encourage guilty pleas by offering substantial benefits in return for the plea.[42]

EXHIBIT
PLEA BARGAIN VERSUS TRIAL

Many Guilty Pleas Are the Result of Plea Negotiations

According to . . . [a] recent study, a negotiated plea occurs when a defendant pleads guilty with the reasonable expectation that the State will give some consideration such as reduction in the number or severity of the charges and/or a more lenient sentence.

Guilty pleas are sometimes explicitly traded for a less severe charge or sentence, but they also result from a straightforward admission of guilt by a defendant. This may result from a hope or impression that such a plea will be rewarded by a lighter sentence or from a concern that a trial will reveal damaging evidence.

The predominance of guilty pleas is not new in the criminal justice system. A study in Connecticut covering the 84 years from 1880 to 1954 concludes that between 1880 and 1910 only 10% of all convictions were obtained by trial.

Some Jurisdictions Have Adopted an Anti-Plea-Bargaining Policy

• • •

A Major Reform Has Been to Increase the Responsibility of Judges for Ensuring Fairness in Plea Negotiations

• • •

Most Felony Cases That Reach Trial Are Tried Before a Jury

• • •

Most Cases That Go to Trial Result in Conviction

• • •

18 States and the District of Columbia Require a Unanimous Verdict in All Trials

Currently, 45 States require unanimity in criminal verdicts, but 26 of these States do not require unanimity in civil verdicts. Five States (Louisiana, Montana, Oregon, Oklahoma, and Texas) do not require unanimous verdicts in criminal or civil trials.

The proportion of jury votes needed to convict varies among jurisdictions that do not require unanimity, ranging from two-thirds in Montana to five-sixths in Oregon.

All States require unanimity in capital cases, and the U.S. Supreme Court does not permit a criminal finding of guilt by less than a six-person majority. Thus, a six-person jury must always be unanimous in a criminal finding of guilty.

Source: Bureau of Justice Statistics, *Report to the Nation on Crime and Justice: The Data* (Washington, D.C.: U.S. Government Printing Office, 1983), p. 65, footnotes omitted.

The Supreme Court has, however, recognized that plea bargaining must have some limitations. Specifically, it has recognized the importance of counsel at the plea-bargaining stage,[43] the need for a public record that would indicate the defendant knowingly and voluntarily entered the plea of guilty,[44] and that the promise made by the prosecuting attorney at the plea-bargaining stage must be kept.[45] But in 1978 the Court, in a five to four decision, upheld the right of the prosecutor to threaten to secure a grand jury indictment against the defendant on a more serious charge if the defendant did not plead guilty to the charge already made. In *Bordenkircher v. Hayes,*[46] the defendant was under indictment for the crime of "uttering a forged instrument" (passing a "hot" check) in the amount of $88.30. The sentence that could be imposed upon conviction of that offense was two to ten years. The prosecutor told the defendant that he would recommend a five-year sentence if the defendant would plead guilty and "save the court the inconvenience and necessity of a trial." If the defendant refused to do so, the prosecutor said he would seek an indictment under the state's Habitual Criminal Act. That act provided that upon conviction of a third felony, a defendant would receive a mandatory sentence of life in prison.

The defendant in *Bordenkircher v. Hayes* refused to accept the plea-bargain offer, went to trial, and was convicted of uttering a forged instrument. In a separate proceeding it was found that he had been convicted of two previous felonies. He was then sentenced to life in prison as required by the Habitual Offender Statute of the state of Kentucky. In a five to four decision, the majority of the Supreme Court recognized the mutual advantages to the state and to the defendant of a system of plea bargaining. The Court emphasized that although the state may not *retaliate* against a defendant who chooses to exercise a legal right, "in the 'give-and-take' of plea bargaining, there is no such element of punishment or retaliation so long as the accused is free to accept or reject the prosecution's offer."[47] The Court continued:

> by tolerating and encouraging the negotiation of pleas, this Court has necessarily accepted as constitutionally legitimate the simple reality that the prosecutor's interest at the bargaining table is to persuade the defendant to forego his right to plead not guilty.[48]

The three dissenting justices argued that the state was being vindictive, that "when plea negotiations, conducted in the face of the less serious charge under the first indictment, fail, charging by a second indictment a more serious crime for the same conduct creates a strong inference of vindictiveness."[49]

In a 1979 case, *Washington v. United States,*[50] the District of Columbia Court of Appeals held that *Bordenkircher* did not apply in a case regarding a defendant who was originally charged with assault after allegedly attacking a person with a knife. The defendant later jumped bail and was indicted for assault with a dangerous weapon and bail jumping. When he was arrested about a year later, a hearing was held on his motion to sever the charges to enable a separate trial on each charge. The court inquired whether there was a chance the case would end in a plea bargain. The U.S. attorney replied that he would be happy to negotiate a plea but that he could not accept the plea offer of the defense—that the defendant plead guilty to bail jumping in return for dropping the assault-with-a-dangerous-weapon charge. The government obtained a continuance on the day of trial and later that day obtained a new indictment. In that indictment, the defendant was charged with the original two counts and, in addition, with assault with intent to kill and assault with intent to kill while armed. The defendant pleaded not guilty to all charges. There was no indication of plea-bargaining attempts after the more serious indictments were filed. The defendant was convicted of assault to kill while armed, although the defendant contended that the prosecutor filed those charges because of vindictiveness.

The District of Columbia Court of Appeals held that this issue had not been settled by the Supreme Court in *Bordenkircher* because when the prosecutor offered a plea bargain to the defendant, he made it clear that if the defendant did not accept that offer, the prosecutor would seek a new and harsher indictment. The defendant, the court asserted, was thus able to make his decision in light of all the facts in the "give and take" of plea negotiation. In *Bordenkircher,* argued the majority in the D.C. Court of Appeals, the prosecutor was using the threat of a harsher indictment as "leverage" in the plea-bargaining process. In *Washington,* however, the prosecutor did not give such notice. The court held that in this situation the prosecutor would have to justify the harsher indictment and that in the future when the government seeks a new and more serious indictment without notice to the defendant and without plea bargaining in good faith, there will be a strong inference of vindictiveness on the part of the prosecution.[51]

ARGUMENTS IN FAVOR OF PLEA BARGAINING

One of the most frequently cited reasons for plea bargaining is that the resources are not available to take all cases to trial. Because over 90 percent of all persons who are accused of criminal offenses plead guilty after the decision is made to prosecute, the present resources are devoted to trying only 10 percent of all criminal cases. Court dockets are already too crowded; thus, the abolition of plea bargaining would exhaust the current resources.

In return for offering defendants the possibility of reduced punishment, defendants who plea bargain offer much to the state. Public money is not spent supporting defendants in jail waiting for trials; prosecutors, public defenders, and assigned counsel limit their courtroom appearances and trial preparation; money is not spent locating witnesses who then must be repeatedly summoned to the courthouse; the police do not spend time in court on the witness stand; money is saved when juries do not have to be summoned or paid; new courtrooms need not be built or staffed with court clerks, bailiffs, or court reporters; and extra judges do not need to be hired to preside over trials.

In support of plea bargaining, it is also contended that not all cases need to go to court. Trials are for the establishment of facts. But when the facts are not in dispute, a trial could be considered a waste of time and resources. Furthermore, some disputes are probably best resolved without the adversary method. For example, consider a defendant charged with acts of open lewdness. A psychiatric examination indicates that he is not legally insane and that he has no serious sexual perversions but that he is suffering from a form of neurosis and needs psychiatric care. He is married, has no previous criminal record, is a college graduate, and is employed by a corporation. If taken to court, the man will receive a criminal record. Even if he is acquitted, such a record would probably result in the loss of his job and social ostracism in the community and endanger his future employment. The prosecutor and the defense attorney get together and decide that in the best interests of society and the defendant, he should be allowed to plead guilty to counts under the Disorderly Conduct Act and to submit to psychiatric treatment, which the psychiatrist thinks will solve his sexual problems. Should this be permitted, or should a trial be held?

The defendant might not only be harmed by the stigma of the trial and resulting conviction but also by the time spent in a criminal trial. But "what is not so often recognized is that to fight a case is also a disruption in the life of the court. Plea bargaining lessens the frequency of those disruptions."[52]

The arguments for plea bargaining were summarized by the U.S. Supreme Court:

> Whatever might be the situation in an ideal world, the fact is that the guilty plea and the often concomitant plea bargain are important components of this country's criminal justice system. Properly administered, they can benefit all concerned. The defendant avoids extended pretrial incarceration and the anxieties and uncertainties of a trial; he gains a speedy disposition of the case, the chance to acknowledge his guilt, and a prompt start in realizing whatever potential there may be for rehabilitation. Judges and prosecutors conserve vital and scarce resources. The public is protected from the risks posed by those charged with criminal proceedings.[53]

ARGUMENTS
OPPOSING
PLEA BARGAINING

The arguments against plea bargaining are becoming more frequent and more severe. Perhaps the most critical has been that judges have not always honored the "deal" made between the defense and prosecution and that defendants may plead guilty, thinking they will receive the agreed-upon bargain, only to discover that they get a more severe sentence from the judge. The courts have, however, placed restrictions of plea bargaining, and the basic test seems to be whether the prosecution has plea bargained in good faith or is reacting vindictively in seeking more serious charges.

The Supreme Court has emphasized the importance of "fundamental fairness" to the defendant in the plea-bargaining process. For example, in a 1971 decision, the Supreme Court held that when a guilty plea rests "in any significant degree" on the prosecutor's promises, the promise must be kept. In that case the defendant had pleaded guilty to a lesser offense on the basis of the prosecutor's promise to make no sentence recommendation. A successor prosecutor recommended the maximum (of one year), which the judge, who said that the original prosecutor's recommendation did not make "a particle of difference" to him, imposed.[54]

Another problem with plea bargaining is that an innocent defendant might be coerced into pleading guilty.[55] In emphasizing the importance of a voluntary guilty plea, the Supreme Court noted that in the case of pleading guilty, the defendant not only admits past conduct but gives up the right to a trial before a jury or judge. "Waivers of constitutional rights not only must be voluntary but must be knowing, intelligent acts done with sufficient awareness of the relevant circumstances and likely consequences."[56]

In determining whether a plea is voluntary the courts consider whether the defendant was represented by counsel, and if so, the plea is less likely to be held involuntary.[57] When the defendant was not represented by counsel, the guilty plea may be ruled involuntary.[58] The Supreme Court, however, has held that defendants who claim that a plea was involuntary because it was entered only to reduce the possible penalty will not prevail. These decisions can still be "the product of a free and rational choice, especially where the defendant was represented by competent counsel whose advice was that the plea would be to the defendant's advantage."[59] The plea cannot be an irrational act based on an apparent but nonexistent advantage to the defendant. Furthermore, plea bargains leading to a guilty plea must not be induced by threats or promises to discontinue improper harassment, misrepresentation, unfilled promises, or promises that have no relation to proper prosecutorial business, such as a bribe.[60]

THE EFFECT OF ABOLISHING PLEA BARGAINING

Opponents of plea bargaining argue that many defendants will still plead guilty in the hope of receiving a better reward, that is, less punishment. Perhaps the best test of the effect of plea bargaining on trials comes from evidence available in jurisdictions that have abolished the plea.

A study of the ban on plea bargaining in Alaska revealed the following: (1) the ban was being followed; plea bargaining has almost disappeared, and along with it, there has been a decline in charge bargaining; (2) defense attorneys claim the ban has increased their work load; they are filing more motions and must spend more time in trial preparation; (3) prosecutors agree it has also increased their work load, but most report they are happy to be out of the "sentencing" process; (4) the average processing time for felony cases has decreased, not increased, as some predicted; (5) trial convictions were up over 11 percent; and (6) sentences were more severe in some types of crime, with the strongest increase seen in the sentencing of drug offenders.[61]

In Arizona, plea bargaining was eliminated for some offenses, but a study concluded that court clogging did not result. After a trial period, it was found that "a ban on plea bargaining failed to cause the widely feared increase of trials in court." One chief prosecutor in Arizona found that "our experience . . . has proved that plea bargaining does not serve any purpose and that its elimination will not disrupt the system of justice."[62]

THE FUTURE OF
PLEA BARGAINING

The Supreme Court has declared that the states and the federal government are free to abolish plea bargaining and guilty pleas,[63] but the future of the system may not depend on the Court. If the system remains, its goal must be that plea-bargained sentences will be close to those that would result from trial, resulting in fairness, the advantages of avoiding delay, and less disparate sentences. To achieve this goal, the parties to the negotiation must accurately perceive the conviction and sentence probabilities; the defendant should not be forced to accept higher bargained sentences because he or she is in jail, cannot afford an attorney, or because his or her public defender does not have the time or resources to go to trial. Finally, prosecutors should not be forced to offer low bargains because of limited resources.[64]

THE ROLE OF
THE JUDGE IN
PLEA BARGAINING

The **judges** also have a role to play in the plea-bargaining process. Although in federal courts, judges generally may not take part in plea negotiations, they do in many state courts. Judicial participation in plea bargaining may take many different forms: judges may indirectly and informally indicate the sentence being considered, may encourage defense lawyers and district attorneys to find an acceptable bargain, may nudge defendants into plea-bargain negotiations, may actively intervene in the plea discussions, or may implicitly bargain by giving lower sentences to defendants who agree to a plea-bargain offer.[65]

Most judges routinely accept guilty pleas, and this practice has been criticized. The defendants may not be examined thoroughly enough to determine whether they understand the charges, the constitutional rights being waived, and the sentencing consequences. In one study, the data showed that plea hearings took approximately three minutes of court time.[66] One commentator noticed trial judges who "look for guilty pleas the way that salesmen look for orders" and who frequently ask one another, "How are your dispositions this month?"[67]

A related criticism is that judges rubber-stamp the plea agreements that are set before them. By the time the plea bargain is submitted to the court, the prosecutor and defense attorney are no longer adversaries but have a common interest in seeing the plea accepted, and the judges do not offer much protection to defendants in these situations.[68]

A final criticism of the judicial role in plea bargaining pertains to the process of sentencing. It is commonly accepted courthouse wisdom that defendants receive more severe penalties after trial than if they accept a plea bargain.[69] This has been defended on two grounds. First, the defendant who pleads guilty saves the system the expense and inconvenience of a trial. In an ideal system, the criminal would not be allowed to bargain with the system, but in reality, courts must deal with a huge volume of criminal cases and defendants, and their attorneys understand that in return for expedient processing of a case, leniency will be granted.[70]

The second justification for higher sentences after a full trial is that the judge has heard all the evidence, has learned the details of the criminal act, and has seen the impact on the victim, all of which give the judge more information about the defendant's character. Furthermore, defendants who show no willingness to admit responsibility for their conduct may convince the judge that the prospects for rehabilitation are lower and that therefore a greater sentence is justified.[71]

THE TRIAL DECISION: JUDGE OR JURY

Although most cases are plea bargained and consequently do not go to **trial**, trials are a crucial part of our system, and they often involve the most difficult and complicated cases as well as the most controversial. We have already examined some of the fundamental rights of defendants at trial, including the right to a trial by jury. But not all cases are tried before a jury, and in most instances, the defendant will be able to choose to be tried before a judge or a jury. Even if the defendant chooses a jury, the judge plays a significant role in the trial.

THE TRIAL JUDGE

The third role of lawyers in the criminal justice system is as a **judge**. Judges are the "referees" in a criminal trial. Theoretically they are neither "for" nor "against" a particular position or issue but, rather, are committed to the fair implementation of the rules of evidence and law. They are charged with making sure that the attorneys play by the rules of the game.

Judges decide whether attorneys' objections to the questions asked of witnesses by other attorneys should be sustained or overruled. They decide whether evidence may be admitted or must be excluded, whether there is sufficient evidence to let the case go to the jury for a decision on the factual question of guilt, or whether a mistrial must be declared as a result of some serious error that would prejudice the case. Judges must have the law, both

"I sentence you to twenty years or until your prison becomes overcrowded, whichever comes first."

Bob Englehart, The Hartford Courant

statutory and case law, at their immediate disposal; they must, in most cases, make instant decisions on the issues in dispute.

Judges must also present the case to the jury with a **charge,** in which they sum up the law in the case and give the jury legal instructions that it must follow in arriving at a verdict. For example, judges must explain to the jury the meaning of the "presumption of innocence" and the state's burden of proving the case beyond a reasonable doubt. They may have great influence over the jury through their attitudes, their rulings, and their charges. They will also have an impact on those who testify and those who are parties in the trial. Few people experience appellate arguments, and their only contact with "justice" may be at the trial. Judges at trial, therefore, should be considerate and uphold the highest standards of justice in their courtrooms. The job is a difficult one and requires great expertise in the law. It is also a powerful position, for although judges may be overruled on appeal, many cases will not be appealed. Finally, judges have tremendous power over defendants at the stage of **sentencing.**

Although some place judges on a pedestal, free from many "human" frailties, others argue that they are only human and therefore subject to all of the prejudices, hostilities, and other human problems that might color their opinions. Judges have traditionally been highly esteemed in America. Even when people have become disillusioned with the courts, their dissatisfaction has usually been focused on the institution of the court, not on the judges, who continued to score high on occupational prestige scales.[72] Recently, however, judges have been criticized regarding **sentencing disparity.**

The prestige of judges is also affected by the quality of the men and women attracted to the position. Because the job has become more complex and salaries have not kept pace with inflation, it has become increasingly difficult to persuade the best-qualified persons to become judges, resulting in "the specter of a judicial 'brain drain,' leading to a judiciary consisting only of the very young, the very old, and the independently wealthy."[73]

Characteristics of judges

The personal characteristics of judges are important. "Brilliant or not so brilliant . . . all judges are human. They thus have values which are shaped by their backgrounds and which are manifested in their decisions."[74] In this country, trial judges and appellate judges have traditionally been white, Anglo-Saxon, Protestant males with middle-class or professional back-grounds and relatively conservative political views.[75]

But some changes have been made. We now have a woman, Sandra Day O'Connor, on the U.S. Supreme Court, and in the past decade, women have been appointed by presidents to the federal judiciary in larger numbers than ever before. But the progress is slow and, some would say, insignificant. Today women occupy only 5 percent of the federal judgeships. Of the 262 appointments made by President Jimmy Carter, 15.3 percent were women; 14.5 percent were black, and 6.1 percent were Hispanic. During the administration of President Ronald Reagan, however, the appointments have been mainly white, male, and conservative Republicans.[76]

Judges are extremely important to our system of criminal justice, and they should be recruited and selected carefully. What qualities do we want in our judges? Judges should be impartial and fair. They should be able to approach a case with an objective and open mind concerning the facts. Judges should be well educated in the substantive law involved in each case as well as in general procedural rules, laws, and evidence. Judges should be able to think and write clearly; their opinions are of great importance to attorneys and other judges who use them to analyze how future cases might be argued and decided. Judges should have high moral standards that enable them to withstand political and economic pressures that might influence decisions. They should be in good physical, mental, and emotional health. They should be good managers, for judges have considerable power over the management of the court system. They should be able to assume power sensibly without abuse and to exercise leadership in social reform when necessary and desirable.[77]

Finally, judges should have what is sometimes called "judicial temperament," as defined by one federal judge: "A judge's comportment must at all times square with the ideals of justice and impartiality that the public projects on us in our symbolic role. A judge must be reflective, perhaps even a bit grave, but must always demonstrate an openness consistent with our tradition of giving each side its say before a decision is rendered." It is also essential that a judge be able to "separate the dignity of the office from a sense of self-importance."[78]

Judicial training   Training for judges in the United States is not so strict as in some other countries.[79] For example, judges in the United States do not necessarily have any specific judicial training. Many have not even practiced criminal law, and others have not practiced any kind of law for more than a few years. A law degree is not required for local judges in some states, although it is required for federal judges.

Steps have been taken to improve the training of trial judges. Most states have some type of training program for new judges, and in 1964, the National Conference of State Trial Judges established a permanent institution for judicial education, providing a place where judges can get training during the summers. In 1969 the National College of Juvenile Justice, the training division of the National Council of Juvenile Court Judges, was established. Located on the campus of the University of Nevada in Reno, the college provides continuing education and training not only for juvenile and family court judges but also for other professionals in the juvenile justice system. Finally, many states now require continuing legal education for judges.[80]

THE JURY   In our system, *capital cases,* or those in which the death penalty may be assessed, must be tried before a jury, but in other cases, defendants may elect to have a nonjury trial in which the judge decides the issue of guilt or innocence. When the case is tried before a jury, however, it is the function of the jury to listen to and weigh the evidence presented by the prosecution and the defense and decide whether the defendant is innocent, in which case there will be an acquittal, or guilty. In some cases, after a finding of guilt, the same or another jury will decide the penalty, but usually the judge determines the sentence.

Analysis of the jury system   Some authorities believe that the **jury** system is among the great achievements of English and American jurisprudence. There are, however, those who have criticized the system. Sociologists have studied the jury in order to gather data on some of the issues, and those studies have become widely recognized in the literature.

Much of the information gathered on the jury comes from the Chicago Jury Project, begun in 1954 and referred to as "the first systematic study of the competence of jurors."[81] Because of opposition to that project, in which jury deliberations were taped without the knowledge of the jurors, Congress passed a statute that prohibits research on juries by that method. Since that time, the studies usually use "simulated" or mock juries. From the jury lists, a mock jury of "similar" jurors is selected, presented with the case, and told to deliberate and decide the issues. Their deliberations are then recorded and analyzed.[82]

The use of mock juries has also been criticized.[83] The main criticism is that the "jurors" in the studies are not involved in a "real trial" and that as a consequence, their responses may not accurately reflect how they would react to the real situation. "In short, the problem with many jury studies is that what has been done in the laboratory simply does not simulate what happens in the real world of the courtroom."[84] The problem has led to the conclusion that the relationship between certain variables and jury verdicts has not yet been tested.

The most recent technique utilized to study jury reactions attempts to get even closer to the actual jury deliberations. This is the use of "shadow juries." The system was devised as an aid in the $300 million antitrust suit brought against the International Business Machines Corporation (IBM) in 1977. An expert was hired to select a panel of six people who were as close as possible to the actual jury in terms of backgrounds and attitudes. They were paid to sit in the courtroom every day of the trial, listen to the evidence, and report their findings each evening. The information was used by the defense in the strategy and preparation of the case. The defense won the case, and the expert went into full-time consulting, forming a company called Litigation Sciences.[85]

Some of the questions for which the investigator used the shadow jury in the IBM case were:

What is the decision-making process among jurors?
What role does social interaction and group influence play in the jury process?
How do jurors use "safe topics?"
What is the sociology of the courtroom?
Why do jurors fail to understand evidence?[86]

Although critics believe that the jury system is an ineffective method for determining facts, the results of empirical research are not clear—there is some support and some lack of support for the system's efficiency and accuracy.[87] The U.S. Supreme Court is convinced that juries do understand the evidence presented at trial,[88] but the research on "shadow juries" questions the Court's conclusion concerning the jury's understanding of the case.[89]

Variables influencing jury decisions   Numerous studies have been made of the variables, both legal and extralegal (those that are not supposed to influence a decision, for example, race, sex, socioeconomic class), that affect jury decisions.[90] First is the variable of the jurors' previous experience. There is some earlier empirical evidence to support the assumption that experienced jurors are more likely than inexperienced jurors are to convict a defendant.[91] A more recent study, however, questioned this assumption but did find that previous experience on juries did influence jurors. This led the investigators to decide that although further research should be conducted, we might reasonably conclude that jury service be restricted to one trial per person.[92]

A second variable that may influence jurors is the witness at trial. A psychologist who is an expert on eyewitness testimony has warned that "eyewitness testimony is so powerful that it can sway a jury even after it has been shown to be largely false. Jurors appear to respond more to the confidence with which an eyewitness responds than to the circumstances surrounding the original event and subsequent recollection of it."[93] Psychological research indicates that when experts testify regarding the problems of memory and the possibility of misassessing eyewitness testimony, jurors are more likely to be critical of the eyewitness testimony.[94]

Third, it is felt that the juror's sex and/or race will influence how he or she views the witnesses and the testimony and, consequently, will influence that juror's decision in the case. There is some evidence that men are more assertive in jury deliberations and more often serve as foremen. They have more influence on other jurors, and they more frequently perceive themselves as having more influence. There is also some evidence that women and blacks are more lenient and less prone to vote for conviction. Women are more likely than men to convict in cases of rape and murder, but when race is considered, black females are significantly more likely than black males to vote for conviction. White females are more likely than white males to convict, but the difference is not statistically significant. When age is controlled, the relation between verdicts of guilt and sex remains about the same for women, but among women, guilty verdicts increase with age.

When education is controlled, guilty verdicts remain at about the same (high) for women, but among male jurors, the rate of acquittals goes up with age. "It appears that females are more conviction-prone across all educational levels, whereas males with post-high school education are less likely to convict than males with less education."[95] There is some evidence that the propensity to prejudge a case is higher among women than men and that the differences are strongest in cases involving the charge of rape.[96]

There is also evidence that decisions regarding guilt or innocence may be related to race. For example, one study found that "black jurors as a whole were . . . more likely to acquit a defendant, regardless of his race. White jurors were found to be less likely to show compassion, particularly toward a black defendant, and were less likely in this instance to be influenced by a group discussion."[97]

JUDGE VERSUS JURY

Should criminal cases be tried before judges or juries? The debate continues, with allegations that juries are too lenient, although there is some recent evidence that they are less lenient than judges are,[98] that they do not understand the evidence,[99] and that jury trials are too time-consuming and too expensive. According to one justice of the Supreme Court, the jury system may well be a "luxury we cannot afford."[100] Still, despite the problems, the system retains great popularity, and in the words of one national news magazine, it may not be perfect, "but it Works."[101]

THE FINAL APPEAL: THE UNITED STATES SUPREME COURT

The most important check we have on the trial process is the process of **appeal**. Earlier, in our brief overview of the court system, we mentioned the appeal process, and here we shall look at the final court of appeal, the United States Supreme Court.

The U.S. Supreme Court, traditionally held in high esteem in this country, began its 1982 term in October, with some of the most widespread criticism in its history. Three law professors, all of whom are former Supreme

The Supreme Court of the United States.

Court clerks, described the Court's opinions as "mediocre," "gobbledy-gook," and "murky." One of the professors concluded that the biggest problem is that the Court just does not have many talented lawyers.[102] A *New York Times* editorial referred to "the diminishing quality of the Court's final product. Wordy opinions ghost written by law clerks get less and less editing by the harried jurists who sign their names to the prose." Yet, the *Times* concluded: "The High Court, despite generations of attack and controversy, remains one of the world's most trusted institutions."[103]

HISTORY
OF THE COURT

The Supreme Court was the only court specifically established by the Constitution. Congress was given the power to establish "such inferior Courts as the Congress may from time to time ordain and establish." The Constitution further specified a few cases in which the Supreme Court would have **original jurisdiction.** It was also to have **appellate jurisdiction** under such exceptions and regulations as determined by Congress.[104]

During the debates of the Constitutional Convention, it was decided that the Supreme Court would have the power to review state court decisions when such decisions affected federal rights. By statute in 1925, Congress "finally settled the dominant principle that should shape the Supreme Court's appellate jurisdiction: that the Court should have almost complete discretionary control of the extent of its appellate business, through grant or denial of the writ of certiorari."[105] A **writ of certiorari** refers to a review or inquiry. When it is granted, the Court is said to have granted *certiorari,* that is, it has agreed to hear and review a case from a lower court. Four of the nine justices who sit on the Supreme Court, must vote in favor of the writ in order for it to be granted.

OPERATION
OF THE COURT

In an average term, the Court hears less than 5 percent of the cases filed. There are two reasons for this limitation. First, because of time, the Court must limit the number of cases heard and decided. But the problem today is that the number of cases the Court is asked to hear has increased significantly, from approximately one thousand per year in 1953 to five thousand or more today. The court also has increased its work load, with the number of signed opinions written per year increasing from around 60 in 1953 to over 120 in 1981.

The second reason the Court hears only some of the cases filed was stated by a former chief justice: "To remain effective, the Supreme Court must continue to decide only those cases which present questions whose resolution will have immediate importance far beyond the particular facts and parties involved."[106] An example would be the *Gideon* case, discussed earlier. The fact that Gideon did not have counsel at his trial in Florida was important only to Gideon, but his case's significance went far beyond the dispute between the prisoner and the state of Florida, as the Court decision handed down in that case established the right of counsel for all criminal defendants in felony cases.

The Court will often hear cases when lower court decisions on the issue in question have differed. The decision of the Supreme Court then becomes the final court resolution of the issue, unless or until it is overruled by a subsequent Supreme Court decision or by a constitutional amendment.

The procedures followed by the Court are also important. Cases that are accepted for review by the Supreme Court must be filed within a specified time before oral argument. The attorneys who "argue" before the Court are under a lot of pressure. They may, for example, be interrupted any time by a justice who wishes to ask a question. In addition, attorneys are expected to argue their cases without reading from prepared **briefs.** They are normally limited to thirty minutes each for oral argument—sometimes an hour—and the time limits are usually strictly enforced. It has been said that one chief justice stopped an attorney in the middle of a word to tell him that his time was up.[107]

When it is in session, the Court hears arguments Monday through Wednesday for two weeks of the month. On Friday, conference day, the justices discuss the cases argued before them and decide which additional ones they will hear. A majority vote is needed for a decision in a case heard by the Court. Should an even number of justices be sitting, resulting in a tie vote, the decision being appealed will be affirmed.

The decision is announced in a written **opinion,** which usually represents a majority opinion. **Concurring opinions** may be written by justices who voted with the majority but who either disagree with the reasons or agree but have additional reasons. Thus, in some cases, the Court's opinion may represent the views of only a plurality of the justices. Opinions "concurring in part, dissenting in part" and **dissenting opinions** may also be written. Those opinions are an important part of the American legal system and are carefully read by lawyers, who may use the arguments in future cases. The justices circulate among themselves drafts of their opinions, which are printed in secret and remain secret until the Court announces its decision in the case. In this way the entire Court participates in the formulation of an opinion, and a written opinion is rarely the sole conclusion of the justice who writes it. Thus, all the justices are to some extent involved in all stages of all cases; that is, the U.S. Supreme Court does not function by committee or by individual assignment.

The Court's decisions are handed down on "opinion days," which are usually three Mondays of each month of the term. The decisions are then made public, and newspapers will pick up portions of those decisions thought to be of general interest.

THE COURT'S
DECISIONS
The principal function of the Supreme Court is to determine whether the litigants' federal constitutional rights have been violated. These constitutional rights must be interpreted in light of changing times and changing needs. "Like a work of artistic creation, the Constitution endures because it is capable of responding to the concerns, the needs, the aspirations of successive generations."[108] But because we differ on our interpretation of the needs, concerns, and aspirations of our society, we also differ on the Court's interpretations, and thus the Court has frequently been accused of "making" rather than "interpreting" law.

Controversial court decisions must, however, be considered in the context of constitutional law and a changing society, with its concomitant need for settling conflicts. If the Constitution is flexible and expected to change as conditions change, while at the same time maintaining some stability and dependability, it is imperative that judicial decisions reflect the changing conditions of the time. And flexibility is one of the Constitution's virtues. Factual situations cannot be foreseen in advance. The law and the Constitution must be flexible enough to deal with different factual situations, which will require adjudication as they arise. If rules had to be clear to everyone before they could be imposed, "society would be impossible."[109] If the rules are not clear, reasonable minds will differ as to their meaning.

The publication of *The Brethren*[110] has raised endless questions about the decision making of the nine justices in black robes who are charged with telling us "what the law is." In this book, the authors portray Chief Justice Warren Burger as an unprincipled man, incapable of leadership, and a legal lightweight who writes weak opinions. Juctice William J. Brennan, Jr., is alleged, in one case that kept a man in prison, to have changed his vote merely to win favor with Justice Harry Blackmun, whose vote he hoped to obtain in future cases. The book has been the subject of much debate, with many authorities taking the position that the frequent references to "anonymous sources" really mean that the authors did not have factual data for many of their allegations and that the book is essentially inaccurate.

The president of the American Bar Association at the time the book was published responded to the controversy by pointing out that most of the allegations about the members of the Court are based on "changes and negotiations in opinions that occur as a case winds its way toward a decision." Noting that these processes are normal when human beings are trying to decide complicated and controversial issues, he insisted that it would be unreasonable to expect justices to have quick and firm decisions and not to be influenced by their colleagues as well as by their reading of other cases. It would also be unreasonable to expect that they would never be wrong.

The Supreme Court is not a mystical, legally omniscient group of Olympians who are able to divine ultimate logic and perfect justice. They are, quite simply, nine human beings striving mightily, if not always perfectly, to resolve disputes that no one else has the responsibility or the authority to resolve. There is no guarantee they will always be popular or even that they will always be right. But there is, despite those human imperfections, an inherent strength in the Court that has allowed it to remain one of our more successful public institutions.[111]

THE COURTS AND THEIR CONGESTION

There is no question but that the courts are overburdened, and that includes the Supreme Court as well as the lower appellate courts and trial courts. The main question, however, is whether we should reduce the amount of litigation or increase the courts' facilities and personnel to handle the increasing volume of cases.

As with most other issues, there is no consensus on this issue, either. Chief Justice Burger leads those who argue that "the problems we now face have resulted from the ... great and increasing litigiousness of our people who historically have a passion for 'taking to the law.'" This is countered by the president of the American Trial Lawyers' Association, who contends that litigation is cost effective and that we are not filing a lot of frivolous lawsuits. He cites the first large-scale empirical study of litigation, the Civil Litigation Research Project: "The propositions that America is a litigious society and that trial lawyers are waxing rich did not stand the test of analysis nor did the assertion that litigation is not cost-effective."[112]

In addition to the argument that we litigate too much is the argument that we appeal too many cases. For example, between 1972 and 1982, the number of petitions from prisoners to federal courts increased from 4,139 to 17,016, an increase of 300 percent. "The statistics reveal that a monster is loose in the federal courts. Fed by 20,000 to 25,000 new cases each year, its rampant growth will not soon slow down."[113] With a total of 5 million law suits filed annually, representing one in ten adults who decided to "tell it to the Judge," we are a long way from Abraham Lincoln's admonition to "discourage Litigation."[114] Several methods have been suggested for relieving the congestion in our courts.

Chief Justice Burger has suggested that one way to discourage litigation is to fine attorneys who file frivolous lawsuits and motions. According to Burger, a few "well-placed $5,000 or $10,000 penalties will help focus attention" on this problem![115] In June 1983, the Supreme Court did order an appellant to pay $500 in damages to the opposing side. The appellant, a black, had brought a series of civil rights suits against a midwestern state university, alleging discrimination in failing to provide him with adequate housing. All of the suits had been dismissed as frivolous by lower federal courts, and a bare majority of five justices voted to impose the penalty under a new rule of procedure passed by the Supreme Court in 1980.[116]

A second method of reducing court congestion is to **decriminalize** the law. Earlier in this text we discussed including within the criminal law some actions that many people do not consider wrong. It was suggested that too many of the resources of our criminal justice system are consumed by this process and that we should remove from the criminal law activities such as prostitution, gambling, and other actions that might properly be regulated by means other than the criminal court process.

A third way to decrease congestion in our courts is to increase the courts' personnel and facilities. The passage of the Omnibus Judgeship Act of 1978[117] was a step in this direction. The act created 152 new federal court positions, representing an increase of 33 percent in the overall size of the federal judiciary. In 1982, the number of federal circuit courts rose from eleven to twelve. Some reorganization of courts as well as changes in the kinds of cases that certain courts may hear has also eased the problem in some places.[118]

A fourth suggestion for relieving court congestion is better internal management of the court systems. Often no provision is made for temporarily replacing judges. For example all of the judges within a jurisdiction could go on vacation at the same time during the summer, leaving little coverage and slowing up criminal trials during those months.

Provisions should also be made for having one judge whose case load is light at a particular time take over some of the load of another. New York State began a program in 1980 that involved shifting judges for a period of one month. The state reported a cut in court congestion of 39 percent.[119] In 1979 New York City began a program of night jury trials of felony cases. This program was to be in effect for a fourteen-month trial period, during which time it was carefully monitored. In March 1980 it was reported that it was still too early to assess the program but that many of the problems had been noted. The attorneys and jurors were often tired, but on the other hand, the jurors did not have to lose income from missing work. Court-rooms, normally vacant at night, could be used without significant additional costs, speeding up the trials of many cases.[120]

The use of computers to manage the case docket has also reduced the backlog of cases.[121] There is also evidence that when the presiding judge improves management techniques, court congestion is reduced. One judge has declared that of every 100 cases in the courts, "10 or 15 simply cry out for a rescue operation by the judge."[122] Another judge believes that "judges are the prime cause of excessive delay, and they have the authority and means to reduce it." They can control the work pace of the attorneys and court reporters; they can set time limits that will expedite trials; and they can penalize attorneys who do not obey the rules.[123]

ALTERNATIVES
TO COURTS

A final suggestion for solving the problems of overcrowded courts is to devise methods for resolving disputes out of court. Chief Justice Burger, speaking in 1976 at the National Conference on the Causes of Popular Dissatisfaction with the Administration of Justice, called for the creation of new systems to handle minor disputes. It is economically unfeasible to settle many disputes in court, and he suggested that we establish a "tribunal consisting of three representative citizens, or two nonlawyer citizens and one specially trained lawyer or paralegal, and vest in them final unreviewable authority to decide certain kinds of minor claims." Burger emphasized that flexibility and informality should be the chief characteristics of these tribunals.[124]

In mid-1977 the Justice Department began in three cities an experimental program offering the public a speedier way to resolve disputes such as domestic quarrels and landlord-tenant problems without taking them to court. Such cases were clogging the courts which, it was argued, should be reserved for more serious problems.[125] This system would use neighborhood justice centers and the process of **mediation**.

Not satisfied with the progress being made in our utilization of noncourt methods for dispute resolution, Chief Justice Burger again emphasized this theme in his annual state of the judiciary given at the midyear meeting of the American Bar Association in Chicago in January 1982. Entitling his presentation "Isn't There a Better Way?" he reminded the attorneys that it was their function to "serve as healers of human conflicts" and that this should

---

HIGHLIGHT

ALTERNATIVES TO COURT: CHINA TRIES MEDIATION

For centuries, the Chinese legal system has relied heavily on mediation to settle disputes. And in China today, we are told, approximately 80 percent of all disputes are settled through mediation. The country has 830,000 mediation committees, with 47,000,000 members. The members of the committees are elected for three-year terms, with three to eleven members, one or two deputy directors, and one director for each committee. These members attend training sessions in mediation, and they are given guidelines by the People's Court. Civil and criminal disputes are included in the mediation process, with the emphasis on avoiding disputes before they arise. Mediation is voluntary, and the decision is not binding. Said the Chinese, "Mediation helps prevent crime and death and helps people live harmoniously. Mediation committee members come from the people; so they know the area, the people, and the problems, and it is therefore easy to conduct investigations and solve the problems as early as possible."

Source: Notes taken by Sue Titus Reid during a tour of the People's Republic of China in August 1982.

be done at reasonable costs, with as little stress as possible on the litigants and in the quickest way possible. Burger emphasized the need to avoid litigation in many cases, quoting an outstanding earlier jurist, "I must say that, as a litigant, I should dread a lawsuit beyond almost anything else short of sickness and of death . . . There must be a better way."[126]

Some progress has been made in developing alternative methods to resolve disputes. For example, Congress passed the 1980 Dispute Resolution Act,[127] under which $1 million will be appropriated annually for five years to create a Dispute Resolution Center, a clearing house for information on dispute resolution. Experiments at the state and local levels will be funded by another $10 million appropriation.[128]

In 1982 the American Bar Association (ABA) authorized a new long-range plan for its Committee on Alternative Means of Dispute Resolution. The committee will establish two working models of multidoor dispute resolution centers, which may include lawyer referral services, public defenders' offices, small claims courts, arbitration or mediation of disputes, use of governmental agencies to settle disputes, advice centers, and social agencies. The ABA's Committee on Lawyer Referral and Information Service is also working on proposals for dispute resolution for consumers, especially the poor, and the ABA Section on Litigation is working on proposals for handling out-of-court disputes at the corporate level.

SUMMARY AND CONCLUSION

The courts may be considered the crux of the criminal justice system, for it is they that supervise not only the trials of criminals but also the controversial processes of plea bargaining and sentencing. In performing some of these functions, the courts involve not only the legal profession but the general public as well, for it is to the public that we turn for jurors. The public's attitude toward that service and toward the courts, attorneys, and judges is also essential to any attempt to improve the system.

This chapter has tried to put the court system in perspective. The system is suffering from congestion and from unethical, unqualified, and inefficient attorneys and judges, but those types unfortunately exist in all professions. It is necessary to understand and evaluate our adversary system, with its emphasis on constitutional rights and fundamental fairness, as distinct from the improper implementation of that system. We have thus attempted to show why we do what we do in our courts as well as examine the criticisms of that institution.

We began with a brief look at the "crisis" in our courts, characterized by long delays and congested court dockets. We then studied each of the three main actors in the court: the prosecutor, the defense, and the judge.

In regard to the prosecutor, we were concerned mainly with the wide discretion that he or she is allowed. Again, we must distinguish between the abuse and the philosophy of the system. We noted that it is impossible to abolish all discretion; it simply is not possible to try all defendants accused of crimes. In many cases, for a variety of reasons, it is more practical to refuse to prosecute or, at a later stage, to dismiss the case. But it is important that all reasonable efforts be made to control prosecutorial discretion to avoid abuses.

Defense attorneys draw more public ire than prosecutors do, as they are often viewed as trying to "get the criminal off." Again, we considered the purpose of the requirement of counsel in criminal cases—that the state must prove its case beyond a reasonable doubt. Most of us would not be able to defend ourselves against the power of the state, and thus, we are entitled to an attorney to be our advocate at trial. If we cannot afford an attorney, the state will provide one for us.

After examining the separate functions of the prosecution and the defense, we looked at the interaction between these two positions in the process of plea bargaining. Often called *bargained justice,* with the implication that defendants do not get a "fair shake," the system must be understood as necessary unless we wish to try all cases. Again, however, the philosophy of the system must be distinguished from its implementation. There is no question but that prosecutors and defense attorneys and, at times, judges violate the rights of defendants during the plea-bargaining process. On the other hand, many complaints by defendants are unjustified. But clearly the process needs scrutinizing. Courts have attempted to place checks on the system, and we looked at some of the court-imposed requirements.

The next section discussed the judge and jury. Either may be the final fact finder in a criminal trial, and in some cases, either may be involved in the sentencing process, although that is more often a judicial function. We studied the role of the judge, considering what qualities that person should have and what training is necessary.

The jury trial is important to our system, as we have a constitutional right to a trial by an impartial jury of our peers. Whether that right should be continued is, however, a matter of debate. We examined some of the issues in that debate, relying on empirical research to find out what goes on in the jury room. We then looked at the final source of appeal of the lower court decisions, the United States Supreme Court.

Finally, we considered some suggestions for improving our court system. The importance of the court system cannot be overemphasized, for it is in the courts that the final determination is made of how problems will be resolved. Once a person has committed an offense for which the state can punish, even if the police's handling of the situation is above question and society has provided all of the necessary resources for "treatment" in whatever setting that may take place, a positive resolution of the problem may easily be thwarted by the courts. The rights of due process guaranteed by the

Constitution may become a farce in the hands of incompetent lawyers and judges, and with long delays in trials, they can easily become meaningless. It is therefore incumbent upon lawyers, judges, probation officers, and all other functionaries of the courts as well as the society in general that the improvement of courts become the prime target in the war against crime.

Disposition of the convicted offender: the concepts of punishment and sentencing

This chapter begins with a brief overview of the philosophy and origin of punishment and then continues with a discussion of the types and methods of punishment. Historical methods now considered "cruel and unusual," such as corporal punishment, mutilation, branding, and flogging are examined before capital punishment, a traditional method discarded temporarily at various times (most recently for legal reasons) and now back in vogue. We shall consider less severe methods of punishment, such as fines, restitution, and community work service, and then the most frequently used method of punishment today—probation. We shall look at probation historically but focus on the current emphasis on intensive probation supervision (IPS), a method of punishment thought to be more severe than traditional probation but, in many cases, as effective as incarceration, with the added "bonus" of relieving some of the problems of prison overcrowding. The final method of punishment we shall discuss is imprisonment. Finally, we shall examine the process of assessing punishment—sentencing, sentencing models, and sentencing disparity as well as suggestions for controlling that disparity. In addition, we shall consider determinate sentencing laws, the impact of the return to this type of sentencing structure, and the constitutional issues of sentencing.

Sentencing is one of the most important stages in the criminal justice system. For offenders, this stage of the process determines the punishments that will be imposed and, thus, how they will spend the coming months or years. For some, sentencing determines whether they will live or die. For society it is a time of decision that necessitates not only action in particular cases but also recognition of the philosophies that underlie the concept of punishment.

Those underlying philosophies have changed recently from an emphasis on **rehabilitation** to one on **deterrence** and **retribution** or, as some say, "just deserts." In Chapter 3 we traced this change in philosophy, looking at the contributions of the classical thinkers and examining their impact on modern thinkers. That historical background indicates to us the changes and fads in punishment and sentencing. As one expert concluded, "It has become almost fashionable now to refer to cycles of change, to conceive of sentencing practices as coming round in circles."[1]

THE CONCEPT AND PHILOSOPHY OF PUNISHMENT

In Graeme Newman's provocative book on punishment, *The Punishment Response,* he outlines the history of punishment. Punishment preceded society, and even in its most brutal forms, it has always been a part of major civilizations; it is inevitable. Punishment "originated in the natural condition of man in relation to the physical world as well as the social world. Man's juxtaposition in this external world has made punishment a necessary and unavoidable part of life."[2] There are many forms of punishment. For example, the pain inflicted on people by the natural environment is punishment. This chapter will, however, have a more narrow focus: the use of punishment in the criminal law.

THE DEFINITION OF PUNISHMENT

Punishment has been defined legally as "any pain, penalty, suffering, or confinement inflicted upon a person by the authority of the law and the judgment and sentence of a court, for some crime or offense committed by him, or for his omission of a duty enjoined by law."[3] This definition includes the infliction of "pain or other consequences normally considered unpleasant"; (1) "inflicted on a person who has violated a rule of law"; (2) "intentionally administered by human beings other than the offender"; and (3) "imposed and administered by an authority constituted by a legal system against which the offense is commited."[4]

Our concern in this chapter is with the state's use of punishment as a method of controlling individual behavior, to punish offenders and to protect society.

THE FUNCTIONALIST PERSPECTIVE: PUNISHMENT AND SOCIAL ORDER

Émile Durkheim, whose writings support the **functionalist** perspective, argued that punishment can be understood only in terms of the social structure.[5] Specifically, he said that punishment varies with the complexity of society's division of labor. The "collective conscience," which is effective in controlling social behavior in less complex societies, loses its force as the **social organization** becomes more complex. For example, religion, an effective form of social control in simple societies, loses much of its force as societies increase in complexity. It thus becomes necessary for them to develop a more formal method of social control and punishment. Durkheim saw both law and punishment as "functionally related to the changing requirements of collective life."[6]

This "collective life" or "collective conscience" was, in Durkheim's view, the basis of society. He believed that the character of social practices and institutions was shaped by beliefs, thus rejecting the position that social institutions and practices shape beliefs. "Accordingly, he argued that transformation in punishment will reflect changes in the strength and nature of shared beliefs."[7] Finally, such punishment is necessary to preserve the social order. "Interdictions, once made, Durkheim observed, must be enforced. Punishment, the bane of human existence, becomes the natural food for the beautiful monster we have created: society."[8]

After testing Durkheim's theory, one social scientist decided that Durkheim's model was a valuable one for studying punishment:

> In linking the nature of control to the organization of society Durkheim makes explicit what too many investigators ignore—the fact that punishment is deeply rooted in the structure of society. Whether we determine that Durkheim's explanation must be specified or completely disregarded, one thing is clear: the investigation of punishment must be sensitive to the present political and economic dimensions of social life.[9]

THE CONFLICT
PERSPECTIVE:
PUNISHMENT
AS REPRESSION

Durkheim's belief that punishment reflects shared beliefs has been questioned by **conflict** theorists, who take the position that punishment is another attempt by the class in power to coerce and control those not in power. "The punishment of crime is a political act. It represents the use of physical force by the state to control the lives of people the state has defined as criminal."[10] The variation in punishment over time is also seen as a political act by the state, and these political decisions are viewed as reflecting the values of the social class in power. Punishment thus is used primarily to punish the types of crime most frequently committed by the lower classes; thus, prisons are filled with lower-class persons, the poor, and the uneducated, and few attempts are made to punish crimes committed by the upper classes, most notably white-collar crimes.[11]

Like the functionalist or the **consensus** position, the conflict perspective assumes that punishment is imposed to maintain order. The difference, however, is that in the conflict perspective, "order is won, not through the extension of social control, but through the radical reorganization of social life."[12]

This radical reorganization of society can never be achieved, claim the conflict theorists, if we are confronted with criminal justice models that "take as given the existing social order" and that "merely justify further repression within the established order." Such solutions "can only exacerbate the conditions of out existence."[13] Under this system, the state uses its power to enforce "the interests of the dominant class in the capitalist state." Efforts at crime control become "the coercive means of checking threats to the social and economic order." Organizations developed for crime control are then "justified" by attempts to apply advanced methods of science and technology, and any activity that threatens the established order of the ruling class is defined as a crime. The only way this system can survive is for the state to increase its repression. "The legal system has long been a means for establishing order, but in the last few years we have experienced its use as the final weapon in protecting the social order. The capitalist system is being perpetuated by the state's use of legal power, not by instituting changes that are necessary for achieving a just and humane society."[14]

TYPES AND METHODS OF PUNISHMENT

CORPORAL PUNISHMENT

Earlier in this text we discussed the emergence of the classical and neoclassical schools of thought, showing that their proponents were reacting against a harsh and arbitrary legal system in which judges had unlimited power in sentencing, a power that they often applied unfairly. In most European countries in earlier days, punishments were harsh, mainly **corporal**, but perhaps the most horrible physical punishment was quartering. The victim would first be put through preliminary torture, such as the burning of limbs. Then the executioner would attach a rope to each of the accused's four limbs and fasten each rope to a bar to which a horse was harnessed. First, the horses would be made to give short jerks, but as the victim cried out in agony, the horses would be suddenly urged on rapidly in different directions. The punishment might, but did not always, continue until the accused died.[15]

Similar physical tortures took place in England, with many physical punishments inflicted in public. People lined the streets to watch the punishments and the executions; they sang ballads while munching on food and sipping on drinks sold by vendors.[16]

Mutilation and branding

Two forms of corporal punishment used frequently were mutilation and branding. These punishments were inflicted to make it impossible for offenders to repeat their crimes and to deter others from committing those crimes. For example, the hand of a thief would be severed; the tongue would be cut out of a person guilty of heresy or treasonous remarks, the eye of a spy would be gouged out; and the male sex offender would be castrated.[17] Mutilation continued as a punishment in England until the eighteenth century,[18] and still is used in some countries today.

Another form of punishment was to *brand* offenders with a letter indicating the type of crime they had committed. In addition to the pain suffered during the process of branding, it was assumed that the social disgrace would have a deterrent effect and that the letter would alert others to the presence of the criminal. The letter M, for example, was used for murderers, T for thieves, F for fighters and brawlers, and A for adulterers.[19]

Although branding and mutilation are not widely used today, at least not in this country, there have recently been some sentences that called for physical castration. In late 1983, three men convicted of a brutal gang rape that left their eighty-pound victim in need of blood transfusions and five days of hospitalization were given the maximum sentence in South Carolina: thirty years. But the judge said he would suspend the sentence if the offenders would voluntarily agree to be castrated. One of the defense attorneys expressed great shock at the sentence, but the defendants were considering the option in order to avoid long years in prison. Castration has not recently been used as a form of punishment in this country. The option was made available in 1975 to two child molesters, but they could not find a surgeon who would perform the operation. That probably will continue to be the case; doctors will be fearful of law suits, and they may also refuse because of ethical reasons, in that the only purpose of the surgery is punishment and mutilation.[20]

On the other hand, some jurisdictions in this country are beginning to use chemical castration as a form of sentencing. The drug Depo-Provera is used to control the sex drive temporarily while the offender also undergoes psychological therapy. Other drugs are also used to control aggression.

Flogging   One of the most popular forms of corporal punishment has been flogging, or whipping. It has been used by parents, schools, and the military, as well as by public officials for punishing criminals. Flogging has ranged from the mild switch a parent might use to the Russian *knout*. The *knout* consisted of several dried and hardened thongs of rawhide that were interwoven with wire, which were often hooked and sharpened so that they tore the flesh. Severe whipping with the *knout* nearly always caused death.[21]

Whipping as a form of punishment can be found in the Bible: Deuteronomy 25:1–3 prescribes forty stripes of whipping, and the Muslim Koran cites one hundred lashes as punishment for prostitutes. Indeed, whipping is one of the forms of corporal punishment traditionally used in this country. In fact, until recently, several statutes relating to whipping were in effect in the state of Delaware. Against a claim that whipping is cruel and unusual punishment, the statutes were upheld by a Delaware court in 1963, though they were repealed in 1973. The use of whipping as a form of punishment within prisons was declared unconstitutional in 1968 by a federal court.[22]

Even though today many criminologists appear to think of corporal punishment as only a traditional punishment or "as a vestigial practice which survives among primitive societies not yet exposed to modern penal ideas," there is evidence that this is not the case. Corporal punishment "has not been abolished throughout the world; rather, it is institutionalized in some societies and there are strong pressures for its reintroduction in others."[23]

CAPITAL
PUNISHMENT

Another form of punishment used extensively in the past and becoming more popular as a method today is **capital punishment.** On March 31, 1984, a rainy cold day in Tulsa, I got up early to begin writing this section of the text. The morning paper arrived two hours later, with two headlines on the front page emphasizing the increasing importance of capital punishment in this country. One referred to an execution scheduled for the following week in Oklahoma (it was later stayed); the other was "Texas 'Candy Man' Executed by Injection." The latter referred to the 12:30 A.M. execution of Ronald Clark O'Bryan, convicted ten years earlier of poisoning his eight-year old son with cyanide-laced Halloween candy.

O'Bryan was executed by lethal injection just hours after a flurry of court activity that at one point appeared to be heading toward a delay of the execution. The previous day, a federal court judge in Washington, D.C., had ordered confiscation of the drugs to be used in the execution, but his ruling was stayed by a federal appeals court, and the Supreme Court refused to intervene. Attorneys had argued that the drugs had not been approved by the Food and Drug Administration for the purpose for which they were to be used: as an injection to kill a human being.

O'Bryan was the sixteenth man to be executed since 1977. The details of those executions and the four since then are found in the Highlight on page 484.

Data on capital punishment

By the end of 1981, the population on death row in this country was 838— 150 more than at the end of the previous year. That was the highest number on death row since the official beginning of data collection in 1953, but by the spring of 1984, death row had almost 1,300 residents. Almost one-half of all inmates on death row are in three states, Florida, Texas, and Georgia, with Florida having the largest number. Approximately 40 percent of the inmates on death row are black; few are women—13 in January 1984.

Methods of capital punishment

Historically, people have been executed in many ways: by ax, by rope, by drawing and quartering, by boiling, by gas, by electricity, and by firearms. Execution by firing squad is a frequently used method in other countries today. In the United States the most popular methods have been hanging, electrocution, and the gas chamber, with death by firing squad used in the state of Utah. More recently, death by lethal injection has been adopted.

Although Oklahoma was the first state to adopt lethal injection as its form of execution, Texas made history as the first to use this method, on December 6, 1982, when Charlie Brooks, Jr., was executed.

Two-tier cell blocks for death row in a maximum-security institution. Inmates are confined in individual cells and are allowed out only a few hours a week. They eat their meals in their cells.

HIGHLIGHT
EXECUTIONS IN THE UNITED STATES, 1977–JULY 1984

Date of Execution	Name	Age	State	Method	Crime	Final Words	Personal Characteristics
1/17/77	Gary Mark Gilmore	36	Utah	Firing Squad	In 1976 robbed and killed a motel clerk.		Refused to appeal. Twice attempted suicide.
5/25/79	John Spenkelink	30	Florida	Electrocution	In 1973 killed an Ohio parole violator.		
10/22/79	Jesse Bishop	46	Nevada	Gas Chamber	In 1977 killed a man while robbing a Las Vegas casino.		Rejected an appeal.
3/9/81	Stephen T. Judy	24	Indiana	Electrocution	In 1979 raped and killed Terry Chasteen and drowned her three children.		
8/10/82	Frank Coppola	38	Virginia	Electrocution	In 1978 robbed, beat, and killed a Newport News woman.		Former policeman.
12/8/82	Charlie Brooks, Jr.	40	Texas	Injection	In 1976 kidnapped and then killed a Ft. Worth car salesman.		
4/22/83	John Louis Evans, III	33	Alabama	Electocution	In 1977 robbed and murdered a Mobile pawnbroker, Edward Nassar, as his two daughters watched.	"I have no malice toward anyone. I have no hatred toward anyone."	During trial admitted guilt. Said he would do it again.
9/2/83	Jimmy Lee Gray	34	Mississippi	Gas Chamber	In 1976 raped and murdered a three-year-old neighbor girl who lived next door to him. He kidnapped her from her apartment, raped, sodomized, and suffocated her in a muddy ditch. Her body was thrown from a bridge.		On parole after serving seven years of a twenty-year term for killing his sixteen-year-old girlfriend. Former computer whiz. Became a Christian in jail and spent last day conferring with ministers, parents, and brother. As a young person was a loner with a violent temper.
12/1/83	Robert Sullivan	36	Florida	Electrocution	In 1973 robbed and shot the assistant manager of Howard Johnson restaurant.	"I hold malice to none. May God bless us all. To all my peers on death row, despite what is about to happen to me, do not quit." He recited the Sixty-second Psalm in tears and thanked the pope for trying to save his life.	A Catholic who grew up in Massachusetts. Adopted son of a surgeon. On death row longer than any other inmate (1973). Claimed he was in a homosexual bar at time of killing. Two other people claimed he was there.

Date of Execution	Name	Age	State	Method	Crime	Final Words	Personal Characteristics
12/14/83	Robert Wayne Williams	31	Louisiana	Electrocution	In 1979 robbed and shot in the face a sixty-seven-year-old security guard of an A & P. Insisted gun was defective and fired by accident.	"I told the truth about what happened. I would like it to be a remembrance for Louisiana and the whole country that would be a deterrence against capital punishment and show that capital punishment is no good and never has been good. I would like all the people who have fought capital punishment to keep on fighting it not just for me but for everybody.	Had attended church regularly as a youth. In teens got with wrong crowd and got on drugs. In the eleventh grade dropped out of school. Wrote his own eulogy. Black.
12/15/83	John Eldon Smith	53	Georgia	Electrocution	In 1974 killed two newly-weds—his wife's former husband and former husband's wife.	No formal statement "Well, the Lord's going to get another one." "Hey, there ain't no point in pulling so tight."	A former insurance salesman. His attorney said he was led astray by "aggressive and ambitious wife."
1/26/84	Anthony Antone	66	Florida	Electrocution	In 1975 arranged murder of a private detective who was gunned down when he answered the doorbell.	"The only thing is 'Forgive them Father, for in their ignorance they know not what they do.' And that's it."	Claimed to be innocent.
2/29/84	Johnny Taylor, Jr.	30	Louisiana	Electrocution	In 1980 stabbed Vogler. Body was found in trunk of car in shopping center.	"Now, warden, you will see that that letter gets to that family."	He wrote a letter to the Vogler family asking forgiveness.
3/14/84	James Autry	29	Texas	Injection	In 1980 murdered a convenience store clerk, age forty-three and the mother of five. He shot her between the eyes when she insisted he pay for his six-pack of beer.	"No" to a request for any last words. Accepted the forgiveness of a priest whose friend he had also killed. Cried. He said "I love you" to a female pen pal and that he was going to a better place.	Maintained he was innocent. Requested live TV coverage of his execution.

Date of Execution	Name	Age	State	Method	Crime	Final Words	Personal Characteristics
3/16/84	James Hutchins	54	North Carolina	Injection	In 1979 murdered two lawmen who had responded to his daughter's call for help because he was drunkenly beating her in an argument over the amount of alcohol in a party punch.	Refused to give any last words. Received final hug from wife.	
3/31/84	Ronald Clark O'Bryan	39	Texas	Injection	In 1974 murdered his eight-year-old son with cyanide-laced Halloween candy in order to collect $31,000 in life insurance.	"We as human beings do make mistakes and errors. This execution is one of those wrongs. But it doesn't mean the whole system of justice is wrong. Therefore, I forgive all—and I do mean all—those who have been involved in my death.... If in any of my thirty-nine years I have offended anyone, I hope they will forgive me as I forgive them. I also pray and ask God's forgiveness for all of us respectively as human beings. To my loved ones, I extend my undying love. To those close to me, know in your hearts I love you one and all. God bless you all and may God's best blessings be always yours."	A former Deer Park optician.
4/5/84	Arthur Goode, III	30	Florida	Electrocution	In 1976 homosexual sex slaying of a nine-year-old boy. Abducted him from school bus stop. After sex acts, strangled him with a belt.	"I apologize to my parents." On the day before, he bragged about his crimes and said he was still eager to molest little boys.	Had been in psychiatric care in Maryland for molesting children. Had been counseled since age five. In March had vowed that if freed "I would kill as many children as I could get my hands on. Why? Because people are prejudiced against me." In 1977 wrote to the Florida governor, "I rejoice every time I hear of a little boy getting murdered."

Date of Execution	Name	Age	State	Method	Crime	Final Words	Personal Characteristics
4/5/84	Elmo Sonnier	35	Louisiana	Electrocution	In 1977 murdered girl, eighteen, and boy, sixteen, on lover's lane by shooting three bullets into back of the heads of each. He and his brother pretended to be law enforcement officers. Both raped the girl while the boy was handcuffed to a tree. Sonnier's brother Eddie, who received a life sentence for abetting the crime, insisted that he was the one guilty of murder. However, at trial each claimed the other pulled the trigger.	"Mr. Le Blanc, I have no hatred in my heart . . . . I have to ask your forgiveness." He insisted his younger brother was guilty.	
5/10/84	James Adams	47	Florida	Electrocution	In 1973 robbed and beat to death with a poker a millionaire rancher and former sheriff's deputy. The victim was at home.	"To all the men on death row, keep on fighting because it's wrong and immoral. I have no animosity toward anyone. I only have love, that's all." Claimed he was innocent.	One of a sharecropper's fourteen children. Studied in prison so that he could read the Bible. Became a confirmed Christian. Black.
6/20/84	Carl Elson Shriner	30	Florida	Electrocution	In 1976 shot and killed convenience store clerk Judith Ann Carter. Mrs. Carter was the mother of four young children.	"Many of my friends have mentioned to me to look for the light, but I already saw the light when I accepted Christ as Lord many years ago. Only now I get to go stand in it and enjoy it with the Lord."	One of ten children. Was released from a Fla. prison only twenty-three days before the murder after serving five years for robbery. Four different courts left Shriner's death sentence intact on appeal.
7/12/84	Ivon Ray Stanley	28	Georgia	Electrocution	In 1976 robbed, beat and buried alive Clifford Floyd, insurance salesman.		Former sawmill worker. IQ of 81.

Date of Execution	Name	Age	State	Method	Crime	Final Words	Personal Characteristics
7/13/84	David Leroy Washington	34	Florida	Electrocution	In 1976 killed three people in Miami, Fla.	"I would like to say to the families of all of my victims, I'm sorry for all the grief and heartache I have brought to them. If my death brings them any satisfaction, so be it. I'd like to say to all the guys on death row, don't bow to defeat, don't bow to a victory, don't bow to a defeat without a fight."	A philosophy-reading former migrant worker. Admitted to the killings. Said that he would rather die than rot in jail.

Compiled by Jill Titus Pickett.

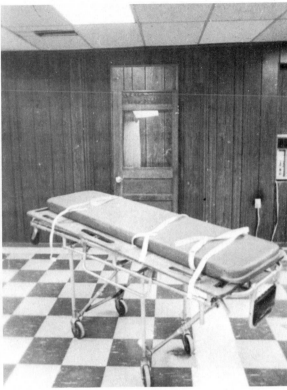

Two popular methods of capital punishment in use today: the electric chair and lethal injection. For the latter, the condemned prisoner is strapped to the table and then rolled to the execution room.

The use of lethal injection, adopted as a more humane method of execution than the others used in this country, has raised some questions. First is the role of medical personnel. The Hippocratic oath contains these words: "I will use treatment to help the sick according to my ability and judgment, but never with a view to injury and wrongdoing. Neither will I administer a poison to anyone when asked to do so nor will I suggest such a course." The prison doctor in the Brooks case indicates that although he would have preferred not to be involved, he has no regrets, despite the bad publicity. "Frankly, I did nothing wrong. I wanted things to go properly."[24]

Another consideration is whether the method really is painless. Some witnesses said Brooks appeared not to be in pain, but a physician disagreed. "It's not like a tetanus shot at the doctor's office. You're inserting a plastic catheter of fairly large dimension inside a vein. If it doesn't go into the vein, it can be excruciating. And in about one in four cases, where there is no decent vein in the hands or arms, it can take hours and be a real bloodbath."[25]

Still another question concerns the use of particular drugs for death by injection, as they have not been tested for this purpose. Consequently, a Washington, D.C., lawyer sued for an injunction to prevent the use of the drugs for lethal injections.

Noting that the government had stopped using certain drugs for killing animals because those drugs had not been tested for that purpose, the attorney retorted: "It seems to me that if the Food and Drug Administration requires that drugs used on dogs and horses be shown to be quick and painless, they ought to do at least as much for drugs used on people."[26]

Finally, it has been argued that execution by lethal injection should be abolished because it is not painful enough: "It's too lenient," said one of the students who demonstrated the night of the Texas execution. "They've got to go out painfully."[27]

Death penalty debate   Debates over the death penalty probably raise more emotions than reason, logic, or evidence does, and the arguments have not changed much over the years. The main arguments center on the issue of deterrence and retribution, discussed in Chapter 3 of this book, but here we shall look at a few other issues in the continuing debate.[28]

First, it has been argued that capital punishment is less expensive than keeping a person in prison for life and, for that reason it should be used for serious crimes. If capital punishment were applied immediately after a person receives sentence, the argument would be accurate. But that is never the case in the United States. The imposition of the death sentence is only the beginning of a long process of appeals,[29] and as a result, capital punishment may actually cost more than life imprisonment. This is because the cost of incarcerating a prisoner on **death row** is also greater than the cost for other prisoners, as there is a need for increased security to ensure that the prisoner does not take his or her own life, is not killed by other prisoners, or is not given a chance to harm others.

Second, it is argued that capital punishment is necessary to secure the safety of guards and inmates. Empirical evidence on the deterrence issue is, as we have already seen, inconclusive.[30] On the other side is the argument that the existence of capital punishment, particularly close to a scheduled execution, enhances the chances of violence within the prison. Death row inmates fear that if one of them is executed by the state, others will follow. They may therefore try to kill the inmate scheduled for execution.

Third, it is argued that the use of capital punishment may hinder the rehabilitative efforts of prison personnel, especially chaplains, who work with those on death row. Further, the living conditions on death row may have a debilitating effect on those awaiting death.

Fourth, it has been argued that because there is always the possibility that an innocent person might be executed, capital punishment should be abolished.

Finally, one of the arguments in favor of retaining the death penalty is that most people support the penalty as a form of punishment. The Supreme Court has recognized public support of punishment as one criterion for deciding whether that punishment is cruel and unusual and therefore unconstitutional. The Court has suggested that if it can be shown that the American people do not favor the death penalty, such evidence might constitute a successful attack on the penalty.[31]

Such evidence is not likely to be produced in the near future, however, with a recent poll revealing that 73 percent of the population support the death penalty for convicted murderers, up from 53 percent in 1972.[32] A recent poll also revealed that two-thirds of the attorneys in the sample believed that death penalties already imposed should be carried out, thus reflecting their "get tough" approach to crime.[33]

It might thus be concluded that none of these reasons is likely to have much impact on the abolition of the death penalty; indeed, it is predicted that the number of executions will increase significantly.

PSYCHOLOGICAL PUNISHMENT AND SOCIAL DISGRACE

Historically, punishments did not always inflict physical pain or death—psychological methods were also used and some of these methods are more effective than corporal or capital punishment. In Scotland, for example, adulterers and fornicators of both sexes were required to stand in front of the church congregation, often held to the wall in iron collars, and questioned by the minister for a half hour every Sunday for a specified number of weeks. The punishment was so feared that some women would commit infanticide and thereby risk capital punishment in preference to suffering the psychological punishment of the social disgrace.[34]

Although we may think of these psychological and social punishments as of historical interest only, a church in a small town near Tulsa, Oklahoma, recently found out otherwise. The elders approached a member and told her that they knew about her affair with the ex-mayor who was not a member of the church. They warned her that unless she ended the affair "and repented" they would have to tell the entire congregation that she had committed the "sin of fornication." The affair ended, but the woman refused to repent. When she was not successful in her pleas with the elders not to tell the congregation, she retained an attorney and sued for the invasion of her privacy and the intentional infliction of emotional distress. She won a $390,000 judgment.

EXILE, BANISHMENT, AND TRANSPORTATION

Among primitive societies, exile or **banishment** from the society is an effective form of punishment. Criminals were often sent to work on galleys as slaves, a practice that continued through the Middle Ages and into the time of Elizabeth I.[35] The conditions under which the criminals worked were deplorable, but fortunately, by the close of the sixteenth century the galley was replaced by vessels that did not need slave labor. This, however, meant that a new method for punishment had to be found, and the solution adopted in many cases was **transportation,** or deportation, to other countries or colonies or islands as a method of controlling crime within the home country. England used this method frequently, and because of an increase in crime at the time the galleys became obsolete, it began transporting criminals to its colonies. Most of the people were sent to the American colonies as indentured servants.

The conditions of transportation were dreadful. The prisoners were chained together and in some cases had only standing room on the ships. Fevers and diseases were rampant, food was meager; sanitary conditions were unbelievable; and homosexuality was extensive. The practice of deportation, like the African slave trade, is one of the most repulsive phases of human history.[36]

The American colonists had tried to stop the deportation of criminals to the United States before the Revolution, but they were told that it was necessary in order to rid England of such evils. It is said that Benjamin Franklin, in response to that argument, suggested that the Americans should send their rattlesnakes to England. By 1821 there were arguments in England that deportation was not an effective treatment, and it was recommended that imprisonment with hard labor be substituted.[37]

Banishment, however, is still used in this country. In 1982 in Florida, a judge told a woman convicted of prostitution that he would suspend her jail sentence if she would leave the state and never return.[38] In 1982 a Houston district judge looked down at the defendant before him and imposed what some natives of that state would consider the ultimate penalty: "Get out of Texas." The defendant could have received twenty years in prison for his conviction of a weapon-possession charge. Said the judge, "Texas is the best place in the world . . . and Judd just doesn't belong here . . . not even in prison." Judd, who had been in Texas only two months, thought that that was a great sentence and did not seem to mind returning to his home state of Michigan. However, the officials who banished him later wanted him back, as he was $840 behind in child support payments, a violation of the terms of his two-year probation sentence that included the banishment. Said the sentencing judge, "The long arm of Texas law kept up with him."[39]

More sophisticated forms of banishment have also been proposed. A distinguished scholar recently reviewed the history of exile, banishment, and transportation and suggested that the United States should consider the use of humane prison colonies now in use in some countries.[40]

FINES, RESTITUTION, AND WORK SERVICE

Two methods of punishment that have been used extensively are the fine paid to the state and restitution paid to the victim. Both of these methods are increasing in popularity and today are often coupled with **community work service.**

The **fine** is a punishment in which the offender is ordered to pay a sum of money to the state in lieu of or in addition to other forms of punishment.

Historically the fine has been frequently used, with those unable to pay the fine being imprisoned as additional punishment. There are, however, some legal problems with this method, highlighted by the 1983 Supreme Court ruling that it is unconstitutional for a state to send a convicted defendant to jail simply because he or she is too poor to pay a fine.[41]

Fines have generally been used in cases involving traffic violations or other nonviolent offenses. Recently, however, with the increasing interest in victim compensation, for both violent and property crimes, some jurisdictions have begun to assess fines to offenders convicted of violent crimes.[42] For violent personal crimes, fines have also been assessed to reimburse the state for its prosecution and incarceration expenses.

Another form of economic punishment is **restitution,** requiring the offender to reimburse the victim financially and/or with service in the community. This form of punishment has had a long history in our country and has, in many instances, received the approval of the Supreme Court.[43] It has also been endorsed by most major crime commissions as well as by the American Law Institute and the American Bar Association, and several states have recently passed legislation providing for restitution. These provisions vary. In some states restitution may be imposed in addition to a fine.[44] In others, restitution may be a condition of probation or conditional discharge but may not be imposed in addition to imprisonment or a fine for a misdemeanor, a less-serious offense.[45] And restitution may be used as a condition of probation or parole or in addition to another type of penalty.[46]

The primary rationale for restitution is to compensate the victim. It is also thought that there is a greater chance of reducing the recidivism of offenders if they participate in some form of restitution, either financial or work services. Through restitution, offenders learn to take responsibility for their own behavior, and it is important to make the offenders accountable to themselves. An appropriate sentence, therefore, will enable them to increase their self-worth as well as compensate their victims and society.[47] Finally, restitution is less expensive than incarceration, an important consideration in light of the already-crowded conditions of our jails and prisons and the increasing expense of building new facilities.

But restitution has raised a number of problems. Although there have been some legal issues in regard to restitution, the main problems are administrative: the victims may overestimate or underestimate losses, and enforcing the payment of restitution may be difficult. Too, it is hard to decide which losses are to be included in the restitution program. For example, there is a controversy over whether to pay the victims for pain and suffering and whether work service should be combined with restitution and, if so, what kind of work service.

PROBATION   The most frequently used method of punishment is **probation,** a sentence imposed by a judge allowing the offender to live in the community under the supervision of a **probation officer.** This type of punishment, like fines and restitution, saves the cost of incarceration, although there is some cost in the administration and supervision of the program.

Historical development of probation Scholars do not agree on the origins of probation, but its use is often traced to English common law.[48] In the United States, probation is traced to John Augustus, the "father of probation," a prosperous shoemaker in Boston. He asked that offenders be given their freedom within the community under his supervision, and Massachusetts responded with a statute in 1878.[49] By 1900 six states had probation statutes; by 1915, thirty-three states had statutes providing for adult probation; and by 1957 all the states had such statutes. And in 1925 a statute authorizing probation in federal courts was passed.

Data on probation As Figure 14.1 indicates, most of the adults in this country who are convicted of crimes are placed on probation, the sentence for 61 percent of the adult offenders in 1982 and one out of every two hundred adults in this country! Only 9 percent were in jail, 19 percent in prison, and 11 percent on

Figure 14.1

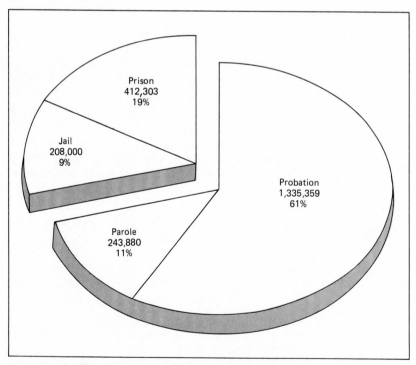

At yearend 1982, 72 percent of adults under correctional supervision were being supervised in the community through probation or parole.

Source: Bureau of Justice Statistics, Probation and Parole 1982 *(Washington, D.C.: Government Printing Office, 1983), p. 2.*

parole. The percentage for probation represented a 9 percent increase over the previous year, with all but three jurisdictions (Illinois, the District of Columbia, and South Carolina) reporting increases in the use of this type of punishment.

Purpose of
probation
In a 1932 case, the U.S. Supreme Court, in considering the revocation of probation, stated that the purpose of probation was to "provide a period of grace in order to aid the rehabilitation of a penitent offender; to take advantage of an opportunity for reformation which actual service of the suspended sentence might make less probable."[50]

Over the years, however, there has been considerable debate and little consensus on whether probation can bring about the **rehabilitation** of offenders. More recently, the concept of intensive probation supervision (IPS) has gained prominence and has focused on another purpose of probation—the **diversion** of defendants from incarceration. For example, in enacting legislation providing for IPS, the Texas legislature specifically stated a goal of diverting at least one thousand persons from incarceration in the Texas Department of Corrections.[51] Diversion is seen as one way to attack the massive problem of overcrowding in our prisons.

Viewing probation as diversion rather than as rehabilitation makes it much easier to determine whether the program has met its "goal." Researchers in Texas have been studying the IPS program since its inception in that state and have tentatively decided that there has been actual diversion.[52]

In addition to diversion, IPS has other objectives. First, in many jurisdictions, probation case loads are so high and probation is considered so ineffective, both in helping the offender and in protecting society, that judges may see no alternative to the incarceration of convicted offenders but IPS.

Second, despite the increased cost of IPS compared with traditional forms of probation, a difference that results from smaller case loads, IPS is still considerably less costly than incarceration. For example, in Texas, regular probation costs about 92¢ a day (of which 58¢ is paid by the state, the rest by the probationer); incarceration costs about $14.57 per day per inmate, and IPS costs about $5.00 per day.

Third, there is some evidence that IPS has eliminated some of the negative public attitude toward probation, as IPS may be viewed as more punitive than traditional probation because of the increased supervision. Finally, there is evidence that IPS is more effective than traditional probation in decreasing recidivism.

Probation
supervision
Authorities have not agreed on important issues in probation, such as whether the size of a probation officer's case load is significantly related to the success or failure of the officer's probationers. But it is clear that we have had trouble with traditional probation. Probation supervision practices and

the conditions of probation vary from jurisdiction to jurisdiction, with little supervision in many cases. For example, in our current nationwide crackdown on driving while intoxicated, many jurisdictions are, in addition to other punishments, placing offenders on probation. But probation often means mailing a card once a month to the probation officer, indicating that the probationer has not violated the terms of probation.

In today's IPS programs, on the other hand, intensive supervision is required. In Georgia, for example, IPS is conducted by "teams." Each team consists of a probation officer and a "surveillance officer" who together have a maximum case load of twenty-five. They see their probationers at least five times a week and may even check on them twice in one evening. The terms of probation are stiff. The probationer is required to get and keep a job, pay both a fine and restitution, fulfill community work service requirements, and meet a 7 P.M. curfew. The only eligible offenders are those who are sentenced to prison; thus, the probationer can look at the terms of probation in light of the alternative—incarceration.[53]

The decision to grant probation

The granting of probation, which may be done only by the court, is technically a form of sentencing. In reality, however, it is usually considered to be a disposition in lieu of sentencing. In some cases the court will sentence a defendant to a term of incarceration but suspend that sentence for a specified period of time during which the offender will be on probation. If the offender does not violate the terms of probation for that period of time, the sentence will never be imposed, but if the offender does violate the probation, he or she will be incarcerated. Because of the close relation of probation to sentencing, which the Supreme Court considers to be a crucial stage in the criminal justice process, the defendant is entitled to due process at the probation hearing. The fundamental idea of due process under the United States Constitution is that a person should not be deprived of life, liberty, or property without reasonable and lawful procedures. This means, among other things, that the judge may not be unreasonable, arbitrary, or capricious in the decision to grant probation. The defendant is entitled to an attorney at this stage, as well as when the probation is revoked and the suspended sentence is imposed.[54]

IMPRISONMENT

Prison as a form of punishment is a relatively recent development. Although we have for a long time confined criminals, for most of the history of civilization, such confinement was not *the* punishment but was a temporary measure—to hold a person awaiting execution, transportation, corporal punishment, or, in some cases, trial.[55]

Today, however, prison is becoming an even more popular method of punishment, with the public supporting longer prison sentences despite our current problems with prison overcrowding.

In historical times, prisoners were often confined in dungeon-type facilities. This grate covers the former entrance to the death row and solitary confinement cells of a maximum security prison.

Today, "stacked" prison cells are common for confinement of inmates.

THE ASSESSMENT OF PUNISHMENT: THE PROCESS OF SENTENCING

SENTENCING MODELS

The three main models of sentencing are legislative, judicial, and administrative, and most systems employ one or more of these types.

In the *legislative model* of sentencing, the **legislature** establishes by statute the length of the **sentence** for each crime. For example, a conviction of burglary carries a sentence of ten years. Under this model no discretion is allowed the judge at the time of sentencing, nor are the prison authorities or parole boards allowed discretion in determining when the inmate will be released. This type of sentence is called the **determinate** or flat-time sentence.

In the *judicial model* of sentencing, the judge decides the length of the sentence within a legislatively established range. For example, the legislature determines that for the crime of burglary the sentence will be from five to ten years, and the judge imposes a sentence within that range. No discretion is given to administrative authorities to reduce that term.

In the *administrative model,* the legislature establishes a wide range of imprisonment for a particular crime, and the judge may or must impose that sentence. For example, the legislature determines that for the crime of armed robbery, the sentence is "one day to life," a sentence that is then imposed by the judge after the defendant is convicted of armed robbery. The decision to release the inmate is later determined by an administrative agency, usually a parole board. The type of sentence imposed in this model is called the **indeterminate sentence.** The idea is that the offender should remain incarcerated only as long as necessary for rehabilitation, but neither a legislature nor a judge can tell in advance how long the sentence should be for a particular individual. Determination to release should therefore be made in individual cases by persons trained to decide when the offender is ready to rejoin society.

There has always been debate over which of the three sentencing models should be used. Today the trend is away from the administrative model and indeterminate sentencing and toward the legislative model and determinate sentences. But even this trend illustrates that most sentencing is actually a combination of the three models. For example, some of the recent legislation permits determinate sentences established by the legislature to be judicially altered if a given case has certain mitigating or aggravating circumstances. This approach has been called **presumptive sentencing.**

Presumptive sentencing assumes that "a finding of guilty of committing a crime would predictably incur a particular sentence unless specific mitigating or aggravating factors are established." It enables the legislature to "retain the power to make those broad policy decisions that can be wisely and justly made about crime and do not involve the particulars of specific crimes and criminals." At the same time, it allows the sentencing judge "some degree of guided discretion to consider and weigh those pertinent factors that cannot be wisely evaluated in the absence of the particular crime and criminal." Finally, the parole board has "some degree of guided discretion to consider and weigh factors that were unavailable at the time of sentencing so that it could tailor its decision regarding release to the needs of the prisoner and society."[56]

Presumptive sentencing differs from flat or determinate sentencing in that it does not remove all judicial discretion. It does, however, check the abuse of that discretion by establishing that a "deviate" sentence will be presumed to be improper. Thus, when the sentence is appealed, the sentencing judge has the burden of proving that there are justifiable reasons for deviating from the recommended sentence.

Finally, various combinations of sentence types are also used. For example, a defendant may be fined and incarcerated, fined and placed on probation, fined and ordered to pay restitution, and so on. There are also combinations of probation and incarceration, including

> *split sentences*—where the court specifies a period of incarceration to be followed by a period of probation
>
> *modification of sentence*—where the original sentencing court may reconsider an offender's prison sentence within a limited time and change it to probation
>
> *shock probation*—where an offender sentenced to incarceration is released after a period of time in confinement (the shock) and resentenced to probation
>
> *intermittent incarceration*—where an offender on probation may spend weekends or nights in jail[57]

Any of the sentencing models or the sentencing combinations may also be affected by other factors. Power may be given to the governor to commute a sentence of life—for example, to a specified term of years. The governor may also have the power to **pardon** an offender (in the case of a federal crime, the president has the pardoning power). It is also possible that sentence length may be reduced in accordance with a **good time** policy. In such cases legislatively or judicially imposed sentences may be reduced because of the inmate's good behavior.

ANALYSIS OF PUNISHMENT ASSESSMENT: SENTENCING DISPARITY

We have seen that (1) it is impossible to abolish all discretion and (2) it is not desirable to try to abolish all discretion. But **discretion** does not, by definition, mean disparity.[58] The existence of discretion in determining sentence length has, however, led to abuses, and criticisms are aimed at parole boards and judges.

Senator Edward M. Kennedy of Massachusetts has labeled judicial sentencing as a "national scandal" and cites situations in which offenders convicted of the same offense are given probation by one judge and a long prison sentence by another.[59]

A study of sentencing undertaken by the Yale Law School also found that sentencing is a national scandal. The authors of that study testified before Congress that "sentencing in the Federal courts is a judicial lottery marked by gross and shocking disparities."[60] A federal judge noted for his analysis of sentencing, concluded: " . . . the almost wholly unchecked and sweeping powers we give to judges in the fashioning of sentences are terrifying and intolerable for a society that professes devotion to the rule of law."[61]

Numerous studies have been conducted on the disparity in judicial sentences. To the extent that race, ethnicity, sex, and socioeconomic status are variables that influence these differences, sentencing disparity is unacceptable. Radical criminologists claim that it is precisely these "extralegal" factors that account for the differences.[62] The basic problem, however, is in isolating the extralegal variables, and until that is done, we cannot really presume that these factors account for the **disparity in sentences.** In addition, most of the studies have serious methodological problems. They usually are not national in scope, and they do not take into account whether counsel was private or court appointed, the defendant's education, the relationship between the defendant and the victim, the defendant's previous record, and his or her potential for rehabilitation. This is not to suggest that differential treatment in the system of criminal justice does not reflect bias and prejudice because of race, age, sex, or socioeconomic status. Rather, the point is to go deeper instead of accepting that conclusion without analyzing the data. It may be that other variables are just as influential, if not more so, than the traditional demographic variables so often associated with differential treatment.

In a review of twenty studies of sentencing, one researcher found that the relationship between sentence imposed and extralegal attributes such as race, age, sex, and socioeconomic status is generally small. He criticized the studies that conclude that the reason for differential sentencing is unjust discrimination, arguing that such a conclusion is often based on a misinterpretation of the results of statistical tests. "While there may be evidence of differential sentencing, knowing of extralegal offender characteristics contributes relatively little (5 percent) to our ability to predict judicial dispositions."[63]

RACE AND SENTENCING

Some earlier researchers who found differential sentencing among blacks and whites convicted of the same offenses concluded that blacks are more likely to get longer sentences and more likely to receive capital punishment. They are also more likely to be executed.[64] Others found that although there was a variation in sentencing by race, "it is a function of intrinsic differences between the races in patterns of criminal behavior. The Negro pattern is a product of the isolative social and historic forces that have molded the larger Negro subculture."[65] Other investigators have detected substantial race differences in sentencing outcomes and decided that the differences originated in the early stages of the sentencing process.[66]

A more recent study of racial discrimination and sentencing determined that blacks were more likely than whites to receive prison terms, more likely to be represented by a public defender rather than a private attorney, more likely to have high bail set, more likely to be detained before trial, and more likely to plea bargain. The investigators noted that these sentencing differentials may be because blacks are less likely to be released pending trial and less likely to have a private attorney. Blacks are also more likely to have a more serious current charge and a more serious past record. But even when controlling for both legal and extralegal factors, there is a statistically significant relationship between race and incarceration. "Black defendants are 20 percent more likely than white defandants to be incarcerated. . . . Black males receive prison sentences more often than white males because they are charged with more serious crimes *and* because they are black." The investigators also found, however, that "while black males *are* more likely than white males to receive prison terms, those who do are, as a group, given lighter sentences than their white counterparts." They interpreted these data as indicating that because whites are more likely to be placed on probation than sentenced to prison, those who are incarcerated are sentenced for longer periods, on the average, than are their black counterparts, because the latter less often receive probation without a prison term.[67] "In short, our findings support, but certainly do not prove, the existence of racial discrimination in sentencing."[68]

Finally, in a study of race and sentencing, two investigators concluded that "the restriction of empirical inquiry to a single dispositional event occurring late in the court process constitutes an inadequate foundation for the evaluation of discrimination in the criminal justice process."[69]

SEX AND SENTENCING

One popular writer contends that women are differentially treated at every stage in the criminal justice system and that this treatment is clearly "sexist"—that is, women are discriminated against merely because of their sex.[70] Others have argued that conversely, the system is more lenient toward women, that it is dominated by men and that they are protective of women.[71] Thus, women receive lighter sentences than men do for the same offenses.[72] That position has, however, been disputed by other researchers who believe that the protective theory is a myth and that in many cases women receive heavier penalties for the same offenses, especially for status offenses. The harsher sentences for women who violate status offenses are seen as a stronger reaction by society to violations of traditional sex-role expectations.[73]

An authority who has written extensively on the subject of women in the criminal justice system reviewed the empirical evidence concerning the differential sentencing of women and determined that although there is preferential treatment, it is insignificant. He feels that "changing sex role definitions and the contemporary women's movement have had little impact on sentencing outcomes of either male or female defendants" and that the differentials by sex have recently been reduced. He concluded that the Supreme Court's decisions, the greater professionalism of court officials, and the bureaucratization of the court have affected discrimination by both sex and race.[74]

It is important, therefore, when analyzing alleged sentencing disparity of women compared with men, to look at the possible influence of legal variables such as offense and prior record, before concluding that sentencing differential is also sentencing disparity. It is also important to look at extralegal variables such as socioeconomic status and race before deciding that sex is the *cause* of sentencing differentials. For example, one study of sentencing of females revealed that the economically disadvantaged woman or the woman with a previous criminal record was more likely to receive a harsh sentence. Lower-income women convicted of forgery received harsher sentences than did higher-income women, but the more important factor was welfare benefits. Indeed, the study revealed that welfare status had a greater impact on sentencing than did either race or income alone. The presence of a previous criminal record also influenced sentence severity. A previous sentence of probation, regardless of the offense, was directly related to harsher sentences for subsequent convictions. The author of this study determined that measurable patterns in sentencing were related to the woman's social position: judicial paternalism and courtroom attitudes toward the role of women in society, the most frequently cited explanations for disparate male and female sentences, do not even have to be considered. Sex per se is not the issue; sentencing patterns can be predicted by using the social indicators of each sex relative to the other.[75]

CONTROL OF SENTENCING DISPARITY

Two approaches are being used to control sentencing disparity. In the first, discretion is left with the judge, but efforts are made to control the discretion. In the second, discretion is removed from the judge and placed with the legislature.

CONTROL OF JUDICIAL SENTENCING DISCRETION

Judges have wide discretion at the sentencing stage, and various methods have been suggested for controlling that discretion. The threat of removal or being pressured to resign is one approach, which has worked in some cases, particularly when citizens have organized "court watches" and publicized controversial sentencing decisions. Recently, however, considerable attention has been given to the establishment of model sentencing guidelines and sentencing councils as means of controlling judicial discretion and sentencing disparity.[76]

Sentencing guidelines are seen as a way to control discretion without abolishing it and while correcting the extreme disparity that can result from individualized sentencing. Suppose that a judge has an offender to sentence. He or she may consider the offender's background, the nature of the offense, or other variables, without any guidelines. When sentencing guidelines are used, the difference is that the relevance of these variables may have been researched. The judge also has a "benchmark" of the reasonable penalty in these circumstances.

There are drawbacks, however, to sentencing guidelines. First, they are just guidelines, and there is nothing (except pressure) to prevent judges from ignoring them. Second, empirical evidence indicates that the presence of such guidelines has not significantly reduced judicial sentencing disparity.[77] Third, there has not been sufficient analysis of the processes in establishing the guidelines.[78] Finally, even if the sentencing guidelines are effective in reducing sentencing disparity among judges, the system has no effect on the prosecutor's virtually unchecked discretion in deciding which charges to file against the defendant, whether to plea bargain, and, if so, how.[79]

If sentencing guidelines are to be effective in accomplishing their goals, it is important that they be developed empirically and based on the accepted philosophy of punishment.[80] Standards for evaluating these guidelines are also essential. Finally, adequate evaluation of the implementation of the guidelines is necessary.[81]

Sentencing councils have also been instituted to control judicial disparity in sentencing. Composed of judges in a specified area, the council meets on a regular basis, and the judges discuss those cases awaiting sentencing. The **presentence report** for each offender is circulated, and each judge recommends a sentence. They then discuss the recommendations, and the judge responsible for that case makes the final sentencing decision. The advantage of the council is that the judges can hear other judges' opinions, which may lead to less sentencing disparity. But the judges are also free to ignore the comments of their colleagues. The assumption, however, is that that will not be the case, and based on a study of sentencing councils in New York and Chicago, there is evidence that sentencing disparity is reduced by about 10 percent as a result of the sentencing councils.[82]

REMOVAL OF
JUDICIAL
SENTENCING
DISCRETION

The second approach to eliminating sentencing disparity is the removal of judicial discretion in sentencing.

The justice model

In Chapter 3, we looked briefly at David Fogel's **justice model** of punishment.[83] Fogel's work has had an important impact on the trend toward determinate sentencing, but unfortunately, the attention to Fogel's approach has centered on his recommendation of determinate sentences and has ignored his other recommendations.

Fogel believes that imprisonment should be viewed only as a "temporary deprivation of liberty. It is the legal cost for the violation of some laws. *The prison is responsible for executing the sentence, not for rehabilitating the convict.*"[84] He argues that the prison's mission must be fairness and justice and that the sentence must be seen by the offender as just, reasonable, and constitutional. The inmate should be deprived only of those freedoms that are incompatible with life in an institution and with the purpose of sentencing. Treatment programs should be voluntary.

The justice model advocates abolishing the traditional types of parole boards and parole agencies and the fortresslike prisons. Such prisons would be replaced by smaller institutions, with a maximum of three hundred persons housed in each, who would be "further divisible into sub-units of 30. The institutions would contain people sentenced to similar terms and release would be determined by a narrow and reviewable system of vested good-time rules."[85]

Finally, in the second edition of his book, Fogel forecast that we would have disastrous results if his plan were implemented piece-meal.

Determinate sentencing   The crux of Fogel's determinate sentencing model is its version of flat-time or determinate sentencing. First, Fogel advises that imprisonment be imposed only as a last alternative, requiring a showing of clear and present danger. Second, Fogel does not recommend sending all felons to prison. Alternatives such as fines, probation, and restitution should be utilized. Third, even "flat" or determinate sentences may be altered. Essentially what

---

EXHIBIT

THE TREND TOWARD MANDATORY SENTENCING

Most States Have Some Mandatory Sentencing Provisions

	Type of Sentencing	*Mandatory Sentencing*	*Mandatory Offenses*
Alabama	Determinate	Yes	Repeat felony
Alaska	Determinate presumptive	Yes	Murder, kidnaping, firearms, repeat felony
Arizona	Determinate presumptive	Yes	Firearms, prior felony convictions
Arkansas	Determinate	Yes	Robbery, deadly weapons
California	Determinate presumptive	No	
Colorado	Determinate presumptive	No	

	Type of Sentencing	Mandatory Sentencing	Mandatory Offenses
Connecticut	Determinate	Yes	Sex assault with firearm, burglary, repeat felony, assault on elderly
Delaware	Determinate	Yes	Murder, kidnaping, prison assault, robbery, narcotics, deadly weapon, habitual criminal, obscenity, others
Florida	Indeterminate	Yes	Drug
Georgia	Determinate	Yes	Armed robbery, burglary, drugs
Hawaii	Indeterminate	No	
Idaho	Determinate	Yes	Firearm, repeat extortion, kidnap or rape with bodily injury
Illinois	Determinate	Yes	Major offenses, specified felonies and offenses, repeaters, weapons
Indiana	Determinate presumptive	Yes	Repeat felony, violent crime, deadly weapons
Iowa	Indeterminate	Yes	Forcible felonies, firearms, habitual offenders, drugs
Kansas	Indeterminate	Yes	Sex offense, firearms
Kentucky	Indeterminate	No	
Louisiana	Indeterminate	Yes	Drugs, violent crime
Maine	Determinate	No	
Maryland	Determinate guidelines	Yes	Repeat violent offenders, handgun
Massachusetts	Indeterminate	Yes	Firearm, auto theft, drug trafficking
Michigan	Indeterminate	Yes	Murder, armed robbery, treason, firearms
Minnesota	Guidelines	No	
Mississippi	Determinate	Yes	Armed robbery, repeat felony
Missouri	Determinate	Yes	Dangerous weapon, repeat felony
Montana	Indeterminate	Yes	Firearms
Nebraska	Indeterminate	No	
Nevada	Determinate	Yes	2nd degree murder, 1st degree kidnaping, sexual assault, firearm repeat felony
New Hampshire	Indeterminate	Yes	Firearms
New Jersey	Determinate presumptive	Yes	Sexual assault, firearms
New Mexico	Determinate presumptive	Yes	Firearms
New York	Indeterminate	Yes	Specified violent and nonviolent felonies
North Carolina	Determinate presumptive	Yes	Armed robbery, 1st degree burglary, repeat felony with firearm
North Dakota	Determinate	Yes	Firearm
Ohio	Indeterminate	Yes	Rape, drug trafficking
Oklahoma	Determinate	Yes	Repeat felony
Oregon	Guidelines, indeterminate	Yes	Drugs
Pennsylvania*	Guidelines, indeterminate	Yes	Selected felonies with firearms, within 7 years of prior convictions, in or near public transportation

	Type of Sentencing	Mandatory Sentencing	Mandatory Offenses
Rhode Island	Indeterminate	No	
South Carolina	Determinate	Yes	Armed robbery, drugs, bomb threat
South Dakota	Indeterminate	No	
Tennessee	Determinate indeterminate	Yes	Specified felonies, firearms, repeat felony
Texas	Determinate	Yes	Repeat felony, violent offenses
Utah	Indeterminate	No	
Vermont	Indeterminate	Yes	Drugs, violent crime
Virginia	Indeterminate	No	
Washington	Indeterminate	Yes	Firearms, rape, repeat felony
West Virginia	Indeterminate	Yes	Firearms in felony
Wisconsin	Indeterminate	No	
Wyoming	Indeterminate	No	

*Pennsylvania updated as of December 1982.

States Primarily Use Three Strategies for Sentencing

- **Indeterminate sentences** usually provide a minimum and a maximum term, either of which may be reduced by "good time" (time credits gained by inmates for good conduct or special achievement) or by a decision of the paroling authorities. The maximum sentence may be set as a range (for example, 5 to 10 years) rather than a specific number of years.
- **Determinate sentences** usually provide a fixed term that may be reduced by good time or parole. Judicial discretion may be available to grant probation or suspend the sentence. Sentencing laws generally provide a maximum (or a range) for sentence duration. Determinate systems are usually based on a definite length for a sentence that can be increased or decreased for aggravating or mitigating factors or on guidelines that define sentence lengths, deviations from which must be justified by sentencing judges.
- **Mandatory prison sentences** are defined by law and must be given upon conviction; the judge is not permitted to grant probation or to suspend the sentence.

Most States Apply a Combination of Sentencing Strategies

Many States may have a predominant orientation toward one strategy (for example, indeterminate) and require another strategy (for example, mandatory sentences) for specific offenses. The strategies utilized by States are constantly evolving, thus complicating overall classification. As of September 1981, for example, some States that required mandatory prison sentences for certain offenses used a predominantly indeterminate strategy while others used a determinate strategy.

Source: Bureau of Justice Statistics, *Report to the Nation on Crime: The Data* (Washington, D.C.: U.S. Government Printing Office, 1983), p. 72.

happens in the Fogel system is that for each type of offense there is a flat-time sentence that may be modified within a specific range, depending on aggravating or mitigating circumstances. After imposition of sentence, however, the sentence can be mitigated *only* by good time credit. Good time credit, Fogel believes, is essential to the system. "With the setting of a flat-time sentence and the abolition of parole, the possibility of this day-for-a-day reduction in the time served is essential to give prisoners a sufficient incentive to behave lawfully while in prison."[87]

Fogel's ideas have been reflected in the recent trend toward mandatory or determinate sentencing.[88] Led by Maine, the first state to return to determinate sentencing, and California, the state that used indeterminate sentencing most extensively, most states now have some form of mandatory sentencing.[89]

Effects of determinate sentencing
Fogel warned about piecemeal implementation of the justice model, but recent studies indicate that his warning was not heeded, at least not in all states. In analyzing the return to determinate sentencing in Illinois, investigators concluded, "In effect, a piecemeal reform was passed which promised to get tough on crime, but whose unanticipated consequences may prove troubling."[90] What might those unanticipated results be? First, there is evidence that criminals will actually serve longer sentences than they served under indeterminate sentencing and that discretion will be even less controlled, as it exists mainly with prosecutors and correctional officials rather than judges.[91]

Second, it is believed that determinate sentencing has and will continue to exacerbate the problems of prison overcrowding, although a study of the situation in California revealed that the increase in prison population there was not the result of the determinate sentencing statute but, rather, the long-term result of harsher sentencing that began in the 1970s before California passed the statute.[92]

Third, it is doubtful whether determinate sentencing will achieve its primary goal of decreasing the crime rate by deterring people from committing crimes. Support for this contention comes from a study that concluded that although obviously those incarcerated for longer periods will not be out on the streets committing crimes, the total effect on the crime rate would be insignificant. "Our analysis indicates that for a one percent reduction in crime, prison populations must increase by three to ten percent, depending on the target population to be sentenced."[93] Nor is it at all clear that sentencing revision will affect the rates of recidivism once the inmates serving those longer terms are released.

Fourth, determinate sentence laws may put pressure on defendants to plead guilty to lesser offenses rather than risk the mandatory sentence of the greater offense. Determinate sentencing established by legislation may also affect the determination of guilt or innocence at trial. Judges and juries might acquit rather than convict in cases in which they are convinced that the defendants are guilty but that the mandatory sentences are too harsh.[94]

A study of the effects of mandatory sentencing in New York and Massachusetts revealed that the "most dramatic effects of the statutory changes" were in the courts. The New York drug law, passed in 1973, provided mandatory and harsh penalties for the sale and possession of illegal drugs.[95] Two years later, Massachusetts legislators, in an effort to reduce the seriousness and also the incidence of street crime, imposed a mandatory penalty for carrying guns.[96] In both states, the penalties for the crimes increased, and the immediate reaction of defendants, according to the study, was to find ways to avoid those penalties. In New York, the result was an increase in the demand for trials, as the statute eliminated plea bargaining in certain felonies. The restriction on plea bargaining was changed in 1976, resulting in a decrease in requests for trials. Another result was a significant increase in motions filed.

In Massachusetts, "defendants facing a year in jail became markedly less cooperative at every step in the process." Some fled rather than face trial. Judicial decisions showed more favor to defendants, with dismissals and verdicts of not guilty increasing. Defendants were more likely to appeal their convictions. In both states, "as the stakes got higher, defendants pursued more dilatory tactics to avoid them."[97]

Finally, those who are critical of judicial discretion often take the position that the disparity created by using that discretion will be eliminated if there are legislatively determined sentences. But this simply is not the case. Aside from the disparity that may result from the displacement of discretion to others in the criminal justice system, disparity will still exist among the states. Two persons convicted of the same offense in different states may receive different sentences because of the differences in state statutes.

Nor will determinate sentencing remove disparity within states. Although that is one of the movement's major goals, "the determinate sentence may not be able to achieve this end due to multiple sources of disparity."[98] Furthermore, determinate sentencing "may seriously undermine our efforts to rehabilitate offenders."[99]

CONSTITUTIONAL ISSUES IN PUNISHMENT AND SENTENCING

The courts have been reluctant to interfere with existing sentencing methods. The courts will, however, hear and decide cases involving *constitutional* issues.

In recent years, the U.S. Supreme Court has taken a closer look at methods of punishment and placed some restrictions on them in regard to its interpretation of the Constitution.

EXHIBIT

AMENDMENT VIII (1791), UNITED STATES CONSTITUTION

. . . nor excessive fines imposed, nor cruel and unusual punishments inflicted.

CRUEL AND UNUSUAL PUNISHMENT

The basis for most of the appeals regarding punishment and sentencing is the Constitution's Eighth Amendment, providing that punishment may not be **cruel and unusual**. The problem, of course, has been the interpretation of that phrase. The U.S. Supreme Court has debated the issue in numerous cases and has declared many forms of punishment as cruel and unusual. For example, in 1879, the Court said that although death by firing squad did not constitute cruel and unusual punishment, death by being burned alive would.[100] On the other hand, death by electrocution is permissible,[101] although it would not be permissible to execute by "burning at the stake, crucifixion, break on the wheel." The Court has said that punishments "are cruel when they involve torture or a lingering death, but the punishment of death is not cruel, within the meaning of that word as used in the Constitution. It implies there is something inhuman and barbarous, something more than the mere extinguishment of life."[102]

The principal issue regarding cruel and unusual punishment has been whether capital punishment itself is cruel and unusual. The Court has ruled that indeed capital punishment is cruel and unusual in some cases, but for

Godfrey v. Georgia

Justice Marshall, joined by Justice Brennan, concurring:

. . . I believe that the death penalty may not constitutionally be imposed even if it were possible to do so in an even-handed manner. . . . The disgraceful distorting effects of racial discrimination and poverty continue to be painfully visible in the imposition of death sentences. . . . The task of eliminating arbitrariness in the infliction of capital punishment is proving to be one which our criminal justice system—and perhaps any criminal justice system—is unable to perform.

I remain hopeful that even if the Court is unwilling to accept the view that the death penalty is so barbaric that it is in all circumstances cruel and unusual punishment forbidden by the Eighth and Fourteenth Amendments, it may eventually conclude that the effort to eliminate arbitrariness in the infliction of that ultimate sanction is so plainly doomed to failure that it—and the death penalty—must be abandoned altogether.

reasons other than the method used. For example, if the punishment is out of proportion to the offense committed or is discriminatory, it is cruel and unusual. Those reasons also apply to other types of punishment. The Court has not, however, been willing to rule that capital punishment itself is cruel and unusual. But not all members of the Court agree, and two of the justices stated their reasons for believing that capital punishment is cruel and unusual, as indicated in the case excerpted on page 509.[103]

Discrimination

Punishments that are not in themselves cruel and unusual may become so if they are imposed unfairly. In the 1972 landmark capital punishment decision, *Furman v. Georgia,*[104] the Court had to decide whether Georgia's capital punishment statute was being arbitrarily and unfairly imposed. According to the Court, the death penalty was "cruel and unusual" because of the arbitrary manner in which it was imposed.

Such arbitrary use of the death penalty would also violate a defendant's right to equal protection under the law. This issue is raised most often in cases involving alleged discrimination against blacks, as compared with whites. Most recently, the issue has been raised in Georgia where a defendant appealed his case on the basis of a study conducted by a University of Iowa law professor who examined nearly 1,000 Georgia cases and 250 variables. This study revealed that the odds of receiving the death penalty were three times greater if the offender had killed a white rather than a black. Similar findings were published by a law professor in California.[105] These findings, however, have not been convincing to the courts.[106]

The issue of sex and discrimination in sentencing has also been raised. A state may not without good reason, have different penalties for women, as compared with men, for the same offense. For example, New Jersey had a statute ruling that female offenders were to be sentenced to an indeterminate sentence for offenses in which male offenders would be given a minimum-maximum term. The result was that women, as a category, could receive longer sentences. The state attempted to justify this difference by arguing that women were better candidates for rehabilitation, which took longer than punishment. But the New Jersey Supreme Court rejected that argument. In analyzing the evidence presented, the court said that the most that it could discern was that there were emotional differences between men and women:

> However, basically, there are no innate differences in capacity for intellectual achievement, self-perception or self-control, or the ability to change attitude and behavior, adjust to social norms and accept responsibility. A female offender must receive the same sentencing treatment a male offender would receive for the same offense.[107]

But if the state can show a good reason for the differences in sentencing, the disparity may be upheld. A federal court in Illinois upheld a state statute that provided for a longer penalty for fathers than for mothers who commit the crime of incest. The court agreed that the state had a "compelling" reason for this differential—the prevention of pregnancy in the case of a female victim of incest. The U.S. Supreme Court refused to hear the case, thus allowing the ruling to stand.[108]

Proportionality   A sentence may also be cruel and unusual and therefore a violation of the Eighth Amendment if it is disproportional in length to the offense for which the defendant was convicted.[109]

Proportionate length generally arises in cases of habitual-offender or **recidivist** statutes, which provide for an increased penalty once a defendant has been convicted of several offenses. The U.S. Supreme Court debated this issue in 1980 in regard to a Texas statute permitting a life sentence to be imposed under the recidivist statute. The case involved a defendant who had previously been convicted in the Texas state courts and sentenced to prison on two separate occasions for two separate felonies. He had been convicted of fraudulently using a credit card to obtain $80 worth of goods or services and, on another occasion, of passing a forged check in the amount of $28.36. Upon conviction of his third felony, obtaining $120.75 by false pretenses, he received a mandatory life sentence. The Supreme Court held that the life sentence was not disproportionate to the offenses and therefore did not constitute cruel and unusual punishment under the Eighth Amendment.[110]

A sentence may also be cruel and unusual and thus unconstitutional if it is disproportional to the type of offense for which the defendant was convicted. The Supreme Court has ruled that capital punishment is disproportionate, for example, to conviction for the crime of rape.[111]

The Court also held unconstitutional the imposition of the death penalty in regard to an accomplice in a felony-murder case, holding that the Eighth Amendment does not permit the imposition of the death penalty on a person who aids and abets a felony during which another person is killed but the defendant does not participate in the killing and does not attempt to kill or intend that a killing will take place or even that lethal force will be used.[112] Finally, the Court has held that states do not have to conduct a study ("proportionality review") of other sentencing decisions before a sentence is imposed.[113]

SUMMARY AND CONCLUSION   The processes of punishment and sentencing present problems in the system of criminal justice. On the one hand, some people believe in the philosophy of individualized treatment, but they encounter insufficient knowledge to implement it successfully, inadequate or insufficient personnel and resources, and, now, attacks by the proponents of the "treatment-does-not-work" philosophy.[114] On the other hand, some believe in "justice" along with the realities of current sentencing disparities. There is no easy answer to the question of how to combine justice and individualization. There must be some discretion, or the system would regress to the mechanical and harsh philosophy of Beccaria, who argued successfully in the eighteenth century that the punishment should fit the crime, a philosophy that made sentencing easy. That system was soon abolished in many countries because it was felt that such justice was cold and cruel and did not take into account mitigating circumstances, which were emphasized by the neoclassical school. In the United States in this century, a philosophy of individualized treatment prevailed, supported by legislatures and recognized by the courts, reaching its most extreme form in the indeterminate sentence. But recently, this philosophy has come under attack. Some states have already returned legislatively to a determinate or presumptive sentencing structure, combined in some cases with the abolition of parole.

This chapter has focused on the problems of the offender's punishment. After an overview of the definition of punishment and its origin, we examined types and methods of punishment, beginning with the harsh types of corporal punishment—including mutilation, branding, and flogging—that we now consider cruel and unusual. More attention was given to capital punishment, as it has once again become widely accepted and more frequently utilized.

We next considered psychological methods and exile, banishment, and transportation, as well as fines, restitution, and community work service. We then turned to the most frequently used method—probation—especially intensive probation supervision (IPS). Lastly we examined the use of prison as punishment.

The assignment of punishment to offenders requires a sentencing decision, either in advance by the legislature or at the time of sentencing by the judge. We looked at sentencing models and sentencing disparity before focusing on methods for controlling sentencing disparity. The use of flat-time, or determinate, sentences is the main approach today, and we studied some of the effects of that approach and the constitutional issues of sentencing.

Throughout this discussion it has become clear that a move toward determinate sentencing does not remove discretion. Indeed, it would be unwise to attempt to do so. The question is where the boundaries of that discretion will lie. The actions of overzealous prosecutors can be checked by judicial sentencing, and judges can take into consideration the circumstances of the crime and of the criminal. And this can be done even if the goal of rehabilitation is abandoned and a philosophy of "just deserts" is adopted. "One need not adopt grandiose rehabilitative goals to think that it should sometimes make a difference whether an armed robbery was committed with a machine gun, a revolver, a baseball bat, a toy gun or a finger-in-the-pocket

... the personal characteristics of offenders may remain as important in a sentencing regime based on desert as in a regime based in part of the goals of rehabilitation and predictive restraint."[115]

It therefore seems reasonable to conclude that the control, not the abolition, of discretion is the issue. The legal profession should recognize and accept the challenge of successful control of judicial and prosecutorial discretion, especially as discretion relates to the sentencing decision. Some of the problems of the criminal justice system, however, cannot be solved by the legal profession alone. Society must take responsibility for offering adequate legal services for all. The whole social structure should be appraised, realizing that the criminal justice system does not exist in isolation from the rest of society. Research must be supported, and the tendency to abandon philosophies, such as treatment, before they have been given a real trial, should be reexamined:

> It is easier to put the offender out of sight than to examine the social structure for cracks. It is easier to punish than to treat. It is easier to abolish the entire system of discretionary sentencing by attacking the abuses than to correct those abuses and provide the resources needed for an adequate implementation of the philosophy of individualized sentencing. It is easier to attack the judges for "leniency" than to examine the need to decriminalize the criminal code or to provide sufficient and trained probation and parole officers or adequate community treatment facilities. It is also easier to lose than to win the war against crime.[116]

PART **V**

Social reaction to crime: corrections

CHAPTER 15

The modern prison

This chapter is the first of three focusing on life in the prison and preparation for release back into the community. Because all important issues relating to prisons are made worse by the extreme overcrowding that exists today, we shall look at its impact on each of the main topics in this chapter. We shall begin with an overview of the problem and then study attempts to cope with it, including double celling and building new facilities. We shall examine prison administration, paying particular attention to the function of guards, the professional treatment staff, and the work supervisors. In the last section we shall consider the impact of overcrowding on inmates, the problem in general, and then the various types of violence exacerbated by overcrowded prisons. Finally, we shall examine the use of civil lawsuits by inmates who are victimized by such violence.

Modern prisons are complex organizations with various groups and sub-cultures, each with a special set of problems. Although most of the media's attention is on the inmates' lawsuits, riots, squalid living conditions, or escapes, the prison administrators and staff who work in the same environment also have problems. All of them are exacerbated by extreme over-crowding of our prisons today.

PRISON POPULATION: THE CRISIS IN NUMBERS

The rapid growth of incarceration, though not accompanied by an equal increase in the construction of **prisons**, has been blamed for the current overcrowding of prison facilities, a problem that exacerbates all other problems in prisons. In Texas, for example, the prison population nearly doubled between 1968 and 1978, even though the housing capacity was expanded by only 30 percent.[1] And since 1978, the number of inmates in the Texas system has continued to grow. The numbers illustrate the problem—12,500 in 1968, 29,892 in 1980,[2] and 36,963 in 1983.[3]

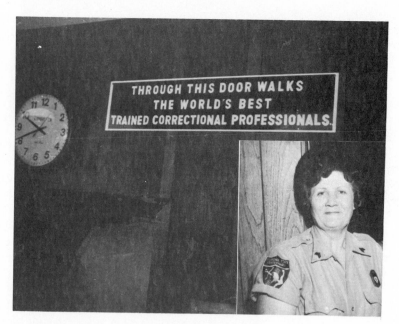

In recent years, the term *guard* has been replaced with *correctional officer,* stressing the more professional approach to the role of the "keepers" of the prison. The recruitment of female correctional officers is also a recent innovation.

Figure 15.1

Number of sentenced state and federal prisoners, yearend 1925–midyear 1983.

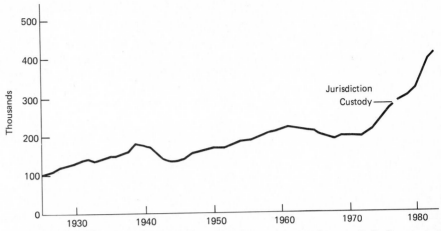

Source: U.S. Department of Justice, Prisoners at Midyear 1983 *(Washington, D.C.: Government Printing Office, October 1983), p. 1.*

Texas is only one example of the burgeoning prison populations in this country. On June 30, 1983, federal and state correctional facilities were incarcerating 431,829 men and women, an increase of 4.2 percent over the previous year. The rapid growth of our prison population in recent years, representing a higher **incarceration** rate than that of all other countries in the world with the exception of the Soviet Union and South Africa,[4] is graphed in Figure 15.1. We currently incarcerate about one out of every 600 Americans.[5]

The increase in the number of prisoners has been attributed to the recent enactment of mandatory and determinate sentencing laws in many states. In addition, many states have adopted stricter parole release guidelines, and some have abolished parole entirely. One other factor contributing to the larger prison population is the emphasis on incarcerating drunk drivers. Finally, in some states, there are more prisoners unable to make bail or post bond for release.[6]

No matter what the reasons for the increase in prison populations, it is a vicious cycle. Crime rates rise, the public cries for more protection, and legislators respond with tougher laws and longer minimum prison sentences. And as prison populations grow, administrative problems multiply, correctional officers feel more pressure, and violence among **inmates** increases.

The overcrowded conditions in prisons have contributed to the dramatic increase in the numbers of inmate lawsuits. These cases challenge prison conditions in all areas of institutional life, and many are based on the administration's inability to provide goods and services to large numbers of inmates. Indeed, although prisoners comprise only about 1.5 percent of our total population, they file 15 percent of the total federal suits.[7] Every region

Figure 15.2

Percentage of prison inmates living in high-density cells or dormitories (less than 60 square feet of floor space per inmate).

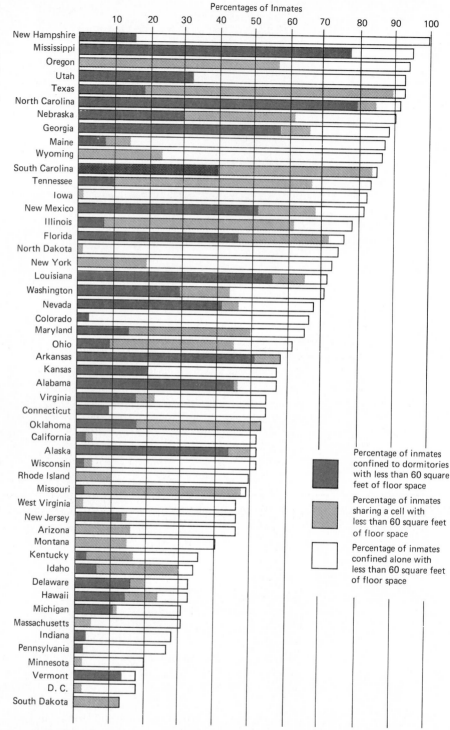

Source: Joan Mullen with Kenneth Carlson and Bradford Smith, American Prisons and Jails, *Vol. I:* Summary Findings and Policy Implications of a National Survey *(Washington, D.C.: U.S. Department of Justice, Government Printing Office, October 1980), p. 161.*

in the United States has been affected by court decisions to eliminate substandard conditions of confinement. Today, most states, territories, and the District of Columbia are under court orders to reduce prison overcrowding or to remedy other confinement conditions.

These court orders have left some administrators in a dilemma. Even though the judicial branch is ordering them to improve conditions and reduce overcrowding, many legislative and executive branches are not providing the necessary funds or support. The result is that prison populations continue to swell, and the problem is no longer limited to a few areas. Figure 15.2 shows the percentages of prison inmates in each state who are living in high-density cells or dormitories. This density of living space overrides all of the problems of prison administration, of which many may be viewed in the context of the Texas prison system, one of the largest in the world.

THE TEXAS PRISON SYSTEM: A CASE ANALYSIS

Texas has the second largest prison system in the nation, and the Texas Department of Corrections (TDC) has also had problems with overcrowding. In 1980, a U.S. district judge detailed the extent of the overcrowding in TDC when he issued his wide-ranging opinion declaring that nearly every aspect of the TDC operation was unconstitutional.[8]

Ruiz v. Estelle

TDC has been, by the admissions of its own officials, severely overcrowded since at least March of 1977. The problem has reached crisis proportions. When Director Estelle testified in August 1979, he reported that approximately 1,000 of the system's 26,000 inmates were sleeping on the floors of TDC institutions. . . . The inmate population continues to increase . . . and the current intolerable situation promises to become even more acute.

The overcrowding at TDC exercises a malignant effect on all aspects of inmate life. Personal living space allotted to inmates is severely restricted. Inmates are in the constant presence of others. . . . Crowded two or three to a cell or in closely packed dormitories, inmates sleep with the knowledge that they may be molested or assaulted by their fellows at any time. Their incremental exposure to disease and infection from other inmates in such narrow confinement cannot be avoided. They must urinate and defecate, unscreened, in the presence of others. Inmates in cells must live and sleep inches away from toilets; many in dormitories face the same situation. There is little respite from these conditions, for the salient fact of existence in TDC prisons is that inmates have wholly inadequate opportunities to escape the overcrowding in their living quarters. . . . Inmates in the cells are provided nothing to sit on, except for the toilet—which has no seat—or bunks. No desk or other flat surface is made available to them for writing purposes. . . . The usable, unobstructed space in the cells amounts to an area approximately seven and one-half feet long and three feet wide, totaling 22.5 square feet. So cramped is such a cell that two standing persons must squeeze by each other to pass, and an average man can stand in the center of the cell and touch both walls with outstretched arms. Barely enough room is present to do bodily exercises, such as push-ups or sit-ups. . . .

When a total of three inmates are confined to a single TDC cell, as is all too often the case, the third must sleep on a mattress in the aisle. These mattresses, and often their occupants, are constantly stepped on by others in the cell attempting to reach the toilet, sink, or door. A third person will usually sleep lengthwise in the aisle, parallel to the bunks, with his head near either the toilet or the barred door. Inmates testified that they were fearful to sleep in the latter location, because they can be injured when the doors are opened. Occasionally, four— and sometimes even five—inmates are assigned to one cell. . . .

The dormitories at TDC units provide even less security and privacy than do the cells. . . .

The population density of inmates confined in dormitories is shocking. At the Central Unit, for example, two rows of double-decker bunks, directly adjacent to each other, run down the middle of the dormitory. The scene was described as resembling one giant bed. . . . Under both of these living arrangements a total deprivation of privacy is insured, since every inmate is in full view of dozens of others at all times. Not even the urinals or toilets are screened or partitioned from the rest of the space. . . .

Furthermore, virtually all inmates are exposed to, and many are victimized by, the concomitants of unguarded, overcrowded cells and dormitories—the ever-present risk of assaults, rapes and other violence—for every day of their incarceration at TDC. In the present state of conditions at TDC, no amount of outside activities assigned to inmates can shield them from these dangerous potentialities for harm.

Even when they are away from the housing areas, inmates are confronted with the inescapable reality that overcrowding is omnipresent within the prison confines.

THE SYSTEM ASPECT

A court order to reduce the prison population is difficult for prison administrators because they do not control the prison population. The number of inmates is determined by the rates of entry and release. Entry into prison is usually controlled at the local level by courts, and release is generally a state function handled by state parole boards or state prison administrators.

The prison population can be affected by changes in several parts of the criminal justice system. For example, changes in the criminal code, such as adding or deleting substantive crimes, will increase or decrease the number of crimes. Social factors may influence the number of crimes reported to the police, as victims may be more likely to report criminal acts if the jurisdiction has legislation for protecting them, providing for restitution and including the victim in the plea-bargaining or sentencing phases of the prosecution.

Improved police methods for investigating and solving crimes may also contribute to higher arrest rates. When more suspects are apprehended and stronger evidence is presented to the district attorney, convictions may rise. Policy changes in prosecutors' offices, especially those concerning initial decisions to prosecute or plea bargain, may also alter prison populations.

Legislative or prosecutorial decisions to use sentencing alternatives such as fines, restitution, or community service will cause variations in commitment rates. A shift to determinate or mandatory prison sentences will also affect the inmate populations.

The court system's work load is also critical: courts attempting to reduce delay between prosecution and adjudication may temporarily increase the number of offenders being sentenced if the backlog is quickly processed. Judges also face the system aspect of prison overcrowding. When the states do not have the funds for alternatives to prison, such as community treatment centers or drug and alcohol rehabilitation programs, the judges must respond to public pressure to "get tough" with criminals, and prison may be the only available answer.[9]

Finally, there is an interdependence between the state and federal correctional systems that is an often-overlooked aspect of reform. It is the combined capacity of both systems that determines how many offenders they can incarcerate. When the state systems have problems, then the federal system often feels the effects, as many federal prisoners are housed in state facilities. On the other side, federal institutions often have to convert long-term facilities into short-term detention units when the local jails are full.[10]

HIGHLIGHT
PRISON IS THE OTHER CRIME

"I used to look at prisons themselves to find out what is wrong with the system, but the problems are much larger. They involve the criminal justice system from top to bottom and society in its entirety. I now see prisons as merely the cesspool, the police as the toilet, and the courts as the plumbing in between."

Source: Richard Lawson, "Prison Is The Other Crime," *Student Lawyer* (April 1982): 18.

SOLUTIONS TO
PRISON
OVERCROWDING

With the various parts of the criminal justice system affecting prison populations, corrections administrators are often at a loss as to how to reduce overcrowded prison populations or how to accommodate extra inmates in existing facilities.

Double celling

Prison administrators often turn to double celling, putting more than one inmate in a single cell, to accommodate the extra prisoners. Nearly 60 percent of federal and state prisoners share their cells with other inmates.[11] The problems associated with double celling and overcrowded conditions are numerous, as the preceding excerpt from *Ruiz v. Estelle,* the Texas prison case, indicated.

***Rhodes v. Chapman*: The Supreme Court on Double Celling.** In *Rhodes v. Chapman,*[12] the U.S. Supreme Court considered issues related to the overcrowding and double celling of inmates. In *Rhodes,* two cellmates at the Southern Ohio Correctional Facility (SOCF), brought a civil rights suit challenging the constitutionality of double celling, alleging that the practice confined cellmates too closely and therefore was a violation of the Eighth Amendment ban against cruel and unusual punishment. The district court and the court of appeals agreed, but the Supreme Court reversed and held that double celling was not unconstitutional. It is important to note, however, that the particular facts of this case were crucial to the decision, and so *Rhodes v. Chapman* should not be interpreted as meaning that double celling is always constitutional.

SOCF is a relatively new facility, with 1,620 cells, several workshops, gymnasiums, schoolrooms, and day rooms, 2 chapels, a hospital ward, a commissary, a barber shop, and a library. SOFC also has a recreation field, a visitation area, and a garden. The cells at SOCF are about 63 square feet large, with a bed (cells with two inmates have a two-tiered bunk bed), a nightstand, a wall-mounted sink, a toilet, a cabinet, a shelf, and a radio. The cells are well heated and ventilated, and many have windows that can be opened. The Court noted that the cells did not have offensive odors and that noise was not a problem.

At the time of the suit, SOCF had approximately fourteen hundred inmates in double cells, and about 75 percent were allowed to spend their waking hours outside the cells. The other 25 percent were under a restrictive classification and spent more time locked in their cells. The Court pointed out that double celling had not put a burden on the availability of space in the day rooms, the visitation facilities, the library, or the schoolrooms. Further, although violence had increased at the prison, the increase was proportional to the increase in population and could not be traced to the double celling.

The Court held, therefore, that the double celling of inmates under the circumstances at SOCF was not **cruel and unusual.** The overcrowded conditions did not lead to deprivation of necessary food, medical care, or sanitation and did not increase violence. Even though the larger prison population meant that inmates had to wait longer before participating in educational programs and that there were fewer job opportunities, "deprivations of this kind simply are not punishments. We would have to wrench the Eighth Amendment from its language and history to hold that delay of these desirable aids to rehabilitation violates the Constitution."

The Court emphasized that the Constitution does not require that conditions in prison be comfortable, although they may not be "cruel and unusual." In determining whether conditions are cruel and unusual, the Court must look to the *totality of circumstances* and determine how they affect the inmates. Following this approach, the Court concluded that double celling at SOCF was not unconstitutional. But one must be cautious when examining the extent of the holding in this case. Should the Court have occasion to consider a facility built before the turn of the century and now having extensive maintenance and repair problems, its conclusion might be different. Similarly, if the Court were looking at the Texas prison system with the documented deficiencies in not only the physical facility but also in problems of health care needs, fire, safety, sewage, sanitation, and staffing standards, the conditions as a whole might be deemed unconstitutional.

Building additional facilities   Some jurisdictions have attacked the problems of prison overcrowding by providing new facilities, either building new prisons or remodeling other facilities. New Jersey for example, recently appropriated $80 million for new prison construction and jail renovations to accommodate the increasing prison population. The New Jersey prison population is projected at 15,000 inmates by 1988, and the current capacity of its prison system is only 7,600.[13] California voters also approved a bond issue for major prison construction of 19,600 beds by 1987, but projections indicate that the new prisons will be double celled and will be "overflowing with convicts as soon as they open."[14]

New prisons, however, are not built without controversy. One argument is that prison cells are so expensive that alternative means of punishment should be created. Building a single cell for a new prisoner can cost from $25,000 to $90,000, not counting the purchase price of the land, and when interest payments on borrowed funds are considered, the final cost is over $200,000 per bed.[15] These figures do, however, vary substantially from state to state. In Tennessee, for example, the estimated cost for a new cell is $25,000, and in New York, the estimates range from $75,000 to $90,000. Adding just four hundred beds to a state prison system can cost as much as $14.5 million.[16]

Typical turn-of-the-century prison; still in use today as a maximum security facility.

The second argument against new prison construction is that we sentence as many criminals as we have room to house. One study reported that building prison space is only a short-term solution. "If prison space is available, it is filled." Although new prisons may reduce acute overcrowding, prison construction is a "bottomless pit."[17] Florida is one example. It has completed one new prison facility on the average of every eight months since 1974, and still its prisons are overcrowded.[18] New prisons fill up, become overcrowded, and society faces the same questions again and again: do we spend more money for new cells, or do we seek alternatives to incarceration?[19]

The final argument against the construction of new prison facilities is the changing nature of our population, which is "getting older" as the birth rate has decreased. Since most offenders are between 18 and 25, we might expect prison populations to decrease as that age group declines.

The expense of building new prisons is more than some jurisdictions can finance, and so they must look for alternative means for providing facilities. Inmates have been housed in trailers, quonset huts, recreation rooms, hallways, classrooms, and storage rooms. New Jersey converted the old Fort Dix stockade into a correctional facility at a cost of $4.6 million.[20] Oklahoma is considering conversion of three state juvenile homes into prisons, and Texas, Arizona, and California have housed inmates in tents to relieve overcrowded conditions.[21] Officials in Washington State leased a surplus federal government prison to house minimum security prisoners.[22] In Arkansas and Alabama, sheriffs of county jails were under agreements to keep state prisoners until inmate populations were reduced in state institutions.[23] And New York has converted military bases, gymnasiums, mess halls, psychiatric facilities, and warehouses into prisons.[24]

Administrative responses to prison crowding

There are also administrative solutions to overcrowded prisons. The state of Georgia turned to probation as a way to reduce the number of offenders sentenced to state prisons, and thus from 1972 to 1981, the number of people on probation doubled. At one point, Georgia announced that 3,000 non-violent offenders would be released during a five-month period in order to reduce overcrowding.[25] In 1980, Michigan passed a law entitled the 1980 Prison Overcrowding Emergency Powers Act,[26] which required the Michigan Department of Corrections to reduce sentences by ninety days when the state prison population reached 12,588 or 95 percent of total capacity. Only inmates who were sentenced under indeterminate sentencing statutes could be released; prisoners serving life sentences or a fixed terms of years were not included in the early parole provisions.[27]

Because corrections officials cannot control the flow of the inmates into the system, court orders to reduce prison populations often leave administrative changes as the only alternative. Most court decisions simply rule that prison populations must be reduced. In Texas, however, a lower court specifically ordered the TDC to reduce overcrowding by using **good time**, **parole**, and **furlough** programs. On appeal, a higher court struck down those orders, saying that they were an unnecessary invasion of the state officials' management responsibility and that the lower court had ordered detailed supervision of programs that did not directly relate to the prison's conditions. The appellate court indicated that the proper course would have been to order the population reduced and to allow state officials to choose the methods. Good time, parole, and furloughs are not the only alternatives, the court said, and Texas officials should be allowed to choose among those programs as well as among **pardons**, use of county institutions, use of minimum security facilities, or changes in sentencing policies in reducing prison populations.[28]

PRISON ADMINISTRATION AND STAFF

Clearly the focus today is on prison overcrowding, and most articles on that subject focus on the effect that overcrowding has on prison facilities, the resulting problems of administration for management, and the problems faced by inmates. A largely ignored group, just as affected by overcrowding as are administrators and inmates, are correctional officers. They have the most extensive contact and perhaps the greatest impact on inmates,[29] but we know very little about them, as they have seldom been the subject of intensive and systematic analyses.[30]

THE FUNCTION OF GUARDS

Traditionally, guards have had two functions: custody and the maintenance of internal order. Earlier studies indicated that guards saw custody and security also as their primary role, with little interest in reforming inmates. Rehabilitation or reformation was "utterly foreign to the average guard."[31] But security has not been a great problem. Few inmates attempt to escape, and only a few who do actually succeed. In reality, then, it is the maintenance of internal order that is the guards' principal function, and this is more difficult today because of prison overcrowding and the increased emphasis on the inmates' rights.

The maintenance of internal order

How do the guards control the inmates' behavior? In the past, physical brutality was used, but that is no longer permissible. Another method, considered by some to be the most effective, is the informal mechanism of the inmate prison community, discussed in detail in the next chapter. The guards permit some of the inmates to have a certain degree of freedom and

Bars on windows and locks on cells indicate the emphasis on security in this Chinese maximum security prison. The windows are designed to permit light to enter the prison, but the inmates cannot see the area beneath the windows.

power over the others and also permit some infractions of the rules. In exchange, these inmates will assist the guards in keeping order within the prison. That is, these inmates will actually control the other inmates' behavior through a rather powerful inmate social system.

Two serious problems arise with the use of informal controls. First, when the guards start "cooperating" with inmates and vice versa, the guards may be corrupted.This corruption can occur in three ways.[32] First, the guards may become corrupted through their friendships with the inmates, as the guards cannot withdraw physically, act through intermediaries, or fall back on their dignity—all methods of controlling friendships with others. If the guards become too friendly with the inmates, they subject themselves to continued pressure from those inmates who can quickly get the upper hand and pressure the guards in a "conflict of loyalties" between the inmates and the administration.

Second, the guards may become corrupted through reciprocity. The guards know that they cannot maintain internal order without the cooperation of at least some of the inmates. But they do not have the usual "rewards" to offer those inmates; thus, the guards may overlook infractions of the rules. The guards also know that a "fund of goodwill" among inmates is important, for in instances of internal disturbance, those guards who have that fund may not be injured by the inmates.

Finally, the guards may lose some of their authority and power in the process of reciprocity, and once that power and authority are lost, they are difficult, if not impossible, to regain.[33]

Administrative attempts to reduce the likelihood of corruption may include frequent rotation of staff, extensive staff training in the proper relationships with inmates, or an information network among the inmates to learn about favors between guards and prisoners. In the prison's essentially closed society, however, there may be no way to eradicate staff corruption, which may extend to treatment personnel as well as correctional officers.

In a study of corruption at Green Haven Prison in New York, investigators uncovered "institutionalized" corruption. The guards allowed prisoners to have drugs, alcohol, and a bookmaking operation. In return, the inmates gave the guards cash, color televisions, watches, and other valuable items. Guards who accompanied inmates on furloughs outside the prison were paid off in cash, sometimes hundreds of dollars, to allow the prisoners to visit with criminal acquaintances, patronize prostitutes, or be unattended. One explanation for the widespread corruption was that Green Haven had the least experienced correctional officers and the most experienced inmates. Another explanation blamed the lax procedures on a familiar pattern:

> The easing of traditional iron-fisted prison management coincides with the entry of prisoners who are young, violent and invested with new legal rights. Prison guards, overwhelmed and resentful, make a cynical deal with the

inmates: to keep the place quiet, they overlook lesser rules, peddle special treatment, ignore traffic in contraband and even participate in it themselves. Before long, the prison slides out of control.[34]

Prison overcrowding increases the opportunities for corruption. Because the correctional officers are less able to control large inmate populations, they may be forced to rely on inmate leaders to "keep the peace." Further, with the expansion of programs and privileges for inmates, there are more rewards that the guards can offer to the prisoners. The guards' time, energy, and attention are scarce resources in the prison environment, but overcrowding increases the demands for them and often leads to circumvention of prison rules.[35]

Prison overcrowding also exacerbates the second problem inherent in the use of informal methods of social control within a prison. Earlier in the book we discussed informal methods of social control outside prison. We noted that these methods were effective mainly in small, closely knit, homogeneous societies. This is also true in prisons. As prisons become overcrowded and populated by offenders with diverse backgrounds, the informal methods of social control lose their effectiveness. At the same time, the federal courts' greater emphasis on the inmates' due process rights complicates formal methods of control. Guards complain that maintaining control today is difficult and, in many cases, dangerous. They are complaining more and more about their working environment and making it impossible for that environment to be ignored.

Working conditions of prison guards

One recent descriptive study of prison guards concluded that although it is impossible to generalize even within one institution, guards have dull jobs—as one said, "We're all doing time, some of us are just doin' it all in eight-hour shifts." There is a high rate of turnover in most institutions; salaries are low; and the minimum qualifications range from a fourth-grade education to a high school diploma and passage of a state civil service test. Some institutions have even lower minimum requirements and virtually no training programs after the guards are hired.[36]

An analysis based on the literature in general and empirical data from the Stateville Prison in Illinois found that the turnover rate of guards was over 100 percent in one institution, with a chronic shortage of applicants for the positions. Among those employed as guards, "absenteeism is staggering, sometimes approaching 40 percent." Guard work is dull, and the guards often work alone.[37] Prison administrators do not stress team work but expect guards to work alone. The guards, therefore, do not depend on other officers for fear of giving prison officials the impression that they lack self-reliance and autonomy. The guards' isolation is reinforced by the prison organization's role expectations: "In short, guards maintain a defensive posture in the social organization of the prison, working neither for the administrators nor for the inmates but for themselves. This condition thus hinders the development of a sense of solidarity or community among guards."[38]

Guards share many of the same fears as inmates do but are afraid to express those fears. Especially in overcrowded institutions, the danger of physical injury or attack is an ever-present threat to the correctional officers. In addition to facing danger daily, they are in a dead-end job and know it. The job has no status in society or even in the prison. The guards are hated by the inmates, and higher prison officials often treat them like inmates. For example, "alleged trafficking in contraband is held to justify periodic shakedowns of the line officers." The treatment personnel often regard the guards with disdain or open contempt and occasionally use them as scapegoats for their own failures.[39]

Guards also have problems outside the prison. One study found that the reaction of family and friends to the choice of prison work was ambivalent. Most thought the job was a dead end, except that it was steady work. Friends often expressed disapproval, and many reported the "fading relationship" syndrome, with fewer and fewer contacts. Many guards responded by moving as far away from the prison as possible, often driving over thirty miles to work. Families also experience stress with correctional work; most reported that the job could not be left at the prison but came home at night. The families feared that anytime the guards did not return home right on time they had been injured or taken hostage at the prison. Many spouses also mentioned the pressure on them to work outside the home in order to supplement the meager pay.[40]

Collective action by guards   Guards have reacted to these working conditions by taking collective action. An increase in strikes and "sick-outs" by guards led to a national study about the impact of unionism by prison employees on the correctional system.[41] This study was the "first comprehensive view of employee unionism in the nation's state prison systems," and it examined the increase in lawsuits and the use of collective bargaining by correctional officers, who argue that such actions are necessary to improve their working conditions and pay. In contrast, administrative officials reply that these actions interfere with the institution's operation and security.[42]

The report noted the rise in prison populations and the court orders that have created changes in prison conditions. It then considered legislative changes that have created problems and conflicts for correctional personnel—for example, the civil rights legislation mandating affirmative action requirements. The employee organizations were dominated by white males, who often resented affirmative action, which heightened the conflict between the administration, which had to implement the affirmative action programs, and the employees, who resist such actions.

In addition to legislative changes, there has been a trend toward establishing one large agency in state government, which typically includes corrections, health, welfare, and social services. Under this organization, the head of corrections does not report directly to the governor but, rather, to the head of the central agency, and so the typical line officer in corrections senses a loss of prestige and authority. Furthermore, for promotion, he or she may have to compete with personnel from other social agencies, and the latter often have more education and training. There has also been a movement toward deinstitutionalization and the use of community-based facilities, which may be a plus for inmates who want to stay near their families and for the community in terms of increased employment opportunities in the facilities, but it must also be viewed in terms of the effect it has had on traditionally rural correctional personnel who see it as a threat to their job security. As a result, their union organizations have grown and have made organized efforts to combat the trend toward community-based corrections.[43]

The report on the study of the guards' collective action also indicated that the 1980s' fiscal crisis in government has affected corrections. Budget problems are even greater than before, bringing with them the inevitable conflicts in decision making. Finally, inmate activism, resulting in an increase in prison riots, prison strikes, and work stoppages and the rise of prisoner's unions and the use of collective bargaining, negotiation, and arbitration have affected correctional personnel.[44]

All of these factors have contributed to the rise of correctional employee unionism, including strikes, lobbying, publicity, lawsuits, and job actions. The report concluded that court decisions have made prisons more humane, but they have also "intensified many of the problems in the nation's jails and prisons. They have stirred up resentment between inmates and correctional employees, and have contributed to the alienation of correctional employees from correctional management."[45] One effect of the labor relations process that has resulted from increased action by guards is that "the state correctional administrator's ability to carry out his traditional administrative responsibilities is being diminished and diffused."[46]

Conflict for guards: the transition to "correctional officers"

Guards have faced increasing role conflicts as a result of the introduction of treatment, educational, and work programs into the prison. They have had to deal not only with inmates but also with professional treatment staff and work supervisors in ways they often find contradictory to their major functions of keeping order and security. Before the introduction of professional services and the emphasis on inmate's legal rights, guards saw themselves as actual guards who controlled the inmates and could enforce the prison's rules for regulating the inmates' daily lives. After the reforms, guards became "correctional officers," and although they were still in charge of security, their jobs took on other functions. The guards were to aid in rehabilitation but were never told how this was to be accomplished.[47]

Most guards remained committed to the goal of security during the reforms, but they found it increasingly difficult to maintain. One problem concerned differing views of the correctional officer's proper role. The older guards tended to follow the security role, and the younger guards tended to believe that some rehabilitation programs would be beneficial.

Studies of prison guard beliefs regarding the rehabilitation of inmates have differing findings. Two studies have shown that guards with longer tenure and higher rankings do not have positive attitudes toward the inmates' treatment-rehabilitation potential,[48] whereas another study found that the rehabilitation perspective increased with age.[49] Another study indicated that even officers who believed it was part of their role to rehabilitate inmates thought this could be done through coercion, such as verbal abuse, intimidation, or other custodial, punitive measures.[50]

Either the rejection of the treatment philosophy or the belief that it can be accomplished through coercion, verbal abuse, and so on, creates problems between correctional officers and the treatment professionals and between correctional officers and inmates.[51] Several suggestions have been made with respect to the elimination or at least the minimization of the stress that officers experience from these conflicting roles. First, of course, is formal training.

Formal training   After analyzing the limited research on prison guards, one writer concluded that guards are "for the most part ordinary human beings with ordinary human failings and virtues. They have in the past been asked to perform impossible tasks without being properly trained to perform even possible ones." No formal training programs for guards were organized until the 1930s, and even today, many guards begin their jobs with no formal training.[52]

It has been suggested, therefore, that one way to establish better relationships between correctional officers and inmates, administration, and treatment personnel is to improve their formal training. The correctional officers spend more time with the inmates than most other prison staff, and so they should be trained in the behavioral sciences. They should be able to understand and assist prisoners with their problems. Correctional officers must draw a tenuous line between maintaining security, at times with very dangerous persons, and trying to establish a rehabilitative atmosphere. And the latter requires skill in human relations.

At the federal penitentiary in Atlanta, an experimental training program for correctional officers attempted to measure whether they could learn to express more respect, empathy, and genuine feeling for the inmates and also to change their own psychological attitudes toward authority and toward themselves. There was some indication that through training, correctional officers could develop the skills needed for more effective interpersonal relationships.[53]

One study evaluated the ability of correctional officers to fill the role of "behavior technician," a person who

1. grasps the basic principles of the social learning approach to the understanding and remediation of human problems;
2. recognizes the role of objectivity, consistency, and reliability in the day-to-day operation of a behavior modification program; and
3. demonstrates the ability to integrate the theoretical orientation and requisite skills by conducting, under the supervision of a qualified professional, an actual behavior change project.[54]

Forty officers at the Draper Correctional Center in Elmore, Alabama, participated in this training. The results indicated that the trained officers increased the number of contacts with inmates and, in addition, increased their use of positive reinforcement. The inmates also rated the trained officers higher, saying, for example, they had become less punitive, improved in their overall ability to work with and supervise inmates, and become more fair. The overall results showed that trained officers could comprehend and use principles of behavior modification. And the officers themselves agreed that the training had benefited their work with prisoners.[55]

Job enlargement   A second way to minimize role conflict of correctional officers is job enlargement. Job enlargement, combining custodial, maintenance, and treatment functions, means allowing correctional officers to set their own pace and take responsibility for the quality of their work, remedying their own mistakes, and generally choosing their own method of working. Reactions to job enlargement have been favorable in the corrections field. Officers report that they like being able to use their skills, the variety, the autonomy, the greater responsibility, and the better feedback. In fact, job enlargement reduced sick days and turnover,[56] two clear signs of tension and role conflict.

Informal helping   Even without formal training in treatment, correctional officers can, if they
networks   are interested, find ways to assist inmates who want treatment. This is known as informal helping networks or grass-roots intervention and is another way to minimize role conflicts, especially those between correctional officers and the professional treatment staff.

Familiarity with inmates and the prison culture puts correctional officers in a unique position to develop intervention strategies for particular individuals and circumstances. Officers may exercise their discretion in removing an inmate from a difficult situation, or they may be the first to recognize a situation difficult for particular inmates and then use their discretion to remove them from that situation.[57] They may also send written reports to the treatment personnel, emphasizing the needs of particular inmates who have requested treatment. If properly done, such intervention may result in a more understanding relationship between the correctional officer and the treatment personnel.

Treatment staff also learn to turn to correctional officers for assistance in pinpointing crisis-prone inmates and for an informal follow-up from correctional officers who are more familiar with the prison system. Once this team approach is working, correctional staff rely on treatment staff to intervene. "Their shared goal, as they see it, is to provide assistance to inmates with adjustment problems."[58]

Human service work

A final method for minimizing role conflict between correctional officers and treatment personnel and between the staff and inmates is human service work. Human service work has three components. First is the provision of goods and services to inmates, depending on their individual needs, which is very much like the informal helping networks. The focus is on individual inmates and current conditions and sometimes involves staff working outside their formal assignments. It includes providing goods, clothing, clean and safe environments, and peace and quiet. When prison distribution services are orderly, inmates receive their daily requirements as well as structure and organizational stability. The staff must recognize the importance of carrying out promises to inmates and developing the inmates' trust. This in turn reduces the inmates' stress and helps control violence.[59]

The second component of human service work is the correctional officer's acting as a referral agent and advocate, including dealing with the prison bureaucracy, such as making appointments with counselors and checking on commissary accounts or delayed mail. The role here is intermediary—a connection between the inmate and the institution. Inmates receive support from staff and know that they have somewhere to turn for help. And when small institutional problems are resolved, the inmates' stress is reduced.

The third component of human service work is aiding inmates with institutional adjustments. The inmates need feedback in areas relating to personal, mental, or physical problems. Although the staff's job here is to offer "caring" to the inmates, the key is confidentiality. Inmates should not be told about the emotional or personal problems of other inmates.[60] The main benefit for correctional officers is the sense of personal satisfaction for meaningful contributions, validation of their authority and ability to get things done, and good feedback for helping. Human service work offers a challenge to officers who are bored with the custodial role. The most important result, however, is a lessening of tension and stress in the institution and an amelioration of the conditions that lead to violent behavior. Not only are the inmates better protected under this approach, but the correctional officers also have less to fear and less dangerous jobs.[61]

But no amount of success in reducing the correctional officers' role conflict by increasing their interest in and ability to handle the inmates' treatment and related problems will substitute for a professional treatment staff.

PROFESSIONAL TREATMENT STAFF

The professional staff includes persons working in education, administration, medicine, psychology, recreation, and social services. They generally do not have responsibility for daily inmate supervision.

There is a basic difference between the goals of correctional officers and those of the professional treatment staff. Correctional officers are concerned with the control of inmates and work best in closed social environments that conform to the rules. Treatment programs, on the other hand, function best in a permissive social climate that allows inmates to make personal decisions and assume responsibility. Treatment personnel and correctional officers may develop "a heightened sense of turf and relate to one another with either open competitiveness or sullen apathy and indifference." In most prisons, correctional officers and treatment personnel are discouraged from attempting to work together. Correctional officers are told to maintain security and confine their inmate assistance activities to referring prisoners to the proper treatment staff. Treatment personnel are told to help the inmates without interfering in prison security.[62]

Prison security measures are the greatest problem for professional staff. All professional staff are told not to do "anything or ask their inmate clients to do anything that would contradict, weaken, or prejudice the security measures that the security authorities have instituted." This admonition may cause interference on both sides: the correctional officers may have to accommodate counseling sessions and the movement of inmates around the prison and the professional staff may be interrupted by lock downs, other security measures, or inmates' work schedules.[63]

Professionals have other problems in a prison setting. Inmates often have to make drastic changes just to be able to cope with institutional life. There is an emphasis on conformity for conformity's sake, and on the notion that "doing time" or just getting by without creating any waves is the only way to survive in prison. Despite this, professional counselors must promote the development of social skills and behavioral changes that will help the inmates upon their release. Whereas the professionals are concerned with helping inmates develop positive responses to themselves and their environment, the correctional staff are supposed to concentrate on the maintenance of rules and of those same positive responses. There is the possibility here for close cooperation between the professional staff and the correctional staff, but traditional institutional barriers to a team approach would have to be broken down first.

One of the main obstacles to cooperation is the different way in which professional personnel and correctional officers perceive education, treatment, and work activities in prison. The correctional staff see these programs as rewards for good inmate behavior, which may be denied for non-conforming behavior. The professional staff, on the other hand, view these programs as vehicles to develop positive responses in inmates and encourage maximum participation, regardless of the institutional behavior record.

Another source of tension concerns the type of interaction with inmates. The professional staff try to establish informal working relationships with the inmates. Because overcrowded institutions mean that not all inmates can be served by formal programs, professional staffers often mingle informally in order to contact as many inmates as possible. They also must concentrate on positive encounters with inmates. The correctional officers, on the other hand, are admonished to maintain distant, formal relations with the inmates; fraternizing and friendliness are not encouraged.[64]

In addition to the conflict between professional personnel and correctional officers, they also have conflicts within their own roles, between the medical model and the service model of delivering programs to inmates. The medical or clinical model assumes that counselors are highly qualified, have extensive training, and should not be associated with the prison's administration. The counselors in this model would not have anything to do with the prisoners' daily lives; they would meet with the inmates only at approved times and places for counseling sessions.

The service model recognizes that the inmates live in a complex environment in prison; the counselors in this system would be involved with the inmates' daily lives. They would assist them with bureaucratic red tape, mix-ups, and minor complaints about everyday prison administration. Their function would be that of troubleshooter, someone who defuses frustrating situations before the inmates resort to violence.

The medical model and the service model might be combined, but in order for that combination to be successful, the professional personnel would have to have a good working relationship with the correctional officers, who may resent any interference by treatment personnel in the inmates' daily lives. If the parameters of the medical and service models were clearly explained to the correctional staff, the probability of conflict would be reduced.[65]

WORK
SUPERVISORS

Despite the treatment personnel's full-time involvement in the inmates' treatment, studies have shown that inmates react more positively to work supervisors than to any other prison staff. Inmates who said they had reformed while in prison often cited the work supervisor as the major influence in their rehabilitation. The traits emphasized by the prisoners were friendliness and fairness, not permissiveness or leniency. The inmates said that the work supervisors who influenced them the most were those who indicated a real and sincere interest in their rehabilitation. This interest was generally seen by the inmates in postrelease gestures that were not required, for example, a work supervisor writing to a former inmate. One study concluded:

> The prison employee who has the greatest reformative influence on an offender is the one who is able to demonstrate sincere and sustained concern for and confidence in the offender's rehabilitation. The prison employee's concern is most effectively manifested by gestures of interest and acts of assistance for the offender which exceed the minimal requirements of the employee's job in the prison.[66]

This positive relationship with inmates is achieved by most work supervisors while encountering very difficult problems. Traditionally, work supervisors have had few incentives to offer the inmates to work. The inmates may be given good time credits for work, resulting in a reduction in time spent in custody, but for the most part, they have dull, routine work with low pay. In addition, the good inmate workers may be socially ostracized by their peers. Finally, work supervisors must shoulder "the burdens of security and internal order which make the simplest job cumbersome through the need for surveillance and control."[67]

PRISON'S IMPACT ON THE INMATES

In recent years, prison overcrowding has created an environment in which inmates are subjected to additional forms of punishment, punishment by other inmates that leads to serious injury or even death. Inmate violence is not new, but this problem, like all other problems in prison, is made worse by extreme overcrowding.

THE GENERAL EFFECT OF OVERCROWDING

Researchers have studied the negative effects of overcrowding in general,[68] but only recently have they paid much attention to the effects of overcrowding in prisons. The general effects of overcrowding only magnify the negative aspects of prison life. Crowded prisons have more violence, deaths, and uncontrolled homosexual assaults, as well as more medical complaints, both physical and mental.[69]

Studies have shown that males undergo great stress when their environment denies adequate personal space and privacy. One response to this stress is hostility and aggressiveness toward other inmates. Because the prison social system rewards those who dominate other prisoners with more resources and freedom of movement, overcrowded prisons encourage aggressiveness. At the least, an inmate will gain status in the system. The administration may encourage violence also by segregating violent prisoners in single cells. Inmates who engage in violent acts thus may be attempting to manipulate their environment; removal from the inmate population by going into segregation is a popular way of coping with overcrowded conditions.[70]

Crowded conditions lead to more contact among inmates; one study found that inmates were more assertive and aggressive, displayed force more often, were more quick-tempered, and were more bothered by minor incidents. "Inmates reported having been witness to, as well as participants in, fights over a cup of coffee, a piece of leftover food, or simply where one happened to be standing." One inmate who did not receive his medication on time stabbed another prisoner several times with a pencil. These kinds of reactions to overcrowded conditions are common in prisons.[71]

Researchers are careful to point out that hostile responses to crowded conditions cannot be attributed solely to the prison environment but that the extreme and intense nature of the reactions is due to the crowding. In *Ruiz v. Estelle,* the court analyzed the effect of the overcrowded conditions in the Texas Department of Corrections.[72]

Ruiz v. Estelle

The present extreme levels of overcrowding at TDC are harmful to inmates in a variety of ways, and the resultant injuries are legion.

The constant threat to the inmates' personal safety posed by overcrowded living conditions in both the multiply-inhabited cells and the packed dormitories presents the most obvious harm. Penologists who testified at trial were virtually unanimous in their condemnation of double and triple celling. Director Estelle himself noted the exigent problems associated with double celling, making reference to the increased opportunity for predatory activities and the enhanced difficulties respecting supervision and control. TDC inmates are routinely subjected to brutality, extortion, and rape at the hands of their cellmates. Some of the most heinous examples have occurred in triple-celling situations, where two-on-one confrontations practically guarantee the capitulation of the abused third cellmate. However, the problems of violence also occur all too frequently in double-celling situations, where one inmate often dominates the other. The evidence made it clear that, even if inmates were doubled up in cells large enough to accommodate two persons, the effects of violence and the climate of fear would remain. . . .

Inmates who live in dormitories are exposed to the same threats of violence endemic to the cells. In several ways, the risks dormitory residents encounter may be greater than those faced by inmates confined in cells. Potentially assaultive inmates are present in great numbers in every dormitory, and since the dormitories are practically unsupervised, violent inmates have free access to their fellows. The record indicates that these risks frequently turn into the repulsive actualities of sex malpractices, barbarous cruelties, and extortions, all of which have been shown to be commonplace in the dormitories. Indeed, some of the correctional experts who testified are of the opinion that abusive violence is inherent and largely uncontrollable in the prison dormitory.

An extensive study of the effects of crowding concluded that "there is a progressive and measurable increase in negative effects with an increase in housing density."[73] Higher illness rates, perceived crowding scores, nonviolent disciplinary infractions, and negative mood states all are more common in double cells, as compared with single cells. Dormitories have the greatest negative effect on inmates, although space itself is not the issue with overcrowded prisons. Instead, the real issue is social density, or the number of occupants in each living unit. Larger dormitories, open and without cubicles or dividers, do not help reduce the negative effects of overcrowding. As one corrections official noted,

> I'm convinced that it's true that the closeness of another human being and the inability to get away and just sit by yourself for a little bit has a lot to do with the way people react. It's like those classic studies about rats—10 in a cage and they're fine; 20 and they're at each other's throats.[74]

In addition to increased violence, overcrowded prisons may induce stress in both inmates and staff and lead to physical and mental problems. Expert witnesses who testified in the Texas Department of Corrections suit stated that the overcrowding in that system caused more physical problems among inmates. Disease spread more quickly, and living conditions were less clean. Some of the additional physical complaints were attributed to more mental health problems among crowded inmates.

In the Texas trial, expert witnesses noted that stress, tension, anxiety, hostility, and depression rose as the prison population rose. As a result of the hostility and depression, experts found higher blood pressures, more aggressive behaviors, greater numbers of disciplinary offenses, and more psychiatric commitments and suicides among inmates.[75]

Another court case produced expert testimony indicating an escalation in homosexual activity, noise, and tension among cellmates when contraband was found in a cell inhabited by more than one prisoner. Friction can also be caused by differences in smoking habits, sleeping habits, or religious practices among cellmates. Furthermore, "overcrowding promotes stealing, tension, fights and animosities among the inmates and these in turn lead to loss of good time and longer stays in prison and substantially lessen the likelihood of any corrective effect in incarceration."[76]

Another contributor to stress in prison is boredom. Most inmates do not work or have access to prison programs. When facilities are overcrowded, the transportation of inmates to and from program sites becomes difficult, and many administrators merely assign inmates more time in their cells rather than cope with moving large numbers around the prison. The prison's educational, recreational, and vocational programs also have long waiting lists. Administrators do not have funds to run enough programs to keep all inmates busy, nor can they hire enough staff to manage large numbers of active inmates. Instead, inmates are expected to spend time in their cells or do menial maintenance work. A high percentage of inmates in United States prisons, both state and federal, are confined to their cells for more than ten hours per day.

Boredom contributes to all prison problems, but inmates react in individual ways. Some feel they must be active constantly in order to survive the prison experience. Their activities may include watching television or listening to the radio or stereo, obtaining and using drugs, making alcoholic beverages, lifting weights or other physical activities, cleaning the cell, scheming, or daydreaming. Inmates may also spend long hours in the prison library researching and writing for court cases. Prisoners in Lakeland, Florida, found a new use for their spare time and dug a 105-foot escape tunnel complete with lights, fans, and support beams underneath the Polk County Correctional Institution. The tunnel was 10 feet below ground, approximately 3 feet high by 2 feet wide, and had a well-camouflaged trap door.[77]

Activities such as these may offer a release for pent-up feelings and a distraction from unpleasant situations, thoughts, or memories. For others, the tedium of prison life causes stress, depression and the feeling that there is nothing to look forward to in the future.[78]

PRISON VIOLENCE   Some people learn to handle stress without acting out their frustrations and feelings in destructive ways, but others are unable to cope and may become violent. In prison, the violent reaction is common, and in many cases, it may lead to physical injury or death.

PRISON RIOTS   After the prison riot at Attica, New York, in 1971, the causes and problems leading to prison riots were studied. Attica had been devastating to both the physical facility, with nearly $2 million in damage, and the people, with forty-three deaths and more than eighty injured persons. Ten years later, the problems associated with prison riots again surfaced when inmates in Santa Fe, New Mexico, went on a rampage, causing $20 million in damage, killing thirty-three inmates and wounding at least ninety persons.[79]

Characteristics of riots   Most prison riots have occurred within the past twenty-five years; only one riot occurred between 1884 and 1888, and only five in that entire century. In addition to being a relatively recent phenomenon, riots usually come in a series. One period was from 1912 through 1915, another from 1927 to 1931, and another from 1939 to 1940. The Jackson, Michigan, riot of 1952 was followed by more than twenty-five riots during 1953. The 1955 riot in Walla Walla, Washington, was followed by a long series of riots, as was the Attica riot in September 1971.[80]

Even in maximum security prisons, prison escape is always a threat.

Most of the earlier riots were isolated incidences, unrelated to influences outside the institution. Most of them fell into the category of *brutal,* as opposed to *collective,* riots. In the earlier, brutal type of riots, prisoners were usually complaining about prison conditions: poor, insufficient, or contaminated food; inadequate, unsanitary, or dirty housing; brutality by prison officials; or some combination of the above.[81] The inmates would complain; the officials would become defensive and resort to disciplinary measures; and the prisoners would complain again and violate internal prison rules, assault others or themselves, and occasionally riot. Most of these earlier riots occurred in essentially unstable institutions. Although order and calm were maintained on the surface, small changes in administrative routines, privileges, or punishments would upset the fragile balance between inmate leaders and inmate followers. Riots in response to these changes were spontaneous and unpredictable and relieved the monotonous calm.[82] Another feature of these riots was the problem of mass escapes. Riots before the twentieth century usually included attempts to escape from the harsh and brutal conditions of prison life.[83]

The second type of riot, the collective riot, first occurred in 1952 and differs sociologically and psychologically from the brutal type. In the 1960s, along with the civil rights protests and student demonstrations on campuses, prisoners' rights groups began to multiply. Criminals were viewed as normal persons except for their backgrounds of excessive discrimination and reduced opportunities. Thus, these groups focused on equalizing the legal rights and social circumstances of the prisoner and the free person.[84]

Riots during this time took a dramatic shift. Although prisoners still demanded improvements in medical care, food services, recreational opportunities, disciplinary proceedings, and educational programs, they also questioned the legitimacy of their incarceration and claimed that they were political victims of an unjust and corrupt political system. By this, prisoners meant that they were imprisoned for breaking laws enacted by a political system reflecting the unequal distribution of power in this country and that the sole purpose of the criminal justice system was to protect the entrenched interests of the wealthy and powerful at the expense of the poor and the weak.[85] Prisoners asserted that their crimes were a justifiable retaliation against a society that had denied them opportunities for social and economic gains and that this denial of basic rights in prison, cruel and disproportionate punishment, racial prejudice, and other violations of the system made prisoners one of America's deprived minorities. Political protest in prisons began as prisoners, like workers and blacks, wanted to be viewed as seeking an effective way of expressing their demands and achieving results from the political system.

Prisoners' rights groups helped inmates focus on the expansion of their constitutional rights, better communication between prisoners and the outside world, development of meaningful work with fair wages, and restoration of their normal rights and privileges upon release. Prisoners wanted to emphasize the poor prison conditions in the hope that community sympathy and support would lead to reform. It worked in some instances. "The image of the politically astute and theoretically well-versed rebel seeking social and economic justice as well as humane prison conditions appealed both to some prisoners and to some members of the community." But this did not lead to substantial prison reform.[86]

Causes of collective riots Collective riots result from the combination of three sociological and social-psychological elements. First is the nature of the maximum custody prison. Although most inmates do not require maximum security, they live in confined quarters in which almost every detail of their lives is monitored and ordered, leaving them with little to do except plan escape. Incarceration under such conditions leads to deprivation and emotional problems.[87]

The second and third components are the aggregation of different types of inmates within one prison and the destruction of the semiofficial, informal inmate self-government by a new administration. When different types of prisoners mingle, the aggressive inmates have an advantage over the more passive ones. The aggressive inmates, including the predatory habitual criminals, take over the leadership of the inmate subculture. The correctional officers' inability to control the inmates means that some of the prison's functions are in the hands of those inmates who hold power over the other inmates and, at times, over the administration. Thus it is they and not the officials who maintain order and discipline within the institution. Those prisoners in control thus form a semiofficial government. They control those few things that make prison life tolerable, and in return for this power, they keep the other inmates under control. This pleases the administration and ensures the continuation of their leadership. But when this inmate control is removed, during periods of administrative reform, and is not replaced with other avenues for inmate self-expression, problems ensue. The aggressive inmates then become a destructive force against the administration, usually with the support of the other prisoners.[88]

An analysis of prison riots noted the importance of the inmates' social structure and its potential for violence when sudden changes were made by the prison administration, along with racial and political tensions. New political activity, the power of minorities, and the increased incidence of violence outside are taken into prison, where the atmosphere strains the tensions between races. Prison officials, therefore, should differentiate between the ordinary militant minority members and the new militants, who are better educated than the black conservatives, more sophisticated politically, and more willing to use any means—including violence—to accomplish their goals. The combination of these two groups in prison has increased the politicization of minorities, and the mingling of these two groups in prison "is the worst possible combination for society."[89]

Prisons in the early 1960s were rigidly segregated, and the prisoners set rules completely separating blacks and whites in dining rooms, movies, and waiting lines. Open racism was common, and any prisoner seen associating with other racial groups was likely to become the target of violence.

Toward the end of the 1960s, Hispanics developed a political identity, and black leaders turned to Marxism. Cooperation with other races was deemed acceptable as long as it was to further political goals. But when this movement died down, the earlier conditions of racial tension again surfaced, and "hate, tension and hostilities between the two races escalated." Prisons were divided into black and white territories; guards condoned and encouraged violence against blacks; gang violence entered the prisons with its perpetrators, along with a renewed emphasis on surviving frequent prison violence and inflicting violence on weaker prisoners. There was a shift from violence among individuals to violence among quasi-political groups, and this new type of violence encouraged mass or collective actions by large groups of prisoners.[90]

The problem of relative deprivation also can lead to prison violence. The prevalence of community awareness of prison conditions and the promise of prison reform have raised expectations that have not been met. Inmates are thus even more dissatisfied with the prison system, not so much because of what they lack but because of their perception of what they lack compared with what others have or with their idea of what they should have.[91]

An exploratory study of prison riots questioned the argument that rising expectations and changes in the informal social-control patterns of prisons are related significantly to prison riots and noted that "the present state of research precludes all but tentative conclusions." The study concluded that

> we may be fairly confident in asserting that there is no close association between rioting and reforms of any particular social conditions, or inmate power structure as it is affected by inmate councils. Similarly, reform periods are not necessarily connected with rioting, nor is there any substantial evidence for a riot-reform cycle in penal administration.[92]

The American Correctional Association Committee on Riots and Disturbances supports this position. Although the committee mentioned many factors as possible causes of prison riots, including the institution's unnatural environment, the prisoners' antisocial characteristics, poor management, inadequate personnel policies and practices, inadequate facilities, insufficient constructive activities for inmates, few legitimate rewards, basic social attitudes of unrest in the outside world, insufficient funding, and inequities in the criminal justice system, they determined that these factors could not be used to explain riots because they had to exist along with other, unknown conditions before a riot would occur.[93]

INDIVIDUAL INMATE VIOLENCE

Riots and mass disturbances in prisons receive wide publicity and sometimes are the basis for prison reform. The inmates, however, live in a less dramatic, but constantly dangerous and violent environment every day.

Physical assaults

Prisons are a concentration of potentially violent individuals, and it is not unreasonable to expect explosive and bloody behavior from them.[94] The violence among inmates is generally underreported, as the inmates are afraid to report incidents for fear of reprisals from other inmates, and the administrators want to avoid the criticism that comes with the public reporting of violence in their prisons. But some studies have indicated that ten to fifteen assaults occur for every one that is noted in prison records. Of the two thousand inmates at Lorton Reformatory near Washington, D.C., one hundred prisoners each year are assaulted and require hospitalization. As many as five inmates have been victims of homicide in a single year. The prisoners carry homemade weapons for protection, and minor skirmishes or disagreements between inmates often erupt into full-scale violence.[95]

Administrators have difficulty coping with violent inmates. The federal government segregates them and houses the most violent in a facility at Marion, Illinois. Marion also houses convicts who are known to be clever escape artists, gang leaders, or troublemakers of any kind. One warden at Marion commented that "judges sentence criminals to prison to protect society. Wardens send prisoners to Marion often to protect other inmates."[96]

The Marion prison is a modern facility, but inside there are no trustees, no honor cells, no prison newspaper, no entertainment visits, few vocational programs, and few if any rehabilitation ideals. Inmates must be counted six times per day, and there is more than one guard for every two prisoners. The average sentence in Marion is thirty-three years; the emphasis is on security and control because there is no good time incentive to offer convicts with two or three consecutive life sentences.

The most violent prisoners who have refused to conform to prison life are in the control unit. The six months of hearings and review required before a prisoner can be sent to the control unit is testimony itself to the harshness of this punishment. The control unit is surrounded by ten steel gates and a metal detector and is monitored by television cameras at all times. The cells are eight feet by six feet and are occupied twenty-three hours per day. During the one hour reserved for exercise and showers, the prisoners are alone or in carefully guarded groups of two or three. Even with extensive supervision, aggression against inmates is random, and small incidents can trigger fatal stabbings.[97]

Most prisons do not have the luxury of so few inmates per correctional officer, nor do they have specially equipped and secure facilities for violent convicts such as the one at Marion. Assaults, then, are commonplace in prisons.

Homosexual assaults One type of physical assault in prison is homosexual, and inmates and prison officials must cope with such assaults as an everyday part of prison life. The lack of heterosexual outlet for sexual tension, combined with other facets of prison experience, including idleness, lack of privacy, lack of classification and segregation procedures, limited or nonexistent ties to the outside world, racial prejudices, gang attempts to gain power, and staff toleration of sexual violence means that inmates are constantly under the threat of homosexual attacks.

Homosexuality is seldom discussed by prison administrators or inmates, and so it is difficult to obtain accurate data on the number of attacks in institutions and the percentage of inmates who engage in such behavior. Despite the imprecise data, there is a growing body of research on male homosexuality in prison,[98] and we shall look briefly at some of the problems.

Accounts of initiation into prison homosexuality fall into two categories. The first are seduction games, a process that starts when a new prisoner arrives at the institution. The most common seduction game is the loan game. An experienced inmate approaches the new prisoner and offers a consumer product that is generally scarce in prison, for example, candy or cigarettes. Eventually the loan is called in, and the inmate is told to pay immediately with double or more interest or become a sexual partner.[99]

The second type of prison violence is much more sudden and unexpected. New inmates may be attacked by two or more prisoners in dormitories or cells upon their arrival. An extensive study of male sexual aggression in prison found that sexual overtures might involve an actual sexual assault, other physical violence, insulting or threatening language, or mere propositions.[100] Violence can be aggressor or victim precipitated. In the first case, the aggressor plans to use violence to coerce his victim before the incident begins. In the second case, the victim reacts violently to a sexual innuendo or proposition seen as threatening. The proposition may be nothing more than a stare, a sideways glance, or any small invasion of privacy or personal space.[101]

The victim may refuse a sexual advance, and the aggressor may react violently to that refusal, interpreting it as an insult or a challenge to fight. Violence may also erupt when homosexual partners disagree; these arguments are similar to disagreements between heterosexual couples and may pertain to terminating the relationship, allocating power, rejection, or pride. Another type of sexual violence in prison concerns arguments between two or more rivals over the sexual favors of a third partner.[102]

Prison homicides   The violence behind bars is unceasing, and the inmates are justified in fearing for their lives. From 1979 to 1980, there was a 7 percent increase in the number of deaths in state and federal penal institutions. Although part of this increase can be attributed to the thirty-three deaths occurring during the New Mexico penitentiary riot, administrators agree that prison violence generally is on the increase. Not all prison deaths are due to violence. A breakdown of the figures reveals that 60 percent of the deaths in 1980 were attributable to illness or natural causes, 14 percent were suicides, and 5 percent resulted from accidental self-injury. Slightly more than 20 percent of the deaths were caused by another person.[103]

Prison homicides are best understood by looking at the relationship between the assailant and the victim. The most prevalent motives for prison homicides in single-assailant cases are homosexuality, arguments, and debts. Most single-assailant cases are based on personal involvement between the murderer and the victim, and over half of the murders are victim precipitated. Single-assailant events tend to occur throughout the prison rather than in the victim's cell and are more likely to occur during the week rather than on the weekend; stabbing is the most common method of killing.

On the other hand, mutiple-assailant cases, known as "ratpacking," are generally motivated by revenge for "snitching" or reporting to the prison officials, gang tensions, drug fights, and homosexuality. Although single-assailant events involve personal relationships, multiple-murder cases appear to be directed toward maintaining the inmates' social order. For example, inmates kill to suppress informants or to maintain the quality or quantity of drugs in the prison. Multiple assailants seek out inmates in their cells and commonly use stabbing or strangulation to kill their victims. Homicides involving more than one assailant seem to be more rational and are planned more carefully.[104]

Certain inmates seem to be "at risk" for homicide. Police informants and snitches who cooperate to convict other criminals generally do not live long behind bars. Child molesters and rapists, known as "short eyes" in prison, are targets for prison violence, as are law enforcement officers who are sent to institutions. Organized crime figures take their criminal associations into prison with them, and members of rival Mafia families are known to order prison killings.

Prison suicides and self-injury

But self-inflicted violence is the most common form of violence in prison. Little attention is paid to this type of violence in prison, but inmates are often successful in their suicide attempts.[105] The problem of self-mutilation is endemic, and if a problem of this magnitude were reported outside prisons, it would "provoke outrage and emergency intervention."[106] On an average day, at least one prison inmate kills himself, and it is estimated that one thousand inmates commit suicide each year.[107] The suicide rate in prisons is sixteen times higher than that of the general population.[108]

The problem is not confined to adult prisoners. Juveniles held in adult detention facilities commit suicide at a rate eight times higher than that for children held in juvenile institutions and four and one-half times the rate for children in the general population.[109]

The reasons for self-inflicted violence and suicides are varied. They have been linked to overcrowded institutions,[110] the extended use of solitary confinement,[111] and the psychological consequences of being a victim in prison.[112] Inmates who are threatened with homosexual rape or other violence in prison often become depressed and desperate about their physical safety. The victims may lack the interpersonal skills and resources that would help fend off would-be aggressors, and they may be socially isolated in prison. Another factor contributing to the victims' psychological state is the often-repeated advice that the only options are "fight or flight." Victims know that if they submit to violence, they will be branded as weak, but if they seek help, they will be branded as snitches or rats. The psychological climate created by violence in prison therefore fosters suicide and self-mutilation.[113]

Inmates who injure themselves are not average prisoners. They are younger and do not have histories of drug addiction, past criminal records, or past prison sentences.[114] The inmates' reaction to suicide attempts is to downplay the events. "Inmates see it as an unmanly and weak thing to do unless it is blatantly manipulative."[115] Correctional staff also downplay this type of violence, because the publicity of self-mutilation, especially when a weapon is used, may reflect lax security measures at the institution. Prison administrators often segregate inmates who threaten or attempt suicide, even though psychologists recommend human contact and communication as the best prevention.[116]

Inmate reaction to individual violence: lawsuits against officials

Inmates who are injured by other inmates in prison (or the families of inmates who are killed) may sometimes bring a civil action against officials for negligence in preventing the attack. They may also sue prison officials under the U.S. Constitution's prohibition against cruel and unusual punishment. As early as 1944, one court declared that prison officials have a duty to protect inmates from other inmates:

> The Government has the absolute right to hold prisoners for offenses against it but it also has the correlative duty to protect them against assault or injury from any quarter while so held. . . . While the law does take his liberty and imposes a duty of servitude and observance of discipline for his regulation and that of other prisoners, it does not deny his right to personal security against unlawful invasion.[117]

When prison conditions are challenged in court, part of the complaint often relates to the lack of physical safety. One of the most recent examples concerns a lawsuit against the Texas Department of Corrections. Along with finding that the TDC prisons were understaffed, the court found other examples of violence against inmates.[118]

Ruiz v. Estelle

In March of 1977, a young inmate at the Clements Unit was confined to a cell already occupied by two older inmates. For the following weeks, his predatory cellmates tortured and preyed upon the youth. A summary of some of the abuses they inflicted on him were as follows: He was forced to clean up the cell by himself, afterwards undergoing beatings, inflicted for no apparent cause. While bound with towels, he was forced to commit unnatural sex acts and to endure blows from fists and a candy can. Still later, burning matches and a lighted cigarette were placed on his unprotected skin. Brandishing a broken glass, the predators threatened to kill him, if he informed on them. To guard further against discovery of their activities, his cellmates followed him to and from the showers and mess hall and physically prevented him from going to the day room. Additionally, they tore up his prescriptions and confiscated his "commissary". When he finally succeeded in reporting his pitiable situation to an officer and was rescued, it was discovered that he had sustained multiple bruises and contusions, multiple second degree burns, a swollen left ankle, and scalp lacerations. . . .

In December of 1978, on the Eastham Unit, a young inmate, sentenced to TDC for a short period of time as "shock probation", was confined in an administrative segregation cell with two inmates who had long histories of violence. Over a period of three days, the young man was repeatedly raped, beaten, and burned by his cellmates, who refused to permit him to eat and forced him to turn his back to the bars whenever an officer passed. Unit officers were alerted to the situation by a building porter. One of the assaulting inmates received a seven year sentence, for his part in these activities. The other inmate who participated in the assaults was merely deprived of his accumulated good time. Three and one-half months after the incident, he was promoted to Class 1 (the highest good time earning status), and a month and a half after that, all of his good time was restored.

In 1980, Congress passed the Civil Rights of Institutionalized Persons Act, which allows the U.S. attorney general to bring suits for civil rights violations on behalf of state prisoners. In March 1983, the Reagan administration filed suit against two Hawaii state prisons, alleging, in part, that state officials had not adequately protected the inmates from assault, rape, and extortion inflicted by other inmates. Although this lawsuit was later dismissed for technical reasons, some prison reform groups are hopeful that the law will be a powerful new weapon in their fight for safe conditions inside prisons.[119]

SUMMARY AND CONCLUSION

This chapter has focused on prison administration and prison violence, in the context of the ways in which overcrowding exacerbates all of the problems in the prison. Prison administration today is much more difficult than it was in earlier times when inmates were confined in solitary cells and never allowed to mingle with other inmates. The inhumaneness of that system has been researched, but in this chapter we have seen that our "modern" prisons, with their overcrowding, may also be inhumane.

We began with an overview of the nature and extent of overcrowding and a discussion of the ways in which prison officials have tried to resolve it, through double celling, building new facilities, and remodeling other structures to be used as prisons. We then looked at prison administration and staff, again in the context of overcrowded facilities. We noted the changing function of the guards' attempts to involve these personnel in the treatment process, and the need for a professional treatment staff. We then considered the role of work supervisors and their impact on inmates.

In the last section, we looked at the impact of prison populations on the inmates, beginning with the effect of overcrowding and then some of its manifestations: prison violence in the form of riots as well as individual inmate aggression against other inmates, leading to physical injury, homosexual rape, or death. Self-inflicted injury or suicide of inmates was also discussed, followed by the use of civil lawsuits to compensate inmates who have been victimized by other inmates in prison when officials have been negligent in preventing such attacks.

In conclusion, it is important to recognize that the "modern prison" is an institution in transition. Prison populations are soaring while budgets are being reduced. Prison administrators feel frustrated with their lack of control over prison populations: Other agencies determine how many inmates will be sent to prison and when they will be released. Many techniques used to accommodate large numbers of prisoners have been challenged in the courts, and in some cases, double celling and mandatory release programs have been declared unacceptable. Administrators often find interim housing for inmates, such as tents, trailers, or other abandoned buildings. But these may cause other problems, such as transferring inmates, maintaining proper staff supervision, and provoking lawsuits.

Even though prison administrators now have information available, new techniques of management are difficult to implement in overcrowded, decentralized, and understaffed facilities. The prison staff may oppose new procedures; in fact, overworked correctional officers are not likely to agree to new job responsibilities when they cannot handle their current assignments. The staff face tremendous problems in prisons, and conditions that have a negative effect on the inmates also affect the staff. Overcrowding means that there is less control over the inmates and that the threat of physical dangers is increased. We looked at forms of corruption in the prison and noted that administrators may not be successful in controlling corruption, at least as long as guards and inmates must interact. Correctional officers and treatment personnel may disagree over treatment and custody and often work at cross-purposes. Whereas correctional officers are concerned with control and conformity, treatment personnel are encouraging individual decisions and responsibility. Both need better role definitions and goals. Even though there have been some improvements in the working relationships between correctional officers and treatment personnel, they have largely been limited in scope and are of little real value to the inmates.

Inmates are constantly exposed to the dangerous environment of overcrowded institutions, and lawsuits challenging the conditions of their confinement have increased as overcrowding has worsened. Their belief is that prison itself is punishment enough and that they should not be subjected to violence from other inmates as well.

Society has not yet made the choices that will be necessary to resolve the problems. Do we want prisons only to punish? Or do we want prisons to educate and train offenders to aid their adjustment in society? Are we going to continue to ignore the problems in prisons until mass riots, with their extensive destruction of property and human life, force us to look at our institutions? Are we willing to acknowledge that as a society, we must punish criminals and that we must punish them in a way that does not wreak havoc on society at the termination of that punishment? Do we want to live in constant fear that our next door neighbor or the person down the block is an ex-convict and that this offender's treatment in prison was so harsh that his or her cynicism and resentment are worse now than before imprisonment? Are we willing to decide to fund correctional systems that will give us back men and women who are less dangerous and better equipped to manage in the free world? It appears that "we must resign ourselves to spending more money on the people we hate most, or find creative, alternative ways to punish criminals who are not so dangerous that they have to be caged with their heads against toilets."[120]

CHAPTER

The inmates' world

This chapter focuses on the prison as experienced by its inmates. We shall discuss the problems of adjustment and whether the inmates' subculture is a product of these problems or is a way of life that they bring with them. We shall then turn to the need for classification systems to determine in what types of facilities particular inmates should be incarcerated and what types of programs would be most beneficial for them. Prison education and prison labor are given particular attention and, finally, the issue of treatment in prison is discussed.

Offenders entering prison for the first time confront a unique and different world. For some, the adjustment is smooth, and for others, the transition to prison life is traumatic. Imprisonment is a series of "status degradation ceremonies" that serve two functions: to destroy the inmates' identities and to assign them new identities of a lower order.[1] The way prisoners are treated when they enter prison exemplifies society's rejection: they are stripped of most of their personal belongings, given a number, examined, inspected, weighed, and documented. To them these acts represent deprivation of their personal identities.

Inmates must cope with the psychological and social problems that result from the worst punishment, the deprivation of liberty. In his study of male inmates, Gresham M. Sykes discussed the moral rejection by the community, which is a constant threat to the inmate's self-concept; the deprivation of goods and services in a society that values material possessions; the deprivation of heterosexual relationships and the resulting threat to the inmate's masculinity; and the deprivation of security in an inmate population that threatens his safety and sometimes his health and life.[2]

"Rejected, impoverished, and figuratively castrated, the prisoner must face still further indignity in the extensive social control exercised by the custodians."[3] Everything the prisoners do, including the showers they can take and the hours they can sleep, is regulated by the prison staff. They have no autonomy and can show no initiative. Thus they are forced to define themselves as weak, helpless, and dependent, which threatens their self-concepts as adults. And the prison system rarely, if ever, permits them to function as adults.

At the same time that the prisoners are adjusting to the inmates and guards, they are also preparing for their release from prison. The prison's isolated **social system**, on the one hand, stresses adaptation to the inmate **subculture** and, on the other, preparation for release.

THE INMATES' SOCIAL SYSTEM

Concern with the negative effects that inmates have on one another led the early **penologists** either to separate the prisoners or to enforce the silent system to avoid verbal and physical contact. With the end of the silent system came the opportunity for inmates to interact verbally. One result has been the opportunity for prisoners to influence one another and even to form a prison subculture, and the reasons for this development have been subjects of debate and study.

PRISONIZATION: SOCIALIZATION INTO THE INMATES' SYSTEM

In 1940, one of the most thorough studies of the prison community was published by Donald Clemmer.[4] Clemmer proposed the concept of prisonization to explain the formation of prisoner subcultures. He defined **prisonization** as "the taking on, in greater or lesser degree, of the folkways, mores, customs, and general culture of the penitentiary." When a new inmate enters prison, he or she also begins the process of prisonization. This process is not the same for all inmates and may be affected by the inmate's personality, environment, and relationships outside prison, whether the inmate joins a primary group in prison, and the degree to which the inmate accepts the codes of prison life.

Clemmer viewed prisonization as the process by which inmates learn about and absorb prison **norms** and values. He also believed that once prisoners accept institutional norms, conventional value systems were ineffective.[5] His theory is essentially a learning theory similar to Sutherland's theory of **differential association** to explain criminal behavior. Like differential association, prisonization is affected by priority, duration, frequency, and intensity of contact with criminal patterns.[6]

EMPIRICAL TESTS OF PRISONIZATION

Clemmer's concept of prisonization was tested empirically by Stanton Wheeler in a study at the Washington State Reformatory. Although Wheeler found strong support for Clemmer's concept of prisonization, he also found that the degree of prisonization varied according to the phase of an inmate's institutional career, developing along a U-shaped curve. Inmates tended to be more receptive to the institutional values of the outside world during the first period of incarceration (measured at the end of the first six months) and the last period (last six months before release) and less receptive during the middle, or prison career, period (more than six months remaining). In the last six months of incarceration, the inmate is anticipating release back into society, and his main reference group shifts from the inmates within the institution to the society outside. Wheeler concluded that Clemmer's concept of prisonization should be reformulated to include the variable of the prison career phase.[7]

Subsequent researchers have found some support for Wheeler's U-shaped curve of attitudes that develop during the inmate's incarceration.[8] In comparing prisonization among male, as compared with female, inmates, researchers have questioned Wheeler's hypothesis. One study found that although time spent in prison was significantly related to prisonization among women inmates, this was not the case among male inmates and that other variables were predictive of prisonization. Among women, attitudes toward race and the police were significant. Among men, the variables of age and attitudes toward law and the judicial system were significant.[9]

The deprivation and importation models

Sociological analyses of the process of prisonization and the emergence of a prison subculture have followed two models. The models have been given various names, but they may be described as (1) the **deprivation model,** and (2) the **importation model.**

Deprivation model. Sykes argued that the inmate subculture is the product of an inmate's attempt to adapt to the deprivations imposed by incarceration. Inmates have few alternatives to reduce their deprivation, loss of status, and degradation. They cannot escape psychologically or physically; they cannot eliminate the "pains of imprisonment." "But if the rigors of confinement cannot be completely removed, they can at least be mitigated by the patterns of social interaction established among the inmates themselves."[10] The inmate has a choice of either uniting with his fellow captives in a spirit of mutual cooperation or withdrawing to seek only the satisfaction of his own needs. In either case, his pattern of behavior is an adaptation to the deprivations of his environment.

According to the deprivation model, the inmates' social system is **functional** in that it enables them to minimize, through cooperation, the pains of imprisonment. For example, if the inmates cooperate in exchanging favors, that not only removes the opportunity for some to exploit others, but it also enables them to accept material deprivation more easily. In addition, those available goods and services can be better distributed and shared if the inmates have a cooperative social system. This system also helps resolve the problem of personal security, alleviate the fear of further isolation, and restore the inmate's sense of self-respect and independence.[11]

These studies were conducted in all-male institutions. A study in an institution housing men and women under similar conditions revealed some differences by sex in the inmates' social structures. Generally "the data seem to justify the conclusion that inmate organization is largely a response to institutional conditions," or, in the words of the model, it is an adaptation to the series of deprivations suffered by inmates in total institutions.[12]

In summary, because of inmates' pains of imprisonment and degradation, which result in a threat to their self-esteem, inmates repudiate the norms of the staff, administration, and society and join forces with one another, developing a social system that enables them to preserve their self-esteem. And rejecting their rejectors, they can avoid having to reject themselves.

Importation model. Another approach to understanding the inmate subculture, say John Irwin and Donald R. Cressey, is that their patterns of behavior are brought with the men to prison.[13] Influences inside the prison are not the only explanations for the inmate social system, and most of the inmate subculture is not peculiar to penal institutions. Irwin and Cressey emphasize the need to distinguish between "prison culture" and "criminal subculture." To do so, they postulate three types of prison subcultures, only two of which are criminal.[14]

The first type, the *thief subculture,* refers to the patterns of values that are characteristic of professional thieves and other career criminals, and this type is found in the prison setting as well as outside.[15] It may also be seen among police, prison guards, college professors, students, and other categories of persons who "evaluate behavior in terms of in-group loyalties."[16]

The second type of inmate subculture is the *convict subculture,* the central value of which is "utilitarianism, and the most manipulative and most utilitarian individuals win the available wealth and such positions of influence as might exist." This type refers to patterns that can be found anywhere that people are incarcerated, and it is "characterized by deprivations and limitations of freedom and in them available wealth must be competed for by men supposedly on an equal footing." Many of the hard-core members of this subculture have spent a lot of time in juvenile institutions.[17]

The final type is the *legitimate subculture,* which is composed of inmates who isolate themselves or are isolated by other inmates. They constitute the largest proportion of the inmate population and are of little or no trouble to the staff. They reject both the criminal and the thief subcultures and are "oriented to the problems of achieving goals through means which are legitimate outside prisons."[18]

A combination of the convict and the thief subcultures form what is usually referred to as the *inmate culture.* All three subcultures bring to the prison past patterns of behavior and attitudes, and the inmate culture is really an "adjustment of accommodation of these three systems within the official administrative system of deprivation and control."[19]

Analysis of the two models
Research on the importation and deprivation models was conducted in 1970 at a maximum security prison in the Southwest. The investigator emphasized that like the rest of us, inmates have a past, a present, and a future and all are related to the process of prisonization. New inmates face two social systems in prison: the formal organization (resocialization) and the inmate society (prisonization), and both compete for the inmate's allegiance. The goals of the formal organization are custody and confinement, and the goal of the inmates is freedom. Because these two social systems conflict, if one succeeds, the other must fail. The prison is not a closed system, and in explaining the inmate culture, we must examine all of these factors: preprison experiences, both criminal and noncriminal; expectations of prison staff and fellow inmates; quality of the inmate's contacts with persons or groups outside the walls; postprison expectations; and the inmate's immediate problems of adjustment. The greater the degree of similarity between preprison activities and prison subculture values and attitudes, "the greater the receptivity to the influences of prisonization." Inmates from the lower, as compared with the higher, social class are more likely to become highly prisonized, and those who have the highest degree of contact with the outside world have the lowest degree of prisonization. Finally, those with a higher degree of prisonization were among those who had the bleakest postprison expectations.[20]

Leo Carroll criticized the deprivation model of prisonization in his study of race relations in an eastern prison. The model "diverts attention from interrelationships between the prison and the wider society . . . and hence away from issues such as racial violence."[21] Carroll also maintains that to try to explain the prison subculture by means of only one of the two models results in undue polarization. The models should not be seen as opposites but may in fact be complementary. "Each may be a representation of the sources and form of inmate organization as it exists under different conditions."[22] According to Carroll, which form of inmate subculture prevails is dependent on the degree of security and deprivation in the institution. In maximum security prisons with a high degree of security, we would expect the deprivation model to prevail, but in prisons with less security and fewer deprivations, the importation model is more likely to predominate. Carroll's research generally supports the importation model, but he concluded that the model was incomplete.

Other researchers have taken the position that the importation and deprivation models should be integrated, that both are important to explaining the process of prisonization. The cross-cultural studies of Ronald Akers and his colleagues are examples. The functional or adaptation model was only partially supported by their data from several countries and one United States jurisdiction. Their data revealed that "the inmate culture varies by whatever differences in organization environment there are from one institution to the next." They also found support for the importation view "because it appears that the level of nonconformity to staff norms is more a reflection of the larger culture from which the inmates are drawn than the specific environment of the prison in which they are currently confined."[23]

This integrative approach has been summarized as follows: "The existence of collective solutions in the inmate culture and social structure is based on the common problems of adjustment to the institution, while the content of those solutions and the tendency to become prisonized are imported from the larger society."[24] It is not reasonable to argue that the importation or deprivation model alone explains the inmate subculture; rather, variables of each are important. "The more relevant issue appears to be how the rather vague propositions associated with each model can be stated more precisely and, more importantly, how they can be merged into a single theoretical framework."[25]

PRISONIZATION:
AN EVALUATION

Empirical tests of Clemmer's concept of prisonization revealed some implications for release from prison and **recidivism** or adequate adjustment to life outside the walls. The inmate subculture may not significantly and permanently alter the inmates' attitudes and thereby hinder their adjustment on parole but might serve as a set of rationalizations they can use when they encounter barriers to parole success.[26]

More important, as a result of prisonization, inmates may define themselves as criminals with "an elaborate set of supporting justifications" and the rejection of society. They may internalize this rejection and as a result place themselves in low esteem. They may then reject their rejectors. Consequently, it may be that the inmate subculture simply functions as a mechanism for improving the inmates' self-concept by increasing their status and offering them acceptance by others.[27]

Finally, it is important to consider the *type* of inmate subculture. Prisonization may not have the same influence on all types and may not have a significant effect on those inmates who belong to the legitimate subculture; they would have low rates of recidivism even if never incarcerated. Nor would it affect those who belong to the convict subculture, for they would remain in a life of crime. Thus, it may not be true "that any particular prison is the breeding ground of an inmate culture that significantly increases recidivism rates."[28]

These studies on prisonization serve to reemphasize the need to look at the total social structure, not only of the prison, but also of the preprison and postprison scenes in order to understand the effects of imprisonment on the inmate.[29]

PRISON PROGRAMS

The need for programs in prison has been emphasized by, among others, Supreme Court Chief Justice Warren E. Burger, who argues that the ultimate paradox is that we spend years and considerable amounts of money to put people in prison, and then we forget them. **Humanitarian** concern disappears when we put prisoners into an "overcrowded, understaffed institution with little or no library facilities, little if any educational programs or vocational training."[30] Burger emphasizes that putting offenders behind bars without attempting to help or change them is an "expensive folly with short-term benefits—a 'winning of battles while losing the war.'"

For years, educational and vocational programs in prisons have had a low priority. Recent data reveal that on the average, a state spends only 1.5 percent of its total correctional budget on inmate education and training programs.[31] One of the arguments in favor of prison education and industry is directed specifically toward the budget problems: inmates could be put to work in prison factories and be required to pay part of their earnings to the state to defray the costs of incarceration. Tax burdens would be reduced for the general public in the short term and in the long term also: by releasing inmates who have skills and can work, welfare payments would be reduced, and at the same time, the ex-offender would be paying taxes.[32] However, there is a great deal of public sentiment against using tax money to start new programs in prison. "The very simple answer to that, is that it costs a lot more money to keep convicts incarcerated than it does to educate them and turn them into productive, taxpaying members of society."[33]

Another argument in favor of education and labor programs concerns their impact on prisons. Most correctional facilities are characterized by pervasive inmate idleness that may lead to destructive behavior and increased

Educational, vocational, and recreational programs are very important to inmates. Prison rodeos are typical of the types of recreational activities in prisons in some parts of the country.

violence. But prison programs would contribute to the institution's stability and would reduce some of the burdens on correctional staff and administrators.[34]

Inmates, as well as correctional staff, would benefit from prison programs. Approximately 95 percent of offenders convicted of serious crimes and sent to prison will eventually return to free society, and their educational level contributes to their unemployment problems. Recent studies indicate that nearly three out of every four inmates do not have a high school diploma.[35] The lack of education, combined with idleness in prison, contributes to low inmate morale and self-esteem. Perhaps the greatest result of prison educational and vocational programs would be an improvement in the institution's morale and a better chance of success upon release.

The first priority for prison programs is sending the offender to the proper institution and choosing the appropriate programs in prison.

CLASSIFICATION The main purpose of prisoner **classification** "is to fit the treatment program of the correctional institution to the requirements of the individual as determined by appropriate diagnostic procedures."[36] For years classification really meant segregation—by race, age, and sex. No attempt was made to assess the problems of a particular offender within the context of a treatment

EXHIBIT

IN WHAT TYPE OF FACILITIES ARE PRISONERS HELD: DESCRIPTION OF PRISONS

What are the characteristics of prisons?	*Federal*	*State*
Number of prisons	38	521
Security level		
Maximum	13	140
Medium	17	207
Minimum	8	174
Inmate population		
Less than 500	10	366
500–999	18	80
1,000 or more	10	75
Year built		
Before 1875	0	25
1875–1924	3	76
1925–1949	16	125
1950–1969	8	156
1970–1978	11	139
Prisoners housed		
Males	31	460
Females	2	40
Coed	5	21
Prison employees		
Number	8,626	83,535
% administrative	2.2	2.2
% custodial	42.4	62.9
% service	23.0	15.9
% other	32.4	19.0

Source: "Prision Facility Characteristics," March 1978, *American Prisons and Jails,* vol. 3, 1980.

State Prisons Are Generally Old and Large

Prisons hold a somewhat less diverse population than do local jails. A large proportion of prisons are old and have many of the maintenace and operational deficiencies associated with other old, high-use buildings.

- Nearly 96% of State and Federal prisoners are sentenced persons with terms of more than 1 year.
- In 1979, more than half of the Nation's inmates resided in facilities with average daily populations of 1,000 or more.
- Nearly 44% of the Nation's prisons are more than 30 years old and these institutions house about 61% of the inmates.
- More than 11% of the imprisoned population resides in facilities built before 1875, and 8 out of 10 inmates in the oldest prisons are in facilities that house more than 1,000 persons.

Prisons Are Often Classified by the Level of Security

- **Maximum or close custody prisons** are typically surrounded by a double fence or wall (usually 18 to 25 feet high) with armed guards in observation towers. Such facilities usually have large interior cell blocks for inmate housing areas. About 41% of the maximum security prisons were built before 1925.

- **Medium custody prisons** typically have double fences topped with barbed wire to enclose the facility. Housing architecture is quite varied, consisting of outside cell blocks in units of 150 cells or less, dormitories, and cubicles. More than 87% of the medium-custody prisons were built after 1925.
- **Minimum custody prisons** typically do not have armed posts and may or may not have fences to enclose the institution. To a large degree, housing consists of open dormitories. More than 60% of the minimum security prisons were built after 1950.

About Half of All Prison Inmates Are in Maximum Security Prisons

In 1979, 52% of all prison inmates were held under maximum security conditions; 37% under medium security; and 11% under minimum security.

The proportion of inmates held in maximum security facilities ranged from 94% in Texas to less than 10% in New Hampshire, North Carolina, and Wyoming. In 14 States, more than half of all prisoners were confined in maximum security institutions. In 1978, about one in five inmates resided in maximum security facilities that housed more than 1,000 inmates and that were built before 1925.

Of the 150 prisons built between 1970 and 1978, 85% hold an average daily population of less than 500 inmates and three-quarters were designed for medium or minimum security.

Inmate Composition and Custody Levels Are Generally Linked to the Age of a Facility

As facility age increases, the proportion of—

- Inmates residing in maximum security custody increases
- Inmates classified as maximum security increases
- Inmates residing in facilities housing 1,000 or more inmates increases
- Younger inmates declines
- Violent offenders increases.

As of March 1978	Date Federal or State Prison Opened					
	Before 1875	1875–1924	1925–1949	1950–1969	1970–1978	Total
Number of inmates	31,361	73,575	66,257	68,272	39,522	278,987
Percent	11	26	24	25	14	100%
% of inmates residing in maximum security	90	69	36	38	35	51%
% of inmates classified as maximum security	61	48	32	32	25	38%

	Date Federal or State Prison Opened					
As of March 1978	*Before 1875*	*1875– 1924*	*1925– 1949*	*1950– 1969*	*1970– 1978*	*Total*
% of inmates residing in facilities greater than 1,000 inmates	77	69	53	52	8	53%
% of inmates less than 25 years old	37	36	37	44	42	39%
% of inmates confined for a violent offense	52	49	40	45	37	45%

Source: *American prisions and jails,* vol. 3, 1980.

Source: Bureau of Justice Statistics, *Report to the Nation on Crime and Justice: The Data* (Washington, D.C.: U.S. Government Printing Office, 1983), p. 79.

program. Today, "classification is a method by which diagnosis, treatment planning and the execution of the treatment programs are coordinated in the individual case."[37] In reality, however, classification decisions may be made according to the institution's needs, available facilities, and so on.

Classification is a process by which an individual is analyzed and a decision is made about the most effective way to apply the institution's treatment resources. The plan should then be executed and revised when necessary. Finally, the program should be coordinated with the activities of the individual on parole or unconditional release.

Classification systems

Classification program. The first element of a classification program should be a *reception* program in which new inmates are segregated for medical tests and orientation. The inmate should also be taken on a tour of the facilities of the institution where he or she will be confined. The institution's rules and regulations should be carefully explained. Personnel should be trained to work with the individual on personal problems, such as the loss of family and friends, as well as with hostilities the individual may have developed toward the police or other elements of the legal process.[38]

It is important to build a case summary of the diagnostic studies. This should contain a legal history of the case; a history of previous criminal record, if any; a social history; physical conditions; vocational abilities and interests; educational and religious background; recreational interest; reports of psychologist and psychiatrist; and the individual's initial reaction to any treatment programs. This initial adjustment phase should be only the beginning of a complete record on the inmate. The final case history should include the case summary and all correspondence about the inmate, a photograph, fingerprints, reports of probation officers and others, progress reports, and legal documents. Staff members should be trained to use these documents effectively, and the documents should be kept confidential from other inmates.[39]

Classification committee.   The classification committee is the key element in classification, and therefore it is important to have well-trained staff members on the board. It should always contain a corrections officer, which allows input by security, reduces the traditional mistrust of classification by security, and cross-trains security people in programs and classification techniques. Other committee members should be staff persons who will help evaluate and work with the inmate. The committee's composition would thus vary from inmate to inmate, to include the appropriate work supervisor and counselor; a staff member from the prison school if the inmate has expressed an interest in education; the psychiatrist, psychologist, and physician who tested and examined the inmate; and so on. Finally, the inmate should be permitted to participate in the initial classification meeting.

A new classification process, which has gained favor among inmates as well as staff, is contract classification. The process is the same, but the findings and recommendations are in writing. This document is kept simple, a behavioral contract that is signed by both the inmate and the classification chair. Basically, it states: You have these needs (for example, alcohol counseling, some social-skill learning and work programming, educational training), and if you do those things required of you in the "needs" portion of the contract, you will be moved to lower security, given additional privileges, recommended for early parole, or offered other rewards.[40]

Reclassification.   If classification is to be effective, it must change as the individual's needs change. The goals set for the inmate may be unrealistic, and he or she may be experiencing too much failure. Or they may be too easily accomplished, and he or she is not challenged.

It is particularly important to consider reclassification before parole or release, and a progress report should be prepared before the inmate goes before the parole board. The institutional staff should cooperate with the parole board, making all necessary records available. In case of parole violation, the parole officer should give adequate information to the institutional staff, who should then reexamine the case and decide which program is most effective for the returning parolee.[41]

Computerized classification. Computers have been used to classify inmates. In Kentucky, for example, a "screening" system was developed to measure the potential for aggressive behavior, depression, and suicide; intellectual status; vocational skills; vocational interests; level of socialization (namely, extent of adoption of middle-class views and values); criminal sophistication; and physical and mental health.

The future of classification   Traditional classification systems are slow and cumbersome. Inmates may spend weeks in a diagnostic center while the staff administer a battery of tests. But the new classification systems are responsive to the budget shortfalls in corrections systems and are basically one of two types.

The first is a *predictive-based* model, which separates inmates according to risk of escape, disciplinary conduct in the institution, and future criminal activity. This system uses explicit criteria to classify inmates and has been called one of the most equitable systems available. There are, however, questions about the validity of the empirical methodologies. The second type is an *equity-based* model, which does not use inmate characteristics or nonlegal variables such as age, race, employment, or education. Instead, the equity-based model uses a few "explicitly designed legal variables reflecting current and previous criminal attributes."

Both of these models have advantages. First, they are more efficient and less costly to operate than are traditional classification models. In addition, they can be used in correctional planning schemes.[42] In fact, the most important future use of classification may be in the area of prison overcrowding. When prison populations are high, overclassification and misclassification are common errors. Because some systems have space in maximum security facilities, inmates may be sent there for administrative reasons unrelated to their needs. This is a critical problem, because the initial classification may not only send the inmate to an inappropriate institution but may also hinder his or her future participation in programs. Inmates sent to maximum security prisons, for example, may never be given the alcohol or drug treatment they need. Further, inmates in maximum security prisons may have more disciplinary problems and, therefore, fewer opportunities to move up through the system and fewer chances to be paroled.

The entire classification system is heavily influenced by overcrowded correctional systems. Thus, classification should be used to plan for population changes and the offenders' needs.[43] The effects of prison can be so destructive that both the inmates and the public suffer, and so classification systems that can objectively assign inmates to the least restrictive level of custody would be in the best interest of the inmates (who would suffer fewer psychological problems from incarceration), the staff (who would not have to contend with misclassified inmates), the administration (who could offer more reintegration programs in less secure facilities), and the public (who would not have to spend tax dollars on expensive maximum security institutions and who would have less to fear from released inmates).[44] Once the inmates are properly classified, the next step is to enroll them in programs to meet individual needs.

PRISON EDUCATION

The data on the educational background of inmates in this country clearly indicate the importance of offering educational programs to incarcerated offenders. Between 20 and 50 percent of all inmates cannot read or write. In most institutions in this country, the majority of inmates over eighteen have had less than an eighth-grade education. Despite the tremendous need for educational programs in prisons, such programs are given a lower priority today than in the past. In the nineteenth century, courses behind the walls were often taught by college professors, public school principals, and lawyers.[45] In this century, on the other hand, few prison systems have attracted qualified professionals as teachers, and not until 1956 did we have our first high school equivalency program in prisons—started in Texas.[46]

Some attempts have been made to improve the extent and quality of educational programs in prisons, particularly in the federal prison system. But even in the federal system, there are more nonparticipants than participants in the educational programs, and the percentages are even higher in state and county institutions.

College education: NewGate programs

The opportunity for inmates to participate in college-level courses, however, has increased. College programs have been created in prisons as well as in colleges and universities, some offering correspondence courses and others offering courses for inmates who are permitted to leave prison to attend classes. The impetus for such programs came from the Office of Economic Opportunity (OEO), which in 1967 funded its first such program in the Oregon State Prison. This program became known as "Project NewGate," designating the purpose of education as giving the inmates a "new gate" out of prison. It also honors the NewGate English penitentiary, which is often given credit for stressing the **rehabilitation** of inmates.[47]

NewGate programs have been instituted throughout the country. Although other college programs have been used in prisons, the NewGate model is more comprehensive. It offers not only quality courses for inmates but also academic and therapeutic counseling and individualized attention from a qualified staff. It was hoped that this comprehensive program would have a positive effect on the total atmosphere of the prison as well as on the attitudes of the inmates who participated. NewGate also offers a postrelease program of follow-up and follow-through assistance to former inmates.

College programs in prisons have problems, nonetheless. The custody and security atmosphere of prisons is not conducive to academic learning, and the average inmate does not have the background and characteristics we most often associate with "college material." Education is further hindered by the population's mobility, inmates arrive and leave the institution at times that do not usually coincide with "semesters" or "quarters." Finally, the lack of financial resources continues to affect the ability of such programs to hire and train qualified staff and to provide adequate facilities. Despite these problems, NewGate programs have had some success.

The Minnesota program

Insight, Inc., is a college degree program in the Minnesota Correctional Facility in Stillwater. It was designed and founded by inmates who now run the program. To be admitted to Insight, Inc., inmates must have the equivalent of a high school diploma and score in the top 60 percent on the same college-bound tests given to all high school students in Minnesota. They must have a perfect disciplinary record for six months before they are allowed to apply. Students are admitted upon signing a contract requiring a full-time prison job, a full-time student load of classes, and maintenance of a C average. Any major disciplinary action means expulsion from Insight. Inmates receive random urinalysis tests, as evidence of drugs also terminates their participation in classes. Further, the contract requires "that there is to be no violence or threat of violence, nor shall there be any loud or boisterous behavior anywhere within the unit" and mandates that the inmate "conduct himself in a manner so as to not discredit fellow residents or the Insight program."

Inmates study in a quiet, nonviolent environment. Hundreds of classes are available through the University of Minnesota's Continuing Education and Extension Program, and about half the credits earned by Insight students are through correspondence classes. Insight furnishes audio-video tapes and equipment and encourages inmates to obtain credits through classes on educational radio and television stations.

The Programmed Logic for Automatic Teaching Operation (PLATO) is also available to Insight students. PLATO offers hundreds of subjects to students through computer terminals in the prison. The lessons are flexible and offer immediate feedback to the user. PLATO offers a message service so that students can leave messages for assistance or questions on the instructor's terminal.

What are the results of this program? Only about 10 percent of the inmates have ever been expelled from the program for disciplinary reasons. Another 10 percent have failed academically. The 134 inmates who have been in the Insight program have earned more than eleven thousand college hours and have a cumulative grade point average slightly above a B. Approximately one hundred Insight inmates have been released from prison, and only six have returned.

The Insight philosophy concentrates on giving inmates a marketable skill and teaching them to be responsible. There is a consensus among the inmates that Insight does help their self-esteem. In fact, they look at Insight as a way to earn back the right to be treated like a human being. One of the keys to this program's success is its voluntary nature. Classes are not forced on any inmate, and in fact, entry to the program is so difficult that it is considered a reward in itself.

The U.S. Department of Education believes that the Insight program is far ahead of other educational offerings in prisons and looks to Insight for guidance in helping other institutions set up college classes.[48]

Legal training in prison

The American Bar Association's BASICS (Bar Association Support to Improve Correctional Services) program funded the Prison Legal Services of Michigan (PLSM) in an effort to train prisoners as **paralegals** at Jackson Prison.[49] The goal of the program was to train prisoners who had demonstrated an interest and ability in the study of law so that they could provide legal services to other inmates.

The inmates studied areas pertinent to many prisoners, such as criminal appellate law and domestic relations, as well as subjects useful outside the prison, for example, probate, welfare, and housing law. Although the students received a salary while attending classes five days a week, the PLSM program also had other incentives, such as high prestige within the prison and job placement assistance upon release.

In the PSLM's beginning stages, the prison staff reacted negatively, fearing that the paralegal program would interfere with prison administration and would "stir up trouble by educating prisoners in the law."[50] A few staff members appeared to resent the paralegals because they had attained a higher educational level of training. But the antagonism of the staff declined as the program progressed.

An independent evaluation of the program concluded that the program had been successful in achieving the main goal of imparting legal knowledge to the trainees and providing legal assistance to other inmates. The evaluators found that the inmate population at Jackson prison had a positive attitude toward the program. The major benefit of the program, however, was that the inmates' training resulted in increased job placement opportunities after release.[51]

Graduate studies

Some prisons also offer opportunities for inmates to pursue graduate work. Ossining Prison in New York is the site of a unique educational program for prisoners: a graduate seminary program leading to a master's degree. The New York Theological Seminary offers the program at no cost to the prison.

Its goal is to prepare inmates to be lay ministers, and the program is designed for long-term inmates who will continue the ministry within the prison. Each morning, the inmates attend classes to learn about history, theology, biblical subjects, and counseling, and each afternoon, they return to their cells for four to five hours of intensive study. Prisoners participate in field work in the prison's crisis center, teach basic adult education classes, and participate in delinquency prevention programs or personal counseling.[52]

PRISON LABOR It has been said that "the most difficult prison to administer is the one in which prisoners languish in idleness. Absence of work leads to moral and physical degradation and corrupts institutional order."[53] Yet prison labor has provoked considerable controversy.[54]

Prison labor Legislation at the federal and state levels has permitted states to prohibit the
legislation sale of prison-made goods within their borders.[55] Such legislation is, however, changing. In 1979, the Prison Industries Enhancement Act (PIE) was passed. This statute permits prison-made goods from several pilot projects to move across state lines as long as the projects meet certain requirements, such as payment of inmate wages that equal the rate paid for similar work in the area, and deductions of up to 80 percent from the inmates' pay for taxes, room and board, family support, and victim restitution. Finally, the prisoners must participate voluntarily.[56]

But other recently enacted federal statutes restrict prison labor. For example, the law that raised the gasoline tax by five cents per gallon prohibited the use of inmate labor in highway construction projects funded by that tax. As a result, several states had to curtail programs for the manufacture of highway and road signs.[57]

Legislation to allow private industries to participate in state prison labor programs has been authorized in at least twenty states. A 1973 Minnesota law allows private companies to lease space in correctional facilities and to hire inmates and parolees.[58] Other states allow inmates to travel to and from work at nearby private companies, provided the business pays up to 75 percent of the salaries of correctional officers who must accompany the prisoners for security reasons.[59] Proposals regarding wage plans vary from requiring that inmates earn not less than 60 percent of the usual wage for work of a similar nature[60] to mandating they earn no more than 50 percent of the minimum wage.[61] Some states allow inmates to be covered by industrial insurance for accidents, but others specifically prohibit eligibility for unemployment compensation.[62]

HIGHLIGHT

THE IMPORTANCE OF LABOR IN THE PEOPLE'S REPUBLIC OF CHINA

If their attitudes are not "right," or they are not obeying their elders, young people in the People's Republic of China may be sent to special institutions to be "reeducated through labor." Those sent for such reeducation are not considered to be delinquent or criminal, and they presumably are not being punished. Therefore, say the Chinese, they do not need to be represented by attorneys when the decision is made to commit them to these special "schools."

The Chinese regulations regarding nonjudicial adjudication, originally published in 1956, were reissued in early 1980. They give nonjudicial committees, which include the local police, the power to confine offenders for one to three years for offenses ranging from brawling and petty thievery to gambling and seduction. The sentences are flexible, however, and the offenders are encouraged to repent. They are not confined with hardened criminals, and, at least in theory, there is no stigma attached to reeducation through labor. The deputy director of one of the prison farms where young people are sent for reeducation said, "Our work here is to educate and reform those offenders whose offenses are not serious enough to require a jail sentence. We ask all our personnel to treat offenders just like doctors treat patients who have an infectious disease, like mothers teaching their children, like teachers instructing their pupils."

Whether the young people are sent for "reeducation through labor" or are incarcerated in jails or prisons after trials, they must work while they are incarcerated. The warden of the Shanghai Municipal Jail emphasized that the inmates spend two hours a day in classes, including English and Japanese, but that most of their time is spent working. The men make watch parts and clothing—mainly shirts—and the women make clothing and knit. The products are sold on the open market at the same price, as are items made outside the prison, but the prison-made products are so labeled.

According to the warden at one of the prisons, the great majority of the inmates "reform themselves" effectively; over 90 percent of them have been praised and rewarded in some way for their good behavior. According to the warden, "We turn a destructive force into workers beneficial to society." Other reports from people who have been in Chinese prisons, however, indicate that the situation is quite different from that pictured by this warden.

Source: Notes taken by Sue Titus Reid during a tour of the criminal justice facilities of the People's Republic of China, August 1982.

Labor in the federal prison system   The Bureau of Prisons' policy calls for assigning all capable inmates to a structured activity, such as educational programs, vocational training, or work details, for eight hours per day, and the inmates are employed in either institutional work or industrial work.

Institutional work includes housekeeping, food preparation and delivery, and maintenance of the prison facility. Approximately 60 percent of working inmates are in institutional jobs receiving nominal pay. The problem with institutional work is that under the policy of keeping all inmates busy, more than necessary are assigned to institutional work. Instead of the ideal eight hour work day, many inmates finish their job assignments in two to

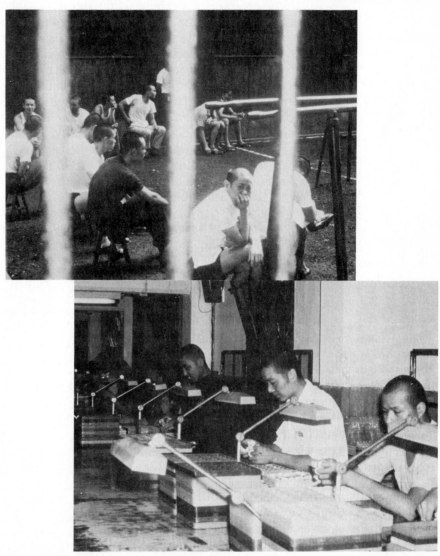

In the People's Republic of China, inmates must work in prison industries. Here the men in a maximum security facility are making watch parts. Some time is provided for recreation, but this prison's limited facilities mean that most of the recreational time is spent just sitting in the prison yard.

three hours and spend the rest of the day idle. Another problem is that with too many inmates, there may not be enough staff for proper supervision. Finally, institutional work does not help prepare inmates for jobs in society.[63]

The second type of employment in federal institutions is industrial work, whose programs generally give inmates work experiences that are closer to outside employment. In contrast with institutional work, industrial work programs sometimes do not have enough inmates assigned to them.

Vocational and industrial programs in the federal system are operated by the Federal Prison Industries, Inc. (FPI), created by Congress in 1934. FPI is a government corporation whose purpose is to employ all able-bodied inmates in federal facilities. FPI is entirely self-sustaining, and all revenues come from the sale of goods made in prison and sold to federal agencies, as well as from services provided for those agencies.

In 1980, the FPI had eighty-two work places in thirty-four facilities. From 1934 to 1970, FPI returned approximately $82 million to the U.S. Treasury. From 1960 to 1980, total sales amounted to about $1.3 billion, and profits exceeded $200 million. Since 1970, approximately $64 million has been used for vocational training programs and incentive payments to inmates in institutional work programs. The FPI's profits are also used to upgrade facilities and equipment.[64]

Strong criticism of FPI has come from those who argue that it has become a prison bureaucracy with the goal of making a profit. Employment is kept down, thus reducing the number of jobs for inmates; low wages are paid; and inmates are trained for jobs that do not exist outside prisons. Attempts to bargain and organize are suppressed. It is claimed that FPI greatly exploits the federal prisons and that only 20 percent of federal prisoners are actually employed.[65]

Prison industry in state systems   Many states and the District of Columbia have prison industry programs, but only about 10 percent of the inmates are employed. Because the programs stress reducing costs to the institution, inmates are channeled into institutional work. Ideally, inmates would be placed in work situations that would challenge them and in which they had some interest. Traditional prison industries, however, are "rarely competitive, practically never teach skills that have marketplace value, and are not calculated to offer the inmate a sense of pride in his work." The most common jobs do not prepare the inmate for living and working in a competitive society heavily dominated by automation. Inmates know that their jobs are not important to society but only to the maintenance of the prison, and many see them as a form of punishment.[66]

The Free Venture Program.   To remedy this situation, the federal government has taken steps to encourage the worthwhile employment of inmates in state institutions. In 1974, the now-defunct Law Enforcement Assistance

Administration (LEAA) began to research the impact of prison industry. What resulted was the **Free Venture Program,** which assists states in turning prison industries into profitable operations through the application of free-world business principles and practices.

Seven states participated in the program, each with a unique form of private participation in prison industries. Some states lease prison space to industries that operate within the walls; others subcontract with private businesses.[67] Private entrepreneurs have served as consultants to programs, provided financial assistance, and served on the board of directors of some prison industries. Free Venture gave grants of money to states to remodel prison industries, and the financial results from these projects have been encouraging.[68]

Evaluation of Free Venture programs. An extensive report analyzes data collected from the various programs in the seven states with Free Venture prison industries.[69] This study used data from institutional records and interviews with industry directors, prison superintendents, corrections officers, Free Venture shop supervisors, prison program staff, and inmates working in both traditional industries and Free Venture programs.

Effect of Free Venture on inmates. Inmates who participated in the Free Venture programs reacted favorably to most aspects of the system. First, they liked the length of the work day, ranging from six to eight hours. Some even wanted to work overtime. The work schedule, however, did present some problems in scheduling other activities such as counseling. Some institutions resolved these scheduling problems by adding a night work shift or offering counseling and other treatment services during evening hours.[70]

Second, inmates responded very favorably to Free Venture's payment of wages.[71] Although the wages were generally low, ranging from $0.20 to $3.74 per hour, they were higher than the average wages in traditional prison industries. Wages are very important to inmates, and over one-half of those in the Free Venture study thought that their wages should be tied to productivity and job performance, which would increase their incentive as well as enhance their self-esteem. Self-esteem is also enhanced when inmates have earned money to use for presents for their families, to pay the expenses of family members who come to visit, and to buy some of their own incidental items in prison. Included in the suggestions concerning wages are proposals for inmates to repay the state for part of the costs of their incarceration, send money to their families to reduce the welfare rolls, and pay restitution to their victims.[72]

A third effect of Free Venture on inmates was increased job satisfaction. One of the program's goals was to create an atmosphere similar to that in the private sector. When supervisors treated inmates like employees, job satisfaction rose. Job satisfaction was also greatest in shops in which wages were tied to productivity and the prisoners felt that their work experience would help them get a better job after release. Inmates also benefited psychologically. Inmates liked the freedom in the Free Venture shops, the lack of tension, the distance from other, troublesome inmates, and the sense of a purpose in life. Seventy-one percent of the inmates said they were satisfied or very satisfied with their jobs, and the majority cited the development of job skills as the most important aspect. Only 15 percent worked primarily for the wages.[73]

A fourth area of impact was on the inmates' behavior. Free Venture workers had fewer disciplinary problems than did nonparticipating inmates. Several reasons were suggested. Inmates who work full time have less time to get into trouble. They are not as bored, and they are not as often involved in the kinds of situations that lead to disciplinary problems. They have money to pay their debts, and therefore they do not have to borrow money or otherwise obligate themselves to other inmates. They have less need to "gain status" with other inmates through aggressive behavior, as they gain status through their jobs. Finally, inmates who used work as a psychological escape from the prison were not as tense, anxious, or aggressive when they returned to their cells at night.

A final effect of Free Venture was on the inmates' job placement after they were released from prison, even though sufficient funds had been set aside for job placement services. The inmates, however, believed that enhanced job opportunities upon release were important, and over half intended to seek similar employment on the outside. Less than one-half of the inmates expected any formal assistance with employment searches on release, although many thought their supervisors could be useful in an informal, personal way.[74]

Effect of Free Venture on the institutions.   Any positive effect of Free Venture on inmates would theoretically have a positive impact on the institution in general. But that has not necessarily been the case, depending on your point of view. Institutions had to make changes in other schedules to accommodate inmates who were working full time during the day. Different arrangements had to be made for family visits, attorney visits, inmate visits to the prison hospital, and so on, and such changes were seen by some administrators as an extreme inconvenience.

The institution also faces problems when some inmates, working in seasonal industries or those that are experiencing changes in production output, do not have enough work. These inmates have to be reassigned to other jobs or left idle. Lengthy security lock downs are also a problem when inmates are supposed to report to work. One solution to that problem has been to provide separate housing for industry workers, but that is another administrative problem.

These administrative problems are perhaps worth Free Venture's positive impact—greater institutional tranquility, less violence and disorder, and better-adjusted inmates. We do need more research on the total impact of prison labor on inmates and the institutions, but as Chief Justice Burger said, "The improvements will cost less in the long run than the failure to make them."[75]

Private industry in state prisons

Use of the prison labor force by strictly private companies without the assistance of grants or funds from the state or federal government is not as common as Free Venture industries are, but it is important for the same reasons. Private businesses bring free-sector expertise into the institutions and offer skills, training, and experiences like those the inmates will encounter upon release. Several programs have been successful in providing meaningful work for inmates.[76]

LEGAL ISSUES IN PRISON EDUCATION AND LABOR

Generally when we talk about education and work opportunities in prisons, we complain that they do not exist or that the programs are inadequate. A recent question has arisen, however, with regard to the institution's right to force an inmate to attend classes or to work. A case in Arkansas answered the question in the affirmative. The case involved an inmate who, because of illness when he was a child, was taken out of school and never returned. He was forty-three years old at the time of the hearing and functionally illiterate, although probably not mentally retarded. He argued that the classes made him extremely nervous but that he was required to attend eight hours of classes one day a week. He contended that he had "a constitutional right to remain ignorant and, indeed, illiterate." The court did not agree. The court said that the nervousness suffered by the inmate while attending classes did not constitute **cruel and unusual punishment.** The court also found that since the inmate had attended classes, he had progressed to reading at a second-grade level. Notice the court's analysis of the constitutional issue:[77]

Rutherford v. Hutto

The question then, is whether in the interest of rehabilitation of convicts a State may constitutionally require adult inmates of a prison to attend classes where they are given an opportunity to learn something which they may or may not be willing or able to turn to their profit. To put it this way, may the State consitutionally lead the horse to water even though it knows that the horse cannot be made to drink?

While it may be doubted that rehabilitation programs in prisons are as effective as we would like for them to be, a State clearly has a right to undertake to rehabilitate its convicts, and indeed most convict complaints in this area are the direct opposite of the complaint made here; most convict complaints involving rehabilitation are either that there are no adequate programs or that the complaining convict is wrongfully denied an opportunity to participate in existing programs.

Granting the right of a State to try to rehabilitate the inmates of its penal institutions, the Court does not think that it should necessarily be left up to an individual convict to determine whether or not he is to participate in a rehabilitative program such as the one involved here. To put it another way, if a State can compel a convict to perform uncompensated labor for the benefit of the State, as can constitutionally be done, a fortiori a State has the constitutional power to require a convict to participate in a rehabilitation program designed to benefit the convict.

There are, of course, constitutional limits to what a State may do in the name or cause of rehabilitation. The Court does not think that a State may subject a convict to a rehabilitative program or procedure that is dangerous to his life or health, or that makes his overall confinement unduly hard or rigorous, or that invidiously discriminates against him on an impermissible ground such as religion or race or that invades federally protected rights that follow the inmate into the institution. But aside from those limitations and perhaps others that do not immediately come to mind, the Court does not consider that a convict has any more right to refuse to be given a chance to benefit from a rehabilitative program than he has to refuse to work or to obey other lawful orders that may be given him by prison personnel.

The "constitutional right to be ignorant" or "the constitutional right to remain uneducated," which petitioner postulates, simply does not exist. On the other hand, the Court holds that a State has a sufficient interest in eliminating illiteracy among its convicts to justify it in requiring illiterate convicts, including adults, to attend classes designed to bring them up to at least the fourth-grade educational level where their exposure to instruction does not affect them adversely in any significant way and where they are not punished simply because they cannot or will not learn. If an illiterate convict can learn to read and write while in prison that achievement itself may give him a degree of self-confidence that he needs to live in the outside world as a law-abiding, productive citizen.

From what has been said it follows that the petition must be dismissed. That means that petitioner can and probably will be required to attend classes again, and if he refuses to do so he may be subjected to reasonable prison discipline. . . .

What has just been said leads the Court to advise petitioner to reconsider his attitude about the school program and to realize that it is designed to benefit him and that it can benefit him if he will let it; certainly, it will not hurt him to have at least some more education than he has.

Along with the inmate's duty to participate in educational programs, some courts have found that prison administrators have a duty to provide these programs. In a case considering the overall conditions in a New Hampshire facility, the court said that "opportunities to stave off degeneration and to minimize impediment to reform" were a proper concern of the court.[78]

On the other hand, a court decision ordering one state to begin programs, jobs, and educational opportunities for inmates was reversed on appeal. The appellate court said that the lack of vocational and educational programs could not be considered a violation of the Eighth Amendment's ban on cruel and unusual punishment.[79]

Finally, the courts have held that inmates do not have a constitutional right to refuse to work while they are incarcerated. Inmates have raised the issue on the basis of several grounds. First, they argue that the wages are too low and that therefore they do not have to work. That issue was settled bluntly by the Eighth Circuit in a case that the Supreme Court refused to review. The court said that any compensation for prison work exists only "by the grace of the state."[80]

The second of the inmates' arguments is that involuntary work assignments constitute cruel and unusual punishment and therefore violate the Eighth Amendment. The courts have also rejected this argument.[81] Finally, inmates have unsuccessfully contended that forced work assignments constitute involuntary slavery and are therefore in violation of the Thirteenth Amendment. A 1914 Supreme Court decision met that issue with these words: "There can be no doubt that the State has authority to impose involuntary servitude as a punishment for crime. This fact is recognized in the Thirteenth Amendment, and such punishment expressly excepted from its terms."[82]

TREATMENT IN PRISON

Our discussion of the world of the inmate has focused on the process of **socialization** within the prison, education, and work opportunities. Although these kinds of opportunities are important, they should be distinguished from *treatment*. Educational and work opportunities, along with other activities such as recreational facilities and religious activities might be called "adjuncts to treatment." They all are important to the prison's total program, and the increase in the availability of these adjuncts may not only be seen as humane but must also be understood in light of federal court cases concerning what types of facilities and programs are required in order for the conditions inside prisons to be constitutional. These programs are not, however, aimed at inmates' particular therapy problems and therefore are not treatment per se. Treatment is broadly considered to include all of those "programs" or approaches that are aimed at reforming or rehabilitating the inmate.

The critical issue today appears to be whether we should be concerned at all with the treatment of inmates. We have already looked at the demise of the "rehabilitative" ideal, noting that it has been replaced with a punishment philosophy of retribution, or "just deserts." Perhaps the most important reason for the change in philosophy was the increasing belief that "nothing works," that there is nothing we can do to rehabilitate offenders.

DOES TREATMENT WORK?

Attempts to measure whether or not treatment has been effective have been made, and the research has been criticized. The impetus for the "nothing-works" approach, which came from a 1974 article, "What Works?—Questions and Answers About Prison Reform,"[83] has been attacked because of its methodology and its lack of coverage of all types of treatment programs.[84] The criticisms did not, however, dim the impact of "nothing works." Perhaps we were just ready to believe that, and the article gave us "evidence" for a conclusion we had already reached.

The conclusions of the 1974 article were supported by other studies. For example, an intensive evaluation of the effects of treatment programs in the California prison system, one of the largest in the nation as well as one of the most progressive, ended with the conclusion that "with rare exceptions ... California's sophisticated programs have little or no effect on recidivism."[85] Treatment personnel in the California system reacted with the argument that even if the rates of recidivism were not reduced, the treatment efforts produced better-adjusted people and that it is quite possible that we just do not know how to measure the real impact of treatment.

The treatment personnel may have a valid point. The use of recidivism to measure the success or failure of the inmates' treatment is questionable. First, researchers do not agree on a definition of that term.[86] Some studies define it as covering those released inmates who are returned to prison; others measure recidivism by arrests, even if the offender is not convicted and incarcerated. Still others consider that an inmate released on parole who violates a parole rule (but not a statute and thus does not commit a crime) and is returned to prison is a recidivist.

Second, it may be that treatment and recidivism, however it is defined, have no relationship. One study of young men in Philadelphia followed the subjects over a specified period of years. The investigators found that most of them were not arrested after their first apprehension by the police; in other words, most were not recidivists. We might conclude, then, that it would be wasteful to launch a treatment program to involve all delinquents after their first official contact with the police. It might even be wise to wait until after the third offense and concentrate efforts on chronic offenders,[87] who, according to this study, had a 70 percent chance of being arrested again. The same might be true for those who are incarcerated. Perhaps some

EXHIBIT
POSTCORRECTIONAL PERFORMANCE IS DIFFICULT TO ASSESS

Some Indicator of a Return to Criminal Activity Is Typically Used to Evaluate Postcorrectional Performance

Rearrest, reindictment, reconviction, and reimprisonment measured over some period of time after release from prison are generally used to gauge the extent of success and failure (recidivism) associated with correctional programs.

The unit of time selected and the level of criminal justice system penetration (that is, more persons are likely to be rearrested than reimprisoned) will substantially affect judgments about the proportion failing or succeeding after a correctional experience.

Moreover, conditionally released populations (that is, parolees) are subjected to supervision requirements that, if violated, may result in a return to prison for noncriminal conduct (such as curfew violation or failure to report to a parole officer). Parolees, also, once discharged from supervision are not followed up further by State or local agencies and, thus, information on new criminal involvements would not generally be available.

Within 1 Year After Release on Parole, About 12% of Those Released Are Likely to Be Back in Prison

It is not possible from available national data to assess the total volume of criminal reinvolvements for all persons released from prison. However, it is possible to assess the extent to which those under parole supervision for up to 3 years are reconfined.

Within the first year of release from prison—

● 12% of the offenders under supervision are returned to prison; about half are returned for violations of their supervision requirements (a technical violation) or for a minor conviction; the other half are returned for new, major convictions.

● About 20% are successfully discharged within 1 year.

● Nearly two out of three releasees are continued on parole after completing the first year successfully.

Within 3 Years After Release on Parole, 24% of the Parolees Are Likely to Be Returned to Prison

Within 3 years of release, 72% of parolees are still considered to be successful, either being discharged (56%) or continued on parole (16%). The proportion returned to prison (24%) is double the 1-year performance; this indicates that half of all parolees who will return to prison within 3 years of release do so in the first year. More than half (55%) of the returns to prison within 3 years are for technical violations of supervision requirements; the remainder are for new, major convictions.

	Parole Status	
	Within 1 Year	Within 3 Years
Discharged	19%	56%
Continued on parole	65	16
Absconded	4	2
Returned to prison	12	24
Died	1	2

Note: Totals may not add to 100% due to rounding.
Source: *Uniform Parole Reports,* 1977.

Most Prison Inmates Report Having Had Prior Sentences to Confinement

Nearly 64% of all adult inmates have experienced prior sentences of incarceration—8% report prior juvenile incarceration only, 29% report prior adult confinements only, and 23% report previous juvenile and adult sentences to a correctional institution (4% did not report whether their prior confinement occurred during their juvenile or adult years).

Offenders admitted to prison in their thirties are more likely than any other age group to be repeat offenders. By contrast, those admitted to prison after age 60 are more likely than other age groups to be experiencing their first confinement.

Age at Current Admission	Number Admitted to Prison	% Serving First Sentence to Confinement
Less than 18	6,254	56%
18–19	29,316	54%
20–29	149,662	44%
30–39	51,727	31%
40–49	15,072	37%
50–59	6,418	36%
60+	2,080	59%

Source: *Survey of Prison Inmates,* 1979.

After Age 30, Many Repeat Offenders Begin to Drop Out of Crime

The decline in the number of admissions after age 30, and the increase in the proportion of persons serving their first confinement sentence after age 40, indicates that substantial dropping-out from imprisonable criminal activity is occurring among repeat offenders as they enter middle age (age 40 or older).

The reasons why repeat offenders end their involvement in crime may be just as important for crime control purposes as the reasons why they begin. Shover's recent research based on interviews with middle-aged men who were criminally active during their younger years suggests that the justice system, in effect, physically "wears down" offenders. The process of repeatedly being arrested, appearing in court, and adjusting to prison life came to be perceived by these offenders as an exhausting ordeal. This suggests the possibility that a deterrent effect may be age-related—that is, as persistent offenders age, the costs of crime become greater, discouraging many from continuing their criminal careers.

Source: Bureau of Justic Statistics, *Report to the Naiton on Crime and Justice: The Data* (Washington, D.C.: U.S. Government Printing Office, 1983), p. 84.

will be recidivists no matter what we do, and others will be law-abiding citizens who do not need treatment.[88]

Third, we need to know more about whether incarceration is a more effective method of punishment than are other methods.[89] There is some evidence that probation is at least as effective in preventing recidivism as a prison term is and that "fines and discharges are much more effective than either probation or imprisonment for first offenders and recidivists of all age groups." Medium-risk offenders are most likely to improve, and there is no evidence that longer institutional sentences are more effective than shorter terms in preventing recidivism. Some studies suggest that open institutions are just as successful as closed ones, and many studies reveal no significant differences between treatment and punishment.[90]

Finally, it is possible that we cannot measure the precise effects of treatment. It can be argued that it makes no difference whether we provide treatment for inmates. The philosophy of just deserts does not preclude treatment; it only precludes forced treatment as well as combining treatment with release procedures. The just deserts approach, as we saw earlier, is based on the assumption that prison *is* the punishment and that offenders will be sentenced to serve only the length of time they deserve to serve in light of the crimes they have committed and the circumstances under which those acts occurred. Offenders are not to be punished beyond what they deserve, nor are they to be forced to become involved in treatment programs. On the other hand, those who want treatment should be given reasonable access to the facilities and programs that will prepare them for a more successful adjustment to life outside the prison.

SUMMARY AND CONCLUSION

Inmates face many problems during incarceration. In this chapter we focused on the world of the inmate, beginning with the inmates' process of socialization into the prison subculture. We discussed whether inmates bring that subculture from the outside or whether it evolves as they attempt to adapt to the pains of imprisonment. We then looked at classification. If inmates are to adjust satisfactorily to life in prison, they first must be classified and then placed in the institutions that are most appropriate to their needs. After classification and assignment, it is important that we offer them educational and work opportunities, and we discussed some of the problems in both of these areas.

In the final section of the chapter, we briefly examined whether treatment programs have been successful and concluded that we do not have an answer. It is, however, clear that we cannot ignore the problems of those we incarcerate. The ways in which inmates adapt to prison life have implications not only for the security of the institution and of society but also for the future of the inmates and of society when the incarcerated individuals are released. As Justice Thurgood Marshall observed with regard to prison life:

> When the prison gates slam behind an inmate, he does not lose his human quality; his mind does not become closed to ideas, his intellect does not cease to feed on a free and open interchange of opinions, his yearning for self-respect does not end; nor is his quest for self-realization concluded. If anything, the needs for identity and self-respect are more compelling in the dehumanizing prison environment.[91]

CHAPTER 17

Corrections
in the community

This final chapter of the text examines the need for community treatment facilities and programs. Most inmates do return to society, and if they are not prepared—or if we refuse to allow them to succeed—we can expect that they will return to a life of crime. Indeed, perhaps some will be criminal no matter what we do. But in this chapter we shall look at programs for reintegration of those who want to become law-abiding citizens. We shall begin with the concept of reintegration and then examine the different types of community correctional facilities. We shall discuss the problems inmates face when they are released from prison, prerelease programs designed to assist them in adjusting to those problems, and, finally, the parole system.

In earlier chapters, we traced the emergence of prisons and the changes in philosophies of punishment and imprisonment. Early reformers thought that offenders should be incarcerated in "total institutions." Removal from home and society was seen as necessary to remove the evil influences that had led to criminal behavior. While incarcerated, the offenders would have time to think and reflect on their behavior and become involved in religious services and other efforts at reformation.

Before long, however, prison reformers were declaring that incarceration in total institutions did not reduce criminal activity after the offenders were released and that it also exacerbated the existing problems of those who had served time. In 1777, reformer John Howard referred to prisons as "seats and seminaries of idleness and every vice," though others were more emphatic. In prison, "by the greatest possible degree of misery, you produce the greatest possible degree of wickedness." In 1864, Jeremy Bentham declared that prisons

> with the exception of a small number, include every imaginable means of infecting both body and mind . . . an ordinary prison is a school in which wickedness is taught . . . weariness, revenge, and want preside over academies of crime. All the inmates raise themselves to the level of the worst.

In 1890 the English prison system was described as "simply a manufactory of lunatics and criminals," and in 1922 the process of imprisonment was described as follows:

> In general the effects of imprisonment are the nature of a progressive weakening of the mental powers and of a deterioration of the character in a way which renders the prisoner less fit for useful social life, more predisposed to crime, and in consequence more liable to reconviction.

These early declarations have been described as conclusions without evidence;[1] yet as we saw in the previous chapter, there is evidence that "modern" prisons, with their emphasis on rehabilitation, brought about by professional treatment as well as educational, vocational, and other programs in prison, also have failed. The impact of incarceration in "total" institutions in this century has been described by sociologists as follows:

> Despite an enormous investment of time, energy, and money, no approach, treatment, or rehabilitative framework has been demonstrably successful in preventing, reducing, and controlling recidivism. So great has been our failure in altering antisocial patterns and life styles that the entire people-changing enterprise has been condemned as both ineffective and, worse, unjust. Many, if not all, seriously concerned behaviorists now firmly believe that the total institution is an historical aberration and must be eliminated with all due haste.[2]

In 1973, the National Advisory Commission on Criminal Justice Standards and Goals called for an increased emphasis on probation, already the most frequently used form of sentencing. The commission concluded: "The most hopeful move toward effective corrections is to continue and strengthen the trend away from confining people in institutions and toward supervising them in the community."[3] During the 1970s, the key word in corrections appeared to be the **reintegration** of the offender into society, a process that "cannot be accomplished by isolating the offender in an artificial, custodial setting."[4] Nevertheless, in the past few years we have moved away from a philosophy of **rehabilitation** and reintegration to one of retribution and "just deserts," and with that movement, we have increased our rates of incarceration in total institutions to the point that most states are currently under court orders to reduce their prison populations. The lack of facilities for incarcerations in prisons has also meant retaining some of the inmates in jails, and so now many of our jails are facing court orders to reduce their populations.

COMMUNITY CORRECTIONS: AN ATTEMPT AT REINTEGRATION

Disillusionment with total institutions, serious problems of prison overcrowding, and, in some cases, concern with treating the offender has led to the current emphasis on reintegrating offenders through **community-based** treatment.

THE CONCEPT OF REINTEGRATION

In contrast with the concept of **incapacitation**—the process of rendering offenders incapable of further criminal activity by removing them from the community and placing them in total institutions, **reintegration** may be defined as:

> the process of preparing both the community and offender for the latter's return as a productive and accepted citizen. . . . the emphasis is on creating the circumstances around him that will enable him to lead a satisfying and law-abiding life. In the reintegration model, corrections must bring about change in the offender, within his family, among his peers, and in the institutions within which he must function successfully—that is, in his social environment.[5]

TYPES OF COMMUNITY CORRECTIONAL FACILITIES

When we talk about community-based facilities in corrections today, we must distinguish such facilities and programs from activities and programs that may be located in the community but are not, strictly speaking, community-based treatment. For example, the old chain gangs worked in the community, but obviously this is not what is meant by community corrections.[6] "Generally, as the frequency, quality, and duration of community relationships increase the program becomes more community-based."[7] The degree to which a correctional system is community based can also be measured by the number of commitments to large state institutions, the extent to which other community services are used, and the degree of involvement by local groups and individuals.[8]

Community corrections should also be distinguished from diversion, a term that is often used to refer to community corrections. Technically, **diversion** means to turn the offender aside from the criminal (or juvenile) justice system. It should not be used to refer to "a different routing within the correctional component of this system." The appropriate term to use for the "development and use of community-based correctional programs as alternatives to institutions" is **deinstitutionalization.**[9]

Community correctional centers are composed of a wide variety of programs, from secure restraint in residential programs to nonsecure residential

---

EXHIBIT

COMMUNITY-BASED FACILITIES

Community-based facilities are operated publicly or privately (under contract) to hold persons for less than 24 hours a day to permit the offender limited opportunities for work, school, or other community contacts. Such facilities are used for a variety of purposes including specialized intervention or assistance (for example, drug or alcohol treatment), graduated release from prison—usually prior to parole—or as a sanction in lieu of prison or jail confinement. In 1979, 11,010 offenders resided in such facilities.

Community-based Facilities House 4% of the Population of State Prison Systems

Relatively few inmates (11,010) in 1979 were housed in 223 community-based facilities.

- Nearly 64% of such inmates were in Southern States; the largest number (1,873) was in Florida.
- Nearly half the facilities reported an average daily population of between 21 and 60 inmates, but about half of all inmates lived in a facility housing 41 to 100 inmates. One in nine such facilities reported that their inmate populations exceeded their rated capacities.
- Only about 16% of community-based residents reside in housing units designed for one person; 42% live in housing units for between two and four persons.
- Community-based facilities reported one employee for every 3.2 inmates, one administrative employee for every 25 inmates, one custodial employee for every 6 inmates, one clerical/maintenance worker for every 18 inmates, and one professional/technical employee for every 17 inmates.

Source: Bureau of Justice Statistics, *Report to the Nation on Crime and Justice: The Data* (Washington, D.C.: U.S. Government Printing Office, 1983), p. 78.

halfway houses. Nonresidential programs are also included in community corrections. The distinguishing characteristics of community correctional centers generally are that (1) the center is not located in a rural area but is in a larger community where participants live and sometimes work; (2) the correctional responsibility rests with a county or municipal political subdivision rather than with the state; (3) the offender has a great deal of responsibility for working out his or her own treatment program; (4) community correctional centers are generally small and have limited budgets; (5) most include representatives from the community who assist in the programs; (6) the emphasis is generally on establishing successful relationships in the community, with family, peers, or employers; and (7) offenders, though not in institutions, do have some degree of restraint.[10]

The Minnesota community corrections plan The correctional system in Minnesota is an example of corrections as a joint effort between the community and the offender to reintegrate or maintain that offender in the community.

Under the Minnesota plan, counties and groups of counties are encouraged to institute local programs for all but the most serious adult offenders and all juvenile offenders. Counties receive a state subsidy determined by a formula based on the county's correctional needs, population, and financial resources, minus the projected costs for the number of people that the county would commit to state institutions. For each eligible offender sent to a state institution, there is a "charge-back" from the state subsidy given to the community, which operates as a powerful incentive to use community corrections rather than commitment to a state institution.[11]

But the community-based corrections program in Minnesota has not been as successful as hoped. First, the extended budget savings to the Department of Corrections did not materialize. Second, there was no improvement in public protection, though the plan did not increase the risks to the community's security. And there were noted improvements in local correctional planning and administration, along with many new community programs with expanded and high-quality services. These included delinquency prevention programs, school programs, group houses, drug and alcohol treatment centers, pretrial services, diversion programs, jail treatment programs, and victim-witness programs. There was a significant drop of 29.5 percent in the rate of commitments to juvenile institutions. There was also an increase in the severity of sentences. The use of probation declined, but the use of probation with a condition of jail time rose, and therefore, there were more commitments to local jails.

The Minnesota plan did not achieve one of its major goals: the reduction of the state's inmate populations. When the plan was instituted, there was a revival in public attitudes favoring incarceration for criminals. This "get-tough" attitude in turn affected the judges, who changed their sentencing practices to conform to community opinion. Thus, a major flaw in the plan was the control given to the judges. Any judge who continued to sentence felons to state institutions could virtually eliminate the county subsidy through the "charge-back" program. To remedy this problem, the Minnesota Sentencing Guidelines Commission provided guidelines for the judges on the length of sentences and whether the sentence should be a state or a community sentence. The guidelines are adjusted each year to reflect the current inmate population and, in effect, set a cap on arrivals at the state's prisons. The guidelines did result in a net decrease in the adult prison population, and the commission is also considering guidelines for the use of local programs, especially jail sentences.[12]

The Des Moines program

The community treatment approach of Des Moines, Iowa, combines a variety of community programs and uses existing facilities with a minimum of expense.[13]

The Des Moines program has four components. First, the pretrial release screening program is an effort to release people before trial and without bond. Objective criteria are used to determine whether an offender has stable roots in the community, and if so, pretrial release is recommended.

The second component is pretrial community supervision of those who are not included in the pretrial release screening. Of those persons, 54 percent are released under careful supervision. Counseling services are available; a complete educational, vocational, and psychiatric evaluation is made of each person within a week of release; and the treatment plan is geared to individual needs.

The third component of the Des Moines program is county- rather than state-supervised probation. As a result, probation officers work more closely with the court in preparing a **presentence report** on each person. They also provide more adequate probation supervision. More people are on probation, and probation officers make extensive use of existing community resources.

Finally, the program offers a community-centered corrections facility, which was established as an alternative to jail but which has also become an alternative to prison. More than 90 percent of the inmates are convicted felons, and about 20 percent are heroin addicts. The program has a contract, an individual treatment plan for each offender, a high use of nonprofessionals, a professional staff of one to every two clients, and a close relationship with other social agencies.

Initial evaluations of the Des Moines program indicated that offenders supervised under the community treatment plan were more likely to appear for their trials than were those released on the traditional form of bail. Costs were reduced by releasing offenders instead of incarcerating them in the local jail. Less than 14 percent of the inmates in the community-centered corrections facility were alleged to have committed another offense, and none of those offenses involved property, public morals, or drug abuse. Most were escapes. After release from the facility, these offenders' rearrest rate was 15 to 36 percent lower than that of most released from traditional institutions.

The Des Moines community program illustrates both the use of minimum sueprvision, as in the pretrial release screening program and county-administered probation, and the more intensive intervention programs for persons who need more than probation supervision or counseling.

One important feature of the Des Moines program is that it has been successfully replicated in at least six other localities in the United States, localities that were considered politically conservative and therefore relatively unreceptive to the community corrections philosophy.[14] Other successful features of the Des Moines program include a reduction in jail overcrowding, improved information for the courts in determinations of pretrial release and sentencing, provision of a residential alternative suitable for large numbers of inmates formerly sent to jail or state prisons, and an improvement in community support for local programs.[15]

On the other hand, one report indicated that the community correctional facility received some offenders who would have been sentenced to probation if the facility had not been available.[16] In one city, investigators found that offenders placed on supervised release would have been **released on bond** or on their own **recognizance** if supervised release had not been available. In other locations, supervised release was not used as much as was pretrial diversion or placement at the community correctional facility while awaiting trial.[17]

Residential versus nonresidential facilities   Many of the earlier community-based treatment facilities, especially those designed for juveniles, were residential centers. Foster homes and group homes were common. A number of these treatment programs have been evaluated.[18]

More recently, however, more attention has been given to the development of nonresidential treatment facilities. The Des Moines program, for example, illustrates the use of supervision in the community at the pretrial stage as well as while on probation. Intensive probation supervision, discussed in Chapter 14, is another type of nonresidential treatment program.

A new proposal for adult nonresidential treatment is the nonresidential state-run work facility (NRWF). This program entails developing a state industrial site where offenders live at home and report for work each day. Part of their wages are withheld for restitution payments to victims. Nonviolent offenders are given the choice of prison or NRWF. If offenders commit crimes or violate work rules, the remainder of their sentences will be served in a prison facility.

Proponents of NRWF argue that it implements the basic philosophies of punishment. The restriction of freedom and the partial use of wages for fines and restitution mean that the plan has deterrent value. The plan also means "just deserts," as the length of the sentence and the extent of the fine or restitution are proportional to the offense. Incapacitation is accomplished because the offenders are under intensive supervision. Finally, unlike many other forms of punishment, NRWF rehabilitates offenders by permitting them to continue working, remain with their families, and assume responsibility for their behavior by paying for the harm they have caused their victims and/or society. Other arguments in favor of NRWF include equity (all offenders have the same working conditions and deduction from their pay), restitution (to individual victims or to a state victim restitution fund), flexibility (the industry can adapt to fewer or more offenders, and judges are not hampered by the lack of prison bed space), reintegration (the offender stays in the community), cost (NRWF is self-supporting), and humaneness (NRWF avoids the overcrowding and violence of prisons).[19]

RELEASE FROM PRISON

The process of reintegration through community treatment programs applies also to offenders who have not been incarcerated; some of these offenders' problems are shared as well by inmates who serve time in institutions and are then released back into society.

INMATES' PROBLEMS UPON RELEASE

Inmates who have been incarcerated have many problems upon their release from prison. Most have limited financial resources; many do not have employment; and some do not even have established residences and families to whom they may return. All receive indifferent and, in many cases, hostile reactions from the community. Those who have been incarcerated for long periods of time have the additional problem of "catching up" on how we do things in our society. All encounter emotional problems in reacting to the new environment, and many feel depressed, estranged, lonely, and rejected. Some institutions offer training sessions to assist inmates in preparing for release; others offer halfway programs for a gradual reentry into society. Most make some attempt to deal with the two most immediate problems: money and jobs.

Financial problems

Institutions react to the financial problems of released prisoners in several ways. The most frequent method of assistance is clothing. Most institutions require that prisoners send their personal clothing home when they enter prison; thus, at the time of release, it is necessary for the institution to replace the prison clothing.

The next most common type of assistance is "gate money," a financial

Once the inmate is paroled, he or she faces many problems.

grant given to each inmate at departure, although some institutions give the money only if the inmate has not acquired a savings account from work assignments during incarceration. Others give very small amounts, some as low as $10. Because most inmates upon release have limited financial resources (and many have no money at all), these funds must pay for transportation, food, clothing, shelter, and other expenses until their first paycheck arrives. And as many do not have jobs when they are released, they may have to wait a long time for a paycheck.

EXHIBIT

TYPES OF PROGRAMS THAT AID EX-OFFENDERS

1. Job Development and Placement: provide assessment, counseling and job development. Clients are matched to jobs and the staff arranges interviews. Staff responsible for analyzing labor market and determining where jobs exist. If the client does not require training, adult basic education, or work experience services, the placement time ranges from two to six weeks.

2. Residential Services: provides 24-hour support during transition time from prison to the community. Both work and non-work time are supervised and counseling is provided to insulate the ex-offender from alcohol, drugs, and active criminals. The typical stay in a residential facility is six months.

3. Supported Work/Work Experience: provides peer support and close supervision to clients with poor work habits, history of substance abuse and adjustment problems. Clients usually receive a stipend or the minimum wage. These programs are targeted for high risk, hard-core unemployed ex-offenders. During the 15 to 50 week program, clients have structured job tasks and frequent performance evaluations on their ability to meet performance standards in commercial jobs.

4. Skill Training: attempts to remedy an ex-offender's lack of skills and education by offering training in colleges, adult basic education classes, vocational schools, apprenticeships and on-the-job training. The training usually lasts 20 weeks.

5. Job Readiness: teaches ex-offenders job-seeking skills, including how to apply for jobs, fill out applications, interview techniques and what is expected in work settings, client work habits through workshops and classes. Training can last from 3 to 60 hours.

6. Financial Assistance: provide weekly or bi-weekly cash payments to ex-offenders and offer assistance in job placement. Financial assistance programs are based on the rationale that cash will give an ex-offender time to adjust to the community and facilitate job-seeking abilities. The financial assistance may last from one to three months.

Source: National Institute of Justice, *Employment Services for Ex-Offenders* (Washington, D.C.: U.S. Government Printing Office, 1980), pp. 9–11.

Add to that a person who is "marked," who is rejected by society and by his or her family. In many cases the ex-offender is also a "handicapped human being, one who needs all the things the rest of us need and a little bit more." Some advocate giving larger subsidies upon release, noting that if an inmate is released without any funds, a return to criminal activity is virtually guaranteed. They argue that it would be cheaper in the long run to support the releasees for a few months than to pay for their arrest, appointed counsel, trial, and incarceration.[20]

Employment   The second major problem of offenders upon their release is employment. The importance of having a job on release is dramatically illustrated by an earlier study of a job placement program for ex-offenders in Seattle. The data indicated that those who were employed full time had an 87 percent chance of successfully completing their parole, compared with only 55 percent for those who were employed half time, and 27 percent for those who worked only occasionally.[21]

There are many explanations of the relationship between employment and recidivism. Some studies find a causal relationship between unemployment and crime, whereas others argue that separate factors such as family influence or personal counseling link the two. Some studies focus on income rather than employment as the major variable affecting recidivism, and there is tentative evidence that the quality of the job may be the most important factor, in both income and work stability.[22]

Several types of programs have been developed to aid ex-offenders in job hunting. One of the most successful programs, the Alston Wilkes Society, is this country's largest private, statewide, nonprofit organization offering services to present and former inmates and their families. Many inmates move from institutions to an Alston Wilkes home where they must find jobs within three weeks, pay rent, and save 20 percent of their income. The program offers classes in filling out job applications and role-playing interview sessions. Donations of clothing and tools for jobs are collected and made available to needy clients.[23]

A national assessment and evaluation of community-based programs that assist ex-offenders in finding and retaining employment concluded that because there was such great variation in the types of employment services offered and the delivery methods, we do not know which services are the most effective. Furthermore, most programs reported that the majority of clients were successfully placed in jobs. Finally, program clients experience lower rates of recidivism than do comparision groups, although outcomes are not consistent, and there is reason to question the methodological adequacy of most evaluations.[24]

PREPARATION
FOR RELEASE   The availability of **prerelease programs** is limited. They differ from institution to institution, ranging from information on etiquette and changing social mores to practical details of how to tie a tie and interview for a job. Some prisons hold prerelease classes, and others have prerelease centers or **halfway houses**.

The reports of success vary, and it is clear that more research into the effectiveness of prerelease programs is needed before definite conclusions can be drawn. Prerelease programs do, however, appear to be a step toward assisting inmates make the difficult adjustments from the restrictive prison environment to the free world.

HIGHLIGHT
RELEASE FROM PRISON IS TRAUMATIC FOR SOME OFFENDERS

In 1977, after spending thirty years in prison in Indiana, Ralph Lobaugh was released. The freedom for which he had fought during fourteen years, however, was too much for him. After two months outside the walls Lobaugh decided he could not cope and went back to prison. Lobaugh "just wanted to live in a cell again and be with his old friends."[1] His case is unusual, but the problems of readjusting to life outside walls are so great that it has been concluded that "the real punishment of prisoners begins when they return to society."[2] That statement may be too extreme, but it is clear that if inmates are not prepared for their return to life outside the walls, if they cannot find jobs, and if they face continued discrimination and harassment, their chances of returning to the institution on another charge will be greatly enhanced.

1. Quoted in *Tulsa World,* October 29, 1977, p. 4, col. 4.
2. Norman C. Colter, "Subsidizing the Released Inmate," *Crime & Delinquency* 21 (July 1974):282

The extensive use of work release and furlough programs in the United States is very recent, stemming from the provision for these programs in the federal system by the Prisoner Rehabilitation Act of 1965. A few states had laws offering work release or furloughs before 1965, but most of the programs in existence today were established by state laws after the 1965 federal law had been passed.

Furloughs   **Furloughs** are brief absences from the institution, usually for a specified purpose other than work or study. Furloughs may be granted to allow inmates to visit sick relatives, attend family funerals, secure employment, obtain a driver's license, meet with future parole officers, arrange for housing, or visit family members. Furloughs may last from several hours to several days.

The main advantage of furlough programs is that the offenders are placed in contact with their families and the outside world. Inmates have a chance to make decisions on their own, away from the closely monitored prison routine, and the community also is given time to adjust to accepting the offender.

An example of a restricted jail furlough program is found in Maine, where

> the sheriff is authorized to establish regulations for and to permit a prisoner under the final sentence of a court furlough from the county jail in which he is confined. Furlough may be granted for not more than 3 days at one time in order to permit the prisoner to visit a dying relative or to obtain medical services, which may be for a period of longer than 3 days if medically required.[25]

Work release   In **work release** programs the inmate is released from incarceration to work or attend school. Inmates may participate in work study, take courses at an educational institution, or work at a job in the community.

Work release programs have different criteria for selecting their participants. In some jurisdictions, the criteria are specified by statute, but in most, the administrative agency that oversees the prison system determines the rules for granting work release. In the past, prison authorities have had almost total discretion in making these decisions, but more recently, the courts have intervened and, in some cases, restricted that discretion. For example, a Delaware inmate, who met the stated criteria for work release but was denied participation in the program, sued and won the right to participate. The federal court stated that although prison authorities have the discretion to grant or deny work release, that discretion must be consistent with the purpose and policy behind work release, including the humane treatment of inmates, rehabilitation, and return to the community as safely and promptly as possible. When an inmate meets all of the regulations' eligibility requirements, prison administrators may not arbitrarily deny the inmate that opportunity.[26]

In many states, inmates are entitled to a hearing before their participation in work release can be terminated. Although the specific requirements vary, inmates generally receive advance written notice of misconduct charges from twenty-four to seventy-two hours before the hearing, a written statement of the evidence used to make the decision, the right to call witnesses and present documentary evidence (when this does not interfere with institutional security), and, sometimes, the right to be assisted in the defense by a prison employee.[27]

Work release programs also have different operating procedures. An example of how the programs operate is the largest and oldest work release program in this country, the North Carolina system. In that program, inmates work each day at a regular job in the community and return to the institution at night. Both misdemeanor and felony inmates are eligible to participate.

Criteria for participation in the work release program, in order of importance, include (1) the nature of the current offense for which the inmate is incarcerated; (2) the length of the sentence and the amount of time served; (3) the inmate's criminal history, including both the number and the seriousness of past offenses; (4) the discipline record in the institution; (5) whether the job plan is appropriate, considering the use of job skills, the retraining potential, the development of good work habits, and the availability of the particular occupation after release; (6) whether the inmate has a family to support; (7) the presence of substance addictions or mental health problems; and (8) previous employment record.

From the work release program, the Department of Corrections receives room, board, and transportation reimbursements; the inmates' families receive support payments; and the state and federal governments receive taxes. Other funds are placed in savings for use after release.

Eighty-five percent of the inmates complete the work release program without any rule violations or escapes. An evaluation found that only 2 percent of work releasees committed new crimes, other than escape, in the community. Conversely, after release, nonwork release inmates were more likely to return to prison during the first twelve months or after two or more years from the date of release. On the other hand, work releasees were more likely to return during their second year after release. "From this it would appear that work release aids individuals primarily during the post-release adjustment period."[28]

Objectively, work releasees had more stable employment records after release, significantly lower unemployment rates, and higher wages. Subjectively, they did not report greater family stability but did say that their ability to send support payments to their families while they were incarcerated was one major positive aspect of the program. Psychological testing revealed that those who participated in work release had attitudes that were significantly less amoral and antisocial and demonstrated less hyperactivity than those who did not participate. This study found that the benefits of work release outweigh any disadvantages and that work release programs should be encouraged because they reduce postrelease criminal activity.[29]

Evaluation of prerelease programs   One of the advantages of furlough and work release programs is that they give the inmates opportunities to be in close contact with their families. Several studies have shown that "those inmates with strong family ties, and who have maintained those ties during incarceration, are more successful on release than those offenders without such ties."[30] Their families also benefit from work release. Inmates generally can provide some support from their work release earnings, so that their families can be relieved of the burden of the bureaucratic red tape in obtaining welfare payments. In addition, work release helps improve the inmates' attitudes toward socially responsible work. Self-esteem, self-image, and self-respect all are frequently mentioned as benefits of work release.

Another possible advantage to work release programs is their cost. Most proponents cite the enormous cost of incarceration to support work release. Researchers have pointed out that inmates on work release may help support their families, that the state can be reimbursed for part of the cost of their incarceration, that governments collect tax money from inmate-employees, and that victim restitution is best accomplished through these programs. Some research, however, has demonstrated the reverse. The hidden costs of the programs lead to longer sentences actually being served before the inmates are totally released, and the contribution of prison staff time may override any economic benefit. This is an area that has not been thoroughly explored, and further studies should be done before deciding that work release programs save money for the state.[31]

Additional problems with work release pertain to the offender-participants in the programs. The releasees may have problems in adjusting to the community during the day and then to the institution at night. Indeed, it might be easier to make a complete break with the institution and attempt to readjust to society without having to return to prison. Also, release during the day may eliminate or interrupt participation in some prison programs that are beneficial to the offender. In addition, problems may arise over the use of the money earned. Transportation is often a problem as well, because many correctional institutions are not located in urban areas where inmates are most likely to find jobs.

A final problem with work release and furlough programs is the possibility that participants may commit additional crimes or escape from supervision. Despite the careful selection of inmates to participate in such programs, some do escape, or attempt to escape, although the rates are very low.

**RELEASE
ON PAROLE**

Most inmates are released from prison on parole before the expiration of their sentences. **Parole** may be defined as "the release of an offender from a penal or correctional institution after he has served a portion of his sentence, under the continued custody of the state and under conditions that permit his reincarceration in the event of misbehavior."[32] Parole is based on the philosophy that the rehabilitation of some individuals might be hindered by further imprisonment and that reintegration can be aided by supervised freedom in the community. The decision to release is usually made by a parole board.[33]

Parole differs from **probation,** a form of sentencing in which the offender is allowed to remain in the community under supervision. Although both permit a convicted person to live in the community under supervision, probation is granted *in lieu of* incarceration and is granted by a judicial officer.

Release in the community with supervision is the most common method of handling adult offenders. At the end of 1982, 72 percent of adults in the correctional system were being supervised in the community through probation or parole. Of those convicted and sent to prison, approximately 75 percent are released on parole, although in some states, the figure is as high as 97 percent. As Figure 17.1 shows, probation has grown faster than parole has, although both are rising.

The cost of maintaining an inmate on parole ranges from $140 per year in Tennessee to $2,310 per year in Hawaii. The average cost in 1982 was $692, a 4.5 percent increase over the cost for 1981.[34] The relative costs of parole and other methods of handling offenders may be seen in Table 17.1.

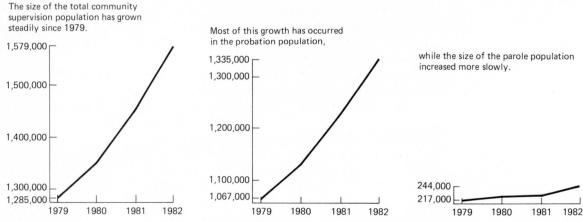

Figure 17.1 *Distribution of offenders supervised in the community.*

Source: U.S. Department of Justice, Bureau of Justice Statistics, Probation and Parole 1982 (Washington, D.C.: Government Printing Office, September 1983), p. 1.

THE PAROLE SYSTEM

The organization of parole is complex. In general, it consists of two main divisions: the **parole board,** responsible for release decisions, and the **parole officers**, who then supervise the parolees in the community. These two parole divisions carry out the four main functions of parole: releasing and placing prisoners on parole, administraton of parole supervision personnel, releasing parolees from supervision upon completion of their sentences or showing that they are no longer a risk to the community, and revoking parole when the parolees have violated the conditions of parole.

THE DECISION TO RELEASE ON PAROLE

Parole boards have had almost total discretionary power to determine which inmates would be released on parole. The assumption was that parole was a privilege, not a right, but the Supreme Court has observed that "nothing in the Constitution requires a State to provide for probation or parole."[35]

Parole board members have a responsibility for individual parole decisions—decisions that have a serious and lasting impact on the inmates' lives—while at the same time they have a responsibility to protect the com-

Table 17.1

Relative costs of corrections operations

Average Annual Cost for One Adult Offender—	
in a Federal prison	$13,000
in a State prison	$5,000–$23,000
in a State "halfway house"	$12,000
in a local community-based facility	$8,000
in a local jail	$8,000
on Federal probation or parole	$1,300
on non-Federal probation or parole	$220–$1,700

Source: Bureau of Justice Statistics, *Report to the Nation on Crime and Justice: The Data* (Washington, D.C.: U.S. Government Printing Office, 1983), p. 92.

munity. Parole boards must work in the confines of legal and administrative restrictions and in the spotlight of public opinion. Parole boards are under tremendous community pressure when well-known prisoners are eligible for parole.

What criteria should be used in the parole decision-making process? Two approaches have been used to predict which applicants for parole would be successful if released. The first type is *statistical* prediction based on **prediction scales.** Criminological research on the use of statistics to predict future criminal behavior began in the 1920s with a study that attempted to relate factors such as age, education, and past criminal record to parole crimes. The resulting table was then used to predict whether other, similar offenders would be suitable candidates for parole.[36]

A review of recent statistical prediction studies yielded mixed results, but there are problems in comparing prediction studies. Some are based on reconviction data, and others are based on arrest data; the latter, of course, include those who are arrested but are not convicted of the crime. The only general conclusion from statistical prediction studies is that it may be easier to predict nonviolent than violent crimes.[37]

The second and most common approach is *clinical* prediction. In this method, an expert examines an inmate and gives a subjective opinion about the likelihood of future crime. Clinical prediction studies also have yielded mixed results. Generally, the studies have shown an overprediction of dangerousness; that is, many offenders who are not violent are predicted to be dangerous and are thus retained in institutions.[38]

Empirical evidence on parole decisions

Some researchers have attempted to gather empirical evidence on parole decisions in order to determine the basis for, as well as the effectiveness of, the parole decision. The results vary, as do their interpretation. For example, earlier studies show that race, age, education, IQ, marital status, sex, or socioeconomic background are variables that influence the decision to grant parole.[39] Some suggest that these variables are used in a discriminatory fashion against blacks, men, the less educated, and people from lower socioeconomic strata. Others found that when controlling for the variable of offense committed as well as the behavior while in prison, the other variables were not relevant. Thus, parole boards do not discriminate in terms of "extralegal" or improper variables such as sex and race.[40]

Control of parole decision making: the use of guidelines

In response to the charge that parole decisions are arbitrary, inconsistent, and inaccurate, guidelines for release decisions have been suggested and, in many jurisdictions, implemented.[41] The United States Parole Commission Guidelines were started in 1970 and implemented in 1974,[42] and they represent a departure from the belief that parole release was justified for its rehabilitative effect and that administrators could predict the proper time to release an inmate.[43] The guidelines partially replace the rehabilitative ideal with the notion of just deserts—that offenders should get what they "deserve." The relationship of the sentence served to the severity of the offense, and factors such as past criminal record and time in prison show the emphasis on the just deserts approach. The guidelines are designed to protect the public by using risk-assessment techniques that reinforce the incapacitation theory of punishment. The rehabilitation ideal is present only in two parts of the guidelines: the measurement of an offender's performance in the institution and the provision for a parole decision made outside the guidelines in certain instances:[44] "The system is designed to contain sufficient structure to provide consistent decision making for similarly situated offenders, yet to be flexible enough to accommodate significant differences among individual offenders."[45]

But the debate over the proper time to release inmates will not go away, despite the adoption of guidelines. Although legislation calling for the abolition of parole has been introduced in Congress, it has never been enacted.* When the Reagan administration realized that parole for federal prisoners would not be eliminated, it issued new and more stringent parole guidelines: "The impact of these changes will be to increase the time customarily served by the most serious offenders. This has been done to further promote respect for the law and to protect society by isolating the serious offender." Again, the incapacitation theory is evident in the new, tougher guidelines.[46]

We should, however, be cautious in assessing the use of guidelines to reduce disparities in sentencing. The guidelines may constrain discretionary parole decisions and lead to more consistency, but their narrowness may lead to an expansion of the judicial role; that is, judges may adjust their sentences to account for parole guidelines.[47]

The removal of parole discretion

The belief that the disparity in parole decision making cannot be controlled has led to the movement to abolish it. Many people believe that parole undermines the long sentences given by judges and juries, and parole boards are seen as too lenient with criminals. When a parolee commits a new crime, the media point to the parole board's decision to release as the main problem with the system. And the public and correctional officials perceive parole boards as gambling with public safety:

> In fact, parole boards are trying to do something that is impossible: predict the future behavior of human beings. They are doing some things that are not valid: basing decisions on the belief that prison training or therapy are effective. They are doing other things that are unjust: keeping people in prison because they may do something bad when they get out.[48]

---

*As this book goes to press, Congress has just enacted a new criminal code. Under this legislation, over a five-year period parole will be phased out entirely.

As a result of these problems, several states have taken discretionary release away from parole boards. Except in Maine and Connecticut, inmates are released to parole supervision in the community after they have completed a fixed term of imprisonment.

What happens when parole boards are abolished? Most states with flat-term or determinate sentencing laws still allow early release based on **good time** credits earned in the institution and still have mandatory supervision for inmates after release. The most obvious result of abolishing release by parole boards has been an increase in time served in institutions, but there have been repercussions in other areas also. Parole boards with limited discretion can no longer act to reduce acute overcrowding in prisons. Where good time provisions still exist, the control of sentence length has moved from the parole board to prison officials. Individual prison guards make the basic decisions about inmate conduct and behavior and therefore control their good time credits. Prosecutors and judges who adjust their charging and sentencing practices also have more discretionary power: "There is just as much discretion in the system as ever. It's just been moved back to a less visible, less measurable point."[49]

PAROLE
SUPERVISION

Most jurisdictions have not, however, abolished parole, and it is therefore important to consider the issue of parole supervision. In Chapter 14, we looked at the recent emphasis on IPS—intensive probation supervision. The use of IPS has come about in reaction to prison overcrowding and is based on the assumption that failure on probation is not inherent in the system but does relate to inadequate supervision.

Various restrictions are imposed on parolees, ranging from prohibitions on the use of alcohol and drugs as well as associating with "questionable" persons, to restrictions on living and job arrangements. Many of the restrictions have been challenged as too vague or as infringing on the offenders' rights. Most parole conditions, however, are upheld as valid if they are legal and moral, and compliance by the parolees is possible. But the restrictions are meaningless unless the parolees are supervised. The key to successful parole, therefore, is the **parole officer**.

The job of parole officer is to assist inmates in coping with the problems of reintegration into the community,[50] and that, of course, includes helping the offender avoid breaking the law. It also includes supervision and assistance in obtaining housing and jobs and in relating to family and friends.

Parole officers attempt to meet these needs through a variety of supervision methods. The most common method is the office visit, in which the parolee is required to talk with the officer at periodic intervals. The visits can be long and detailed or brief and cursory.

Another supervision technique is the unannounced home or employment visit. Home visits are often conducted when the officer has reason to believe

---

EXHIBIT
HOW EFFECTIVE IS PAROLE?

Within 1 Year After Release on Parole, about 12% of Those Released Are Likely to Be Back in Prison

It is not possible from available national data to assess the total volume of criminal reinvolvements for all persons released from prison. However, it is possible to assess the extent to which those under parole supervision for up to 3 years are reconfined.

Within the first year of release from prison—

- 12% of the offenders under supervision are returned to prison; about half are returned for violations of their supervision requirements (a technical violation) or for a minor conviction; the other half are returned for new, major convictions.
- About 20% are successfully discharged within 1 year.
- Nearly two out of three releasees are continued on parole after completing the first year successfully.

Within 3 Years After Release on Parole, 24% of The Parolees Are Likely to Be Returned to Prison

Within 3 years of release, 72% of parolees are still considered to be successful, either being discharged (56%) or continued on parole (16%). The proportion returned to prison (24%) is double the 1-year performance; this indicates that half of all parolees who will return to prison within 3 years of release do so in the first year. More than half (55%) of the returns to prison within 3 years are for technical violations of supervision requirements; the remainder are for new, major convictions.

	Parole Status	
	Within 1 Year	Within 3 Years
Discharged	19%	56%
Continued on parole	65	16
Absconded	4	2
Return to prison	12	24
Died	1	2

Note: Totals may not add to 100% due to rounding.

Source: Bureau of Justice Statistics, *Report to the Nation on Crime and Justice: The Data* (Washington, D.C.: U.S. Government Printing Office, 1983), p. 84.

---

the parolee has not submitted a correct report of his or her activities and living situation.

The least restrictive method of supervision is by mail. This is used when the parolee has been allowed to move to another jurisdiction and face-to-face interviews are not possible, or when case loads are too large to accommodate office visits by each parolee.[51]

The critical question for most people is whether offenders released on supervised parole will commit additional crimes. Earlier studies attempted to define the relationship between parole supervision and crime, but the studies have been criticized on methodological grounds.[52]

A recent study attempted to remedy the methodological problems of the earlier studies. Juveniles were randomly assigned to discharge from parole supervision or continued under parole programs and were followed for twenty-six months. This study found no differences in the extent of arrests or convictions but did find that the parolees were charged with fewer drug and alcohol offenses and more property, homicide, and rape offenses. The researchers theorized that the police treat parolees more harshly than they do other suspects or that parolees avoid drug and alcohol problems because they can be so easily detected and can be the basis for a return to prison.[53]

PAROLE REVOCATION

Regardless of the type of supervision on parole, it is clear that some parolees do commit additional crimes or at least violate one or more of their parole conditions. When that occurs, their parole officers are responsible for instituting parole revocation proceedings. Historically, parole could be revoked easily and without **due process** protections. Revocation was justified on the theory that parole was a "privilege" or an "act of grace"—that parole was a "contract" in which the parolees agreed that if they violated the conditons of parole or committed any more crimes, their parole would be revoked, and they would be sent back to prison. Another view was that parole was a matter of "continuing custody" in which the parolees were subject to the same rules and regulations governing daily conduct as they were before being released from prison.[54]

In 1972, the U.S. Supreme Court applied the due process theory to parole revocations, stating that (1) the purpose of parole was rehabilitation; (2) until the rules were violated, an individual could remain on parole; (3) full due process rights used in criminal trials did not apply to parole revocation; (4) the termination of liberty by revocation resulting in "grievous loss" mandated some due process protection; (5) informal parole revocation hearings were proper; (6) parole should not be revoked unless the rules were violated; and (7) the requirements of due process would change with particular cases.

The Supreme Court required the following elements of due process at all parole revocation proceedings:

1. Written notice of the alleged violations of parole;
2. Disclosure to the parolee of the evidence of violation;
3. Opportunity to be heard in person and to present evidence as well as witnesses;
4. Right to confront and cross-examine adverse witnesses unless good cause can be shown for not allowing this confrontation;

Morrissey v. Brewer

The parolee is not the only one who has a stake in his conditional liberty. Society has a stake in whatever may be the chance of restoring him to normal and useful life within the law. Society thus has an interest in not having parole revoked because of erroneous information or because of an erroneous evaluation of the need to revoke parole, given the breach of parole conditions. And society has a further interest in treating the parolee with basic fairness: fair treatment in parole revocations will enhance the chance of rehabilitation by avoiding reactions to arbitrariness.

5. Right to judgment by a detached and neutral hearing body;
6. Written statement of reasons for revoking parole as well as of the evidence used in arriving at that decision.[55]

The importance of fairness in the revocation of parole is emphasized by the Supreme Court in the brief excerpt given above.[56]

Parole revocations should not be arbitrary, but it is possible to grant parolees a fair hearing on parole revocation and still revoke parole because of some minor infraction of the rules. For example, in some jurisdictions, any violation of the terms of parole will result in revocation and return to prison. In deciding what actions are serious enough to warrant parole revocation, we should keep in mind the potentially harmful effects of incarceration as well as the increased cost of incarceration compared with that of parole. As budget problems continue to plague the corrections system and prisons continue to be overcrowded, we must consider the costs when deciding how to punish. Violent offenders are one issue, but violation of a minor parole condition, such as driving a car without permission from the parole officer, is quite another.

SUMMARY AND CONCLUSION

This chapter has focused on the offender in the community. We began with a look at the concept of reintegration, the guiding philosophy behind most community programs for offenders. In response to claims that treatment in prison did not work and that incarceration costs too much, community programs were proposed as the answer to both problems. We reviewed the Minnesota Community Corrections Act, a statutory attempt to foster community programs, and the Des Moines program, and we also examined residential versus nonresidential community facilities and programs.

We then turned to offenders who are released from traditional institutions. We first discussed the general problems faced by these offenders and then their financial and employment needs. The need to prepare inmates for release from prison was studied, particularly two programs: furlough and work release.

In the final section we looked at the issue of release on parole. In regard to the parole system, we discussed the decision to parole and noted the debate over discretion in parole decisions and the problem of attempting to predict future behavior. We considered guidelines designed to make parole decisions less discretionary and found that removing discretion in one part of the system usually meant transferring it to another part, rather than an actual reduction in the use of discretion.

We examined the role of the parole officer who attempts to assist parolees in adjusting to life outside prison while still playing the role of "police" when parolees violate the terms of parole. Finally, we discussed parole revocation.

Treatment in prison has been called a failure, and some community programs have not shown promising results. Both parole boards and parole supervision have been called wasteful and unnecessary. It is clear that not all offenders need traditional secure confinement in prison; many offenders complete community treatment programs successfully. But it is also clear that those offenders who are sent to prison develop severe problems after release, during their adjustment to freedom. In both cases, the trend in corrections is to seek support in the community. Prisons will not be abolished, however, and as long as we are releasing offenders from institutions, the protection of society demands that we have services to assist their reintegration.

EPILOGUE:

Crime and criminology: an assessment

On March 23, 1981, two national news magazines dramatized the nation's growing concern with violent crime. The cover of *Time,* picturing a grotesque face and a gun, was headlined "The Curse of Violent Crime." *Newsweek,* also picturing a gun on its cover, carried the headline "The Epidemic of Violent Crime." The series of articles in these two magazines highlighted many of the issues, fears, concerns, problems, and unanswered questions about crime in this country.

Newsweek described the "Plague of Violent Crime" in these words: "Defying any cure, it overwhelms the police, the courts and the prisons—and warps U.S. life."[1] With pictures of some of the victims who were murdered during one recent week and a graph of the "Trend in Terror," giving rates of murder, rape, robbery, and assault in this country, *Time* declared that "a pervasive fear of robbery and mayhem threatens the way America lives."[2] These articles were published only a few weeks after Chief Justice Warren E. Burger spoke to the American Bar Association's annual meeting. Burger referred to the "reign of terror" in American cities and declared that crime is reducing this country to "the status of an impotent society whose capability of maintaining elementary security on the streets, in schools, and for the homes of our people is in doubt."

According to a *Newsweek* poll, these statements accurately reflect some of the concerns of Americans, over one-half of whom reported that they are afraid to walk alone at night in some areas within one mile of their homes. The respondents also indicated their lack of confidence in the police and courts to handle the problems of rising crime.[3]

The *Time* and *Newsweek* articles indicated that most Americans fear being victimized by violent crime. Many respond by buying handguns and other weapons, bar their doors with deadbolts, avoid carrying much cash or wearing expensive jewelry when going out, and, in many cases, become prisoners in their own homes, afraid to go out at night. Some are even afraid to be on the streets during the day.

Since 1981, however, the official picture of crime in this country has changed. As we saw in Chapter 2, a downward trend began in 1982, with reductions in both property and violent crimes, as measured by the *Uniform Crime Reports* and the National Crime Survey data on victims. In June 1984, the Justice Department announced its tentative crime figures for 1983, indicating that serious crimes were down by 7 percent and that household burglaries had hit record lows. Violent crimes were down by 9.8 percent. The data represented the lowest rate of victimization for personal larceny in the eleven years that the department has been collecting data on victimization. The official crime data collected by the FBI also reported in its preliminary report in April 1984 that serious crimes had dropped in 1983. The FBI data, covering crimes "known to the police," in contrast with the Justice Department's data based on interviews with victims, reported a 7 percent decline in the 1983 crime rate, as compared with the 1982 rate of serious offenses.[4]

What are the variables that might explain the changes in the crime rate between 1981 and 1983, and what are the implications? In this Epilogue, we shall look briefly at the four major areas of criminology, as represented by the four parts of this text, in order to assess "where we are" and "where we are going" in criminology.

THE MEASUREMENT OF CRIME

In Chapter 2 we looked at the two most frequently used measures of crime, the *Uniform Crime Reports* collected by the FBI, and the National Crime Surveys of the Justice Department's Bureau of Justice Statistics. We also considered less frequently used self-reports of crime and the problems with each of these methods. And we looked at the recent decline in the crime rates, as indicated by the official data. Now we have another year of declining rates—1983—to explain. Is crime actually going down, or does the "explanation" of the data rest with the methods of collection and analysis?

In the 1970s some experts predicted that the crime rates would begin to fall in the 1980s because of the decline in the population between the ages of eighteen and twenty-five. Some believe that this has occurred because the post-World War II baby boom generation has moved out of the most crime-prone age bracket. Others have argued that the declining crime rates are the direct result of our "get-tough" attitudes toward sentencing and punishment. That is, with record numbers of people now behind bars, we are not only deterring those persons from preying on the public, but also our harsh stand on crime has created a sufficient fear of punishment that others are being deterred from engaging in crime.

Critics of the success of the get-tough position contend that we must analyze the data more carefully. In so doing, there is evidence that some jurisdictions with the toughest sentencing laws and highest rates of incarceration continue to have the highest crime rates, whereas some jurisdictions that have not moved so far in the get-tough direction continue to have lower rates of crime.

Which is correct? Most analysts say it is too soon to tell, that we cannot draw conclusions about crime trends on the basis of a two-year period. The data will have to be watched and studied for a longer period before it is reasonable to decide that crime rates actually are declining and will continue to do so in the future. Even if that occurs, it will be difficult—if not impossible—to determine what has influenced that trend. We still do not know enough about what causes criminal behavior, and until we do, we will not be able to decide what deters people from engaging in that behavior.

Even if the official data reflect an actual and significant decline in crime rates that will continue for some time, we still have to deal with the problem of the public's perception of crime. In our earlier discussion of fear of violent crime, we noted that the fears of women and the elderly are not based on fact; that is, their fear of being victimized by violent personal crime is generally out of proportion to the probability that they will actually be victims. But many people react according to possibilities, not probabilities.

The impact of fear of crime is a serious problem. Recently, the National Institute of Justice (NIJ) awarded almost $2 million to the Police Foundation to begin experimental programs in two cities (Houston, Texas, and Newark, New Jersey) that will try to reduce such fear.[5]

It is unlikely that the recent downward trend in crime rates will alleviate our fear of crime, especially violent crime, even though violent personal crimes are committed far less often than are property crimes that do not involve personal contact. It is probably the randomness of highly publicized violent personal crimes that contributes to our fear of being victims of violent crime. And this fear, coupled with the public's perception that the criminal justice system is inadequate to handle the problem of crime, creates problems that will not be alleviated easily, if at all.

THE CRIMINAL JUSTICE SYSTEM AND CORRECTIONS

Discussions on crime today most frequently focus on the criminal justice system and corrections. Criticisms have come from the legal profession as well as from the public. In 1981, Supreme Court Chief Justice Warren E. Burger, again in his annual address to the American Bar Association, directed his criticisms to the criminal justice system and corrections. Burger asked, "Is a society redeemed if it provides massive safeguards for accused persons" but does not provide "elementary protection for its decent, law-abiding citizens?" Specifically, he called for stricter bail release laws and policies, speedier trials, speedier appellate review of convictions, and some limitations on appellate review.

Burger also called for improvement in the educational and vocational opportunities for inmates, increased opportunities for family visitations with inmates, broad-scale improvement of the prisons' physical facilities, and reexamination of the treatment of nonviolent first offenders. Burger realized that his suggestions "will be costly in the short run and the short run will not be brief," but he warned that such measures are necessary if we are to avoid the "dismal paths of the past."

In his 1984 annual address to the Bar, Chief Justice Burger noted that recent public opinion polls show that the public's confidence in lawyers in this country is declining sharply, though at the same time, the number of lawyers is increasing dramatically. The United States now has two-thirds of all the lawyers in the world, and one-third of those entered practice within the past five years. We might think that the increase in lawyers would create healthy competition, resulting in better service and more reasonable fees;

yet, as pointed out by Derek Bok, the former dean of the Harvard Law School and now the president of that university, "The blunt, inexcusable fact is that this nation, which prides itself on efficiency and justice, has developed a legal system that is the most expensive in the world."[6]

Despite the cost of our legal system and the abundance of lawyers, we are faced with a backlog in the courts, resulting in long delays for many trials. During this delay, many defendants wait in jail, and with the move toward using bail for preventive detention, even more defendants will be jailed awaiting their trials.

The movement toward bail for the preventive detention of defendants thought to be dangerous raises what is perhaps the most difficult problem of the criminal justice system—the conflict between the rights of defendants and the rights of the rest of us to be protected from crime. That conflict is seen in many of the issues we have discussed in this book. The exclusionary rule is one example. This rule was instituted by the Supreme Court to prevent police from violating the rights of persons suspected of crimes. If the evidence is seized illegally, it may not be used at the trial of that suspect. But in 1984, the Court relaxed the rule. Under the new holdings, the Court will permit the use of illegally seized evidence if it can be shown that that evidence would have been discovered by the police anyway,[7] or if the police, in good faith, acted on the basis of a warrant issued by a magistrate later found to be invalid.[8] It will thus become more difficult for defendants to win a favorable ruling on a motion to suppress illegally seized evidence. But perhaps it will become easier for police to seize evidence illegally, thus eroding the freedom from unreasonable searches and seizures that our Constitution guarantees.

But the main result may be increased litigation over whether the evidence would have been found by the police later, without the illegal seizure, or whether the police acted in good faith. These possibilities illustrate an important element of the criminal justice system, and one that is frequently ignored—the effect that a change in one part of the system may have on the other parts. The refusal to confront this issue is one of the most dramatic failures in our attempts to reform the system. Throughout the book we have seen examples. Increasing the lengths of sentences and moving from indeterminate to mandatory sentencing usually result in prison overcrowding, leading to court orders to reduce prison populations or to build more prisons (at a phenomenal cost) to house the inmates. Removing discretion from the judge at the time of sentencing may increase the discretion of the prosecutor (who may refuse to prosecute because the mandatory sentence upon conviction is so high) or the jury, who may refuse to convict for the same reason.

Most of the changes that we have made in the criminal justice system and corrections may be viewed as short-term efforts to solve the problem of crime. One authority has termed our recent efforts "barbed wire justice," concluding,

> Prisons do prevent crime: imprisonment keeps prisoners from committing additional crimes, and capital punishment assures us that they won't commit another crime. It is not clear, however, whether this strategy really stops crimes or whether it merely postpones them, at great public expense until the "over-corrected" and embittered inmate is finally released.[9]

That comment, made by a clinical psychologist in a correctional institution, emphasizes our real problem, which can only be solved, if at all, by social scientists, for they are the only ones in a position to tell us what causes crime.

CRIMINOLOGY AND THE CAUSES OF CRIME   In Part 2 of this text we looked at the social scientists' contributions to our understanding of the causes of criminal behavior, as well as the recent developments in psychology, biology, and genetics. The importance of research on the causes of criminal behavior was emphasized in a provocative article published in 1978 by criminologist Donald R. Cressey, who discussed his concern with the need for sociologists and criminologists to become more involved in developing and testing theories of human behavior. Referring to a 1967 prediction he made about the future content of criminology courses as combining legal and social science knowledge, Cressey expressed his concern that such has not occurred. Rather, he declared, "there seems to have been a *smothering* of social science knowledge as criminology has expanded."[10]

In his 1967 prediction, Cressey had hoped that criminologists would use their knowledge of social science not only to further their understanding of why criminals behave as they do but also to apply this knowledge to analyze why courts, police, prosecutors, judges, and legislators behave as they do. Instead, many criminologists have moved toward a policy orientation. Some have abandoned attempts to find cause-and-effect relationships in human behavior and have become antagonistic to such scientific efforts, as they spend an increasing amount of time attempting to "do something" about crime. The administration of the criminal law, rather than an understanding of crime and criminals, has become the focus. "The typical modern criminologist is a technical assistant to politicians bent on repressing crime, rather than a scientist seeking valid propositions stated in a causal framework. If cause—and with it the search for generalizations—goes out the window, criminology will become even more of a hodgepodge than it is now. In the long run, the nation will be worse off as a result."[11]

The concern with the failures of criminology and criminal justice was also discussed by C. R. Jeffery. The Jeffery and Cressey articles appeared with others in a symposium issue of *Criminology,* entitled "Criminology: New Concerns and New Directions." Jeffery outlined the failure of psychiatry and psychology between 1920 and 1950, when these disciplines were the basis for the treatment model in penal institutions. This failure he compared with the "failure of the sociological model as found in the war against poverty program in the 1960 era. The notion that the opportunity structure could be altered through education and job training, thus altering poverty and delinquency, was also a total disaster. The failure of criminology as a science of the individual was matched by its failure as a science of the social offender."[12]

On the other hand, Jeffery noted, the government's "war on crime," which resulted in the 1967 appointment of the president's crime commission, passage of the Safe Streets Act, and development of the Law Enforcement Assistance Administration, has been a failure. Even the government recognized the failure of LEAA, described by former Attorney General Griffin Bell as a "paper-shuffling operation which had failed to come up with new and innovative means to combat the ever-growing crime problem."[13] Jeffery warned that increasing the police force and developing new types of "hardware" for combating crime would not be effective. He concluded that the treatment model has been abandoned "at a time when the behavioral sciences are about to make a major contribution to our knowledge of human behavior. It is ironic that in the 1970s, when we are returning to an eighteenth-century punishment model of crime control, twenty-first-century breakthroughs are occurring in our understanding of human behavior."[14] Jeffery emphasized the need for a major research effort "to join biology, medicine, psychology, criminology, and criminal law into a new crime prevention model. We must approach the crime problem as a behavioral problem and not as a political problem."[15]

A similar position was taken by criminologist Simon Dinitz when he referred to

> the propensity for modern scholars to forego hard scholarly work in order to assume leadership roles in the intoxicating world of social and ideological movements. Such has too often occurred to the detriment of the scholars and the field. In only a few historical periods was it considered inappropriate for intellectual types to get involved in sociopolitical movements. In these periods scholarly productivity frequently blossomed, in stark contrast to the present when the media consume ideas like prisons consume people.[16]

In contrast, recall our discussion in Chapter 5 of Richard Quinney's conflict or critical approach to criminology. Quinney calls for abandoning the search for causality in criminology. The attempt to discover "what is" should be replaced with an attempt to understand and implement "what should be." In several chapters in this text, we compared the conflict perspective with the functional approach in criminology. Clearly these two approaches, described as "two dramatically different theoretical perspectives," continue to battle for the support of criminologists as well as policy makers. But there is a "disturbing similarity between these competing paradigms," and that is their "tendency to reduce important *empirical* issues to questions of *moral* judgment."[17]

In conclusion, regardless of their position on values and policy issues, if criminologists expect to be taken seriously, they must find some ideas based on scientific findings. Cressey's warning should be heeded:

> Criminologists should not abandon science to become policy advisors in this repressive war on crime. Neither should they retreat into broad intellectualizing, accompanied by political proselytizing. . . . They . . . should sharpen their scientific research tools and put them to work on studies designed to secure comprehension of the conditions under which criminal laws are enacted, enforced, and broken. If they do so, and come up with some reasonable generalizations, politicians might listen to them, just as politicians listened to Bentham, Beccaria, Voltaire, and even Freud.[18]

CONCLUSION The greatest danger we face now is to conclude, without further evidence, that the decreasing crime rate is *caused* by the recent return to determinate and longer sentences, with the accompanying punishment philosophy of "just deserts." Such a conclusion would lead to an even larger reduction in the prison educational, vocational, and treatment programs designed to allow inmates who wish to reform to do so. A few years ago, Chief Justice Burger warned: "We take on a burden when we put a man behind walls, and that burden is to give him a chance to change. If we deny him that, we deny his status as a human being, and to deny that is to diminish our own humanity and plant the seeds of future anguish for ourselves."[19]

Burger's fear, however, is reflected in the current "lock 'em up and throw away the key" attitude of many Americans. This punitive reaction to crime may keep more convicted persons off the streets for a longer period of time, in which case it would provide temporary relief, but the price we would pay in the long run might not warrant the short-term "solution." Americans need to face the issue of crime in terms of long-range solutions. We may not have all of the answers, but we will never have any of them if we continue to hide behind a punitive policy of longer sentences without carefully studying and assessing what happens to those on whom those sentences are imposed. The next decade will be a critical one in this country, and attorneys and social scientists must confront the complicated problems of the criminal justice system. Citizens must realize that the answers are not simple; indeed, they are complex and costly and require the understanding and cooperation of us all.

Glossary

Administrative Law regulations governing public administrative agencies, which affect private persons as the agencies make rules, investigate problems, and decide cases.

Adversary System a legal system that involves a contest between two opponents, the prosecuting attorney and the defense attorney, who each attempt to convince the judge and/or jury of their version of the case.

Aggravated Assault the unlawful use of force by one person against another with a deadly weapon, with the intent to commit a violent personal crime such as murder or rape, or, in some states, with a hood or mask to conceal one's identity.

Anomie a state of normlessness in society, which may be caused by decreased homogeneity and which provides a setting conducive to crimes and other antisocial acts.

Appeal a step in a judicial proceeding, petitioning a higher court to review a lower court's decision. A case that has been so transferred is "on appeal."

Appellant the losing party in a lower court who appeals to a higher court for review of the lower court's decision.

Appellate Jurisdiction a higher court's power to rehear or review cases and to alter the lower court's decision.

Appellee the winning party in a lower court who argues on appeal that the lower court's decision was correctly made.

Arraignment in criminal practice, the stage in the criminal justice system when the defendant appears before the court, hears the indictment, and pleads guilty or not guilty to the charges.

Arrest depriving a person of his or her liberty; taking a person into custody for the purpose of formally charging him or her with a crime; or initiating juvenile proceedings.

Arson the willful and malicious burning of structures. Modern statutes often have a more severe penalty for the burning of a dwelling house than of other real property.

Bail a system of posting bond to guarantee a defendant's presence at trial while allowing the accused to be released until that time.

Bail Bondsman one who in return for a fee posts the bond for the accused and theoretically forfeits the money to the state if the defendant does not appear in court.

Banishment historically, the punishment of exile from a particular city, area, or country for a set period of time or for life. A modern form is banishment parole, in which an inmate is released from prison on the condition that he or she leave a particular state.

Behavior Theory theory based on the belief that all behavior is learned and can be unlearned. It is the basis for behavior modification, the approach used in both institutionalized and noninstitutionalized settings for changing behavior.

Booking the process of officially recording an arrest and entering the suspect's name, the offense charged, the place, time, arresting officer, and reason for the arrest. Usually done at a police station by the arresting officer.

Briefs written documents filed with the court, which give the basic arguments in a case and are used not only as a statement of information for the courts but also to persuade the court to make a particular ruling in the case.

Burden of Proof in a legal sense, the duty or necessity of proving a disputed fact as a case progresses. For example, in a criminal case the state has the burden of proving the defendant's guilt beyond a reasonable doubt.

Burglary breaking and entering any type of enclosed structure without consent and with the intent to commit a felony.

Capital Punishment the imposition of the death penalty for an offender convicted of a capital offense.

Career Criminal persons who commit a variety of offenses over an extended period of time; also refers to offenders who specialize in particular types of crime, for example, burglary.

Cartographic School an approach to criminology that uses population data to ascertain the influence of social conditions and geographical phenomena, such as climate, location, and topography, on criminal behavior.

Case Law the aggregate of reported judicial decisions, which are legally binding court interpretations of written statutes and previous court decisions or rules made by courts in the absence of written statutes or other sources of law. See also Common Law.

Causation the idea that the occurrence of events is determined by cause-and-effect relationships. Causation assumes a relationship between two phenomena in which the occurrence of the former brings about changes in the latter. A *necessary cause* is one without which a given effect cannot occur; a *suffi-*

cient cause is always followed or accompanied by a given effect and may or may not be a necessary cause. Indirect causation involves a chain of events leading to a final effect. In the legal sense, causation is the element of a crime that requires the existence of a causal relationship between the offender's conduct and the particular harmful consequences.

Change of Venue a change in the place of a trial, generally from one county or district to another. One purpose is to ensure the jury will not be biased by pretrial publicity.

Charge the formal allegation that a suspect has committed a specific offense. The term also means instructions on matters of law given by a judge to the jury.

Child Stealing the abduction of a child by one parent, in violation of a court custody order, when that child is in the legal custody of the other parent.

Civil Law that part of the law concerned with the rules and enforcement of private or civil rights, as distinguished from criminal law. In a civil suit, an individual who has been harmed seeks personal compensation in court rather than seeking criminal punishment through state prosecution.

Classical Theorists writers and philosophers who argued that the punishment should fit the crime. The popularization of this school of thought led to the abolition of the death penalty and torture in some countries and generally to more humane treatment of criminals.

Classification the allocation of prisoners to the custodial level and the treatment program within the correctional institution that best fits the individual's needs.

Closure Theory an explanation of criminal behavior based on the idea that social isolation reduces an individual's perception of available behavior alternatives so that criminal activity is then seen as a way to reduce the tensions of isolation.

Cognitive Development Theory psychological theory of behavior based on the belief that people organize their thoughts into rules and laws and that the way in which those thoughts are organized results in either criminal or noncriminal behavior. This organization of thoughts is called *moral reasoning* and, when applied to law, *legal reasoning.*

Common Law broadly defined, common law is the body of law and legal theory that originated in England and was adopted in the United States; it is distinguished from Roman law, civil law, and canon law by its emphasis on the binding nature of interpretative court decisions. In a narrower sense, common law refers to the customs, traditions, judicial decisions, and other materials that guide courts in decision making, as opposed to the courts' use of written statutes or the Constitution. See also Case Law.

Community-Based Corrections an approach to punishment that stresses reintegration of the offender into the community through the use of local facilities. As an alternative to incarceration, the offender may be placed in the community on probation or, in conjunction with imprisonment, in programs such as parole, furlough, work release, foster homes, or halfway houses.

Community Service a type of punishment in which the offender is ordered to participate in community service or work projects, sometimes in conjunction with probation or restitution.

Computer Crime commission of any crime involving the use of a computer.

Concentric Circle Theory an ecological theory that divides cities into zones based on environmental qualities and attempts to find a relationship with crime and delinquency rates.

Concurring Opinion a judge's written opinion that agrees with the result in a case but disagrees with the majority opinion's reasoning.

Conduct Norms usually unwritten rules developed by a group and governing ways of acting. They may vary from group to group and are formulated through social interaction and based on the group's social values. Members recognize the group point of view, which labels an action as normal and right or abnormal and wrong.

Conflict Approach in contrast with the consensus approach, the conflict approach views values, norms, and laws as creating dissension, clash, conflict. Conflict thinkers do not agree on the nature or the source of the conflict; nor do they agree on what to call this perspective. The *pluralistic* approach sees conflict emerging from multiple sources, and the *critical* approach assumes that the conflict reflects the political power of the society's elite groups. Also called *Marxist, new conflict approach, New Criminology, materialist criminology,* and *socialist criminology.*

Consensus Approach an explanation of the evolution of law that considers law to be the formalized views and values of the people, arising from the aggregate of social values and developing through social interaction. Criminal law, then, is a reflection of societal values broader than the values of special interest groups and individuals.

Constitutional Causes of Crime a theory of criminal behavior that assumes that behavior is influenced by the structure or physical characteristics of a person's body.

Containment Theory an explanation of criminal behavior that focuses on two insulating factors that help prevent a person from turning to criminal behavior; first, the individual's favorable self-concept and commitment to long-range legitimate goals and, second, the pressure of the external social structure against criminal activity.

Control Group in an experiment with two or more groups, the control group is used as a standard and is not introduced to the experimental variable. The control group is similar to the experimental group in all other relevant factors. Investigators can then measure the differences between the control and experimental groups before and after the variable is used with the experimental group.

Corporal Punishment infliction of penalites on the physical body rather than on the mind.

Corporate Crime an intentional act or omission of an act that violates criminal statutory or case law and that is committed by individuals in a corporate organization for its benefit.

Corrections all the official ways in which society reacts to persons who have been convicted of committing criminal acts, including persons handled by the juvenile courts.

Crime an intentional act or omission of an act that violates criminal statutory or case law and for which the state provides a specified punishment.

Crime Rate in the *Uniform Crime Reports,* the number of offenses recorded per 100,000 population.

Crimes Known to the Police the record of those serious offenses for which the police find evidence that the crime actually occurred.

Criminal Justice System the agencies responsible for enforcing criminal laws, including legislatures, police, courts, and corrections. Their decisions pertain to the prevention, detection, and investigation of crime; the apprehension, accusation, detention, and trial of suspects; and the conviction, sentencing, incarceration, or official supervision of adjudicated defendants.

Criminal Law the statutes and norms whose violation will subject the accused person to government prosecution. In general, criminal laws encompass those wrongs considered to be so serious as to threaten the welfare of the entire state.

Criminologists those professionals who study crime, criminals, and criminal behavior.

Cruel and Unusual Punishment punishment prohibited by the Eighth Amendment of the United States Constitution. The interpretation rests with the courts. Some examples are the death penalty for rape without homicide, torture, and excessive lengths or conditions in sentences.

Culture Conflict Theory an analysis of crime resting on clash-of-conduct norms, both of which are partially accepted and lead to contradictory standards and opposing loyalties. *Primary conflict* refers to the clash-of-conduct norms between two different cultures, and *secondary conflict* refers to the clash-of-conduct norms between groups in a single culture.

Death Row those prison cells housing inmates convicted of capital crimes and sentenced to capital punishment.

Decriminalization the process of removing from the criminal law acts defined as crimes. The term is generally used to refer to acts that many people do not consider "criminal."

Defendant in criminal law, the party charged with a crime and against whom a criminal proceeding is pending or has commenced.

Defense Attorney the attorney who represents the accused in criminal proceedings before, during, and after trial and whose main function is to protect the legal rights of the accused.

Deinstitutionalization the process of developing and using community-based facilities as alternatives to "total" institutions.

Deprivation Model a theory of prisonization based on the idea that the inmate subculture arises from prisoners' adaptation to the severe physical and psychological losses imposed by incarceration.

Determinate Sentence the length of the sentence is determined by the legislature with no variation allowed by the judge, the correctional institution, or the parole board.

Determinism a doctrine holding that one's options, decisions, and actions are decided by inherited or environmental causes acting upon one's character.

Deterrence a justification for punishment based on the prevention or discouragement of crime through fear or danger, as by punishing offenders to serve as examples to potential criminals or by incarcerating offenders to prevent them from committing further criminal acts.

Diagnostic Classification Centers units within the correctional system to which persons in custody are sentenced to allow the professional staff to determine which treatment program and correctional facility are appropriate for the individual's rehabilitation.

Differential Anticipation Theory explains criminal behavior by postulating that when people consider the available legitimate and the illegitimate behaviors, they select the alternative that is perceived or anticipated to be the best. It makes no difference which actually is the best—it is the anticipation or perception of it that determines the choice.

Differential Association Reinforcement Theory a crime-causation theory based on the idea that criminal behavior is learned through associations with criminal behaviors and attitudes combined with a social-learning theory of operant conditioning. Criminal behavior, then, is learned through associations and is continued or not as a result of the positive or negative reinforcement received.

Differential Association Theory denotes a person's associations that differ from those of other persons; a theory of crime causation resting on the idea that criminal behavior is learned through associations with criminal behavior and attitudes. A person who engages in criminal behavior can be differentiated by the quality or quantity of his or her learning through associations with those who define criminal activity favorably and the relative isolation from lawful social norms.

Differential Identification Theory explains criminal behavior by using the perspectives of others in determining one's own choices of behavior. Those others may be real or imaginary people.

Differential Opportunity a theory that attempts to combine the concepts of anomie and differential association by analyzing both the legitimate and the illegitimate opportunity structures available to individuals. Criminal behavior is possible because the environment has models of crime as well as opportunities to interact with those models.

Discretion in the criminal justice system, the authority to make decisions and choose among options according to one's own judgment rather than to specific legal rules and facts. Discretionary decision making can result in actions tailored to individual circumstances and in inconsistent handling of offenders at several stages.

Dissenting Opinion a judge's written opinion that disagrees with the result and the reasoning of the majority decision.

Diversion correctly used, diversion removes the offender from the criminal justice system and channels him or her into, for example, a social welfare agency. Diversion has also been used to describe the handling of juveniles in a system separate from the adult criminal justice system and the sentencing of offenders to community-based correctional facilities rather than to prison.

Double Celling the practice of housing two (or more) inmates in a room designed for one.

Double Jeopardy the Fifth Amendment of the United States Constitution prohibits a second prosecution after a first trial for the same offense; the pertinent part reads, "nor shall any person be subject for the same offense to be twice put in jeopardy of life or limb."

Dual Court System the separate judicial structure of various levels of courts within each state in addition to the national structure of federal courts. The origin of the laws violated usually dictates whether the state or federal court is an appropriate forum for the case. The state system generally consists of lower and higher trial courts, appellate courts, and a state supreme court that governs the interpretation of laws within a state. The federal system consists of district trial courts, circuit appellate courts, and the United State Supreme Court. Trial courts hear factual evidence, and the issues are decided by a judge or a jury. Appellate court judges review the decisions of lower courts.

Dualistic Fallacy in criminological studies, the assumption that a population has two mutually exclusive subclasses, such as criminals and noncriminals.

Due Process a fundamental idea under the United States Constitution that a person should not be deprived of life, liberty, or property without reasonable and lawful procedures. The exact interpretation of what is required by due process rests with the courts.

Ecological School an approach to criminology that studies the quantitative relationship between geographic phenomena and crime to ascertain the geographic and spatial distribution of crime.

Economic Determinism a doctrine used to explain the relationship between economics and crime caused by the capitalist system's social situation. Economic determinism rests on the assumption that acquiring material goods is the basic source of human motivation and that human behavior is rational. The argument is that private ownership creates poverty for some who then turn to crime as a result of this economic need.

Embezzlement obtaining rightful possession of property with the owner's consent and subsequently wrongfully depriving the owner of that property.

Enjoin a court order that requires or commands the performance or cessation of an action.

Entrapment a defense alleging that a government agent instigated a crime by making false representations, appealing to the defendant's sympathy or friendship, or offering an inducement to the defendant to commit a crime.

Exclusionary Rule   the Fourth Amendment of the U.S. Constitution provides that "the right of the people to be secure in their persons, houses, papers and effects, against unreasonable searches and seizures shall not be violated and no warrants shall issue, but upon probable cause. . . . " Evidence seized in violation of the Fourth Amendment is excluded from criminal trials; the most common examples of excluded evidence are statements made or property seized during an illegal arrest, search, or line-up. In 1984, the Supreme Court ruled that some illegally seized evidence may be used at trial.

Felony   a serious type of offense, such as murder, armed robbery, or rape. Punishments for felonies range from imprisonment for one year to death.

Felony-Murder Doctrine   used to hold a defendant liable for murder if a human life is taken during the commission of another felony, such as armed robbery, kidnapping, or arson.

Fine   a type of punishment in which the offender is ordered to pay a sum of money to the state in lieu of or in addition to other forms of punishment.

Folkways   norms of acting that arise from unconscious habits or routine ways of doing things. Folkways are the correct way of doing things because they are the traditional customs, habits, and behavior of a given group, tribe, or nation. Mild ridicule or ostracism follows the infringement of a folkway, whereas severe disapproval results from the infringement of mores.

Fornication   from the Latin word for brothel *(fornix)*, meaning unlawful sexual intercourse between two unmarried persons.

Free Venture Program   started by the federal government to encourage worthwhile employment of inmates incarcerated in state institutions. The program assists states in turning prison industries into profitable operations through the application of free-world business principles and practices.

Free Will   a philosophy urging punishment severe enough for people to choose to avoid criminal acts. It includes the idea that a certain criminal act warrants a certain punishment without any variation.

Functional Consequences   a social system's beneficial and harmonious results from changes in one part of the system that have positive effects on another part.

Furlough   an authorized, temporary leave from prison, during which the inmate may be attending a funeral, visiting his or her family, or attempting to secure a job.

General Deterrence   the philosophy of punishment resting on the belief that punishment in an individual case will inhibit others from committing the same offense.

Good Time   credit resulting in a reduction of prison time, awarded for satisfactory behavior in prison.

Grand Jury   a group of citizens convened by legal authority to conduct secret investigations of evidence, evaluate accusations against suspects for trial, and issue indictments.

Granny Bashing   physical abuse of elderly parents.

Habeas Corpus   a written court order to bring the accused before the court to determine whether the defendant's custody and confinement are lawful under the constitutional due process of law.

Halfway House   a prerelease center used to help the inmate in changing from prison life to community life, or a facility that focuses on special adjustment problems of offenders, such as a drug or alcohol treatment center. The term is also used to describe a residential facility used as an alternative to prison for high-risk offenders considered unsuitable for probation.

Hedonism   the idea that people choose pleasure and avoid pain. In law, its proponents advocate clearly written laws and certainty of punishment without any departure from the prescribed penalty.

Homicide   the killing of a human being. Homicide is a criminal act when it is committed without any legal justification, and the defendant may be charged with murder or manslaughter.

Humanitarianism   the doctrine that advocates the removal of harsh, severe, and painful conditions in correctional institutions.

Immunity, Civil   exemption for certain public officials from the liability or penalty for tortious acts that the law generally imposes on other citizens.

Importation Model   a theory of prisonization based on the idea that the inmate subculture arises not only from internal prison experiences but also from external patterns of behavior that the inmate brings to the prison.

Incapacitation   a theory of punishment and goal of sentencing, generally implemented by incarcerating an offender in order to prevent him or her from committing any other crimes.

Incarceration   imprisonment in an institution. Jails usually contain those sentenced to less than one year, whereas state and federal prisons house those sentenced to custody for more than one year.

Incest   sexual relations between members of the immediate family, other than husband and wife. The most common type is between father and daughter.

Indeterminate Sentence   the length of the sentence is determined not by the legislature or the court but by professionals at the institution or by parole boards that decide when an offender is ready to return to society. The actual sentence given by the judge may range from one day to life.

Index Offenses the serious crimes as reported by the FBI's *Uniform Crime Reports:* murder and non-negligent manslaughter, forcible rape, robbery, aggravated assault, burglary, larceny-theft, motor vehicle theft, and arson.

Indictment the grand jury's written accusation formally charging the named suspect with a criminal offense. An indictment arises from matters placed before the grand jury by the prosecutor, as opposed to a presentment.

Individual (or Specific) Deterrence a philosophy of punishment based on the idea that the threat of punishment may prevent an individual from committing any crimes. The use of incarceration is an example.

Infanticide the murder of infants, a common practice in some primitive societies, when, for example, babies were born deformed.

Information the most common formal document used to charge a person with a specific offense. The prosecutor, acting on evidence from police or citizens, files this document with the court, and it is tested at the preliminary hearing. Unlike the indictment, this procedure does not require participation by the grand jury.

Inmate a person confined in a prison, asylum, or similar institution.

Inquisitorial System a system in which the accused is presumed to be guilty and must prove his or her innocence.

Intent in the legal sense, intent is the design, determination, or purpose with which a person uses a particular means to effect a certain result; it shows the presence of will in the act that consummates a crime.

Jail a locally administered confinement facility used to detain persons awaiting a trial or those serving sentences of less than one year.

Judge a judicial officer, elected or appointed to preside over a court of law. Judges are to be neutral and final arbiters of law with primary responsibility for all court activities, ranging from monitoring the attorneys and instructing the jury to deciding cases and sentencing those found guilty.

Judicial Review the courts' power to determine whether legislative and executive acts infringe on the rights guaranteed by state constitutions and the U.S. Constitution. This power may be limited by statutes, case holdings, the U.S. Constitution itself, or by restrictions placed on federal courts with regard to interference in state matters.

Jurisdiction the lawful right to exercise official authority, whether executive, judicial, or legislative; the territory of authority within which such power may be exercised. For the police, it refers to the geographical boundaries of power; for the courts, it refers to the power to hear and decide cases.

Jury in a criminal case, a number of persons summoned to court and sworn to hear the trial, determine certain facts, and render a verdict of guilty or not guilty. In some jurisdictions, juries recommend or determine sentences.

Just Deserts the idea that an individual who commits a crime deserves to suffer for it. Also called *retribution.*

Justice Model a philosophy holding that justice is achieved when offenders receive punishments based on what is deserved by their offenses, as written in the law; the crime determines the punishment. In sentencing, this model presumes that prison should be used only as a last resort. Flat-time sentences are set for each offense; parole is abolished; and early release can be achieved only through good time credit.

Juvenile a person subject to the jurisdiction of the juvenile court through operation of a statutorily imposed age limit.

Juvenile Court the courts with original jurisdiction over persons defined by the state as juveniles and over cases concerning dependent or neglected persons, status offenses, and delinquent acts.

Labeling Theory an attempt to explain deviance as a social process by which some people who commit deviant acts come to be known as deviants and others do not. Deviance is seen as a consequence of society's decision to apply that term to a person, and deviant behavior is behavior that society labels as deviant.

Larceny the taking of personal property without the owner's consent and with the intent to deprive the owner of it permanently. Historically, *petit larceny* involved small amounts with imprisonment as punishment, and *grand larceny* involved larger amounts and the death penalty. Most modern theft statutes abolish the common law distinctions, and courts have ruled that the death penalty may not be imposed for larceny alone.

Legislature the segment of government that drafts and enacts laws for a particular level of government with a certain jurisdiction.

Magistrate a lower judicial officer in the state or federal court system.

Mala in Se acts morally wrong in themselves, such as rape, murder, or robbery.

Mala Prohibita acts that are wrong because they are prohibited by positive law, that is, legislation.

Manslaughter, Involuntary causing the death of another while acting in a criminally negligent manner that shows a disregard for human life. Also called negligent manslaughter.

Manslaughter, Voluntary an intentional killing under mitigating circumstances of adequate provocation, mistaken justification, or diminished capacity, which reduce the offense from murder to manslaughter. Also called nonnegligent manslaughter.

Mediators those persons who attempt to settle claims between parties outside the courtroom; programs for noncourt settlement of disputes were instituted to help reduce the backlog of cases in the court systems.

Mens Rea criminal intent, the guilty or wrongful purpose of the defendant at the time he or she committed a criminal act.

Miranda Warning the rule from *Miranda v. Arizona*, which mandates that before the interrogation of a person in custody, he or she must be told of the right to remain silent, or the fact that anything said may be used as evidence against him or her, and of the right to an attorney who will be appointed if the accused cannot afford to hire one.

Misdemeanor an offense less serious than a felony, such as disorderly conduct, prostitution, or public drunkenness, and generally having a penalty of short-term incarceration in a local facility, or a fine.

M'Naghten Rule frequently used test of insanity in American courts. For the insanity defense to be effective, the defendant at the time of the crime must have suffered from a defect of reason and consequently not have known the nature and quality of the act or that the act was wrong. In some jurisdictions, knowing the difference between right and wrong is still a defense if defendants can show that they had an "irresistible impulse" and therefore could not control their behavior.

Model Penal Code the American Law Institute's codification of basic and general criminal law; often used as the basis for drafting new criminal laws.

Mores the social norms that give a group or society its moral standards of behavior and that are considered essential to its preservation and welfare. Nonconformity with mores is severely sanctioned by the group, even though the term generally refers to those standards that have not been enacted as part of the formal criminal law.

Murder the unlawful and unjustified killing of a human being with malice aforethought: the intent to kill, the intent to do great bodily harm, an act done in willful disregard of the strong likelihood that death or great injury would result, or a killing done during the commission of another felony.

Neoclassical Theorists those who argued that situations or circumstances that made it impossible to exercise free will were reasons to exempt the accused from conviction.

Nolle Prosequi literally, "I refuse to prosecute," describing the prosecutor's discretion to refuse to file a case.

Norms the rules or standards of behavior shared by members of a group or society and defined by the common expectations of the group with regard to types of appropriate behaviors.

Offender a person who commits an offense; used in statutes to describe a person implicated in the commission of a crime.

Offense an act committed or omitted in violation of a statute forbidding or mandating it.

Opinion the written statement by a judge or a court of the decision reached in a case that explains the law and gives detailed reasons for the decision.

Organization Crime the illegal commission or omission of an act by an individual or group in a legitimate formal organization, usually a business, which has a harmful physical or economic effect on employees, consumers, or the general public.

Organized Crime a regimented and disciplined social framework for carrying out illegal acts or legal acts by illegal means, usually for economic gain and with force.

Original Jurisdiction the power of a court to hear an initial case, to try the facts and make a decision on the law and the facts, as opposed to appellate jurisdiction.

Overcriminalization the misuse of criminal sanctions by declaring illegal behavior considered by many to be legitimate.

Overrule to make void. A judicial decision is overruled when a later decision by the same court or by a superior court sets down a ruling directly opposite to the earlier decision. The first decision then has no value as binding precedent.

Paralegals individuals who do not have the specific academic credentials of an attorney, but who have skills related to the law.

Pardon an act by the head of state that exempts an individual from punishment for a crime he or she committed and removes the legal consequences of the conviction. Pardons may be absolute or have conditions attached; may be individual or granted to a group or class of offenders; or may be partial, in which case the pardon remits only part of the punishment or removes some of the legal disabilities resulting from conviction.

Parole the continued custody and supervision in the community by federal or state authorities after an offender is released from an institution before expiration of the sentenced term. Parolees who violate the conditions of parole may be returned to the institution.

Parole Boards the panels at the state and federal levels that decide how much of a sentence an offender will serve in the institution and whether he or she is ready to return to society with continued supervision in the community.

Parole Officer the government employee responsible for counseling and supervising inmates released on parole in the community.

Penologists those professionals who study the science of punishment, prevention of crime, and management and administration of correctional facilities.

Phrenology a theory of behavior based on the idea that the exterior of the skull corresponds to the interior and to the brain's conformation; thus a propensity toward certain types of behavior may be discovered by examining the "bumps" on the head.

Plea Bargaining the negotiation between the prosecution and the defense for reduction of the punishment. Normally, the charge is reduced in return for the defendant's plea of guilty to a lesser charge or a promise of cooperation with the prosecutor in providing evidence or testimony in other cases.

Police local law enforcement officials within the department of government that maintains and enforces law and order throughout a geographical area.

Positivists theorists who thought that the study of crime should emphasize the individual, scientific treatment of the criminal, not the postconviction punishment. They believed that the punishment should fit the criminal, not the crime.

Posttraumatic Stress Disorder (P-TSD) legally recognized defense to criminal behavior in some countries; refers to severe trances or flashbacks characteristic of some men who fought in the war in Vietnam.

Prediction Scales statistical measurements of antecedent factors used to identify those variables that make more probable the occurrence of a future event or behavior. The scales are then used to predict the

success or failure of persons, based on the presence or absence of these variables. These scales or tables have been used to predict results in such areas as marriage, parole, and delinquent or criminal behavior.

Preliminary Hearing an open court proceeding before a judge, used to determine if there is probable cause to believe that the defendant committed a crime and should be held for trial.

Premenstrual Tension Syndrome (PMS) tension suffered by some women before and during menstruation; in some countries, a legally recognized defense to criminal behavior.

Prerelease Programs a system of programs within institutions that assists inmates in adjusting to life in normal society. The programs cover subjects such as money management, interviewing for jobs, and basic social skills.

Presentence Report a recommendation of punishment or treatment, generally prepared by a probation officer, based on the life history of the offender, and given to the judge to assist him or her in making a sentencing decision.

Presentment a written accusation issued by the grand jury on the basis of its own investigation, as opposed to an indictment.

Presumptive Sentences a method for determining punishment in which the legislature sets a standard sentence in the statute, but the judge may vary that sentence if the case has mitigating or aggravating circumstances.

Pretrial Detention placing the accused in jail before trial. This may be due to an inability to raise money for bail.

Preventive Detention a practice of holding the accused in jail before trial to ensure that he or she will not commit further crimes and will be present at trial. This may be done illegitimately through setting the bail so high that the accused cannot raise the money or legitimately by statutory provision.

Prison a state or federal custodial facility for the confinement of adults sentenced to more than one year.

Prisonization the process by which a prison inmate assimilates the customs, norms, values, and culture of prison life.

Proactive the police's response to criminal behavior in which they actively detect crimes and seek offenders rather than relying on citizen's reports of crimes.

Probable Cause an evidentiary standard; a set of facts and circumstances that justifies a reasonably intelligent and prudent person's believing that an accused person had committed a specific crime.

Probation   a form of sentencing in which the offender is allowed to remain in the community under conditioned supervision. The term also refers to the component of the criminal justice system that administers all phases of probation.

Probation Officer   the official employed by a probation agency who is responsible for preparing presentence reports, supervising offenders placed on probation, and helping them integrate into society as lawful citizens.

Property Crimes   those crimes not directed toward the person, such as burglary, larceny-theft, motor vehicle theft, or arson.

Prosecuting Attorney   a government official whose duty is to initiate and maintain criminal proceedings on behalf of the government, against persons accused of committing crimes.

Prostitution   the act or practice of granting sexual favors in return for money or something else of value.

Psychiatry   a field of medicine that specializes in the understanding, diagnosis, treatment, and prevention of mental problems.

Psychoanalysis   a special branch of psychiatry, based on the theories of Sigmund Freud and employing a particular personality theory and method of treatment; the approach concentrates on individual case study.

Public Defender   an attorney (a government officer) whose function is to represent defendants who cannot afford to hire private lawyers.

Publisher-only Rule   an institutional security rule that inmates can receive hardback books only if mailed directly from publishers.

Rape   unlawful intercourse; called *forcible rape* if committed against the victim's will by the use of threats or force. Statutory rape refers to consensual sexual intercourse with a consenting person who is below the legal age of consent.

Ratio Decidendi   the ground of a decision; the point in a case that determines the judgment.

Reactive   the police's response to criminal behavior in which they rely on notification by citizens that a crime has been committed, instead of actively detecting crimes and seeking offenders.

Recidivism   may be used to mean violations of the law by released inmates in terms of arrests or convictions for further crimes, or it may denote noncriminal violations of conditions by probationers and parolees.

Rehabilitation   the rationale for reformation of offenders, based on the premise that human behavior is the result of antecedent causes, which may be known by objective analysis and permit scientific control of human behavior. The focus is on treatment, not punishment, of the offender.

Reintegration   a philosophy of punishment that focuses on returning the offender to the community with restored education, employment, and family ties.

Release on Recognizance   the process of releasing the accused before trial without requiring a money bond. This is used for defendants with strong ties in the community and who present little risk of flight to avoid prosecution.

Respondeat Superior   literally, "let the master answer"; a doctrine that holds the master liable for certain wrongful acts of his or her servants. The master need not participate in the act or even have knowledge of it.

Restitution   a type of punishment in which the offender must reimburse the victim financially or with services. This may be required in lieu of or in addition to a fine or other punishment, or as a condition of probation.

Retribution   a theory of punishment that contends that an offender should be punished for the crimes committed because he or she deserves it.

Revenge   a doctrine under which a person who violates the law should be punished in the same way the victim was.

Robbery   taking personal property from the possession of another against his or her will by the use of force or fear.

Routine Activity Theory   a theory explaining crime by means of three elements: (1) likely offenders (people who are motivated to commit crimes), (2) suitable targets (presence of things that are valuable and that can be transported fairly easily), and (3) absence of capable guardians (people that can prevent the criminal activity).

Sampling   the technique of choosing a representative group or a subject group, not the total population, to measure and observe in order to estimate the quality or nature of the whole.

Scienter   the term used to describe the defendant's guilty knowledge of the cause that led to an injury, or the facts upon which the defendant should have acted.

Selective Incapacitation   a sentencing procedure whereby objective data are used to identify the offenders who are the greatest risks to our society.

Such offenders are then incarcerated, and those who present only slight risks may be placed on probation or in community treatment programs.

Self-Concept Theory see Containment Theory.

Sentence the decision of the judge or jury, according to statutory law, fixing the punishment for an offender after conviction.

Sentence Disparity a term used to describe the variations and inequities that result when defendants convicted of the same crime receive sentences of different types or lengths.

Sentencing the postconviction stage in the criminal justice system that includes all those decisions the court makes with regard to the official handling of a person who pleads guilty or is convicted of a crime.

Sentencing Council a panel of judges that reviews presentence reports, discusses individual cases, and makes advisory recommendations on the length and type of sentence.

Serial Murderers persons who commit more than one murder but at different times, in contrast with mass murderers, who murder a number of people at one time.

Social-Control Theory an explanation of criminal behavior that focuses on the control mechanisms, techniques, and strategies for regulating human behavior and leading to conformity or obedience to the society's rules, and that argues that deviance results when social controls are weakened or break down so that individuals are not motivated to conform to them.

Social Organization a general term referring to the organizational aspects of societies, institutions, communities, and groups. The study of social organization focuses on the function of the particular group and the ways in which that functioning is maintained through systems of social roles and norms. A social organization's basis is a common understanding or shared meaning among members as to the social reality that provides regularity and predictability in social interaction.

Social System the interrelationship of acts, roles, and statuses of the various people who make up the social structure. A social group or set of interacting persons or groups considered a unitary whole because it reflects the common values, social norms, and objectives of the individuals who comprise it, even though it is considered distinct from those individuals.

Socialization the basic lifelong social process by which an individual is integrated into a social group by learning its culture, values, and social roles.

Sodomy historically, a term that referred to both bestiality (intercourse between a human and an animal) and buggery (intercourse by a man with another man or with a woman by the anus) and that was called the *crime against nature.* In more modern statutes, the term is often used to refer to any type of sexual relations considered to be "unnatural," including buggery and bestiality as well as oral sex.

Specific Deterrence see Individual Deterrence.

Statutory Law law created or defined in a written enactment by the legislature, as opposed to case law.

Strict Liability liability without fault; a legal concept that holds a defendant liable even if he or she did not intend the consequences of the act, was not negligent, was not acting in bad faith, or did not have knowledge of the act. Often used in tort law to hold the master liable for the acts of servants.

Subculture an identifiable segment of society or group having specific patterns of behavior, folkways, and mores, that sets that group apart from the other groups within a culture or society.

Tort the area of law referring to civil wrongs such as slander and libel and automobile, industrial, or another type of accident caused by negligence, medical malpractice, and trespassing on property. Some actions, such as trespassing on property and assault and battery, are crimes as well as torts.

Transportation the historical practice of deporting criminals to other countries as punishment.

Trial the formal fact-finding process in court, in which all evidence in a case is presented and a decision is made by the judge or jury as to whether the defendant is guilty, beyond a reasonable doubt, of criminal charges.

Utilitarianism the ethical theory that makes the happiness of the individual or society the end and the criterion of the morally good and right. In politics, this means that the greatest happiness of the greatest number is the sole end and criterion of all public action.

Victimless Crimes offenses that interfere with the normative order of society; also called public order crimes. Examples are vagrancy, disorderly conduct, gambling, narcotics offenses, public drunkenness, and some types of sexual behavior.

Victims' Compensation Programs plans for providing a variety of services to victims to assist them in facing the emotional, social, and economic consequences of crime.

Voir Dire literally, "to speak the truth"; the preliminary questioning of prospective jurors by the attorneys and/or the judge.

Warden the chief administrative officer in a prison or other correctional facility.

Warrant a writ issued by a court authorizing specific acts by law enforcement officials, for example, the arrest of a person or the search of a specific place.

White-Collar Crime the term used to describe violations of the law by persons with higher status; it usually refers to corporate or individual crime in connection with businesses or occupations regarded as a legitimate part of society.

Work Release an authorized absence that allows the inmate to hold a job or attend school but that requires him or her to return to the institution during nonworking hours.

Writ of Certiorari a document issued to a lower court directing that the record of a case be transferred to the superior court for review.

XYY Chromosome Theory a constitutional theory of criminal behavior based on the premise that there is a relationship between the extra Y chromosome found in some males and a propensity toward criminal activity.

Appendix
Guide to legal citations of reported decisions

Furman v. Georgia 408 U.S. 238, 308 (1972).

The name of the case [*Furman v. Georgia*] is followed by the volume number [408] and the abbreviated title of the reporter [U.S.]; next is the page number on which the case begins [238]; the second number [308] denotes the page on which the cited material or quotation appears; the date follows in parentheses [(1972)]. This basic format is used for all case citations. Following is a list of reporter abbreviations, later case history, and explanatory abbreviations:

At., At.2d: Atlantic Reporter, Atlantic Reporter Second Series
Cal. Rptr: California Reporter
F.2d: Federal Reporter Second Series
F.Supp: Federal Supplement
N.Y.S.2d: New York Supplement Second
N.W., N.W.2d: North Western Reporter, North Western Reporter Second Series
N.E., N.E.2d: North Eastern Reporter, North Eastern Reporter Second Series
P., P.2d: Pacific Reporter, Pacific Reporter Second Series
S.E., S.E.2d: South Eastern Reporter, South Eastern Reporter Second Series
S.Ct.: Supreme Court Reporter
U.S.: United States Reports
Wis.: Wisconsin Reporter
Aff'd: affirmed; the appellate court confirms and ratifies the decision of the lower court. *Aff'd sub nom* means that the name of the case is not the same at the appellate court as it was in the lower court. *Aff'd per curiam* means that the opinion was written by the court as opposed to being written by a single judge.
cert. denied: certiorari denied; the U.S. Supreme Court refused to grant the writ of certiorari thereby refusing to hear and decide the case.
concurring opinion: an opinion of a judge which agrees with the result but disagrees with the reasoning of the majority opinion.
dissenting opinion: an opinion of a judge which disagrees with the result and the reasoning of the majority opinion.
reh. denied: rehearing denied; the court refuses to consider the case a second time.
remanded: sent back to the lower court for another decision.
rev'd: reversed; overthrown, set aside, made void, changed to the contrary or to a former decision. The court on appeal may reverse the lower court decision *and* remand the case for the lower court to give another decision.
vacated: annulled, set aside, rendered void.

Notes

Chapter 1

1. D. F. Aberle et al., "The Functional Prerequisites of a Society," *Ethics 60* (January 1950): 100.
2. William Graham Sumner, *Folkways* (New York: Dover, 1906), pp. 1–79.
3. W. Page Keeton, Gen. ed., *Prosser and Keeton on The Law of Torts,* 5th ed., (St. Paul: West Publishing, 1984), p. 1. For a brief introduction to tort law, see pp. 1–7, and for a discussion of the distinction between torts and crime, see pp. 7–8.
4. Paul Tappan, *Crime, Justice and Correction* (New York: McGraw-Hill, 1960), p. 10.
5. People v. Beardsley, 113 N.W. 1128, 1131 (Mich. Sup. Ct. 1907).
6. Jones v. State, 43 N.E. 2d 1017 (Ind. Sup. Ct. 1942).
7. American Law Institute, *Model Penal Code,* § 2.02.
8. Commonwealth v. Pierce, 138 Mass. 165, 174 (1884).
9. U.S. v. Dotterweich, 320 U.S. 277 (1943).
10. For a recent limitation to the felony-murder doctrine, see Enmund v. Florida, 458 U.S. 782 (1982).
11. Hazel B. Kerper, *Introduction to the Criminal Justice System* (St. Paul: West Publishing, 1972), p. 27.
12. Southern Pacific Co. v. Jensen, 244 U.S. 205, 222 (1917).
13. Oliver W. Holmes, *The Common Law* (Boston: Little, Brown, 1881), pp. 1–2.
14. For a discussion of this case, see *American Bar Association Journal* 59 (January 1973): 92.
15. Sherman v. United States, 356 U.S. 369 (1958).
16. "Husband Faces Murder Charge in Mercy Killing of Wife," *Tulsa World,* March 20, 1983, p. B6, col. 1.
17. "Florida Jury Condones Mercy Slaying," *Tulsa World,* April 2, 1983, p. 2, col. 3.
18. Thorsten Sellin, "A Sociological Approach," in Marvin E. Wolfgang et al., eds., *The Sociology of Crime and Delinquency,* 2d ed. (New York: John Wiley, 1970), p. 6.
19. Paul W. Tappan, "Who Is the Criminal?" *American Sociological Review* 21 (February 1947): 99.
20. "Battle in Chinatown over Peking Duck Heating Up," *Los Angeles Times,* March 3, 1982, p. 1, col. 5.
21. See, for example, Peter H. Rossi, Emily Waite, Christine E. Bose, and Richard E. Berk, "The Seriousness of Crimes: Normative Structure and Individual Differences," *American Sociological Review* 39 (April 1974): 224–237. See also the discussion in Hyman Gross, "A Model of Criminal Justice," in Hyman Gross and Andrew von Hirsch, eds., *Sentencing* (New York: Oxford University Press, 1981), pp. 37–42.
22. Stephen Schafer, *Theories in Criminology* (New York: Random House, 1969), pp. 63–64.
23. Schafer, p. 72.
24. For a general discussion of the use of the criminal law to control morality, as well as particular applications to our early history, see William E. Nelson, "Emerging Notions of Modern Criminal Law in the Revolutionary Era," in Abraham S. and Joseph Goldstein, eds., *Crime, Law and Society* (New York: Free Press, 1971); Kai T. Erikson, *Wayward Puritans: A Study in the Sociology of Deviance* (New York: John Wiley, 1966); Patrick Devlin, *The Enforcement of Morals* (New York: Oxford University Press, 1965); Norval Morris and Gordon P. Hawkins, *The Honest Politician's Guide to Crime Control* (Chicago: University of Chicago Press, 1969); Morris R. Cohen, "Moral Aspects of the Criminal Law," *Yale Law Journal* 49 (April 1940): 987–1026; Troy Duster, *The Legislation of Morality: Law, Drugs and Moral Judgment* (New York: Free Press, 1970); and Lon L. Fuller, *The Morality of Law* (New Haven, Conn.: Yale University Press, 1964).
25. Morris and Hawkins.
26. Sanford H. Kadish, "Overcriminalization," in Leon Radzinowicz and Marvin Wolfgang, eds., *Crime and Justice: The Criminal in Society,* vol. 1, (New York: Basic Books, 1971), p. 57.
27. For an excellent discussion of the various theories used to analyze the origins of laws regulating alcohol and drugs, as well as a review of empirical studies, see John Hagan, "The Legislation of Crime and Delinquency: A Review of Theory, Method, and Research," *Law & Society Review* 14 (Spring 1980): 603–628.
28. These figures and most of the historical account come from an editorial by John Barbour of the Associated Press, reprinted in the *Tulsa World,* "50 Years Ago, America Opened the Bottle Again," December 4, 1983, p. D3, col. 1.

29. See the recent report by Joseph A. Califano, former secretary of health, education and welfare, commissioned by Governor H. L. Carey of New York, to head the study reported in *The 1982 Report on Drug Abuse and Alcoholism* (Warner).

30. John Barbour, "50 Years Ago . . ."

31. See Raymond T. Nimmer, *Two Million Unnecessary Arrests: Removing a Social Service Concern from the Criminal Justice System* (Chicago: American Bar Foundation, 1971).

32. President's Commission on Law Enforcement and Administration of Justice, *Challenge of Crime in a Free Society* (Washington, D.C.: U.S. Government Printing Office, 1967), p. 233.

33. For a discussion of this trend in Canada, see H. M. Annis, "The Detoxification Alternative to the Handling of Public Inebriates: The Ontario Experience," *Journal of Studies on Alcohol* 40 (March 1979): 196–210. For a survey on the implementation of public policies on public drunkenness and an examination of alternative policies, as well as reports on recent innovations in dealing with the problem, see *Decriminalization of Public Drunkenness,* stock number 027–000–1661616, available for $7.50 from the Superintendent of Documents, U.S. Government Printing Office, Washington, D.C. 20402. See also David E. Aaronson, C. Thomas Dienes, and Michael C. Musheno, "Changing the Public Drunkenness Laws: The Impact of Decriminalization," *Law & Society Review* 12 (Spring 1978): 405–436; Paul C. Friday, "Issues in the Decriminalization of Public Intoxication," *Federal Probation* 42 (September 1978): 33–39; and "Note: Alcohol Abuse and the Law," *Harvard Law Review* 94 (May 1981): 1660–1712.

34. Ga. Code Ann. § 99–3901 (1982).

35. *Justice Assistance News* 3 (March 1982).

36. David Margolis, quoted in "President's Antidrug Task Forces Are Falling Behind in Organizing," *New York Times,* May 1, 1983, p. 1, col. 5.

37. Morris and Hawkins, *The Honest Politician's Guide,* p. 15. For a more recent source on sex crimes, see Donal E. J. MacNamara and Edward Sagarin, *Sex, Crime and the Law* (New York: Free Press, 1977).

38. "Note: Fornication, Cohabitation, and the Constitution," *Michigan Law Review* 77 (December 1978): 253. See this article for an extensive analysis of the constitutional issues involved in statutes that proscribe consensual, private sexual behavior.

39. *Black's Law Dictionary,* 4th rev. ed. (St. Paul: West Publishing, 1968), p. 781.

40. For a case upholding a statute that makes it a misdemeanor for an unmarried man and woman to associate lewdly and lasciviously and to bed and cohabit together, see Ensminger v. Commissioner of Internal Revenue, 610 F. 2d 189 (4th Cir., 1979), *cert. denied,* 446 U.S. 941 (1980). For a case rejecting that type of statute as grounds for prohibiting a woman of good character and honest demeanor and found to be professionally competent from taking the state bar exam, see Cord v. Gibb, 254 S.E. 2d 71 (Sup. Ct. Va., 1979).

41. Idaho Criminal Code, 18–6603.

42. Wisconsin Criminal Code, 944.17; later this crime was classified as a class A misdemeanor with a maximum penalty of $10,000 or imprisonment for nine months or both. Wisconsin Criminal Code, 939.51.

43. For a discussion, see Steven A. Rosen, "Police Harassment of Homosexual Women and Men in New York City, 1960–1980," *Columbia Human Rights Law Review* 12 (Fall–Winter 1980–1981): 159–190.

44. Idaho Criminal Code, § 18–6605.

45. State v. Altwater, 157 P. 256, 257 (Idaho Sup. Ct. 1916).

46. For a reaction from the police, see "A.I.D.S.: A New Threat to Cops," *National Centurion* 1 (October 1983): 23–26 (a police magazine).

47. "Cuomo Signs AIDS Bill," *New York Times,* August 6, 1983, p. 9, col. 6.

48. Illinois Criminal Code, 38 sec. 11-2.

49. See Edwin M. Schur, *Crimes Without Victims: Deviant Behavior and Public Policy* (Englewood Cliffs, N.J.: Prentice-Hall, 1965).

50. See Troy Duster, *The Legislation of Morality: Law, Drugs and Moral Judgment* (New York: Free Press, 1970); Joseph R. Gusfield, *Symbolic Crusade: Status Politics and the American Temperance Movement* (Urbana: University of Illinois Press, 1963); Stuart L. Hills, *Crime, Power, and Morality: The Criminal Law Process in the United States* (Scranton, Pa.: Ray Chandler, 1971).

51. Schur, *Crimes Without Victims,* p. 4.

52. "Prisoners and Alcohol," U.S. Department of Justice, *Bureau of Justice Statistics Bulletin* (Washington, D.C.: U.S. Government Printing Office, January, 1983). See also Jeremy Coid, "Alcoholism and Violence," *Drug and Alcohol*

Dependence, February 1982, pp. 1–13. Kathryn Graham et al., "Aggression and Barroom Environments," *Journal of Studies on Alcohol* 41 (March 1980): 277–292; James J. Collins, Jr., *Drinking and Crime* (London and New York: Tavistock, 1982); and James J. Collins, *Alcohol Use and Criminal Behavior: An Executive Summary.* U.S. Department of Justice, National Institute of Justice (Washington, D.C.: U.S. Government Printing Office, 1981).

53. Facts on Alcoholism, National Council on Alcoholism, Inc., 2 Park Avenue, New York, N.Y. 10016.

54. Robert P. Gandossy et al., *Drugs and Crime: A Survey and Analysis of the Literature.* U.S. Department of Justice, National Institute of Justice (Washington, D.C.: U.S. Government Printing Office, 1980), p. xiii.

55. James A. Inciardi, "Heroin Use and Street Crime," *Crime and Delinquency* 25 (July 1979): 335–346.

56. For a detailed discussion of deterrence, see Chapter 3 of this text. For a series of essays on the effects of types of intervention with alcohol and drug problems, see D. A. Ward, ed., "Use of Legal and Non-Legal Coercion in the Prevention and Treatment of Drug Abuse," *Journal of Drug Issues* 12 (Winter 1982): complete issue. For a series of essays concerning law as a mechanism for social control, see Jack P. Gibbs, ed., *Social Control: Views from the Social Sciences,* vol. 51 (Beverly Hills, Calif.: Sage Focus Editions, 1982).

57. "Female Alcoholism Studied," *New York Times,* May 18, 1982, p. 10, col. 1.

58. "Alcoholism Among Nuns: A Long-Neglected Illness," *Los Angeles Times,* March 11, 1982, p. V1, col. 1.

59. For an extensive evaluation of one of these programs, see Richard W. Hall, "An Alternative to the Criminality of Driving While Intoxicated," *Journal of Police Science and Administration* 5 (June 1977): 138–144.

60. 23 U.S.C. § 408.

61. All of the above are discussed in "The War on Drunk Driving: Getting Tough with the Killers of 26,000 Americans a Year," *Newsweek,* September 13, 1982, 34–39. For more information on Ross's position, see his *Deterring the Drinking Driver; Legal Policy and Social Control* (Lexington, Mass.: Lexington Books, 1982). See also Ross, "Drinking and Driving," in Sanford H.

Kadish, editor in chief, *Encyclopedia of Crime and Justice,* vol. 2. (New York: Free Press, 1983), pp. 632–636.

62. For a case holding unconstitutional this practice of excluding aliens just because they are homosexuals, see Lesbian/Gay Freedom Day Committee, Inc. v. United States Immigration and Naturalization Service, 541 F. Supp. 569 (N. Dist. Ca., 1982).

63. Concerning the effect of such variables on arrests for drug violations, see B. K. Singh and G. W. Joe, "Substance Abuse and Arrests: Variations in Pretreatment Arrests of Clients in Drug Treatment Programs," *Criminology* 19 (November 1981): 315–327.

64. Morris and Hawkins, *The Honest Politician's Guide,* p. 2.

65. The President's Commission on Law Enforcement and Administration of Justice, *Task Force Report: The Courts* (Washington, D.C.: U.S. Government Printing Office, 1967), p. 107.

66. Andrew von Hirsch, "Desert and Previous Convictions in Sentencing," *Minnesota Law Review* 65 (April 1981): 607.

67. Edwin M. Schur, *Law and Society: A Sociological View* (New York: Random House, 1968).

Chapter 2

1. For a more detailed discussion, see James O. Finckenauer, "Crime As a National Political Issue: 1964–76: From Law and Order to Domestic Tranquility," *Crime & Delinquency* 24 (January 1978): 13–27.

2. *Newsweek,* March 23, 1981, p. 46.

3. The study was conducted by Drs. Linda and Robert Lichter of George Washington University. They viewed a six-week sample of prime-time entertainment programing for 1981, in order to count the number of incidences of violent crime that come into our living rooms. *Tulsa Tribune,* January 10, 1983, p. A9, col. 4.

4. See, for example, Terance D. Miethe, "Public Consensus on Crime Seriousness: Normative Structure or Methodological Artifact?" *Criminology* 20 (November 1982): 515–526; and Peter Rossi and J. P. Henry, "Seriousness: A Measure for All Purposes?" in M. Klein and J. Teilman, eds. *Handbook of Criminal Justice Evaluation* (Beverly Hils, Calif.: Sage Publications, 1980).

5. See, for example, Richard Quinney, *The Social Reality of Crime* (Boston: Little Brown, 1970);

and J. E. Conklin, *The Impact of Crime* (New York: Macmillan, 1975).

6. James Garofalo, "Crime and the Mass Media: A Selective Review of Research," *Journal of Research in Crime and Delinquency* 18 (July 1981): 319–350. See also Drew Humphries, "Serious Crime, News Coverage, and Ideology: A Content Analysis of Crime Coverage in a Metropolitan Paper," *Crime & Delinquency* 27 (April 1981): 191–205.

7. See D. A. Graber, *Crime News and the Public* (New York: Praeger, 1980).

8. Anthony N. Doob and Glen E. Macdonald, "Television Viewing and Fear of Victimization: Is the Relationship Causal?" *Journal of Personality and Social Psychology* 37 (February 1979): 175.

9. Mark Warr, "The Accuracy of Public Beliefs About Crime: Further Evidence," *Criminology* 20 (August 1982): 185–204.

10. For a recent analysis of the relationship between climate and crime, see Ehor O. Boyanowsky et al., "Toward a Thermoregulatory Model of Violence," *Journal of Environmental Systems* 11 (1981–1982): 81–87.

11. George B. Vold, *Theoretical Criminology* (New York: Oxford University Press, 1958), pp. 164, 165. See also Harwin L. Voss and David M. Petersen, eds., *Ecology, Crime and Delinquency* (New York: Appleton-Century-Crofts, 1971).

12. Terence Morris, "Some Ecological Studies of the 19th Century," reprinted as chap. 2 in Voss and Petersen, *Ecology, Crime and Delinquency,* pp. 65–76. For a recent analysis of the contributions of Quételet, see Sawyer F. Sylvester, "Adolphe Quételet: At the Beginning," *Federal Probation* 46 (December 1982): 14–19.

13. Yale Levin and Alfred Lindesmith, "English Ecology and Criminology of the Past Century," chap. 1 in Voss and Petersen, eds., *Ecology, Crime and Delinquency,* pp. 59, 60, 61, referring to the works of Henry Mayhew and Joseph Fletcher.

14. Morris, "Some Ecological Studies of the 19th Century," p. 66. For a more recent analysis of crime and spatial distribution, see Lynn A. Curtis, *Criminal Violence* (Lexington, Mass.: Heath, 1974), pp. 119–158.

15. See Keith D. Harries, "Crime Rates and Environmental Denominators," *Journal of Environmental Systems* 11 (1981–1982): 3–15.

16. For a complete listing of data sources, see Timothy Flanagan and Maureen McLeod, eds., *Sourcebook of Criminal Justice Statistics—1982,* U.S. Dept. of Justice, Bureau of Justice Statistics (Washington, D.C.: U.S. Government Printing Office, 1983). An excellent introduction to the various federal data and the agencies can be found in U.S. Department of Justice, Bureau of Justice Statistics: *Federal Justice Statistics* (Washington, D.C.: U.S. Government Printing Office, March 1982).

17. For the legislative history of the creation of the Bureau of Justice Statistics, see Roland Chilton, "Criminal Statistics in the United States," *Journal of Criminal Law and Criminology* 71 (Spring 1980): 56–67.

18. "BJS Announces Five-Year Program Plan," *Justice Assistance News,* October 1982, p. 3.

19. *Criminal Justice Newsletter,* June 6, 1983, pp. 1–2.

20. This procedure is used in all states except five that do not have state-level UCR programs.

21. See Hans Zeisel, "The Disposition of Felony Arrests," *American Bar Foundation Research Journal* (Spring 1981): 409–462; and Don W. Brown, "Arrest Rates and Crime Rates: When Does a Tipping Effect Occur?" *Social Forces* 57 (December 1978): 671–682.

22. See, for example, Michael J. Hindelang, "Variations in Sex-Race-Age-Specific Incidence Rates of Offending," *American Sociological Review* 46 (August 1981): 461–474; Donald J. Black, "Production of Crime Rates," *American Sociological Review* 35 (August 1970): 1–16; and David F. Greenberg, Ronald C. Kessler, and Charles H. Logan, "A Panel Model of Crime Rates and Arrest Rates," *American Sociological Review* 44 (October 1979): 843–850. For a study on the problems in reporting crime, see Robert A. Silverman, "Measuring Crime: More Problems," *Journal of Police Science and Administration* 8 (September 1980): 265–274.

23. "Burying Crime in Chicago," *Newsweek,* May 16, 1983, p. 63; and "Chicago Police Audit Finds Many Crimes Passed Over," *New York Times,* May 2, 1983, p. 11, col. 5. For a recent analysis of the factors that influence police behavior in detection, arrest, service, and violence, see Lawrence W. Sherman, "Causes of Police Behavior: The Current State of Quantitative Research," *Journal of Research in Crime and Delinquency* 16 (January 1980): 69–100.

24. For an analysis of the decisions of victims to report a crime to the police, see Michael R. Gottfredson and Michael J. Hindelang, "A Study of the Behavior of Law," *American Sociological Review* 44 (February 1979): 3–18.

25. David Seidman and Michael Couzens, "Getting the Crime Rate Down: Political Pressure and Crime Reporting," *Law & Society Review* 8 (Spring 1974): 457–493.

26. Gwynn Nettler, *Explaining Crime,* 3rd ed. (New York: McGraw-Hill, 1984), p. 41.

27. Thorsten Sellin and Marvin E. Wolfgang, *The Measurement of Delinquency* (New York: John Wiley, 1964), p. 294.

28. Other kinds of crime that are not included but that affect all of us are what one author calls "mundane crime, petty vice and public disorder offenses, folk crime, work place crime, and environmental abuse offenses." Only the first type is included in the UCR. For a discussion, see Don C. Gibbons, "Mundane Crime," *Crime & Delinquency* 29 (April 1983): 213–227.

29. See Michael R. Gottfredson and Don M. Gottfredson, *Decisionmaking in Criminal Justice: Toward the Rational Exercise of Discretion* (Cambridge, Mass.: Ballinger, 1980), pp. 21–59.

30. Gottfredson and Gottfredson, *Decisionmaking in Criminal Justice,* pp. 22, 23, 35.

31. For a discussion of early victimization surveys, see Michael Hindelang, *Criminal Victimization in Eight American Cities: A Descriptive Analysis of Common Theft and Assault* (Cambridge, Mass.: Ballinger, 1976).

32. See Phillip H. Ennis, "Crime, Victims and the Police," *Trans-action* 4 (June 1967): 39; and Richard L. Block, "Police Action As Reported by Victims of Crime," *Police,* November–December 1970, p. 43.

33. See National Criminal Justice Information and Statistics Service, *Crime in the Nation's Five Largest Cities: Advance Report* (Washington, D.C.: U.S. Government Printing Office, 1974).

34. Larry J. Cohen and Mark I. Lichback, "Alternative Measures of Crime: A Statistical Evaluation," *Sociological Quarterly* 23 (Spring 1982): 253–266.

35. Cohen and Lichback; Robert M. O'Brien, David S. Shichor, and David L. Decker, "An Empirical Comparison of the Validity of UCR and NCS Crime Rates," *Sociological Quarterly* 21 (Summer 1980): 391–401; Paula Holzman Kleinman and Irving Faber Lukoff, "Official Crime Data: Lag in Recording Time As a Threat to Validity," *Criminology* 19 (November 1981): 449–454.

36. James S. Wallerstein and C. J. Wyle, "Our Law-Abiding Lawbreakers," *Probation* 25 (April 1947): 107–112.

37. See Austin Porterfield, "Delinquency and Its Outcome in Court and College," *American Journal of Sociology* 49 (November 1943): 199–208; and Austin Porterfield, *Youth in Trouble* (Ft. Worth: Leo Potishman Foundation, 1946).

38. James F. Short and F. Ivan Nye, "Extent of Unrecorded Juvenile Delinquency: Tentative Conclusions," *Journal of Criminal Law, Criminology, and Police Science* 49 (November–December 1957): 296–302.

39. Michael J. Hindelang, Travis Hirschi, and Joseph G. Weis, *Measuring Delinquency* (Beverly Hills, Calif.: Sage Publications, 1981), p. 23.

40. For a discussion of the method they have used for correcting some of the problems, by means of self-reports to measure delinquency, along with an analysis of delinquency and social class, see Delbert S. Elliott and David Huizinga, "Social Class and Delinquent Behavior in a National Youth Panel: 1976–1980," *Criminology* 21 (May 1983): 149–177. For a discussion of the self-report method as well as other methods of measuring crime, see Gordon P. Waldo, ed., *Measurement Issues in Criminal Justice* (Beverly Hills, Calif.: Sage Publications, 1983).

41. See Albert J. Reiss, Jr., "Measurement of the Nature and Amount of Crime," in the President's Commission on Law Enforcement and Administration of Justice, *Studies in Crime and Law Enforcement in Major Metropolitan Areas: Field Surveys III,* vol. 1 (Washington, D.C.: U.S. Government Printing Office, 1967), pp. 1–183.

42. Michael J. Hindelang, Travis Hirschi, and Joseph G. Weis, "Correlates of Delinquency: The Illusion of Discrepancy Between Self-Report and Official Measures," *American Sociological Review* 44 (December 1979): 995–1014. For a review of these and other criticisms of self-report studies, see Delbert S. Elliott and Suzanne S. Ageton, "Reconciling Race and Class Differences in Self-reported and Official Estimates of Delinquency," *American Sociological Review* 45 (February 1980): 95–110.

43. For an article using NYS data to determine sex differences in delinquent behaviors, see Rachelle J. Canter, "Sex Differences in Self-Report Delinquency," *Criminology* 20 (November 1982):

373–393. For an article finding few sex differences in a self-report study, see Pamela Richards, "Quantitative and Qualitative Sex Differences in Middle-Class Delinquency," *Criminology* 18 (February 1981): 453–470.

44. "Criminal Victimization in the United States: 1973–82 Trends," Bureau of Justice Statistics Special Report, U.S. Department of Justice, September 1983. All 1982 data on victimization and the data on trends between 1973 and 1982 come from this report.

45. William H. Webster, Foreword, "Crime in the United States," *Uniform Crime Reports,* 1982. Federal Bureau of Investigation (Washington, D.C.: U.S. Government Printing Office), p. iii.

46. *Uniform Crime Reports, 1982,* p. 33.

47. *Uniform Crime Reports,* p. 36.

48. See Charles R. Tittle, "Labelling and Crime: An Empirical Evaluation," pp. 241–270 in Walter Gove, ed., *The Labelling of Deviance: Evaluating a Perspective,* 2d ed. (Beverly Hills, Calif.: Sage Publications, 1980).

49. Michael J. Hindelang, "Variations in Sex-Race-Age-Specific Incidence Rates of Offending," *American Sociological Review* 46 (August 1981): 462. See also Michael J. Hindelang, Travis Hirschi, and Joseph G. Weis, "Correlates of Delinquency: The Illusion of Discrepancy Between Self-Report and Official Measures," *American Sociological Review* 44 (December 1979): 955–1014; and Delbert S. Elliott and David Huizinga, "Social Class and Delinquent Behavior in a National Youth Panel: 1976–1980," *Criminology* 21 (May 1983): 149–177.

50. John Braithwaite, "The Myth of Social Class and Criminality Reconsidered," *American Sociological Review* 46 (February 1981): 36.

51. *Uniform Crime Reports, 1982,* p.165.

52. *Uniform Crime Reports, 1982,* p. 176.

53. *Uniform Crime Reports, 1982,* p. 174.

54. *Uniform Crime Reports, 1982,* p. 177.

55. "Old Enough to Know Better: A Stunning Rise in Crime by Senior Citizens Creates a Quandary," *Time,* September 20, 1982, p. 77.

56. U.S. National Commission on the Causes and Prevention of Violence, *Violent Crime: Homicide, Assault, Rape, Robbery,* introduction by Daniel Patrick Moynihan (New York: Braziller, 1969).

57. Marvin Wolfgang, Robert M. Figlio, and Thorsten Sellin, *Delinquency in a Birth Cohort* (Chicago: University of Chicago Press, 1972).

58. *Uniform Crime Reports,* 1982, p. 184.

59. See, for example, The Rand Corporation study of inmates in California, Michigan, and Texas, report R-2947-NIC, available for $10 from Rand's publications department, 1700 Main Street, Santa Monica, Calif. 90406, published in 1983 and noted in *Justice Assistance News* 4 (October 1983): 4, finding that blacks and Hispanics are imprisoned longer than whites are. See also Margaret Farnworth and Patrick M. Horan, "Separate Justice: An Analysis of Race Differences in Court Processes," *Social Science Research* 9 (December 1980): 381–399; Cassia Spohn, John Gruhl, and Susan Welch, "The Effect of Race on Sentencing: A Re-examination of an Unsettled Question," *Law & Society Review* 16 (1981–1982): 71–89; R. L. McNeely and Carol E. Pope, eds., *Race, Crime and Criminal Justice* (Beverly Hills, Calif.: Sage Publications 1981); Joel Peter Eigen, "Punishing Youth Homicide Offenders in Philadelphia," *Journal of Criminal Law & Criminology* 72 (Fall 1981): 1072–1093; Daniel J. Bell, "Criminal Justice Administration in Black America," *Journal of Crime & Justice,* 1979, pp. 42–57; and Pamela Irving Jackson and Leo Carroll, "Race and the War on Crime: The Sociopolitical Determinants of Municipal Police Expenditures in 90 Non-Southern U.S. Cities," *American Sociological Review* 46 (June 1981): 290–305.

60. *Uniform Crime Reports,* 1976, Table 27, pp. 176, 178, 184.

61. *Uniform Crime Reports, 1982,* p. 175. See chap. 1, "The Extent and Nature of Female Crime," in Susan K. Datesman and Frank R. Scarpitti, eds., *Women, Crime and Justice* (New York: Oxford University Press, 1980), pp. 3–64. See also James A. Inciardi, "Women, Heroin, and Property Crime," pp. 214–222, in Datesman and Scarpitti.

62. But see Hans von Hentig, *The Criminal and His Victim* (New Haven, Conn: Yale University Press, 1948); and also von Hentig, "Remarks on the Interaction of Perpetrator and Victim," *Journal of Criminal Law, Criminology, and Police Science* 31 (March–April 1941): 303–309; Margery Fry, *Arms of the Law* (London: Victor Gollancz, 1951); and Stephen Schafer, *The Victim and His Criminal* (New York: Random House, 1968). See also Schafer, *Compensation and Restitution to Victims of Crime and Victimology: The Victim and His Criminal* (Reston,

Va.: Reston, 1977); and Marvin Wolfgang, "Victim-Precipitated Homicide," *Journal of Criminal Law, Criminology, and Police Science* 48 (1957): 1–11

63. For a recent analysis of this phenomenon, see H. M. Rose, *Black Homicide and the Urban Environment.* Final Report. U.S. Department of Health and Human Services, National Institute of Mental Health/Center for Minority Group Mental Health Programs, 1981, available from the National Institute of Justice/National Criminal Justice Reference Service, Microfiche Program, Box 6000, Rockville, MD 20850, microfiche free.

64. For a detailed discussion of the history of rape, along with an analysis of racism as it relates to the crime, see Jennifer Wriggins, "Rape, Racism, and the Law," *Harvard Women's Law Journal* 6 (Spring 1983): 103–141.

65. Paul E. Joubert, J. Steven Picou, and W. Alex McIntosh, "U.S. Social Structure, Crime, and Imprisonment," *Criminology* 19 (November 1981): 354–355.

66. All of the quotations in the preceding two paragraphs are from Lee A. Daniels, "Black Crime, Black Victims," *New York Times Magazine,* May 16, 1982, p. 92.

67. See Samuel L. Gaertner, John F. Dovidio, and Gary Johnson, "Race of Victim, Nonresponsive Bystanders, and Helping Behavior," *Journal of Social Psychology* 117 (June 1982): 69–77.

68. See Joel Peter Eigen's study of the processing of youth offenders. "Punishing Youth Homicide Offenders in Philadelphia," *Journal of Criminal Law & Criminology* 72 (Fall 1981): 1072–1093.

69. "Crime and the Elderly," Bureau of Justice Statistics *Bulletin.* U.S. Department of Justice (Washington, D.C.: U.S. Government Printing Office, 1981). See also the 1981 publication of that organization, E. Hochstider, *Crime Against the Elderly in 26 Cities;* and F. P. Morello, *Juvenile Crimes Against the Elderly* (Springfield, Ill.: Chas. C Thomas, 1982).

70. See John H. Lindquist and Janice M. Duke, "The Elderly Victim at Risk," *Criminology* 20 (May 1982): 115–126. These authors also analyze the rate of victimization of the elderly, as compared to their fear of crime.

71. See Jackson Toby, "Violence in School," in Michael Tonry and Norval Morris, eds., *Crime and Justice: An Annual Review of Research,* vol. 4 (Chicago: University of Chicago Press, 1983),

pp. 1–47. See also Joan McDermott, "Crime in the School and in the Community: Offenders, Victims, and Fearful Youths," *Crime & Delinquency* 29 (April 1983): 270–282.

72. Marvin Wolfgang, *Patterns in Criminal Homicide* (Philadelphia: University of Pennsylvania Press, 1958) p. 252.

73. For a detailed analysis of violent crimes involving friends, neighbors, family members, or work associates, as compared with strangers, see *Intimate Victims—A Study of Violence Among Friends and Relatives.* Bureau of Justice Statistics (Washington, D.C.: U.S. Government Printing Office, 1980). See also Curtis, *Criminal Violence,* pp. 45–64.

74. *Criminal Victimization in the United States,* 1980, p. 10.

75. Keith Bottomley, *Decisions in the Penal Process* (South Hackensack, N.J.: Fred B. Rothman, 1973), p. 21.

76. John I. Kitsuse and Aaron V. Cicourel, "A Note on the Uses of Official Statistics," *Social Problems* 11 (Fall 1963): 137.

77. Aaron V. Cicourel, *The Social Organization of Juvenile Justice* (New York: John Wiley, 1968), p. 37.

78. See Donald J. Black, "Production of Crime Rates," *American Sociological Review* 35 (August 1970): 733–748. See also Kitsuse and Cicourel, "A Note on the Uses of Official Statistics," 131–139.

79. Kitsuse and Cicourel.

80. Stanton Wheeler, "Criminal Statistics: A Reformulation of the Problem," *Journal of Criminal Law, Criminology, and Police Science* 58 (September 1967): 317–324.

Chapter 3

1. George A. Lundberg, *Can Science Save Us?* (New York: Longman, 1961), p. 134.

2. Philip M. Hauser, "Social Science and Social Engineering," *The Bobbs-Merrill Reprint Series in the Social Sciences,* S-114, p. 213, reprinted from *Philosophy of Science* 16 (July 1949).

3. Daniel Glaser, "A Review of Crime-Causation Theory and Its Application," in Norval Morris and Michael Tonry, eds., *Crime and Justice: An Annual Review of Research,* vol. 1 (Chicago: University of Chicago Press, 1979), pp. 204, 205.

4. Attorney General William French Smith, "Federal, State, Local Law Enforcement Must Cooperate to Fight Crime in America," *Justice Assistance News,* August 1981, p. 2.

5. For examples of the use of this method, see Clifford Shaw, *Brothers in Crime* (Chicago: University of Chicago Press, 1938); Shaw, *The Jack-Roller* (Chicago: University of Chicago Press, 1930); Shaw, *The Natural History of a Delinquent Career* (Chicago: University of Chicago Press, 1931); and Edwin H. Sutherland, ed., *The Professional Thief* (Chicago: University of Chicago Press, 1937). A more recent example of a case study is Carl B. Klockars, *The Professional Fence* (New York: Free Press, 1974).

6. For an example of the use of this design, see Delbert S. Elliott and Harwin L. Voss, *Delinquency and Dropout* (Lexington, Mass.: Lexington Books, 1974). See also Marvin E. Wolfgang, Robert M. Figlio, and Thorsten Sellin, *Delinquency in a Birth Cohort* (Chicago: University of Chicago Press, 1972).

7. See Leon Festinger, Henry W. Riecken, and Stanley Schacter, *When Prophecy Fails* (Minneapolis: University of Minnesota Press, 1956); Kai T. Erikson, "A Comment on Disguised Observation in Sociology," *Social Problems* 14 (Summer 1966): 366–373. See also William F. Whyte, *Street Corner Society* (Chicago: University of Chicago Press, 1943); Hans Toch, "Cast the First Stone: Ethics As a Weapon," *Criminology* 19 (August 1981): 185–194; and Marvin E. Wolfgang, "Confidentiality in Criminological Research and Other Ethical Issues," *Journal of Criminal Law & Criminology* 71 (Spring 1981): 345–361.

8. Lundberg, *Can Science Save Us?* pp. 143–144.

9. *On Crimes and Punishments,* trans. Henry Paolucci (Indianapolis: Bobbs-Merrill, 1963), pp. ix–xxxiii.

10. Eliott Monochese, "Cesare Beccaria," in Herman Mannheim, ed., *Pioneers in Criminology* (Montclair, N.J.: Patterson Smith, 1973), p. 48.

11. Monochese, p. 49.

12. Stephen Schafer, *Theories in Criminology* (New York: Random House, 1969), p. 106.

13. Roscoe Pound, quoted in Frank Tannenbaum, *Crime and the Community* (New York: Ginn, 1938), p. 4.

14. Coleman Phillipson, *Three Criminal Law Reformers: Beccaria, Bentham, and Romilly* (New York: Dutton, 1923), p. 234.

15. Gilbert Geis, "Jeremy Bentham," in Mannheim, *Pioneers,* p. 57.

16. George B. Vold, *Theoretical Criminology* (New York: Oxford University Press, 1958), p. 25.

17. See Raffaele Garofalo, *Criminology,* trans. Robert W. Millar (Boston: Little, Brown, 1914); Francis Allen, "Raffaele Garofalo," in Mannheim, *Pioneers,* pp. 318–340; Enrico Ferri, *The Positive School of Criminology* (Chicago: Kerr, 1913); and Enrico Ferri, *Criminal Sociology,* trans. Joseph Killey and John Lisle (Boston: Little, Brown, 1917). For a discussion and an evaluation of Ferri's contributions, see Thorsten Sellin, "Enrico Ferri," in Mannheim, *Pioneers,* pp. 316–384.

18. Schafer, *Theories in Criminology,* p. 123.

19. Marvin E. Wolfgang, "Cesare Lombroso," in Mannheim, *Pioneers,* pp. 232–291. See also Cesare Lombroso, *Crime, Its Causes and Remedies,* trans. H. P. Horton (Boston: Little, Brown, 1911), p. 33.

20. Edwin H. Sutherland and Donald Cressey. *Criminology,* 10th ed. (Philadelphia: Lippincott, 1978), p. 59.

21. Wolfgang. "Cesare Lombroso," p. 288. For a discussion of the attempts of the Englishman George Buckman Goring (1870–1910), to test Lombroso's theories, see Charles Goring, *The English Convict* (London: H. M. Stationery Office, 1913). See also Edwin D. Driver, "Charles Buckman Goring," in Mannheim, *Pioneers,* p. 429, with a reference to Thorsten Sellin. E. R. A. Seligman and A. Johnson, eds., "Charles Buckman Goring," *Encyclopedia of the Social Sciences,* vol. 6, (New York: Macmillan, 1931), p. 703. Although Goring's empirical work was probably superior to that of Lombroso, Goring also made some serious errors. For a detailed discussion, see "Charles Goring's *The English Convict:* A Symposium," *Journal of Criminal Law & Criminology* 5 (1914–1915): 207–240, 348–363.

22. Wolfgang, "Cesare Lombroso," p. 271.

23. Thorsten Sellin, "The Lombrosian Myth in Criminology," *American Journal of Sociology* 42 (May 1937): 898–899. For a scathing criticism of Lombroso, see Alfred Lindesmith and Yale Levin, in the same issue, pp. 653–671.

24. Schafer, *Theories in Criminology,* p. 123.

25. For a discussion, see Richard A. Posner, "Retribution and Related Concepts of Punishment," *Journal of Legal Studies* 9 (January 1980): 71–92.

26. Francis Edward Devine, "Cesare Beccaria and the Theoretical Foundation of Modern Penal Jurisprudence," *New England Journal of Prison Law* 7 (Winter 1981): 13. See also Beccaria, *On Crimes and Punishments,* pp. 10–13, 53–54, 66–67.

27. See Herbert L. Packer, *The Limits of the Criminal Sanction* (Palo Alto, Calif.: Stanford University Press, 1968).

28. *Time,* September 13, 1982, p. 38.

29. Francis Allen, "Criminal Justice, Legal Values and the Rehabilitative Ideal," *Journal of Criminal Law, Criminology, and Police Science* 50 (September-October 1959): 226–232.

30. President's Commission on Law Enforcement and Administration of Justice. *The Challenge of Crime in a Free Society* (Washington, D.C.: U.S. Government Printing Office, 1967).

31. For a more detailed discussion of the indeterminate sentence, see Sue Titus Reid, "A Rebuttal to the Attack on the Indeterminate Sentence," *Washington Law Review* 51 (July 1976): 565–606; Alan Dershowitz, "Indeterminate Confinement: Letting the Therapy Fit the Harm," *University of Pennsylvania Law Review* 123 (December 1974): 297–339; and Frankel, *Criminal Sentences: Law Without Order.*

32. David A. Ward, "Evaluation Research for Corrections," in Lloyd E. Ohlin, ed., *Prisoners in America* (Englewood Cliffs, N.J.: Prentice-Hall, 1973), p. 196.

33. Ward, p. 198.

34. See, for example, Alfred Blumstein and Jacqueline Cohen, "Sentencing of Convicted Offenders: An Analysis of the Public's View," *Law & Society Review* 14 (Winter 1980): 223–261. On determinate sentencing, see Kathleen J. Hanrahan, "Determinate Penalty Systems in America: An Overview," *Crime & Delinquency* 27 (July 1981): 289–316. See also Leonard Orland, "From Vengeance to Vengeance: Sentencing Reform and the Demise of Rehabilitation," *Hofstra Law Review* 7 (Fall 1978): 29–56; Franklin E. Zimring, "Making the Punishment Fit the Crime," *Hastings Center Report* 6 (December 1976): 13–17; Determinate Sentencing: Reform or Regression," Proceedings of the Special Conference on *Determinate Sentencing,* June 2-3, 1977 (Washington, D.C.: U.S. Government Printing Office, 1978).

35. *Time,* September 13, 1982, p. 38.

36. See, for example, Martin R. Gardner, "The Renaissance of Retribution—An Examination of Doing Justice," *Wisconsin Law Review* 1976 (Fall 1976): 781–815.

37. Furman v. Georgia, 408 U.S. 238 (1972).

38. Gregg v. Georgia, 428 U.S. 153, 184–185 (1976).

39. 428 U.S. 153, 183.

40. Jack P. Gibbs, "The Death Penalty, Retribution and Penal Policy," *Journal of Criminal Law & Criminology* 69 (Fall 1978): 294.

41. Ernest van den Haag, "Punishment As a Device for Controlling the Crime Rate," *Rutgers Law Review* 33 (Spring 1981): 719–730.

42. Andrew von Hirsch, *Doing Justice: The Choice of Punishments* (New York: Hill & Wang, 1976).

43. David Fogel, " . . . We Are the Living Proof . . . " *The Justice Model for Corrections* (Cincinnati, Ohio: W. H. Anderson, 1975).

44. Fogel, pp. 183–184.

45. Fogel, p. 184.

46. Fogel, p. 192, emphasis in the original.

47. Fogel, p. 202, emphasis deleted.

48. Fogel, p. 206.

49. Rich J. Carlson, *The Dilemma of Corrections* (Lexington, Mass.: Heath, 1976), p. 126.

50. Richard Quinney, *Criminology,* 2d ed. (Boston: Little, Brown, 1979), pp. 108–109.

51. "An Eye for an Eye," *Time,* January 24, 1983, p. 32.

52. "An Eye for an Eye," p. 32.

53. Jack P. Gibbs, *Crime, Punishment and Deterrence* (New York: Elsevier North-Holland, 1975), p. 11.

54. Gibbs, p. ix. For a recent discussion of methodological problems of research in this area, see John Hagan, ed., *Deterrence Reconsidered: Methodological Innovations* (Berkeley, Calif.: Sage Publications, 1982).

55. See Robert F. Meier, "Correlates of Deterrence: Problems of Theory and Method," *Journal of Criminal Justice* 7 (Spring 1979): 18–19.

56. See Robert F. Meier, Steven R. Burkett, and Carol A. Hickman, "Sanctions, Peers, and Deviance: Preliminary Models of a Social Control Process," *Sociological Quarterly* 25 (Winter 1984): 67–82. See also Meier, "Perspectives on the Concept of Social Control," *Annual Review of Sociology* 8 (1982): 35–55; and William Minor and Joseph Harry, "Deterrent and Experiential Effects in Perceptual Deterrence Research: A Replication and Extension," *Jour-*

nal of Research in Crime and Delinquency 19 (1982): 190–203.

57. Thorsten Sellin, "The Death Penalty," in Thorsten Sellin, ed., *Capital Punishment* (New York: Harper & Row, 1967).

58. Richard O. Lempert, "Desert and Deterrence: An Assessment of the Moral Bases of the Case for Capital Punishment," *Michigan Law Review* 79 (May 1981): 1202.

59. See Lempert, 1203–1206.

60. Lempert, 1205–1206.

61. Daniel Glaser and Max S. Zeigler, "Use of the Death Penalty v. Outrage at Murder," *Crime and Delinquency* 20 (October 1974): 337.

62. William C. Bailey, "Use of the Death Penalty v. Outrage at Murder: Some Additional Evidence and Considerations?" *Crime & Delinquency* 22 (January 1976): 37, referring to Thorsten Sellin, *The Death Penalty* (Philadelphia: American Law Institute, 1959).

63. For research on these distinctions, see Jack P. Gibbs, "Crime, Punishment and Deterrence," *Southwest Social Science Quarterly* 48 (March 1968): 515–530; and Franklin Zimring and Gordon Hawkins, *Deterrence: The Legal Threat in Crime Control* (Chicago: University of Chicago Press, 1973).

64. Daniel Glaser, "A Response to Bailey: More Evidence on Capital Punishment As Correlate of Tolerance for Murder," *Crime & Delinquency* 22 (January 1976): 43.

65. Isaac Ehrlich, "The Deterrent Effect of Capital Punishment: A Question of Life and Death," *American Economic Review* 65 (June 1975): 397–407.

66. Lempert, "Desert and Deterrence," 1206.

67. Lempert, 1206. For other reactions to Ehrlich's work, see David C. Baldus and James W. L. Cole, "A Comparison of the Work of Thorsten Sellin and Isaac Ehrlich on the Deterrent Effect of Capital Punishment," *Yale Law Journal* 85 (December 1975): 170–186. See also Richard M. McGahey, "Dr. Ehrlich's Magic Bullet: Econometric Theory, Econometrics, and the Death Penalty," *Crime & Delinquency* 26 (October 1980): 485–502. For Ehrlich's reaction to these critics, see Ehrlich, "Deterrence: Evidence and Inference," *Yale Law Journal* 85 (December 1975): 209–227.

68. Lempert, "Desert and Deterrence," 1207. For detailed criticisms of Ehrlich's work, see pp. 1210–1215. For his analysis of other economet-

ric approaches, see 1215–1224. For further evidence in support of the death penalty as a deterrent, see David P. Phillips, "The Deterrent Effect of Capital Punishment: New Evidence on an Old Controversy," *American Journal of Sociology* 86 (July 1980): 139–148.

69. Johannes Andenaes, "Determinism and Criminal Law," *Journal of Criminal Law, Criminology, and Police Science* 47 (November-December 1956): 406–413.

70. See H. Laurence Ross, *Deterring the Drinking Driver: Legal Policy and Social Control* (Lexington, Mass.: Lexington Books, 1982).

71. John Braithwaite and Gilbert Geis, "On Theory and Action for Corporate Crime Control," *Crime & Delinquency* 28 (April 1982): 305.

72. Marshall B. Clinard and Robert F. Meier, *Sociology of Deviant Behavior,* 5th ed. (New York: Holt, Rinehart and Winston, 1979), p. 248, cited in Braithwaite and Geis, p. 302.

73. See the discussions of Gibbs, "Crime, Punishment, and Deterrence"; and Johannes Andenaes, "General Prevention Revisited: Research and Policy Implications," *Journal of Criminal Law, Criminology, and Police Science* 66 (September 1975): 338–365.

74. See Assembly Committee (1968) *Deterrent Effects of Criminal Sanctions,* Progress Report of the Assembly Committee on Criminal Procedure. California Legislature; N. Walker, *Sentencing in a Rational Society* (Hammondsworth, England: Penguin Books, 1969), cited in Jerry Parker and Harold G. Gransmick, "Linking Actual and Perceived Certainty of Punishment," *Criminology* 17 (November 1979): 366–379.

75. See Gibbs, "Crime, Punishment, and Deterrence"; and Andenaes, "General Prevention Revisited." For a critique of these proposals, see Parker and Gransmick, "Linking Actual and Perceived Certainty," pp. 368–369.

76. For examples of early studies attempting to measure this relationship, see Gibbs, "Crime, Punishment and Deterrence"; and Charles R. Tittle, "Crime Rates and Legal Sanctions," *Social Problems* 16 (Spring 1969): 409–423. For a study concluding that there is "no consistent support for the hypothesis that severe punishment deters crime," see Theodore G. Chiricos and Gordon P. Waldo, "Punishment and Crime: An Examination of Some Empirical

Evidence," *Social Problems* 18 (Fall 1970): 200–217.

77. Harold G. Grasmick and Donald E. Green, "Legal Punishment, Social Disapproval and Internalization As Inhibitors of Illegal Behavior," *Journal of Criminal Law & Criminology* 71 (Fall 1980): 325–335. See also Grasmick and Green, "Deterrence and the Morally Committed," *Sociological Quarterly* 22 (Winter 1981): 1–14.

78. See for example, the works of Johannes Andenaes, "The General Preventive Effects of Punishment," *University of Pennsylvania Law Review* 114 (May 1966): 949–983; Charles Tittle, "Sanction Fear and the Maintenance of Social Order," *Social Forces* 55 (1977): 569–596; and Franklin Zimring, "Perspective on Deterrence." Public Health Science Publication No. 2056 (Washington, D.C.: U.S. Government Printing Office, 1971).

79. Grasmick and Green, "Deterrence and the Morally Committed," 2, 13. For similar findings, see Ronald Akers et al., "Social Learning and Deviant Behavior: A Specific Test of a General Theory," *American Sociological Review* 44 (August 1979): 636–655; Gary F. Jensen, Maynard L. Erikson, and Jack P. Gibbs, "Perceived Risk of Punishment and Self-reported Delinquency," *Social Forces* 57 (September 1978): 57–78; and Matthew Silberman, "Toward A Theory of Criminal Deterrence," *American Sociological Review* 41 (June 1976): 442–461.

80. Raymond Patternoster, Linda E. Saltzman, Gordon P. Waldo, and Theodore G. Chiricos, "Perceived Risk and Social Control: Do Sanctions Really Deter?" *Law & Society Review* 17 (1983): 477. See also an article by the same authors, "Estimating Perceptual Stability and Deterrent Effects: The Role of Perceived Legal Punishments in the Inhibition of Criminal Involvement," *Journal of Criminal Law & Criminology* 74 (Spring 1983): 270–297.

81. Richard A. Posner, *Economic Analysis of Law* (Boston: Little, Brown, 1972), p. 1, quoted in John E. Monzingo, "Economic Analysis of the Criminal Justice System," *Crime & Delinquency* 23 (July 1977): 262.

82. Monzingo, p. 263.

83. Gary S. Becker, "Crime and Punishment; An Economic Approach," *Journal of Political Economy* 2 (March-April 1968): 176.

84. For a compilation of essays on economic theories of criminal behavior and administration, see Kevin N. Wright, ed., *Crime and Criminal Justice in a Declining Economy* (Cambridge, Mass.: Oelgeschlager, Gunn & Hain, 1981). See also Steven Stack, "Social Structure and Swedish Crime Rates," *Criminology* 20 (November 1982): 499–513; and Peter Schmidt and Ann D. Witte, *The Economics of Crime: Theory, Methods, and Applications* (New York: Academic Press, 1983).

85. Ann Dryden Witte, "Crime Causation: Economic Theories," in Sanford H. Kadish, editor in chief, *Encyclopedia of Crime and Justice,* vol. 1 (New York: Free Press, 1983), p. 318.

86. Isaac Ehrlich, "The Deterrent Effect of Criminal Law Enforcement," *Journal of Legal Studies* 1 (1972): 259.

87. Isaac Ehrlich, "Participation in Illegitimate Activities: A Theoretical and Empirical Investigation," *Journal of Political Economy* 81 (May/June 1973): 521–565. For a discussion of the application of economic theory to an explanation of crime among females, see Ann P. Bartel, "Women and Crime: An Economic Analysis," *Economic Inquiry* 17 (January 1979): 29–51.

88. Ann Dryden Witte, "Estimating the Economic Model of Crime with Individual Data," *Quarterly Journal of Economics* 94 (February 1980): 57. For an excellent but brief explanation of the economic theory of crime, as well as a discussion of some of the criticisms of the theory, see Witte, "Crime Causation: Economic Theories." For a thorough discussion of the empirical tests of the theory, see Philip J. Cook, "Research in Criminal Deterrence: Laying the Groundwork for the Second Decade," in Norval Morris and Michael Tonry, eds., *Crime and Justice: An Annual Review of Research,* vol. 2 (Chicago: University of Chicago Press, 1980), pp. 211–268. This article contains an excellent bibliography on economic theory and pictures the empirical research in chart form, on pp. 246–249.

89. Colin Loftin and David McDowall, "The Police, Crime, and Economic Theory: An Assessment," *American Sociological Review* 47 (June 1982): 399, 400.

90. Herbert Jacob, "Rationality and Criminality," *Social Science Quarterly* 59 (1979): 584, quoted in Cook, "Research in Criminal Deterrence:

Laying the Groundwork for the Second Decade," p. 219.

91. From "An Outline of Intellectual Rubbish," in Bertrand Russell, *Unpopular Essays* (New York: Simon & Schuster, 1962), p. 71, quoted in Michael R. Gottfresdon and Don M. Gottfresdson, *Decisionmaking in Criminal Justice: Toward the Rational Exercise of Discretion* (Cambridge, Mass.: Ballinger, 1980), p. 3.

92. Stephen S. Brier and Stephen E. Fienberg, "Recent Econometric Modeling of Crime and Punishment: Support for the Deterrence Hypothesis?" *Evaluation Review* 4 (April 1980): 147.

93. Monzingo, "Economic Analysis of the Criminal Justice System," p. 261.

94. Witte, "Crime and Causation: Economic Theory," 321.

95. Witte, 322. For an excellent review and analysis of economic theory and deterrence, see Jan Palmer, "Economic Analyses of the Deterrent Effect of Punishment: A Review," *Journal of Research in Crime and Delinquency* 14 (January 1977): 4–21.

96. Cook, "Research in Criminal Deterrence," p. 262.

97. Daniel P. King, "Criminal Deterrence: Some Implications for Policy," *Police Journal* 54 (January 1981): 80, quoting Nils Christie, "Utility and Social Values in Court Decisions on Punishment," in Roger Hood, ed., *Crime, Criminology and Public Policy* (New York: Free Press, 1974), p. 285.

98. King, 82.

99. For a debate on this issue, see John Braithwaite, "Challenging Just Deserts: Punishing White-Collar Criminals," *Journal of Criminal Law & Criminology* 73 (Summer 1982): 723–763; and Andrew von Hirsch, "Desert and White-Collar Criminality: A Response to Dr. Braithwaite," *Journal of Criminal Law & Criminology* 73 (Fall 1982): 1164–1175. See also John Collins Coffee, Jr., "Corporate Crime and Punishment: A Non-Chicago View of the Economics of Criminal Sanctions," *American Criminal Law Review* 17 (Spring 1980): 419–476.

100. Norval Morris and Gordon Hawkins, *The Honest Politician's Guide to Crime Control* (Chicago: University of Chicago Press, 1969), p. 119. For a compilation of essays on the death penalty both pro and con, see Hugo Adam Bedau, ed. *The Death Penalty in America,* 3rd. ed. (New York: Oxford University Press, 1982), and in *Crime & Delinquency* 26 (October 1982). See also David P. Phillips, "The Deterrent Effect of Capital Punishment: New Evidence in an old Controversy," *American Journal of Sociology* 86 (July 1980): 139–148. For evidence that increasing arrest rates do not deter crime, see Roland Chilton, "Analyzing Urban Crime Data: Deterrence and the Limitations of Arrests per Offense Ratios," *Criminolgy* 19 (February 1982): 590–607.

101. David L. Bazelon, "Street Crime and Correctional Potholes," *Federal Probation* 41 (March 1977).

102. Bazelon, "Street Crime," 3.

103. *Seattle Times,* June 18, 1975, p. A10, col. 1.

104. Norval Morris, *The Future of Imprisonment* (Chicago: University of Chicago Press, 1974), pp. 13, 15, 27. Emphasis in the original.

105. Francis A. Allen, *The Decline of the Rehabilitative Ideal: Penal Policy and Social Purpose* (New Haven, Conn.: Yale University Press, 1981).

106. Francis T. Cullen and Karen E. Gilbert, *Reaffirming Rehabilitation* (Cincinnati: Anderson Publishing, 1982).

Chapter 4

1. Sarnoff A. Mednick and Jan Volavka, "Biology and Crime," in Norval Morris and Michael Tonry, eds., *Crime and Justice: An Annual Review of Research,* vol. 2 (Chicago: University of Chicago Press, 1980), p. 86. For an annotated bibliography of recent works on the biological aspects of criminal violence, see Marvin E. Wolfgang and Neil Alan Weiner, comps., *Criminal Violence: Biological Correlates and Determinants: A Selected Bibliography.* U.S. Department of Justice. National Institute of Justice, December 1981.

2. Stephen Schafer, *Theories in Criminology* (New York: Random House, 1969), pp. 27, 112, 113.

3. Arthur E. Fink, *Causes of Crime: Biological Theories in the United States, 1800–1915* (Philadelphia: University of Pennsylvania Press, 1938), pp. 2, 3.

4. Schafer, *Theories in Criminology,* p. 115. See also Fink, pp. 17–19.

5. Leonard Savitz, Stanley H. Turner, and Toby Dickman, "The Origin of Scientific Criminology: Franz Joseph Gall As the First Criminologist," in Robert F. Meier, ed., *Theory in Criminology: Contemporary Views* (Beverly Hills, Calif.: Sage Publications, 1977), pp. 53, 54, 55.

6. Schafer, *Theories in Criminology,* p. 123.

7. Schafer, p. 24, quoting Marvin E. Wolfgang, "Cesare Lombroso," in Herman Mannheim, ed., *Pioneers in Criminology,* 2d ed. (Montclair, N.J.: Patterson Smith, 1973). Unless otherwise noted, the information on Lombroso's background and theories is based on this excellent essay by Wolfgang, pp. 232–291.

8. Cesare Lombroso, *Crime, Its Causes and Remedies,* trans. H. P. Horton (Boston: Little, Brown, 1911), p. 365.

9. Wolfgang, "Cesare Lombroso," pp. 269–270, 288.

10. Raffaele Garofalo, *Criminology,* trans. Robert W. Millar (Boston: Little, Brown, 1914), p. 79.

11. For an excellent discussion of Garofalo, see Francis Allen, "Raffaele Garofalo," in Mannheim, *Pioneers,* p. 326.

12. Garofalo, *Criminology,* pp. 95, 96.

13. Garofalo, p. 24.

14. Thorsten Sellin, "Enrico Ferri" in Mannheim, *Pioneers,* pp. 370–371.

15. Enrico Ferri, *The Positive School of Criminology* (Chicago: Kerr, 1913), p. 93.

16. Enrico Ferri, *Criminal Sociology,* trans. Joseph Killey and John Lisle (Boston: Little, Brown, 1917), p. 209. Ferri called these changes "penal substitutes" or "equivalents" of punishment. Among them he listed freedom of emigration, changes in the tax structure, public improvements to supply work for the indigent, substitution of metal for paper money to reduce counterfeiting, cheap workingmen's houses, sanitary police regulations for dwellings in the city and country, and improved street lighting. He also suggested economic and electoral reforms, provision for marriage of the clergy, changes in marriage and divorce laws, and an intelligent regulation of prostitution, pp. 242–277.

17. Schafer, *Theories in Criminology,* p. 183.

18. Schafer, p. 184.

19. Ernst Kretschmer, *Physique and Character,* trans. W. J. H. Sprott (New York: Harcourt, Brace, 1926), p. xiv.

20. W. H. Sheldon. *The Varieties of Human Physique: An Introduction to Constitutional Psychology* (New York: Harper & Row, 1940), pp. 8–9.

21. Sheldon, pp. 3, 221, 237. See also W. H. Sheldon, *The Varieties of Temperament* (New York: Harper & Row, 1942); *Varieties of Delinquent Youth: An Introduction to Constitutional Psychiatry* (New York: Harper & Row, 1949); and *Atlas of Men* (New York: Harper & Row, 1954).

22. Juan B. Cortés, with Florence M. Gatti, *Delinquency and Crime: A Biopsychosocial Approach* (New York: Seminar Press, 1972), p. 8.

23. Albert K. Cohen, Alfred Lindesmith, and Karl Schuessler, *The Sutherland Papers* (Bloomington: Indiana University Press, 1956), p. 289.

24. Sheldon, *Atlas of Men,* p. 15.

25. Sheldon, *Varieties of Temperament,* p. 438.

26. See Sheldon Glueck and Eleanor Glueck, *Physique and Delinquency* (New York: Harper & Row, 1956), pp. 2, 249. Glueck and Glueck, *Five Hundred Criminal Careers* (New York: Knopf, 1930); Glueck and Glueck, *Later Criminal Careers* (New York: Commonwealth Fund, 1937); Glueck and Glueck, *Criminal Careers in Retrospect* (New York: Commonwealth Fund, 1943); and Glueck and Glueck, *Unraveling Juvenile Delinquency* (New York: Commonwealth Fund, 1950).

27. Hermann Mannheim, *Comparative Criminology* (Boston: Houghton Mifflin, 1965), p. 241.

28. Cortés. *Delinquency and Crime,* p. 19. See also Mannheim.

29. Edwin H. Sutherland and Donald R. Cressey, *Criminology,* 9th ed. (Philadelphia: Lippincott, 1970), p. 120, quoting S. L. Washburn.

30. Glueck and Glueck, *Physique and Delinquency,* pp. 2, 249.

31. Cortés, *Delinquency and Crime,* pp. 5–6.

32. Cortés, p. 158.

33. See Richard L. Dugdale, *The Jukes: A Study in Crime, Pauperism, Disease, and Heredity,* 4th ed. (New York: Putnam's, 1942), for a report on the "jukes," and Henry H. Goddard, *Feeblemindedness, Its Causes and Consequences* (New York: Macmillan, 1914), for a report on the "Kallikaks."

34. L. D. Zeleny, "Feeblemindedness and Criminal Conduct," *American Journal of Sociology* 38 (January 1933): 569; Carl Murchison, *Criminal*

Intelligence (Worcester, Mass: Clark University Press, 1926), chap. 4; and Edwin H. Sutherland, "Mental Deficiency and Crime," in Kimball Young, ed., *Social Attitudes* (New York: Holt, Rinehart & Winston, 1931), pp. 357–375. See also Samuel Hopkins Adams, "The Juke Myth," *Saturday Review,* April 2, 1955, pp. 48–49.

35. Sheldon Glueck and Eleanor Glueck, *Of Delinquency and Crime* (Springfield, Ill: Chas. C Thomas, 1974). The same conclusion was reached in the classic study by Lee N. Robins, *Deviant Children Grown Up* (Baltimore: Williams & Wilkins, 1966).

36. Charles Goring, *The English Convict* (London: H.M. Stationery Office, 1913).

37. For a general discussion, see chap. 9, "Heredity: Human Sterilization," in Fink, *Causes of Crime.* These statutes were upheld. For example, in 1927 the United States Supreme Court affirmed a sterilization order in the case of eighteen-year-old Carrie Buck. According to the Court, Buck was the mentally retarded daughter of a feebleminded woman and had given birth to a retarded, illegitimate child. She had been committed to a state institution, and a Virginia statute provided for the sterilization of persons committed to mental institutions when the superintendent of the institution decided that such was in the best interests of society and of the patient. The Supreme Court held that the rights of due process of the woman were not violated. According to Justice Holmes, writing for the Court, "We have seen more than once that the public welfare may call upon the best citizens for their lives.... The principle that sustains compulsory vaccination is broad enough to cover cutting the Fallopian tubes.... Three generations of imbeciles are enough." Buck v. Bell, 274 U.S. 200, 207 (1927). Later evidence indicated that Ms. Bell's daughter was not retarded.

38. For a discussion of fifteen major family studies published between 1874 and 1926, including a chart picturing the author and original date of publication, the family or tribe name, and the principal sponsor of the research, see Nicolas F. Hahn, "Too Dumb to Know Better: Cacogenic Family Studies and the Criminology of Women," *Criminology* 18 (May 1980): 3–25.

39. See, for example, the works of J. Lange, *Crime As Destiny,* trans. C. Haldane (London: Allen & Unwin, 1931). For a detailed study of these early studies, see Karl O. Christiansen, "A Review of Studies of Criminality Among Twins," in Sarnoff A. Mednick and Karl O. Christiansen, eds., *Biosocial Bases of Criminal Behavior* (New York: Gardner Press, 1977); and Christiansen, "A Preliminary Study of Criminality Among Twins," in Mednick and Christiansen, pp. 89–108.

40. Mednick and Volavka, "Biology and Crime," p. 97.

41. Odd S. Dalgaard and Einar A. Kringlen, "A Norwegian Twin Study of Criminality," *British Journal of Criminology* 16 (1976): 213–232.

42. Mednick and Volavka, "Biology and Crime," p. 97.

43. For a review of the studies, see Mednick and Volavka, "Biology and Crime," pp. 98–101.

44. Mednick and Volavka, pp. 103–104. See also Barry Hutchings and Sarnoff A. Mednick, "Criminality in Adoptees and Their Adoptive and Biological Parents: A Pilot Study," in Mednick and Christiansen, eds., *Biosocial Bases of Criminal Behavior,* pp. 127–142; and Sarnoff A. Mednick, "Some Considerations in the Interpretation of the Danish Adoption Studies," in Mednick and Christiansen, pp. 159–164.

45. P. A. Jacobs et al., "Aggressive Behavior, Mental Subnormality, and the XYY Male," *Nature* 208 (December 1965): 1351.

46. See, for example, N. Maclean et al., "A Survey of Sex Chromosome Abnormalities Among 4,515 Mental Defectives," *Lancet* 1 (February 1962): 293; A. A. Sandbury et al., "XYY Genotype," *New England Journal of Medicine* 268 (March 1963): 585; P. L. Townes et al., "A Patient with 48 Chromosomes XYYY," *Lancet* 1 (May 1965): 1401; W. H. Price et al., "Criminal Behavior and the XYY Male," *Nature* 213 (February 1967): 815; and T. R. Sarbin and J. E. Miller, "Demonism Revisited: The XYY Chromosomal Anomaly," *Issues in Criminology* 5 (1970): 195–207.

47. Mednick and Volavka, "Biology and Crime," p. 93. See also Jan Volavka and Sarnoff A. Mednick, Joseph Sergeant, and Leif Rasmussen, "EEGs of XYY and XXY Men Found in a Large Birth Cohort," in Mednick and Christiansen, pp. 189–198.

48. Vicki Pollock et al., "Crime Causation: Biological Theories," in Sanford H. Kadish, editor in chief, *Encyclopedia of Crime and Justice,* vol. 1. (New York: Macmillan, 1983), p. 311. For a

discussion of genetic theories and crime, see Lee Ellis, "Genetics and Criminal Behavior: Evidence Through the End of the 1970s," *Criminology* 20 (May 1982): 43–66.

49. Unless otherwise indicated, the basic information in this and the following sections on neuroendocrinology and neurochemistry and the autonomic nervous system studies are taken from Pollock et al., "Crime Causation," pp. 311–315.

50. Pollock et al., p. 311, referring to the study of Sarnoff A. Mednick et al., "EEG As a Predictor of Antisocial Behavior," *Criminology* 19 (August 1981): 219–229. See that study for details of the findings as well as for a discussion of the methods by which this type of research is conducted. See also Volavka et al., "EEGs of XYY Men Found in a Large Birth Cohort."

51. Mednick and Volavka, "Biology and Crime," p. 143. For a more extensive analysis, see pp. 130–132. See also Pollock et al., "Crime Causation," pp. 311–312.

52. Pollock et al., "Crime Causation," p. 312.

53. Pollock et al.

54. Quoted in Ashley Montagu, "The Biologist Looks at Crime," *Annals of the American Academy of Social and Political Science* 217 (September 1941): 55.

55. Montagu, pp. 54–55.

56. Saleem A. Shah and Loren H. Roth, "Biological and Psychophysiological Factors in Criminality," in Daniel Glaser, ed., *Handbook of Criminology* (Chicago: Rand McNally, 1974), pp.101, 123.

57. See, for example, Anke A. Ehrhardt and Heino F. L. Meyer-Bahlburg, "Effects of Prenatal Sex Hormones on Gender-Related Behavior," *Science* 211 (March 1981): 1312–1318.

58. See L. E. Kreuz and R. M. Rose, "Assessment of Aggressive Behavior and Plasma Testosterone in a Young Criminal Population," *Psychosomatic Medicine* 34 (1972): 321–332; and C. H. Doering et al., "Negative Affect and Plasma Testosterone: A Longitudinal Human Study," *Psychosomatic Medicine* 37 (1975): 484–491, cited in Mednick and Volavka, "Biology and Crime."

59. Shah and Roth, "Biological and Psychophysiological Factors in Criminality," pp. 124–125.

60. Mednick and Volavka, "Biology and Crime," p. 138. See also Robin Room, "Alcohol and Crime: Behavioral Aspects," in Kadish, ed., *Encyclopedia of Crime and Justice*, vol. 1, pp.

35–42 and James J. Collins, ed., *Drinking and Crime: Perspectives on the Relationships Between Alcohol Consumption and Criminal Behavior* (New York: Guilford Press, 1981).

61. Mednick and Volavka, p. 142. See also M. Douglas Anglin, "Drugs and Crime: Behavioral Aspects," in Kadish, ed., vol. 2, pp. 626–643; and Duane C. McBride and Clyde B. McCoy, "Crime and Drug-Using Behavior: An Area Analysis," *Criminology* 19 (August 1981): 281–302.

62. Alexander G. Schauss, "Poor Nutrition Blamed in Antisocial Behavior," *Tulsa World,* April 11, 1981, p. A4, col. 1. For information on the studies of hypoglycemia (low blood sugar) and crime, see a brief review in Mednick and Volavka, "Biology and Crime," pp. 135–136.

63. Mednick and Volavka, "Biology and Crime," p. 106.

64. Pollock et al., "Crime Causation," p. 315. See Sarnoff A. Mednick et al., "Biology and Violence," in Marvin E. Wolfgang and Neil A. Weiner, eds., *Criminal Violence* (Beverly Hills, Calif.: Sage Publications, 1982), pp. 21–81.

65. Hans Toch, "Perspectives on the Offender, in Toch, ed. *Psychology of Crime and Criminal Justice* (New York: Holt, Rinehart & Winston, 1979), p. 157.

66. Fink, *Causes of Crime,* p. 178. For greater detail on Healy's work, see William Healy, *The Individual Delinquent* (Boston: Little, Brown, 1915); Franz Alexander and William Healy, *Roots of Crime* (New York: Knopf, 1935); and William Healy and Augusta Bronner, *New Light on Delinquency and Its Treatment* (New Haven, Conn.: Yale University Press, 1931).

67. For more detail on the contributions of Freud, see Sigmund Freud, *An Outline of Psycho-Analysis* (1940). In J. Strachey, ed., *Standard Edition of the Complete Psychological Work of Sigmund Freud,* vol. 23 (London: Hogarth Press, 1953), pp. 144–207.

68. Vold, *Theoretical Criminology,* p. 125.

69. Herbert C. Quay, "Crime Causation: Psychological Theories," in Kadish, ed., *Encyclopedia of Crime and Justice,* vol. 1, p. 332.

70. Toch, ed., *Psychology of Crime and Criminal Justice,* p. 172.

71. See, for example, Cyril Burt, *The Young Delinquent* (New York: D. Appleton, 1925); Sheldon Glueck and Eleanor Glueck, *One Thousand Juvenile Delinquents: Their Treatment by Court and Clinic* (Cambridge, Mass.: Harvard

University Press, 1934); and Healy and Bronner, *New Light on Delinquency.*

72. See, for example, Karl F. Schuessler and Donald R. Cressey, "Personality Characteristics of Criminals," *American Journal of Sociology* 55 (March 1950): 476–486. One of the earlier researchers, Cyril Burt, was later accused of altering the data he reported. See *Psychology Today* 10 (February 1977): 33. For a follow-up to the Schuessler and Cressey study, see Gordon Waldo and Simon Dinitz, "Personality Attributes of the Criminal: An Analysis of Research Studies, 1950–1965," *Journal of Research in Crime and Delinquency* 4 (July 1967): 185–201.

73. Vold, *Theoretical Criminology,* pp. 137–138. For information on using the objective personality measure MMPI (Minnesota Multiphasic Personality Inventory), see Starke A. Hathaway and Elio D. Monachesi, *Analyzing and Predicting Juvenile Delinquency with the MMPI* (Minneapolis: University of Minnesota Press, 1953).

74. For a discussion, see M. Q. Warren, "The Case for Differential Treatment of Delinquents," *Annals of the American Academy of Political and Social Science* 381 (1969): 47–59.

75. See the discussion in Helen M. Annis and David Chan, "The Differential Treatment Model: Empirical Evidence from a Personality Typology of Adult Offenders," *Criminal Justice and Behavior* 10 (June 1983): 159–173.

76. Annis and Chan. For a study of the psychological characteristics of four types of female criminals (addicts, addict-prostitutes, prostitutes, and nonaddict nonprostitute offenders), see Brenda D. Townes, Jennifer James, and Donald C. Martin, "Criminal Involvement of Female Offenders: Psychological Characteristics Among Four Groups," *Criminology* 18 (February 1981): 471–480.

77. See Jean Piaget, *The Moral Judgment of the Child* (New York: Harcourt Brace Jovanovich, 1932).

78. Lawrence Kohlberg, "The Development of Modes of Moral Thinking and Choice in Years 10 to 16," (Ph.D. diss., Harvard University, 1958).

79. Lawrence Kohlberg et al., *The Just Community Approach to Corrections: A Manual* (Niantic: Connecticut Department of Corrections, 1973). For a recent report on the experiments in this area, see Joseph E. Hickey and Peter Scharf, *Towards a Just Correctional System* (New York: Josey Bass, 1980.)

80. Merry Ann Morash, "Cognitive Developmental Theory: A Basis for Juvenile Correctional Reform?" *Criminology* 19 (November 1981): 362, 363.

81. William B. Nagel, *The New Red Barn: A Critical look at the Modern American Prison* (New York: Walker, 1973), pp. 131–134. For a discussion of the empirical, practical, and ethical issues of behavior modification treatment programs that are based on operant-learning principles, see Curtis J. Braukmann et al, "Behavioral Approaches to Treatment in the Crime and Delinquency Field," *Criminology* 13 (November 1975): 299–331.

82. Albert Bandura, "The Social Learning Perspective: Mechanisms of Aggression," in Toch, ed., *Psychology of Crime and Criminal Justice,* p. 201.

83. For a discussion of learning theory and punishment among juveniles, see Terrie E. Moffitt, "The Learning Theory Model of Punishment: Implications for Delinquency Deterrence," *Criminal Justice and Behavior* 10 (June 1983): 131–158.

84. For the social-learning theory perspective on the impact of the family, see E. Mavis Hetherington and Barclar Martin, "Family Interaction," in Herbert C. Quay and John S. Werry, eds., *Psychopathological Disorders of Childhood,* 2d ed. (New York: John Wiley, 1979), pp. 247–302. Concerning the impact of television, see Bandura, "The Social Learning Perspective."

85. Quay, "Crime Causation," p. 339.

86. H. J. Eysenck, *Crime and Personality* (London: Routledge & Kegan Paul, 1977). For a study indicating that the Eysenck model is not applicable, at least for American black and Hispanic criminal groups, see Curt, R. Bartol and Howard A. Holanchock, "Eysenck's Theory of Criminality: A Test on an American Prison Population," *Criminal Justice and Behavior* 6 (September 1979): 245–249.

87. Gwynn Nettler, *Explaining Crime,* 3rd ed. (New York: McGraw-Hill, 1984), p. 207.

88. Eysenck, *Crime and Personality,* p. 13.

89. Nettler, *Explaining Crime,* p. 297.

90. Nettler.

91. Julian B. Roebuck, *Criminology Typology* (Springfield, Ill.: Chas. C Thomas, 1967), p. 39.

92. Mednick and Volavka, "Biology and Crime," pp. 143–144, emphasis in the original. For a compilation of recent essays on biology and crime, see C. R. Jeffery ed., *Biology and Crime* (Beverly Hills, Calif.: Sage Publications, 1979).

93. Edward O. Wilson, *On Human Nature* (Cambridge, Mass.: Harvard University Press, 1978).

94. Edward O. Wilson, *Sociobiology: The New Synthesis* (Cambridge, Mass.: Harvard University Press, 1975), p. 4. See also Boyce Rensberger, "The Nature-Nurture Debate II: On Becoming Human," *Science* 83 (April 1983): 40, 41.

95. See for example, Sociobiology Study Group of Science for the People, "Sociobiology—Another Biological Determinism," in Arthur L. Caplan, ed., *The Sociobiology Debate: Readings on the Ethical and Scientific Issues Concerning Sociobiology* (New York: Harper & Row, 1978), pp. 280–290. See this collection of essays for other criticisms as well as for scholarly articles in support of sociobiology.

96. Rensberger, "The Nature-Nurture Debate I," p. 41.

97. C. Ray Jeffery, *Crime Prevention Through Environmental Design* (Beverly Hills, Calif.: Sage Publications, 1971), pp. 184, 185.

98. Mednick and Volavka, "Biology and Crime," p. 144.

99. Marvin E. Wolfgang, Foreword to Mednick and Christiansen, eds., *Biosocial Bases of Criminal Behavior,* pp. v, vi.

100. "Hinckley: Trial and Error," *Newsweek,* April 5, 1982, p. 83.

101. *New York Times,* May 5, 1982, p. 1, col. 3, and May 6, 1982, p. 11, col. 4.

102. *New York Times,* June 8, 1982, p. 13, col. 1, and *Tulsa World,* June 13, 1982, p. A15, col. 1. Quotation is from the *Tulsa World.*

103. *New York Times,* May 19, 1982, p. 15, col. 1; May 25, 1982, p. 14, col. 1; May 29, 1982, p. 10, col. 1; June 2, 1982, p. 13, col. 4; June 4, 1982, p. 4, col. 1; June 9, 1982, p. 6, col. 5; and June 12, 1982, p. 10, col. 1.

104. *New York Times.* June 17, 1982, p. 17, col 1; and June 18, 1982, p. 13, col. 1.

105. *Time,* July 5, 1982, p. 22.

106. M'Naghten's case, 8 Eng. Rep. 718 (1843).

107. For the beginnings of this rule, see State v. Thompson, Wright's Ohio Rep. 617 (1834) and Commonwealth v. Rogers, 48 Mass. 500 (1844).

108. *National Law Journal,* May 3, 1982, p. 11.

109. See, for example, the estimated figures in *Time,* July 5, 1982, p. 27; and *New York Times,* June 27, 1982, p. 4E, col. 3.

110. See *Newsweek,* November 23, 1981, p. 103.

111. *National Law Journal,* February 15, 1982, p. 12.

112. *National Law Journal,* p. 12.

113. *National Law Journal,* p. 13. The cases discussed above are detailed in the following: *New York Times,* May 29, 1982, p. 20, col. 4; July 12, 1982, p. 18, col. 2; July 22, 1982, p. 20, col. 1, and August 22, 1982, p. 23, col. 1.

114. For a more thorough discussion of these and other cases, see Note: "The XYY Syndrome: A Challenge to Our System of Criminal Responsibility," *New York Law Forum* 16 (Spring 1970): p. 232. For a more recent analysis, see Lawrence E. Taylor, "Genetically-influenced Antisocial Conduct and the Criminal Justice System," *Cleveland State Law Review* 31 (1982): 61–75.

115. 372 N.Y.S.2d 313 (Sup. Ct. N.Y., 1975).

116. 372 N.Y.S.2d 313, 317, 319, 320 (citations omitted).

Chapter 5

1. Richard A. Berk, Kenneth J. Lenihan, and Peter H. Rossi, "Crime and Poverty: Some Experimental Evidence from Ex-Offenders," *American Sociological Review* 45 (October 1980): 770.

2. Ronald L. Akers, *Deviant Behavior: A Social Learning Approach,* 2d ed. (Belmont, Calif: Wadsworth, 1977).

3. Yale Levin and Alfred Lindesmith, "English Ecology and Criminology of the Past Century," *Journal of Criminal Law, Criminology and Police Science* 27 (March–April 1937): 801–816; reprinted in Harwin L. Voss and David M. Petersen, eds., *Ecology, Crime and Delinquency* (New York: Appleton-Century-Crofts, 1971), pp. 47–48.

4. David Matza, *Becoming Deviant* (Englewood Cliffs, N.J.: Prentice-Hall, 1969), p. 31.

5. Nels Anderson, *The Hobo* (Chicago: University of Chicago Press, 1923). See also Harvey Zorbaugh, *The Gold Coast and the Slum* (Chicago: University of Chicago Press, 1929); and Paul Cressey, *The Taxi-Dance Hall* (Chicago: University of Chicago Press, 1932).

6. For a discussion of Burgess's theory, see Noel P. Gist and Sylvia Fleis Fava, *Urban Society,* 5th ed. (New York: Thomas Y. Crowell, 1964), pp. 108–109, from which the quotations in this paragraph are taken.

7. Clifford R. Shaw and Henry D. McKay, *Juvenile Delinquency and Urban Areas,* rev. ed. (Chicago: University of Chicago Press 1972), p. 21 (first published in 1942).

8. One of the problems with this method is that square-mile area units are drawn geographically, not in terms of neighborhoods. It is therefore likely that the square-mile areas do not capture "natural areas," the segregated-by-choice areas. It was assumed that these areas were formed because of people's tendency to elect to live near those with whom they share values and goals pertaining to occupation, race, nationality, education, and so on. They were called *natural areas* because they were not designed according to any preconceived plan. See Gist and Fava, *Urban Society,* pp. 106–107.

9. Shaw and McKay, p. 106.

10. Shaw and McKay, pp. 140, 141, 384.

11. Shaw and McKay, pp. 315, 316.

12. See, for example, Solomon Kobrin, "The Formal Logical Properties of the Shaw-McKay Delinquency Theory," chap. 5, in Voss and Petersen, *Ecology, Crime and Delinquency,* pp. 101–131; and Christen T. Jonassen, "A Reevaluation and Critique of the Logic and Some Methods of Shaw and McKay," chap. 6, in Voss and Petersen, *Ecology, Crime and Delinquency,* pp. 133–145.

13. Jonassen, p. 145. For information on earlier attempts to test the theory of ecology in Baltimore, see Bernard Lander, *Towards an Understanding of Juvenile Delinquency* (New York: Columbia University Press, 1954). For a critical analysis of the basic methodology of Lander's study, see Lawrence Rosen and Stanley H. Turner, "An Evaluation of the Lander Approach to Ecology of Delinquency," *Social Problems* 15 (Fall 1967): 189–200. See also Robert A. Gordon, "Issues in the Ecological Study of Delinquency," *American Sociological Review* 32 (December 1967): 924–944.

14. Emile Durkheim, *The Rules of Sociological Method* (New York: Free Press, 1964), p. 66 (first published in 1938).

15. Durkheim, p. 70.

16. Durkheim, p. 71.

17. Durkheim, pp. 71–72.

18. For a discussion of Durkheim's theory of anomie, see Émile Durkheim, *The Division of Labour in Society,* paper ed. (New York: Free Press, 1964), pp. 374–388.

19. See Myron Boor, "Effects of United States Presidential Elections on Suicide and Other Causes of Death," *American Sociological Review* 46 (October 1981): 616–618, for the results of his studies and citations to related research. Quotation is on p. 618.

20. Robert K. Merton, *Social Theory and Social Structure,* enlarged ed. (New York: Free Press, 1968).

21. Merton, p. 185.

22. Merton, p. 189.

23. Merton, pp. 190, 192–193.

24. Merton, p. 200.

25. Merton, p. 201.

26. Merton, p. 208.

27. Merton, p. 241.

28. Edward Sagarin, *Deviants and Deviance: An Introduction to the Study of Disvalued People and Behavior* (New York: Holt, Rinehart & Winston, 1975), pp. 108–109.

29. Josefina Figueira-McDonough, "On the Usefulness of Merton's Anomie Theory: Academic Failure and Deviance Among High School Students," *Youth & Society* 14 (March 1983): 276, 277.

30. Frederic M. Thrasher, *The Gang,* abbrev. ed. (Chicago: University of Chicago Press, 1927, 1963). William F. Whyte, in his classic study, *Street Corner Society* (Chicago: University of Chicago Press, 1943), disputed the social disorganization theory.

31. Albert K. Cohen, *Delinquent Boys: The Culture of the Gang* (New York: Free Press, 1955).

32. Cohen, *Delinquent Boys,* pp. 59–65 (emphasis in the original).

33. See, for example, Frank E. Hartung, *American Sociological Review* 20 (December 1955): 751–752; Donnell M. Poppenfort, *American Journal of Sociology* 62 (July 1956): 125–126; and Hermann Mannheim, *British Journal of Sociology* 7 (July 1956): 147–152.

34. John I. Kitsuse and David C. Dietrick, "Delinquent Boys: A Critique," in Harwin L. Voss, ed., *Society, Delinquency, and Delinquent Behavior* (Boston: Little, Brown, 1979), pp. 238–245. Quotation is on p. 238.

35. Cohen, *Delinquent Boys,* p. 123.

36. Kitsuse and Dietrick, "Delinquent Boys," p. 240. For the results of a study questioning the

relationship between "status deprivation" and delinquency, see Albert J. Reiss, Jr., and A. Lewis Rhodes, "Status Deprivation and Delinquent Behavior," *Sociological Quarterly* 4 (Spring 1963): 135–149.

37. Cohen, *Delinquent Boys,* p. 117.
38. Kitsuse and Dietrick, "Delinquent Boys," pp. 244–245.
39. Gresham M. Sykes and David Matza, "Techniques of Neutralization: A Theory of Delinquency," in Marvin E. Wolfgang et al, eds., *The Sociology of Crime and Delinquency,* 2d ed. (New York: John Wiley, 1970), pp. 292–299.
40. Sykes and Matza, pp. 295 (emphasis omitted), p. 298.
41. See Joseph W. Rogers and M. D. Buffalo, "Neutralization Techniques: Toward a Simplified Measurement Scale," *Pacific Sociological Review* 17 (July 1974): 313–331; and Buffalo and Rogers, "Behavioral Norms, Moral Norms, and Attachment Problems of Deviance and Conformity," *Social Problems* 19 (Summer 1971): 101–113.
42. W. William Minor, "The Neutralization of Criminal Offense," *Criminology* 18 (May 1980): 103–120. See this article for a brief review of other empirical tests of the Sykes and Matza theory. See also W. William Minor, "Techniques of Neutralization: A Reconceptualization and Empirical Examination," *Journal of Research in Crime and Delinquency* 18 (July 1981): 295–318.
43. Albert K. Cohen and James F. Short, Jr., "Research in Delinquent Subcultures," *Journal of Social Issues* 14 (1958): 20–37.
44. David Matza, *Delinquency and Drift* (New York: John Wiley, 1964), p. 28.
45. Richard A. Cloward and Lloyd E. Ohlin, *Delinquency and Opportunity: A Theory of Delinquent Gangs* (New York: Free Press, 1960). This book is an extension of Cloward's earlier article, "Illegitimate Means, Anomie, and Deviant Behavior," *American Sociological Review* 24 (April 1959): 164–176.
46. Cloward and Ohlin, pp. 150, 152.
47. Clarence Schrag, "Delinquency and Opportunity: Analysis of a Theory," in Voss, ed., *Society, Delinquency, and Delinquent Behavior,* p. 259.
48. Schrag, p. 261.
49. James F. Short, Jr., Ramon Rivera, and Ray A. Tennyson, "Perceived Opportunities, Gang Membership, and Delinquency," *American*

Sociological Review 30 (February 1956): 56–67. Quotation is on p. 56.
50. Delbert S. Elliott and Hawrin L. Voss, *Delinquency and Dropout* (Lexington, Mass.: D.C. Heath, 1974).
51. Elliott and Voss, pp. 5, 204–205.
52. Elliott and Voss, pp. 206–207.
53. Walter B. Miller, "Lower Class Culture As a Generating Milieu of Gang Delinquency," in Wolfgang et al, ed., *Sociology of Crime and Delinquency,* p. 358.
54. Kenneth Polk, "Urban Social Areas and Delinquency," *Social Problems* 14 (Winter 1967): 320–325; reprinted in Voss and Petersen, eds., *Ecology, Crime and Delinquency,* pp. 273–281. Quotation is on p. 281.
55. Richard E. Johnson, "Social Class and Delinquent Behavior: A New Test," *Criminology* 18 (May 1980): 91.
56. See, for example, James F. Short, Jr., "Differential Association and Delinquency," *Social Problems* 4 (January 1957): 233–239; F. Ivan Nye, *Family Relationships and Delinquent Behavior* (New York: John Wiley, 1958); James F. Short, Jr., and F. Ivan Nye, "Reported Behavior As a Criterion of Deviant Behavior," *Social Problems* 5 (Winter 1957–1958): 207–213; and F. Ivan Nye, James F. Short, Jr., and Virgil J. Olson, "Socio-Economic Status and Delinquent Behavior," *American Journal of Sociology* 63 (January 1958): 381–389.
57. John P. Clark and Eugene P. Wenninger, "Socio-Economic Class and Area As Correlates of Illegal Behavior Among Juveniles," in Wolfgang et al., eds., *Sociology of Crime and Delinquency,* p. 459.
58. William M. Rhodes and Catherine Conly, "Crime and Mobility: An Empirical Study," in Paul L. Brantingham and Patricia L. Brantingham, eds., *Environmental Criminology* (Beverly Hills, Calif.: Sage Publications, 1981), pp. 182–183.
59. Rhodes and Conly, p. 172.
60. Oscar Newman, *Defensible Space* (London: Architectural Press, 1972). See also Newman, *Architectural Design for Crime Prevention* (Washington, D.C.: U.S. Government Printing Office, 1973); and *Design Guidelines for Creating Defensible Space* (Washington, D.C.: U.S. Government Printing Office, 1976).
61. See, for example, Jane Jacobs, *The Death and Life of Great American Cities* (New York: Random House, 1961); and C. R. Jeffery, *Crime*

Prevention Through Evironmental Design, rev. ed. (Beverly Hills, Calif.: Sage Publications, 1977).

62. John Baldwin, "Ecological and Area Studies in Great Britain and the United States," in Norval Morris and Michael Tonry, eds., *Crime and Justice: An Annual Review of Research,* vol. 1 (Chicago: University of Chicago Press, 1979), p. 54.

63. Newman, *Defensible Space,* p. 3, quoted in Baldwin, pp. 54–55.

64. Barbara B. Brown and Irwin Altman, "Territoriality and Residential Crime: A Conceptual Framework," in Brantingham and Brantingham, eds., *Environmental Criminology,* p. 66. See also Patricia L. Brantingham and Paul J. Brantingham, "Mobility, Notoriety, and Crime: A Study in the Crime Patterns of Urban Nodal Points," *Journal of Environmental Systems* 11 (1981–1982): 89–98.

65. Jeffery, *Crime Prevention,* p. 224, quoted in Baldwin, "Ecological and Area Studies," p. 55.

66. Baldwin, p. 57, referring to the research of Brantingham and Brantingham. See P. J. Brantingham and P. L. Brantingham, "The Spatial Patterning of Burglary," *Howard Journal* 14 (1975): 11–23; and "Residential Burglary and Urban Form," *Urban Studies* 12 (1975): 273–284.

67. H. L. Nieburg, "Crime Prevention by Urban Design," *Society* 12 (1974): 42, quoted in Baldwin, p. 57, n. 57.

68. See A. R. Gillis and John Hagan, "Density, Delinquency, and Design: Formal and Informal Control and the Built Environment," *Criminology* 19 (February 1982): 514–529.

69. Lawrence E. Cohen, Marcus Felson, and Kenneth C. Land, "Property Crime Rates in the United States: A Macrodynamic Analysis, 1947–1977; with Ex Ante Forecasts for the Mid-1980s," *American Journal of Sociology* 86 (July 1980): 90–118.

70. Dennis W. Roncek, "Dangerous Places: Crime and Residential Environment," *Social Forces* 60 (September 1980): 74–96.

71. See the study of Robert D. Crutchfield et al., "Crime Rate and Social Integration: The Impact of Metropolitan Mobility," *Criminology* 20 (November 1982): 468–478.

72. See Cecil L. Willis, "Durkheim's Concept of Anomie: Some Observations," *Sociological Inquiry* 52 (Spring 1982): 106–113.

73. Claude S. Fischer, "The Public and Private Worlds of City Life," *American Sociological Review* 46 (June 1981): 315.

74. Albert K. Cohen, "Crime Causation: Sociological Theories," in Sanford H. Kadish, editor in chief, *Encyclopedia of Crime and Justice,* vol. 1 (New York, Macmillan, 1983), p. 351.

75. Lawrence E. Cohen and Marcus Felson, "Social-Change and Crime Rate-Trends: A Routine Activity Approach," *American Sociological Review* 44 (August 1979): 604. See also Lawrence C. Cohen, "Modeling Crime Trends: A Criminal Opportunity Perspective," *Journal of Research in Crime and Delinquency* 18 (January 1981): 138–164.

76. See, for example, Peter H. Rossi, Richard A. Berk, and Kenneth J. Lenihan, *Money, Work and Crime* (New York: Academic Press, 1980).

77. Steven Stack, "Social Structure and Swedish Crime Rates: A Time-Series Analysis, 1950–1979," *Criminology* 20 (November 1982): 510.

78. Leo Carroll and Pamela Irving Jackson, "Inequality, Opportunity, and Crime Rates in Central Cities," *Criminology* 21 (May 1983): 181, 192.

79. See, for example, David L. Decker, David Shichor, and Robert M. O'Brien, *Urban Structure and Victimization* (Lexington, Mass.: Lexington Books, 1982).

80. Lawrence E. Cohen and David Cantor, "Residential Burglary in the United States: Life-Style and Demographic Factors Associated with the Probability of Victimization," *Journal of Research in Crime and Delinquency* 18 (January 1981): 125. See also Lawrence E. Cohen, James R. Kluegel, and Kenneth C. Land, "Social Inequality and Predatory Criminal Victimization: An Exposition and Test of a Formal Theory," *American Sociological Review* 46 (October 1981): 505–524; Lawrence E. Cohen, David Cantor, and James R. Kluegel, "Robbery Victimization in the U.S.: An Analysis of a Nonrandom Event," *Social Science Quarterly* 62 (December 1981): 644–657; and James F. Nelson, "Multiple Victimization in American Cities: A Statistical Analysis of Rare Events," *American Journal of Sociology* 85 (January 1980): 870–891.

81. Michael R. Gottfredson, "On the Etiology of Criminal Victimization," *Journal of Criminal Law & Criminology* 72 (Summer 1981): 725–726. See also Joseph Harry, "Derivative Devi-

ance: The Cases of Extortion, Fag-Bashing, and Shakedown of Gay Men," *Criminology* 19 (February 1982): 546.

82. *U.S. News & World Report,* December 22, 1975, p. 49.

83. See Nicholas Gage, *The Mafia Is Not an Equal Opportunity Employer* (New York: McGraw-Hill, 1971). See also Alan Block, "Searching for Women in Organized Crime" in Susan K. Datesman and Frank R. Scarpitti, *Women, Crime and Justice* (New York: Oxford University Press, 1980), pp. 192–213.

84. Freda Adler, *Sisters in Crime: The Rise of the New Female Criminal* (New York: McGraw-Hill, 1975) pp. 19–20.

85. See, for example, Richard Deming, *Women: The New Criminals* (Nashville: Thomas Nelson, 1977); Nanci Koser Wilson, "The Masculinity of Violent Crime—Some Second Thoughts," *Journal of Criminal Justice* 9 (1981): 111–123. For a critique, see Darrell Steffensmeier, "Flawed Arrest 'Rates' and Overlooked Reliability Problems in UCR Arrest Statistics: A Comment on Wilson's 'The Masculinity of Violent Crime—Some Second Thoughts,'" *Journal of Criminal Justice* 11 (1983): 167–171. For Wilson's response to Steffensmeier, see Wilson, "Masculinity and Violent Crime: A Response to Steffensmeier's Comment," *Journal of Criminal Justice* 11 (1983): 173–176. For a general discussion on women and violent crime, see David A. Ward, Maurice Jackson, and Renee E. Ward, "Crimes of Violence by Women," in Datesman and Scarpitti, *Women, Crime, and Justice,* pp. 171–191.

86. These studies are reviewed briefly in Rachelle J. Canter, "Sex Differences in Self-Report Delinquency," *Criminology* 20 (November 1982): 373–393.

87. Rita James Simon, *Women and Crime* (Lexington, Mass.: D.C. Heath, 1975), p. 47. See also Freda Adler and Rita James Simon, *The Criminology of Deviant Women* (Dallas: Houghton Mifflin, 1979). For evidence attacking the opportunity theory as an explanation for the differences in criminality between white and black females, see Vernetta D. Young, "Women, Race, and Crime," *Criminology* 18 (May 1980): 26–34. For a discussion of property crimes of women compared with those of men, see Dorothy Zietz, *Women Who Embez-*

zle or Defraud—A Study of Convicted Felons (New York: Praeger, 1981). For an analysis of crime patterns among females, see Nicolette Parisi, "Exploring Female Crime Patterns: Problems and Prospects," in Nichole Hahn Rafter and Elizabeth Anne Stanko, eds., *Judge, Lawyer, Victim, Thief: Women, Gender Roles and Criminal Justice* (Boston: Northeastern University Press, 1982). For a discussion of a study of property crimes among females, finding support for the economic theories of criminal behavior and no support for the opportunity theory, see Ann P. Bartel, "Women and Crime: An Economic Analysis," *Economic Inquiry* 17 (January 1979): 29–51.

88. Rita J. Simon, "Women and Crime in Israel," chap. 7, in Simha F. Landau and Leslie Sebba, eds., *Criminology in Perspective* (Lexington, Mass.: D.C. Heath, 1977), p. 81. See also Rita J. Simon, *Women and Crime* (National Institute of Mental Health, Center for Studies of Crime and Delinquency (Washington, D.C.: U.S. Government Printing Office, 1975).

89. Weis, "Liberation and Crime," p. 19

90. Darrell J. Steffensmeier, "Crime and the Contemporary Woman: An Analysis of Changing Levels of Female Property Crime, 1960–75," *Social Forces* 57 (December 1978): 566–584. See also Steven Box and Chris Hale, "Liberation and Female Criminality in England and Wales," *British Journal of Criminology* 23 (January 1983): 35–49. See also Carol Smart, "The New Female Criminal: Reality or Myth?" *British Journal of Criminology* 19 (January 1979): 50–59; and Ilene H. Nagel and John Hagan, "Gender and Crime: Offense Patterns and Criminal Court Sanctions," in Michael Tonry and Norval Morris, eds., *Crime and Justice: An Annual Review of Research,* vol. 4 (Chicago: University of Chicago Press, 1983), pp. 91–144. See also Joan McCord and Laura Otten, "A Consideration of Sex Roles and Motivations for Crime," *Criminal Justice and Behavior* 10 (March 1983): 3–12.

91. Darrell J. Steffensmeier, "Trends in Female Crime: It's Still a Man's World," *USA Today,* September 1979, p. 44

92. Darrell J. Steffensmeier, "Organization Properties and Sex-Segregation in the Underworld: Building a Sociological Theory of Sex Differences in Crime," *Social Forces* 61 (June 1983): 1010–1032. See also Darrell J. Steffensmeier,

"Assessing the Impact of the Women's Movement on Sex-Based Differences in the Handling of Adult Criminal Defendants," *Crime & Delinquency* 26 (July 1980): 344–357 and Darrell J. Steffensmeier, Alvin S. Rosenthal, and Constance Shehan, "World War II and Its Effect on the Sex Differential in Arrests: An Empirical Test of the Sex-Role Equality and Crime Proposition," *Sociological Quarterly* 21 (Summer 1980): 403–416.

93. Darrell J. Steffensmeier and Renee Hoffman Steffensmeier, "Trends in Female Delinquency: An Examination of Arrest, Juvenile Court, Self-Report, and Field Data," *Criminology* 18 (May 1980): 62–85.

94. Lee H. Bowker, *Women, Crime, and the Criminal Justice System* (Lexington, Mass.: D.C. Heath, 1978), p. 277. Bowker was referring to the work of David A. Ward, Maurice Jackson, and Renee E. Ward, "Crimes of Violence by Women," in Donald J. Mulvhill and Melvin M. Tumin, eds., *Crimes of Violence* vol. 13 (Washington, D.C.: U.S. Government Printing Office, 1969), pp. 867, 906. Similar results were found by Eddyth P. Spears, Manual Vega, and Ira J. Silvermann, "The Female Robber." (Paper presented at the annual meeting of the American Society of Criminology, Atlanta, 1977).

95. Weis, "Liberation and Crime," p. 24

96. Canter, "Sex Differences in Self-Report Delinquency," p. 389, references omitted.

97. Stephen Norland and Neal Shover, "Gender Roles and Female Criminality," *Criminology* 15 (May 1977): 95.

98. Neal Shover and Stephen Norland, "Sex Roles and Criminality: Science or Conventional Wisdom?" *Sex Roles* 4 (1978).

99. See C. Ronald Huff, "Conflict Theory in Criminology," in James A. Inciarci, ed., *Radical Criminology: The Coming Crises* (Beverly Hills, Calif.: Sage Publications, 1980), pp. 61–77, for a brief but excellent overview of conflict theory.

100. Ronald L. Akers, *Deviant Behavior: A Social Learning Approach,* 2d ed. (Belmont, Calif.: Wadsworth, 1977), p. 15.

101. Thorsten Sellin, *Culture, Conflict, and Crime,* Social Science Research Council, Bulletin no. 41, New York, 1938, p. 105.

102. Solomon Kobrin, "The Conflict of Values in Delinquency Areas," *American Sociological Review* 467 (January 1962): 167–175.

103. George B. Vold with T. J. Bernard, *Theoretical Criminology* 2d ed. (New York: Oxford University Press, 1978).

104. George B. Vold, *Theoretical Criminology* (New York: Oxford University Press, 1958), p. 208.

105. Austin T. Turk, "Law As a Weapon in Social Conflict," *Social Problems* 23 (February 1976): 288.

106. See Austin T. Turk, *Criminality and the Legal Order* (Chicago: Rand McNally, 1971).

107. Turk, p. 48.

108. Ian Taylor, Paul Walton, and Jock Young, *The New Criminology: For a Social Theory of Deviance* (London: Routledge & Kegan Paul, 1973), p. 243.

109. Austin T. Turk, *Political Criminality: The Defiance and Defense of Authority* (Beverly Hills, Calif.: Sage Publications, 1982), p. 15.

110. Ronald L. Akers, "Theory and Ideology in Marxist Criminology: Comments on Turk, Quinney, Toby, and Klockers," *Criminology* 16 (February 1979): 537. For a brief but excellent article on the distinctions between radical criminology and the conflict perspective, see Robert M. Bohm, "Radical Criminology: An Explication," *Criminology* 19 (February 1982): 565–589. See also Thomas J. Bernard, "The Distinction Between Conflict and Radical Criminology," *Journal of Criminal Law & Criminology* 72 (Spring 1981): 362–379.

111. James A. Inciardi, "Editorial," *Criminology* 16 (February 1979): 443–444. For a collection of articles on radical criminology, see James A. Inciardi, ed., *Radical Criminology: The Coming Crises* (Beverly Hills, Calif.: Sage Publications, 1980).

112. See Karl Marx, *Critique of Political Economy* (New York: International Library, 1904, originally published in 1859).

113. Frank Tannenbaum, *Crime and the Community* (Boston: Ginn, 1938), p. 25.

114. W. A. Bonger, *Criminality and Economic Conditions,* trans. Henry P. Horton (Boston: Little, Brown, 1916).

115. Bonger, p. 669.

116. Richard Quinney, "The Production of Criminology," *Criminology* 16 (February 1979): 445, 455.

117. Richard Quinney, *Critique of Legal Order: Crime Control in a Capitalist Society* (Boston: Little, Brown, 1974).

118. Quinney, pp. 11–13.

119. Quinney, p. 165.

120. Richard Quinney, *Criminology: Analysis and Critique of Crime in the United States* (Boston: Little, Brown, 1974), pp. 37–41.

121. Quinney, p. 41.

122. Richard Quinney, *Class, State and Crime: On the Theory and Practice of Criminal Justice* (New York: D. McKay, 1977), pp. 61–62, 165. See also Quinney, *Critique of Legal Order..*

123. See Richard Quinney, *Social Existence: Metaphysics, Marxism, and the Social Sciences* (Beverly Hills, Calif.: Sage Publications, 1982); and *Providence: The Development of Social and Moral Order* (New York: Longman, 1980). For an analysis of the development of Marxism in the 1970s, see Ronald Hinch, "Marxist Criminology in the 1970s: Clarifying the Clutter," *Crime and Social Justice* 19 (Summer 1983): 65–74.

124. Gresham N. Sykes, "The Rise of Critical Criminology," *Journal of Criminal Law and Criminology* 65 (June 1974): 212.

125. Richard Quinney, ed., *Criminal Justice in America: A Critical Understanding* (Boston: Little, Brown, 1974), p. 8.

126. Sykes, "The Rise of Critical Criminology," 213. See also the recent critique of critical criminology by Jackson Toby, "The New Criminology Is the Old Baloney," in Inciardi, ed., *Radical Criminology*, pp. 124–132.

127. See, for example, the works of William J. Chambliss and Robert B. Seidman, *Law, Order, and Power* (Reading, Mass.: Addison-Wesley, 1971); Chamblis, ed., *Sociological Readings in the Conflict Perspective* (Reading, Mass.: Addison-Wesely, 1973); and Inciardi, ed., *Radical Criminology*. This work contains articles by a number of scholars some of whom are conflict theorists and some of whom are analyzing that approach. Included are articles by some of the radical theorists, such as David O. Friedrichs, Steven Spitzer, and Harold E. Pepinsky. See also Anthony Platt, "Prospects for a Radical Criminology in the United States," *Crime and Social Justice* 1 (Spring-Summer 1974): 2–10; Herman Schwendinger and Julia Schwendinger, "Defenders of Order or Guardians of Human Rights?" *Issues in Criminology* 5 (Summer 1970): 123–157; Barry Krisberg, *Crime and Privilege: Toward a New Criminology* (Englewood Cliffs, N.J.: Prentice-Hall, 1975); and Raymond J. Michalowski and Edward W. Bohlander, "Repression and Criminal Justice in Capitalist America," *Sociological Inquiry* 46 (1976): 99–107. For a discussion of the rise of radicalism in the United States, see David F. Greenberg, ed., "Introduction," *Crime and Capitalism* (Palo Alto, Calif.: Mayfield, 1980). For an analysis of conflict theory, see Franklin P. Williams, III, "Conflict Theory and Differential Processing: An Analysis of the Research Literature," in Inciardi, ed., *Radical Criminology*, pp. 213–232.

128. Akers, "Theory and Ideology," pp. 528, 529, 537, 538, 543.

129. Akers, 529.

130. Sykes, "The Rise of Critical Criminology," p. 213.

131. Theodore H. Chiricos and Gordon P. Waldo, "Socioeconomic Status and Criminal Sentencing: An Empirical Assessment of a Conflict Proposition," *American Sociological Review* 40 (December 1974): 770.

132. Richard F. Sparks, "A Critique of Marxist Criminology," in Norval Morris and Michael Tonry, eds., *Crime and Justice: An Annual Review of Research*, vol. 2 (Chicago: University of Chicago Press, 1980), p. 203.

133. See Ronald Bayer, "Crime, Punishment, and the Decline of Liberal Optimism," *Crime & Delinquency* 27 (April 1981): 173, 175.

134. R. N. Davidson, *Crime and Environment* (New York: St. Martin's Press, 1981), p. 93.

135. Glenn E. Weisfeld and Roger Feldman, "A Former Street Gang Leader Reinterviewed Eight Years Later," *Crime & Delinquency* 28 (October 1982): 567.

Chapter 6

1. See, for example, John Hagan, "Labeling and Deviance: A Case Study of the 'Sociology of the Interesting,'" *Social Problems* 20 (Spring 1973): 447–458; and Charles Wellford, "Labeling Theory and Criminology: An Assessment," *Social Problems* 22 (February 1975): 313–332.

2. Albert K. Cohen, Alfred Lindesmith, and Karl Schuessler, *The Sutherland Papers* (Bloomington: Indiana University Press, 1956), p. 19.

3. Cohen, Lindesmith, and Schuessler, p. 18.

4. Edwin H. Sutherland and Donald R. Cressey, *Principles of Criminology*, 10th ed. (Philadelphia: Lippincott, 1978), pp. 81–82. (emphasis omitted)

5. James F. Short, Jr., "Differential Association and Delinquency," *Social Problems* 4 (January 1957): 233.

6. James F. Short, Jr., "Differential Association As a Hypothesis: Problems of Empirical Testing," *Social Problems* 8 (Summer 1960): 14–25.

7. Albert J. Reiss, Jr., and A. Lewis Rhodes. "An Empirical Test of Differential Association Theory," *Journal of Research in Crime and Delinquency* 1 (January 1964): 12.

8. Cohen, Lindesmith, and Schuessler, *Sutherland Papers*, p. 37. For a more recent collection of these papers by Sutherland, with a new introduction, a short autobiographical statement by Sutherland, and a bibliographic update, see Edwin H. Sutherland, *On Analyzing Crime*, ed. and with an introduction by Karl Schuessler (Chicago: University of Chicago Press, 1973).

9. Donald R. Cressey, "The Theory of Differential Association: An Introduction," *Social Problems* 8 (Summer 1960): 3.

10. Edwin H. Sutherland and Donald R. Cressey, *Criminology*, 9th ed. (Philadelphia: Lippincott, 1974), p. 78. This position was retained in the tenth edition, published in 1978.

11. Sutherland and Cressey, *Criminology*, 10th ed., p. 84. In particular, Cressey is referring to the comment by Sheldon Glueck that if differential association is the key to explaining criminal behavior, "the biggest criminals of all would be professors of criminology, prison guards, and prison chaplains" because of the time they spend with criminals. Sheldon Glueck, "Theory and Fact in Criminology: A Criticism of Differential Association," *British Journal of Delinquency* 7 (October 1956): 97.

12. Sutherland and Cressey, p. 85.

13. Sutherland and Cressey, p. 90.

14. Sutherland and Cressey, 9th ed., p. 86.

15. Sutherland and Cressey, p. 90.

16. Melvin L. DeFleur and Richard Quinney, "A Reformulation of Sutherland's Differential Association Theory and a Strategy for Empirical Verification," *Journal of Research in Crime and Delinquency* 3 (January 1966): 1–22.

17. Donald R. Cressey, "The Language of Set Theory and Differential Association," *Journal of Research in Crime and Delinquency* 3 (January 1966): 23.

18. Robert L. Burgess and Ronald L. Akers, "A Differential Association-Reinforcement Theory of Criminal Behavior," *Social Problems* 14 (Fall 1966): 128–147. See Akers's discussion in Ronald L. Akers, *Deviant Behavior: A Social Learning Approach*, 2d ed. (Belmont, Calif.: Wadsworth, 1977), pp. 39–60.

19. Ronald L. Akers, Marvin D. Krohn, Lonn Lanza-Kaduce, and Marcia Radosevich, "Social Learning and Deviant Behavior: A Specific Test of a General Theory," *American Sociological Review* 44 (August 1979): 637–638.

20. Akers et al., 638–639.

21. Akers et al., 651.

22. Donald R. Cressey and David A. Ward, *Delinquency, Crime and Social Process* (New York: Harper & Row, 1969), p. xi.

23. Reed Adams, "Differential Association and Learning Principles Revisited," *Social Problems* 20 (Spring 1973): 458–470.

24. See, for example, Ronald L. Akers et al., "Social Learning and Deviant Behavior: A Specific Test of a General Theory," *American Sociological Review* 44 (August 1979): 636–655; and Kenneth H. Andrews and Denise B. Kandel, "Attitude and Behavior: A Specification of the Contingent Consistency Hypothesis," *American Sociological Review* 44 (April 1979): 298–310.

25. Gary F. Jensen, "Parents, Peers and Delinquent Action: A Test of the Differential Association Perspective," *American Journal of Sociology* 78 (November 1972): 562–575, quoted in Susan M. Jaquith, "Adolescent Marijuana and Alcohol Use: An Empirical Test of Differential Association Theory," *Criminology* 19 (August 1981): 277.

26. Jaquith, "Adolescent Marijuana and Alcohol Use," referring to Jensen's study, pp. 277–278.

27. Jaquith.

28. Daniel Glaser, "Differential Association and Criminological Prediction," *Social Problems* 8 (Summer 1960): 13.

29. Daniel Glaser, *The Effectiveness of a Prison and Parole System* (Indianapolis: Bobbs-Merrill, 1964), p. 29.

30. Albert Bandura, "The Social Learning Perspective: Mechanisms of Aggression," in Hans Toch, ed., *Psychology of Crime and Criminal Justice* (New York: Holt, Rinehart & Winston, 1979), p. 204.

31. Bandura, p. 205.

32. George Gerbner et al., "Television Violence, Victimization, and Power," *American Behavioral Scientist* 23 (June 1980): 710–711.

33. Gerbner et al., 715.

34. "Boy Accused of Sex Assault: Barroom Rape Case Cited," *Tulsa World,* April 18, 1984, p. 1A, col. 3.

35. David Pearl et al., *Television and Behavior: Ten Years of Scientific Progress and Implications for the Eighties.* National Institute of Mental Health (Washington, D.C.: U.S. Government Printing Office, 1982). The full report has now been published: J. Ronald Milavsky et al., *Television and Aggression: A Panel Study* (New York: Academic Press, 1983).

36. See Albert J. Reiss, "Delinquency As the Failure of Personal and Social Control," *American Sociological Review* 16 (April 1951): 196–207.

37. Gwynn Nettler, *Explaining Crime,* 3rd ed. (New York: McGraw-Hill, 1984), p. 290. (emphasis in the original)

38. Walter C. Reckless and Simon Dinitz, "Pioneering with Self-Concept As a Vulnerability Factor in Delinquency," *Journal of Criminal Law, Criminology, and Police Science* 58 (December 1967): 522.

39. Walter C. Reckless, "Containment Theory," in Marvin E. Wolfgang et al., eds., *The Sociology of Crime and Delinquency,* 2d ed. (New York: John Wiley, 1970), p. 402.

40. Reckless, "Containment Theory," p. 402.

41. Richard A. Ball, "Development of Basic Norm Violation: Neutralization and Self-Concept Within a Male Cohort," *Criminology* 21 (February 1983): 90.

42. Walter C. Reckless, *The Crime Problem,* 5th ed. (Englewood Cliffs, N.J.: Prentice-Hall, 1973), pp. 55–57, reprint of his article from *Federal Probation* 25 (December 1961), pp. 42–46.

43. Herbert A. Bloch and Gilbert Geis, *Man, Crime, and Society: The Forms of Criminal Behavior,* 2d ed. (New York: Random House, 1970), p. 100. For an attempt to test containment theory, see Gordon P. Waldo, "Boys' Perceptions of Outer Containment and Delinquency Potential" (Ph.D. diss., Ohio State University, 1967). For an analysis of the work of Reckless and his associates on self-concept, see Michael Schwartz and Sandra S. Tangri. "A Note on Self-Concept As an Insulator Against Delinquency," *American Sociological Review* 30 (December 1965): 922.

44. For a discussion of these and other criticisms, see Sandra S. Tangri and Michael Schwartz, "Delinquency Research and the Self-Concept Variable," *Journal of Criminal Law, Criminology and Police Science* 58 (June 1967): 183. See also Jim Orcutt, "Self-Concept and Insulation Against Delinquency: Some Critical Notes," *Sociological Quarterly* 11 (Summer 1970): 381–390.

45. Harwin L. Voss, "Differential Association and Containment Theory: A Theoretical Convergence," in Harwin L. Voss, ed., *Society, Delinquency and Delinquent Behavior* (Boston: Little, Brown, 1970), pp. 198, 206. For examples of recent research, see Arnold Meadow, Stephen I. Abramowitz, and Arnold De La Cruz, "Self-Concept, Negative Family Affect, and Delinquency: A Comparison Across Mexican Social Classes," *Criminology* 19 (November 1981): 434–448; and L. Edward Wells and Joseph H. Rankin, "Self-Concept As a Mediating Factor in Delinquency," *Social Psychology Quarterly* 46 (March 1983): 11–22.

46. See Nettler, *Explaining Crime,* 3rd ed., p. 293.

47. Travis Hirschi, *Causes of Delinquency* (Berkeley and Los Angeles: University of California Press, 1969), p. 10.

48. Hirschi, p. 34.

49. Émile Durkheim, *Suicide,* trans. John A. Spaulding and George Simpson (New York: Free Press, 1951), p. 209, quoted in Hirschi, *Causes of Delinquency,* p. 16.

50. See Hirschi, *Causes of Delinquency,* pp. 16–34. For a discussion, see Michael J. Hindelang, "Causes of Delinquency: A Partial Replication and Extension," *Social Problems* 20 (Spring 1973): 473.

51. Hirschi, p. 229.

52. Hirschi, pp. 54, 56.

53. Hirschi, p. 72.

54. Hirschi, pp. 132, 134.

55. Hirschi, p. 108.

56. Hindelang, "Causes of Delinquency," 471–487.

57. Rand D. Conger, "Social Control and Social Learning Models of Delinquent Behavior: A Synthesis," *Criminology* 14 (May 1976): 19.

58. Conger, 35.

59. See Delbert S. Elliott and Harwin L. Voss, *Delinquency and Dropout* (Lexington, Mass.: Lexington Books, 1974).

60. Eric Linden and James C. Hackler, "Affective Ties and Delinquency," *Pacific Sociological Review* 16 (January 1973): 27–46.

61. Hirschi, *Causes of Delinquency,* pp. 230–231. For another critique of the social-control theory approach, see Akers, *Deviant Behavior,* pp. 37–38.

62. Michael D. Wiatrowski, David B. Griswold, and Mary K. Roberts, "Social Control Theory and Delinquency," *American Sociological Review* 46 (October 1981): 525.

63. Wiatrowski et al., "Social Control Theory and Delinquency"; see also Lamar T. Empey, *American Delinquency* (Homewood, Ill.: Dorsey Press, 1978).

64. Wiatrowski et al., "Social Control Theory and Delinquency," p. 537.

65. Robert Richard Lyerly and James K. Skipper, Jr., "Differential Rates of Rural-Urban Delinquency: A Social Control Approach," *Criminology* 19 (November 1981): 389, 396–398.

66. Nettler, *Explaining Crime,* p. 314 (emphasis in the original)

67. Kai T. Erikson, "Notes on the Sociology of Deviance," *Social Problems* 9 (Spring 1962): 308. See also Kai T. Erikson, *Wayward Puritans* (New York: John Wiley, 1966).

68. Edwin Lemert, *Social Pathology* (New York: McGraw-Hill, 1951).

69. Edwin M. Lemert, *Human Deviance, Social Problems, and Social Control* (Englewood Cliffs, N.J.: Prentice-Hall, 1967), p. 17.

70. Erikson, "Notes on the Sociology of Deviance," p. 311.

71. For a summary of the development of labeling theory, see Walter R. Gove, ed., *The Labelling of Deviance: Evaluating a Perspective,* 2d ed. (Beverly Hills, Calif.: Sage Publications, 1980). For a discussion and analysis of the major assumptions of labeling theory, see Charles Wellford, "Labelling Theory and Criminology: An Assessment," *Social Problems* 22 (February 1975): 332–345.

72. Becker, *Outsiders,* p. 14. For a discussion of the processes involved in labeling, see Edwin M. Schur, *Radical Nonintervention: Rethinking the Delinquency Problem* (Englewood Cliffs, N.J.: Prentice-Hall, 1973), pp. 120–126.

73. Richard D. Schwartz and Jerome H. Skolnick, "Two Studies of Legal Stigma," *Social Problems* 10 (Fall 1962): 136.

74. Schwartz and Skolnick, 138–139.

75. Schwartz and Skolnick, 139, 141.

76. D. L. Rosenhan, "On Being Sane in Insane Places," *Science* 179 (January 1973): 250.

77. Craig Haney, Curtis Banks, and Phillip Zimbardo, "Interpersonal Dynamics in a Simulated Prison," *International Journal of Criminology and Penology* 1 (1973): 69–97; reprinted in Darrell J. Steffensmeier and Robert M. Terry, eds., *Examining Deviance Experimentally* (Port Washington. N.Y.: Alfred University Press, 1975), p. 223. See also F. K. Heussentamm, "Bumper Stickers and the Cops," *Transaction* 8 (February 1971): 32–33; reprinted in Steffensmeier and Terry, pp. 251–259.

78. Anne Rankin Mahoney, "The Effect of Labeling Upon Youths in the Juvenile Justice System: A Review of the Evidence," *Law & Society Review* 8 (Summer 1974): 583–614. Quotation is on p. 609. See this article for a listing and discussion of the empirical studies.

79. Charles T. Tittle, "Labelling and Crime: An Empirical Evaluation," chap. 6, in Walter R. Gove, ed., *The Labelling of Deviance,* 1st ed. (New York: Holsted Press, 1975), pp. 157–179. Quotation is on p. 158, citations omitted.

80. Tittle, p. 176.

81. See, for example, Paul G. Schervish, "The Labeling Perspective: Its Bias and Potential in the Study of Political Science," *American Sociologist* 8 (May 1973): 47–57.

82. See John Hagan, "Labelling and Deviance."

83. Wellford, "Labelling Theory and Criminology," 337.

84. Ronald L. Akers, "Problems in the Sociology of Deviance: Social Definitions and Behavior," *Social Forces* 46 (June 1968): 463.

85. Bernard A. Thorsell and Lloyd D. Klemke, "The Labeling Process: Reinforcement and Deterrent?" *Law & Society Review* 6 (February 1972): 393–403.

86. Mary Owen Cameron, *The Booster and the Snitch* (New York: Free Press, 1964).

87. Robert Rosenthal and Lenore Jacobson, "Teacher Expectations for the Disadvantaged," *Scientific American* 218 (1968): 19.

88. George A. Lundberg, *Can Science Save Us?* (New York: Longman, 1961), pp. 143, 144.

Chapter 7

1. See, for example, Marshall B. Clinard and Richard Quinney, *Criminal Behavior Systems: A Typology,* 2d ed. (New York: Holt, Rinehart & Winston, 1973).

2. Don C. Gibbons, "Offender Typologies—Two Decades Later," *British Journal of Criminology* 15 (April 1975): 148.

3. Gibbons, 152, 153. For a thorough discussion of Gibbons's approach see his *Society, Crime, and Criminal Careers: An Introduction to Criminology,* 4th ed. (Englewood Cliffs, N.J.: Prentice-Hall, 1983). For a listing and discussion of several of the other typologies developed by social scientists, see Vernon Fox, *Introduction to Criminology* (Englewood Cliffs, N.J.: Prentice-Hall, 1976), pp. 328–345. See also Abraham S. Blumberg, "Typologies of Criminal Behavior," in Blumberg, ed., *Current Perspectives on Criminal Behavior: Essays on Criminology,* 2d ed. (New York: Knopf, 1981), pp. 25–55. For a critique of typologies, see Clayton A. Hartjen and Don C. Gibbons, "An Empirical Investigation of Criminal Typology," *Sociology and Social Research* 54 (October 1959): 56–62.

4. Bureau of Justice Statistics, *Report to the Nation on Crime and Justice* (Washington, D.C.: U.S. Government Printing Office, 1983), p. 2.

5. *Report to the Nation on Crime and Justice,* p. 10.

6. "The Plague of Violent Crime," *Newsweek,* March 23, 1981, p. 46.

7. Milton S. Eisenhower, "Preface," in Hugh Davis Graham and Ted Robert Gurr, eds., *Violence in America: Historical & Comparative Perspectives,* rev. ed. (Beverly Hills, Calif.: Sage Publications, 1979), p. 10.

8. Richard Maxwell Brown, "Historical Patterns of American Violence," chap. 1 in Graham and Gurr, pp. 20, 21.

9. Brown, p. 41.

10. Émile Durkheim, *The Rules of Sociological Method* (New York: Free Press, 1964), p. 71. (First published in 1938)

11. Edith E. Flynn, "Crime and Violence in American Society—An Overview," *American Behavioral Scientist* 23 (May–June 1980): 643–645.

12. U.S. Department of Justice, *Violent Crime in the United States,* National Indicators System, Briefing Book, 1981 (Washington, D. C.: U.S. Government Printing Office, 1981), p. 8. For an extensive analysis of trends in violent crime, see Ted Robert Gurr, "Historical Trends in Violent Crime: A Critical Review of the Evidence," in Michael Tonry and Norval Morris, eds., *Crime and Justice: An Annual Review of Research,* vol. 3 (Chicago: University of Chicago Press, 1981), pp. 295–353.

13. Federal Bureau of Investigation, *Uniform Crime Reports,* 1982 (Washington, D.C.: U.S. Government Printing Office, 1983), p. 40.

14. "U.S. Crime Reports Decline 7% in Year, F.B.I. Data Indicate," *New York Times,* April 20, 1984, p. 1, col. 6.

15. "'82 Drop in Crime Victims Was Largest in Decade," *New York Times,* August 5, 1983, p. 8, col. 6.

16. *Uniform Crime Reports,* 1982, p. 20.

17. *Uniform Crime Reports,* 1982, pp. 21–22.

18. *Uniform Crime Reports,* 1982, p. 6.

19. Ali E. R. 801 (House of Lords, 1954).

20. Hollis v. Kentucky, 652 S.W. 2d 61 (Ky. 1981).

21. *Uniform Crime Reports,* 1982, p. 12.

22. See Manfred Guttmacher, "The Normal and the Sociopathic Murderer," in Marvin Wolfgang, ed., *Studies in Homicide* (New York: Harper & Row, 1967), pp. 114–123. For a contrary view, see Stuart Palmer, *A Study of Murder* (New York: Thomas Y. Crowell, 1960).

23. Marvin E. Wolfgang, "A Sociological Analysis of Criminal Homicide," *Federal Probation* 23 (March 1961): 48–55, reprinted in Wolfgang, ed., *Studies in Homicide,* pp. 15–28. Quotation is on p. 15. Wolfgang's study on which these conclusions are based was conducted in Philadelphia. He gathered data from police files from January 1, 1948, through December 31, 1952. Richard Block, in his study of homicides in Chicago between 1965 and 1973, found similar patterns to those of the Wolfgang study. In general, homicides increased during that period and represented two patterns: homicides involving arguments between spouses or friends and homicides based on robbery, with the second type increasing more rapidly than the first. Richard Block, "Homicide in Chicago: A Nine-Year Study (1965–1973)," *Journal of Criminal Law & Criminology* 66 (December 1975): 496–510.

24. *Uniform Crime Reports,* 1982, p. 12.

25. David F. Luckenbill, "Criminal Homicide As a Situated Transaction," *Social Problems* 25 (December 1977): 176–186.

26. See the study of Ken Levi, "Becoming a Hit Man: Neutralization in a Very Deviant Career," *Urban Life* 10 (April 1981): 47–63.

For a discussion of "reframing," see Erving Goffman, *Frame Analysis* (Cambridge, Mass.: Harvard University Press, 1974).

27. "Officials Cite a Rise in Killers Who Roam U.S. for Victims," *New York Times,* January 21, 1984, p. 1, col. 5.

28. "Police from 19 States Study Evidence on Mass Murderer," *Tulsa World,* October 13, 1983, p. 1, col. 4.

29. 3 Co. Inst. *68 quoted in Rollin M. Perkins, *Perkins on Criminal Law,* 2d ed. (Mineola, N.Y.: Foundation Press, 1969), p. 280.

30. *Uniform Crime Reports,* 1982, p. 16.

31. See, for example, Ill. Crim. Code § 12-6.

32. 369 N.E.2d 131, 134 (Ill.App.1st Dist. 1977), citations omitted.

33. "Homicides Involving Robbery in New York Rising, Study Shows," *New York Times,* February 9, 1982, p. 1, col. 4.

34. Robbery that results in murder or serious injury is the subject of a study to be conducted by Duke University and funded by the National Institute of Justice.

35. *Uniform Crime Reports,* 1982, p. 12.

36. *Uniform Crime Reports,* 1982, p. 17.

37. Cummings v. State, 382 N.E.2d 605 (Ind. 1979).

38. Reported in "Thugs Who Don't Use Guns Are Most Likely to Injure," *New York Times,* January 1, 1979, p. 6, col. 6.

39. *Uniform Crime Reports,* 1982, p. 18.

40. Joan Petersilia, Peter W. Greenwood, and Marvin Lavin, *Criminal Careers of Habitual Felons,* National Institute of Law Enforcement and Criminal Justice (Washington, D.C.: U.S. Government Printing Office, 1978). Quotations are on pp. vii and xiii. See André Normandeau, "Patterns in Robbery," *Criminologica* 6 (November 1968): 12, cited in Charles H. McCaghy, *Deviant Behavior: Crime, Conflict & Interest* (New York: Macmillan, 1976), p. 148. For a discussion of the characteristics of robbers, see McCaghy, pp. 145–150. See also John E. Conklin, *Robbery and the Criminal Justice System* (Philadelphia: Lippincott, 1972); Werner J. Einstadter, "The Social Organization of Armed Robbery," *Social Problems* 17 (Summer 1969): 64–83; and Peter Letkemann, *Crime As Work,* chap. 4, "Overt Crimes (Victim Confrontation): The Technical Dimensions of Robbery, with Special Attention to Bank Robbery," pp. 90–116. For a discussion

of both general and specific deterrence and robbery, see James F. Haran and John M. Martin, "The Imprisonment of Bank Robbers: The Issue of Deterrence," *Federal Probation* 41 (September 1977): 27–30.

41. Lawrence E. Cohen, David Cantor, and James R. Kluegel, "Robbery Victimization in the United States: An Analysis of a Nonrandom Event," *Social Science Quarterly* 62 (December 1981): 654, 655.

42. Cohen et al., p. 655. For a study of the relationship between geography and the crimes of burglary and robbery, see Leon E. Pettiway, "Mobility of Robbery and Burglary Offenders: Ghetto and Nonghetto Spaces," *Urban Affairs Quarterly* 18 (December 1982): 255–270.

43. Charles W. Dean and Mary deBruyn-Kops, *The Crime and the Consequences of Rape* (Springfield, Ill.: Chas. C Thomas, 1982), pp. 18–19.

44. See Mary Ann Largen, "History of Women's Movement in Changing Attitudes, Laws, and Treatment Toward Rape Victims." chap. 7, pp. 69–74, in Marcia J. Walker and Stanley L. Brodsky, eds., *Sexual Assault: The Victim and the Rapist* (Lexington, Mass.: Heath, 1976). See also William B. Sanders, "New Consciousness of Rape," pp. 22–23 in *Rape and Woman's Identity* (Beverly Hills, Calif.: Sage Publications, 1980). For an earlier but widely publicized book on rape, see Susan Brownmiller, *Against Our Will: Men, Women and Rape* (New York: Simon & Schuster, 1975).

45. For a discussion of the development of rape crisis centers, see H. Elizabeth King and Carol Webb, "Rape Crisis Centers: Progress and Problems," *Journal of Social Issues* 37 (Fall 1981): 93–104.

46. 373 N.E.2d 538, 593–643 (Ill.App.Ct. 1978), *rehearing denied,* March 3, 1978.

47. Mich. Comp. Laws Ann. § 750.520j(1). See also Fed. R. Evid. 412. And see Paul F. Rothstein, "New Federal Evidence Rule 412 on Sex Victim's Character," *Criminal Law Bulletin* 4 (July–August 1979): 353–366. For a critique of statutory changes in the area of rape, see Lawrence Herman, "What's Wrong with the Rape Reform Laws?" *Civil Liberties Review* 3 (December 1976-January 1977): 60–73.

48. People v. McKenna, 585 P.2d 275 (Colo. Sup.Ct. 1978).

49. *Uniform Crime Reports,* 1982, p. 13.

50. *Uniform Crime Reports,* 1982, pp. 14–15.
51. The literature on forcible rape is extensive. For references, see Barbara M. Pawloski, "Forcible Rape: An Updated Bibliography," *Journal of Criminal Law & Criminology* 74 (Summer 1983): 601–625.
52. For a review of the literature on these findings, see R. Lance Shotland and Lynne Goodstein, "Just Because She Doesn't Want to Doesn't Mean It's Rape: An Experimentally Based Causal Model of the Perception of Rape in a Dating Situation," *Social Psychology Quarterly* 46 (September 1983): 220–232.
53. Neil M. Malamuth, "Rape Proclivity Among Males," *Journal of Social Issues* 37 (Fall 1981): 138–157.
54. Mary Beard Deming and Ali Eppy, "The Sociology of Rape," *Sociology and Social Research* 65 (July 1981): 373.
55. Paul H. Gebhard, John H. Gagnon, Wardell B. Pomeroy, and Cornelia V. Christenson, *Sex Offenders* (New York: Harper & Row, 1965), pp. 197–205.
56. See Manachem Amir, "Forcible Rape," *Federal Probation* 31 (March 1967): 51–58; and Amir, *Patterns in Forcible Rape* (Chicago: University of Chicago Press, 1971).
57. Gibbons, *Society, Crime and Criminal Careers,* p. 388.
58. A. Nicholas Groth, *Men Who Rape: The Psychology of the Offender* (New York: Plenum, 1979).
59. Groth, pp. 13–58.
60. Ann Wolbert Burgess and Lynda Lytle Holmstrom, "Rape: Its Effect on Task Performance at Varying Stages in the Life Cycle," pp. 23–33, in Walker and Brodsky, *Sexual Assault.* Quotation is on p. 32. For a discussion of the adjustment of rape victims, see Thomas W. McCahill et al., *The Aftermath of Rape* (Lexington, Mass.: Heath, 1979), pp. 21–78.
61. For a discussion of these issues, along with citations of empirical studies, see Charles W. Dean and Mary deBruyn-Kops, *The Crime and the Consequences of Rape* (Springfield, Ill.: Chas. C Thomas, 1982), pp. 105–106.
62. Dane G. Kilpatrick, Patricia A. Resick, and Lois J. Veronen, "Effects of a Rape Experience: A Longitudinal Study," *Journal of Social Issues* 37 (Fall 1981): 105–122. See also Joyce E. Williams and Karen A. Holmes, *The Second Assault: Rape and Public Attitudes* (Westport,

Conn.: Greenwood Press, 1981).
63. McCahill et al., *The Aftermath of Rape,* p. 4. The book later tells us, however, that a "successful home visit was completed for 790" of the 1,401 women, and most of the results are based on a sample of 790. See p. 11.
64. McCahill et al., p. 26.
65. McCahill et al., p. 31.
66. McCahill et al., p. 35.
67. L. L. Holstrom and A. W. Burgess, "Rape: The Husband's and Boyfriend's Initial Reactions," *Family Coordinator* 28 (1979): 321, quoted in Priscilla N. White and Judith C. Rollings, "Rape: A Family Crisis," *Family Relations* 30 (January 1981): 104.
68. McCahill et al., *The Aftermath of Rape.* For a critique of this study, see the book review by Martin D. Schwartz and Todd R. Clear in *Crime and Delinquency* 27 (January 1981): 137–142.
69. Joyce E. Williams and Karen A. Holmes, *The Second Assault: Rape and Public Attitudes* (Westport, Conn.: Greenwood Press, 1981), p. 106.
70. Williams and Holmes, p. 49.
71. "'Adoptable' Doll Brings Out the Crowds," *New York Times,* November 29, 1983, p. 7, col. 1.
72. "The Shooting of the President: American Nightmare," *Newsweek,* April 13, 1981, p. 29.
73. See Walter B. Miller, "Lower Class Culture As a Generating Milieu of Gang Delinquency," *Journal of Social Issues* 14 (1958): 5–19.
74. Wolfgang, "A Sociological Analysis of Criminal Homicide," p. 27. See also Marvin E. Wolfgang and Franco Ferracuti, *The Subculture of Violence: Towards an Integrated Theory in Criminology* (Beverly Hills, Calif.: Sage, 1982). (Originally published in 1967)
75. *Uniform Crime Reports,* 1982, pp. 7, 14, 21.
76. See, for example, William G. Doerner, "A Regional Analysis of Homicide Rates in the United States," *Criminology* 13 (May 1975): 90–101; and Raymond D. Gastil, "Homicide and a Regional Culture of Violence," *American Sociological Review* 36 (June 1971): 412–427.
77. Brochure for James D. Wright, Peter H. Rossi, and Kathleen Daly, *Under the Gun: Weapons, Crime, and Violence in America* (Hawthorne, N.Y.: Aldine, 1983).
78. See Marvin Wolfgang, "A Sociological Analysis of Criminal Homicide," *Federal Probation* 23

(March 1961): 48–55, reprinted in Wolfgang, ed., *Studies in Homicide* (New York: Harper & Row, 1967), p. 27. For a replication of Wolfgang's study and similar findings, see Harwin L. Voss and John R. Hepburn, "Patterns in Criminal Homicide in Chicago," *Journal of Criminal Law, Criminology and Police Science* 59 (December 1968): 499–508.

79. Judith R. Blau and Peter M. Blau, "The Cost of Inequality: Metropolitan Structure and Violent Crime," *American Sociological Review* 47 (February 1982): 126. For a reaction to this study, see Robert M. O'Brien, "Metropolitan Structure and Violent Crime: Which Measure of Crime?" *American Sociological Review* 48 (June 1983): 434–437.

80. Sandra J. Ball-Rokeach, "Values and Violence: A Test of the Subculture of Violence Thesis," *American Sociological Review* 38 (December 1973): 478.

81. Howard S. Erlanger, "The Empirical Status of the Subculture of Violence Thesis," *Social Problems* 22 (December 1974): 280–292. See also William G. Doerner, "The Index of Southernness Revisited: The Influence of Wherefrom upon Whodunnit," *Criminology* 16 (May 1978): 47–66; and James F. O'Connor and Alan Lizotte, "The 'Southern Subculture of Violence' Thesis and Patterns of Gun Ownership," *Social Problems* 26 (April 1978): 420–429.

82. Steven F. Messner, "Regional and Racial Effects on the Urban Homicide Rate: The Subculture of Violence Revisted," *American Journal of Sociology* 88 (March 1983): 1006.

83. At the time these defendants pleaded guilty, the maximum sentence that could be imposed on persons pleading guilty was thirty years; but a new statute was passed in June 1983, permitting a maximum of fifty years: "New York Extends Terms for Violent Crime Sprees," *New York Times,* June 4, 1983, p. 10, col. 1.

84. "Five Get 30-Year Terms for Crime Spree on L.I." *New York Times,* December 8, 1982, p. 18, col. 5. See also *New York Times,* May 30, 1982. In one of the reports, police indicated that although the customers were told to engage in sexual activities in front of one another, none actually did; instead they "simulated sex."

85. "The Plague of Violent Crime," *Newsweek,* March 23, 1981, p. 46.

86. "The Curse of Violent Crime: A Pervasive Fear of Robbery and Mayhem Threatens the Way America Lives," *Time,* March 23, 1981, p. 16.

87. Frank F. Furstenberg, Jr., "Fear of Crime and Its Effects on Citizen Behavior" (Paper presented at the Symposium on Studies of Public Experience, Knowledge and Opinion of Crime and Justice, Bureau of Social Science Research, Washington, D.C.), quoted in James Garofalo, "The Fear of Crime: Causes and Consequences," in National Institute of Justice, *Victims of Crime: A Review of Research Issues and Methods* (Washington, D.C.: U.S. Government Printing Office, 1982), p. 113.

88. President's Commission on Law Enforcement and the Administration of Justice, *The Challenge of Crime in a Free Society* (Washington, D.C.: U.S. Government Printing Office, 1967), p. 52.

89. See, for example, Kenneth Friedman et al., *Victims and Helpers: Reactions to Crime.* U.S. Department of Justice, National Institute of Justice (Washington, D. C.: U.S. Government Printing Office, 1982).

90. Wesley G. Skogan and Michael G. Maxfield, *Coping with Crime: Individual and Neighborhood Reactions* (Beverly Hills, Calif.: Sage Publications, 1981), chap. 4, "Victimization and Fear," p. 59.

91. See the research of Mary Holland Baker et al., "The Impact of a Crime Wave: Perceptions, Fear, and Confidence in the Police," *Law & Society Review* 17 (1983): 319–335.

92. For an analysis of public perceptions of crime, see Mark Warr, "The Accuracy of Public Beliefs About Crime," *Criminology* 20 (August 1982): 185–204.

93. Baker et al., "The Impact of a Crime Wave."

94. Wesley G. Skogan et al., *The Reactions to Crime Project: Executive Summary.* U.S. Department of Justice. National Institute of Justice (Washington, D.C.: U.S. Government Printing Office, 1982), p. 3; and "The Impact of Media and Neighborhood Networks on Fear," chap. 10, pp. 163–182. See also "Crime in the Media," chap. 8, pp. 127–144, in Skogan and Maxfield, *Coping with Crime.*

95. Stephanie Riger, "On Women," in Dan A. Lewis, ed., *Reactions to Crime* (Beverly Hills, Calif.: Sage Publications, 1981), pp. 47–52.

96. Riger, "On Women."
97. For an analysis of the elderly and their fear of crime, see Jane C. Ollenburger, "Criminal Victimization and Fear of Crime," *Research on Aging* 3 (March 1981): 101–118.
98. For a discussion, see Herb Rubenstein, *The Link Between Crime and the Built Environment: The Current State of Knowledge,* vol. 1, U.S. Department of Justice, National Institute of Justice (Washington, D.C.: U.S. Government Printing Office, 1980).
99. "The New Fortress America," *Time,* September 12, 1983, p. 51.
100. Dan A. Lewis and Michael G. Maxfield, "Fear in the Neighborhoods: An Investigation of the Impact of Crime," *Journal of Research in Crime and Delinquency* 17 (July 1980): 160.
101. See Michael J. Hindelang et al., *The Victims of Personal Crime* (Cambridge, Mass.: Ballinger, 1978).
102. Skogan and Maxfield, *Coping with Crime,* p. 205.
103. Skogan et al., *The Reactions to Crime Project,* p. 4.
104. John E. Conklin, *The Impact of Crime* (New York: Macmillan, 1975), p. 99.
105. For a discussion, see Dan A. Lewis and Gerta Salem, "Community Crime Prevention: An Analysis of a Developing Strategy," *Crime & Delinquency* 3 (July 1981): 405–421.
106. "Fear of Crime Leads in Survey on Reasons to Leave Big Cities," *New York Times,* May 16, 1981, p. 8, col. 1.
107. Skogan et al., *The Reactions to Crime Project,* pp. 3–4. See also "Flight to the Suburbs," chap. 14, pp. 241–255, in Skogan and Maxfield, *Coping with Crime.*
108. See, for example, Steven Balkin and Pauline Houlden, "Reducing Fear of Crime Through Occupational Presence," *Criminal Justice and Behavior* 10 (March 1983): 13–33.
109. Skogan and Maxfield, *Coping with Crime,* p. 12.

Chapter 8

1. This information is taken from that broadcast on January 20, 1984.
2. Dierde A. Gaquin, "Spouse Abuse: Data from the National Crime Survey," *Victimology* 2 (1977–1978): 632.
3. Stanley Kramer, *History Begins at Sumer* (Toronto: Doubleday, 1959), p. 12.
4. For a discussion of Roman law, see Robert E. Shepard, "The Abused Child and the Law," *Washington and Lee Law Review* 22 (Spring 1965): 182–195. For a discussion of English common law, see Mason P. Thomas, "Child Abuse and Neglect: Historical Overview, Legal Matrix and Social Perspectives," *North Carolina Law Review* 50 (February 1972): 223–249; both cited in Stephen J. Pfohl, "The 'Discovery' of Child Abuse," *Social Problems* 24 (1977): 310–323. See this article for a brief but excellent history of the recognition of child abuse in this country.
5. Richard J. Gelles, *Family Violence* (Beverly Hills, Calif.: Sage Publications, 1979), p. 11.
6. *President's Task Force on Victims of Crime, Final Report* (Washington, D.C.: U.S. Government Printing Office, 1982), pp. 49–50.
7. "Panel Formed to Study Family Violence," *New York Times,* September 19, 1983, p. 13, col. 1.
8. OK. Rev. Stat. tit. 22 § 60.1.
9. Bureau of Justice Statistics, *Intimate Victims: A Study of Violence Among Friends and Relatives.* A National Crime Survey Report. (Washington, D.C.: U.S. Government Printing Office, 1980), p. 3.
10. Gelles, *Family Violence,* p. 11.
11. Sergeant Dick Ramon, head of the sex-crimes unit of the Seattle Police Department, quoted in "Child Abuse: The Ultimate Betrayal," *Time,* September 5, 1983, p. 22.
12. "Light on Child Abuse," *New York Times,* April 30, 1984, p. 1, col. 1.
13. Matter of Shant T, N.Y.L.J., August 20, 1981, p. 14, cited in *American Bar Association Journal* 68 (November 1982): 1362.
14. See T. Riede et al., *A Texas Study of Child Sexual Abuse and Child Pornography* (Huntsville, Tex.: Sam Houston State University, 1979), cited in Glen Kercher and Marilyn McShane, "Characterizing Child Sexual Abuse on the Basis of a Multi-Agency Sample," forthcoming in *Victimology.*
15. See Suzanne Sgroi, *Handbook of Clinical Intervention in Child Sexual Abuse* (Lexington, Mass.: Heath, 1982), cited in Kercher and McShane.

16. Allen D. Sapp and David L. Carter, *Child Abuse in Texas: A Descriptive Study of Texas Residents' Attitudes* (Huntsville, Tex.: College of Criminal Justice, Sam Houston State University), p. 7. For a symposium of articles on child abuse, see the *Chicago-Kent Law Review* 54 (1978): 635–826.

17. "Reports of Child Abuse on Rise," *Justice Assistance News* 4 (May 1983): 4.

18. David Finkelhor, "Sexual Abuse: A Sociological Perspective," *Child Abuse and Neglect* 6 (1982): 95–102.

19. "Studies Find Sexual Abuse of Children Is Widespread," *New York Times,* May 13, 1982, p. 20, col. 1.

20. "A Senator Recounts Her Own Experience As an Abused Child," *New York Times,* April 27, 1984, p. 1, col. 4.

21. Edward P. Sarafino, "An Estimate of Nationwide Incidence of Sexual Offenses Against Children," *Child Welfare* 58 (February 1979): 127–134. For a discussion of the need for accurate data on child sexual abuse, see V. De Francis, *Protecting the Child Victim of Sex Crimes Committed by Adults* (Denver: Children's Division, American Humane Association, 1969).

22. John H. Gagnon, "Female Child Victims of Sex Offenses," *Social Problems* 13 (Fall 1965): 176–192.

23. For a discussion of these and other problems with collecting data on the sexual abuse of children, see Sarafino, "An Estimate of Nationwide Incidence of Sexual Offenses Against Children."

24. C. Shift, "Sexual Assault of Children and Adolescents," testimony before a subcommittee of the U.S. House of Representatives on January 11, 1978, in New York City. Cited in Sarafino, 132.

25. Kercher and McShane, "Characterizing Child Sexual Abuse."

26. See Kercher and McShane, p. 2, referring to the research of David Finkelhor, *Sexually Victimized Children* (New York: MacMillan, 1979); Kercher and McShane, "The Prevalence of Child Sexual Abuse Victimization in an Adult Sample of Texas Residents," *Child Abuse and Neglect: An International Journal,* in press; and A. Sapp and David Carter, *Child Abuse in Texas* (Huntsville, Tex.: Criminal Justice Center, Sam Houston State University, 1978).

27. Kercher and McShane, "Characterizing Child Sexual Abuse."

28. See, for example, Richard Gelles, "Violence Towards Children in the United States," *American Journal of Orthopsychiatry* 48 (October 1978): 580–592; and Gelles, *Family Violence,* pp. 23–26.

29. Judith Miller and Mark Miller, "Protecting the Rights of Abused and Neglected Children," *Trial* 19 (July 1983): 69. See also Gelles, *Family Violence,* pp. 34–35.

30. "Child Sexual Abuse: A Pioneering Study," *New York Times,* February 7, 1983, p. 15, col. 5, referring to the study by Dr. David Finkelhor of the Family Violence Research Program at the University of New Hampshire.

31. Kercher and McShane, "Characterizing Child Sexual Abuse." Quotation is on p. 23 of the unpublished manuscript. For a review of the literature and a discussion of the findings of the authors' empirical research on pedophiles (adults who have sexual relations with children), see W. L. Marshall and M. M. Christie, "Pedophilia and Aggression," *Criminal Justice and Behavior* 8 (June 1981): 145–158.

32. Laura Meyers, "Incest: No One Wants to Know," *Student Lawyer* 9 (November 1980): 30.

33. Meyers, "Incest."

34. For a study that found cases of incest to be highest among siblings, see Finkelhor, *Sexually Victimized Children.* For a discussion of reasons that women are not usually offenders in cases of incest, see Finkelhor, "Sexual Abuse."

35. Robert L. Geiser, *Hidden Victims: The Sexual Abuse of Children* (Boston: Beacon Press, 1979), p. 52.

36. Sandra Butler, "Incest: Whose Reality, Whose Theory?" pp. 323–333, in Barbara Raffel Price and Natalie J. Sokoloff, *The Criminal Justice System and Women: Offenders, Victims, Workers* (New York: Clark Boardman, 1982). Quotation is on p. 331.

37. "The Child Victim of Incest," *New York Times,* June 15, 1982, p. 22, col. 1. For a discussion of the biosocial view of incest, see the recently published work of Joseph Shepher, *Incest: A Biosocial View* (New York: Academic Press, 1983).

38. Geiser, *Hidden Victims,* p. 68. For a discussion of male incest victims, see Maria Jasjleti, "Suf-

fering in Silence: The Male Incest Victim," *Child Welfare* 59 (May 1980): 269–276. For a discussion of reactions of victims to incest, see Roxane L. Silver, Cheryl Boon, and Mary H. Stones, "Searching for Meaning in Misfortune: Making Sense of Incest," *Journal of Social Issues* 39 (1983): 81–102.

39. For a review of such theories, see Richard Gelles and Murray Straus, "Determinants of Violence in the Family: Toward a Theoretical Integration," pp. 549–581, in Wesley Burr et al., eds., *Contemporary Theories About the Family,* vol. 1 (New York: Free Press, 1979); and Blair and Rita Justice, *The Abusing Family* (New York: Human Sciences Press, 1976).

40. See, for example, Gerald T. Hotaling and Murray Straus, "Violence and the Social Structure As Reflected in Children's Books from 1850–1970," in M. Straus and G. Hotaling, eds., *The Social Causes of Husband-Wife Violence* (Minneapolis: University of Minnesota Press, 1979): and Murray Straus, "A Sociological Perspective on the Prevention and Treatment of Wife-Beating," pp. 194–238 in Maria Roy, ed., *Battered Women: A Psychosociological Study of Domestic Violence* (New York: Van Nostrand Reinhold, 1977), cited in Gelles, *Family Violence.*

41. Study by psychiatrists Brant Steele and Carl Pollock, cited in Ruth Inglis, *Sins of the Fathers: A Study of the Physical and Emotional Abuse of Children* (New York: St. Martin's Press, 1978), p. 69.

42. Richard Gelles, "Child Abuse As Psychopathology: A Sociological Critique and Reformulation," *American Journal of Orthopsychiatry* 43 (1973): 611–621, cited in Anderson and Lauderdale, p. 286. See also Stephen C. Anderson and Michael L. Lauderdale, "Characteristics of Abusive Parents: A Look at Self-Esteem," *Child Abuse and Neglect* 6 (1982): 285–293.

43. See Gelles, *Family Violence,* pp. 32–37.

44. Gelles, *Family Violence;* and also his chapter, "The Social Construction of Child Abuse," pp. 43–53.

45. Geiser, *Hidden Victims,* referring to "The Battered Children," *Newsweek,* October 10, 1977, p. 112B.

46. See J. Verterdal, "Etiological Factors and Long Term Consequences of Child Abuse," *Interna-*

tional Journal of Offender Therapy and Comparative Criminology 27 (1983): 25–54.

47. "Studies Find Sexual Abuse of Children Is Widespread."

48. "Helping to Heal the Scars Left by Incest," *New York Times,* January 9, 1984, p. 15, col. 2.

49. Michael W. Agopian, "Parental Child Stealing: Participants and the Victimization Process," *Victimology: An International Journal* 5 (1980): 263.

50. Agopian, pp. 263–273. See also Agopian, *Parental Child-Stealing* (Lexington, Mass.: Heath, 1981).

51. 42 U.S. Code § 534 (1982).

52. 28 U.S. Code § 534 (1982).

53. "Unveiling a Family Secret," *Newsweek,* February 18, 1980, p. 104.

54. "Unveiling a Family Secret," p. 104.

55. Michael D. A. Freeman, *Violence in the Home: a Socio-Legal Study* (Westmead, Farnborough, Hampshire, England: Gower, 1980), p. 239. (First published 1979 by Saxon House.)

56. Murray Straus, Richard J. Gelles, and Suzanne Steinmetz, *Behind Closed Doors: Violence in the American Family* (New York: Doubleday, 1980).

57. "Unveiling a Family Secret," p. 106. See Conn. Gen. Stat. Ann. § 46a–14.

58. "Unveiling a Family Secret," p. 106. For a general discussion of the issue of domestic abuse of the elderly, see Marilyn R. Block, "Violence in The Family: Abuse of the Elderly," in Sanford H. Kadish, ed., *Encyclopedia of Crime and Justice,* vol. 4 (New York: Free Press, 1983), pp. 1635–1637. See also Marilyn R. Block and Jan D. Sinnott, eds., *The Battered Elder Syndrome: An Exploratory Study* (College Park: University of Maryland, Center on Aging, 1979).

59. R. Emerson Dobash and Russell Dobash, *Violence Against Wives: A Case Against the Patriarchy* (New York: Free Press, 1979), quoted in a book review by Elaine Hillberman, *Crime & Delinquency* 27 (April 1981): 265.

60. Kersti Yllo and Murray A. Straus, "Interpersonal Violence Among Married and Cohabiting Couples," *Family Relations* 30 (July 1981): 345.

61. Marjorie Fields, *Notes from the Women's Rights Project, Abused Women,* ACLU, vol. 1, November 1977, cited in Donna M. Moore,

"Editor's Introduction: An Overview of the Problem," p. 8, in Donna M. Moore, ed., *Battered Women* (Beverly Hills, Calif.: Sage Publications, 1979).

62. Culmer v. Wilson, 44 P. 833, 836-837 (Utah Sup.Ct. 1896).

63. Del Martin, "Battered Women: Society's Problem," in Price and Sokoloff, *The Criminal Justice System and Women,* p. 266. See this source for other references on this topic. For other historical accounts, see Freeman, *Violence in the Home: A Socio-Legal Study,* pp. 177–178; and Gelles, *Family Violence,* pp. 91, 93.

64. See Gelles, *Family Violence,* p. 96.

65. Bailey v People, 130 P. 832, 835, 836 (Colo. Sup. Ct. 1913). Footnotes and citations omitted.

66. One study, for example, revealed that only two out of every ninety-eight cases of wife assaults were reported to the police. R. Emerson and Russell P. Dobash, "Wives: The 'Appropriate' Victims of Marital Violence," *Victimology* 2 (1978): 437.

67. "Study Details Family Violence," *New York Times,* April 23, 1984, p. 5, col. 1. The attorney general's remarks were published in *Justice Assistance News* 5 (February-March 1984): 2.

68. "Wife Beating: The Silent Crime," *Time,* September 5, 1983, p. 23.

69. See Gelles, *Family Violence,* p. 92. See also Straus, Gelles, and Steinmetz, *Behind Closed Doors.*

70. "Wife Beating," *Time,* p. 23.

71. "Wife Beating," *Time,* p. 24.

72. See presentation of Del Martin, author of *Battered Wives* (San Francisco: Glide Publications, 1976), before the U.S. Commission on Civil Rights in its hearings on *Battered Women: Issues on Public Policy* (Washington, D.C.: U.S. Government Printing Office, 1978), pp. 4–5. See also Moore, "Battered Women," p. 15.

73. Moore, p. 16.

74. "Wife Beating: The Silent Crime," *Time,* p. 26.

75. According to *Time,* although unemployment is not the cause of battering, it may be related. "In Youngstown, Ohio, for example, where the unemployment rate in 1982 reached 21 percent, domestic violence increased a staggering 404 per cent over 1979." "Wife Beating: The Silent Crime," p. 24.

76. Moore, *Battered Women,* p. 17.

77. *Report from the Conference on Intervention Programs for Men Who Batter,* sponsored by Special Programs Division, Law Enforcement Assistance Administration, U.S. Department of Justice (Washington, D.C.: U.S. Government Printing Office, 1981), p. 11.

78. Gelles, *The Violent Home* (Beverly Hills, Calif: Sage Publishing, 1972).

79. Moore, *Battered Women,* p. 19.

80. Mildred Daley Pagelow, *Women-Battering: Victims and Their Experiences* (Beverly Hills, Calif.: Sage Publications, 1981), p. 54. For a discussion of these myths, see pp. 54–88.

81. Moore, *Battered Women,* p. 20.

82. For a discussion of the results of interviews with over one hundred battered women who revealed how they reacted to domestic violence, see Kathleen J. Ferraro and John M. Johnson, "How Women Experience Battering: The Process of Victimization," *Social Problems* 30 (February 1983): 325–339.

83. Gelles, *The Violent Home.*

84. Richard Gelles, "Abused Wives: Why Do They Stay?" *Journal of Marriage and the Family* 38 (1976): 659. See also this chapter by the same title, in Gelles, *Violent Home,* chap. 5, pp. 95–110.

85. Gelles, *Violent Home,* pp. 100–101.

86. Pagelow, *Women-Battering,* p. 163.

87. Gelles *Violent Home,* pp. 101–102.

88. Pagelow, *Women-Battering,* p. 169.

89. Gelles, *Family Violence,* pp. 103–104.

90. For a discussion of the common law exemption from rape of marital sexual relations, see Thomas R. Bearrows, "Abolishing the Marital Exemption for Rape: A Statutory Proposal," *University of Illinois Law Review* 1983 (1983): 202–203.

91. Tex. Penal Code Ann. § 21.02(a).

92. Sir Matthew Hale, quoted in Note: "Rape in Marriage: The Law in Texas and the Need for Reform," *Baylor Law Review* 32 (Winter 1980): 109.

93. By Diana E. H. Russell (Briarcliff Manor, N.Y.: Stein & Day, 1975).

94. Lee H. Bowker, "Marital Rape: A Distinct Syndrome?" *Social Casework* 64 (June 1983): 347. See this source for a listing of the research papers.

95. A. Nicholas Groth and H. Jean Birnbaum, *Men Who Rape: The Psychology of the Offender*

(New York: Plenum, 1979); and Lenore Walker, *The Battered Woman* (New York: Harper & Row, 1979).

96. David Finkelhor and Kersti Yllo, "Forced Sex in Marriage: A Preliminary Research Report," *Crime & Delinquency* 28 (July 1982): 459. See also Richard Gelles, "Power, Sex, and Violence: The Case of Marital Rape," in Gelles, *Family Violence*, pp. 121–135.

97. Yllo, quoted in *New York Times,* November 29, 1982, p. 20, col. 1.

98. Report of Dr. Diana Russell, presented to the American Sociological Association and quoted in the *New York Times.*

99. Or. Rev. Stat. §§ 163.375 (repealed 1977). For a discussion of recent changes in state statutes, see Martin D. Schwartz and Todd R. Clear, "Toward a New Law on Rape," *Crime & Delinquency* 26 (April 1980): 129–151. For a discussion of many of the issues on spousal rape, see the excellent collection of essays in Duncan Chappell, Robley Geis, and Gilbert Geis, eds., *Forcible Rape: The Crime, the Victim, and the Offender* (New York: Columbia University Press, 1977).

100. State v. Rideout, 5 *Family Law Reporter* (BNA) 2164 (1979).

101. Commonwealth v. James K. Chretien, Supreme Judicial Court of Massachusetts, Essex Mass. Adv. Sh. (1981) 661, December 2, 1980; March 9, 1981.

102. Cited in "Wife Beating: The Silent Crime," p. 23.

103. Gelles, "The Truth About Husband Abuse," chap. 8, in Gelles, *Family Violence*, p. 137.

104. "Jury Acquits Woman Who Admits Slaying, Hiding Mate," *Tulsa World,* March 9, 1983, p. C1, col. 4. For discussions on the self-defense doctrine, see Lenore E. Walker, Roberta K. Thyfault, and Angela Browne, "Beyond the Juror's Ken: Battered Women," *Vermont Law Review* 7 (Spring 1982): 1–14. For an analysis of the use of the self-defense argument in cases involving the victim's use of deadly force to avoid rape, see Don B. Kates, Jr., and Nancy Jean Engberg, "Deadly Force Self-Defense Against Rape," *U.C. Davis Law Review* 15 (Summer 1982): 873–906.

105. See W. Page Keeton, *Prosser and Keeton on Torts,* 5th ed. (St. Paul: West Publishing, 1984), pp. 901–904, for a discussion of the common law doctrine of spousal immunity from tort liability.

106. See Edward J. Kionka, *Torts: Injuries to Persons and Property* (St. Paul: West Publishing, 1977), pp. 413–416. For a recent case, see Tevis v. Tevis, 400 A.2d 1189 (N.J Sup. Ct. 1979).

107. Quoted in "Comment: Spouse Battering and Ohio's Domestic Violence Legislation," *University of Toledo Law Review* 13 (Winter 1982): 358.

108. Ohio Rev. Code Ann. §§ 2919.25, 2919.26, 3113.31.

109. Ohio Rev. Code Ann. §§ 2919.25.

110. For a discussion of the advantages and disadvantages of the Ohio provision, see "Comment: Spouse Battering and Ohio's Domestic Violence Legislation," pp. 358–368.

111. See Ohio Rev. Code Ann. § 3113.31 (c).

112. For a discussion of this attitude, see the collection of essays edited by Jane Roberts Chapman and Margaret Gates, *The Victimization of Women* (Beverly Hills, Calif.: Sage Publications, 1978).

113. "Wife Beating: The Silent Crime," p. 24.

114. Linda A. Labell, "Wife Abuse: A Sociological Study of Battered Women and Their Mates," *Victimology* 4 (1979): 266.

115. For a survey of national facilities, see *Monograph on Services to Battered Women,* Colorado Association for Aid to Battered Women, U.S. Department of Health and Human Services Office of Human Development Services, available free from Project Share, P. O. Box 2309, Rockville, MD. 20852. See also *Under the Rule of Thumb: Battered Women and the Administration of Justice,* A Report of the United States Commission on Civil Rights (Washington, D.C.: U.S. Government Printing Office, 1982).

116. "Wife Beating: The Silent Crime," p. 24.

117. For a discussion of these problems, see Alan McEvoy, Jeff B. Brookings, and Clifford E. Brown, "Responses to Battered Women: Problems and Strategies," *Social Casework* 64 (February 1983): 92–96.

118. See Gelles, *Family Violence*, pp. 102–108, for a discussion and citations. For a brief overview of the reaction of police, courts, and prosecutors in cases of domestic violence, see "Spouse Battering and Ohio's Domestic Violence Leg-

islation," *University of Toledo Law Review* 13 (Winter 1982): 347–355.

119. Richard A. Berk et al., "Bringing the Cops Back In: A Study of Efforts to Make the Criminal Justice System More Responsive to Incidents of Family Violence," *Social Science Research* (September 1980): 194, referring to the works of Martin, *Battered Wives;* and Martin, *Battered Women.*

120. For a discussion of reasons why some victims refuse to cooperate with prosecutors in cases of domestic violence, along with a bibliography on this subject as well as police and prosecutorial noncooperation in such cases, see Maureen McLeod, "Victim Noncooperation in the Prosecution of Domestic Assault: A Research Note," *Criminology* 21 (August 1983): 395–416.

121. "Assailant's Arrest Found to Deter Domestic Violence," *Justice Assistance News* 4 (May, 1983): 5.

122. "The Effects of Going Public on Sexual Abuse," *New York Times,* May 5, 1984, p. 1, col. 3.

123. "Many Family Violence Victims Suffer," *Justice Assistance News* 4 (April 1983): 6.

Chapter 9

1. Rollin M. Perkins, *Criminal Law,* 2d ed. (Mineola, N.Y.: Foundation Press, 1969), p. 231.

2. Perkins, p. 232.

3. Perkins, p. 233. For a history of the development of the law of theft, see Jerome Hall, *Theft, Law and Society,* rev. ed. (Indianapolis: Bobbs-Merrill, 1952), chaps. 1–4.

4. Cal. Penal Code § 484.

5. "Stopping Fraud and Theft of Credit Cards," *New York Times,* March 13, 1982, p. 20, col. 2.

6. "ABC News," December 13, 1982, special assignment.

7. Federal Bureau of Investigation, *Uniform Crime Reports, 1982* (Washington, D.C.: U.S. Government Printing Office, 1983), p. 27.

8. *Uniform Crime Reports,* p. 28.

9. *Uniform Crime Reports,* p. 29.

10. Edwin M. Lemert, "An Isolation and Closure Theory of Naive Check Forgery," *Journal of Criminal Law, Criminology and Police Science* 44 (September-October 1953): 301–304.

11. Lemert, p. 298. For a later study confirming these findings, see Maurice Gauthier, "The Psychology of the Compulsive Forger," *Canadian Journal of Corrections* 1(July 1959): 62–69. See also Irwin A. Berg, "A Comparative Study of Forgery," *Journal of Applied Psychology* 28 (June 1944): 232–238; John L. Gillin, *The Wisconsin Prisoner* (Madison: University of Wisconsin Press, 1946), pp. 167–173; Norman S. Hayner, "Characteristics of Five Offender Types," *American Sociological Review* 16 (February 1961): 96–102.

12. Mary Owen Cameron, "An Interpretation of Shoplifting," in Marshall B. Clinard and Richard Quinney, eds., *Criminal Behavior Systems: A Typology* (New York: Holt, Rinehart & Winston, 1967), p. 109; reprinted from Mary Owen Cameron, *The Booster and the Snitch: Department Store Shoplifting* (New York: Free Press, 1964).

13. A fence is a person who disposes of stolen goods. In many cases, fences are professionals and are connected with organized crime. For a discussion of fences, see Duncan Chappell and Marilyn Walsh, "Receiving Stolen Property: The Need for Systematic Inquiry into the Fencing Process," *Criminology* 11 (February 1974): 484–497; Walsh, *The Fence: A New Look at the World of Property Theft* (Westport, Conn.: Greenwood Press, 1977); and Carl B. Klockars, *The Professional Fence* (New York: Free Press, 1974).

14. For an analysis of the variables involved in the prosecution of shoplifters, see Audrey Feuerverger and Clifford D. Shearing, "An Analysis of the Prosecution of Shoplifters," *Criminology* 20 (August 1982): 285–286.

15. Cameron, "An Interpretation of Shoplifting," p. 118.

16. D. P. Walsh, *Shoplifting—Controlling a Major Crime* (New York: Macmillan, 1978).

17. *Time,* November 17, 1980, p. 94.

18. For a discussion of the historical development of the law of burglary, see Wayne R. LaFave and Austin W. Scott, Jr., *Handbook on Criminal Law* (St. Paul, Minn.: West 1972), pp. 708–717, from which this summary has been taken.

19. *Uniform Crime Reports, 1982,* p. 23.

20. *Uniform Crime Reports, 1982,* pp. 24–25.

21. See Don C. Gibbons, *Changing the Lawbreaker: The Treatment of Delinquents and*

Criminals (Englewood Cliffs, N.J.: Prentice-Hall, 1965), pp. 106–108.

22. See Chris W. Eskridge, "Prediction of Burglary: A Research Note," *Journal of Criminal Justice* 11 (1983): 74.

23. See Jack L. Nasar, "Environmental Factors and Commercial Burglary," *Journal of Environmental Systems* 11 (1981–1982): 56.

24. See Michael J. Hindelang, *Criminal Victimization in Eight American Cities: A Descriptive Analysis of Common Theft and Assault* (Cambridge, Mass.: Ballinger, 1976); T. A. Reppetto, *Residential Crime* (Cambridge, Mass.: Ballinger, 1974); *Criminal Victimization in the United States: A Report of a National Survey, Field Surveys II.* (Washington, D.C.: U.S. Government Printing Office, 1967); Lawrence E. Cohen and David Cantor, "Residential Burglary in the United States: Life-Style and Demographic Factors Associated with the Probability of Victimization," *Journal of Research in Crime and Delinquency* 18 (January 1981): 113–128; and Lawrence E. Cohen and David Cantor, "The Determinants of Larceny: An Empirical and Theoretical Study," *Journal of Research in Crime and Delinquency* 17 (July 1980): 140–159.

25. For a more complete discussion of these issues, along with numerous citations of sociological works on professional criminals, see Gregory R. Staats, "Changing Conceptualizations of Professional Criminals: Implications for Criminology Theory," *Criminology* 15 (May 1977): 49–65.

26. Edwin H. Sutherland, *The Professional Thief* (Chicago: University of Chicago Press, 1937).

27. Robert Winslow, *Society in Transition: A Social Approach to Deviancy* (New York: Free Press, 1970).

28. For an example of some of the earlier works, see the works of David Maurer, who was a linguist, not a sociologist, and who called his work "an experiment in what might be called the social structure of language." Quoted in Andrew Walker, "Sociology and Professional Crime," in Abraham Blumberg, ed., *Current Perspectives on Criminal Behavior: Original Essays on Criminology* (New York: Knopf, 1974), p. 17. The books by Maurer are *The Big Con* (New York: Signet, 1962) and *Whiz Mob: A Correlation of the Technical Argot of Pick-pockets with Their Behavior Pattern* (Gainesville, Fla.: American Dialect Society, 1955).

29. Don C. Gibbons, *Society, Crime, and Criminal Careers: An Introduction to Criminology,* 3rd ed. (Englewood Cliffs, N.J.: Prentice-Hall, 1977), pp. 284–288.

30. See George M. Camp, "Nothing to Lose: A Study of Bank Robbery in America" (Ph.D. diss., Yale University, 1967); Leroy C. Gould, "The Changing Structure of Property Crime in an Affluent Society," *Social Forces* 48 (September 1969): 50–59.

31. See Richard A. Peterson, David J. Pittman, and Patricia O'Neal, "Stabilities in Deviance: A Study of Assaultive and Non-Assaultive Offenders," *Journal of Criminal Law, Criminology, and Police Science* 53 (March 1962): 44–48; and Harold S. Frum, "Adult Criminal Offense Trends Following Juvenile Delinquency," *Journal of Criminal Law, Criminology, and Police Science* 49 (May–June 1958): 29–49.

32. Reppetto, *Residential Crime.*

33. Julian B. Roebuck and Mervyn L. Cadwallader, "The Negro Armed Robber As a Criminal Type: The Construction and Application of a Typology," *Pacific Sociological Review* 4 (Spring 1961): 21–26. For additional studies of conventional criminals, see Donald MacKenzie, *Occupation: Thief* (Indianapolis: Bobbs-Merrill, 1955); Hutchins Hapgood, *Autobiography of a Thief* (New York: Fox, Duffield, 1930); John E. Conklin, *Robbery and the Criminal Justice System* (Philadelphia: Lippincott, 1972); Werner J. Einstadter, "The Social Organization of Armed Robbery," *Social Problems* 17 (Summer 1969): 64–83; Peter Letkemann, *Crime As Work* (Englewood Cliffs, N.J.: Prentice-Hall, 1973); Sheldon Glueck and Eleanor Glueck, *500 Criminal Careers* (New York: Knopf, 1930); and John L. Gillin, *The Wisconsin Prisoner* (Madison: University of Wisconsin Press, 1946). For additional discussions of typologies related to conventional criminals, see Clarence C. Schrag, "Some Foundations for a Theory of Correction," in Donald R. Cressey, ed., *The Prison* (New York: Holt, Rinehart & Winston, 1961), pp. 346–356; Clarence Schrag, "A Preliminary Criminal Typology," *Pacific Sociological Review* 4 (Spring 1961): 11–16; Norman S. Hayner,

"Characteristics of Five Offender Types," *American Sociological Review* 26 (February 1961): 96–102; Marshall B. Clinard and Robert F. Meier, *The Sociology of Deviant Behavior,* 5th ed. (New York: Holt, Rinehart and Winston, 1979); Clinard and Quinney, *Criminal Behavior Systems;* James Inciardi, "Vocational Crime," in Daniel Glaser, ed., *Handbook of Criminology* (Skokie, Ill.: Rand McNally, 1974), pp. 299–401; Ronald Akers, *Deviant Behavior: A Social Learning Approach* (Belmont, Calif.: Wadsworth, 1973); and Gibbons, *Society, Crime, and Criminal Careers.*

34. Peter W. Greenwood with Allan Abrahams, *Selective Incapacitation,* prepared for the National Institute of Justice, U.S. Department of Justice (Santa Monica, Calif.: Rand Corporation, 1982). Earlier reports are by Mark Peterson, Jan Chaiken, Patricia Ebener, and Paul Honig, *Survey of Prison and Jail Inmates: Background and Method* (1982); Kent Marquis with Patricia Ebener, *Quality of Prisoner Self-Reports: Arrest and Conviction Response Errors* (1981); Jan Chaiken and Marcia Chaiken with Joyce Peterson, *Varieties of Criminal Behavior: Summary and Policy Implications* (1982); Jan Chaiken and Marcia Chaiken, *Varieties of Criminal Behavior* (1982); Joan Petersilia and Paul Honig with Charles Hubay, *The Prison Experience of Career Criminals* (1980); and Joan Petersilia, Peter W. Greenwood, and Marvin Lavin, *Criminal Careers of Habitual Felons* (1978).

35. Greenwood, *Selective Incapacitation,* p. vii.

36. Michael J. Hindelang, Travis Hirschi, and Joseph G. Weis, "Correlates of Delinquency: The Illusion of Discrepancy Between Self-Report and Official Measures," *American Sociological Review* 44 (December 1979).

37. Marvin E. Wolfgang, Robert M. Figlio, and Thorsten Sellin, *Delinquency in a Birth Cohort* (Chicago: University of Chicago Press, 1972).

38. For a report of this study, see Petersilia, Greenwood, and Lavin, *Criminal Careers of Habitual Felons.*

39. Mark A. Peterson and Harriet B. Braiker with Suzanne M. Polich, *Who Commits Crimes: A Survey of Prison Inmates* (Cambrdige, Mass.: Oelgeschlager, Gunn & Hain, 1981).

40. Greenwood, *Selective Incapacitation.*

41. Petersilia et al., *Criminal Careers of Habitual Felons.*

42. Greenwood, *Selective Incapacitation,* p. 19.

43. Mark A. Peterson and Harriet B. Braiker with Suzanne M. Polich, *Doing Crime: A Survey of California Prison Inmates* (Santa Monica, Calif.: Rand Corporation, 1980), pp. vii–xii.

44. Patrick A. Langan and Lawrence A. Greenfeld, "Career Patterns in Crime," Bureau of Justice Statistics Special Report (Washington, D.C.: U.S. Department of Justice, June 1983).

45. C. M. Kelley, *Crime in the United States: Uniform Crime Reports,* 1974.

46. Marvin E. Wolfgang, "From Boy to Man—From Delinquency to Crime," in *The Serious Juvenile Offender: Proceedings of a National Symposium,* (Washington, D.C.: Office of Juvenile Justice and Delinquency Prevention, U.S. Department of Justice, 1978), p. 165. A later study of the Philadelphia cohort is being conducted but is not yet complete.

47. For a discussion on the accuracy of such self-reports, see K. H. Marquis, *Quality of Prisoner Self-Reports: Arrest and Conviction Response Errors,* prepared for the National Institute of Justice (Santa Monica, Calif.: Rand Corporation, 1981).

48. Edwin H. Sutherland, *White Collar Crime* (New York: Holt, Rinehart & Winston, 1961), originally published in 1949 by the Dryden Press. See also Sutherland, *White Collar Crime: The Uncut Version,* with an introduction by Gilbert Geis and Colin Goff (New Haven, Conn.: Yale University Press, 1983).

49. Donald R. Cressey, foreword to Sutherland, p. iii.

50. See Gibbons, *Society, Crime and Criminal Careers,* p. 322; and Gilbert Geis, "Toward a Delineation of White-Collar Offenses," *Sociological Inquiry* 32 (Spring 1962); 160–171.

51. Clinard and Quinney, eds., *Criminal Behavior Systems,* p. 131.

52. Clinard and Quinney, pp. 206–223.

53. August Bequai, *White-Collar Crime: A 20th-Century Crisis* (Lexington, Mass.: Heath, 1978), p. 2.

54. 42 U.S. Code §§ 3701 et seq.

55. Herbert Edelhertz, *The Nature, Impact and Prosecution of White-Collar Crime,* U.S. Department of Justice, Law Enforcement Assistance Administration (Washington, D.C.: U.S. Government Printing Office, 1970), pp. 19–20.

56. Albert J. Reiss, Jr., and Albert D. Biderman, *Data Sources on White-Collar Law-Breaking,* U.S. Department of Justice, National Institute of Justice (Washington, D.C.: U.S. Government Printing Office, 1980), p. xxiii.

57. Reiss and Biderman, p. xxviii.

58. Reiss and Biderman, p. i.

59. August Bequai, "Wanted: The White Collar Ring," *Student Lawyer* 5 (May 1977): 45.

60. "Crime in the Suites: On the Rise," *Newsweek,* December 3, 1979, p. 114.

61. Marshall B. Clinard, *Illegal Corporate Behavior*, National Institute of Law Enforcement and Criminal Justice (Washington, D.C.: U.S. Government Printing Office, 1979), pp. xv, xvi. See also Marshall B. Clinard and Peter C. Yeager, *Corporate Crime* (New York: Free Press, 1980).

62. See Sutherland, *White Collar Crime* and "Is White Collar Crime Crime?" *American Sociological Review* 10 (April 1947): 132–139. For a discussion of public reaction to prosecutions of white-collar criminals in the 1961 Electrical Conspiracy Case, see Gilbert Geis, "The Heavy Electrical Equipment Antitrust Cases of 1961," in Gilbert Geis, ed., *White-Collar Criminal* (New York: Atherton, 1968), pp. 103–117.

63. Laura Shill Schrager and James F. Short, Jr., "How Serious a Crime? Perceptions of Organizational and Common Crimes," chap. 1 in Gilbert Geis and Ezra Stotland, eds., *White-Collar Crime: Theory and Research* (Beverly Hills, Calif.: Sage Publications, 1980), p. 15.

64. Francis T. Cullen, Bruce G. Link, and Craig W. Polanzi, "The Seriousness of Crime Revisited: Have Attitudes Toward White-Collar Crime Changed?" *Criminology* 20 (May 1982): 83–102. These investigators were replicating the earlier work of Peter H. Rossi et al., "The Seriousness of Crimes: Normative Structure and Individual Differences," *American Sociological Review* 39 (April 1974): 224–237. See also Cullen et al., "Public Support for Punishing White-Collar Crime: Blaming the Victim Revisited?" *Journal of Criminal Justice* 11 (1983): 481–493.

65. See, for example, the classic study of Donald R. Cressey, *Other People's Money: A Study in the Social Psychology of Embezzlement* (New York: Free Press, 1953).

66. Marshall B. Clinard and Peter C. Yeager, "Corporate Crime: Issues in Research," *Criminology* 16 (August 1978): 257–258.

67. Clinard, *Illegal Corporate Behavior,* abstract.

68. Clinard, p. 18.

69. "Developments in the Law—Corporate Crime: Regulating Corporate Behavior Through Criminal Sanctions," *Harvard Law Review* 92 (April 1979): 1229.

70. Clinard and Yeager, "Corporate Crime: Issues in Research," 261–262.

71. Clinard, *Illegal Corporate Behavior,* abstract.

72. See "Corporate Crime: The Untold Story," *U.S. News & World Report,* September 6, 1982, p. 25; and Irwin Ross, "How Lawless Are Big Companies," *Fortune,* December 1, 1980, p. 57.

73. Leonard Orland, "Reflections on Corporate Crime: Law in Search of Theory and Scholarship," *American Criminal Law Review* 17 (Spring 1980): 508.

74. T. R. Young, "Corporate Crime: A Critique of the Clinard Report," *Contemporary Crises* 5 (July 1981): 323–336. See also Harold C. Barnett, "Corporate Capitalism, Corporate Crime," *Crime & Delinquency* 27 (January 1981): 4–23.

75. See Clarence C. Walton, ed., *The Ethics of Corporate Conduct* (Englewood Cliffs, N.J.: Prentice-Hall, 1977); and Marshall B. Clinard, *Corporate Ethics and Crime: The Role of Middle Management* (Beverly Hills, Calif.: Sage Publications, 1983).

76. Clinard, *Illegal Corporate Behavior,* p. 214. For a discussion of each approach, see pp. 214–228. See also Ralph Nader, Mark Green, and Joel Seligman, *Forming the Giant Corporation* (New York: Norton, 1976).

77. Quoted in John C. Coffee, Jr., "'No Soul to Damn: No Body to Kick': An Unscandalized Inquiry into the Problem of Corporate Punishment," *Michigan Law Review* 79 (January 1981): 386.

78. Robert W. Ogren, "The Ineffectiveness of the Criminal Sanction in Fraud and Corruption Cases: Losing the Battle Against White-Collar Crime," *American Criminal Law Review* 11 (Summer 1973): 960. Concerning the kinds of sentences imposed on corporate offenders, see Stanton Wheeler, David Weisburd, and Nancy Bode, "Sentencing the White-Collar Offender: Rhetoric and Reality," *American Sociological Review* 47 (October 1982): 641–659; and John L. Hagan and Ilene H. Nagel, "White-Collar Crime, White-Collar Time: The Sentencing of

White-Collar Offenders in the Southern District of New York," *American Criminal Law Review* 20 (Fall 1982): 259–289.

79. Andrew Hopkins, "Controlling Corporate Deviance," *Criminology* 18 (August 1980): 198–214. Quotations are on pp. 198, 212.

80. See Alfred S. Pelaez, "Of Crime—and Punishment: Sentencing the White-Collar Criminal," *Duquesne Law Review* 18 (Summer 1980): 823–835. For a discussion of the philosophy of punishment with regard to the white-collar criminals, see John Braithwaite, "Challenging Just Deserts: Punishment of White-Collar Criminals," *Journal of Criminal Law & Criminology* 73 (Summer 1982): 723–763.

81. For a statement supporting this position and arguing in favor of criminal prosecution for corporate actions that endanger life and limb, see W. Allen Spurgeon and Terence P. Fagan, "Criminal Liability for Life-Endangering Corporate Conduct," *Journal of Criminal Law & Criminology* 72 (Summer 1981): 400–433.

82. Published in *Justice Assistance News* 3 (October 1982): 7.

83. "Millions Suffer from Computer Phobia," *Chicago Tribune,* reprinted in the *Tulsa World,* November 20, 1983, p. F22, col. 4.

84. "Beware: Hackers at Play: Computer Capers Raise Disturbing New Questions About Security and Privacy," *Newsweek,* September 5, 1983, p. 42.

85. "F.B.I. Is Studying Computer 'Raids,'" *New York Times,* August 12, 1983, p. 9, col. 6.

86. August Bequai, *Computer Crime* (Lexington, Mass.: Heath, 1978), p. xiii.

87. "Computer Crimes Called Rising Problem," *Tulsa World,* September 6, 1980, p. A5, col. 1.

88. U.S. Congress, Senate, 97th, Cong. 1st sess, (daily), 10 January 1979, *Congressional Record* vol. 125: S-726, quoted in Bill D. Colvin, "Computer Crime Investigators: A New Training Field," *FBI Law Enforcement Bulletin* 48 (July 1979): 9.

89. "Crackdown on Computer Capers: Companies Scramble to Safeguard Their Electronic Brains," *Time,* February 8, 1982, p. 60. See also D. B. Parker, *Computer Security Management* (Reston, Va.: Reston, 1981); U.S. Department of Justice, Bureau of Justice Statistics, *Computer Security Techniques* (Washington, D.C.: U.S. Government Printing Office).

90. Bequai, *Computer Crime,* p. 4.

91. Discussed in *Computer Crime: Criminal Resource Manual,* National Criminal Justice Information and Statistics Service (Washington, D.C.: U.S. Government Printing Office, 1979), pp. 9–29.

92. National Criminal Justice Information and Statistics Service, *Computer Crime,* pp. 53–57.

93. "Electronic Fund Transfer and Crime," Bureau of Justice Statistics. Special Report, February 1984, p. 2.

94. U.S. Department of Justice, *The Investigation of Computer Crime: An Operational Guide to White Collar Crime Enforcement* (Washington, D.C.: U.S. Government Printing Office, 1980), p. 5.

95. See Jay Bloombecker, "The Trial of a Computer Crime," *Criminal Defense* 8 (January–February 1981): 7–13.

96. U.S. Code § 552a (1976).

97. Dr. Joseph Weizenbaum, professor of computer science at the Massachusetts Institute of Technology, quoted in "Laws to Bar Computer Misuses Remain Scarce," *New York Times,* August 8, 1983, p. 1, col. 4.

98. Bequai, *Computer Crime,* p. 181. See also U.S. Department of Justice Statistics, *Computer Crime: Electronic Fund Transfer Systems and Crime* (Washington, D.C.: U.S. Government Printing Office, 1982).

99. See Robert T. Anderson, "From Mafia to Cosa Nostra," *American Journal of Sociology* 71 (November 1965): 302–310. See also Donald R. Cressey, *Theft of the Nation: The Structure and Operations of Organized Crime* (New York: Harper & Row, 1969); and Donald R. Cressey, *Criminal Organization* (New York: Harper & Row, 1972). For recent studies of organized crime that failed to reveal a connection between the local organized crime and a national organization, see John A. Gardiner, *The Politics of Corruption: Organized Crime in an American City* (New York: Russell Sage, 1970); and William J. Chambliss, "Vice, Corruption, Bureaucracy, and Power," *Wisconsin Law Review* 4 (1971): 1130–1155.

100. See Giovanni Schiavo. *The Truth About the Mafia* (New York: Vigo Press, 1962). Also see Frederick Sondern, Jr., *Brotherhood of Evil: The Mafia* (New York: Farrar, Straus & Giroux, 1959); Ed Reid, *Mafia* (New York: Random House, 1952); Edward J. Allen, *Merchants of Menace—The Mafia* (Springfield, Ill.:

Chas. C Thomas, 1962); Norman Lewis, *The Honored Society* (New York: Putman, 1964); and Francis A. J. Ianni with Elizabeth Reuss-Ianni, *A Family Business* (New York: Russell Sage, 1972).

101. For a history of organized crime, see Daniel Bell, "Crime as an American Way of Life," *Antioch Review* 13 (June 1953): 131–154; Frederic D. Homer, *Guns and Garlic: Myths and Realities of Organized Crime* (West Lafayette, Ind.: Purdue University Press, 1974); and Donald Cressey, *Theft of the Nation: Organized Crime: Report on the Task Force on Organized Crime,* National Advisory Committee on Criminal Justice Standards and Goals (Washington, D.C.: U.S. Government Printing Office, 1976). See also Guy Tyler, ed., *Organized Crime in America* (Ann Arbor: The University of Michigan Press, 1962); Howard Abadinsky, *The Mafia in America: An Oral History* (New York: Praeger, 1981); and Jonathan Kwitny, *Vicious Circles: The Mafia in the Marketplace* (New York: Norton, 1979).

102. President's Commission on Law Enforcement and Administration of Justice, *The Challenge of Crime in a Free Society* (Washington, D.C.: U.S. Government Printing Office, 1967), p. 187.

103. Francis A. J. Ianni and Elizabeth Reuss-Ianni, "Organized Crime: An Overview," in Sanford H. Kadish, ed. in chief, *Encyclopedia of Crime and Justice,* vol. 3, p. 1095.

104. Ianni and Reuss-Ianni, "Organized Crime."

105. Ianni and Reuss-Ianni, p. 1097.

106. Ianni and Reuss-Ianni, p. 1096.

107. Ianni and Reuss-Ianni, "Organized Crime."

108. For a discussion, see P. Reuter, J. Rubinstein, and S. Wynn, *Racketeering in Legitimate Industries—Two Case Studies—Executive Summary,* U.S. Department of Justice, National Institute of Justice (Washington, D.C.: U.S. Government Printing Office, 1982.

109. "Illegal Dumping of Toxins Laid to Organized Crime," *New York Times,* June 5, 1983, p. 1, col. 1.

110. "How the Mob Really Works," *Newsweek,* January 5, 1981, p. 34.

111. See Joy S. Albanese, "What Lockheed and La Cosa Nostra Have in Common: The Effect of Ideology on Criminal Justice Policy," *Crime & Delinquency* 28 (April 1982): 211–232.

112. As of Janury 31, 1983, organized crime reportedly took its 1,081st murder victim (with the counting starting in 1919), "A Gangland Hit in Chicago," *Newsweek,* January 31, 1983, p. 27. For a discussion on the use of violence in organized crime, see Gilbert Geis, "Violence and Organized Crime," *Annals of the American Academy of Political and Social Science* 364 (March 1966); 85–95; Burton B. Turkus and Sid Feder, *Murder, Inc.* (New York: Farrar, Straus & Giroux, 1952).

113. Cressey, *Theft of the Nation,* p. 7.

Chapter 10

1. See Herbert L. Packer, *The Limits of the Criminal Sanction* (Stanford, Calif.: Stanford University Press, 1968).

2. For an analysis of the developments in the system since 1964, see James O. Rinckenauer, "Crime As a National Political Issue: 1964–76: From Law and Order to Domestic Tranquility," *Crime & Delinquency* 24 (January 1978): 13–27.

3. For a historical account of the development of the accusatorial system, the development of the inquisitorial system, and a comparison of the two systems, see Pendleton Howard, *Criminal Justice in England* (Littleton, Colo.: Fred B. Rothman, 1981), pp. 381–394.

4. See Jerome Frank, *Courts on Trial: Myth and Reality in American Justice,* 1949, reprinted ed. (New York: Atheneum, 1963); and Marvin E. Frankel, *Partisan Justice* (New York: Hill & Wang, 1980).

5. Joint Anti-Fascist Refugee Committee v. McGrath, 341 U.S. 123, 162–163 (1951), Justice Felix Frankfurter concurring.

6. Tehan v. Schott, 382 U.S. 406, 415 (1966).

7. Schmerber v. California, 384 U.S. 767, 772 (1966). On the issue of a reasonable expectation of privacy from governmental intrusion into one's privacy, see Katz v. United States, 389 U.S. 347 (1967); Griswold v. Connecticut, 381 U.S. 479 (1965); and Eisenstadt v. Baird, 405 U.S. 438 (1976).

8. Johnson v. United States, 333 U.S. 10, 13–14 (1948). See also Coolidge v. New Hampshire, 403 U.S. 443 (1971), *reh. den.,* 404 U.S. 874 and Katz v. United States, 389 U.S. 346 (1967).

9. Katz v. United States, 389 U.S. 346, 357. See also Weeks v. United States, 232 U.S. 383; Trupiano v. United States, 334 U.S. 699 (1948); Chi-

mel v. California, 395 U.S. 752 (1969); Harris v. United States, 390 U.S. 234 (1968); and Coolidge v. New Hampshire, 403 U.S. 443. For a recent limitation of Coolidge, see Texas v. Brown, 51 LW 4361 (1983). See also Terry v. Ohio, 392 U.S. 1 (1968).

10. 103 Sup. Ct. 2317 (1983).

11. See Aguilar v. Texas, 378 U.S. 108 (1964) and Spinelli v. United States, 393 U.S. 410 (1969).

12. 342 U.S. 165, 166, 172 (1952).

13. Lee v. Winston, 717 F.2d 888 (4th Cir., 1983), referring to Schmerber v. California, 384 U.S. 767 (1966).

14. Venner v. State, 367 A.2d 949 (Md. Sup. Ct. 1977), cert. denied, 431 U.S. 932 (1977).

15. "Outrage in the Station House: Some Police Strip-Search Women Even for Traffic Violations," Time, March 19, 1979, p. 36.

16. Mary Beth G. v. City of Chicago, 723 F. 2d 1263 (7th Cir. 1983), footnotes omitted.

17. 441 U.S. 520 (1979).

18. Roscom v. City of Chicago, 570 F.Supp. 1259, 1262 (N.D.Ill., E.D., 1983).

19. United States v. United States District Court, 407 U.S. 297, 313 (1972).

20. Coolidge v. New Hampshire, 403 U.S. 443, 474–475.

21. 367 U.S. 643 (1961).

22. 367 U.S. 643, 644.

23. Payton v. New York, 445 U.S. 573 (1980).

24. 455 U.S. 573, 589–590.

25. Welsh v. Wisconsin, U.S. Law Week 52 (May 15, 1984): 4581. See also "Fourth Amendment Cases Dominated High Court's Criminal Law Decisions," U.S. Law Week 52 (September 13, 1983): 1039–1040. For a brief summary of the recent cases decided by the Court in this area, see "Nine Key Decisions Expand Authority to Search and Seize," American Bar Association Journal 69 (November 1983): 1740–1748.

26. Edward Bennett Williams, quoted in Alexander B. Smith and Harriet Pollack, Crime and Justice in a Mass Society (Waltham, Mass.: Xerox College Publishing, 1972), p. 194.

27. 297 U.S. 278 (1936).

28. 384 U.S. 436 (1966).

29. 384 U.S. 436, 445–458 (footnotes and citations omitted).

30. Des Moines Register, October 12, 1968.

31. Abraham S. Blumberg, "Law and Order: The Counterfeit Crusade," in Blumberg, ed., The Scales of Justice (Chicago: Aldine, 1970), p. 16.

32. For a review of United States Supreme Court cases under the Miranda ruling, see Alan N. Lane and Richard D. Grossman, "Miranda: The Erosion of a Doctrine," Criminal Defense 8 (July–August 1981): 23–27. These authors argue that later court decisions have undermined the Miranda doctrine.

33. Oregon v. Mathiason, 429 U.S. 492 (1977).

34. Minnesota v. Murphy, U.S. Law Week 52 (February 21, 1984): 4246.

35. New York v. Quarles, 104 S. Ct. 2626 (1984): Nix v. Williams, U.S. Law Week 52 (June 12, 1984), and Massachusetts v. Sheppard, U.S. Law Week 52 (July 1984).

36. Betts v. Brady, 316 U.S. 455 (1942).

37. 372 U.S. 335 (1963). See also Argersinger v. Hamlin, 407 U.S. 25 (1972).

38. For a general discussion of the issues on effective assistance of counsel, see Geoffrey P. Alpert, "Effective Assistance of Counsel: The Exchange Theory," Criminal Law Bulletin 17 (September–October 1981), 381–404; David Bazelon, "The Defective Assistance of Counsel," University of Cincinnati Law Review 42 (Winter–Spring 1973): 1–46. See also United States v. DeCoster, 487 F.2d 1197, rehearing 598 F.2d 311 (D.C.Cir. 1979), cert. denied; 444 U.S. 944 (1979); David Bazelon, "The Realities of Gideon and Argersinger," Georgetown Law Journal 64 (Summer–Fall 1976): 811–838.

39. United States v. Ash, 413 U.S. 300 (1973); and see United State v. Wade, 388 U.S. 218, 227 (1967).

40. Anders v. California, 386 U.S. 738, 744 (1967).

41. McMann v. Richardson, 397 U.S. 759, 771 (1970). See also Wainwright v. Torna, 455 U.S. 586 (1982).

42. Javor v. United States, 724 F.2d 831 (9th Cir. 1984).

43. Strickland v. Washington, 52 U.S. Law Week, (May 15, 1984).

44. See David W. Neubauer and John Paul Ryan, "Criminal Courts and the Delivery of Speedy Justice: the Influence of Case and Defendant Characteristics," Justice System Journal 7 (Summer 1982): 213–235.

45. On the issue of the right to a public trial, see the following recent cases: Globe Newspaper Company v. Superior Court, etc., 102 S.Ct. 2613 (1982), holding that "to justify the exclusion of the press and public from criminal trials, the state must show that closure is necessitated by a compelling governmental interest and is nar-

rowly tailored to serve that interest." This case involved a Massachusetts statue requiring the trial judges to exclude the press and the general public from trials that pertained to specified sexual offenses with victims under the age of eighteen. The Court did not preclude excluding the public except on a routine basis without compelling reasons for the exclusion.

46. Taylor v. Louisiana, 419 U.S. 522, 530 (1975). For a recent interpretation, see United States v. Nelson, 718 F.2d 315 (9th Cir., 1983).

47. Jury Selection and Service Act of 1968, 28 U.S. Code §1861.

48. See United States v. Bearden, 659 F.2d 590 (5th Cir. 1981), *cert. denied,* 456 U.S. 936 (1982). Rather, the "essence of randomness is the absence of any arbitrary attempt to exclude a class of persons from the jury," McClendon v. United States, 587 F.2d 384 (8th Cir. 1978), *cert. denied,* 440 U.S. 983 (1979). See also United States v. Hawkins, 566 F.2d 1006, 1014 (5th Cir. 1978), *cert. denied,* 439 U.S. 848 (1978).

49. Taylor v. Louisiana, 419 U.S. 522, 538 (1975).

50. See Smith v. Texas, 311 U.S. 128, 130 (1940). See also Peters v. Kiff, 407 U.S. 493 (1972).

51. See Taylor v. Louisiana, 419 U.S. 522; and Duren v. Missouri, 439 U.S. 335 (1979).

52. See, for example, Michael J. Saks, *Jury Verdicts* (Lexington, Mass.: Lexington Books, 1977); and Robert T. Raper, "The Effect of a Jury's Size and Decision Rule on the Accuracy of Evidence Recall," *Social Science Quarterly* 67 (June 1981): 352–361.

53. Williams v. Florida, 399 U.S. 78 (1970).

54. Ballew v. Georgia, 435 U.S. 223 (1978).

55. Burch v. Louisiana, 441 U.S. 130, 138 (1979).

56. Apodaca v. Oregon, 406 U.S. 404 (1972).

57. 391 U.S. 510, 512–514, 518–523 (1968).

58. Sheppard v. Maxwell, 384 U.S. 333 (1966).

59. 384 U.S. 333, 349 (1966), citations omitted.

61. For a discussion of this controversy, see Joseph R. Weisberger, "The Supreme Court and the Press: Is Accommodation Possible?" *The Judges' Journal* 19 (Winter 1980): 14–15.

62. "Private Justice, Public Injustice," *New York Times,* July 5, 1979, p. A16, col. 1.

63. "Slamming the Courtroom Doors," *Time,* July 16, 1979, p. 66.

64. Richmond Newspapers, Inc. v. Virginia, 448 U.S. 555 (1980).

65. See Globe Newspaper Co. v. Superior Court, etc., 102 S.Ct. 2613 (1982), mentioned earlier. See also the Court's recent holding concerning the right of the public, except in rare instances, to attend jury selection proceedings. Press-Enterprise Co. v. Superior Court of California, Riverside County, *U.S. Law Week* 52, (January 18, 1984): 4113.

66. Lana Istnick, "Research and Resources: Room 707," *Gusher* (December 1982): 18.

67. "Judges Examine Victim Participation In Court Proceedings," *Justice Assistance News* (December 1983–January 1984): 11.

68. For a history of the development of victim compensation programs and analysis of the need for such programs see Sue Titus Reid and Lorna Keltner, *Criminal Justice,* (N.Y.: Holt, Rinehart and Winston, 1985), Chapter 3.

69. 18 U.S. Code § 1501, sec. 2.

70. 18 U.S. Code § 3579.

71. 18 U.S. Code §§ 3579 and 3580.

72. United States v. Welden, 568 F.Supp. 516, 536 (N.D.Ala., 1983). Another federal court however, upheld the constitutionality of the Act. See U.S. v. Brown, Crim. No. 83-372, 7/10/84 (E.D.Pa.).

73. Cal. Const. Art. I, 28.

74. Brosnahan v. Brown, 186 Cal. Rptr. 30 (Ca.Sup.Ct. 1982).

75. Robert Bolt, *A Man for All Seasons* (New York: Vintage Paperbacks, Random House, 1962), pp. 37–38.

Chapter 11

1. For an overview of the development of police systems, see David H. Bayley, "Police: History," in Sanford H. Kadish, editor in chief, *Encyclopedia of Crime and Justice,* vol. 3 (New York: Free Press, 1983), pp. 1120–1125; and Richard J. Lundman, *Police and Policing: An Introduction* (New York: Holt, Rinehart and Winston, 1980) For information on the English system, see also W. L. Melville Lee, *A History of Police in England* (London: Methuen, 1901). For information on the history of the police system in this country, see James F. Richardson, *The New York Police: Colonial Times to 1901* (New York: Oxford University Press, 1970); Roger Lane, *Policing the City: Boston, 1822–1885* (Cambridge, Mass.: Harvard University Press, 1967); Kenneth G. Alfers, *"The Washington Police: A History, 1800–1886"* (Ph.D. diss., George Washington University, 1975); and Jonathan Rubinstein, *City Police* (New York: Ballantine, 1973).

2. For a discussion of state police, see Robert Borkenstein, "Police: State Police," in Kadish, ed., *Encyclopedia of Crime and Justice,* vol. 3, pp. 1131–1135. For a discussion of urban police, see Egon Bittner, "Police: Urban Police," in Kadish, ed., pp. 1135–1139.

3. For the history of the FBI, see Richard E. Morgan, "Federal Bureau of Investigation: History," in Kadish, ed., *Encyclopedia of Crime and Justice,* vol. 2, pp. 768–775. For the enforcement of federal laws, see Norman Abrams, "Federal Criminal Law Enforcement," in Kadish, ed., pp. 779–785.

4. See Arthur Niederhoffer, *Behind the Shield: The Police in Urban Society* (Garden City, N.Y.: Doubleday, 1969).

5. President's Commission on Law Enforcement and the Administration of Justice, *The Challenge of Crime in a Free Society* (Washington, D.C.: U.S. Government Printing Office, 1967), p. 109.

6. U.S. Congress, House, 97th, Cong. 2nd sess., (daily), 24 March 1983, *Congressional Record,* vol. 128: E 1256.

7. Larry T. Hoover, *Police Educational Characteristics and Curricula,* U.S. Department of Justice, LEAA, and National Institute of Law Enforcement and Criminal Justice (Washington, D.C.: U.S. Government Printing Office, July 1975), pp. 217–218.

8. See, for example, Paul Chevigny, *Police Power* (New York: Vintage Books, 1969), pp. 272–273.

9. For a variety of articles on police education, see the symposium on education and training of police in *Police Chief* 50 (October 1983). See also R. Thomas Dull, "Current Issues in Criminal Justice Education: Aftermath of the Sherman Report," *Journal of Police Science and Administration* 10 (September 1981); 315–325; and L. Sherman, *The Quality of Police Education* (San Francisco: Jossey-Bass, 1978).

10. *Who Is Guarding the Guardians? A Report on Police Practices.* A Report of the United States Commission on Civil Rights (October 1981), p. 153.

11. "L.I. Police Force Sued by the U.S. for Bias on Jobs: Hiring Termed Unfair to Women and Minorities," *New York Times,* June 25, 1983, p. 11, col 6. For a discussion of the variable of race and its relationship to allocation of resources within police departments, see Pamela Irving Jackson and Leo Carroll, "Race and the War on Crime: The Sociopolitical Determinants of Municipal Police Expenditures in 90 Non-Southern U.S. Cities," *American Sociological Review* 46 (June 1981); 290–305; and Lee Carroll and Pamela Irving Jackson, "Minority Composition, Inequality and the Growth of Municipal Police Forces, 1960–71," *Sociological Focus* 15 (October 1982): 327–345.

12. Bratton v. City of Detroit, 704 Fed.2d 878 (6th Cir., 1983), Rehearing and Rehearing En Banc *denied* August 4, 1983, *cert. denied,* No. 83–551, *U. S. Law Week* 52 (1984): 3499.

13. "Spotlight" Lee Brown," *The National Centurion* 1 (August 1983), 15. See also "Houston's New Police Chief," *Newsweek,* March 22, 1982, p. 38.

14. For a discussion of the history of women in policing, see Barry D. Mishkin, "Female Police in the United States," *The Police Journal* 54 (January 1981): 22–33, and Daniel J. Bell, "Policewomen: Myths and Reality," *Journal of Police Science and Administration* 10 (March 1982): 112–120.

15. The actions are brought under Title VII of the 1964 Civil Rights Act, 42 U.S.C. § 20000 (1964), amended by 42 U.S.C. § 20000 (1972).

16. See Horace v. City of Pontiac, 625 F.2d 765 (6th Cir. 1980).

17. Costa v. Markey, 706 F.2d 1 (1st Cir., 1983).

18. Robert J. Homant, "The Impact of Policewomen on Community Attitudes Toward Police," *Journal of Police Science and Administration* 11 (March 1983): 17–22.

19. For an interesting discussion of this issue, see Susan E. Martin, "Policewomen and Policewomen," *Journal of Police Science and Administration* 7 (September 1979): 314–323.

20. For a discussion see Michael T. Charles, "Women in Policing: The Physical Aspect," *Journal of Police Science and Administration* 10 (June 1982): 194–205.

21. Charles, p. 198.

22. See J. J. Preiss and J. J. Ehrlich, *An Examination of Role Theory: The Case of the State Police* (Lincoln: University of Nebraska Press, 1966); and Niederhoffer, *Behind the Shield.*

23. Robert M. Regoli and Eric D. Poole, "Measurement of Police Cynicism: A Factor Scaling Approach," *Journal of Criminal Justice* 7 (Spring 1979): 37–51. Quotation is on p. 46.

24. Robert M. Regoli, Eric D. Poole, and John D. Hewitt, "Exploring the Empirical Relationship between Police Cynicism and Work Alienation," *Journal of Police Science and Administration* 7 (September 1979): 336–339.

25. Dennis Jay Wiechman, "Police Cynicism toward the Judicial Process," *Journal of Police Science and Administration* 7 (September 1979): 340–345. See also Ernest V. Chandler and Claude S. Jones, "Cynicism—An Inevitability of Police Work?" *Journal of Police Science and Administration* 7 (March 1979): 65–68.

26. See John H. McNamara, "Uncertainties in Police Work: The Relevance of Police Recruits' Backgrounds and Training," in David J. Bordua, ed., *The Police: Six Sociological Essays* (New York: Wiley, 1967), pp. 163–252, and Niederhoffer, *Behind the Shield,* p. 160.

27. *Who is Guarding the Guardians?,* pp. 154–155. For studies on the relationship between personality and effective policing, see K. Robert C. Adlam, "The Police Personality: Psychological Consequences of Being a Police Officer," *Journal of Police Science and Administration* 10 (September 1982): 344–349; David Lester et al., "The Personality and Attitudes of Female Police Officers: Needs, Androgyny, and Attitudes Toward Rape," *Journal of Police Science and Administration* 10 (September 1982): 357–360; and John A. Johnson and Robert Hogan, "Vocational Interests, Personality and Effective Police Performance," *Personnel Psychology* 34 (Spring 1981): 49–53.

28. Michael K. Brown, *Working the Street: Police Discretion and the Dilemmas of Reform* (New York: Russell Sage Foundation, 1981), pp. xii, 7.

29. Herman Goldstein, *Policing A Free Society,* (Cambridge, Mass.: Ballinger, 1977), p. 263.

30. Clarence Schrag, *Crime and Justice American Style,* National Institute of Mental Health Center for Studies of Crime and Delinquency (Washington, D.C.: U.S. Government Printing Office, 1972), pp. 125–126.

31. Peter K. Manning, "The Police: Mandate, Strategies, and Appearances," in Jack D. Douglas, ed., *Crime and Justice in American Society* (Indianapolis, Ind.: Bobbs-Merrill, 1971), p. 176.

32. The President's Commission on Law Enforcement and Administration of Justice, *Task Force Report: The Police* (Washington, D.C.: U.S. Government Printing Office, 1967, p. 1.

33. Herbert L. Packer, *The Limits of the Criminal Sanction* (Stanford, Calif.: Stanford University Press, 1968), p. 283.

34. James F. Richardson, *Urban Police in the United States* (Port Washington, N.Y.: Kennikat Press, 1974), p. x.

35. Discussed in Hoover, *Police Educational Characterstics and Curricula.*

36. James Q. Wilson, *Varieties of Police Behavior: The Management of Law and Order in Eight Communities* (Cambridge, Mass.: Harvard University Press, 1968), p. 21.

37. See, for example, Eva S. Buzawa, "Police Officer Response to Domestic Violence Legislation in Michigan," *Journal of Police Science and Administration* 10 (December 1982): 415–424.

38. *Tulsa World,* October 8, 1977, p. 1, col. 5.

39. Hoover, *Police Educational Characteristics and Curricula,* p. 9.

40. Rubinstein, *City Police,* p. 350.

41. See Wilson, *Varieties of Police Behavior,* p. 18.

42. Albert J. Reiss, Jr., *The Police and the Public* (New Haven, Conn.: Yale University Press, 1971), pp. 63, 64, 71. For a discussion of these and other studies, see Goldstein, *Policing a Free Society,* pp. 24–25. See also Jerome H. Skolnick, *Justice Without Trial,* 2nd ed. (New York: John Wiley, 1975).

43. Richard J. Lundman, "Police Patrol Work: A Comparative Perspective," in Lundman, ed., *Police Behavior,* p. 55.

44. Goldstein, *Policing a Free Society,* p. 29.

45. Lundman, "Police Work," in Lundman, ed., *Police Behavior,* p. 64.

46. See R. I. Mawby, "Overcoming the Barriers of Privacy: Police Strategies Against Nonvisible Crime," *Criminology* 18 (February 1981): 501–521.

47. Wilson, *Varieties of Police Behavior,* p. 53. See also M. Michael Fagan and Kenneth Ayers, Jr., "The Life of a Police Officer: A Developmental Perspective," *Criminal Justice and Behavior* 9 (September 1982): 273–285.

48. Wilson, *Varieties of Police Behavior,* pp. 19, 29.

49. Wilson, p. 25.

50. Russell Golesh, "Thank God for a Wife Who Cares," *Police Stress* 1 (Spring 1979): 17, quoted in James D. Sewell, "Police Stress," *FBI Law Enforcement Bulletin* 50 (April 1981): 7. See also Peter E. Maynard and Nancy E.

Maynard, "Stress in Police Families: Some Policy Implications," *Journal of Police Science and Administration* 10 (September 1982): 302–314.

51. Terry Eisenberg, "Job Stress and the Police Officer: Identifying Stress Reduction Techniques," in William H. Kroes and Joseph J. Hurrell, eds., *Job Stress and the Police Officer: Identifying Stress Reduction Techniques* (Proceedings of Symposium, Cincinnati, Ohio, May 8–9, 1975), (Washington, D.C.: U.S. Government Printing Office).

52. Jerry Dash and Martin Reiser, "Suicide Among Police in Urban Law Enforcement Agencies," *Journal of Police Science and Administration* 6 (March 1978): 18, quoted in W. Clinton Terry, III, "Police Stress: The Empirical Evidence," *Journal of Police Science and Administration* 9 (March 1981): 70. See also Judie Graffin Wexler and Deana Dorman Logan, "Sources of Stress Among Women Police Officers," *Journal of Police Science and Administration* 11 (March 1983): 46–53; and David Lester, Fred Gronau, and Kenneth Wondrack, "The Personality and Attitudes of Female Police Officers: Needs, Androgyny, and Attitudes Toward Rape," *Journal of Police Science and Administration* 10 (September 1983): 357–360.

53. For a bibliography and discussion of these studies, see Terry, "Police Stress," pp. 67–68.

54. Christina Maslach and Susan E. Jackson, "Burned-out Cops and Their Families," *Psychology Today* 12 (May 1979): 59.

55. Peter E. Maynard and Nancy E. Maynard, "Stress in Police Families: Some Policy Implications," *Journal of Police Science and Administration* 10 (September 1982): 312.

56. Maslach and Jackson, "Burned-Out Cops," 61–62.

57. For a review of the research, see Terry, "Police Stress," 68–69. See also Leonard Territo and Harold J. Vetter, "Stress and Police Personnel," *Journal of Police Science and Administration* 9 (June 1981): 199–201.

58. Quoted in Anne Choen, "I've Killed That Man Ten Thousand Times," in *Police Magazine* (July 1980): 17–23. On stress in general, see John M. Violanti, "Stress Patterns in Police Work: A Longitudinal Study," *Journal of Police Science and Administration* 11 (June 1983): 211–216; Sam E. White and Kenneth E. Marino, "Job Attitudes and Police Stress: An Exploratory Study of Causation," *Journal of Police Science and Administration* 11 (September 1983): 264–274; and W. Clinton Terry, III, "Police Stress as an Individual and Administrative Problem: Some Conceptual and Theoretical Difficulties," *Journal of Police Science and Administration* 11 (June 1983): 156–165.

59. Dr. Martin Reiser, who holds an Ed.D. degree, has written extensively about police psychology. His latest book is a collection of papers in the field: *Police Psychology: Collected Papers* (Los Angeles: Lehi Publishing, 1982).

60. This information comes from two articles in the February 4, 1982 issue of the *Los Angeles Times*, pt. V, sec. 1. Some courts have recognized the relationship between stress in policing and physical problems, including heart attacks and other physical problems resulting in death, and have awarded pensions to the survivors of the officer. See, for example, Borough of Aliquippa v. Workmen's Compensation Appeal Board, 336 A.2d 450 (Pa. 1975), (officer suffered heart attack while trying to break up a gang fight), Gaughan v. Comm. State Police, 67, Lack. Jur. 9 (Pa. 1966), heart attack of officer caused by severe emotional strain suffered while attending a serious accident; and Oklahoma v. Schooner, 535 P.2d 688 (Okla. 1975), peptic ulcer resulting in death of officer because of work-related stress.

61. Bill Sommerville, "Double Standards in Law Enforcement with Regard to Minority Status," *Issues in Criminology* 4 (Fall 1968):39.

62. Arthur I. Waskow, "Community Control of the Police," *Trans-Action* 6 (December 1969): 4.

63. Ronald K. Tauber, "Danger and the Police: A Theoretical Analysis," *Issues in Criminology* 3 (Summer 1967): pp. 72, 74, 79.

64. Foreword by Charles R. Gain, Chief of Police, Oakland, Calif., in Hans Toch, J. Douglas Grant, and Raymond T. Galbin, eds., *Agents of Change: A Study in Police Reform* (New York: John Wiley, 1975).

65. Mary Jeanette C. Hageman, "Who Joins the Force for What Reasons: An Argument for 'The New Breed,'" *Journal of Police Science and Administration* 7 (June 1979): 206–210. Quotation is on p. 210.

66. Rubinstein, *City Police*, pp. 262–264.

67. Nathan Goldman, *The Differential Selection of Juvenile Offenders for Court Appearance* (New York: National Council on Crime and Delinquency, 1963). See also Irving Piliavin and Scott Briar "Police Encounters with Juveniles,"

American Journal of Sociology 70 (September 1964): 206–214. These studies relate to juveniles only.

68. Cal. Penal Code § 645 (e).
69. Kolender et al. v. Lawson, *U. S. Law Week* 51 (1983): 4532.
70. *U. S. Law Week* 51: 4533.
71. Mallory v. United States, 354 U.S. 449, 456 (1957). This case involved a rape by a masked black man. All three blacks who had access to the basement where the rape occurred and who fit the general description of the rapist were arrested.
72. Goldman, *The Differential Selection of Juvenile Offenders.*
73. See William J. Chambliss and John T. Liell, "The Legal Process in the Community Setting," *Crime and Delinquency* 12 (October 1966): 310–317. See also T. C. Esselstyn, "The Social Role of the County Sheriff," *Journal of Criminal Law, Criminology, and Police Science* 44 (July–August 1953): 177–184.
74. Rubinstein, *City Police,* pp. 151–152.
75. Richard J. Lundman, "Routine Arrest Practices: A Commonweal Perspective," *Social Problems* 22 (October 1974): 127–141; Lundman, "Organizational Norms and Police Discretion: An Observational Study of Police Work with Traffic Law Violators," *Criminology* 17 (August 1979): 159–171. See also Lundman, *Police and Policing.*
76. Donald Black, "The Social Organization of Arrest," *Stanford Law Review* 23 (June 1971): 1104–1109, emphasis omitted.
77. Mattis v. Schnarr, 547 F.2d 1607, 1016 (8th Cir. 1976), vacated, Ashcroft v. Mattis, 431 U.S. 171 (1977).
78. Tenn. Code Ann. § 40–808 (1975).
79. Garner v. Memphis Police Dept, 710 F.2d 240, 244, 266 (6th Cir. 1983). The U.S. Supreme Court has agreed to hear two cases on this issue. Tennessee v. Garner, No. 83–1035; and Memphis Police Dept. v. Garner, No. 83–1070, during the 1984–85 term.
80. United States v. City of Philadelphia, 482 F.Supp. 1248 (E.D.Pa. 1979), aff'd, 644 F.2d 187 (3rd Cir. 1980).
81. "Philadelphia Accord Set on Suit on Police Hiring," *New York Times,* August 13, 1983, p. 6, col. 6.
82. CBS News "60 Minutes," June 24, 1984.
83. In March, 1984, a police officer was acquitted by an all-white jury of the charge of manslaughter in the shooting death of a black. The shooting led to three days of rioting in Miami, Florida, in 1982. The acquittal of the Hispanic officer was also followed by rioting by black youths.
84. "Koch Defends the Police at Hearing on Brutality," *New York Times,* November 29, 1983, p. 1, col. 1.
85. Arnold Binder and Peter Scharf, "Deadly Force in Law Enforcement," *Crime & Delinquency* 28 (January 1982): 1, 23. See also James J. Fyfe, "Blind Justice: Police Shootings in Memphis," *Journal of Criminal Law & Criminology* 73 (Summer 1982): 721.
86. See Catherine H. Milton et al., *Police Use of Deadly Force* (Washington, D.C.: Police Foundation, 1977), pp. 3–4, for a discussion of such findings.
87. See National Minority Advisory Council on Criminal Justice, *The Inequality of Justice: A Report on Crime and the Administration of Justice in the Minority Community* (October 1980); pp. 15–16.
88. President's Commission on Law Enforcement and Administration of Justice, *Task Force Report: The Police* (Washington, D.C.: U.S. Government Printing Office, 1967), pt. II, chap. 4, as quoted in *Who Is Guarding the Guardians?,* pp. vi–vii.
89. Nicholas Pileggi, "The War on the Cops," *New York,* March 17, 1980, pp. 31, 32.
90. Mona Margarita, "Killing the Police: Myths and Motives," *The Annals of the American Academy of Political and Social Science* 452 (November 1980): 63.
91. *Justice Assistance News,* May 19, 1983, p. 15.
92. Milton et al., *Police Use of Deadly Force,* p. 3. See also David Lester, "Civilians Who Kill Police Officers and Police Officers Who Kill Civilians: A Comparison of American Cities," *Journal of Police Science and Administration* 10 (December 1982): 384–387.
93. William A. Westley, "Violence and the Police," *American Journal of Sociology* 49 (July 1953): 39, 161, 163.
94. Paul Chevigny, *Police, Power: Police Abuses in New York City* (New York: Random House, 1969), p. 283.
95. Hans Toch, *Police, Prisons, and the Problems of Violence* (Washington, D.C.: U.S. Government Printing Office, 1977), pp. 31–32.
96. Westley, "Violence and the Police," pp. 35–38, 62–63.

97. *The Knapp Commission Report on Police Corruption* (New York: Braziller, 1972), p. 13.
98. *Knapp Commission Report*, p. 260.
99. "Police Say Isolated Cheating Has Replaced Corruption Found By Knapp Inquiry," *New York Times,* January 26, 1981, p. 2, col. 1.
100. Goldstein, *Policing a Free Society,* p. 218.
101. "Drug Abuse by Police Called New York Force's Key Worry," *New York Times,* June 26, 1983, p. 15, col 1. For reports on police corruption in Chicago, see Herbert Beigel and Allan Beigel, *Beneath the Badge: A Story of Police Corruption* (New York: Harper & Row, 1977). For a more recent report of police corruption that is still under investigation, see "A True Prince of the City: In Chicago a Cop Goes Undercover to Crack a Police Dope Ring," *Time,* July 26, 1982, p. 17.
102. Lawrence W. Sherman, ed., *Police Corruption: A Sociological Perspective* (Garden City, N.Y.: Doubleday, 1974), p. 6.
103. Wilson, *Varieties of Police Behavior,* Chapters 5–7, pp. 140–226.
104. Sherman, *Police Corruption,* pp. 7–8.
105. *Knapp Commission Report,* p. 4.
106. Sherman, *Police Corruption,* pp. 1–39.
107. Sherman, p. 31, referring to the work of Alvin Gouldner.
108. Sherman, pp. 196–201. See Ellwyn R. Stoddard, "'The Informal Code' of Police Deviancy: A Group Approach to 'Blue-Coat Crime,'" *Journal of Criminal Law, Criminolgy, and Police Science* 59 (June 1968): 204, 212, 213.
109. Niederhoffer, *Behind the Shield,* p. 74.
110. Rubinstein, *City Police,* pp. 392–393.
111. Weeks v. United States, 232 U.S. 383 (1914).
112. Mapp v. Ohio, 367 U.S. 643 (1961).
113. Yale Kamisar, "The Search and Seizure of America," *Human Rights* 10 (Winter 1982): 14, referring to the analysis of Stanford law professor John Kaplan, a critic of the exclusionary rule.
114. Olmstead v. United States, 277 U.S. 438, 485 (1928), Justice Brandeis, dissenting. See also Stephen H. Sachs, "The Exclusionary Rule: A Prosecutor's Defense," *Criminal Justice Ethics* 1 (Summer–Fall 1982). This journal contains a symposium on the pros and cons of the exclusionary rule and is an excellent source on the topic.
115. Elkins v. United States, 364 U.S. 206, 217 (1960).
116. Sachs, "The Exclusionary Rule," 31. See also United States v. Janis, 428 U.S. 433, 499–53 (1976), referring to the methodological problems of these studies.
117. Sachs, p. 32.
118. People v. Defore, 150 N.E. 585, 587 (N.Y. Ct. App., 1926).
119. A study in California reported that less than one-half of 1 percent of the felony cases resulted in dismissal because of the exclusionary rule—that is, without the illegally seized evidence, there was not sufficient evidence to convict the defendant. Cited by Paul J. Cleary, "The Exclusionary Rule: Criminal Law's Best-Known, Most Controversial, Least-Understood Provision," *Tulsa World,* May 29, 1983, sec. I, p. 1, col. 1.
120. See Comptroller General of the United States, *Impact of the Exclusionary Rule on Federal Criminal Prosecutions* (Washington, D.C.: United States Government Printing Office, April 19, 1979), p. 1.
121. See United States v. Williams, 622 F.2d 830 (5th Cir. 1980 (en banc) Alternative holding, *cert. denied,* 449 U.S. 1127 (1981).
122. Gates v. Illinois, 103 S.Ct. 2317 (1982).
123. Massachusetts v. Sheppard, 441 N.E.2d 725 (Sup.Jud.Ct.Mass. 1982), *reversed U.S. Law Week* 52 (June 26, 1984): 5177. In June of 1984 the Court ruled that illegally seized evidence is admissible if the police would have found it anyway, later, by legal methods. The Court calls this the "inevitable discovery exception to the exclusionary rule." Nix v. Willams, *U.S. Law Week* 52 (June 14, 1984): 4732.
124. *Knapp Commission Report,* p. 90.
125. *Knapp Commission Report,* p. 132.
126. Don R. Derning, "Police and Public Cooperation," in H. Cohn and E. Viano, eds., *Police Community Relations: Images, Roles, Realities* (Philadelphia: Lippincott, 1976), p. 25.
127. See Arthur I. Waskow, "Community Control of the Police," *Trans-Action* 7 (December 1969): 4–7.
128. Timothy D. Naegele, "Civilian Complaints Against the Police in Los Angeles," *Issues in Criminology* 3 (Summer 1967): 7–25. Civil suits against police officers are, however, difficult to win. It is difficult to get police to report other police for violations of civil rights or to testify against their co-workers when suits are filed. See Chevigny, *Police Power,* pp. 249–251.

129. *U.S. News & World Report,* November 1, 1982, p. 43.
130. For a series of articles on the balance between police power and individual rights and liberties, see the symposium in *University of Toledo Law Review* 13 (1983).
131. Skolnick, *Justice Without Trial,* pp. 238–239.
132. James Leo Walsh, "Professionalism and the Police: The Cop As Medical Student," *American Behavioral Scientist* 13 (May–August 1970): 705–725.
133. Peter K. Manning, "The Police: Mandate, Strategies, and Appearances," in Jack D. Douglas, ed., *Crime and Justice in America: A Critical Understanding* (Boston: Little, Brown, 1974), pp. 171, 186–191.
134. Manning, pp. 171, 186–191. See also Peter K. Manning, *Police Work: The Social Organization of Policing* (Cambridge, Mass.: Ballinger, 1978).
135. President's Commission on Law Enforcement and Adminstration of Justice, *The Challenge of Crime in a Free Society* (Washington, D.C.: U.S. Government Printing Office, 1967), p. ix.
136. *Knapp Commission Report,* p. 32.
137. Manning, "The Police: Mandate, Strategies and Appearances," pp. 198–199.
138. Jerome Skolnick, *Politics of Protest* (New York: Touchstone Books, 1969), pp. 290–291.
139. Morton Bard, "Family Intervention Police Teams as a Community Mental Health Resource," *The Journal of Criminal Law, Criminology, and Police Science* 60 (1969): 247–250.
140. See Kenneth Culp Davis, *Police Discretion* (St. Paul, Minn.: West Publishing, 1975).
141. Milton et al., *Police Use of Deadly Force,* p. 47.
142. Arthur L. Kobler, "Police Homicide in a Democracy," *Journal of Social Issues* 31 (1975): 167. See also *Police Use of Deadly Force: What Police and the Community Can Do About It.* A Workshop Conducted by the Community Relations Service at the 1978 Annual Conference of the National Association of Human Rights Workers. U.S. Department of Justice (Washington, D.C.: U.S. Government Printing Office, 1978). See also the symposium on the use of deadly force and firearms training, *Police Chief* 50 (May 1983).
143. See Lawrence C. Sherman's article for a more detailed discussion, along with an excellent bibliography: "Causes of Police Behavior: The Current State of Quantitative Research," *Journal of Research in Crime and Delinquency* 16 (January 1979): 69–100.

Chapter 12

1. Powell v. Alabama, 287 U.S. 45, 57 (1932).
2. Gerstein v. Pugh, 420 U.S. 103, 112 (1975).
3. See, for example, Anne Rankin, "The Effect of Pre-Trial Detention," *New York University Law Review* 39 (June 1964): 641. See also Patricia Wald, "Foreword" to Rankin, p. 631. See also Caleb Foote et al., "Compelling Appearance in Court: Administration of Bail in Philadelphia," *University of Pennsylvania Law Review* 102 (June 1954): 1031–1079; Foote, ed., *Studies on Bail* (Philadelphia: University of Pennsylvania Law School, Institute of Legal Research, 1966). See also Paul B. Wice, *Freedom for Sale: A National Study of Pretrial Release* (Lexington, Mass.: Heath, 1974).
4. A. Keith Bottomley, *Decisions in the Penal Process* (South Hackensack, N.J.: Fred B. Rothman, 1973), pp. 88–92.
5. Gerald R. Wheeler and Carol L. Wheeler, "Reflections on Legal Representation of the Economically Disadvantaged: Beyond Assembly Line Justice," *Crime & Delinquency* 26 (July 1980): 319–332. See also John S. Goldkamp, "Pretrial Custody and Later Judicial Outcomes," chap. 9, in Goldkamp, ed., *Two Classes of Accused: A Study of Bail and Detention in American Justice* (Cambridge, Mass.: Ballinger, 1979).
6. The President's Commission on Law Enforcement and Administration of Justice, *Task Force Report: Corrections* (Washington, D.C.: U.S. Government Printing Office, 1967), p. 25.
7. For a more detailed discussion, see National Advisory Commission on Criminal Justice Standards and Goals, *Corrections* (Washington, D.C.: U.S. Government Printing Office, 1973), pp. 107, 109. For a recent analysis of ROR, see Tim S. Bynum, "Release on Recognizance: Substantive or Superficial Reform?" *Criminology* 20 (May 1982): 67–82.
8. For a discussion of the bail system in England, see in Pendleton Howard, *Criminal Justice in England* (Littleton, Colo.: Fred B. Rothman, 1981), pp. 336–342.
9. In re Underwood, 508 P.2d 721, 723 (Cal. Sup. Ct. 1973). For a brief overview on the right to

bail, see Wayne R. LaFave, "Bail: The Right to Bail," in Sanford Kadish, editor in chief, *Encyclopedia of Crime and Justice,* vol. 1 (New York: Free Press, 1983), pp. 99–107.

10. Stack v. Boyle, 342 U.S. 1, 5 (1951).

11. Lewis Katz, Lawrence Litwin, and Richard Bamberger, *Justice Is the Crime* (Cleveland: Case Western Reserve University Press, 1972), p. 138.

12. District of Columbia Court Reform Act of 1970, D.C. Code Encyl. §§ 23-1321 et. seq.

13. Calif. Const. Art. I §28. See also Nebr. Const. Art. I, § 9; Wis. State Stats. § 969.035; and Mich. Const. Art. I § 15.

14. U.S. v. Edwards, 430 A.2d 1321 (D.C.Ct.App. 1981).

15. Hunt v. Roth, 648 F.2d 1148 (8th Cir. 1981), *vacated on other grounds*, Murphy v. Hunt, 455 U.S. 478 (1982).

16. Government of Virgin Islands v. Leycock, 678 F.2d 467 (3d Cir. 1982).

17. See Jerome Skolnick, "Judicial Response in Crisis," in Skolnick, ed., *The Politics of Protest* (New York: Simon & Schuster, 1969).

18. For a study of the influence of extralegal as well as legal variables on the decision whether to grant bail, see Ilene H. Nagel, "The Legal/Extra-Legal Controversy: Judicial Decisions in Pretrial Release," *Law & Society Review* 17 (1983): 481–515.

19. For an analysis of the criticisms, along with a discussion of the positive aspects of the bondsman system and the possible adverse effects of eliminating this system, see Mary A. Toborg, "Bail Bondsmen and Criminal Courts," *Justice System Journal* 8 (Summer 1983): 141–156.

20. Pannel v. U.S. 320 F.2d 699 (D.C.Cir. 1963) (Judge Skelly Wright, concurring).

21. Ky. Rev. Stat. §§ 431.510 et. seq. This statute was upheld in Benboe v. Carroll, 625 F.2d 737 (6th Cir. 1980).

22. Or. Rev. Stat. §§ 135.230 et. seq. See Stephen Gettinger, "Has the Bail Reform Movement Stalled?" *Corrections Magazine* 6 (February 1980): 30.

23. For a history of bail reform, see Malcolm M. Feeley, *Court Reform on Trial* (New York: Basic Books, 1983): and Caleb Foote, "Bail: Bail Reform," in Kadish, ed., *Encyclopedia of Crime and Justice,* vol. 1, pp. 107–111.

24. Charles E. Ares, Anne Rankin, and Herbert Sturz, "The Manhattan Bail Project," *New York University Law Review* 38 (January 1963): 68. See this article, which is the basis for the comments in this section, for a more detailed discussion of the project. For other discussions of early bail reform plans, see Thomas P. O'Rourke and Richard G. Salem, "A Comparative Analysis of Pretrial Procedures," *Crime & Delinquency* 14 (October 1968): 367–373; and Gerald S. Levin, "The San Francisco Bail Project," *American Bar Association Journal* 55 (February 1969): 135–137.

25. "12% of Those Freed on Low Bail Fail to Appear," *New York Times,* December 2, 1983, p. 1. col. 2.

26. 11 U.S. Code §§ 3152-3156.

27. Pretrial Services Act, Pub. L. 97-267, 96 Stet. 1136–1139 (1982) amending 18 U.S. Code §§ 3152-3155.

28. 18 U.S. Code § 3146.

29. "The Bail Reform Act of 1966, *Iowa Law Review* 53 (August 1967): 170.

30. "Burger Seeks Study of Bail Releases in Major Crime," *New York Times,* February 12, 1979, p. A14, col. 3.

31. Hans Mattick, "The Contemporary Jails of the United States: An Unknown and Neglected Area of Justice," in Daniel Glaser, ed., *Handbook of Criminology* (Skokie, Ill.: Rand McNally, 1974), pp. 777–848.

32. Mattick, p. 781.

33. Mattick, p. 777.

34. Mattick, p. 778.

35. Edith Elisabeth Flynn, "Jails and Criminal Justice," chapter 2, in Lloyd E. Ohlin, ed., *Prisoners in America* (Englewood Cliffs, N.J.: Prentice-Hall, 1973), p. 49.

36. Jerome Hall, *Theft, Law and Society* (Boston: Little, Brown, 1935), p. 108. See also John Howard, *State of Prisons,* 2d ed. (Warrington, England: Patterson Smith, 1792).

37. Inmates of the Suffolk County Jail v. Eisenstadt, 360 F.Supp. 676 (1973), *aff'd.* 494 F.2d 1196, *cert. denied.* 419 U.S. 977 (1974).

38. Joseph F. Fishman, *Crucible of Crime: The Shocking Story of the American Jail* (New York: Cosmopolis Press, 1923), p. 82.

39. Fishman, p. 82.

40. Fishman, pp. 13–14. For a more extensive history of jails, see Mattick, "The Contemporary Jails of the United States," pp. 782–785; Edith E. Flynn, "Jails," in Kadish, ed., *Encyclopedia of Crime and Justice,* vol. 3, pp. 915–917; and David J. Rothman, *The Discovery of the Asylum:*

Social Order and Disorder in the New Republic (Boston: Little, Brown, 1971).

41. National Commission on Law Observance and Enforcement, *Report on Penal Institutions, Probation, and Parole.* Report of the Advisory Committee on Penal Institutions, Probation, and Parole (Washington, D.C.: U.S. Government Printing Office, 1931), p. 273.

42. Daniel Fogel, quoted in "The Scandalous U.S. Jails," *Newsweek,* August 18, 1980, p. 74.

43. Norman Carlson, quoted in *New York Times,* January 5, 1982, p. B10.

44. See Ronald L. Carlson and Mark S. Voelpel, "Material Witnesses and Material Injustice," *Washington University Law Quarterly* 58 (1980): 1–53.

45. *Justice Assistance News* 4 (April 1983): 7.

46. Bureau of Justice Statistics, *Profile of Jail Inmates: Sociodemographic Findings From the 1978 Survey of Inmates of Local Jails* (Washington, D.C.: U.S. Government Printing Office, 1980), p. 1.

47. *Profile of Jail Inmates.*

48. For a collection of articles on jail administration, see "Jail Management," *Prison Journal* 41 (Spring-Summer 1981). For an analysis of rural jails, see Shanler D. Cronk, Joanne Jankovic, and Ronald K. Green, eds., *Criminal Justice in Rural America* (Washington, D.C.: U.S. Department of Justice, 1982).

49. "Jail Business: Private Firm Breaks in," *American Bar Association Journal* 69 (November 1983): 1611.

50. "NIC's Board Endorses a Model for Building, Managing Jails," *Justice Assistance News* 15 (March 1, 1984): 4.

51. See Suzanne Charlé, "Suicide in the Cellblocks," *Corrections Magazine* 4 (August 1981): 6–16.

52. *American Prisons and Jails, vol. III: Conditions and Costs of Confinement.* Department of Justice, National Institute of Justice (Washington, D.C.: U.S. Government Printing Office, 1980), p. 90. See also Thomas C. Neil and Paul Katsampes, "Training and Staff Development for Jails: What is and What Can Be," *The Prison Journal* 41 (Spring-Summer 1981): 13–22.

53. Bureau of Justice Statistics, *Report to the Nation on Crime and Justice: The Data* (Washington, D.C.: U.S. Government Printing Office, 1983), p. 92.

54. Henry Weiss, "Strategies for Maintaining Social Service Programs in Jails," *Federal Probation* 46 (March 1982): 56.

55. Charles L. Newman and Barbara R. Price, *Jails and Drug Treatment* (Beverly Hills, Calif.: Sage Publications, 1977), p. 11.

56. U.S. Department of Justice, Law Enforcement Assistance Administration, National Criminal Justice Information and Statistics Service, *Survey of Inmates of Local Jails* (Washington, D.C.: U.S. Government Printing Office, 1972).

57. Newman and Price, *Jails and Drug Treatment.*

58. Newman and Price, pp. 21–30.

59. Newman and Price, p. 31.

60. Newman and Price, p. 31.

61. Newman and Price, p. 186.

62. See James Austin and Paul Litsky, "Promises and Realities of Jail Classification," *Federal Probation* 46 (March 1982): 1–67.

63. "The Scandalous U.S. Jails," p. 74.

64. *American Prisons and Jails, vol. III: Conditions and Costs of Confinement,* p. 82. See also Advisory Commission on Intergovernmental Relations, *Jails: Intergovernmental Dimensions of a Local Problem: A Commission Report* (Washington, D.C.: U.S. Government Printing Office, 1984).

65. "The Scandalous U.S. Jails," p. 77.

66. "Punishment: Jailhouse Suicides Are Neither Remorseful Nor Depressed," *Psychology Today* (August 1982): 13, referring to the study by the National Center on Institutions and Alternatives.

67. Bruce L. Danto, "Approaches to the Violent Criminal," *International Journal of Offender Therapy and Comparative Criminology* 23 (1979): 11–20. See also the series of articles in Danto, ed., *Jail House Blues* (Orchard Lake, Mich.: Epic Publications, 1973). See also Katharine Hooper Brier, "Jails: Neglected Asylums," *Social Casework* 64 (September 1983): 387–393.

68. See the series of articles on jail fires in *Corrections Magazine* 9 (February 1983). Quotation is on p. 21. See also N. E. Schafer, "Fire Safety in Jails," *Federal Probation* 46 (September 1982): 41–45.

69. Miller v. Carson, 401 F.Supp. 835, 869, 871-72 (S.D.Fla. 1975); Lowery v. Metropolitan Dade Co., 43 Fla.Supp. 84 (Fla.11th Jud.Cir. 1971).

70. Inmates of the Suffolk County Jail v. Eisenstadt, 360 F.Supp. 676, 679 (D.Mass. 1973), aff'd, 494 F.2d 1196, cert. denied, 419 U.S. 977 (1974). See also Strachan v. Ashe, 548 F.Supp. 1193 (D.Mass. 1982).

71. Inmates of the Suffolk County Jail v. Eisenstadt, 360 F.Supp. 678, 680–681, note 8.

72. Block v. Rutherford, *U.S. Law Week* 52 (June 26, 1984): pp. 5067–5076.

73. "U.S. Charges Nebraska Jail Is Biased Against Female Officers," *Justice Assistance News* 13 (February 15, 1984): 6.

74. For details, see W. Donald Pointer and Marjorie Kravitz, *Prison and Jail Health Care: A Selected Bibliography,* U.S. Department of Justice, National Institute of Corrections (Washington, D.C.: U.S. Government Printing Office, 1981).

75. Estelle v. Gamble, 429 U.S. 97 (1976).

76. Quoted in "U.S. Says Newark's Jails Violate Prisoners' Rights," *Criminal Justice Newsletter* 16 (February 1, 1984); p. 6.

77. 441 U.S. 520 (1979).

78. 441 U.S. 520, 563.

79. 441 U.S. 520, 567, 570.

80. 441 U.S. 520, 557–578 (Justice Marshall, dissenting).

81. For a recent case discussing what might constitute punishment, see Putnam v. Gerloss, 639 F.2d 415 (8th Cir. 1981).

82. Kincaid v. Rusk, 670 F.2d 737 (7th Cir. 1982).

83. "Jail Will Reopen with a New Look," *New York Times,* October 17, 1983, p. 1, col. 6.

84. See Blair v. Anderson, 325 A.2d 94 (Del.S.Ct. 1974); and Dezort v. Village of Hinsdale, 342 N.E.2d 648 (Ill.App.Ct. 1976).

85. Harrell v. City of Belen, N.M. Valencia County District Court, no. 21230, December 22, 1977, reported in *American Trial Lawyers Association Law Reporter* (May 1978): 170.

86. *Student Lawyer* 7 (April 1979): 5.

87. Richard A. McGee, "Our Sick Jails," *Federal Probation* 35 (March 1971): 4–5.

88. Ronald Goldfarb, *Jails: The Ultimate Ghetto* (Garden City, N.Y.: Doubleday, 1975), pp. 420–421, 450–451.

89. "Drunks, U.S. Detainees Tied to Jail Crowding," *ABA Journal* 68 (December 1982): 1553. But see also David Whitford, "Despite Decriminalization, Drunks Still Clog Our Nation's Jails," *Corrections Magazine* 9 (April 1983): 31–39.

90. *American Bar Association Journal* 68 (December 1982): 1560.

91. "Weekend Jail: Doing Time on the Installment Plan," *Corrections Magazine* 4 (March 1978): 28–38.

92. "Home Detention Gaining Support," *Justice Assistance News* 14 (November 21, 1983): 3.

93. For a discussion, see David B. Rothman and John R. Kimberly, "The Social Context of

Jails," *Sociology and Social Research* 59 (July 1975): 344–361.

94. Quoted in Goldfarb, *Jails: The Ultimate Ghetto,* p. 21.

Chapter 13

1. Earl Warren, "Delay and Congestion in the Federal Courts," quoted in Hans Zeisel, Harry Kalven, Jr., and Bernard Buckholz, eds., *Delay in Court* (Boston: Little, Brown, 1959), p. xxi.

2. Remarks of attorney general of the United States, William French Smith, before the fifth annual Brookings Institution meeting on the Administration of Justice, reprinted in the *Congressional Record*—Senate, vol.,128 (97th Cong.; 2nd sess.) February 2, 1982, p. 265.

3. Warren E. Burger, "Isn't There a Better Way?" *American Bar Association Journal* 68 (March 1982): 275.

4. See the results of the study commissioned by the National Center for State Courts, summarized by Edward B. McConnell, director of that organization, in "Why People Today Distrust the Courts," *The Judges' Journal* 17 (Summer 1978): 12–16.

5. Harold J. Spaeth, *An Introduction to Supreme Court Decision Making* (San Francisco: Chandler, 1972), p. 72.

6. Robert H. Jackson, "The Supreme Court as a Unit of Government," in Alan F. Westin, ed., *The Supreme Court: Views from Inside* (New York: Norton, 1961), pp. 22–23.

7. Marbury v. Madison, 5 U.S. (1 Cranch) 137 (1803).

8. For a discussion of federal courts, see Charles McC. Mathias, Jr., "The Federal Courts Under Siege," *Annals,* AAPSS 462 (July 1982): 26–33.

9. For more information on the state and federal court systems, see Fannie J. Klein, *Federal and State Court Systems: A Guide* (Cambridge, Mass: Ballinger, 1977).

10. For a discussion of trial courts, see Herbert Jacob, "Presidential Address: Trial Courts in the United States: The Travails of Exploration," *Law & Society Review* 17 (1983): 407–423. See also "The American Judiciary: Critical Issues," special edition of *Annals* 462 (July 1982), with special editors, A. Leo Levin and Russell R. Wheeler 462 (July 1982); Richard Nelly, *How Courts Govern America* (New Haven, Conn.: Yale University Press, 1981); and Richard A. L. Gambitts, et al., *Governing*

Through Courts (Beverly Hills, Calif.:, Sage Publications, 1981).

11. Alexis de Tocqueville, "The Temper of the Legal Profession in the United States," in John J. Bonsignore et al., eds., *Before the Law: An Introduction to the Legal Process* (Boston: Houghton Mifflin, 1974), p. 154.

12. James Willard Hurst, *The Growth of American Law* (Boston: Little, Brown, 1950), pp. 251–252.

13. For an excellent discussion of public opinion about lawyers in colonial America, see Leon Jaworski, "The Lawyer in Society," *Baylor Law Review* 33 (Winter 1981): 9–13.

14. See Peter H. Rossi, "Occupational Prestige in the United States, 1925–1963," *American Journal of Sociology* 70 (November 1964): 286–302. See also Quintin Johnstone and Don Hopson, Jr., *Lawyers and Their Work: An Analysis of the Legal Profession in the United States and England* (Indianapolis: Bobbs-Merrill, 1967).

15. Bailey Morris, "Lawyers' Images of Yesteryear Are Crumbling Fast," *Washington Star,* September 13, 1976, p. Al, col. 1.

16. "Those #⋆X!!! Lawyers," *Time,* April 10, 1978, p. 56.

17. *New York Times,* May 4, 1981.

18. For a recent study of prosecutors, see Joan E. Jacoby, *The American Prosecutor: A Search for Identity* (Lexington, Mass.: D. C. Heath and Company, 1980). For a brief discussion of prosecutors' careers see Sue Titus Reid and Lorna Keltner, "Careers in Criminal Justice: Law," in Sanford H. Kadish, editor in chief, *Encyclopedia of Crime and Justice,* vol. 1 (New York: Free Press, 1983); and Reid and Keltner, *Criminal Justice* (New York: Holt, Rinehart and Winston, forthcoming), chap. 7. See also Abraham S. Goldstein, "Prosecution: History of the Public Prosecutor," in Kadish, ed., *Encyclopedia of Crime and Justice,* vol. 3, pp. 1286–1290. For a comparison with other countries, see Thomas Weigend, "Prosecution: Comparative Aspects," in Kadish, ed., *Encyclopedia of Crime and Justice,* pp. 1296–1304.

19. See June Louin Tapp and Felice J. Levine, eds., *Law, Justice, and the Individual in Society* (New York: Holt, Rinehart and Winston, 1977). See also Leonard R. Mellon, Joan E. Jacoby and Marion A. Brewer, "The Prosecutor Constrained by His Environment: A New Look at Discretionary Justice in the United States," *Journal of Criminal Law and Crimi-*
nology 72 (Spring 1981): 53; and Leslie Donovan, "Justice Department's Prosecution Guidelines of Little Value to State and Local Prosecutors," *Journal of Criminal Law and Criminology* 72 (Fall 1981): 955–992.

20. See Oyler v. Boles, 368 U.S. 448, 456 (1962); U.S. v. Batchelder, 442 U.S. 114, 123–4 (1979); and U.S. v. Nixon, 418 U.S. 683, 693 (1974).

21. Herman Schwartz and Bruce Jackson, "The Prosecutor," *Student Lawyer* 4 (March 1976): 17. See also Norman Abrams, "Prosecution: Prosecutorial Discretion," in Kadish, ed., *Encyclopedia,* vol. 3, pp. 1271–1286.

22. General Accounting Office, *Reducing Federal Judicial Sentencing and Prosecuting Disparities: A Systemwise Approach Needed* (Washington, D.C.: U.S. Government Printing Office, March 1979), p. 18.

23. See Imbler v. Pachtman, 424 U.S. 409 (1976). For a discussion of suggested methods for controlling prosecutorial discretion, see Reid and Keltner, *Criminal Justice,* chap. 7.

24. See J.D. Pflaumer, Inc. v. U.S. Department of Justice, 450 F.Supp. 1125 (E.D.Pa. 1978), Briggs v. Goodwin, 569 F.2d 10 (D.C. Cir. 1977), *cert. denied,* 437 U.S. 904 (1978).

25. Murray A. Schwartz, quoted in John Kaplan, *Criminal Justice* (Mineola, N.Y.: Foundation Press, 1973), p. 261.

26. For a discussion of attorneys' careers, see Reid and Keltner, "Careers in Criminal Justice," pp. 149–152.

27. See Leonard Downie, Jr., *Justice Denied: The Case for Reform of the Courts* (New York: Praeger, 1971), pp. 174–75.

28. See Robert I. Weiland and Ward Bower, "Where the Earnings Are," *Barrister* 7 (Winter 1980): 45–48.

29. Jerome E. Carlin, *Lawyers on Their Own: A Study of Individual Practitioners in Chicago* (New Brunswick, N.J.: Rutgers University Press, 1962); Carlin, *Lawyers' Ethics: A Survey of the New York City Bar* (New York: Russell Sage, 1966); Jack Ladinsky, "Careers of Lawyers, Law Practice, and Legal Institution," in Rita James Simon, ed., *The Sociology of Law* (San Francisco: Chandler, 1968); Ladinsky, "The Impact of Social Backgrounds of Lawyers on Law Practice and the Law," *Journal of Legal Education* 16 (1963): 127–144.

30. Arthur Lewis Wood, *Criminal Lawyer* (New Haven, Conn.: College and University Press, 1967).

31. Paul B. Wice, *Criminal Lawyers: An Endangered Species* (Beverly Hills, Calif.: Sage Publications, 1978), Foreword by Fred Cohen, pp. 9, 10.

32. Wice, p. 214. For a history of the development of services for the poor, see Robert Hermann, Eric Single, and John Boston. *Counsel for the Poor: Criminal Defense in Urban America* (Lexington, Mass.: Heath, 1977).

33. Quoted in Jonathan D. Casper, *American Criminal Justice: The Defendant's Perspective* (Englewood Cliffs, N.J.: Prentice-Hall, 1972), p. 101.

34. "The Right to Counsel, Argersinger v. Hamlin: An Unmet Challenge," *Criminal Law Bulletin* 11 (January-February 1975): 67, 72.

35. Warren E. Burger, Foreword to L. Ray Patterson and Elliott Cheatham, *The Profession of Law* (Mineola, N.Y.: The Foundation Press, 1971), p. v.

36. See Geoffrey P. Alpert, "Inadequate Defense Counsel: An Empirical Analysis," *American Journal of Criminal Law* 7 (March 1979): 1–21.

37. See, for example, Henry H. Rossman, William F. McDonald, and James A. Cramer, "Some Patterns and Determinants of Plea-Bargaining Decisions: A Simulation and Quasi-Experiment," in William F. McDonald and James A. Cramer, eds., *Plea-Bargaining* (Lexington, Mass.: Lexington Books, 1980), p. 77.

38. For the classic sociological study of plea bargaining, see Donald J. Newman, "Pleading Guilty for Consideration: A Study of Bargain Justice," *Journal of Criminal Law, Criminology, and Police Science* 46 (March-April 1956): 780–790. See also Donald J. Newman, *Conviction: The Determination of Guilt or Innocence without Trial* (Boston: Little, Brown, 1966). See also Arthur Rossett and Donald Cressey, *Justice by Consent* (Philadelphia: Lippincott, 1976); and James E. Bond, *Plea Bargaining and Guilty Pleas* (New York: Clark Boardman, 1975).

39. Albert W. Alschuler, "Plea Bargaining and Its History," *Columbia Law Review* 79 (January 1979): 1.

40. See, for example, John H. Langbein, "Understanding the Short History of Plea Bargaining," *Law & Society Review* 13 (Winter 1979): 261, where he notes that "[p]lea bargaining is a *nontrial* mode of procedure." (Emphasis in the original.)

41. Santobello v. New York, 404 U.S. 257, 260–261 (1971). Plea bargaining must be encouraged, however, without any actual or threatened physical harm or mental coercion which makes the plea involuntary. See Brady v. U.S., 397 U.S. 742, 750 (1970).

42. Corbitt v. New Jersey, 429 U.S. 212 (1978). For a discussion of Corbitt, see Malvina Halberstam, "Towards Neutral Principles in the Administration of Criminal Justice: A Critique of Supreme Court Decisions Sanctioning the Plea Bargaining Process," *Journal of Criminal Law and Criminology* 73 (Spring 1982): 13–14.

43. Brady v. United States, 397 U.S. 742 (1969).

44. Boykin v. Alabama, 395 U.S. 238 (1968).

45. Santobello v. New York, 404 U.S. 257.

46. Bordenkircher v. Hayes, 434 U.S. 357 (1978).

47. Bordenkircher v. Hayes, 434 U.S. 357, 363.

48. Bordenkircher v. Hayes, 434 U.S. 357, 364.

49. Bordenkircher v. Hayes, 434 U.S. 357, 367.

50. Washington v. United States, 404 A.2d 926 (D.C.App. 1979). This case was later withdrawn from publication by order of the court.

51. See also United States v. Litton Systems, Inc., 573 F.2d 195 (4th Cir.), *cert. denied,* 439 U.S. 383 (1978), stating that retaliatory motive must be shown to prove prosecutorial vindictiveness; and United States v. Vaughn, 565 F.2d 283 (4th Cir. 1977).

52. Maureen Mileski, "Courtroom Encounters: An Observation Study of a Lower Criminal Court," *Law & Society Review* 5 (May 1971): 21.

53. Blackledge v. Allison, 431 U.S. 63, 71 (1977).

54. Santobello v. New York, 404 U.S. 257.

55. For results of an experiment concluding that innocent defendants were much less likely to accept plea bargains than the guilty, see W. Larry Gregory, John C. Mowen, and Darwyn E. Linder, "Social Psychology and Plea Bargaining: Applications, Methodology, and Theory," *Journal of Personality and Social Psychology* 36 (December 1978): 1521–1530.

56. Brady v. U.S., 397 U.S. 742, 748.

57. See Bordenkircher v. Hayes, 434 U.S. 357, 363.

58. See State v. Swindell, 607 P.2d 852 (Wash.Sup.Ct. 1980).

59. North Carolina v. Alford, 400 U.S. 25, 31 (1970).

60. Brady v. U.S., 397 U.S. 742.

61. M. L. Rubinstein and T. J. White, "Plea Bargaining—Can Alaska Live Without It?" *Judi-*

cature 62 (December-January 1979): 266–279. See also D. C. Anderson, "You Can't Cop a Plea in Alaska Anymore," *Police* 2 (January 1979): 4–12; and Michael L. Rubinstein and Teresa J. White, "Alaska's Ban on Plea-Bargaining," in William F. McDonald and James A. Cramer, eds., *Plea-Bargaining* (Lexington, Mass.: Lexington Books, 1980), pp. 25–56; and Michael L. Rubinstein, Stevens H. Clarke, and Teresa J. White, *Alaska Bans Plea Bargaining,* U.S. Department of Justice (Washington, D.C.: U.S. Government Printing Office, 1980).

62. Moise Berger, "The Case against Plea Bargaining," *American Bar Association Journal* 62 (May 1976): 621–624.

63. Corbitt v. New Jersey, 439 U.S. 212 (1978).

64. Stuart S. Nagel and Marian Neef, "The Impact of Plea Bargaining on the Judicial Process," *American Bar Association Journal* 62 (August 1976): 1020–1022.

65. James A. Cramer, Henry H. Rossman and William F. McDonald, "The Judicial Role in Plea-Bargaining," in McDonald and Cramer, eds., *Plea-Bargaining*, pp. 139, 141.

66. James A. Cramer, "Judicial Supervision of the Guilty Plea Hearing," in Cramer, ed., *Plea Bargaining* (Beverly Hills, Calif.: Sage Publications, 1981), p. 193.

67. Albert W. Alschuler, "The Changing Plea Bargaining Debate," *California Law Review* 69 (May 1981): 690.

68. Lee Sheppard, "Disclosure to the Guilty Pleading Defendant: Brady v. Maryland and the Brady Trilogy," *Journal of Criminal Law and Criminology* 72 (Spring 1981): 173.

69. See David Brereton and Jonathan D. Casper, "Does It Pay to Plead Guilty? Differential Sentencing and the Functioning of Criminal Courts," *Law & Society Review* 16 (February 1981): 45; Brady v. U.S., 397 U.S. 742, 751; and Donald M. Barry and Alexander Greer, "Sentencing Versus Prosecutorial Discretion: The Application of a New Disparity Measure," *Journal of Research in Crime and Delinquency* 18 (July 1981): 254–271.

70. See U.S. v. Wiley, 278 F.2d 500 (7th Cir. 1960).

71. Frank v. Blackburn, 646 F.2d 873 (5th Cir. 1980) *cert. denied*, 454 U.S. 840 (1981).

72. See James Willard Hurst, "The Functions of Courts in the United States, 1950–1980," *Law & Society Review* 15 (1980–81): 401–471.

73. "Courts Face Threat of 'Brain Drain' As Judges Seek Greener Pastures," *American Bar Association Journal* 66 (January 1980): 19.

74. Stuart Nagel, "Off-the-Bench Judicial Attitudes," in Glendon Schubert, ed., *Judicial Decision-Making* (New York: Free Press, 1963), pp. 43–44.

75. See Nagel. Also see A. Keith Bottomley, *Decisions in the Penal Process* (South Hackensack, N.J.: Fred B. Rothman, 1973), pp. 143–144.

76. "The Reagan Brand on the Judiciary: His Choices Are White, Male, Conservative and Solidly Competent," *Time,* February 28, 1983, p. 74.

77. For a more detailed discussion of these qualities, see Sheldon Goldman, "Judicial Selection and the Qualities that Make a 'Good' Judge," *Annals of the American Academy of Political and Social Sciences* 462 (July 1982): 113–114.

78. Irving R. Kaufman, "An Open Letter to President Reagan on Judge Picking," *American Bar Association Journal* 67 (April 1981): 443.

79. See Honorable Roberta Ralph and Robert I. Manuwal, "Training (?) of the American Judiciary," *University of West Los Angeles Law Review* 12 (Spring 1980): 34–40, for a discussion of the training of judges in England, France, Japan, West Germany, and the Scandanavian countries.

80. For a discussion of the programs of various states, see Ralph and Manuwal, pp. 29–34.

81. Howard S. Erlanger, "Jury Research in America: Its Past and Future, *Law & Society Review* 4 (February 1970): 345.

82. Harry Kalven and Hans Zeisel, *The American Jury* (Boston: Little, Brown, 1966). For a review of earlier research on juries, see Erlanger, "Jury Research in America."

83. See K. C. Gerbasi, M. Zuckerman, and H. T. Reis, "Justice Needs a New Blindfold: A Review of Mock Jury Research," *Psychological Bulletin* 84 (March 1977): 323–345.

84. J. L. Bernard, "Interaction Between the Race of the Defendant and That of Jurors in Determining Verdicts," *Law and Psychology Review* 5 (Fall 1979): 104. For a discussion of jury deliberations as a group process, see Murray Levine, Michael P. Farrell and Peter Perrotta, "The Impact of Rules of Jury Deliberation on Group Developmental Processes," pp. 263–304, in Bruce Dennis Sales, ed., *The Trial Process* (New York: Plenum Press, 1981).

85. Lori B. Andrews, "Mind Control in the Court-room," *Psychology Today* (March 1982): 66–73.

86. Donald E. Vinson, "The Shadow Jury: An Experiment in Litigation Science," *American Bar Association Journal* 68 (October 1982): 1243.

87. For a recent analysis, see Stuart Nagel, David Lamm, and Marian Neef, "Decision Theory and Juror Decision-Making," in Sales, ed., *The Trial Process*, pp. 353–386.

88. Duncan v. Louisiana, 391 U.S. 145, 156 (1968).

89. Vinson, "The Shadow Jury," 1246.

90. See Reid Hastie, Steven D. Penrod and Nancy Pennington, "What Goes On in a Jury Delib-eration: Jury Size, Juror Gender and the Requirement of Unanimity Make a Difference in the Way a Jury Deliberates," *American Bar Association Journal* 69 (December 1983): 1848–1853.

91. Jerome H. Skolnick, *Justice Without Trial: Law Enforcement in Democratic Society,* 2nd ed. (New York: Wiley, 1975).

92. Dennis H. Nagao and James H. Davis, "The Effects of Prior Experience on Mock Juror Case Judgments," *Social Psychology Quarterly* 43 (June 1980): 190–199. Quotation is on pp. 197–198.

93. Elizabeth F. Loftus, "The Eyewitness on Trial," *Trial* 16 (October 1980): 31.

94. Loftus, "Impact of Expert Psychological Testi-mony on the Unreliability of Eyewitness Iden-tification," *Journal of Applied Psychology* 65 (February 1980): 9–15. See also Clive R. Hollin and Brian R. Clifford, "Eyewitness Testimony: The Effects of Discussion on Recall Accuracy and Agreement," *Journal of Applied Social Psy-chology* 13 (May-June 1983): 234–244; and Donna M. Murray and Gary L. Wells, "Does Knowledge That a Crime Was Staged Affect Eyewitness Performance," *Journal of Applied Social Psychology* 12 (1982): 42–53.

95. Carol J. Mills and Wayne E. Bohannon, "Juror Characteristics: to What Extent Are They Related to Jury Verdicts?" *Judicature* 64 (June-July 1980): 28.

96. Edmond Costantini and Joel King, "The Par-tial Juror: Correlates and Causes of Prejudg-ment," *Law & Society Review* 15 (1980): 9–40.

97. Bernard, "Interaction," p. 10.

98. See, for example, James P. Levine, "Jury Toughness: The Impact of Conservatism on Criminal Court Verdicts," *Crime & Delin-quency* 29 (January 1983): 71–87.

99. According to an attorney who also served as a juror, the rest of the jurors did not understand the case. "It concerns me deeply that all eleven of my fellow jurors had only vague or imperfect notions of the true nature of the process in which they were required to play such a crucial part. I cannot agree that it is healthy for citizens of a democracy to dispense justice within a miasma of ignorance." Ivor Kraft, "Happy New Year—You're a Juror," *Crime & Delin-quency* 28 (October 1982): 599. For a listing of his specific ways in which to improve the jury system, see p. 600.

100. "Juries May be Luxury in Future, Says Ste-vens," *American Bar Association Journal* 65 (September 1979): 1292.

101. *U.S. News & World Report,* November 1, 1982, p. 45.

102. "Supreme Court Dissension," *Tulsa World,* October 3, 1982, sec. I, p. 1, col. 1, quoting Wil-liam Van Alstyne of Duke, Thomas Kratten-maker of Georgetown University and A. E. Dick Howard of the University of Virginia.

103. "Supreme Court Blues," *New York Times,* October 4, 1982, p. 18, col. 1.

104. *Article III [2] United States Constitution.*

105. Hurst, *Growth of American Law,* pp. 120–121.

106. Chief Justice Fred M. Vinson, quoted in Ron-ald L. Carlson, *Criminal Justice Procedure,* 2d ed. (Cincinnati: W. H. Anderson, 1978), p. 243.

107. Henry J. Abraham, *The Judicial Process,* 2d ed. (New York: Oxford University Press, 1968), p. 194.

108. Paul A. Freund, *On Law and Justice* (Cam-bridge, Mass.: Harvard University Press, 1968), p. 54.

109. Edward H. Levi, *An Introduction to Legal Rea-soning* (Chicago: University of Chicago Press, 1968), p. 1.

110. Bob Woodward and Scott Armstrong, *The Brethren: Inside the Supreme Court* (New York: Simon & Schuster, 1979).

111. Leonard S. Janofsky, "Court Reigns Supreme," *American Bar Association Journal* 66 (March 1980): 242. For an earlier study on the Supreme Court justices, see John R. Schmidhauser, "The Background Characteristics of United States Supreme Court Justices," in Glendon Schubert, ed., *Judicial Behavior* (Skokie, Ill.: Rand McNally, 1965).

112. David S. Shrager, "The Myth of the Litigious Society," *Trial* 20 (February 1984): 4. See also Jethro K. Lieberman, *The Litigious Society* (New York: Basic Books, 1981).

113. Robert S. Want, "The Caseload Monster in the Federal Courts," *American Bar Association Journal* 69 (May 1983): 615.

114. "U.S. Legal System: Victim of Its Success," *Tulsa World,* April 3, 1983, p. 12, col. 3.

115. "Challenging the 'Hired Guns,'" *Time,* February 27, 1984, p. 103.

116. "'Frivolous' Appeals Prompt Court to Make First Use of Penalty Rule," *New York Times,* June 14, 1983, p. 1, col. 1.

117. 28 U.S. Code § 44.133.

118. See the discussion of the Federal Courts Improvement Act of 1982 in David Schwartz, "Two New Federal Courts," *American Bar Association Journal* 68 (September 1982): 1091–1093. For information on reorganization of state courts, see Ron Roach, "State Seeks to Retool Clogged Justice System," *San Diego Tribune,* August 24, 1981, p. 3, col. 3. This article notes that the California Judicial Council estimated that a 5 percent improvement in efficiency would result in a $25 million savings in the annual criminal justice budget in California. See also Ca. Const. art. VI, § 5, amended June 23, 1982.

119. "New York State Says Shifting of Judges Cut Court Calenders 39%," *New York Times,* February 10, 1980, p. A16, col. 3.

120. See "The Jury Is Still Out on Test of Felony Trials at Night," *New York Times,* March 20, 1980, p. B1, col. 2.

121. See John F. Grady, quoted in "Judge Urges Cutting Needless Costs, Delays," *American Bar Association Journal* 68 (May 1982): 526.

122. Thomas B. Marvell, "Appellate Court Delay Reduction: Judges First," *Appellate Court Administration Review* 3 (1980–1981): 28.

123. See David W. Neubauer and John Paul Ryan, "Criminal Courts and the Delivery of Speedy Justice: The Influence of Case and Defendant Characteristics," *Justice System Journal* 7 (Summer 1982): 213–235.

124. "The Direction of the Administration of Justice," *American Bar Association Journal* 62 (June 1976): 728. For a detailed discussion of alternative methods of settling disputes, see Benedict S. Alper and Lawrence T. Nichols, *Beyond the Courtroom: Programs in Commu-*

nity Justice and Conflict Resolution (Lexington, Mass.: Lexington Books, 1981).

125. *Washington Post,* June 13, 1977, p. A5, col. 1. For a discussion of a similar program in Orlando, Florida, see Ross F. Conner and Ray Surette, *The Citizen Dispute Settlement Program: Resolving Disputes Outside the Courts* (American Bar Association, 1977).

126. Burger, "Isn't There a Better Way?", pp. 274, 275.

127. Public Law 96-190, February 12, 1980, 94 Stat. 17.

128. For a discussion of the Act and some possible problems with its implementation, see Paul Nejelski, "The 1980 Dispute Resolution Act," *The Judges' Journal* 19 (Winter 1980): 33–35, 44–45.

Chapter 14

1. David J. Rothman, "Sentencing Reforms in Historical Perspective," *Crime & Delinquency* 29 (October 1983): 631.

2. Graeme Newman, *The Punishment Response* (Philadelphia: Lippincott, 1978), chap. 2, pp. 13–25. Quotation is on p. 13.

3. *Black's Law Dictionary,* 4th ed. (St. Paul: West Publishing, 1968), p. 1398.

4. H. L. A. Hart, *Punishment and Responsibility* (New York: Oxford University Press, 1968), pp. 4–5, cited in Newman, *The Punishment Response*, pp. 7–9.

5. Émile Durkheim, *The Rules of Sociological Method* (New York: Free Press. 1964); *The Division of Labour in Society,* enlarged ed. (New York: Free Press, 1964).

6. Steven Spitzer, "Punishment and Social Organization: A Study of Durkheim's Theory of Penal Evolutuion," *Law & Society Review* 9 (Summer 1975): 613–637. Quotation is on p. 617.

7. Spitzer, 631–632.

8. Newman, *The Punishment Response,* p. 25.

9. Spitzer, "Punishment and Social Organization," 634.

10. Erik Olin Wright, *The Politics of Punishment: A Critical Analysis of Prisons in America* (New York: Harper & Row, 1973), p. 22.

11. See George Rusche and Otto Kircheimer, *Punishment and the Social Structure* (New York: Russell and Russell, 1968); and William J. Chambliss, "A Sociological Analysis of the Law

of Vagrancy," *Social Problems* 12 (Fall 1964): 67–77.

12. John Horton, "Order and Conflict Theories of Social Problems," reprinted in Frank Lindenfeld, ed., *Radical Perspectives on Social Problems: Readings in Critical Sociology,* 2d ed. (New York: Macmillan, 1973), p. 25.

13. Richard Quinney, *Class, State and Crime: On the Theory and Practice of Criminal Justice* (New York: D. McKay, 1977), p. 17. See also Quinney, 2d ed., 1980.

14. Richard Quinney, *Criminology,* 2d ed. (Boston: Little, Brown, 1979), pp. 79, 107. See his chapter "Legal Order and Crime Control," pp. 77–113, for a more detailed analysis of his position on this issue.

15. See Paul Lacroix, *France in the Middle Ages* (New York: Frederick Ungar, 1963), p. 394.

16. See William and Ariel Durant, *The Story of Civilization,* vol. 9., *The Age of Voltaire* (New York: Simon & Schuster, 1965).

17. Harry Elmer Barnes, *The Story of Punishment* 2d ed. (1930; reprinted, Montclair, N.J.: Patterson Smith, 1972), p. 61.

18. Gerald Leinwand, ed., *Prisons* (New York: Simon & Schuster, 1972), p. 13.

19. See Alice Morse Earle, *Curious Punishments of Bygone Days* (New York: Duffield, 1907), pp. 138–149, for a detailed discussion of branding.

20. "Castration or Incarceration?" *Time,* December 12, 1983, p. 70.

21. Barnes, *Story of Punishment,* p. 58.

22. State v. Cannon, 190 A.2d 514 (Del. S.Ct.1963). Whipping in the Arkansas prison system was declared unconstitutional in Jackson v. Bishop, 404 F.2d 571 (8th Cir.1968). But whippings are permitted under some circumstances, in schools. See Ingraham v. Wright, 430 U.S. 651 (1977).

23. James O. Midgley, "Corporal Punishment and Penal Policy: Notes on the Continued Use of Corporal Punishment with Reference to South Africa," *Journal of Criminal Law & Criminology* 73 (1982): 402.

24. "A 'More Palatable' Way of Killing," *Time* December 20, 1982, p. 28.

25. Quoted in Tamar Lewin, "Execution by Injection: A Dilemma for Prison Doctors," *New York Times,* p. EY8, col. 1. The U.S. Supreme Court has agreed to hear an Oklahoma case on this issue.

26. Quoted in Lewin.

27. "The First 'Humane' Execution?" *Newsweek,* December 20, 1982, p. 41.

28. Tom R. Tyler and Renee Weber, "Support for the Death Penalty: Instrumental Response to Crime, or Symbolic Attitude," *Law & Society Review* 17 (1982): 21–45. For arguments for and against capital punishment, see Ernest van den Haag and John P. Conrad, *The Death Penalty: A Debate* (New York: Plenum, 1983). See also Jan Gorecki, *Capital Punishment: Criminal Law and Social Evolution* (New York: Columbia University Press, 1983).

29. See Barry Nakell, "The Cost of the Death Penalty," *Criminal Law Bulletin* 14 (January–February 1978): 69–80.

30. See William J. Bowers and Glenn L. Pierce, "Deterrence or Brutalization: What Is the Effect of Executions?" *Crime & Delinquency* 26 (October 1980): 453–484; and Richard Lempert, "The Effect of Executions on Homicide: A New Look in an Old Light," *Crime & Delinquency* 29 (January 1983): 88–115.

31. Gregg v. Georgia, 428 U.S. 153 (1976).

32. "Support Grows for Death Penalty," *Justice Assistance News,* September 26, 1983, p. 8.

33. Law Poll, "Lawyers Strongly Favor the Death Penalty," *American Bar Association Journal* 69 (September 1983): 1218.

34. F. H. Taylor, cited in Herbert A. Bloch and Gilbert Geis, *Man, Crime, and Society: The Forms of Criminal Behavior* (New York: Random House, 1962), p. 499.

35. Barnes, *Story of Punishment,* p. 68.

36. Barnes, p. 92.

37. Jerome Hall, *Theft, Law, and Society* (Boston: Little, Brown, 1935), p. 106.

38. *Los Angeles Times,* February 10, 1982, p. 2, col. 2.

39. *San Antonio Express,* May 7, 1982, p. A9, col. 1.

40. Lee H. Bowker, "Exile, Banishment and Transportation," *International Journal of Offender Therapy and Comparative Criminology* 24 (1980): 78.

41. Bearden v. Georgia, 103 S.Ct. 2064 (1983).

42. See Okla. Stat. Ann. Tit. 22 § 991 (a), (e).

43. See Bradford v. U.S., 228 U.S. 446 (1913).

44. See, for example, New Jersey Stat. § 2A:93-5.1.

45. See, for example, Ill. Ann. Stat. ch. 38 § 1005-6-3.

46. See Md. Ann. Code art. 27 § 640.

47. "Turning Society's Losers into Winners," *The Judges' Journal* 19 (Winter 1980): 4–9, 48–51.

48. For the history of probation in European countries, see Sue Titus Reid and Lorna Keltner, *Criminal Justice* (New York: Holt, Rinehart and Winston, forthcoming), chap. 14.

49. For a more detailed discussion of the contributions of Augustus, see Dressler, *Practice and Theory of Probation and Parole*, pp. 21–27.

50. Burns v. United States, 276 U.S. 216, 220 (1932).

51. Tex. Code Crim. Pro. 42.121. § 1.01.

52. See Frank P. Williams, III, Charles M. Friel, Charles B. Fields, and William V. Wilkinson, *Assessing Diversionary Impact: An Evaluation of the Intensive Supervision Program of the Bexar County Adult Probation Department* (Huntsville, Tex.: Sam Houston State University Criminal Justice Center, 1982); and Charles B. Fields. "The Intensive Supervision Probation Program in Texas: A Two-Year Assessment" (Ph.D. diss., Sam Houston State University Criminal Justice Center, 1984).

53. Stephen Gettinger, "Intensive Supervision: Can It Rehabilitate Probation?" *Corrections Magazine* 9 (April 1983): 7–8.

54. Mempha v. Rhay, 389 U.S. 128 (1967). In 1973 the Supreme Court ruled that the probationer is entitled at probation revocation (even when that proceeding is not combined with sentencing) to the same type of hearing required at parole revocation by an earlier decision, Morrissey v. Brewer, 408 U.S. 471. But the right to counsel at probation revocation would be determined on a case-by-case basis. For the details of this holding, see Gagnon v. Scarpelli, 411 U.S. 778 (1973). Courts have also placed some restrictions on conditions that may be imposed. For a general discussion, see Reid and Keltner, *Criminal Justice*, chap. 14.

55. For a history of the development of prisons, see Barnes, *The Story of Punishment*. See also Michael Ignatieff, *A Just Measure of Pain: The Penitentiary in the Industrial Revolution 1750–1850* (New York: Pantheon Books, 1978); John Irwin, *Prisons in Turmoil* (Boston: Little, Brown, 1980); Dario Melossi and Pavarini, *The Prison and the Factory: Origins of the Penitentiary System,* trans. Glynis Cousin (Totowa, N.J.: Barnes & Noble, 1981); *New England Journal on Prison Law* 7 (Winter 1981) has a series of articles on the emergence of prisons in Europe and in this country. See also David J. Rothman, *Conscience and Convenience: The Asylum and Its Alternatives in Progressive America* (Boston: Little, Brown, 1980).

56. *Fair and Certain Punishment.* Report of the Twentieth Century Fund Task Force on Criminal Sentencing, with a background paper by Alan M. Dershowitz (New York: McGraw-Hill, 1976), pp. 19–20.

57. Bureau of Justice Statistics Bulletin, *Probation and Parole 1982* (Washington, D.C.: U.S. Government Printing Office, 1983), p. 2. For a discussion of all these sentencing combinations, see Reid and Keltner, *Criminal Justice*, chap. 14.

58. See Robert L. Thomas, "Court—Prosecutor—Probation Officer: When Is Discretion Disparity in the Criminal Justice System?" *Federal Probation* 46 (June 1982): 57–62.

59. Edward M. Kennedy, "Justice in Sentencing," *New York Times*, July 29, 1977, p. A21, col. 5.

60. U.S. Courts Sentencing Called Judicial Lottery," *New York Times*, June 10, 1977, p. A28, col. 5.

61. Marvin E. Frankel, *Criminal Sentences: Law Without Order* (New York: Hill & Wang, 1973), p. 5.

62. See, for example, Robert Lefcourt, ed., *Law Against the People* (New York: Random House, 1971), p. 22; William J. Chambliss and R. B. Seidman, *Law, Order and Power* (Reading, Mass.: Addison-Wesley, 1971); and Richard Quinney, *The Social Reality of Crime* (Boston: Little, Brown, 1970), pp. 141–142.

63. John Hagen, "Extra-Legal Atrributes and Criminal Sentencing: An Assessment of a Sociological Viewpoint," *Law & Society Review* 8 (Spring 1974): 379.

64. Sol Rubin, "Disparity and Equality of Sentences—A Constitutional Challenge," *Federal Rules Decisions* 40 (1966), pp. 65–67.

65. Edward Green, "Inter- and Intra-Racial Crime Relative to Sentencing," *Journal of Criminal Law, Criminology and Police Science* 55 (1964): 356–358.

66. James D. Unnever, Charles E. Frazier, and John C. Henretta, "Race Differences in Criminal Sentencing," *Sociological Quarterly* 21 (Spring 1980): 197–206.

67. Cassia Spohn, John Gruhl, and Susan Welch, "The Effect of Race on Sentencing: A Re-Examination of an Unsettled Question," *Law & Society Review* 16 (February 1981): 71–88. Quotations are on pp. 78, 83, 85. For other studies indicating that black offenders are less likely than whites to be placed on probation, see Martin A. Levin, *Urban Politics and Criminal Courts* (Chicago: University of Chicago Press, 1977); and Unnever, Frazier, and Henretta, "Race Differences in Criminal Sentencing," pp. 197–205.

68. Spohn et al., 86.

69. Margaret Farnworth and Patrick M. Horan, "Separate Justice: An Analysis of Race Differences in Court Processes," *Social Science Research* 9 (December 1980): 381–399. Quotation is on p. 384.

70. Karen DeCrow, *Sexist Justice* (New York: Vintage Books, 1974).

71. This view can be traced back to the early influential sociologist, W. I. Thomas, *Sex and Society* (Boston: Little, Brown and Company, 1970). See also Otto Pollak, *The Criminality of Women* (Philadelphia: University of Pennsylvania Press, 1950).

72. See Rita James Simon, "American Women and Crime," *Annals* 423 (January 1976): 31–46.

73. See E. A. Anderson, "The Chivalrous' Treatment of the Female Offender in the Arms of the Criminal Justice System: A Review of the Literature," *Social Problems* 23 (February 1976): 350–357; and G. Armstrong, "Females Under the Law—'Protected' but Unequal," *Crime & Delinquency* 23 (April 1977): 109–120. For a review of these and other studies, see Peter G. Sinden, "Offender Gender and Perceptions of Crime Seriousness," *Sociological Spectrum* 1 (January–March 1981): 39–52.

74. Darrell J. Steffensmeier, "Assessing the Impact of the Women's Movement on Sex-Based Differences in the Handling of Adult Criminal Defendants," *Crime & Delinquency* 26 (July 1980): 344–357.

75. Candace Kruttschnitt, "Social Status and Sentences of Female Offenders," *Law and Society Review* 15 (1980–1981): 247–265. See also Nicolette Parisi, "Are Females Treated Differently? A Review of the Theories and Evidence on Sentencing and Parole Decisions," in Nicole Hahn Rafter and Elizabeth Anne Stanko, eds., *Judge, Lawyer, Victim, Thief: Women, Gender Roles, and Criminal Justice* (Boston: Northeastern University Press, 1982).

76. See Sheart S. Nagel and Robert Geraci, "Effects of Reducing Judicial Sentencing Discretion," *Criminology* 21 (August 1983): 309–331.

77. See John D. Hewitt, Robert M. Regoli, and Todd R. Clear, "Evaluating the Cook County Sentencing Guidelines: A Replication and Extension," *Law & Policy Quarterly* 4 (April 1982): 259–261.

78. Kenneth M. Flaxman, "The Hidden Dangers of Sentencing Guidelines," *Hofstra Law Review* 7 (Winter 1979): 279–280.

79. See William M. Rhodes and Catherine Conly, "Federal Sentencing Guidelines: Will They Shift Sentencing Discretion from Judges to Prosecuters?" chap. 8, in James A. Cramer, ed., *Courts and Judges* (Beverly Hills, Calif.: Sage Publications, 1981), p. 200.

80. See Brian Forst and Charles Wellford, "Punishment and Sentencing: Developing Sentencing Guidelines Empirically from Principles of Punishment," *Rutgers Law Review* 33 (Spring 1981): 799–837. For a lengthy but excellent analysis of the issues, see David Crump, "Determinate Sentencing: The Promises and Perils of Sentence Guidelines," *Kentucky Law Journal* 68 (1979–1980): 1–100.

81. See Andrew von Hirsch, "Commensurability and Crime Prevention: Evaluating Formal Sentencing Structures and Their Rationale," *Journal of Criminal Law & Criminology* 74 (Spring 1983): 209–248.

82. Shari Siedman Diamond and Hans Zeisel, "Sentencing Councils: A Study of Sentence Disparity and Its Reduction," in Marcia Guttentag and Shalom Saar, eds., *Evaluation Studies Review Annual,* vol. 2 (Beverly Hills, Calif.: Russell Sage, 1977), pp. 481–622.

83. See David Fogel, *We Are the Living Proof: The Justice Model for Corrections* (Cincinnati: Anderson Publishing, 1975).

84. Fogel, p. 202. Emphasis in the original.

85. Fogel, p. 204.

86. Fogel, 2d ed., 1979, p. 274.

87. Fogel, 1975, p. 255.

88. For a history of the trend toward determinate sentences, see R. S. Morrelli, C. Edelman, and R. Willoughby, *Survey of Mandatory Sentencing in the U.S.—A Summary and Brief Analysis of Mandatory Sentencing Practices in the United States* (Harrisburg: Pennsylvania Com-

mission on Crime and Delinquency Division of Criminal Justice Statistics, 1981). See also Andrew von Hirsch and Kathleen J. Hanrahan, "Determinate Penalty Systems in America: An Overview," *Crime & Delinquency* 27 (July 1981): 289–316.

89. For a discussion of the California plan, see Jonathan D. Casper, David Brereton, and David Neal, "The California Determinate Sentence Law," *Criminal Law Bulletin* 19 (September–October 1983): 405–433. For a thorough analysis of the implementation and impact of the determinate sentencing statute in Indiana, see John D. Hewitt and Todd R. Clear, *The Impact of Sentencing Reform: From Indeterminate to Determinate Sentencing* (New York: University Press of America, 1983).

90. Francis T. Cullen, Karen E. Gilbert, and John B. Cullen, "Implementing Determinate Sentencing in Illinois: Conscience and Convenience," *Criminal Justice Review* 8 (Spring 1983): 1–16.

91. See also David Brewer, Gerald E. Beckett, and Norma Holt, "Determinate Sentencing in California: The First Year's Experience," *Journal of Research in Crime and Delinquency* 18 (July 1981): 200–231; David Crump, "Determinate Sentencing: The Promises and Perils of Sentence Guidelines," *Kentucky Law Journal* 68 (1979–1980): 1–100; and Frederick A. Hussey and Stephen P. Lagoy, "The Impact of Determinate Sentencing Structures," *Criminal Law Bulletin* 17 (May–June 1981): 197–225.

92. See Jonathan Casper, "Determinate Sentence Law Did Not Increase Imprisonments," *Justice Assistance News* 3 (April 1982): 4.

93. Joan Petersilia and Peter W. Greenwood, "Mandatory Prison Sentences: Their Projected Effects on Crime and Prison Populations," *Journal of Criminal Law & Criminology* 69 (Winter 1978): 615.

94. See the study of Benedict S. Alper and Joseph W. Weiss, "The Mandatory Sentence: Recipe for Retribution," *Federal Probation* 41 (December 1977): 15–20.

95. N.Y. Penal Law § 220 (McKinney Supp. 1973). L. 1973 c. 276, 277, 278, 676, 1051.

96. Mass. Gen. Laws Ann. ch. 269 § 10 (West 1972 & Supp. 1979).

97. Kenneth Carlson, *Mandatory Sentencing: The Experience of Two States.* Policy Briefs, National Institute of Justice (Washington D.C.: United States Government Printing Office, 1982), pp. 7, 8, 15.

98. Hewitt and Clear, *The Impact of Sentencing Reform,* p. 101.

99. Leonard Orland, "Is Determinate Sentencing an Illusory Reform?" *Judicature* 62 (March 1970): 381.

100. Wilkerson v. Utah, 99 U.S. 130, 135 (1879).

101. In re Kemmler, 136 U.S. 436 (1890).

102. 136 U.S. 436, 446, 447. See also Francis v. Resweber, 329 U.S. 459, 460 (1947), holding that the electrocution, after an unsuccessful attempt in which there was a mechanical failure when the switch was pulled on the electricity going to the electric chair, was not cruel and unusual punishment.

103. Godfrey v. Georgia, 446 U.S. 420, 433 (Justice Marshall, concurring, joined by Justice Brennan), footnotes and citations omitted.

104. 408 U.S. 238 (1972).

105. "Courts Study Link Between Victim's Race and Imposition of Death Penalty," *New York Times,* January 5, 1984, p. 8, col. 1.

106. See the discussion in "Journal of Proceedings," *U.S. Law Week* 52 (January 17, 1984): 3530–3531.

107. State v. Chambers, 307 A.2d 78, 82 (N.J. Sup. Ct. 1973).

108. Weeks v. Illinois, 372 N.E.2d 163 (Ill. App. Ct. 4th Dist., 1977), *cert. denied,* 439 U.S. 809 (1978).

109. See in re Rodriquez, 537 P. 2d 384, 392 (Cal. Sup. Ct. 1975); and Weems v. United States, 217 U.S. 349, 367 (1910). For a general discussion of the proportionality issue, see Hyman Gross, "Proportional Punishment and Justifiable Sentences," in Hyman Gross and Andrew von Hirsch, eds., *Sentencing* (New York: Oxford University Press, 1981), pp. 272–283.

110. Rummel v. Estelle, 445 U.S. 263 (1980).

111. Coker v. Georgia, 433 U.S. 584 (1977).

112. Enmund v. Florida, 458 U.S. 782 (1982).

113. Pulley v. Harris, 104 S. Ct. 871 (1984).

114. See Robert Martinson, "What Works? Questions and Answers About Prison Reform," *Public Interest* 35 (Spring 1974): 22–54.

115. Alschuler, "Sentencing Reform and Prosecutorial Power," pp. 64–65.

116. Sue Titus Reid, "A Rebuttal to the Attack on the Indeterminate Sentence," *Washington Law Review* 51 (July 1976): 606.

Chapter 15

1. Garvin McCain, Verne C. Cox, and Paul B. Paulus, *The Effect of Prison Crowding on Inmate Behavior* (Washington, D.C.: U.S. Department of Justice, U.S. Government Printing Office, 1980), p. 103.

2. U.S. Department of Justice, *Prisoners in State and Federal Institutions on December 31, 1980* (Washington, D.C.: U.S. Government Printing Office, 1982), p. 2.

3. "Numbers Game Shows Need for Change in Corrections," *Tulsa Tribune,* January 31, 1983, p. 11C, col. 1.

4. James Austin and Barry Krisberg, "Wider, Stronger and Different Nets: The Dialectics of Criminal Justice Reform," *Journal of Research in Crime and Delinquency* 18 (January 1981): 179. See also Stephen Gettinger, "The Prison Population Boom: Still No End in Sight," *Corrections Magazine* 9 (June 1983): 6–11, 47–49.

5. "What Are Prisons For? No Longer Rehabilitation, but to Punish—And Lock the Worst Away," *Time,* September 13, 1982, p. 38.

6. For a comprehensive review of suggested reasons for increasing prison populations, see Todd R. Clear, Patricia M. Harris, and Albert I. Record, "Managing the Cost of Corrections," *Prison Journal* 62 (Spring–Summer 1982): 9–14.

7. Lawrence Muhammed, "Suits from the Slammer," *Barrister* 9 (Winter 1981): 55.

8. Ruiz v. Estelle, 503 F.Supp. 1265, 1277–1279 (S.D. Texas 1980), *aff'd.,* in part 679 F.2d. 1115 (5th cir. 1983), footnotes and citations omitted. We shall use examples of the problems in Texas throughout this chapter to illustrate modern problems in corrections.

9. Peter Finn, "Judicial Responses to Prison Crowding," *Judicature* 67 (February 1984): 318–325.

10. *Justice Assistance News* 4 (May 1983): 2.

11. U.S. Department of Justice, *Justice Assistance News* 2 (May 1981): 8.

12. Rhodes v. Chapman, 452 U.S. 337 (1981).

13. *New York Times,* April 12, 1983, p. 19, col. 4, and June 16, 1983, p. 26, col. 1.

14. Dennis Dunne, deputy director of planning and construction for the California Department of Corrections, quoted in "California Prison Construction Isn't Solving Population Woe," *Tulsa World,* June 30, 1983, p. 4ZA, col. 1. See also

Gettinger, "The Prison Population Boom," p. 10.

15. Finn, "Judicial Responses, p. 320.

16. *New York Times,* January 5, 1982, p. 1, col. 1; *Tulsa World,* June 27, 1982, p. 13, col. 3; and *Los Angeles Times,* April 6, 1982, p. 3, col. 1.

17. *New York Times,* March 26, 1981, p. A17, col. 1; *Tulsa World,* February 20, 1983, p. I1, col. 1; and *Tulsa World,* December 7, 1981, p. 12A, col. 1.

18. *Time,* September 13, 1982, p. 39. See also "California Prison Construction Isn't Solving Population Woe," p. 4A, col. 1.

19. Alfred Blumstein and Soumyo Moitra, "An Analysis of the Time Series of the Imprisonment Rate in the States of the United States: A Further Test of the Stability of Punishment Hypothesis," *Journal of Criminal Law & Criminology* 70 (Fall 1979): 376–390.

20. *New York Times,* May 23, 1982, p. 8E, col. 3, and August 12, 1981, p. 13, col. 3.

21. *Tulsa Tribune,* May 5, 1983, p. F1, col. 1; *San Diego Union,* April 25, 1982, p. A-9, col. 2; and Dennis Holder, "High Noon for Texas Prisons," *Student Lawyer* 11 (November 1982): 30.

22. Bruce Ramsey and Stephen Gettinger, "Washington State Seeks a Return to Normalcy," *Corrections Magazine* 7 (June 1981): 34.

23. *Tulsa Tribune,* May 5, 1983, p. 10D, col. 6, and July 16, 1981, p. 11A, col. 1.

24. *New York Times,* January 16, 1983, p. 7, col. 4; and *Tulsa World,* April 13, 1983, p. 16A, col. 6.

25. *Tulsa World,* July 29, 1982, p. 4C, col. 6, and April 19, 1981, p. C23, col. 4.

26. Mich. Comp. Laws Ann. § 800.71–800.79 (1981).

27. *New York Times,* September 29, 1983, p. 11, col. 1; and Clear, Harris, and Record, "Managing the Cost of Corrections," p. 47.

28. Ruiz v. Estelle, 679 F.2d 1115, 1148.

29. Roy R. Roberg, "Turbulence in Corrections: Implications for Management Practice," chap. 9, in Roy R. Roberg and Vincent J. Webb, eds., *Critical Issues in Corrections: Problems, Trends and Prospects* (St. Paul: West Publishing, 1981), p. 255. See also Daniel Glaser, *The Effectiveness of a Prison and Parole System* (Indianapolis: Bobbs-Merrill, 1969).

30. Kelsey Kauffman, "Prison Officers' Attitudes and Perceptions of Attitudes: A Case of Pluralistic Ignorance," *Journal of Research in Crime*

and Delinquency 18 (July 1981): 273. See also David Duffee, "The Correction Officer: Subculture and Organizational Change," *Journal of Research in Crime and Delinquency* 11 (July 1974): 155–172; James B. Jacobs and Harold G. Retsky, "Prison Guard," *Urban Life* 4 (April 1974): 5–29. For a recent collection of materials on prison guards, see Ben M. Crouch, ed., *The Keepers: Prison Guards and Contemporary Corrections* (Springfield, Ill.: Chas. C Thomas, 1980).

31. Donald Clemmer, *The Prison Community* (New York: Holt, Rinehart & Winston, 1958), p. 84. See also Gresham Sykes, *Society of Captives* (Princeton, N.J.: Princeton University Press, 1958); J. Roucek, "Sociology of the Prison Guard," *Sociology and Social Research* 20 (November 1935): 145–151.

32. For a discussion of this process, see Lloyd W. McCorkle, "Social Structures in a Prison," in Norman Johnston et al., eds., *The Sociology of Punishment and Correction,* 2d ed. (New York: John Wiley, 1979), p. 431.

33. McCorkle.

34. *New York Times,* June 12, 1983, p. 1, col. 5, and June 27, 1981, p. 16, col. 1.

35. See Lucien X. Lombardo, "Stress, Change, and Collective Violence in Prison," chap. 5, in Robert Johnson and Hans Toch, eds., *The Pains of Imprisonment* (Beverly Hills, Calif.: Sage Publications, 1982), p. 81.

36. Edgar May, "Prison Guards in America: The Inside Story," *Corrections Magazine* 2 (December 1976): 3–5, 40, 45.

37. Jacobs and Retsky, "Prison Guard," p. 11. See also the articles by Ben M. Crouch and Geoffrey P. Alpert: "Prison Guards' Attitudes Toward Components of the Criminal Justice System," *Criminology* 18 (August 1980): 227–236; "Sex and Occupational Socialization Among Prison Guards: A Longitudinal Study," *Criminal Justice and Behavior* 9 (June 1982): 159–176; and James B. Jacobs, "What Prison Guards Think: A Profile of the Illinois Force," *Crime & Delinquency* 24 (April 1978): 185–196.

38. Eric D. Poole and Robert M. Regoli, "Alienation in Prison: An Examination of the Work Relations of Prison Guards," *Criminology* 19 (August 1981): 254, 258–259.

39. Jacobs and Retsky, "Prison Guard," pp. 11–13. For further discussions of job satisfaction among correctional officers, see Hans Toch and John Klofas, "Alienation and Desire for Job Enrichment Among Correctional Officers," *Federal Probation* 46 (March 1982): 35–44; Boas Shamir and Amos Drory, "Occupational Tedium Among Prison Officers," *Criminal Justice and Behavior* 9 (March 1982): 79–99; and Lucien X. Lombardo, *Guards Imprisoned: Correctional Officers at Work* (New York: Elsevier North-Holland, 1981).

40. T. C. Willett, "Prison Guards in Private," *Canadian Journal of Criminology* 25 (January 1981): 1–17.

41. John M. Wynne, Jr., *Prison Employee Unionism: The Impact on Correctional Administration and Programs,* National Institute of Law Enforcement and Criminal Justice et al. (Washington, D.C.: U.S. Government Printing Office, 1978), pp. 3, 4, 5.

42. Wynne.

43. Wynne, pp. 31–34.

44. Wynne, pp. 35–38.

45. Wynne, p. 27

46. Wynne, p. 153.

47. Leo Carroll, *Hacks, Blacks and Cons: Race Relations in a Maximum Security Prison* (Lexington, Mass.: Heath, 1974), pp. 47, 52. For further discussion, see John R. Hepburn and Celesta Albonetti, "Role Conflict in Correctional Institutions: An Empirical Examination of the Treatment-Custody Dilemma Among Correctional Staff," *Criminology* 17 (February 1980): 445–459. Crouch, *The Keepers;* and Richard A. McGee, *Prisons and Politics* (Lexington, Mass.: Lexington Books, 1981).

48. See Raymond H. D. Teske, Jr., and Harold E. Williamson, "Correctional Officers' Attitudes Toward Selected Treatment Programs," *Criminal Justice and Behavior* 6 (March 1979): 62–63; and Boas Shamir and Amos Drory, "Some Correlates of Prison Guards' Beliefs," *Criminal Justice and Behavior* 8 (June 1981): 242–243. See also Crouch and Alpert, "Prison Guards' Attitudes Toward Components of the Criminal Justice System."

49. Toch and Klofas, "Alienation and Desire for Job Enrichment," p. 41.

50. Peter O. Peretti and Margaret Hooker, "Social Role Self-Perceptions of State Prison Guards," *Criminal Justice and Behavior* 3 (June 1976): 193–194. For a study describing how role conflicts in correctional officers' jobs contribute to

stress, see Shamir and Drory, "Occupational Tedium Among Prison Officers," pp. 79–99; and P. A. Hansen, *Creative Stress Management for Law Enforcement and Corrections* (Longmont, Colo.: Creative Stress Management, 1981).

51. Kelsey Kauffman, "Prison Officers' Attitudes and Perceptions of Attitudes: A Case of Pluralistic Ignorance"; and Lombardo, *Guards Imprisoned*. See also Lucien X. Lombardo, "Stress, Change and Collective Violence in Prison," chap. 5 in Johnson and Toch, eds., *The Pains of Imprisonment*.

52. Gordon Hawkins, *The Prison: Policy and Practice* (Chicago: University of Chicago Press, 1976), p. 106.

53. William L. Megathlin and Sherman R. Day, "The Line Staff As Agents of Control and Change," *American Journal of Correction* 34 (May-June 1972): 12–16.

54. Robert R. Smith, Michael A. Milan, Larry F. Wood, and John M. McKee, "The Correctional Officer As a Behavioral Technician," *Criminal Justice and Behavior* 3 (December 1976): 346–347.

55. Smith et al., "The Correctional Officer," pp. 345–360. For a discussion of ineffective training attempts, see Willett, "Prison Guards in Private." Willett reports on one experiment in removing officers from the institution for college training and finding that on their return, the prisons had absolutely no interest in the program. Prison staff and senior officers said the status quo should be maintained, regardless of what the trainees had learned.

56. Roberg, "Turbulence in Corrections," pp. 247–278.

57. See Hans Toch, "Is a 'Correctional Officer,' by Any Other Name, a 'Screw'?" *Criminal Justice Review* 3 (Fall 1978): pp. 24–28. See also Herbert A. Rosefield, "Mental Health Professionals Train Correctional Co-workers," *Corrections Today* 42 (May–June 1980): 44, 79.

58. Johnson, "Informal Helping Networks," p. 63.

59. Lucien X. Lombardo, "Alleviating Inmate Stress," in Johnson and Toch, eds., *The Pains of Imprisonment*, pp. 287–289.

60. Lombardo, pp. 290–292.

61. Lombardo, pp. 292–296. See also Roberg, "Turbulence in Corrections." pp. 255–256.

62. See Robert Johnson and Shelley Price, "The Complete Correctional Officer: Human Service and the Human Environment of Prison," *Criminal Justice and Behavior* 8 (September 1981): 343–346.

63. See Walter Y. Quijano and Steven A. Logsdon, "Some Issues in the Practice of Correctional Psychology in the Context of Security," *Professional Psychology* 9 (May 1978): 228–239. Quotation on p. 228. See also Robert Johnson, "Informal Helping Networks in Prison: The Shape of Grass-Roots Correctional Intervention," *Journal of Criminal Justice* 7 (Spring 1979): 56.

64. For a complete discussion of these issues, see Quijano and Logsdon, "Some Issues," pp. 232–238.

65. James B. Jacobs, "The Stateville Counselors: Symbol of Reform in Search of a Role," *Social Service Review* 50 (March 1976): 138–147. For more information about professional staff in prisons, see Jerry K. Kiessling and Donald A. Andrews, "Behavior Analysis Systems in Corrections: A New Approach to the Synthesis of Correctional Theory, Practice, Management and Research," *Canadian Journal of Criminology* 22 (October 1980): 412–427; and Phillip A. Belcastro, Robert S. Gold, and Justice Grant, "Stress and Burnout: Physiologic Effects on Correctional Teachers," *Criminal Justice and Behavior* 9 (December 1982): 387–395.

66. Glaser, *The Effectiveness of a Prison and Parole System*, pp. 146–148. See also James B. Jacobs, ed., *New Perspectives on Prisons and Imprisonment* (Ithaca, N.Y.: Cornell University Press, 1983), p. 137.

67. Gresham M. Sykes, *The Society of Captives* (Princeton, N.J.: Princeton University Press, 1958), p. 30.

68. For a discussion of the studies of social scientists on the effects of overcrowding in general, see Allan D. Vestal and Sue Titus Reid, "Toward Rational Land Use Planning, an Interdisciplinary Approach," *Florida State University Law Review* 1 (1973): 276–286.

69. An excellent review of the general problems resulting from overcrowded prisons may be found in *Overcrowded Time: Why Prisons are So Crowded and What Can Be Done* (New York: Edna McConnell Clark Foundation, 1982). See also Peter Suedfeld, "Environmental Effects on Violent Behavior in Prisons," *International Journal of Offender Therapy and Comparative Criminology* 24 (1980): 107–116.

70. Carl B. Clements, "Crowded Prisons: A Review of Psychological and Environmental Effects," *Law and Human Behavior* 3 (1979): 217–225.

71. Dale E. Smith, "Crowding and Confinement," chap. 3, in Johnson and Toch, eds., *The Pains of Imprisonment,* pp. 45–62.

72. Ruiz v. Estelle, 503 F. Supp. 1265, 1281–1282.

73. Garvin McCain, Verne C. Cox, and Paul B. Paulus, *The Effect of Prison Crowding on Inmate Behavior* (Washington, D.C.: U.S. Government Printing Office, 1980).

74. James A. Lieber, "The American Prison: A Tinder Box," *New York Times Magazine,* March 8, 1961, p. 60. For a study indicating that social density causes more stress than spatial density does, see Garvin McCain, Verne C. Cox, and Paul B. Paulus, "The Relationship Between Illness Complaints and Degree of Crowding in a Prison Environment," *Environment and Behavior* 8 (June 1976): 283–290.

75. Ruiz v. Estelle, 503 F.Supp. 1265, 1282.

76. Smith v. Fairman, 528 F.Supp. 186, 197. For more information on prison stress, see Hans Toch, "Studying and Reducing Stress," chap. 2, in Johnson and Toch, eds. *The Pains of Imprisonment,* pp. 25–44; and Carl B. Clements, "The Relationship of Offender Classification to the Problems of Prison Overcrowding," *Crime & Delinquency* 28 (January 1982): 72–81. For an excellent review of many types of complaints by inmates that relate to crowded conditions, see Hans Toch, *Living in Prision: Ecology of Survival* (New York: Free Press, 1977), pp. 20–38.

77. Reported in the *Tulsa Tribune,* May 29, 1980, p. 14A, col. 4.

78. Toch, *Living in Prison,* pp. 22–26.

79. For an account of these two riots, see Sue Titus Reid and Lorna Keltner, *Criminal Justice* (New York: Holt, Rinehart and Winston, forthcoming), chapter 15.

80. See John Irwin, *Prisons in Turmoil* (Boston: Little, Brown, 1980), p. 24.

81. Frank E. Hartung and Maurice Floch, "A Social-Psychological Analysis of Prison Riots: An Hypothesis," *Journal of Criminal Law, Criminology and Police Science* 47 (May–June 1956): 51.

82. Irwin, *Prisons in Turmoil,* pp. 25–26. See also the analysis of earlier riots in Vernon Fox, *Violence Behind Bars* (New York: Vantage Press, 1955).

83. For an analysis of the role of escapes in earlier riots, see John J. Gibbs, "Violence in Prison: Its Extent, Nature and Consequences," chap. 5, in Roy R. Roberg and Vincent J. Webb, eds., *Critical Issues in Corrections: Problems, Trends and Prospects* (St. Paul: West Publishing, 1981), pp. 110–145.

84. Irwin, *Prisons in Turmoil,* pp. 94–98.

85. For a more detailed discussion of this viewpoint, see C. Ronald Huff, "The Discovery of Prisoners' Rights: A Sociological Analysis," chap. 2, and Alvin J. Bronstein, "Prisoners' Rights: A History," chap. 1, in Geoffrey P. Alpert, ed., *Legal Rights of Prisoners* (Beverly Hills, Calif.: Sage Publications, 1980), pp. 47–65.

86. Gibbs, "Violence in Prison," pp. 127–128. Quotation is on p. 128. See also Irwin, *Prisons in Turmoil,* p. 94. For an extensive analysis of this area, see "The Prisoners' Rights Movement and Its Impacts," chap. 2 in Jacobs, ed., *New Perspectives on Prisons and Imprisonment,* pp. 33–60. For an interesting article detailing the differences in patterns of historical riots as compared with more recent uprisings, see Frederick J. Desroches, "Anomie: Two Theories of Prison Riots," *Canadian Journal of Criminology* 25 (April 1983): 173–190.

87. Hartung and Floch, "A Social-Psychological Analysis," 52.

88. Hartung and Floch, p. 52.

89. Edith Elisabeth Flynn, "Sources of Collective Violence in Correctional Institutions," in *Prevention of Violence in Correctional Institutions,* pp. 17–28.

90. Irwin, *Prisons in Turmoil,* pp. 72–77, 183–193. Quotation is on p. 183. For a detailed explanation of the rise of political prisoners and racism, see Ronald Berkman, *Opening the Gates: The Rise of the Prisoners' Movement* (Lexington, Mass.: Heath, 1979). For further information on the changing nature of prison inmates see John Irwin, "The Changing Social Structure of the Men's Prison," chap. 1, in David F. Greenberg, ed., *Corrections and Punishment* (Beverly Hills, Calif.: Sage Publications, 1977), pp. 21–40; Joan W. Moore et al., *Homeboys: Gangs, Drugs, and Prison in the Barrios of Los Angeles* (Philadelphia: Temple University Press, 1978); and Charles Stastny and Gabrielle Tynaruer, *Who Rules the Joint? The Changing Political Culture of Maximum-Security Pri-*

sons in America (Lexington, Mass.: Heath, 1982).

91. Flynn, "Sources of Collective Violence," pp. 17–28.

92. G. David Garson, "The Disruption of Prison Administration: An Investigation of Alternative Theories of the Relationship among Administrators, Reformers, and Involuntary Social Service Clients," *Law & Society Review* 6 (May 1972): 531–561. See also American Correctional Association, *Riots and Disturbances in Correctional Institutions* (Washington, D.C: American Correctional Association, 1970), p. 1.

93. See also Desroches, "Anomie: Two Theories of Prison Riots," pp. 174–177.

94. See Paul W. Keve, "The Quicksand Prison," *Prison Journal* 63 (Spring-Summer 1983): 47–58; and Peter Scharf, "Empty Bars: Violence and the Crisis of Meaning in the Prison," *Prison Journal* 63 (Spring–Summer 1983): 114–124.

95. Lawrence White, "Lifting Invisible Bars," *District Lawyer* 5 (November-December 1980): 36. See also "U.S. Prisons: Myth v. Mayhem," *Time,* May 5, 1980, pp. 64–65; Donald J. Shoemaker and George A. Hillery, Jr., "Violence and Commitment in Custodial Settings," *Criminology* 18 (May 1980): 94–102; and Lee H. Bowker, *Prison Victimization* (New York: Elsevier North-Holland, 1980).

96. Michael Satchell, "The End of the Line," *Parade,* September 28, 1980, p. 4. For a typology of prison violence, see Lee H. Bowker, "An Essay on Prison Violence," *Prison Journal* 63 (Spring–Summer 1983): 24–31.

97. Satchell, "The End of the Line," pp. 5, 6.

98. See, for example, Joseph Fishman, *Sex in Prison* (New York: National Library Press, 1934); Peter C. Buffum, *Homosexuality in Prisons* (Washington, D.C.: U.S. Government Printing Office, 1972); John Gagnon and William Simon, "The Social Meaning of Prison Homosexuality," *Federal Probation* 32 (March 1968): 23–29; Susan Brownmiller, *Against Our Will: Men, Women and Rape* (New York: Simon & Schuster, 1975); Bowker, *Prison Victimization;* Alice Propper, *Prison Homosexuality* (Lexington, Mass.: Heath, 1980); Daniel Lockwood, *Prison Sexual Violence* (New York: Elsevier North-Holland, 1980); and Carroll, *Hacks, Blacks, and Cons.*

99. For an extended discussion of introductory homosexual rituals, see Carl Weiss and David James Friar, *Terror in the Prisons: Homosexual Rape and Why Society Condones It* (Indianapolis: Bobbs-Merrill, 1974), pp. 68–79. See also Gibbs, "Violence in Prison"; Roberg and Webb, eds., *Critical Issues in Corrections,* pp. 110–149, in which he points out that aggressive inmates usually move in on their intended victims within the first eight weeks of incarceration; and see Alan J. Davis, "The Sheriff's Vans," *Trans-Action* 6 (December 1968): 12.

100. Lockwood, *Prison Sexual Violence,* pp. 16–23.

101. Daniel Lockwood, "Reducing Prison Sexual Violence," chap. 15 in Johnson and Toch, eds., *The Pains of Imprisonment.* pp. 257–265.

102. Gibbs, "Violence in Prison," p. 132. See also Daniel Lockwood, "Issues in Prison Sexual Violence," *Prison Journal* 63 (Spring–Summer 1983): 73–79.

103. U.S. Department of Justice, *Prisoners in State and Federal Institutions on December 31, 1980,* p. 9.

104. Sawyer F. Sylvester, John H. Reed, and David O. Nelson, *Prison Homicide* (New York: Halsted Press, 1977), p. xxii. See also Randy Atlas, "Crime Selection for Assaults in Four Florida Prisons," *Prison Journal* 63 (Spring–Summer 1983): 59–72.

105. Hans Toch, *Peacekeeping: Police, Prisons, and Violence* (Lexington, Mass.: Heath, 1976), p. 61.

106. Hans Toch, *Men in Crisis: Human Breakdown in Prison* (Chicago: Aldine, 1975), p. 127.

107. Suzanne Charlé, "New Programs Attack the No. 1 Killer of Jail Inmates," *Corrections Magazine* 7 (August 1981): 7.

108. *New York Times,* November 22, 1981, p. 18, col. 1.

109. *Justice Assistance News* 2 (February 1981): 3.

110. McCain, Cox, and Paulus, *The Effect of Prison Crowding on Inmate Behavior.*

111. Ruiz v. Estelle, 503 F.Supp. 1265, 1334.

112. Hans Toch, "A Psychological View of Prison Violence," chap. 4, in Albert K. Cohen, George F. Cole, and Robert C. Bailey, eds., *Prison Violence* (Lexington, Mass.: Heath, 1976), pp. 43–51.

113. Toch, "A Psychological View," p. 45.

114. Gibbs, "Violence in Prison." See also Richard H. Anson, "Inmate Ethnicity and the Suicide Connection: A Note on Aggregate Trends,"

Prison Journal 63 (Spring–Summer 1983): 91–99; and Leon Hankoff, "Prisoner Suicide," *International Journal of Offender Therapy and Comparative Criminology* 24 (1980): 162–166.

115. Toch, "A Psychological View," p. 49.

116. Toch, *Living in Prison.*

117. Coffin v. Richard, 143 F.2d 443, 445 (6th Cir. 1944).

118. Ruiz v. Estelle, 503 F.Supp. 1265, 1293.

119. The statute is found in Title 42 United States Code 1997. See also "Hawaii Prisons Sued: First 'Institutionalized Persons Act' Case," *Corrections Magazine* 9 (June 1983): 4; and U.S. v. Hawaii, 564 F.Supp. 189 (D. Hawaii 1983).

120. Richard Reeves, "High Price of Punishing Criminals," *Tulsa World,* June 27, 1982, p. 13, col. 3.

Chapter 16

1. See Harold Garfinkel, "Conditions of Successful Degradation Ceremonies," *American Journal of Sociology* 61 (March 1956): 420–424.

2. Gresham M. Sykes, *The Society of Captives* (Princeton, N.J.: Princeton University Press, 1958), pp. 63–83. See also Gordon Trasler, "The Social Relations of Persistent Offenders," in Robert M. Carter, Daniel Glaser, and Leslie T. Wilkins, eds., *Correctional Institutions* (Philadelphia: Lippincott, 1972), p. 207.

3. Gresham M. Sykes and Sheldon L. Messinger, "The Inmate Social System," in Richard A. Cloward et al., eds., *Theoretical Studies in Social Organization of the Prison* (New York: Social Science Research Council, 1960), p. 15.

4. Donald Clemmer, *The Prison Community,* 1940 reprint ed. (New York: Holt, Rinehart & Winston, 1958).

5. Clemmer, pp. 298–301.

6. Edwin H. Sutherland and Donald R. Cressey, *Principles of Criminology,* 10th ed. (New York: Lippincott, 1978), p. 76.

7. Stanton Wheeler, "Socialization in Correctional Communities," *American Sociological Review* 26 (October 1961): 697–712. For a discussion of changing references of inmates, see John R. Stratton. "The Measurement of Inmate Change During Imprisonment" (Ph.D. diss., University of Illinois, 1963).

8. See for example, Peter G. Garabedian, "Social Roles and Processes of Socialization in the Prison Community," *Social Problems* 11 (Fall 1963): 139–152: Daniel Glaser, *The Effectiveness of a Prison and Parole System,* abridged ed. (Indianapolis: Bobbs-Merrill, 1969). Other researchers have seriously questioned the findings of Wheeler's study, although these critics have acknowledged that the differences between their findings and Wheeler's and others' who have found that a U-shaped curve of attitudes during imprisonment may be due to the particular organization system of the institutions from which the data were secured. See Robert Atchley and M. Patrick McCabe, "Socialization in Correctional Communities: A Replication," *American Sociological Review* 33 (October 1968): 774–785; and Gene Kassebaum, David Wilner, and Daniel Wilner, *Prison Treatment and Parole Survival: An Empirical Assessment* (New York: John Wiley, 1971), chap. 2, "Doing Time in a Pastel Prison."

9. Geoffrey P. Alpert, George Noblit, and John J. Wiorkowski, "A Comparative Look at Prisonization: Sex and Prison Culture," *Quarterly Journal of Corrections* 1 (Summer 1977): 29–34. See also Geoffrey P. Alpert, "Patterns of Change in Prisonization: A Longitudinal Analysis," *Criminal Justice and Behavior* 6 (June 1979): 159–174.

10. Sykes, *The Society of Captives,* p. 82, emphasis deleted.

11. Sykes and Messinger, "The Inmate Social System," p. 17. For a discussion of "structural accommodation" in prison, see Cloward et al., *Theoretical Studies,* pp. 21, 35–41. For information about the effect of total institutions on previous experiences, see Erving Goffman, "On the Characteristics of Total Institutions," chap. 2, in Donald R. Cressey, ed., *The Prison: Studies in Institutional Organization and Change* (New York: Holt, Rinehart & Winston, 1961), pp. 22–47. See also Nicolette Parisi, *Coping with Imprisonment* (Beverly Hills, Calif.: Sage Publications, 1982).

12. Charles R. Tittle, "Inmate Organization: Sex Differentiation and the Influence of Criminal Subcultures," *American Sociological Review* 34 (August 1969): 503. See also Charles R. Tittle and Drollene P. Tittle, "Social Organization of Prisoners: An Empirical Test," *Social Forces* 43 (December 1964): 216–221.

13. John Irwin and Donald R. Cressey, "Thieves, Convicts and the Inmate Culture," *Social Prob-*

lems 19 (Fall 1962): 143. Clemmer agreed that part of the prison subculture depended on the men's experiences outside the prison. See Clemmer, *The Prison Community,* pp. 229–302; and see also Clarence C. Schrag, "Social Types in a Prison Community," (M.A. thesis, University of Washington, 1944).

14. Irwin and Cressey, "Thieves, Convicts and the Inmate Culture," 142.

15. See, for example, Walter C. Reckless, *The Crime Problem,* 2d ed. (New York: Appleton, 1945), pp. 114–145, 148–150; Edwin H. Sutherland, *The Professional Thief* (Chicago: University of Chicago Press, 1937).

16. See, for example, William Foote Whyte, "Corner Boys: A Study of Clique Behavior," *American Journal of Sociology* 46 (March 1941): 647–663; and Walter B. Miller, "Lower Class Culture As a Generating Milieu of Gang Delinquency," *Journal of Social Issues* 14 (1958): 5–19, for his discussion of the focal concerns of toughness, smartness, and autonomy, which he maintains are characteristic of the lower class. They are also characteristic of this category of prison subculture, according to Irwin and Cressey.

17. Irwin and Cressey, "Thieves, Convict, and the Inmate Culture," 148.

18. Irwin and Cressey. For Clemmer's support of this type, see *The Prison Community,* p. 130.

19. Irwin and Cressey, "Thieves, Convicts and the Inmate Culture," 153. For a discussion of the impact that traditional roles of women in our society have on the inmate culture of women's prisons, see Rose Giallombardo, *Society of Women: A Study of a Woman's Prison* (New York: John Wiley, 1966).

20. Charles W. Thomas, "Prisonization or Resocialization: A Study of External Factors Associated with the Impact of Imprisonment," *Journal of Research in Crime and Delinquency* 10 (January 1975): 13–21. See also Charles W. Thomas, "Toward a More Inclusive Model of the Inmate Contraculture," *Criminology* 8 (November 1970): 251–262; Geoffrey P. Alpert, "Prisons As Formal Organizations: Compliance Theory in Action," *Sociology and Social Research* 63 (October 1978): 112–128. See also Barry C. Field, "A Comparative Analysis of Organizational Structure and Inmate Subcultures in Institutions for Juvenile Offenders," *Crime & Delinquency* 27 (July 1981): 336–363. For a discussion of inmate adaptation to the formal prison orga-

nization, see Lynne Goodstein, "Inmate Adjustment to Prison and the Transition to Community Life," *Journal of Research in Crime and Delinquency* 16 (July 1979): 246–272.

21. Leo Carroll, "Race and Three Forms of Prisoner Power: Confrontation, Censoriousness, and the Corruption of Authority," in C. Ronald Huff, ed., *Contemporary Corrections: Social Control and Conflict* (Beverly Hills, Calif.: Sage Publications, 1977), p. 40. For more information, see Geoffrey P. Alpert, "Institutional Diversity and Prisonization: A Longitudinal Analysis," *LEA Journal of the American Criminal Justice Association* 42 (Winter-Spring 1979): 31–39. See also Matthew T. Zingraff and Rhonda M. Zingraff, "Adaptation Patterns of Incarcerated Female Delinquents," *Juvenile and Family Court Journal* 31 (May 1980): 35–47.

22. Leo Carroll, *Hacks, Blacks, and Cons: Race Relations in a Maximum Security Prison* (Lexington, Mass.: Heath). See also John R. Hellburn and John R. Stratton, "Total Institutions and Inmate Self-Esteem," *British Journal of Criminology* 17 (July 1977): 237–250. Other researchers have argued that the importation and deprivation models should be integrated. See, for example, Barry Schwartz, "Pre-Institutional vs. Situational Influence in a Correctional Community," *Journal of Criminal Law, Criminology, and Police Science* 62 (Winter 1971): 532–542. See also Ronald L. Akers, "Type of Leadership in Prison: A Structural Approach to Testing the Functional and Importation Models," *Sociological Quarterly* 18 (Summer 1977): 378–383: Clemens Bartollas, Stuart J. Miller, and Simon Dinitz, *Juvenile Victimization: The Institutional Paradox* (New York: John Wiley, 1976).

23. Ronald L. Akers, Norman S. Hayner, and Werner Gruninger, "Prisonization in Five Countries: Type of Prison and Inmate Characteristics," *Criminology* 14 (February 1977): 538.

24. Charles W. Thomas, quoted in Akers, Hayner, and Gruninger, p. 548. For a discussion of the use of the integrative approach to explain drug usage in prison, see Ronald L. Akers, Norman S. Hayner, and Werner Gruninger, "Homosexual and Drug Behavior in Prison: A Test of the Functional and Importation Models of the Inmate System," *Social Problems* 21 (1974): 410–422.

25. Charles W. Thomas, David M. Petersen, and Rhonda M. Zingraff, "Structural and Social Psy-

chological Correlates of Prisonization," *Criminology* 16 (November 1978): 390–391; Charles W. Thomas and David M. Petersen, *Prison Organization and Inmate Structures* (Indianapolis: Bobbs-Merrill, 1977); Matthew T. Zingraff, "Prisonization As an Inhibitor of Effective Resocialization," *Criminology* 13 (November 1975): 366–388. Another study supporting the combination of theories is William M. Bumberry and J. Thomas Grisso, "Importation Versus Inmate Socialization As the Primary Determinant of Perceptions of Halfway House Residents," *Journal of Community Psychology* 9 (April 1981): 177–187.

26. Wheeler, "Socialization in Correctional Communities."

27. Wheeler, p. 711. For a discussion of the process of rejecting the rejectors, see Lloyd W. McCorkle and Richard Korn, "Resocialization Within Walls," *Annals of the American Academy of Political and Social Science* 293 (May 1954): 88–98.

28. Irwin and Cressey, "Thieves, Convicts and the Inmate Culture," 155.

29. For a discussion of criticisms of prisonization, see Gordon Hawkins, *The Prison: Policy and Practice* (Chicago: University of Chicago Press, 1976), pp. 63–80. For an excellent review of the literature on prison communities or subcultures, see Lee H. Bowker, *Prisoner Subcultures* (Lexington, Mass.: Heath, 1977).

30. Warren E. Burger, "Annual Report to the American Bar Association by the Chief Justice of the United States," *American Bar Association Journal* 67 (March 1981): 293. See also Warren E. Burger, "More Warehouses, or Factories with Fences?" *New England Journal on Prison Law* 8 (Winter 1982): 111–120.

31. U.S. Congress, Senate, 98th Cong., 1st sess., (daily) 1 March 1983, *Congressional Record* 129: S1847.

32. See Burger, "More Warehouses," p. 119; and George E. Sexton, "The Industrial Prison: A Concept Paper," *Prison Journal* 62 (Autumn-Winter 1982): 13–24. For a critique of the argument that prison labor programs would be economically beneficial, see Todd R. Clear, Patricia M. Harris, and Albert L. Record, "Managing the Cost of Corrections," *Prison Journal* 62 (Spring-Summer 1982): 22–23.

33. Dr. Joseph Burchac quoted in *New York Times,* January 4, 1981, p. 22, col. 1.

34. U.S. General Accounting Office, *Report to the Attorney General: Improved Prison Work Programs Will Benefit Correctional Institutions and Inmates* (Washington, D.C.: U.S. Government Printing Office, June 29, 1982), pp. 1–2. See also Vergil L. Williams and Mary Fish, *Convicts, Codes and Contraband: The Prison Life of Men and Women* (Cambridge, Mass.: Ballinger, 1974).

35. Joan Petersilia, *Racial Disparities in the Criminal Justice System* (Washington, D.C.: U.S. Government Printing Office, 1983), p. 54.

36. Paul Tappan, *Crime, Justice and Correction* (New York: McGraw-Hill, 1960), p. 623.

37. Frank Loveland, "Classification in the Prison System," in Paul W. Tappan, ed., *Contemporary Correction* (New York: McGraw-Hill, 1951), p. 91. See also Richard W. Hanson et al., "Predicting Inmate Penitentiary Adjustment: An Assessment of Four Classificatory Methods," *Criminal Justice and Behavior* 10 (September 1983): 293–309.

38. Loveland, p. 95.

39. "Classification," in George Killinger and Paul Cromwell, eds., *Penology* (St. Paul: West Publishing, 1973), pp. 281–283.

40. Warden A. I. Murphy, private correspondence. For more information on classification programs, see Carl B. Clements, "Test-Trait Fallacies: Prison Style," *American Psychologist* 35 (May 1980): 476–478; Timothy J. Flanagan, "Correctional Policy and the Long-Term Prisoner," *Crime & Delinquency* 28 (January 1982): 82–95; and Hans Toch, "Inmate Classification As a Transaction," *Criminal Justice and Behavior* 8 (March 1981): 3–14.

41. American Correctional Association, *Manual of Correctional Standards* (Washington, D.C. Commission on Accreditation for Corrections 1966).

42. James Austin, "Assessing the New Generation of Prison Classification Models," *Crime & Delinquency* 29 (October 1983): 561–576.

43. For an extensive discussion, see Carl B. Clements, "The Future of Offender Classification: Some Cautions and Prospects," *Criminal Justice and Behavior* 8 (March 1981): 15–38. See also Stephen Gettinger, "'Objective' Classification: Catalyst for Change," *Corrections Magazine* 8 (June 1982): 24–27; and Clear, Harris, and Record, "Managing the Cost of Corrections," pp. 24–26.

44. See the series of articles in *Classification As a Management Tool: Theories and Models for Decision Makers* (College Park, Maryland: American Correctional Association, 1982).

45. Elmer Hubert Johnson, *Crime, Correction, and Society,* 4th ed. (Homewood, Ill.: Dorsey Press, 1978), pp. 371–372.

46. Michael V. Reagen and Donald M. Stoughton, eds., *School Behind Bars: A Descriptive Overview of Correctional Education in the American Prison System* (Metuchen, N.J.: Scarecrow Press, 1976). See also William B. Nagel, *The New Red Barn: A Critical Look at the Modern American Prison* (New York: Walker, 1973), pp. 123–127.

47. For a fascinating discussion of an early Connecticut prison called New-Gate, see Charles W. Dean, "The Story of New-Gate," *Federal Probation* 43 (June 1979): 8–14. New-Gate was the first state prison in this country and is now a museum, open to the public.

48. Extensive information about Insight can be found in Eric Black, "Doing Time by the Book," *Student Lawyer* (January 1983): 23–27, 41–42. Quotations are from pp. 25, 41, 42. Information on the PLATO system can be found in National Clearinghouse for Criminal Justice Planning and Architecture, "PLATO: Computer-Based Education," bulletin issued in November 1976.

49. Robert S. Baer, *A Guide to Training and Employment of Prisoners as Paralegals* (Washington, D.C.: American Bar Association, 1979).

50. Baer, p. 25.

51. Ross F. Connor and James Emshoff, *Legal Aid and Education for Prisoners, An Evaluation of the State Bar of Michigan's Prison Project, BASICS* (Washington, D.C.: American Bar Association, 1978). See also Ross F. Conner, W. Davidson, and James Emshoff, *Legal Aid and Legal Education for Prisoners—An Evaluation of the State Bar of Michigan's Prison Project* (Washington, D.C.: U.S. Government Printing Office, 1978).

52. "Convicts in New York Study to Be Ministers," *New York Times,* December 4, 1982, p. 13, col. 1.

53. Elmer Hubert Johnson, *Crime, Correction, and Society* (Homewood, Ill.: Dorsey Press, 1978), p. 559.

54. For a discussion of the history of prison labor in Europe and America, see Sue Titus Reid and Lorna Keltner, *Criminal Justice* (New York: Holt, Rinehart & Winston, 1985).

55. For a discussion of this legislation, see Barbara Auerbach, "New Prison Industries Legislation: The Private Sector Re-enters the Field," *Prison Journal* 62 (Autumn-Winter 1982): 25–36.

56. 18 U.S. Code 1761. For further information, see Jack Schaller, "Work and Imprisonment: An Overview of the Changing Role of Prison Labor in America," *Prison Journal* 62 (Autumn–Winter 1982): 8.

57. Warren E. Burger, "Ex-Prisoners Can Become Producers, Not Predators," *Nation's Business* (October 1983): 38.

58. Minn. Stat. Ann. 243.88.

59. See Kansas Stat. Ann. 47-7-108 through 44-7-112.

60. Rev. Code of Wash. Ann., 72.09.100 (1).

61. Alaska Stat. 33.32.015, et. seq.

62. Rev. Code of Wash. Ann., 72.60.102; and Indiana Stat. Ann. 11-10-7-3.

63. See General Accounting Office, *Report to the Attorney General: Improved Prison Work Programs Will Benefit Correctional Institutions and Inmates* (Washington, D.C.: U.S. Government Printing Office, 1982), p. 13.

64. General Accounting Office, *Improved Prison Work Programs,* pp. 16, 17, 53. For further information on the financial aspects of FPI, see U.S. Department of Justice, Office of Management and Budget, *The Budget of the United States Government: Fiscal Year 1981, Appendix* (Washington, D.C.: U.S. Government Printing Office, 1982). For a fascinating account of industry in China's prisons, see E. Eugene Miller, "Prison Industries in the People's Republic of China," *Prison Journal* 62 (Autumn-Winter 1982): 52–67.

65. Robert Mintz, "Federal Prison Industry—The 'Green Monster': Part One—History and Background," *Crime and Social Justice* 6 (Fall-Winter 1976): 61–48.

66. Seymour Halleck, *Psychiatry and Dilemmas of Crime* (Berkeley and Los Angeles: University of California Press, 1971), pp. 284–285. See also Paul W. Keve, *Prison Life and Human Worth* (Minneapolis: University of Minnesota Press, 1974), pp. 30–31; Neal Miller and Walter Jensen, Jr., "Reform of Federal Prison Industries: New Opportunities for Public Offenders," *Justice System Journal* 1 (Winter 1974): 5–6.

67. For further information on the state use of grant money, see Gail S. Funke, Billy L. Wayson, and Neal Miller," The Future of Correctional Industries," *Prison Journal* 62 (Autumn-Winter 1982): 39–41; and Michael Fedo "'Free Venture': Seed Money to Revitalize Industries," *Corrections Magazine* 7 (April 1981): 11.

68. "Burger Urges Prison Reform, Pleads for Additional Judges," *Criminal Justice Newsletter,* January 17, 1984, p. 7.

69. Grant R. Grissom, *Impact of Free Venture Prison Industries Upon Correctional Institutions* (Washington, D.C.: U.S. Government Printing Office, January 1981). See also Gail S. Funke, Billy L. Wayson, and Neal Miller, *Assets and Liabilities of Correctional Industries* (Lexington, Mass.: Heath-Lexington Books, 1982).

70. Grissom, *Impact of Free Venture,* pp. ii, 23, 26, 68. For the issues surrounding vocational education in prisons, see National Advisory Council on Vocational Education, *Vocational Education in Correctional Institutions* (Washington, D.C.: U.S. Government Printing Office, 1981); and for the problems in obtaining qualified teachers for vocational training programs in prisons, see Richard A. Holodick, Milton E. Larson, and Ivan E. Valentine, "Vocational Instructors in Corrections, *Corrections Today* 42 (May–June 1980): 62–64.

71. Warren E. Burger, "More Warehouses, or Factories with Fences?" *New England Journal on Prison Law* 8 (Winter 1982): 118.

72. For a discussion, see Sexton, "The Industrial Prison," pp. 13–24.

73. Grissom, *Impact of Free Venture,* pp. 43, 45. See also Paul Gendreau, Doretta Burke, and Brian A. Grant, "A Second Evaluation of the Rideau Inmate Volunteer Program," *Canadian Journal of Criminology* 22 (January 1980): 66–77.

74. Grissom, *Impact of Free Venture,* p. 38.

75. Burger, "More Warehouses, p. 115.

76. See Burger, "Ex-Prisoners," p. 39; Michael Fedo, "Free Enterprise Goes to Prison," *Corrections Magazine* 7 (April 1981): 5–13; and Sharon Goodman, "Prisoners As Entrepreneurs: Developing a Model for Prisoner-Run Industry," *Boston University Law Review* 62 (November 1982): 1163–1195.

77. Rutherford v. Hutto, 377 F. Supp. 268, 270, 271, 272, 273 (E.D. Ark. 1974). See also Jackson v. McLemore, 523 F. 2d 838 (8th Cir. 1975).

78. Laaman v. Lelgemoe, 437 F. Supp. 269, 317 (D.N.H. 1977).

79. Hoptowit v. Ray, 682 F.2d 1237 (9th Cir. 1982).

80. Sigler v. Lowrie, 404 F. 2d 659, 661 (8th Cir.) *cert. denied,* 395 U.S. 940 (1969).

81. See Shields v. Hopper, 519 F. 2d 1131 (5th Cir. 1975).

82. U.S. v. Reynolds, 235 U.S. 133 (1914). For a review of other legal issues in this area, see Neal Miller and Walter Jenson, Jr., "Inmate Labor Practices and Laws: A Preliminary Analysis," in Alpert, ed., *Legal Rights of Prisoners,* pp. 217–242.

83. Robert Martinson, "What Works?—Questions and Answers About Prison Reform," *Public Interest* 35 (Spring 1974): 22–54. The complete report is published in Douglas Lipton, Robert Martinson, and Judith Wilks, *The Effectiveness of Correctional Treatment: A Survey of Treatment Education Studies* (New York: Holt, Rinehart & Winston, 1975).

84. See Carl B. Klockars, "The True Limits of the Effectivenss of Correctional Treatment," *Prison Journal* 55 (Spring-Summer 1975): 53–54; Ted Palmer, "Martinson Revisited," chap. 2, in Robert Martinson, Ted Palmer, and Stuart Adams, *Rehabilitation, Recidivism, and Research* (Hackensack, N.J.: National Council on Crime and Delinquency, 1976), pp. 41–62. This article was originally published in the *Journal of Research in Crime and Delinquency* 12 (July 1975): 133–152. See also Kevin N. Wright, "A Re-Examination of Correctional Alternatives," *International Journal of Offender Therapy and Comparative Criminology* 24 (1980): 179–192.

85. Michael S. Serrill, "California: More Prisoners, More Programs, More Problems," *Corrections Magazine* 1 (September 1974): 4.

86. See Vincent J. Webb et al., "Recidivism: In Search of a More Comprehensive Definition," *International Journal of Offender Therapy and Comparative Criminology* 20 (1976): 144–147. For a technical discussion of the models used to predict recidivism, see Michael R. Lloyd and George W. Joe, "Recidivism Comparisons Across Groups: Methods of Estimation and Tests of Significance for Recidivism Rates and Asymptotes," *Evaluation Quarterly* 3 (February 1979): 105–117; Stephen Stollmack, "Comments on 'The Mathematics of Behavioral Change,'" *Evaluation Quarterly* 3 (February

1979): 118–123; Michael D. Maltz, Richard McCleary, and Stephen P. Pollock, "Recidivism and Likelihood Functions: A Reply to Stollmack," *Evaluation Quarterly* 3 (February 1979): 124–131; and William E. Stein and Michael R. Lloyd, "The Maltz-McCleary Model of Recidivism: A Reexamination," *Evaluation Review* 5 (February 1981): 132–144.

87. Marvin E. Wolfgang, Robert M. Figlio, and Thorsten Sellin, *Delinquency in a Birth Cohort* (Chicago: University of Chicago Press, 1972), p. 254.

88. For a series of studies indicating traits that might promote rehabilitation in various groups of prisoners, see the following articles by Robert V. Heckel and Elizabeth Mandell in *Journal of Clinical Psychology* 37 (April 1981), "A Factor Analytic Study of the Demographic Characteristics of Incarcerated Males," 423–425; "A Factor Analytic Study of the Demographic Characteristics of Incarcerated Male and Female Juvenile Offenders," 426–429; and "A Factor Analytic Study of the Demographic Characteristics of Adult and Juvenile Incarcerates," 430–433. See also the article by the same authors, "A Factor Analytic Study of the Demographic Characteristics of Incarcerated Females," *Journal of Clinical Psychology* 37 (July 1981): 678–680.

89. See Gordon P. Waldo and Theodore G. Chiricos, "Work Release and Recidivism: An Empirical Evaluation of a Social Policy," *Evaluation Quarterly* 1 (Feburary 1977): 87–108; and James Austin and Barry Krisberg, "The Unmet Promise of Alternatives to Incarceration," *Crime & Delinquency* 28 (July 1982): 374–409.

90. Roger Hood and Richard Sparks, *Key Issues in Criminology* (New York: World University Library, 1970).

91. Procunier v. Martinez, 416 U.S. 396, 428 (1974), Justice Marshall, with whom Justice Brennan joins, concurring.

Chapter 17

1. Gordon Hawkins, *The Prison: Policy and Practice* (Chicago: University of Chicago Press, 1976), pp. 56–59.

2. Harry E. Allen et al., "Sociopathy: An Experiment on Internal Environmental Control," *American Behavioral Scientist* 20 (November–December 1976):215.

3. National Advisory Commission on Criminal Justice Standards and Goals, *A National Strategy to Reduce Crime* (Washington, D.C.: U.S. Government Printing Office, 1973), p. 121.

4. Nora Klapmuts, "Community Alternatives to Prison," chap. 15, in John Monahan, ed., *Community Health and the Criminal Justice System* (New York: Pergamon Press, 1976), p. 206. For an article supporting the trend toward community corrections, see John P. Conrad, "There Has to Be a Better Way," *Crime & Delinquency* 26 (January 1980): 83–90.

5. Robert M. Carter et al., *Program Models: Community Correctional Centers* (Washington, D.C.: U.S. Government Printing Office, 1980), p. 3.

6. Lloyd E. Ohlin, Alden D. Miller, and Robert B. Coates, *Juvenile Correctional Reform in Massachusetts. A Preliminary Report of the Center for Criminal Justice of the Harvard Law School*, National Institute for Juvenile Justice and Delinquency Prevention, LEAA (Washington, D.C.: U.S. Government Printing Office, 1977), p. 23.

7. Andrew Rutherford and Osman Bengur, *Community Based Alternatives to Juvenile Incarceration*, National Evaluation Program, Phase I, Summary Report, National Institute of Law Enforcement and Criminal Justice, LEAA (Washington, D. C.: U.S. Government Printing Office, 1976), p. 11.

8. E. K. Nelson et al., *Program Models: Unification of Community Corrections* (Washington, D.C.: U.S. Government Printing Office, 1980), p. 13.

9. Robert D. Vinter et al., *Juvenile Corrections in the States: Residential Programs and Deinstitutionalization: A Preliminary Report* (Ann Arbor: University of Michigan Press, 1975), National Assessment of Juvenile Corrections, pp. 48–49.

10. See James McSparron, "Community Correction and Diversion: Costs and Benefits, Subsidy Modes, and Start-Up Recommendations," *Crime & Delinquency* 26 (April 1980): 226–247.

11. Minn. Stat. Ann. 401.01 et. seq. The law was later amended so that charge-backs applied only to juveniles and those adults sentenced before 1980.

12. For a discussion of the Minnesota Plan, see Kenneth F. Schoen, "The Community Corrections Act," *Crime & Delinquency* 24 (October 1978): 458–464. See also "Minnesota's Community Corrections Act Takes Hold," *Corrections Magazine* 4 (March 1978): 54; and John Blackmore,

"Evaluating the Minnesota Evaluation," *Corrections Magazine* 7 (August 1981): 24–32. See pp. 34–38 in the same issue for an evaluation and report on the Oregon plan, a community corrections plan modeled on the Minnesota Community Corrections Act. For a discussion of the criticisms of the Minnesota plan, see McSparron, "Community Correction and Diversion." For a discussion and critique of the California Community Treatment Project, see Paul Lerman, *Community Treatment and Social Control: A Critical Analysis of Juvenile Correctional Policy* (Chicago: University of Chicago Press, 1975), pp. 19–104.

13. Information on this program may be found in the LEAA publication, *Community Based Corrections in Des Moines: An Exemplary Project,* National Institute of Law Enforcement and Criminal Justice (Washington, D.C.: U.S. Government Printing Office, 1976). See also Carter et al., *Program Models,* pp. 11–48.

14. For a report on similar programs, see Robert Rice, *Evaluation of the Des Moines Community-Based Corrections Replication Programs: Summary Report* (Washington, D.C.: U.S. Government Printing Office, 1979).

15. Carter et al., *Program Models,* p. 49.

16. See Richard R. Lancaster, *The Residential Corrections Facility at Fort Des Moines: A Cost-Effectiveness Analysis* (Des Moines: Iowa Bureau of Correctional Evaluation, 1978).

17. See Rice, *Evaluation of the Des Moines Community-Based Corrections,* pp. 12, 23.

18. For information on some of these programs, see Lloyd W. McCorkle, Albert Elias, and F. Lovell Bixby. *The Highfields Story: An Experimental Treatment Project for Youthful Offenders* (New York: Holt, Rinehart & Winston, 1968); H. Ashley Weeks, *Youthful Offenders at Highfields* (Ann Arbor: University of Michigan Press, 1958); LaMar T. Empey and Jerome Rabow, "The Provo Experiment in Delinquent Rehabilitation," *American Sociological Review* 26 (October 1961): 683. See also Richard M. Stephenson and Frank R. Scarpitti, "Essexfields: A Non-Residential Experiment in Group Centered Rehabilitation of Delinquents," *American Journal of Correction* 31 (1969): 12–18. LaMar T. Empey and Maynard L. Erickson, *The Provo Experiment Evaluation of Community Control of Delinquency* (Lexington, Mass.: 1972); Joan McCord, William McCord, and Emily Thurber,

"The Effects of Foster-Home Placement in the Prevention of Adult Antisocial Behavior," in John R. Stratton and Robert M. Terry, eds., *Prevention of Deliquency Problems and Programs,* (New York: Macmillan, 1968); LaMar T. Empey and Steven G. Lubeck. *The Silverlake Experiment: Testing Delinquency, Theory and Community Intervention* (Chicago: Aldine, 1971).

19. See Steven Balkin, "Prisoners by Day: A Proposal to Sentence Non-Violent Offenders to Non-Residential Work Facilities," *Judicature* 64 (October 1980): 154–164.

20. Norman C. Colter, "Subsidizing the Released Inmate," *Crime & Delinquency* 241 (July 1975): 285. For a review of the mixed results from the Transitional Aid Research Project (TARP), which gave unemployment benefits to 2000 releasees each in Georgia and Texas, see Peter H. Rossi, Richard A. Berk, and Kenneth J. Lenihan, *Money, Work, and Crime: Experimental Evidence* (New York: Academic Press, 1980); and Jeffrey K. Liker, "Wage and Status Effects of Employment on Affective Well-Being Among Ex-Felons," *American Sociological Review* 47 (April 1982): 264–283.

21. Richard J. Simmons, "M-2 (Man-to-Man) Job Therapy," chap. 9, in Calvert R. Dodge, ed., *A Nation Without Prisons: Alternatives to Incarceration* (Lexington, Mass.: Heath, 1975), p. 175.

22. See, for example, the following: Mary A. Toborg et al., *The Transition from Prison to Employment: An Assessment of Community-Based Assistance Programs,* National Institute of Law Enforcement and Criminal Justice, LEAA (Washington, D.C.: U.S. Government Printing Office, 1978); Michelle Sviridoff and James W. Thompson, "Links Between Employment and Crime: A Qualitative Study of Rikers Island Releasees," *Crime & Delinquency* 29 (April 1983): 195–212; James L. Beck, "Employment, Community Treatment Center Placement, and Recidivism: A Study of Released Federal Offenders," *Federal Probation* 45 (December 1981):3–8; and Liker, "Wage and Status Effects." For the opposite view that improved economic status does not result in decreased criminal activity, see Thomas Orsagn and Ann Dryden Witte, "Economic Status and Crime: Implications for Offender Rehabilitation," *Criminology* 72 (Fall 1981): 1055–1071.

23. Marc R. Levinson, "In South Carolina, Community Corrections Means the Alston Wilkes

Society," *Corrections Magazine* 9 (June 1983): 41–46. For information on programs in Iowa and Illinois, see "The Safer Foundation: 'Find Them a Job or They'll Do a Job," *Corrections Magazine* 8 (June 1982): 18–19. For a review of the practical problems in starting a program for ex-offenders, see Stanley S. Nakamura, "An Experimental Focus on the Development of Employment for Ex-Offenders," *Federal Probation* 26 (March 1982): 31–34.

24. See Toborg et al., *The Transition from Prison to Employment,* p. iii.

25. Maine Stat. Ann. tit. 34 §1008.

26. Winsett v. McGinnes, 617 F. 2d 996, 999 (3rd Cir. 1980), *cert denied,* 449 U. S. 1093 (1981). Because the Supreme Court refused to hear this case, the Third Circuit's decision stands. The Supreme Court has never addressed the issue of inmates' access to work release programs, and until it does, decisions in the various areas of the country will probably differ. For a thorough analysis, see Lawrence P. Margolis, "Inmate's Liberty Interest in Work Release Program—Winsett v. McGinnes," *Wake Forest Law Review* 17 (April 1981): 273–292. For a contrasting decision, see Johnson v. Stark, 717 F.2d 1550 (8th Cir. 1983).

27. See, for example, State ex rel Kaus v. McManus, 238 N.W.2d 596, 602, 603 (Minn. 1976); People v. Metz, 403 N.Y. Supp. 2d 330 (1978); Tracy v. Salamack, 572 F.2d 393 (2nd Cir. 1978); and Perrote v. Percy, 465 F. Supp. 112 (W.D.Wisc. 1979).

28. Ann D. Witte, "Work Release in North Carolina—A Program That Works!" *Law and Contemporary Problems* 41 (Winter 1977): 230–251. Quotation is on p. 242.

29. Witte, 243–251.

30. John D. Case, "'Doing Time' in the Community," *Federal Probation* 31 (March 1967): 9.

31. For a review of the research on this subject, see Jonathan F. Katz and Scott H. Decker, "An Analysis of Work Release: The Institutionalization of Unsubstantiated Reforms," *Criminal Justice and Behavior* 9 (June 1982): 229–250.

32. Attorney General's Survey of Release Procedures, *Parole,* vol. 4 (Washington, D.C.: U.S. Government Printing Office, 1939), p. 4, quoted in Vincent O'Leary, "Parole Administration," chap. 25, in Daniel Glaser, ed., *Handbook of*

Criminology (Skokie, Ill.: Rand McNally, 1974), pp. 909–949. Quotation is on p. 909.

33. For a general discussion of parole, see A. B. Smith and L. Berlin, *Introduction to Probation and Parole* (St. Paul: West Publishing, 1979). For information about the history and development of parole, see Michael R. Gottfredson and Don M. Gottfredson, *Decisionmaking in Criminal Justice: Toward the Rational Exercise of Discretion* (Cambridge, Mass.: Ballinger, 1980), pp. 281–372; Neil Morgan, "The Shaping of Parole in England and Wales," *Criminal Law Review* (March 1983): 137–151.

34. Bureau of Justice Statistics, *Probation and Parole 1982* (Washington, D.C.: U.S. Government Printing Office, 1982). See also George Camp et al., *The Corrections Yearbook 1983* (South Salem, N.Y.: Criminal Justice Institute, 1983), pp. 34–35; and National Council on Crime and Delinquency, *Parole in the United States, 1980–1981* (Washington, D.C.: U.S. Government Printing Office, 1983).

35. Greenholtz v. Inmates of Nebraska Penal and Correctional Complex, 442 U.S. 1, 19 (1979). See also Morrissey v. Brewer, 433 F. 2d 942 (8th Cir. 1971), *rev'd,* 408 U.S. 471 (1972) and Tarlton v. Clark, 441 F.2d 384, 385 (5th Cir. 1971), *cert. denied,* 403 U.S. 934 (1972).

36. U.S. Department of Justice, *Sentencing and Parole Release, Classification Instruments for Criminal Justice Decisions,* vol. 4 (Washington, D.C.: U.S. Government Printing Office, 1979), p. 7.

37. See, for example, John S. Carroll, "Judgments of Recidivism Risk: The Use of Base-rate Information on Parole Decisions," in Paul D. Lipsitt and Bruce D. Sales, eds., *New Directions in Psycholegal Research* (New York: Van Nostrand Reinhold, 1980), pp. 66–86; Don M. Gottfredson, Leslie T. Wilkins, and Peter B. Hoffman, *Guidelines for Parole and Sentencing: A Policy Control Method* (Lexington, Mass.: Heath 1978); Alfred Blumstein and Soumyo Moitra, "The Identification of 'Career Criminals' from 'Chronic Offenders' in a Cohort," *Law and Policy Quarterly* 2 (July 1980): 321–334; and Penny R. Lukin, "Recidivism and Changes Made by Delinquents During Residential Treatment," *Journal of Research in Crime and Delinquency* 19 (January 1981): 101–112.

38. See, for example, Harry L. Kozol et al., "The Diagnosis and Treatment of Dangerousness,"

Crime & Delinquency 18 (October 1972): 371–392; and Carroll, "Judgments of Recidivism Risk."

39. See, for example, Leo Carroll and Margaret E. Mondrick, "Racial Bias in the Decision to Grant Parole," *Law & Society Review* 11 (Fall 1976): 93–107; and David M. Peterson and Paul C. Friday, "Early Release from Incarceration: Race As a Factor in the Use of 'Shock Probation,'" *Journal of Criminal Law & Criminology* 66 (March 1975): 79–87.

40. Joseph E. Scott, "The Use of Discretion in Determining the Severity of Punishment for Incarcerated Offenders," *Journal of Criminal Law & Criminology* 65 (March 1974): 214–224. For an in-depth study of the interplay of factions within a parole board membership, see John A. Conley and Sherwood E. Zimmerman, "Decision Making by a Part-Time Parole Board: An Observational and Empirical Study," *Criminal Justice and Behavior* 9 (December 1982): 396–431.

41. "'Dramatic Changes' Seen in Sentencing, Parole," *Justice Assistance News* 4 (September 1983): 8.

42. For examples of the grids, see 28 Code of Federal Regulations § 2.20 (1981). For further information on the process of instituting guidelines in a management context, see Thomas J. Bernard, "The Development of Federal Parole Guidelines," *Criminal Justice Review* 8 (Spring 1983): 24–28.

43. For a detailed explanation of the U.S. Parole Commission guidelines, see Payton v. U.S., 363 F.2d 132 (5th Cir. 1981).

44. James L. Galvin and Kenneth Polk, "Parole Guidelines: Suggested Research Questions," *Crime & Delinquency* 27 (April 1981): 213–224; and Payton v. U.S., 636 F.2d 132, 142.

45. Barbara Stone-Meierhoefer and Peter B. Hoffman, "Presumptive Parole Dates: The Federal Approach," *Federal Probation* 46 (June 1982): 41–57. For an article examining the use of guidelines to reduce sentence disparity, see Michael R. Gottfredson, "Parole Guidelines and the Reduction of Sentencing Disparity," *Journal of Research in Crime and Delinquency* 16 (July 1979): 218–231.

46. "U.S. Parole Commission Guidelines Revised," *Justice Assistance News* 4 (March 1983):9.

47. For a discussion of sentencing disparity and parole, see Edward M. Kennedy, "Toward a New System of Criminal Sentencing: Law with Order," *American Criminal Law Review* 16 (Spring 1979): 353–382. For a discussion of the judicial role in sentencing and parole, see U.S. v. Addonizio, 442 U.S. 178 (1979).

48. David T. Stanley, *Prisoners Among Us: The Problems of Parole* (Washington, D.C.: Brookings Institute, 1976), p. 185. See also "The Problem of Parole," *Justice Assistance News* 4 (May 1983): 14; Andrew von Hirsch and Kathleen J. Hanrahan, *The Question of Parole: Retention, Reform, or Abolition:* (Cambridge, Mass.: Ballinger, 1979); and Keven Krajick, "Abolishing Parole: An Idea Whose Time Has Passed," *Corrections Magazine* 9 (June 1983): 32–40.

49. Sheldon Messinger, quoted in Krajick, "Abolishing Parole," 36. For further discussion of the displaced discretion problem, see Leslie T. Wilkins, "Sentencing Guidelines to Reduce Disparity?" *Criminal Law Review* (April 1980): 204–214; Andrew von Hirsch and Kathleen J. Hanrahan, "Abolish Parole Release?—The Choice of Decisionmaker," in Hyman Gross and Andrew von Hirsch, eds., *Sentencing* (New York: Oxford University Press, 1981), pp. 352–368; Frederick A. Hussey and Stephen P. Lagoy, "The Determinate Sentence and Its Impact on Parole," *Criminal Law Bulletin* 19 (March-April 1983): 101–130; and Robert G. Culbertson, "Achieving Correctional Reform," chap. 11, in Roy R. Roberg and Vincent J. Webb, eds., *Critical Issues in Corrections: Problems, Trends and Prospects* (St. Paul: West Publishing, 1981), pp. 308–345.

50. For more information, see Doug Thomson and David Fogel, *Probation Work in Small Agencies: A National Study of Training Provisions and Needs* (Chicago: University of Illinois at Chicago Press, 1980): Richard McCleary, *Dangerous Men: The Sociology of Parole* (Beverly Hills, Calif.: Sage Publications, 1978). For the results of a two-year study reporting that ex-offenders were just as effective as parole officers in the supervision function of parole, see Joseph E. Scott, *Ex-offenders As Parole Officers* (Lexington, Mass.: Heath, 1980).

51. See Joan D. Kelinman, "Guess Who's Coming to Dinner: A Critical Look at Home Visits by Parole Officers," *Columbia Human Rights Law Review* 14 (Fall-Winter, 1982–1983): 355–381.

52. See Howard R. Sacks and Charles H. Logan, *Does Parole Make a Difference?* (West Hartford:

University of Connecticut School of Law Press, 1979).

53. Patrick G. Jackson, "Some Effects of Parole Supervision on Recidivism," *British Journal of Criminology* 23 (January 1983): 17–34. See also John P. Conrad, "Who Needs a Door-Bell Pusher? The Case for Abolishing Parole," *Prison Journal* 59 (Autumn–Winter 1979): 17–26.

54. See John W. Palmer, *Constitutional Rights of Prisoners,* 2nd ed. 1977, with 1981 supplement. (Cincinnati: Anderson Publishing, 1973), p. 114.

55. Morrissey v. Brewer, 433 F.2d 942 (8th Cir. 1971), *rev'd* 408 U.S. 471 (1972). For a later case holding that there is no constitutional right to counsel at all parole revocation hearings, see Gagnon v. Scarpelli, 411 U.S. 778 (1973). For an overview of the parole revocation process, see John S. Carroll and R. Barry Ruback, "Sentencing by Parole Board: The Parole Revocation Decision," chap. 13, in Bruce Dennis Sales, ed., *The Trial Process* (New York: Plenum, 1981), pp. 459–480.

56. Morrissey v. Brewer, 408 U.S. 471, 484, citations and footnotes omitted.

Epilogue

1. "The Plague of Violent Crime," *Newsweek,* March 23, 1981, p. 46.

2. "The Curse of Violent Crime," *Time,* March 23, 1981, p. 16.

3. "The Plague of Violent Crime," p. 46.

4. *Tulsa World,* June 11, 1982, p. 1, col. 1.

5. "News Release," United States Department of Justice, January 12, 1983.

6. Chief Justice Warren E. Burger, "The State of Justice," *American Bar Association Journal* 70 (April 1984): 63, quoting Derek Bok.

7. Nix. v. Williams, *U.S. Law Week* 52 (June 12, 1984):4732.

8. Massachusetts v. Sheppard, *U.S. Law Week* 52 (June 26, 1984): 5177 and U.S. v. Leon, *U.S. Law Week* 52 (June 26, 1984): 5155.

9. Aris T. Papas, "Barbed Wire Justice," *Corrections Today* 46 (June 1984): 56.

10. Donald R. Cressey, "Criminological Theory, Social Science, and the Repression of Crime," *Criminology* 16 (August 1978): 173.

11. Cressey, 177.

12. C. R. Jeffery, "Criminology As an Interdisciplinary Behavioral Science," *Criminology* 16 (August 1978): 153–154.

13. Quoted in Jeffery, p. 154.

14. Jeffery, p. 156.

15. Jeffery, p. 166.

16. Simon Dinitz, "Nothing Fails Like a Little Success," *Criminology* 16 (August 1978): 230–231.

17. John Hagan, "The Legislation of Crime and Delinquency: A Review of Theory, Method, and Research," *Law & Society Review* 14 (Spring 1980): 603, emphasis in the original.

18. Cressey, "Criminological Theory," pp. 188–189.

19. Warren E. Burger, "No Man Is an Island,"*American Bar Association Journal* 56 (April 1970): 328.

Acknowledgments

(Continued from p. iv)

Photos p. 24 (left), Michael Weisbrot and family/Stock, Boston; (middle), Arthur Tress/Woodfin Camp and Associates; (right), Eugene Gordon/Photo Researchers, Inc.

Photo p. 52, courtesy of The University of Tulsa/Stephen Crane.

Photo p. 125, Associated Press/Wide World Photos.

Photo p. 153, Associated Press/Wide World Photos.

Photo p. 159, Matthew Klein/Magnum Photos.

Photo p. 257, United Press International/Bettmann Archive.

Photo p. 264, Associated Press/Wide World Photos.

Photo p. 295, courtesy of Leslie Kennedy.

Photo p. 314, Woodfin Camp and Associates. Copyright © Dick Durrance II 1981.

Photo p. 337, Dennis Lake/Photo Researchers, Inc.

Photo p. 355, courtesy of Mary Collins.

Photos p. 374 (left), Daniel S. Brody/Stock, Boston; (right), United Press International/Bettmann Archive.

Photo p. 397, courtesy of Sue Titus Reid.

Photo p. 426, courtesy of The University of Tulsa/Stephen Crane. Center of New York City.

Photo p. 429, courtesy of the South Carolina Department of Corrections.

Photo p. 466, The Supreme Court Historical Society.

Photo p. 483, courtesy of The University of Tulsa/Stephen Crane.

Photos p. 489 (left), courtesy of The University of Tulsa/Stephen Crane; (right), courtesy of Oklahoma State Penitentiary.

Photos pp. 497, 518, 526, courtesy of The University of Tulsa/Stephen Crane.

Photo p. 528, courtesy of Leslie Kennedy.

Photo p. 542, courtesy of The University of Tulsa/Stephen Crane.

Photo p. 562, courtesy of Oklahoma State Penitentiary.

Photos p. 573, courtesy of Geoffrey Grant.

Photo p. 595, Tyrone Hall from Stock, Boston.

General Index

Case Index